THE DAYS OF MARTIN LUTHER KING, JR.

THE DAYS OF MARTIN LUTHER KING, JR.

by Jim Bishop

G. P. PUTNAM'S SONS

NEW YORK

Contents

For the Record

HE WAS SHORT and chubby, a man with a boy's grin, the mentality of a sophisticated prophet, and the voice of a hollow log drum booming in the Congo. Dr. Martin Luther King, Jr., was, on the surface, a typical black preacher who called down fire and brimstone on sinners but thought it would happen in the next world rather than this one. A black woman who refused to move to the back of a bus propelled Dr. King into world prominence. Fearful and pessimistic, he fought her cause and was stunned when he won. In time, he was to lead the Southern black man to fresh freedoms after hundreds of years of servitude. In a span of thirteen years the preacher saw himself as a black Mohandas Gandhi, perhaps a Jesus, because he won victory after victory by advocating nonviolence and the unselfish love for the hating whites.

Nonviolence was not only his credo, but his rationale. He reminded the militants that 22,000,000 blacks had neither the weapons nor the possibility of winning a fight against a white government of 180,000,000 people. He was shrewd; he was naïve. He was courageous; he was cowardly. He was a leader, but not a strategist. Almost always, he was willing to settle for less than he asked for his people, but he got more for them than they had been able to achieve in three centuries of servitude.

At times, his attitude was almost saintly. His life became a series of violent confrontations, each different from the others. To the historian, the joke was on the white man because King was asking for equality in what was considered a classless society. It was demeaning to both sides to acknowledge the fact that America, the puritanical democracy, fostered a caste system, every bit as rigid as India's, of at least four main classes—white, "poor white trash," Spanish-speaking people, and blacks.

The black leadership was aware of this but refused to admit it. The men on Capitol Hill and in the White House were born into it and contented themselves with pious promises. This broad blessed land of sparkling streams and tall forests had sparrows living on one branch and swallows on another, but men pretended not to be aware of it.

Dr. King was given a short time to accomplish a brotherhood of many kinds of birds, and his indictments of his enemies left ruffled feathers and bloody beaks. He asked equal pay for equal skills, voting rights for blacks, the extermination of ghettos, an antidistinctive status called equality; but his true goal was social acceptibility of all blacks by all whites. When he spoke of "brotherhood," the reverend intended more than the integration of schools and buses. It also appears that he favored interracial marriage; otherwise he felt the blacks and the whites would always remain separate and distinct. It is incredible, he said, to believe that the black man can ask for equality in all respects except one.

It was the so-called poor whites of the South who feared this segment of the Freedom Movement most. It was the ignorant farmer who warmed his hate and fright of the black on the body of his wife. His male forebears had warned him that the black man had superior sexual endowments and must, at all cost, be "kept in his place." The white sharecropper is not aware that military doctors in three wars have issued reports that there is no essential difference anatomically between the blacks, the whites, the browns, reds, and yellows. The white Southerner referred to the black as a "buck."

The white man living on the red clay roads learned that the best way of keeping the black man "in his place" was to beat him, jail him, lynch him. Innocent or guilty, the black was hanged, burned, and emasculated as an example to other blacks. The black learned to drop his head when he passed a white woman and often to step off the sidewalk so that he might not accidentally brush against her. Almost any infraction, a misunderstood smile, a word of admiration, could lead to a charge of rape by a hysterical white woman. Often, there was no trial, no investigation, just a band of white men in cotton fields who shouted to one another, hurried to their unpainted shacks, got their hunting rifles, and went off to stage a lynch party.

In the latter part of the nineteenth century and the first half of the twentieth, there were many lynchings. White farmers and hooded members of the Ku Klux Klan offered a cornered black his life if he would "confess." Innocent or guilty, he often confessed to save his skin but always lost it.

No one, it seems, was able to protect the black woman from the sexual aggression of the white man. In those rare cases where the girl or her parents brought the matter to court, the same solemn words were heard again and again: "It is impossible to rape a nigger woman." Often as not, this brought laughter from the jury, a concomitant of acquittal.

Both sides have distorted the history of race in America. The blacks do not want to admit that it was black chieftains in Africa who sold men and women to the white man. The white man does not want to concede that once slavery was abolished, he hoped with all his heart that the black man would return to Africa. The South was terrified by the fact that the blacks were proliferating faster than the whites in some Southern states. Mississippi, for example, cannot be called a "white" state. There are two dark faces for every light one in any public square.

The municipal and state laws of the South, in the criminal code, were targeted at the black man. Something which might be classified as a misdemeanor for the white man became a felony when a black was charged. In one section of the criminal code the black was favored. This, ironically, was in the realm of murder. If black killed black, the indictment was swift, the trial was brief, and the sentence was light. The philosophy behind this kind of law is that "a dead nigger is a good nigger." Often, the legal latitude for sentencing ranged from a year in prison to life or execution.

Most of the policemen and sheriffs who enforced these laws were drawn from the "poor whites." This imparted to the sadistic law enforcement officer the right to brutalize any black. It was incumbent on the black to explain to his child, as early as possible, the lack of justice and equality he must expect. "If a white boy hits you, don't hit back."

This situation might have endured through the second half of the twentieth century except for two things; Rosa Parks would not move to the back of a bus; and the United States Supreme Court handed down its monumental decision that equal but separate facilities in schools were a violation of the Constitution.

The head of the black began to peer above the windrows of corn and cotton in December, 1955. It looked around, and no one shot at it. The head lifted higher and higher, and a boldness beset the man whose grandfather was a slave, a chattel with no name. The heads and faces became more numerous, and leaders such as Roy Wilkins of the National Association for the Advancement of Colored People, the hard and ageless A. Philip Randolph of the Pullman porters, Martin Luther King, James Farmer, Eldridge Cleaver, Medgar Evers, Floyd McKissick, Rap Brown, Elijah Muhammad, Malcolm X, and many others now stood in plain view to demand the material and social equalities which should have been theirs since Abraham Lincoln signed the Emancipation Proclamation in 1863.

In 1956 the white South became frightened. Truly frightened. The Supreme Court and Congress were granting liberties to blacks which, they felt, would lead to bloodshed. The South was fond of proclaiming to the rest of the nation that "we take better care of our Negroes than you do yours." In arrogant sectionalism, it claimed that the rest of the country did not understand its "problems." It was hardly a matter of understanding them; they had been enumerated so many times in the halls of Congress that legislators and listeners could no longer detect the difference between a new expiation and an old echo. The ever-growing number of blacks was but one of the problems. The South needed industry, cheap labor, needed to revise its archaic thinking and join the twentieth century, to excommunicate its flowing-haired, pandering politicians and exchange them for young progressive men whose eyes, unlike those of Senator James Eastland and Judge Leander Perez, were in front of their heads and not in back. The sacred word was "tradition." The real tradition, the jasmine-scented custom of good manners, spirited horses, and mint juleps, expired when William Tecumseh Sherman cut a swath of smoldering ashes through the South in the Civil War. The tradition was gone, dead, deceased, a litany of archaic customs.

In this atmosphere the cold volcano erupted. White Citizens Councils were organized to hold the blacks in check; police chiefs refused parade permits to black men; blacks sat at lunch counters in five-and-ten-cent stores demanding to be served. There were sit-ins, stand-ins, hunger strikes, boycotts, bombings, shootings, the use of high-pressure fire hoses on crowds, picket fences of bayonets, calls for help to Washington from both sides, arrests which sometimes amounted to 600 a day in one town, looting riots which were referred to as "long hot summers," campus riots between students of the left against students of the right, book burnings, the clank of tanks in the night. The cry for "law and order" became an antiblack phrase.

Those who thought that the national convulsion was a momentary matter were mistaken. Dr. King said, "The American racial revolution is a revolution to 'get in' rather than to overthrow. We want a share in the American economy, the housing market, the educational system and the social opportunities. This goal itself indicates that a social change in America must be nonviolent."

Some leaders asked the government to carve out a black state, or province, in the Southwest. This would give blacks their own merchants, professions, mayors, and governors. It was a hackneyed notion long ago broken on the wheel of logic. Others started a Back-to-Africa movement, but this brought no more substantive support than tolerant smiles because the protesters knew that Africa, itself convulsed in a struggle to climb out of the hole of colonialism, was engaged in deadly fratricidal strife with blacks killing blacks. The American ghetto, in a material way, was much more livable than the lonely thatched huts of the jungle villages. The majority of the 22,000,000 American blacks, who remained aloof from activism, synthesized their wishes in an almost wistful way: "We want the fence between us torn down right now. We aren't ready to cross over to your side of the street yet—it may take another generation before it can happen—but we want those fences down now."

American blacks, especially those in the North, had worked hard for at least fifty years to become as near white as possible. Some who were born with light skin "passed" as whites. Others, who subscribed to black magazines such as *Ebony,* found the pages replete with advertisements selling hair-straightener products. Other ads promised to "lighten" dark skin. The mark of humiliation and shame was in the fact that the products sold well.

The hair straighteners began to disappear from the market shortly after the racial struggle began. Black men and women paid beauticians to kink their hair and make it bushy. The Afro hairdo was in. Possibly it was the first sign of defiant pride in being a black.

Martin Luther King sometimes assailed his people in anger and sometimes in poor taste. "Our crime rate is far too high," he said. "Our level of cleanliness is frequently far too low. Too often those of us who are in the middle class live above our means, spend money on nonessentials and frivolities, and fail to give to serious causes, organizations, and educational institutions that so desperately need funds. We are too often loud and boisterous, and spend far too much on drink. Even the most poverty-stricken among us can purchase a ten-cent bar of soap; even the most uneducated among us can have high morals."

On that occasion, he was speaking with the white man's tongue because uncleanliness, illiteracy, immorality, drunkenness, laziness, and one unmentioned item—venereal disease—are the crutches of the white supremacist, remove them and he becomes paralyzed. It occurred to few that the government in Washington, through a succession of thirteen administrations, could have assisted the black man to a curriculum of education which might have eradicated much of the ugliness of his life. The best the government could think of was to single out an outstanding black now and then and refer to him as "a credit to his race."

At no time were the American blacks united in aspiration or action. The most insidious enemy was not the white racist—he exposed himself for all to see—it was the middle-class black. To use the vernacular, he "had it made" and he fought the "troublemakers" among his people.

He was the professional man—the physician, the pastor, the attorney, the engineer, the politician—the man who owned a home, had a sizable income and an automobile, and lived on a hill overlooking the ghetto. Negro clerics decried the efforts of Martin Luther King and some ran to the white mayor to denounce King to the press. The middle-class black had something to protect, something his brethren did not have, and he had no intention of risking it to fight for equality for all.

I find it impossible to write a biography of Dr. Martin Luther King, Jr., without including the elements which surrounded his lifework. Such a book must include those who helped him, those who hurt him, those who inspired him, even those of his own race who called him "Uncle Tom." It must also include the fragmentation of the Black Revolution, even the small fact that blacks in Harlem pelted his limousine with eggs.

Most of all, Dr. King's story is emotional, rather than intellectual or logical. These were days, not of love, not of the sweet waters of reason, but of blood. These were days of hard hearts and stone heads.

My gratitude is extented to Ralph Abernathy, Bernard Lee, Martin Luther King, Sr., the members of King's official staff, his friends and supporters, and those who opposed him in many cities for their patience in granting interviews, in reconstructing conversations. For the "thoughts" of characters, I thank them for the revealing books, articles, and tracts they wrote. For the million and a quarter words of concise notes from which the book was written, I thank my wife, Kelly Bishop, who serves with distinction and without pay.

JIM BISHOP

Hallandale, Florida

I. SUNSET

1

HE STARED THROUGH THE WINDOW, the commiserating brown eyes looking at the concrete runway but not seeing it. The jet motors whined, but the plane did not move. It was pinned to John F. Kennedy Airport like a tin butterfly. The stubby fingers passed back and forth across the safety belt, and he said, "We're going to be late in Memphis." The cheerful clergyman was always late. People begged him to come to Los Angeles, to Washington, to Detroit, to Chicago, and all the invitations were imperative. Nothing would go right unless Dr. Martin Luther King, Jr., was present.

The work, the time, the 10,000 miles each month in planes, the meetings, the disputes, the persuasions, the marches, the press conferences, the speeches—all of it depressed him. He was thirty-nine years of age and he was Methuselah. The exterior was young, jaunty; the cheeks round with tiny burls of whiskers; swift-moving feet on short legs; full lips which could summon the speech of the intellectual or could resurrect a down-home form of conversation—"Hi, man! Press the flesh!"—but it seemed to him that although all his magnificent efforts had taken him to the top of a hill, he was now, for some reason, walking down the cool side. He was like this jet plane, designed to fly at high speed, now incapable of leaving the ground.

"It isn't our style of operation," said the twin sitting in the aisle seat. There was no response. The Reverend Bernard Lee, bodyguard and companion, looked like Dr. Martin Luther King, Jr., talked like him, and, in minor key, thought like him. Lee could get on a phone, call Atlanta, and convince Coretta King that he was her husband. "When the President of the United States visits someplace, his men go there and see what the situation is. We got no intelligence on Memphis." Dr. King was not President of the United States, but Bernard Lee had uttered a truth. Sporadically, America kills Presidents, but a black preacher with his head above all other black preachers makes a better target.

Usually, Dr. King's personal staff, in conference with the hierarchy of the Southern Christian Leadership Conference, worked on matters of personal safety weeks ahead of each march, sending advance men to wet their fingers and hold them against the breeze of discontent, asking police protection, working out the timing of the line of march, and deciding which units were welcome and which could not participate. This time there was, as Lee stated, no advance work.

If there was a weakness in the system, it could be laid at the feet of King himself. It was difficult for him to say the word "no." Weeks before, he had been at a convention of preachers in Miami, and he had been entreated, not once, but three times, to go to Memphis and attend a rally for striking Negro garbage men. He had lounged in the warm sun of Florida, planning a gigantic Poor People's March on Washington, knowing that he had better make it a good one, especially convincing to Congress and Lyndon Johnson. He needed a victory desperately.

He had felt the whip of the militants, Rap Brown, Eldridge Cleaver, Malcolm X, and he had referred to them as "the crazies." King represented the mildest, and therefore the least dolorous, faction that White America could hope for in the struggle between 22,000,000 blacks and 180,000,000 whites. He preached nonviolence and he was sincere. Dr. King was conscious of the fact that odds of 8 to 1 against a cause does not permit violence as an option. His mind, his heart were concentrating solely on the Poor People's March—not on Memphis. Memphis was an entr'acte. Still, smiling in the sun of Miami, he had said yes to the Reverend Ralph Jackson; he had said yes to Jim Lawson, who with a handful of followers, represented the only Southern Christian Leadership Conference strength in Memphis; he had said yes, most of all, to the Reverend Samuel B. Kyles.

"Come to Memphis for the protest march," they had begged. Kyles, tall, skinny, swift, and blunt, said that it was imperative for Dr. King to join them and lock arms with the marchers in the front line. Dr. King had nodded agreeably and said, "Billy, I'll be there." And now, with the early sun yellow and cold over Jamaica Bay, he was sitting in a jet, anxious to get to Memphis, anxious to get it over with. A half hour passed, and still the plane did not move.

He had left the Hilton in New York too early to call his wife. She was in Washington trying to get support from women's organizations for the

Poor People's March. Coretta, the talented, the pretty, would be the star at a press conference and there, in her controlled, schoolteacher diction, she would call for peace in Asia, just as Dr. King had done recently. Many Americans felt it was a subversive cry for defeat. Others applauded his stand. Dr. King was plunging from Southern politics into the international arena. He had been criticized by the press for braiding the problems of race with the problems of the war in Vietnam. His call for peace in Asia had cost him friendships, memberships, and donors to his cause.

It did not change his attitude, he was repeating the words through his wife. And yet he was neither a Communist nor a radical. Martin Luther King was a political shopper. He would accept any candidate who would lend his office to the cause of blacks. Eisenhower had listened to him, smiled, shaken hands, and ignored him. Kennedy had fenced with King, displaying great personal interest in the safety of the preacher, calculatedly cadging black votes, but fighting only feebly for civil rights bills. Johnson had tried to give King status by inviting him to the White House and nailing down two civil rights bills in Congress, but King thought he detected the kiss of Judas and was both surprised and happy when Lyndon Johnson declared that he would not seek a second term.

The shriek of the jet engines grew louder, and the plane lumbered down the runway. The Memphis march was going to have to start without Martin Luther King. There was no chance he could be in line by 11 A.M.

The protest march had been originally scheduled for March 22, 1968. An unseasonal foot of snow had fallen on Memphis, and the protest had been postponed six days. Black groups not associated with the sanitation workers began to volunteer to join them. As days passed, there were more and more of them. Pledges came in from 6,000 people. A young group called the Invaders, originally organized in Chicago, had a branch in Memphis, and their leaders complained that they had not been consulted about the march or the limits of the protest.

To mollify them, a group of ministers agreed to a meeting. The sedate sat facing the seditious. The Invaders, with Afro coiffures and dashikis hanging from their shoulders, asked why the march should not be turned into a violent demonstration of power and destructiveness at some point along Beale Street. The elders were shocked. With restraint, they argued that Martin Luther King was committed to nonviolence, that he would not come to Memphis if he knew of this proposal. "Man," one of the Invaders said, "you know, we want to get something done. I mean, all this stuff about marching downtown, all these bourgeoisie wanting to march downtown to get their pictures on national television doing their civil rights thing—man, that's nothing. That ain't digging. That ain't going to help my brothers."

The ministers were unified. They told the Invaders that this march was going to be peaceful. The Invaders could stay out of it. At one point, a violent young man said that the Invaders would be invited or maybe there would be no march at all. The threat was real, but the march leaders still declined the endorsement of the Invaders. The young men, retreating slightly, asked if they could use the church mimeograph machines to reproduce the formula for making Molotov cocktails. The ministers refused and made a fist-pounding decision: "You can join the rest of us in a nonviolent march, or you can boycott it."

"Man," one Invader said, "if you expect honkies to get the message, you got to break some windows." The meeting adjourned with no decision on either side. The Invaders found a mimeograph machine and ran off hundreds of sheets defining the ingredients of a Molotov cocktail. Many of these papers reached Hamilton High School, where black students waited impatiently for lunchtime, when they could run through the exits like a stream of lava and move downtown to join the march. When the moment arrived, on Thursday the twenty-eighth, they were met by Mayor Henry Loeb's riot police on the school grounds. The boys retreated, then returned with a torrent of rocks and bottles.

The Memphis Police Department did not respond with guns; they advanced in metal-helmeted rows with clubs. In the melee a black girl was injured. The Invaders quietly passed the word that she had been killed by "the pigs."

Downtown, at the Clayborne Temple Methodist Church, thousands of adults were gathering. They moved in dark currents around the church grounds, and well-dressed black women passed among the young, asking, "Are you with the older folks or the young?" If they answered, "The young," the ladies requested them to leave the area. The leaders of the Invaders waited at the edge of the crowd. They too had a message for "Whitey," but it could wait until their parents began the dignified minuet of the march.

The Invaders waited for the arrival of "Martin Luther Coon," the Uncle Tom. Some said he did not belong in Memphis, that his presence would not solve their problems. They chatted in bitterness and in laughter. King wouldn't know Beale Street from W. C. Handy Park. He was an elegant stranger, a Nobel Prize winner for Peace, an internationally renowned adherent of Gandhi and Jesus—"For an encore, he's gonna lay down in front of a squad car." He was a fat figure in an expensive suit, a black who was supposed to be sacred. The Invaders were ready to bet coins that he didn't even know what the whole demonstration was for. The Invaders were also willing to bet that the only aspect of the matter known by the superduper Dr. King was the name of the mayor—Loeb. He had probably been well filled in on Loeb's background, because the mayor was tough and intractable.

Did King know anything else really? Or was he so monumental that Memphis was just a wayside stop on the way to the Poor People's March in Washington? The day before, the mayor and the council had sat in session. When a mild liberal member tried to mediate the matter, Loeb had shouted him into silence. Further, he had managed to recruit white truck drivers and helpers for twenty-three of the garbage trucks and was in the process of catering only to white neighborhoods. This left "Colored Town" with a bad odor, real and symbolic.

The jet, in time, sat down at Memphis Airport. "Chilly," Dr. King said, buttoning his coat. Memphis, to him, was country music, the blues, a municipality sitting on the edge of the broad cocoa of the Mississippi, a city of old black farm customs and manners, but also a city of shell-food, blaring bands with trombone sleeves in motion, and the high high wail of trumpets.

Memphis was that and more. It was a city with a heritage. It was the home and the pride of a slave trader named Nathan Bedford Forrest, who later became a general in the Civil War. "If I ain't fightin' to keep my niggers," Forrest shouted, "then what the hell am I fightin' for?" When the war was done, after the young men of the South had left a fine scarlet carpet from Atlanta to Gettysburg, he watched the Northern politicians come in and invite the black man to vote, to elect legislatures and governors. General Forrest of Memphis became the first Imperial Wizard of the Knights of the Ku Klux Klan.

Fifteen years later, in the 1880's, a Jewish family named Loeb moved into Memphis. They started a hand laundry business with black employees and prospered. Eighty years later, the Loebs were rich, affluent, and political. In this generation some had become Episcopalians and married Christians. Mayor Loeb was one of these, when he took office, he did what the white constituency wanted done: He gave the blacks as little as possible. They constituted 40 percent of the population, but with the exception of a few who had "musical talent," they represented to the white people a vast agglomerate of dark skins masking troublemakers, thieves, rapists, and indolents.

Mayor Henry Loeb resolved that no black alien, especially one named Dr. Martin Luther King, Jr., was going to alter the situation between whites and blacks in Memphis. Loeb would not hesitate to call upon his Police Department to club heads; nor would he deem it an evil deed to phone Governor Buford Ellington for national guardsmen. This, without Dr. King's knowledge, pitted the peaceful pacifier against the mad fist of City Hall. This, coupled with the Invaders' planned violence, was more than anyone could overcome.

This cherubic man, riding into town in style, was fated to lose the battle. His august position in the world as a fighter for human dignity was more than just threatened. He was fighting for his political life. His career as the "Jesus" of the blacks led to his staff referring to him as "De Lawd." This was an "in" joke, but he and Coretta made reference, publicly and privately, to his "Gethsemane" and his "Crucifixion." Yet he knew that he was on the cool side of the hill, and that he and his staff must plan bigger and ever bigger victories. In truth, the Poor People's March planned for Washington in a few weeks was a retreat, because King had found it necessary to enlist the support of other oppressed groups such as Mexicans and Indians.

The march in Memphis had started. It was orderly, rank on rank of blacks linking arms with their fellows to spread from curb to curb. King got out of the limousine. He backed into the front row of marchers, held his elbows out, and grinned with the delight of a child who knows that he is not breaking any law, but that he is breaking a will to resist.

There was so much that no one told him about Memphis. A few days earlier, the ministers, trying to placate the Invaders, permitted one of them to address a rally. "I'm a radical," he had said, eyes racing over the group, reading faces. "Before Henry Loeb will listen, the garbage has to be in the street, not in your backyard. . . . Preaching and raising money are fine. Somebody has to do it. But there are *men* out there. We've got to do some fighting. Not marching—*fighting!* And when you talk about a city with as many cops as this city's got, you'd better have some guns. You're going to need them before it's over." As the young man concluded, a minister stepped up, smiled forgivingly, and said, "We have chosen our weapons. These are the weapons of nonviolence."

There were many thousands more nonviolent marchers than violent ones, but Martin Luther King, unknowingly, was leading a gigantic walking time bomb. He had heard the cry in Watts—"Burn, baby, burn!"—and he had countered with the Christian ethic: "Build, baby, build!" Congressman Adam Clayton Powell of Harlem had, a month earlier, stated: "The white man is finished and the day of Martin Luther King has come to an end."

Powell, in his effrontary, was a prophet. But so, too, was Dr. King. He had called his secretary in Atlanta to ask for a rundown of his appointments, and she said he was killing himself. Sometimes, when a tragic truth is uttered, the victim laughs. Dr. King did just that and said, "You are all going to kill me anyway, and I'd just as soon die at an early age."

Increasingly, in speeches, Dr. King referred to his own death as though it were a ghostly bird whose talons he could feel on his shoulder. It was as though he were trying to convince himself that it didn't matter. In Sunday sermons, he opened his mouth to emit those deep tolling bells of words and said, "If a man has not found something worth giving his life for, he is not fit to live." He once said to his aides, whom he could lift to the heights or plunge to despair at will, "I cannot live in fear. I have to function. If there is one fear I have conquered, it is the fear of death." Sometimes, when his aides criticized him for morbidity, Dr. King said, "I'm just being realistic." He knew that he had gone too far, grown too big. To someone, somewhere, on a certain day as yet unknown, he would be a target.

On this day, he marched with a façade of happiness. The grin was turned on full; some whites were in the line of march. The people on the curbs shouted encouragement and applauded. Once more, the man standing at his side was wrong. Bernard Lee had looked back over the ranks of marchers and had seen snow-white hair, smiling middle-aged faces, younger men and women locked happily arm in arm, and he felt relieved. Dr. King had apologized to the leaders in the front rank for being late, but he felt elated to be in the midst of his kind of people: the overpowering majority of sensible blacks, who could move mountains in any state by smiling, asking politely and unendingly for justice, inaugurating the peaceful march of power, and, at the same time, putting the white municipality in a bad light because the television cameras always picked up the grim police on each curb, following the march with billy clubs in their hands and revolver holsters whacking their hips.

The television cameras were dead ahead, the cars moving at a walking pace with cameramen on top, grinding out one more benign march in the history of the black man. Someone came up behind Martin Luther King, Jr., and shoved him forward. He kept himself from falling and looked back. His assailant was a very young man. Dr. King was pushed again. This time he turned backward and found that black teen-agers on the curbs were moving in on the marchers. Behind him the first doleful music of shattered glass tinkled. He saw signs reading BLACK POWER and the young fighting the police to break up the ranks of marchers.

Lee tightened his grip on Dr. King's arm. The Reverend Ralph Abernathy, second-in-command to King, the stout mustachioed joker, the roaring Southern preacher of fire and brimstone and fun, looked to his leader for guidance. The Reverend Jackson, who wouldn't wear a tie for anybody, the young man from Chicago who was in charge of Operation Breadbasket, the uncommon common man in the group, thought he could bring the adolescents into line. Lee, always looking for signs of danger to King, said, "Things look shitty."

The early afternoon was now sunny and warming; the chill had left the breeze. A half dozen blocks behind the march, the broad muddy reaches of the Mississippi tried to capture the sunbeams and, having lost, picked up the shadow of the new bridge to Arkansas on the other shore. The march was on Main Street now and Lee looked very unhappy indeed. He said to Jim Lawson, "We're pulling out. We denounce this march." A sports store named York Arms had its front windows broken; blacks walked in on the shattered glass, and police began to swing clubs.

Scalps were split, and the blood of blacks ran red down the sides of their faces. The Reverend Samuel "Billy" Kyles grabbed a radio from a black marshal. A monotonous voice kept asking: "Permission to break up the march. Permission to break up the march. Permission. . . ."

Permission was granted from police hadquarters, and the police formed ranks in front of the line of march. In a moment, as Billy Kyles fled down to a street corner and leaned panting against a telephone pole, the marchers had reversed themselves and were fleeing in the opposite direction. The police, who had grown up believing that the good black man is the one who knows "his place," struck out with clubs and tear gas, hurled high over the fleeing mob. Dr. King, the believer, the trusting man, said, "Bernard, what do you think?" King was frightened, King was shocked; but he didn't want it said that he had left the line of march under fire. He required someone to force him to leave. Abernathy stood, braving the jostling, and said, "I don't know." Lee was positive. He clenched the arm of the preacher tighter until the sleeve was bunched. "I know," he said. "If they're breaking glass back there, the only next thing

is for the police to take action to protect property and, Doctor, we have
to pull out."

Bernard Lee didn't wait for an answer. He yanked King forward and
down a side street. The screams of the hurt became a mass roar, like
flames licking an old tenement. King appeared to have momentarily lost
control. His features were slack with horror. He followed the pulling
arm, but his flowered tie was askew; his jacket twisted to one side. His
breath was coming in gasps as they trotted away from the frightfulness.
The belly belch of tear gas guns was clear. The few ministers who
remained screamed, with arms high, "Go back. Go back to the church."
Mrs. Kyles was standing on a sidewalk watching. A young policeman
approached her and her child. He pulled a gun. The only thing she could
think of to say was: "You'd better know what you're doing with that
thing." His hands were shaking, and he stared at her, and all the fear of
the white South for the black man was in his eyes.

Kyles rescued his family and, with other divines, got some of the
crowd back to Clayborne Temple. The people stood shaking and crying,
and the police walked around them with guns drawn. Some picked up
the bleeding and those who were tear-gassed. A march leader phoned
police headquarters breathlessly and said, "Get the police away from
Clayborne Temple and we'll handle this thing. Get them the hell out of
here." The police were ordered to surround the area at a distance. As
they began to leave, the Invaders threw pop bottles and rocks. The cops
returned and shot tear gas through the doors of the church.

The blacks were badly frightened by the police. They had no way of
knowing that the police, who had never experienced anything like this,
were no less afraid. The mere size of the black crowd, unarmed, could in
concert, have overwhelmed the officers of the law. The ambulances from
John Gaston Hospital and St. Joseph's were making round trips to pick
up the injured. The police went into a black market called the Big M,
beat up the owner behind the counter, and then beat his customers.
There was rage enough for everyone. Black shops, no matter what products they sold, were ordered to close at once.

Martin Luther King was still trotting behind Bernard Lee when Lee
saw a car with two black women in it. "Please," he begged. "Stop. Stop.
This is Dr. Martin Luther King. Please stop." The car stopped. King
stumbled into the back seat with Abernathy and Lee. "Take us to the
Rivermont Motel," Lee said softly. "You know, the Holiday Inn on the
river." The women looked back at the figure with his chin on his chest
and said nothing. They drove him to the motel.

The riot didn't stop, and now the firing of pistols was heard and people ran. With sundown, Memphis became quiet. The toll was 60 persons injured, 280 arrested, and 1 dead. The one killed was a black boy who, when cornered by police in a dead-end alley, held his hands above his head and was shot to death.

Billy Kyles took his wife and child up a side street, got in the family car and drove home. Few minds were functioning properly. Some remembered the previous month, when King had promised a crowd of 15,000 roaring cheering blacks: "We will have a march and a one-day work stoppage. I can promise you that Memphis will not function that day." Thousands of blacks milled about the church grounds, trying to decide what it was that had destroyed the day, what exactly could have made Mayor Loeb look good and the faithful look bad. Some shook their heads dolefully and said: "It was Dr. King. Nobody else. He led us in a violent march, and that gave the police an excuse to break us." Some said, "It was the teen-agers. Nobody asked them, but they broke into our ranks and ran riot through the stores." Others said, "He ran, didn't he? That man ran."

Henry Loeb now had the ideal excuse for asking Governor Buford Ellington of Tennessee to send 4,000 national guardsmen to protect the city from riot and flame. Ellington not only agreed, but placed an additional 4,000 troops on alert.

The police, assessing damage, counted 155 stores with windows smashed; about a third had had their contents stolen. Of those arrested, forty-one were charged with looting. Lyndon Johnson, shocked at the news coming onto the White House Telex machine, phoned to offer federal assistance to the city. He was in the awkward position of pushing fresh civil rights legislation through Congress and, at the same time, making a televised growling announcement: "We will not let violence and lawlessness take over the country." A few black ministers issued statements claiming that the police had "overreacted," but the television tapes showed clearly that the teen-agers, many armed with sticks, had run through the ranks of marchers to smash windows on the other side, while the marchers closed the distance between ranks so that law enforcement officers could not get through.

A sundown to sunrise curfew was imposed at once. Sniper shots were heard at the W. C. Handy Park at 9 P.M. National guardsmen walked the streets in groups, carbines at the ready. In New York City, Congressman Adam Clayton Powell referred to the leader of the march as

"Martin Loser King." Roy Wilkins, head of the NAACP, advised King to cancel his Poor People's March on Washington because it was obvious that he could no longer lead peaceful rallies. Members of the Black Panthers, SNCC, and other militant organizations said that Memphis proved that the day of nonviolence was over. Had King not proved beyond argument, in Birmingham and Albany, Georgia, that where he led in peaceful piety, violence and death followed? If there was anything more disastrous than the Memphis march, it was the opening he gave to his black as well as white adversaries to reject his presence in their communities. All of those who envied or despised this man now had a legitimate excuse to spurn him.

The shiny car cooled in front of the Rivermont. King was in a room on an upper floor, bent forward in a chair. His elbows on his knees, he studied the plain rug on the floor. Members of his staff came in quietly, whispered the latest news, and left noiselessly. King was in shock. Now and then he shook his head from side to side, as though he did not believe what he was thinking.

Abernathy, the optimist, phoned his wife, Juanita, in Atlanta and said that everything was going to be all right, no matter what she heard on radio or television. King arose, glancing angrily from silent face to silent face, and walked out on the balcony with Bernard Lee. "First of all," said his bodyguard twin, "you should come back to Memphis. That's first of all. You have to come back here to prove that you can lead a nonviolent march."

"Yes," the minister said vacantly. "Yes, we must come back. Nonviolence as a concept is now on trial."

"We should have had some intelligence work done before we came here," Lee said. "We walked right into this thing."

"We're coming back soon," Martin King said grimly. "We're coming back, and it's going to be as nonviolent as the old days."

Bits and pieces of the ugly puzzle began to take shape for him. The boys from Hamilton High School had fought the police with rocks and bottles before the march started. The Invaders had planned their strategy better than he had his; they had walked along the sidewalks on each side of the line of march until they were ready to attack. Others lifted placards which proclaimed: DAMN LOEB—BLACK POWER IS HERE! Many middle-aged marchers arrived too early and began drinking at 10 A.M. The police carried cans of Mace.

King returned to his room. No newspaper was going to blame Jim

Lawson or Billy Kyles or anybody but King. Jesse Jackson, standing in rolled-up denims, and Ralph Abernathy, silent and staring, heard Martin Luther King say that maybe he should withdraw from all public appearances for a period of meditation and fasting, as Mohandas Gandhi had done in India. Perhaps if he said he was about to fast "unto death," the black people would forswear violence. If he did this and was sincere about it, King might unite the Rap Browns, the Stokely Carmichaels, the Whitney Youngs, the Roy Wilkinses, even the Eldridge Cleavers.

He spoke like a man in a trance. No matter that the leaders assured him that the police had done more damage today than the blacks; it didn't matter who started it and who finished it—the onus was on Martin Luther King, Jr. He knew it.

His people, he heard, were mocking him for living in a white motel on the banks of the Mississippi. Was he now so rich, so affluent, that he preached black and lived white? A man down in the parking lot sent an anonymous note. "History," it read, "has passed you by."

His friends, his staff advised him to pay no heed to criticism. The thing was done and over. It couldn't be undone. Partial penance was to put on a black silk jacket and go down into the lobby and face the press. The victory smile of many marches would not be on his face. He had lost a small battle at a time when he had to win, in a place that didn't matter. The big thing in his mind was Resurrection City in Washington, and there, with the white dome of the Capitol standing tall at the far end of the Mall, he would again preach peace and civil rights and he would be the hero of old.

He took the elevator down. The lobby and the grounds were thick with grinning hostile bees. He said that he would issue a statement, but he wasn't going to respond to questions. The lights were as bright as high noon in a desert; the whirling ball-point pens danced like dervishes.

"I ask you to draw a distinction," he said in his slow, deep tone, "between the conduct of the marchers and the misbehavior of the militant interlopers. I thought"—he looked up from a chair with gloom locked in his gaze—"I thought the march itself was basically a very dignified one." Then he altered direction and stated that he was disappointed, deeply regretful. Another turn. "There are consultations scheduled in Washington regarding the Poor People's Campaign, but I am going to delay them to sort out the troubles in the black community of Memphis."

It was confused and confusing. Newspaper reporters wanted to ask questions, but Dr. King excused himself. The holy man was making a disorderly retreat. When he returned to his room, he said, "I want to meet with the leaders of those Invaders in the morning. Set it up for me."

Abernathy was worried. "We ought to get out of here," he said.

King paced the floor. He appeared to be calm, but desolation was there, too. "See if you can get us on a noon flight tomorrow or maybe in the afternoon." A phone call came in from Atlanta; he took it in the bedroom. Coretta's voice, musical and sweet, came to him. She had seen the headlines and watched the riots on television. She tried to comfort her husband, but Dr. King was beyond logic. He kept telling her not to worry about it; but he knew she would, and both voices were unconvincing. He returned to the living room and held his hand up as though to stave off Abernathy's concern. "Don't worry," he said. "I'll pull out of it."

He asked the Memphis group to prepare a release at once that Dr. Martin Luther King, Jr., would lead a peaceful march in Memphis within a week. Abernathy knew that King did not want to come back to Memphis. So did Kyles and Lee. And yet, each of them understood that it was necessary, it was urgent, that Loeb and Ellington be shown that King was still king.

He walked the floor through the early hours of the morning. Physical violence was sickening to Martin Luther King. Whenever he was arrested, he went along not only quietly, but meekly and with fear. In such cases, he permitted personal abuse, such as being lifted off his feet by his coat collar or having his face held down against a precinct desk, without protest.

In the morning, four timid young men presented themselves. Dr. King was shaving. He used a powder, instead of shaving cream. It was a depilatory of such obnoxious odor that it became a rude staff joke. Bernard Lee often asked, through the closed bathroom door, "My God, Doc. You shaving or having a bowel movement?" King asked Ralph Abernathy to go down to the lobby and take care of the morning press conference. He wanted a firsthand talk with the leaders of the Invaders.

The Reverend Mr. Abernathy was willing, but not happy. For a long time, he had been the number two man in the hierarchy of the Southern Christian Leadership Conference, but the number was much more remote than it seemed. People who came to meet or listen to Dr. King wanted no substitute. The round eyes of Abernathy saw disappointment whenever he entered a room. In his own church, he could shout his Come-to-Jesus amens in thunderclaps, and avert his face slightly, look purposefully sly, and say something so funny that it rocked the congregation with laughter. He was a lifter of spirits, a joker, a man who adored Martin Luther King, Jr.

King sat with the youths. He looked at them, but they didn't want to look at him. They felt respect for this great leader of their people, but they said that he was "off the rails" as far as those nonviolent goals were concerned. Quietly, King asked them to speak up. A young man named Smith was the leader, and he said that, first of all, they wanted Dr. King to know that they were sorry about yesterday. Very sorry. They knew what he wanted; but he didn't know what they wanted, and that's how the trouble had started.

One said that none of the reverends would listen to them. After all, they represented the young people. They had a right to be heard. Long before King arrived in Memphis, they had fought the Black Establishment. The Black Establishment? "Yes, sir. All those old kinkies." A month earlier, the older group invited two Invaders to become members of the steering committee. How long did that last? One meeting. That's all. Just one meeting. An Invader had stood at the meeting to say that the black garbage men were really hurting because they had struck, and they represented 90 percent of all sanitation drivers and helpers, but that Mayor Loeb had white drivers taking garbage from white homes. "We have to stop them trucks," the Invader had said.

That had ended the alliance between old and young. The steering committee had dropped the militants at once. One teen-ager said that the Invaders, unlike their parents, did not have cars or money. The four of them sat looking at Dr. King. He asked them if an automobile and a little money would mean that much to them. They beamed their smiles at him. The black leader began to sense the distillation of bribery. He said that he had been a growing boy once, and he knew how important that first car was. The smiles deepened.

"Well," he said, "I want you to pledge that you and your followers will either practice nonviolence or stay away from the demonstrations." They promised. "I will try to get you fellows a car," he said, "and a little money." He said he couldn't promise much, but he would keep his promise if they kept theirs. "You don't have to follow my philosophy," he said, almost with sorrow, "but we've got to stick together and follow the same tactics."

In the lobby of the hotel, Dr. King burst in on the press conference. While still walking toward the group, he frowned and growled: "You know my best friend, Ralph Abernathy, I'm sure. Ladies and gentle-

men. . . ." Ralph had been talking. He was surprised at King's attitude, because he usually exhibited impeccable manners and insisted on a
high-blown kind of protocol, where the lowest in rank introduces the
next highest and so on up to himself.

He did not wait for cameras or reporters to adjust. He looked like a
stocky young bull confronting the whole bullring. "We're coming back
next week," he said at once. This time, he declared, the police would not
stop the march. The march would be nonviolent all the way. The SCLC
was about to open the eyes of Memphis to the true plight of the sanitation workers. If the march did not achieve this, he said with finger
jabbing the air, there would be more demonstrations. A reporter spoke
up and asked if it was possible, after yesterday's events, to stage a
nonviolent march. "Once a riot takes place," Dr. King snapped, "it is
very difficult to bring reason to the situation." He was asked the cause of
the riot yesterday. "I was completely caught in a miscalculation," he
said.

His group had had no hand in the plans for the demonstration, he
said. "None of us was aware that there had been talk of violence among
the youthful militants." This would not happen again, he could assure
everyone. He was ahead in this game of editorial thrust and riposte, but
King began to weasel. "It is not my fault," he said, "that there was a
breakdown in communication between young militants and the Negro
leadership." At once, he seemed to realize that these words would not
endear him to the Invaders or even to older fighters. "We cannot ex-
clude the possibility of civil disobedience," he said. "Increased militancy
is necessary because we have learned in the last few years how deeply
rooted racism is in America. . . .

"Riots are here," he almost shouted, waving his arms. "They are part
of the ugly atmosphere of our society. If they take place, they aren't my
responsibility." His clever and often calculated words seemed to have
deserted Dr. King in his anger and frustration. He was guaranteeing a
nonviolent march, then admitting the possibility of civil disobedience,
disavowing any responsibility for a possible second riot, and blaming all
of it on the blacks of Memphis and the aura of violence throughout
White America. "Our government and most white people have done
nothing to remove the conditions that produce riots."

He was breathing heavily. "Even if we don't have a single march," he
said irritably, "most experts agree that this summer will be worse than
last." The voice began to soften, almost in exhaustion Dr. King
solemnly assured his audience that "I am a riot preventer. My position

is to take the energies of potential rioters and move them into the field of creative protest. Anyway," he said, "this will disrupt and change society much more swiftly than street fighting."

Abernathy took him by the arm. He was grinning. They left the lobby, and when the elevator door closed, he grabbed King by the shoulder and squeezed. "You know," he said, "in all these years we've been together, I knew you had some lion in you. I just knew it. But I never saw it until just now." King was not in a mood for compliments. He asked Abernathy to summon some of the local people for lunch. Then they would get on the plane for home.

The lunch was almost a monologue. It was served in King's room. For the first time in his public career, he was unhappy with everyone— including himself. These men, who had pleaded with him to come to Memphis, had betrayed him consciously or unconsciously. He had walked into this inferno bowing and smiling, locking arms in the front ranks with the local people.

Now he knew the insurmountables of Memphis. Now, too late. The Invaders were a fraction of the opposition. Immature and easily won over. "Loeb—now there's a man to watch. Hell, he's tougher than Bull Connor was in Birmingham." The police acted like police dogs waiting to be unleashed. He couldn't even muster a majority of the blacks in Memphis to help their own garbage men. They were sitting at home, watching television, waiting to see what would happen. If it was trouble, they were not in it. If the march won justice for workers, they wanted their share of it. King knew he was regarded by some as a "trouble-maker." Governor Ellington was openly training special units of the National Guard to quell riots. Someone at the table said that this was because of the trouble in North Nashville last year.

Perhaps. But what gave the governor the right to proclaim: "There are people who would like to see riots, and they are not all in the North Nashville area. Martin Luther King is training three thousand people to start riots, and when we say that we are going to train the guard to protect the lives of people and their property, there is a big hullabaloo about it."

King wasn't training anybody for rioting. He had been publicly disowned and disavowed by the Black Panthers, SNCC, members of the Urban League, even segments of the mild NAACP. His own organization, the SCLC, was beginning to splinter in some cities. These people had believed in him and his mission and his methods, but thirteen years of token results is a long, long time.

He said good-bye cheerfully. "We'll be back," he kept saying, shaking hands. "We'll be back." The staff in Atlanta would be in touch with Memphis, and if the march were to take place on Friday, April 5, King would probably arrive on Wednesday, the third, for private consultations and public church rallies. Abernathy and Bernard Lee got into the car with King, and the driver swung along the edge of the Mississippi to get to the airport.

The smile died. "Maybe," Dr. King said for the first time in his life, "maybe we ought to let violence run its course." No one responded. The car sped through the late bronze haze, and there was peace inside. No one disagreed with him; these were the close disciples. They would rise to glory together, or they would fall to oblivion—or worse, even death—together.

The plane left a little late. In Atlanta, Coretta King received a phone call that it would arrive at 6:20 P.M. That meant that he would be home about 7, and no one had to explain to her that he was going to need all the comforting, all the commiseration a woman can give. She was ready.

Sometimes on a flight between Memphis and Atlanta, the city of Birmingham can be seen shining in the sun far off to the right. Even if King could have seen Birmingham in the distance, he could not have distinguished buildings and people. He could not have seen the slender smiling white man entering the Aeromarine Supply Company at 5701 Birmingham Airport Highway. The Smiler was there to make several purchases, among them a two-by-seven riflescope. James Earl Ray was anxious to look at Dr. King through that scope.

It was dark when the jet turned to its final leg and flashed on its moon-monster eyes to find the runway at Atlanta. The three men walked down the ramp and through the corridor. Abernathy said, "How about a movie later?" The three bucked the tide of transients and reached the parking lot. "There's your car," King said, pointing to a 1955 Ford. "If you'll just take me home now, we'll go to the movie later." In the car, he changed his mind. "How about going over to the health club?" This was a part of the Young Men's Christian Association. No, Abernathy said. He'd drive King to the health club, but he'd rather hurry right home to show himself to his wife. Just telling her over the phone that he was all right, unhurt, was not enough for her. She was the kind who had to see. "I'll go home," Abernathy said, "and then I'll join you at the health club."

King, nude, sat alone in the 145-degree heat of the steam room, perspiration dripping from his eyebrows, and this gave him more time to dwell upon the depressing aspects of his life. He wrapped a big towel around his middle, cinched it, and phoned Abernathy. "I don't feel up to a movie," he said. "I don't want to be with anybody but you and Juanita and Coretta. We'll come out to your house, and I'll bring some fish."

A taxicab brought King to his spacious home on Sunset Avenue, and as always, when he burst through the front door, the words were the same: "Where's Coretta?" He wanted to tell her what had happened, but he didn't want to relive it. This was Atlanta—big, safe, home. Memphis was a light-year away, a wicked comet in flames. He talked anyway. The story came in bursts. Coretta King sat by his side and listened and consoled.

They drove over to the Abernathy home, and as they walked into the house, Dr. King began to sniff. His nose twitched, and he smiled. "Soul food, man!" he said. "Soul food!" Juanita Abernathy knew that old-time sharecropper food was really his favorite. It was also her husband's, but it required so much boiling in the kitchen that in recent years she had seldom prepared it. Coming up were collard greens, a casserole of boiled pigs' feet, pigs' ears and pigs' tails, and, to tantalize the tongue, croaker fish.

The mood began to rise. His aide Lilie Hunter and Bernard Lee were also there. King phoned his father and mother to tell them that he was home safe and would probably see them the next day. He called the late workers at the office and ordered them to set up a staff meeting of the Southern Christian Leadership Conference in his study at the Ebenezer Baptist Church for 10 A.M. He ate. He teased Juanita Abernathy about her scrumptious cooking; Abernathy felt happily silly and made everybody laugh. The sentences began to lapse into the patois of the Southern black, which consists of regional slang terms abutting one another so closely that, to an outsider, it is like a foreign tongue.

To the black, there is a special warmth in it, a communion, a relief of tension. This is the time when the intelligent black permits himself to refer to other blacks as "niggers," using a white man's term without intending offense any more than an Irish group, referring to one of their own, uses the derogatory word "harp." The conversation moved into the den.

The first pale streaks of light were touching the spires of downtown Atlanta when the Kings got home. He was sleepy, but as promised, he had "come out of it all right." He would get little rest before the morning meeting, but the darkness in his mind had dissipated, and Mrs. King could sense, without mentioning it, that her man was once more in command of himself and his career. It was a bright morning indeed.

Business seemed always to be good at Robert E. Wood's Aeromarine Supply Company. His sports goods shop was spacious, and his prices were reasonable. It appeared to be an odd choice to set up shop just off the big Birmingham Airport with the shriek of jet engines forever rising to a crescendo and then diminishing like summer thunder. Mr. Wood did well amid the noise and the traffic. He sold almost anything a sportsman might need from a length of strut wire for a small private plane on up to boat accessories, tent pegs, and rifles.

Birmingham is big and rigid. It works hard to draw outside business, but it declines outside advice. The men speak quietly and hospitably, but the alien from another state detects suspicion in the smile. The city wears a faded scent of the Old South, but between Tarrant City and Bessemer, Birmingham is modern and industrious, catering to the needs of Alabama all the way from Decatur to Mobile. Years ago black residents called it "Big Bummingem." It still is.

Sportsmen were in and out of Mr. Wood's store all day on Friday, March 29. It was the beginning of the weekend, and the cold air had begun to soften. This caused camping equipment to be dusted and brought down from attics, hunting boots to be surveyed, and sportsmen to become shoppers. The Smiler came in quietly, almost timidly. He looked around until he saw a rack of rifles and approached U. L. Baker, the only clerk without a customer.

The Smiler said that he wanted to look over some rifles. Baker asked what kind. The customer said he didn't really know. He was going to go hunting with his brother, and he thought they'd be after deer. Could be up around the Sand Mountains or over to Arkadelphia. Donald Wood, son of the owner, heard part of the conversation, but kept walking to assist other clerks. He was shown several types, and the Smiler hefted them as though he understood their varied uses and spoke laconically now and then about deer. He excited no interest in anyone except Baker and Wood, who felt that this man knew very little about rifles, ammunition, and deer.

He wasn't an easy man to serve. He took his time. John De Shazo, another customer, came into buy a gun case, and even though he had to wait, he fell into a conversation with the deer hunter, who said he might hunt deer with his brother in Wisconsin. The geography had been altered. Mr. De Shazo watched the Smiler finally settle on a Remington 700, caliber .243 Winchester. He asked if he could have twenty rounds of .243 ammunition, an amount which might last an hour or two in good hunting territory, and—oh, yes, he wanted a scope mounted on it, Baker showed him a few types, and the Smiler decided on a two-by-seven Redfield and asked that it be mounted.

No gunsmith wants the labor of mounting and calibrating a gunsight until he knows how he's going to be paid, because it requires time. The Smiler said that he would pay in cash. A two-by-seven scope means that, by looking through it at the cross hairs, the target has a narrow side-to-side range but is magnified seven times in size. A deer, for example, at a distance of 250 feet would appear to be about 36 feet away.

The customer gave his name as Harvey Lowmeyer. Donald Wood looked him over and decided that Aeromarine Supply had a novice on its hands, but one does not counsel customers unless they ask for it. What he saw was a small man wearing a plain brown suit with a plain face, one who appeared to be perpetually amused at something. He had a Southern accent, but Mr. Wood knew that it was not Alabama. It had a slow, sweet drawl which matched the grin.

He didn't blanch when he was told that the rifle, with its shiny walnut stock, would come to $134.95; the scope was priced at $74.60, the convex metal base for the scope and the rings to hold it were $20.32, and the little box of cartridges $4.65. This, with a tax of $14.07, came to $248.59, a lot of money for an unemployed man who wasn't sure what state he would be hunting in.

He gave his address as 1907 South Eleventh Street, Birmingham, Alabama. It is remarkable that the Smiler could remember some of his lies. His habit was to lie most of the time, and he was lying now, even though it wasn't necessary. Usually, when he visited Birmingham, James Earl Ray rented a room at 2608 Highland Avenue. That day he was registered at the TraveLodge Motel, 821 South Twentieth Street as Eric Galt, of 5533 Hollywood Boulevard, Los Angeles, California. At the moment, he was not Ray, not Galt, but Lowmeyer. His fingerprints were on every rifle he handled.

The cash was paid, the gun and ammunition were dropped on the floor behind the front seat of a white Mustang, and the Smiler backed away from the store and disappeared. A short time later he phoned. Donald Wood answered. The voice said he was "Harvey Lowmeyer—remember?—the man who purchased the Remington?" Well, it turned out that the rifle was not heavy enough, and could he come back and

exchange it? Mr. Wood said it was too late in the day, but if he would
return the firearm in the morning, with the ammunition, he'd see what
he could do.

Saturday at 9 A.M. the Smiler returned. He was apologetic about the
exchange of rifles but said that his brother figured that this one wasn't
heavy enough. This time the novice knew exactly what he wanted. It was
as though, between his ignorance of yesterday and his knowledge of this
morning, someone had ordered him to ask for a type of gun which must
have been unknown to him the day before. "Let me see a Remington
760," he said. "30.06 caliber." Wood had the gun but said that there
would be an additional cost. "Don't matter," the Smiler said.

He was shown the rifle, heavier to level against the eye. "I can't adjust
the scope right now," the clerk said. "How about three o'clock?" Mr.
Ray returned in the white Mustang on time. He sighted through the
scope and turned his smile up. The box of .243 cartridges was placed on
the counter. It was exchanged for twenty Remington-Peters shells. Each
weighed twice as much as the other bullets. The new ones would leave
the muzzle at 2,670 feet per second, about three and a half times the
speed of sound. James Earl Ray had something that would stop an
elephant.

The baked red brick of the Ebenezer Baptist Church has been reaching toward God since 1886. It is old without decay, ancient with honor,
aloof from all except the 4,000 blacks who walk or drive down Auburn
Avenue in Atlanta in their Sunday best to sing, to pray, to listen, to
believe. The vaulted interior gives an impression of gleaming mahogany
and cathedral windows. The carpet, which steps up to the altar, is plain
and well kept. The huge basement room can hold services for an additional 1,500 while Pastor Martin Luther King, Sr., is at the pulpit on the
main floor.

When the old man spoke, he faced a big white clock below the rim of
the choir loft in back, and its silent face told him when he was going on
too long. Behind him were red draperies, rich hanging and slightly ajar,
to show Jesus in prayer at Gethsemane. Ebenezer Baptist was never a
"fun" church, where parishioners could stand and shout and stomp. It
was, as far as history can disclose, a place where everyone was expected
to walk in humility, where collection plates were never passed, where
committees were elected to assess the monies required by the church,
where the preacher would go to a funeral home—if requested—to pray
over the body of a sinner who never attended church. All the pastors

were Fundamentalists; Jonah and the whale were as real as the apple in the Garden of Eden. Women with white hats conducted Bible classes for children; men in black suits placed the books of psalms in the holders behind each pew; Ebenezer maintained an air of dignity in the world of a black section of Atlanta where cheap grocery stores and summer flies abounded.

Many years ago Martin Luther King, Jr.'s maternal grandfather was pastor of that church. Pastor Williams was succeeded by Martin Luther King, Sr. It was the elder King's constant prayer that his sons—Martin, Jr., and A.D.—would go to Morehouse College as he had, become ordained, and become the righteous, God-fearing man he was. Neither of them made the grade. The brilliant son arced the daylight skies like a dark comet; A.D. wanted a wife, a swimming pool, a car, a church of his own, and no criticism from his father.

As co-pastor, Martin, Jr., had his own study in the newer wing of the church, an administrative building of pale brick with a walkway into the old church. There he called a meeting of his personal staff and the officers of the Southern Christian Leadership Conferences at 10 A.M. Saturday, March 30, 1968. In addition, he asked Jim Lawson, the man from Memphis, to be present.

The participants picked up chairs and set them around the smooth dark desk and the high-backed leather chair. Jesse Jackson lounged against a wall. King was late. The men chatted, some speaking softly, enunciating the options; others were loud in denouncing Memphis and what it had done to the movement. No one polled an opinion, although Ralph Abernathy was sitting in his friend's big chair, trying to channel the dialogue of frustration into something which might please the Reverend Dr. King when he arrived.

He walked in with Bernard Lee, glancing at the faces with barely a greeting. He tossed his automobile keys onto the green blotter and took a chair next to Ralph. The cherubic face scowled. This time—perhaps the first time—King was sufficiently angry to flog his friends. The Reverend Mr. Abernathy took a look and quietly rose from the big leather chair, motioning King to switch with him.

"Mike," said Abernathy, "sit where you belong." "Mike," of course, was not King's name. Blacks in the South often use names other than their real ones. For example, King always called Abernathy David. It is a part of the black Southern culture to assume special names, different names, names they affectionately give to one another as a show of special friendship. These names are never used by anyone else.

King sat in his proper chair, and once he had attained a deafening silence in the room, he began cutting and shredding the staff with words. The men accepted the rebukes. The staff had failed miserably in not preparing Memphis for the march. The entire matter had been left up to Jim Lawson, the SCLC's man in the town, and he had not been up to it. Dr. King had seen on television what he had not seen leading the march: the violence, the looting, the swinging nightsticks. It was wrong—all of it. He had read the newspapers, too, and there were dozens of editorials demanding that he cancel the Poor People's March—the blacks could not control themselves in Memphis; they were sure to make a shambles of the capital of the United States.

The men in the room kept their silence. "This is no longer a race war," King shouted. "It's a class war." The word "war" was anathema to him, and now he was using it as though he were admitting, unconsciously perhaps, that the struggle for quality was never intended to be nonviolent. His deep voice rambled on, sometimes falling from one unconnected thought to another. Suddenly he began to turn those penetrating brown eyes from one man to another, demanding to know: "What do you think, Jesse? . . . What do you think, Jim? . . . What do you think, Lee?" He did not seem to be interested in their opinions because he barely listened before calling the next name.

The responsibility was theirs. King had not failed them; they had failed him. His anger and his hurt reached a peak when he said solemnly, "Before we go to Washington, something has to happen within this staff. This staff," he said, pointing a finger at front row center, "is not as spiritually and intellectually involved as it should be." He said he was considering not returning to Memphis and calling off the Poor People's March in the face of "the rising tide of hate in America."

The president of SCLC stood up. He left without saying good-bye. Abernathy followed him. He didn't like the way King was acting. "What is wrong? What is bothering you?" he said in the corridor.

King paused, looking at his car keys. "I'll be all right. I just need to think. I'll tell you about it some other time."

The men he left behind felt that they had been placed on trial. It was up to them to draw up a plan of action, one guaranteed to restore the prestige of the group. Some, like Hosea Williams and Jesse Jackson, were willing to acknowledge King's leadership but were troubled about nonviolence as a doctrine. It was inequitable to expect peaceable blacks to march in ranks, only to be beaten by violent police. Possibly the movement was dying because it was committed to nonviolence and those who confronted the demonstrators knew that they did not have to fear retaliation. Morally, it was wrong to strike first, but what was wrong about defending oneself against clubs and guns? Some of the marches had the aspects of lynchings.

The road to Washington was closed. The only way it could be opened was by marching through Memphis again. No one appeared to be excited at the prospect, because Memphis was not intended, at any time, to be more than a gesture to Jim Lawson and the sanitation workers.

Slowly, inexorably, the staff worked toward Memphis the next week, Washington after that. The decision would have to be ratified by King, but Abernathy moved ahead as though he already had it. Three men—Jim Orange, Hosea Williams, and Jesse Jackson—were delegated to be in Memphis the following day, Sunday, March 31. They were ordered to work with Lawson and to call meetings of all the group leaders who would be in the parade and to make certain, above all, that their people would be under control. The Reverend Andrew Young, who had political ambitions, would arrive on Monday. Dr. King and the Reverend Mr. Abernathy would be in Memphis on Tuesday.

To stop the complaints about their staying at a white man's hotel, Abernathy suggested that Lawson find a nice black one. "The Lorraine," he said. "It's a nice place."

The logistics were worked out. Suggestions were made and noted. An élan began to pervade the room. One man suggested that Ralph call Dr. King back at once. "Tell him come back and see the esprit de corps here—the oneness." The call was put in, and King said he would come right over. He drove back, but he did not get to the room. The men waited. And waited. A call was put into SCLC headquarters. He wasn't there. Another call went to his home. Mrs. King said he had left some time before. Where could he be? His officers sat and waited.

A girl distributing mail walked in and said that Dr. King was downstairs in the hall talking to his father. The elder King was pleading with his son not to go back to Memphis, not to go to Washington. "Daddy" King had a way of staring through shiny bifocals so that he didn't appear to blink. Once upon a time he could have spanked this little boy, but he had lost him in a spiral of world renown, and now all he could say was that all his life he had found church work, the saving of souls, to be the most important of all.

He was worried about Martin's personal safety, and so was his mother. Hadn't Martin done enough for the blacks? Couldn't others hold the bright torch? No, and no, and no. The young pastor loved his father, but he had outgrown him, outgrown this solid old church with its ancient promises of happiness and equality in a life hereafter.

When he rejoined the staff, King reminded the men that he had been invited to preach the next day in the big Washington Cathedral. He had promised Dean Francis Sayre that he would be there, and King hadn't prepared a sermon. Someone said timidly: "Make it on hope."

Abernathy said, "Mike, while you were gone, the Holy Spirit came into this room."

The plan was submitted to him with enthusiasm, and he listened gravely, nodding assent. "I want the entire staff in Memphis by Wednesday"—he looked at the calendar on his desk—"the third of April. And we're going to hold church meetings at night and meet the people and talk to them. The march will take place on Friday, April fifth. Any objections?"

There were none. This time he thanked everyone as he left and said he had a great deal of work to do before going to Washington. He met his longtime personal aide Lilie Hunter on the way out. "Man," he said to her, "Birmingham and Bull Connor was one thing—this man Loeb is something else."

Surely it must have occurred to King that even if the next march were peaceful, the mayor's Police Department could provoke blacks into an act of violence, and this in turn would lead to the plea on the radios: "Permission to break up the march. Permission. . . ." Loeb could afford to sit back in innocence as the protector of persons and property and, knowing that the Southern Christian Leadership Conference was now at its weakest—in disrepute with blacks as well as whites—could break up the march and break the spine of the Movement, without leaving his office in City Hall.

That Saturday night King, Abernathy, and Lee flew from Atlanta to Washington. There wasn't much conversation. The doctor worked over his notes on the tray before him, crossing out phrases and substituting others. He was fond of figures of speech to illustrate points in his address, and his tendency was to overdo them.

The next morning was Passion Sunday. The National Cathedral was filled, mostly with the well-nourished white faces of Episcopalians when Dean Sayre greeted the little party in the sacristy. King was assisted in robing in dark cassock and white surplice. It was prestige of the noblest type for a black preacher from the Deep South to be invited to deliver a sermon in the holy bastion of the Establishment.

He spoke well, and his audience gave him complete attention. His eyes flickered across the faces of the people who made decisions for the nation. This was no place for "down-home" talk; his theme was going to be racial equality.

"The aims of this movement," he said, "can never be fulfilled until we eradicate the last vestige of racial injustice." In time, he got around to the Poor People's March on Washington. He was not addressing his audience now; he was taking dead aim on the White House of Lyndon Johnson and Congress. "This will not be a dramatic gesture," he said, "but a demand for long-overdue compensation." The slow booming voice echoed off the lofty vault of the cathedral. Three or four times Dr. King repeated the assertion: "It will be an orderly, nonviolent demonstration.

"Many times," he said, "I have been advised to slow down, that time would correct evils. But time is neutral," he said. The Poor People's March would "call attention to the gap between promises and fulfillment—to make the invisible visible. The seat of power of this nation is unmoved by the plight of the poor, so the poor would come in person." Congress, he was sure, "would not move unless confronted with demands in a massive show of determination." It was, in essence, a fair sermon, but it tried too hard to be statesmanlike and not enough to be specific. King might have displayed enormous courage had he stated what he must have known to be true: that he had been seduced by invitations to the White House by three Presidents, who, in his estimation, gave him and other black leaders sympathetic hearings but did little—except in the case of Johnson—to ram civil rights legislation down the throat of Congress.

Actually, the sermon was a failure. King had doled out a basketful of generalities—worst of all, old generalities—and he had not pinned down or indicted any of the leaders of the country. But King flew home to Atlanta content that it was good. The evening was spent in the gray reflective gloom of the television set. He and Coretta listened to President Johnson's address—Vietnam, domestic tensions—and King slouched and clasped his fingers across his waist. At the end of the speech the President announced that he would not seek reelection and would decline if nominated. The shock was stunning.

The reaction of the black pastor was hard to understand. He decided to cancel the Poor People's March. It was a way out of a high-risk operation and he could concentrate on Memphis.

He phoned Abernathy and reminded him that in 1964 he had ordered a moratorium on racial demonstrations to "elect Johnson." He had now decided that immediately after a peaceful victory in Memphis he would announce that the March on Washington was no longer necessary; the Southern Christian Leadership Conference would announce that it would wait and see whether the Democrats nominated a McCarthy, a Humphrey, or a Kennedy and whether the Republicans nominated a Rockefeller, a Reagan, or a Nixon. His personal choice would be Humphrey. The Vice President, King felt, was free of the shackles of Vietnam and domestic strife imposed upon him by Lyndon Johnson— Hubert Humphrey would be his own man.

The man he would least like to see nominated and elected was the Republican Richard Nixon. He told Abernathy that if they staged the Poor People's March and it turned into a riotous mob, this alone would compel the Republicans to nominate Nixon, a reactionary. Abernathy was not to spread the word to the staff; Dr. King would do it himself the next weekend.

He was certain that he was a kingmaker; like most chiefs of state, he surrounded himself with men who told him so. A modest man can disbelieve his minions for a length of time, but after a while it becomes easier and easier to subscribe to a position of power which isn't real. Martin Luther King, Jr., read even deeper substance into the resignation of Lyndon Johnson. He felt that although he had been severely rebuffed for his stand on Vietnam, Johnson's announcement had reopened the subject of foreign affairs for King to examine publicly.

It was a whole new ball game.

Sometimes there is a day when the telephone claims almost all attention, all time. Monday, April 1, 1968, was such a day for Dr. King. He was in his paneled study at home most of the time, either dialing numbers or answering the phone. First of all, he wanted to know what each man thought of Lyndon Johnson's abdication. Didn't he think it reopened the whole field of civil rights and foreign affairs to the SCLC? Yes, everyone agreed. Everyone had been shocked by the Presidential announcement but felt it would redound to the benefit of the Movement. Even though Johnson had been their hero in 1964, he had become their devil in 1968.

There was a lilt in the voice of Martin Luther King. It was as though he felt that he were being bailed out of prison. The depressed mood was gone. Ordinarily, he did not question the minutiae of a march; now he insisted upon knowing who was doing what in Memphis and what guarantees he had that this was going to be nonviolent, nondrinking. Everything he heard on the phone reassured him. All staff members were working harder than ever to ensure that this march would be a model of passivity.

Jesse Jackson suggested that if the march could be postponed from Friday until Monday, April 8, he could bring some really "big people" to its front line, people with sufficient prestige to make Mayor Loeb and the police feel the awe of their presence—senators, judges, the fat cats. The idea was being discussed by a diverse group on the staff.

In the afternoon, Dr. King went to the headquarters of the Southern Christian Leadership Conference, an old Masonic building where the first two floors were rented and filled with pretty black clerks and ugly file cabinets. This time—this one time—Dr. King had arranged his schedule so he could check over every aspect of the march; he even knew, ahead of time, that the city would seek an injunction in federal court against him.

This was a pretty day. The air in Atlanta had a cool freshness which promised warmer weather. Crocuses had begun to bud in bright colors; dogwood was as colorful in "Colored Town" as it was in white Atlanta. Forsythia, a lacy yellow and chartreuse a week ago, had discarded the seductive gown and was back to plain green. There was time to be with his two daughters and two sons, in the past few years there had been precious little time to play with them, and that fact scarred Dr. King's conscience.

The languid days were rare, and he used them to "tease." He love-mocked his little boys, his daughters, his wife, his staff, his parents. Sometimes he phoned his mother and told her that he was A.D. At others, he pointed to his attractive wife and said, "Now look at this poor little colored girl. Where would she be if I hadn't taken her out of the cotton fields of Alabama and married her?" He never "teased" his father, because "Daddy" King was the monarch, the righteous Christian.

Few noticed that in Dr. King's demonstrations throughout the South and in the North, Atlanta had escaped almost unscathed. SNCC had had a few sit-ins at restaurants and soda fountains, and Martin Luther King, Jr., had made a token display of himself for the cameras, but he did not seriously fight the white structure of Atlanta. He shook up other municipal nests from Mississippi to Chicago, but not his own. Segregation was rigorous in Atlanta—the blacks were weakened by the fact that they did not live in a single ghetto but were scattered throughout several in the city. They further segregated themselves into strata of society. No black banker or owner of an insurance company fought the system. Only the young militants, inside Morehouse College or unemployed, felt the urge to ask the Southern Christian Leadership Conference why, when its headquarters were in Atlanta, the Queen City of the South was the only one spared marches and rock throwing.

Atlanta was root and trunk of the Reverend Dr. King. The city and his father were, in his mind, one. He averted a confrontation with both whenever possible. Here he had no heart for the dispute. At the Ebenezer Baptist Church, he often walked softly down the hallway to his study, not stopping to see if his father was in his office. Often, even casual conversation was painful for both.

It was on Tuesday, April 2, 1968, that King stopped at the church for his mail, and "Daddy" caught him on the inside steps, coming up. The conversation between the white-haired oak and the splendid sapling began on a family note. A.D. was at a convention in Miami. The younger brother was somewhat of a disappointment to "Daddy." The father's heart's desire was to raise God-fearing preachers who would cling to the oak until it fell. A.D. was rebellious; he had no desire to be Martin Luther King, Sr. or Jr. As an ordained minister of the Southern Baptist Church he knew that he could not drink or partake of sins of the flesh, but he could enjoy life much more if he was away. He declined his father's offer to be an assistant pastor at Ebenezer and selected a church in Ansley, Alabama. He got along well with Martin and "Daddy," but he separated himself from their professional lives.

The conversation in the hallway moved to the Poor People's March in Washington, and "Daddy" stared through those shiny bifocals, pursing and unpursing his lips, loving this God-given gift from his loins and fearing the mountains his son felt impelled to climb. Now it was worse—Memphis again. He hoped that Martin wasn't seriously considering returning to Tennessee—the issue wasn't that big so far as the cause was concerned. The old man began to push back the cuticles on his fingers and yank at them with the other hand. This was his "tic."

"Daddy" King did not upbraid Martin; he did not beg him to get out of the Movement and turn it over to others. Both men understood the chances a black takes when he fights whites—no matter on what level—and both understood that the slender shadow of death could have been awaiting on any of the many roads Martin marched. It could still be waiting, around any corner in any city at any time.

They talked in the hall above the top step for more than an hour. Nothing was accomplished on either side except the respectful evasions of reality. Martin was too far away for "Daddy" to reclaim him; "Daddy" was too close to his own neighborhood and his own business to look up and see the distant clouds light up under a setting sun. He wanted what he could touch, and nothing more. He said good-bye to Martin, and the young reverend went on to his office.

The sun wasn't up when the Reverend Mr. Abernathy squeezed himself behind the wheel of his 1955 Ford, put the lights on, and started for King's house. They were booked on an early flight to Memphis, and he knew that King, who normally awakened at nine, had lately become restless and could not sleep beyond dawn. Sometimes, as Coretta King and the children slept, he sat in a robe in his study penciling notes or reading. This time he would be washed, shaved, and dressed, probably on the stoop waiting in a black silk suit and carrying that attaché case he swung from hand to hand.

Abernathy was wrong. Dr. King was still in bed when he arrived. He rang the bell, and, in a trice, Mrs. King was up, offering juice and coffee and toast to both men, who said they didn't have time. Dr. King dashed into the bathroom and out, sorry that he had overslept, and told Abernathy that he had to stop by the SCLC office for a moment to pick up something before they headed for the airport. This squeezed time. The coffee was percolating; the children still slept. There was no time for either.

The good-bye kiss was quick and perfunctory, and the men hurried down the flight of stairs to the car. As a dictator Martin Luther King was a "suggester." The car pulled away, and King said, "Take this street to the right."

"Michael," Abernathy said, "I know where the office is."

"David," King said. Abernathy had turned the car to the right, "I want you to know another way to drive there." King used his keys to get inside and came out minutes later saying, "Let's go."

They checked in at the airport and walked swiftly down the long corridor for the flight to Memphis. Aboard the plane, one of the crew said, "This plane has been under guard all night. We have had a bomb threat. The Reverend Martin Luther King is aboard." King glanced at Abernathy. Both shook their heads.

Memphis was only an hour away, but the weather was bone-chilling and rainy. The sky was dark and low; the clouds moved eastward fast enough for the eye to see; water swept in uneven ranks across the concrete of the airport to die in an ominous code against the big windows. The usual big car was waiting for them. King told the driver, "Take us to the Lorraine." He had been there once before, and the rooms had been big and square and plain, some with twin beds and a dresser, a night table, an end table, and a television set. The bathrooms were well kept. King was making sure this time that there would be no criticism by the blacks of Memphis that he was staying at a white motel.

Room 306 was a good one. It was on the second floor, facing the parking lot below and the covered swimming pool. A porch ran the length of the floor, and the Reverend Dr. King wasn't more than ten or twelve feet from the outside stairway. His staff had rooms upstairs and down, and the minister appeared frightened. He organized meetings in the various rooms, upstairs and down, and assigned various aspects of the march to each of them. This was Wednesday. Dr. King had made up his mind to hold the march on Monday. He was edgy. The unexpected slam of a door or someone shouting a greeting from the porch to a new arrival in the parking lot made him jump.

The City of Memphis was in federal court asking for an injunction against all "nonresidents of the city acting in concert" from organizing or starting a street demonstration. Andy Young was ordered to hurry to federal court to find out what was going on and to report back to King. It didn't matter, in a way, because King had been preaching for some time that a man's conscience could discern the difference between a good law and a bad one and that he, King, would obey none but the good ones.

He said to Abernathy, "Whether the injunction is granted or not, I am going to lead that march." He stepped out on the porch, and the big eyes, troubled, looked at the sky. The stranger standing beside him was Joseph Louw, a producer of films. A thin vein of bluish lightning snapped down on Memphis, and a crackling sound rolled over the Mississippi.

"Hey, Doc," said Louw, "now we really see who's boss."

"Yes, sir," King said, turning back to the room, "He sure is." The television set was on, and Memphis had had a tornado warning. Nothing, nothing was going right. The committees were debating and disagreeing with one another; the rain was torrential, which meant that few would be at the Mason Street Temple that evening to listen to Dr. King speak; it was the consensus of the attorneys in the group that the federal court would stop the march of "nonresidents"; Dr. King, a small man with a fine mentality and a massive ego, had no desire to address a small crowd. He felt he had something to say, and he wasn't going to waste his talent on small groups. "David," he said, "if this rain keeps up, will you go in my place?"

Abernathy agreed. He knew better than King that there was no substitute for King, but if it was his wish, Ralph would go and, in his basso tone, would deliver the message to the faithful. He could see the disappointment on the damp faces before him, but he would obey without question. King tossed the local newspapers on the bed. The accent was anti-King; further, they quoted the abusive remarks of Rap Brown and other militants, who were taking dead aim at King. A television announcer, concluding the midday news, heard the lash of wind, rain, and thunder outside the studio and said over the air, "Maybe God is trying to tell us something."

King shut the set off. He went out on the porch with Abernathy and Jesse Jackson, and, from the parking lot below, a cinematographer took his picture for television. Over his head were clearly pictured the numbers of his room, 306. King said nothing, except to exchange greetings with those he knew. Looking straight ahead, he could see the clapboard fences and the tall weeds behind the cheap hotels on South Main Street. The back windows stared blankly from old brick. There the alcoholics could hole up for a week in a room for $8.50. A man with that money could snore on a cheap bed until sweet unconsciousness deserted him. Then he could walk down the long flight of inside stairs to the front and huddle inside his collar, begging money for a trip "home" —to Nashville, Jackson, Birmingham, Atlanta, Macon—any city that came to mind. Sometimes, when suckers were rare, the drunks slept on the lawn next to the hotel, the cold rain beating them slowly to death. Dr. King saw none of that because it was a full block away from the respectability of the Lorraine. What his eyes saw were the backs of these run-down buildings, rain blackening the bricks and boards, and a car or two coming in through the Lorraine gate and stopping at the little office on the left side, where transients registered.

Abernathy looked at his watch. "You have a meeting of all the ministers at Jim Lawson's church. Time to go." The Reverend Mr. Kyles, tall, thin and sharp, presided. Jesse Jackson spoke. Andy Young returned from federal court, where an injunction against the demonstration had been issued—and he forgot to tell Dr. King about it. Young spoke. Last of all, King.

There was no dais, just a table. King grabbed it with both hands and hoped aloud that all the reports he had been receiving were correct. The ministers had assured him, one and all, that this would be a different march, orderly, unostentatious, prayerful. Someone in a back row slapped a hymnbook at odd intervals. All the ministers saw Martin Luther King, Jr., jump each time the sound came. No one wanted to make an issue of it by asking the slapper to stop, but King reached a point of nervousness where he stopped in mid-sentence to look around, sometimes behind him.

As the meeting broke up, a federal marshal served a paper on King enjoining him from marching on Monday. He thanked the man and said to Kyles: "Somebody could really make money off white folks. Every time they enjoin me from marching, they insure the success of the march. Somebody could make money by telling them what not to do."

King needed cheering. So Kyles said that Mrs. Kyles was working up a real soul food dinner for the next night and she wanted him to be the guest of honor. A bright smile came to the doctor's mouth, and he said, "Sam, can you guarantee that she really knows how to make it?" Kyles said he was positive, that the pigs' ears and feet and the collard greens would be delectable and the time would be 6 P.M.

Something about the dinner sounded like home, like better days. "Can I bring some of the others?" King asked. Kyles said that he could bring a dozen—Mrs. Kyles would be prepared. Someone else told King that his brother, A.D., was flying into Memphis from Miami and would be at the Lorraine soon. This jacked the mood up a little.

In the Lorraine, he said, "Order some fish. See if they have any croaker." They didn't. He took the fish they had and sat with a few of his staff and ate. His appetite returned. There had been no breakfast, and there was much to do in a short time. First of all, he wanted to meet those militants again—"those Invaders." He barked sarcastically at Jesse Jackson for not telling him about the injunction before it was handed to him. "No matter," he said. "We march Monday." The Reverend Mr. Kyles missed the meeting with the Invaders. Even if he had been invited, it is doubtful that he would have attended, because he knew these young men and he didn't trust them. Nor would he tell Dr. King a very important fact: The Invaders had asked the Memphis ministerial group for $100,000 to implement their own program of riot and arson. Kyles and his group had told them they wouldn't get one dollar.

The march would be peaceful. The Invaders would make it so. If any of the older men drank, the Invaders were to haul them out of the march. One thing was certain: Martin Luther King had better come through with the car and the money, or he would find himself in deep,

deep trouble. Nor had they given up on the assignment of cowering their own ministers. A little polite blackmail—executed in a nice respectful manner—might bring them to their senses so that a little of the dollars that were being dropped into collection plates could buy new suits and new girls for the Invaders.

It was after 4 P.M. when the Invaders arrived at the Lorraine. Dr. King had warned the youths that he would not have this final meeting with them unless they permitted some of his staff to sit in and listen. Jim Orange was present. So were Jim Bevel and Andy Young. A dozen of the young men came in. They smiled hello. No smiles were returned. "We want a part in this thing," one of them said. "See, nobody ever asks us. You're the first one." King told them that they had an important part in the march. They were to be the peace-keepers. Through the lightning and the roar of wind and bowling alley thunder, the young men talked to the older ones.

At one point they made an almost plaintive point: "We want to belong. We're tired of being outside; bring us inside once and see what happens." No one knew Dr. King's thoughts, and he confided them to no one. One thing was certain: Without the goodwill and obedience of the Invaders, there would be no march. The Southern Christian Leadership Conference faced a federal injunction against marching and faced a first-class police department which had already laid out a plan to stop the blacks from marching—preferably with clubs and guns this time. They also faced Mayor Loeb, who was determined that Memphis was going to have racial peace, and a governor who had 4,000 men armed with rifles and bayonets.

King faced brute strength from outside and within. And yet he talked softly for an hour, clenching his hands between his knees and studying them, looking up now and then to caress the wild young faces with his eyes, and telling them that he was counting on them all the way. He had made promises to them; they had made vows to him.

He excused himself when he heard A.D. had arrived and went down to his brother's room on the ground floor. They hugged and wrestled, and Billy Kyles, who watched it, felt that the mood was up, the march was on, and this time they couldn't lose. The optimism was as infectious as the earlier pessimism. Dr. King, who was not an attorney, issued a statement to the press calling the restraining order of Judge Bailey Brown "illegal and unconstitutional. There is a real possibility," he said, "that I will not obey it." His lawyers would be in court tomorrow to have the order dissolved. His belligerence, in the face of a United States court, was unprecedented for him. "It is a matter of conscience," he proclaimed. "We have a moral right and responsibility to march."

The Smiler's face was distorted by the metronomic windshield wipers. He was on his way to Memphis. Darkness overcame him as he passed the interchange of Routes 78 and 240 at Robert O'Brien Park. He was in no hurry. The thing he had to do in Memphis could wait. So far as is known, no one was with him. In the car was his little bag—James Earl Ray was always particular about his shirts and socks and shorts—and the long cardboard package with the rifle and the scope. He had one thing more: somebody's money in his pocket. Somebody from Atlanta or Birmingham kept him fairly well staked.*

Days earlier, Ray was in a motel outside Selma, Alabama, when Dr. King had scheduled meetings in the town. The white man had missed seeing the black one, but this time it seemed certain that the pastor would spend a day or two in Memphis—maybe more. The work of James Earl Ray was simple. Get a room, buy a newspaper, locate the quarry, and rent a nearby duck blind. That—and patience—would ensure the work. There would be no more tracking, no more problems, just a matter of getting out of Memphis safely and back to the payoff point. There he would have to abandon the white Mustang he enjoyed so much and then fly first to Canada, then to Great Britain, and finally to Africa.

And yet there were built-in weaknesses. The slim Smiler lacked intelligence. It would not be fair to state that he was stupid, but his history was one of ignorance and failure. He had elected to lead a life of crime, but he had been caught many times and knew more about the inside of prison bars than the outside. He grew up in Quincy, Illinois, and in Ewing, Missouri—towns about twenty miles apart on opposite sides of the Mississippi River.

The father of the family, James Gerald Ray, was an ex-convict. The mother, Lucille, was an alcoholic. He had a difficult time trying to find work because of his record; Lucille could give birth to children but couldn't rear them. Sometimes, in despair, they moved in with her

---

* After intensive research, the author found nothing to substantiate Ray's story of meeting a man named "Raoul" in Canada, a man Ray could not identify with a last name, an address, or even a plausible motive for selecting a witless person to kill Dr. Martin Luther King, Jr. Almost 2,000,000 words of correlated notes would indicate, with little room for doubt, that: (1) James Earl Ray had a financial backer and (2) the man who financed the assassination, working alone or representing a group, ordered Ray where to go and when and promised to help him get to Rhodesia. The United States had no extradition treaty with Rhodesia, which had recently seceded from the Commonwealth of Nations.

family in Alton, Illinois; sometimes they returned to Quincy or Ewing. All the luck they had was hard. James Ray altered his name so many times that it was difficult for him to remember which one he was using at present: James Ray; Gerry Ray; George Ray; Gerry Rayn; Gerry Raynes; Gerry Raines; or Gerry Ryan.

Lucille clung to her Roman Catholicity and spurned contraceptives. She gave birth to James Earl Ray in 1928; Marjorie Raynes in 1930; John Larry the following year; Gerald in 1935—in time, a total of nine. It is incredible that one large family should sustain so much anguish and sit in clapboard houses waiting for matters to get worse. For less than $1,000 Lucille Ray's mother bought the Rays a 63-acre farm outside Ewing in the summer of 1935. It seemed sensible that if the father could not find work, then he could become his own employer. But seed cost money; crops were poor; cash was nonexistent. The babies had big bellies and hungry eyes.

When they reached the farm bought by Lucille's mother, they found that only 35 acres could be tilled and worked; the rest was rocky ravines and old hummocks.

The year was 1935, and Ewing, which had a population of 350, had two banks. Both closed down. A street of shops died. Anyone with $350 in cash could buy a house. A laborer, if he could find work, would be paid one dollar a day. It was dirt poor and white Protestant all the way. "The only time we ever saw a nigger," a businessman said, "was when they was building the highway. They kept him in a special camp." There was a public relief office for the proven poor. Lucille came into town once a week in shabby clothes to get salt, cornmeal, and flour. Once in a while, she bought a pint of gin and buried it in her shopping bag.

The father barely tried to work the farm. Standing on the squeaky porch, looking at it, he knew that it would not pay. It would break his back. So he got aboard an ancient pickup truck, called to his eldest son, James Earl Ray, that he was going to town, and the boy would hop up beside his father. If there was any conversation, no one remembers it. They bounced over hard dirt ruts and stopped at Cason's Pool Hall. The father played. The hungry boy sat on a tall stool in the rear, smiling at everybody. The boy wore cut-down overalls; his father bought "used" motor oil for the truck.

Day by day Lucille Ray began to surrender her soul. It was like walking down a long stairway with a feeble light at the top and none at the bottom. The retrogression was steady. She cuddled her children, but she had no words for them. For a period of eight years she did not visit the woman on the next farm. Her husband didn't even take care of the swaybacked horse they owned. There was a cow and a cringing German shepherd. Lucille took care of them, but her silences grew longer and longer.

There was no animosity. Quarrels were few. At thirty, she was a drunken drudge. Her hair was unwashed and stiffened away from her ears. She had a vegetable garden, and wearing a dirty old dress and sometimes, in the chill, a worn-out tweed coat, she bent down stiff-kneed to mulch the ground. Dinner was often the same night after night: a pot of navy beans with suet and onions.

But time had not finished its work with Lucille Maher Ray. Of the nine children, Marjorie, at the age of six, walked off the porch to play with a box of matches. She came screaming into the house with her long black hair a mass of flames, the little face bright with horror. Lucille wrapped her little girl in a blanket, but nothing could help. Marjorie Ray, mother's favorite, was buried in an unmarked grave. When the cold weather came and the icy wind tore through the cracks of the farmhouse, Mrs. Ray often kept all her children home from school.

They didn't have the proper clothes. She drank and pulled all of them into bed with her. Noses barely above the quilts, they lay there in silence.

James got a single-shot .22 rifle and went out for squirrel; but he was a poor marksman, and shells cost money. He shot pool, chalking the cue in blue-green and sizing up the rail shots, and he was better than his father. Lucille begged her husband to rip the floor and tear the sidings from the house to make firewood. He did it, and his boys helped him.

The house was open to the elements when James Ray, Sr., found a one-room shack which he could buy with no down payment. He trucked it back to the farm with a used potbelly stove. The family moved in, and Lucille hung a dirty blanket between the children and the parents. The Rays were nothing, emanating from nothing. It wasn't until World War II started that the father found work with the Chicago, Burlington and Quincy Railroad. James Earl Ray graduated from elementary school; his brother Gerry ran away from home. All of them, half alive, realized that the basic commodity in life was money. Toward the end of the war James got a job with International Shoe Company. He was diligent, neat, smiling, a good clerk. For two years, it appeared that the Ray family had spawned an energetic and law-abiding son.

The war ended. The government cut back on shoe orders. James Earl Ray was fired. He stopped to say a polite good-bye to the only man in the company who had befriended him—a German immigrant. He was sorry about the war, but James Ray assured the older man that he now admired all things German. The boy had done an astonishing thing in two years of work: He had $1,180 in a bank account.

On February 19, 1946, James Earl Ray enlisted in the U.S. Army at East St. Louis. He chose Germany for his assignment and became a military policeman in the 382d Battalion, stationed at Nuremberg. He was a member of the occupying forces in the city where the Nazi leaders were being tried and hanged. Most of the MP's rode jeeps with white batons, white gloves, and an imperious attitude impervious to a congenial smile. James Earl Ray was small and thin and silent. He had developed a shyness which extended to the limit—when a *Fräulein* smiled at him, he averted his face. When he wanted sex, he would buy it with cash. He could not bear a free friendship or a free love affair.

He was, according to the records, a model soldier until he began drinking. He was transferred out of the Military Police to Company B, Sixteenth Regiment. James Earl Ray felt insulted and humiliated. He accepted the transfer and shortly thereafter was arrested for being drunk in quarters. After three days in a stockade he tried to escape and failed. A court-martial gave James Earl Ray three months. He was not a model prisoner. The United States Army had not divulged anything regarding the young man's behavior in prison, but there is no doubt that a vicious streak began to show. Before half his sentence was up, Army officers said that he was not fit for service, and he was sent home. On his final papers they wrote "inept." He came home holding his arm up and yelling, "Heil Hitler!"

Ray got a job in Chicago, bought a Mercury, lost the job, and saw the car repossessed. He was twenty-one years of age and broke, fearful of anything except a vacuous smile. When he had a few dollars, he bought sexy paperback books and rented a room in a cheap boardinghouse. He had tried, and tried hard, to make a better life for himself than that his mother and father had. In the Army he had sent allotment checks home. In sum, considering the family background, James Earl Ray had been a good son.

The pleasant side of the law hadn't worked out, so Ray decided to try the unpleasant side. He hitchhiked to Los Angeles and, on October 7, 1949, was caught trying to rob the Forum Cafeteria at night. He got away from the assistant night manager, leaped through a window, ran down a fire escape, and was almost caught by a parking attendant. In the grappling, the burglar dropped an Army discharge certificate and an account passbook from a bank. Both bore the name James Earl Ray. An office typewriter was found on the top step of the fire escape.

A few days later, Ray displayed the chronic witlessness which was to stain his life by walking on a street near the cafeteria. The assistant manager identified him and called the police. James Earl Ray said that he had not entered the cafeteria to steal; he knew nothing about the typewriter: "I had a few beers, and sometimes when I have a few beers I end up in the wrong place. Of course I ran when that man scuffled with me. I had this happen once before back home when I had a few beers. I tried to open a door in the wrong house. Someone had to take me home." The law subscribes to infinitesimal doubts. The Smiler got off with a slap on the wrist.

Matters were worse back home. Younger brother Gerry was in and out of prison. John Larry was in the Indiana Reform School. In Quincy, Lucille worked making salads in the Lincoln-Douglas Hotel. Her husband washed dishes. One worked nights; the other, days. They were also registered for unemployment relief. James Gerald Ray stood on a street corner one night and watched Lucille walk the streets from bar to bar. He left her and disappeared.

Juvenile authorities took the children away. Carol Jean, her father's favorite, escaped and found him in St. Louis. Some of the children were in a Catholic home under the name of Ryan. It is doubtful that they knew their names. Uncle Earl drifted off to Buffalo, where he was found dead beneath a railroad trestle.

In prison, convicts made sport of James Earl Ray. They called him a "hard luck character," a "stupo," a natural loser in the field of crime. Sometimes, walking the cobbles in the prison yard, he opened his mouth to say that when he got out he was going to make one "big lick." He was in and out of prison so frequently that some wardens referred to James Earl Ray as the "commuter."

It is beyond credence to trace the history of the Ray family. James Earl Ray, in a bright straw hat, managed to get his picture taken by an automatic camera while robbing a supermarket. The police were looking for the Smiler in the straw hat when, five weeks later, he robbed another market with the same hat and smile. In this case, a safe had to be opened in the back room. James Ray and an old prison friend held the customers at bay with guns, and Ray went back to flush the manager. Ray again made a small error. He came up one grocery aisle while permitting his quarry to come up an adjoining one. The manager stooped low, found a phone, and called the police. After the call was made, Ray walked upstairs to the office and yanked the phone wire from the wall. The two crooks backed out the front door with guns in hand, and a breadman, carrying a large package, didn't see them and almost knocked both men down.

Police arrived. Ray and pal got into a car and, with tires squealing, made a U-Turn. James Ray, driving, forgot to close his door and was almost flung to the pavement. The police of Alton, Illinois, conceded that they had not seen anything like it since the days of the silent movies and the Keystone Kops. The robbers had $2,200, but they had overlooked $15,000 in cash in the safe. Corporal Raymond Dooley, who was closest in the chase out of town, was transfixed when he saw the getaway car racing back into town.

He watched the blue car go by and turned to give chase. The robbers ran it into an empty lot, hit a barn, and escaped on foot. In the wreck, police found $342, two revolvers, an assortment of license plates on the floor, and a straw hat. Ray got away. His aged accomplice came out of the woods and said he wanted to return to prison because he was tubercular.

Ray stole money orders and cashed them, but it wasn't until he arrived at Leavenworth Prison that the convicts explained to him that a crook never uses the same handwriting to make out the front side and then to endorse it. Once he refused to transfer to a model prison farm because he heard that there were blacks in it. He said he hated blacks; he never said he had a desire to kill one. James Earl Ray thought that they all should be deported to Africa.

Tonight the Smiler fought the splatter of heavy rain up Route 78 along Lamar Avenue to a well-lighted place near Huguenot Street called the New Rebel Motor Hotel. The hour was early. He parked the Mustang and, with his equipment, walked in. Behind the desk stood Henrietta Hagemaster, a woman who had worked at the New Rebel for nine years. Cheerlessly, she asked Ray if he had a reservation. He didn't. It made no difference. There were some empty rooms. She turned the registration card in his direction and he wrote:

Eric S. Galt
2608 Highland Avenue,
Birmingham, Alabama

On the line where it said "Representing," James Earl Ray left a blank. A boy went out in the lot and certified the car's license plate as

138993 Alabama. The arrival date was jotted as "4/3/68" and the departure date as "7." This was Wednesday, so it would appear that Ray was allowing himself until Sunday to finish his assignment. The room cost $6.24, and the guest paid in advance. The night clerk, Ivan Webb, came on duty and he noticed that Ray's car had Mexican *Turista* stickers on it. A light was on in Room 34 all night. It was an improvement on all those jails. In some of them, he had passed the word to "cons" that there ought to be a million dollars waiting for someone to kill Dr. Martin Luther King, Jr., and he would like a "big lick" at it.

At the same time that James Earl Ray was checking into the New Rebel, Martin Luther King, Jr., was resigning himself to a dark and lonely night. Abernathy and some of the others on the staff had gone to the Mason Street Temple to address, admonish, and cheer as many blacks as might show up for the first public meeting designed to whip up a contained fury against the injustices of the Memphis administration. He picked up the phone and called his wife in Atlanta. It was after 8 P.M. in the Queen City of the South, and the children were in bed. He missed them. He missed her. They talked about the injunction Loeb had obtained against "nonresidents" demonstrating. It made no difference, the pastor said. He had made up his mind to lead the march anyway. She begged him to be careful. They spoke about Lyndon Johnson's sudden call for peace talks with North Vietnam. King said good-night after promising her he would call the next night.

The car carrying Ralph Abernathy and Jesse Jackson pulled up in front of the temple. At once, big television globes lighted the side alley, and the rain swept diagonally across the beams like snow. The men walked heads down and could hear the whir of cameras. When Abernathy got inside, he shook the rain from his collar and looked around. Amazement froze his features. The temple was crowded, and the ministers were on the altar, waiting. People stood to look behind him, waiting for King. They were polite; no one expressed disappointment.

Abernathy knew that this was not his crowd. It belonged to King; it had come to see King; it had come to hear him raise their spirits. "Where's a phone?" he asked. Jackson told Abernathy to follow him. He and some others formed a phalanx, and they jostled down the aisle to the pay booth in the front of the church.

"Michael?" said Ralph. "You must come over here. I'm not saying the church is full to overflowing, but there has got to be two thousand people here waiting in wet clothes."

Dr. King said, "You don't have to sell me, David. I'm on my way." In ten minutes the stocky figure of Dr. King, head down, came in from the rain, and the crowd gave him a standing ovation.

The presiding minister of the meeting began to feel better. He was jocular. "Now," he said into a silvery microphone, "which one of you fellows is going to speak first?" Ralph stepped up. He had no prepared statement. Dr. King had none. For years they had worked a silent agreement that if the crowd was dull, Abernathy would speak first because the rotund mustachioed man could make parishioners laugh, as well as make them think.

Dr. King sat in a row of ministers, fingers clasped, waiting. "So often," Abernathy said, waving an arm in dismissal, "we take our leaders for granted. The President of the United States is never introduced as anything but just the President of the United States. Now tonight—tonight, I want to introduce to you the leader of the Southern Christian Leadership Conference." That might have concluded the introduction, if Ralph were prepared to follow the supreme simplicity of the introduction he had cited.

He became derailed and began a lengthy recitation of the life of Dr. Martin Luther King, Jr. "He came from the loins of Southern Baptist preachers," he shouted, as though no one in the church knew it.

"His father is a Baptist preacher. His brother is a Baptist preacher. His granddaddy was a Baptist preacher." A frown, half irritation, half amusement, wrinkled the forehead of Dr. King. Abernathy was winging, and no one could stop him. Abernathy pointed to his chest. "His friend is a darned good Baptist preacher." The communicants burst into laughter. On and on he flew, oratorically, for twenty-five minutes. People fidgeted.

At last, Abernathy turned and escorted Dr. King to the microphone. For a moment—a very brief moment—King smiled the rich warm smile that belonged to him. "My friend," he said softly, "has the eloquence of Demosthenes, the ability of Plato, and the mentality of an Aristotle." The people laughed and shuffled their feet. The myopic eye of each camera caught Dr. King looking as he always looked—well dressed; in charge of his audience; pausing to think the next sentence before uttering it.

The words were lachrymose, honed with sorrow, self-pity, and death. It did not dominate the crowd; it appealed to their mercies. He told his audience that the injunction granted today was a "violation of First

Amendment privileges." Shaking a finger high over his head, he shouted that he would "lead the march on Monday," and the people cheered and stomped. It is possible that Dr. King was speaking more directly to the cameras and, through them, appealing to Americans everywhere. He exhorted everyone to be nonviolent at all times. There must not be any overt act or sign among the marchers that would encourage a clash with law officers.

At times, the voice was soft, almost tender—a man ruminating aloud. He told how he had been stabbed in the chest by a demented black woman in Harlem. Later the doctors told him that the tip of the blade had lodged against his aorta, and if he had so much as sneezed, he would have been a dead man. "I left Atlanta this morning and as we got on the plane. . . ." He told the story of the bomb plot.

"And then I got into Memphis, and someone began to talk about the threats that were out or what would happen to me from some of our sick brothers." The speaker looked up at the ceiling. The feet of rain walked noisily. The big side window shutters slammed, one by one, and opened again. He held one hand in the other, and he looked like a child who is emerging from a frightening dream and isn't sure which is real and which is dream.

Billy Kyles read the face and ordered someone to put on the big fans so that the shutters would remain open to the night. "It is no longer a question of violence or nonviolence in this day and age," King shouted. "It is nonviolence or nonexistence." In retrospect, his followers felt that Dr. King was overwhelmed with the thought of nonexistence. He spoke for an hour, but the gloom was introspective, highly personal. The row of silent ministers behind him, and the shouting people before him, wanted to hear about that great big glorious march, but the speaker was preaching his funeral oration all the way.

For a month, Ralph Abernathy had been whispering to friends: "Martin is not himself." Andy Young told friends that Dr. King had developed a habit of looking behind him, suddenly and without reason. Kyles saw what the flapping of shutters did to him. That afternoon the discordant slapping of a book of psalms on a bench had unnerved him.

He grasped the lectern. Dr. King was ready to close his talk. The people looked at one another. "I don't know what will happen now," he said. "We have got difficult days ahead." He shook his head from side to side and gathered his breath in the manner of a man stifling a sob. "But it doesn't matter to me because I have been to the mountaintop. Like anyone else, I would like to live a long life. But I'm not concerned with that."

The great head came up and his eyes searched the faces below. "I just want to do God's will, and He has allowed me to go up the mountain." The palm of his hand shot upward. "I see the Promised Land. I may not get there with you, but I want you to know tonight that we, as a people, will get to the Promised Land. I am happy tonight that I am not worried about anything." The voice lowered, almost growling. "I'm not fearing any man. Mine eyes have seen the glory. . . ."

He did not finish the words "of the coming of the Lord." Instead, he stopped, turned, picked his coat from a chair, and walked out the side entrance. He did not remain to see the people stand and cheer, to see tears which have no color, to listen to the cheers of amen, to say good-night to the ministers, who were shocked into silence. Head down, he walked through the alley to his car, some of his entourage trotting behind.

Back at the Lorraine, he worked in silence for a while on a vituperative sermon he planned to deliver at the Ebenezer Baptist Church on Sunday. Half of it was already written. The title was "Why America May Go to Hell."

2

MULBERRY STREET sparkled with sunlit puddles. The air was fresh and clear, coming across from Arkansas, sweeping the dirt of last night under the rug of the vast Mississippi River, humming off-key around downtown Memphis, to caress Mulberry and the tired, fading buildings of the blacks. Along Mulberry, only the Lorraine Motel appeared to be fresh and bright.

The hour was 9 A.M., and the wall in front of the two-story building was gray and gray-black with last night's storm. The car entrance at the left was designed so that guests could enter or leave by car, but not without passing the little office, with its leather sofa, the rack of maps and, behind a half railing, the switchboard. Mrs. Lorraine Bailey sat there. Never in her life had she seen lights blink on and off as yesterday and this morning. Those Southern Christian people used the phone from a clutch of rooms on the main floor diagonally across from her office and from upstairs, too.

They called local a hundred or more times—and long distance, too. Her hand ached from penciling the calls; often, she had to say, "Please hold a minute," as more lights kept flashing. Scores of additional calls were incoming, and she had no time to register incoming customers, who leaned against the little railing staring and waiting. Mrs. Bailey had ambition, initiative, and a face with the same sweet smoldering fire of Coretta King. Lorraine Bailey was older. She and her husband had slaved and saved to get this place. It was popular among blacks who could afford it, and she named the place after herself and hired only black girls who knew how to make a bed properly, dust, clean ashtrays, and rub a gleam onto the tiles of the bathroom walls.

Mrs. Bailey* paid special attention to the switchboard light on Room 306. If Martin Luther King, Jr., lifted that telephone, Lorraine Bailey wanted to be ready—all other calls would have to wait. He had been here once before, in 1966, and she had been disappointed the last week when he had stayed at the white Holiday Inn on the river.

She was not privy to anything Dr. King planned, except that she had heard that last night he had braved a torrential rain to speak at the Mason Street Temple, and the newspapers stated that he was ordering a one-day work stoppage for tomorrow. Her concern was to sign guests in, to watch to see that no one left without paying, and to mind that switchboard. There was an old section of the motel down near the next corner, at Huling Avenue, but she had clerks there who could take care of semipermanent residents at a cheaper rate. In the new section, she had installed wall fixtures for making instant coffee.

The light glowed from 306, and her heart raced to take care of the call. It was not Dr. King. Another voice asked her to phone Dr. Samuel Kyles and please ask him to come over. A phone call for 306 came in from a voice which sounded like a young boy with a down-home accent. She didn't listen, but it was a leader of the Invaders who just wanted to tell Dr. King, "You can count on us. There isn't going to be any trouble."

In the room, Abernathy had been out of bed, padding around the room in a robe, wondering why it should be that for two days in a row he had been out of bed before King. In all the years of their association, he had been first awake, first washed and dressed, and sometimes had had to jostle Abernathy to arouse him. He made a whispered phone call, and King sat up in bed.

Wherever he woke up, Dr. King looked around the room to establish himself. Then he slipped his feet over the side of the bed, squirmed into his slippers, and went to the bathroom. April 4, 1968, had begun. "You want juice and coffee?" Abernathy asked through the closed door.

"No, thank you. See if you can get Jesse and some of the staff to come up here at ten."

Andy Young was ordered back to court to find out what the United States was going to do about the Monday march. Dr. King came out of the bathroom unshaved, the little black burls spotting his jowls. The mood was no better than that of yesterday. In the room directly below, Bernard Lee was out of bed, had finished his coffee, and was wandering

---

* She had five days to live. Mrs. Bailey died of a cerebral hemorrhage after the events of this day.

up and down the porch, visiting rooms, chatting, trying to reassure the staff (before King called them) that matters would go much easier this time in Memphis, even though "Doc's" mood was down. Someway, somehow, they were going to have to assure him and reassure him.

The staff sat on chairs, on arms of chairs, on the two single beds in Room 306 and on the floor. Reassurance expired with the opening words: "Some of my staff are committed to violence, and they will have to go." The black faces looked at one another in consternation with an ancient correlation: "Is it I, Jesus? Is it I?" King spoke at length, but the words cleared no path for his ministers; he rambled as he had at the Mason Street Temple the night before. For ten minutes, he dwelt upon the patient suffering of Jesus and Gandhi. His followers, especially his staff, must be totally committed to this principle, or America's soul could not be redeemed.

"Some of you may have a worry," he said. "Not me. I faced the question of death a long time ago." To Jackson, Abernathy, Kyles, Lawson, Lee, and the others, he was proving the opposite. He was now obsessed with death, and they were powerless to ameliorate it. There was an inbred attitude of superiority in the statement, as though he were resigned to eternal darkness—and they were not. Sometimes, in the discourse, he indicted the emerging militants in his group without naming names or even looking at faces. At other times, he wandered in his thinking, a man hating violence but ready to concede that its time had come and America would be inundated with fists, fire, and guns.

"Perhaps it is inevitable. No matter what happens, I just cannot remain silent; I can't take a back seat; I must be right in it even if I am the sole voice crying that nonviolence is the answer to social change. Some of you, I feel, are changing your attitudes." He looked up at Ralph Abernathy, "I want Ralph to drop these people from our staff."

Then King turned to talking about the big march. The organization, the work still to be done. The meetings were going to be interminable. There were big meetings in one room, and sections held in another; there were confidential conversations on the porch; there were phone calls all over the United States asking the prominent, the respected, even government officials please to come to Memphis to march. The tactic of calling upon the "big people" had a purpose beyond the prestige of having them in the march. Its primary purpose was to make Loeb and Police Chief Holloman cautious about deliberately precipitating a riot.

The Smiler slept late. He had been up until the early hours in the New

Rebel, doing whatever he felt was necessary to the accomplishment of his mission. It is doubtful that he could, in retrospect, assess the almost comical succession of failures of his life. There is no doubt that he had a visitor that night—even though it cannot be documentarily proved—because he was not a man to sit up all night looking at street maps and reexamining a rifle. The Smiler was indolent and ignorant; he would need someone to tell him where to go to do the thing he had to do.

The trunk of his car held a bundle of soiled clothes which would fit a man of about 125 pounds, smaller than James Earl Ray. The Mustang ashtray was full of dead cigarettes, and Ray was never known to smoke. The car carpet was heavy with mud under the right front seat, and the Smiler was known to be neat to the point of obsession with an automobile. On April 1 he was known to have had $10.50 in cash. That morning he had $1,050. Alone now, he asked a bellman to bring a copy of the Memphis Commercial Appeal. The newspaper stated that Dr. Martin Luther King, Jr., was staying at the Lorraine Motel on Mulberry Street.

There was time, and to spare. No hurry. He checked out of the New Rebel at noon and cruised the city in the Mustang. He must have passed the Lorraine; he may even have read the room numbers on the second floor until he found "306." A stupid man works twice as hard as an intelligent one to achieve success. He must have seen the backs of the sleazy rooming houses on Main. They were elevated; a marksman would be looking down at his target. The distance could not have been more than 225 feet. With a two-by-seven scope, the distance would be about 32 feet. Black men and black waitresses moved along the Lorraine's porch. Customers drove in; others checked out.

It was possible for the Smiler to study the serious black faces up and down Mulberry and to feel truly superior—because he had a surprise. It might be sprung in a couple of hours; it might not occur until tomorrow; it might have to wait until Monday morning. Whatever the time and the day, this time the Smiler could not bungle the job because he had twenty shells and, even if he could shoot only four, it would be more than enough.

He would have to find a room on Main—a room, let us say, with a view. Then he could do his job, go up a few blocks to the Arkansas-Riverside Drive, turn left and go down Route 55, turn right and go across the Memphis-Arkansas Bridge into the state of Arkansas and roll smoothly through West Memphis out into the country; or he could remain on Route 55 and roll fast down into the state of Mississippi before an alarm was sounded; or he could go east down Lamar Avenue toward Mineral Wells, Mississippi; or he could push the Mustang north up Thomas Street onto Route 51. The options were endless.

Best of all, easiest of all, would be to get on Route 78, a few minutes from the friendly state of Mississippi, and cut diagonally down through Tupelo into Birmingham, where the last big payoff would be waiting, in addition to an airplane ticket to Canada, thence abroad to England and finally the sanctity of Rhodesia, where blacks, although more numerous than here, knew their "place" and kept it.

The Mustang moved up and down the neighborhood, a mechanical animal prowling for a lair. Ray may have been alone. His employer may have been with him. It was imperative that the neighborhood be studied with care. Main Street must have seemed ideal. The rooming house was a cheap no-questions-asked-cash-in-advance place. Any room in the back would look east at the Lorraine. A chair, some patience. An easy assignment. If there could be a problem, it would be parking the car. The second most important part of his work would be to get into that Mustang, pull away from the curb, make a right turn on Huling Avenue, and he would be exactly four streets from the big busy highway which ran north and south along the edge of the river. Any automobile could be lost in a stream of hundreds of cars southbound. Total elapsed time from the squeeze of a trigger to total anonymity on Route 55—between four and five minutes; 360 heartbeats.

A little after noon, Room 306 had been emptied of all except King and Abernathy. Dr. King grumbled that he didn't know whether he had done any good, but he had warned the neo-militants in his official family that he was aware of them and that they could go elsewhere, or they could abide by his peaceful principles. Dr. Abernathy reminded him that they had a big dinner date at Billy Kyles' house, and King said that reminded him that he was hungry. He picked up the phone and ordered salad and catfish.

The order was taken by Mrs. Lorraine Bailey, and she left the switchboard to do the cooking herself. A few minutes later, a slender waitress brought one salad and set it on a tray before Dr. King. "Hey," said Abernathy, "where's my salad?" The two men engaged in small talk as King ate. When the second salad arrived, two forks dipped into it, and Abernathy was amused. "First you eat your salad," he said; "then you eat mine." The catfish came up—one plate—and Ralph Abernathy put on his hurt expression. The waitress had left before there was time to protest. "I'm hungry, Michael. I didn't even have breakfast."

"Eat from my plate," King said. There were two forks. "I'm tired of all these meetings," he said. He was more than tired; he was a steel gear worn smooth, spinning at top speed without engaging other gears. Abernathy reminded him that someone at the meeting had suggested that the organization hire one of the Invaders as a permanent employee. "No," King said sharply. "No."

"The idea, Michael, is that maybe they can be taught and disciplined. We must be able to communicate."

King shook his head adamantly. The mule in him surfaced. "No. Ralph," he said, using that name as he always did on serious occasions, "I want you to see to it and be responsible: that never in the history of this organization will we employ anyone who will use violence." He poked a finger against Abernathy's chest. "I want you to see to that."

At 2:30 P.M., King said that he was going downstairs to A.D.'s room. For Abernathy, it was time to drop onto the bed for a nap. There was music coming from Jesse Jackson's room. He had brought the Operation Breadbasket band down from Chicago, and they were rehearsing as a limited combo. Kyles heard the sad high wail of the blues and walked in. "Hey, man," Jackson said, "would it be all right if this band played in your church?"

Kyles nodded. "Yeah. Fine. No problem." Another mass meeting was scheduled for the Mason Street Temple that night.

The Mustang pulled to the curb a few doors away from the rooming house. The Smiler got out, looked around lazily, and removed his gear. Then he locked the car and walked toward the north entrance of the rooming house. The door had been painted green on green, and in time, chunks had fallen off. There was a small sign DRINK WINK—THE SASSY ONE. Another sign read: APARTMENTS—ROOMS. Ray walked into the hallway, dismal and odoriferous with an unblinking light bulb hanging from two dusty wires. He started up the long flight of stairs. At the top was a double doorway and one more wall sign: NO CURSEING [sic] OR FOUL TALK.

At the sound of footsteps, Mrs. Bessie Brewer emerged from her room near the desk. It was her rooming house, and she had been long accustomed to the unwashed drunks, the thick indecipherable tongues, the hands digging to the bottom of an assortment of pockets trying to find the $1.25 for a roof and a mattress. As she sat behind the little registry desk, she looked up at the man in surprise. He was not a drifter; he wore a brown suit and a nice figured tie. His face was shaved, and his hands looked clean. His hair was neatly combed, and he sat his bundles down gently and looked around. The little smile absorbed her interest; it was frozen to his mouth. It was—well, silly. A silly sort of smile. He asked for a room. She thought he had a Memphis drawl; it had a soft dragging sound, as though the Smiler were in no particular hurry to say what he had to say.

She said she had a real nice room, with a kitchenette, too, for $10 a week. "Can I look?" he said. James Earl Ray was shown a big front room looking right down at his white car. No, he said slowly; no. He wouldn't need kitchenette privileges; he might only stay overnight, you see. Mrs. Brewer explained that, really, this was her nicest room, and she felt that no gentleman of his caliber would want to be back among men who snored and moaned all night and who sometimes cried aloud from the depths of deep wells full of snakes.

He was taken back past the desk and down the hall to number 8. This was a clean room, not as big as the front room, but the windows faced a blank wall. He rolled up a shade and shook his head. Didn't she have something farther back? He was looking at the other half of Mrs. Brewer's rooming house. Yes, she had something farther back; but it was in the other wing and not much to look at. Ray turned the small smile on her. He didn't mind. He'd like to be far back, away from the street noise and people walking up and down the halls.

She led him through a door, past a shorter stairway, and down a dingy hall. They passed rooms numbered 2-B, 3-B, and 4-B. When they came to 5-B, Mrs. Brewer said it was the only room she had vacant in the back. There was one farther back, 6-B, but it was occupied by a man and a lady. The Smiler wanted to know what that door was, all the way back, at the head of an alley stairway. That, said Mrs. Brewer, was the bathroom. Ray nodded. He examined the premises, touching the bed with his fingertips and showing interest in the sofa, the two chairs, and the dresser. Casually, he lifted the shade next to the sofa, and found himself looking at a wall. He walked to the other window, on the easterly side, and lifted curtains. He was looking diagonally across the back edge of the main wing of the rooming house at the Lorraine Motel.

It wasn't much of a look, but there it was, a little more than 200 feet away. Directly below was another stairway, leading to the weedy back lot with a single tree shivering under the late sun. "How much?" said the Smiler.

"This one is eight fifty a week," Mrs. Brewer said.

He nodded. "That will be fine," he said, and followed her to the front and across to the other wing. She gave him a guest register, and he gave her a brand-new $20 bill. He signed his name "John Willard" and put $11.50 change in his pocket. Mrs. Brewer looked at her watch and wrote 3:15 P.M. next to his name.

He assured her that he knew the way back, accepted a key, and lifted his packages. When he had settled in the room, he drew a chair up next to the window and looked diagonally across at the Lorraine. At once, Ray realized that he had failed to anticipate one thing: he could see Room 306, and he could see blacks on the porch and down in the parking lot, but at 200 feet, how would he know Martin Luther King? Any stocky well-dressed Negro going into that room or coming out might look like King; the Smiler could not afford to kill the wrong man. Why hadn't he thought of binoculars when he was buying all this stuff? Why indeed?

James Earl Ray locked the room and left hurriedly. It was 3:30 now, and the sun would be down at 6:30 P.M. He had to get those binoculars. Somehow he had a lifelong habit of forgetting some one thing—messing up everything. At 4 P.M. he parked his car in front of the York Arms Company not far from Beale Street. The smile was fainter now; he told the clerk briskly that he wanted a pair of binoculars—not expensive, please. Cordra York, Sr., had several models. Ray selected a Bushnell which sold for $41.55. He put them to his eyes and looked across the street. Their power was 7 by 35; he watched pedestrians 200 feet away and more, and they appeared to be close, the legs pumping up and down, but not appearing to draw much closer.

Time was running out. He was back in front of the rooming house in fifteen minutes. The time was 4:30 P.M. Ray slowed the white Mustang down, looking for a parking space near his wing of the rooming house. He found one, a squeeze, but he got the car in and carried a grayish-blue paper sack upstairs. He unlocked the room, hurried inside. There was a strap on the leather case. It wasn't needed. He ripped it off and threw it on the bed. There was a neck strap around the glasses. He didn't need that either; if he sighted his man, he didn't want something swinging across his chest as he put the rifle to his right shoulder.

He lifted the glasses to his eyes and started to correct the individual lenses to his vision, using the edge of the wall of the other wing of the rooming house to focus on. The bathroom—if it had a back window—

should look almost directly across at the Lorraine porch. He moved the binoculars a fraction. It had a back window.

It was a solid nap for Ralph Abernathy. He awakened, scowled at his gold watch, and saw that it was 5 P.M. No one was in 306 with him. He sat up, called the switchboard, and Mrs. Bailey connected him with A.D.'s room. Martin Luther King answered. "David," he said happily, "I wish you were here. Come on down." There were several men in the room, but conversational gambit was only between the brothers. They "teased," shouted, and "remembered."

Abernathy walked in, and King said, "We had such a good time this afternoon. Would you believe we called Mother and spoke a whole hour? A whole hour on the phone?" Abernathy marveled that the mood had changed. The presence of the younger brother had achieved the impossible; it had switched the older brother's thoughts to family, to mother, to childhood, to carefree times. The only solemn thought to come to Martin was when someone mentioned the hour and he wondered what had happened to Andy Young. "He's been in court all day on that injunction suit, and we haven't heard a word."

Abernathy and King left the room and walked up the outside stairway to 306. If there was a man in a rooming-house window watching Dr. King, he did nothing. The two men used a key to get into 306, pausing in the doorway. "David," said Dr. King, "I must shower and shave before Billy gets here."

They were barely inside when Billy Kyles arrived. "OK, guys," he shouted, clapping his big hands together. "Let's go. I said dinner at five. It's five." It struck King funny. Everyone knew that he made a habit of being late—the minor affectation of the snob—and King, hurrying into the bathroom, said, "Can't fool me. We called Gwen and she said dinner at six."

Kyles flopped into a chair. "I told you guys five because I *know* how slow you are."

The bathroom door opened, and Dr. King came out, patting the horrible-smelling shaving powder on his face. "Hey," he said, lapsing into dialect, "what you folks havin' for dinner anyway? Is this soul food? I don't want it to be like when I went to one preacher's house in Atlanta, and he said they was havin' soul food and they had ham and it was cold. Ham and Kool-Aid. Your Gwen is too pretty to know how to cook anyway. Did you get the church members to cook, Billy?"

"No, man. Don't you worry about it. We got soul food. Don't worry about it, just get ready and let's go."

"We don't want no filet mignon, Billy."

Dr. King's lawyer, Chauncey Eskridge, came into the room. The odor of the shaving powder was unbearable. Bernard Lee came in holding his nose. "The car's downstairs," he said.

King emerged from the bathroom in underwear, looking for his clothing. "Chauncey," he said, "will you go tell Jesse to get ready? And tell him to put on a tie." The Reverend Jesse Jackson would refuse. He thought of himself as a new breed of minister, one who wore turned-up levis, and a turtleneck sweater. Sometimes he wore a dashiki.

In Room 306 the ministers chattered. School was out. The important meetings, the strategy, the discipline were behind them. The men felt a sense of release; a chance to be together in one dining room, talking, shouting, telling stories, eating, kidding, feeling a kinship, letting the clock march its minutes by without attention—these are golden hours to any man who has a friend. It was present now, upstairs and down, a gentle massage to the muscles of the mind, an opportunity to be silly and irresponsible.

"This shirt is too tight," said Dr. King, trying to bring the collar together.

"You're getting too fat," Kyles said, and everybody chuckled.

"I am getting too fat," said King, unbuttoning the shirt.

Dr. Abernathy bugged his eyes and pretended to be insulted. "You mean you ain't gonna wear that shirt I washed for you last night?"

King found another white shirt. "Somebody stole my tie," he said, rummaging through his small suit case.

"Mike," said Ralph, "why don't you look down at that chair in front of you?" King picked the tie up and began to knot it. Kyles glanced at his watch. The drive down to South Parkway East wouldn't take more than fifteen minutes, but Kyles was an electric wire of a man, always in motion and on time. Abernathy watched the suppressed impatience. "When we called Gwen," he said, "we asked how many can we bring, and she said many as you like. She gonna have plenty of greens, black-eyed peas, pigs' ears. Takes a little time to get all that stuff ready."

Downtown Memphis began to come alive. Hundreds of cars pulled out of parking lots, away from department stores and offices. Thousands were homeward bound. Although the sun was still up, lights were on in show windows, and the rattle of place settings in restaurants clanged for early diners. David Wood, a patron of Jim's Grill, pulled his car slowly along the front of the rooming house. He found a parking space in front of a white Mustang, but the space was so small that the cars were close to touching bumpers. Lloyd Jowers, who owned the tavern, drew his car close behind the rear bumper of a white Mustang. He had to pull in close because the rear end of his Coup de Ville was blocking a hydrant. Across the street, Mrs. Elizabeth Copeland paused in her work to glance at the parked cars. She saw the white one and said to Mrs. Peggy Hurley, "Your husband is here for you."

Mrs. Hurley glanced out the window. "No," she said. "We have a white Falcon."

In the rooming house, Charles Stephens, in 6-B, heard furniture being moved in the next room. He was an industrious man who was ill with tuberculosis and had been forced to retire. His room was between the bathroom and the Smiler's room. Ray was resetting a chest of drawers so that he could watch the Lorraine from a wing chair. There was a woman with Stephens, his common law wife. Both heard the scraping sounds of wood on wood. There was the sound of a window being raised. It is possible—even probable—that the Smiler was at the window when Abernathy and King walked upstairs from A.D.'s room. If this were true, and Ray were able to use the binoculars and identify his target, he would have found that it required too much time to drop the glasses and adjust the sights of the rifle.

The Smiler looked up and down the dim hallway. He took his rifle and his binoculars and went into the bathroom at the back of the house. He passed the Stephens room, and since the door was open, the man and woman saw someone pass. They heard the bathroom door close, and the lock was snapped. Inside, Ray found a single window. It straddled the right edge of the old-fashioned tub and the floor. It would be impossible to keep one foot on the floor and one in the tub, so he stood in the tub, raised the window partway, and found that by crouching a little, he found not only that he could see that porch more clearly, but that there was also a ledge which could be used as an ideal rest for a rifle. An old screen was outside the window. The Smiler lifted it from its hinges and dropped it into the yard. Standing in the tub, he watched black men move in and out of Room 306. He must have realized that there would not be this much traffic unless Dr. King was in the room. A life of failures confronted a life of successes.

There were some footsteps outside the bathroom door. Someone turned the knob, found it locked, and walked away. In a few minutes, the steps returned, and someone knocked. James Earl Ray did not respond. The thought of losing the "big lick" because of some possible drunk who had to use the lavatory must have been irritating. He could go back to his room and return a few minutes later, but those might be the important few minutes.

William Anchues was knocking on the door. He passed Stephens' room and said, "Who's hogging the john?"

Stephens was trying to repair a radio. "I don't know," he said. "A man checked into Five-B this afternoon. Maybe him." A moment later the Smiler unlocked the door, peeked out, saw no one, and returned to his room with his equipment.

Anchues used the bathroom and came out. It is probable that Ray had his ear to his door to listen to the footsteps. When they receded, he picked up his rifle and binoculars and returned to the bathroom. For the second time, Charles Stephens and the woman with whom he shared the room watched him go by. The doorway was three feet wide, and the Smiler and his equipment could pass the door in one stride. Stephens was drunk, drunk but still fairly alert. In his illness, liquor appeared to restore his strength for a while, and the coughing did not trouble him.

"Call us a cab," he said to his woman. She went up front and phoned the Veterans Cab Company. The dispatcher said he would send a man over right away.

"Pick us up in Room Six-B," the woman said. The sick man relaxed in a painless unconsciousness. Ray was in the bathroom, his fingerprints and palm prints all over the window ledge with matching prints back in his room.

Either it had not occurred to him that his prints were on file from United States Army days, or he did not care. He was up here in a bathroom facing a man who could not see him. He would shoot him to death and care nothing what the police might do because it would require minutes for them to gather their strength, and he had a car standing below at the curb which could whisk him out of the state of Tennessee into Mississippi, Alabama, and eventually Georgia.

By the time they found out the name of the man they were looking for that eight-hour flight to Canada and Great Britain would be completed, and he would be on another plane to Africa. There was a lot of money in it, and it was one assignment where he had nothing to fear. Just squeeze a trigger once, twice, four times—whatever it required—and care not how many were killed as long as you bagged the big peaceful "nigger." Of one thing he was certain: He was not going to unlock that bathroom door between now and sundown.

There were steps in the hall. James M. McCraw was the cabdriver. He looked in 6-B. Charles Stephens was on the bed, legs drawn up, arms across his chest. McCraw smiled. He looked at the woman. "He's in no shape to go anywhere."

"Wake him up," she said. She did not know that the taxicab driver and Charles Stephens had been drinking buddies for seven years and the driver knew that his friend would not awaken.

"I didn't know the call was from Charlie," he said, shaking him gently and listening to the moans. Some men are meant to die swiftly; some slowly. Once Charlie had been a good engineer. Now he was waiting out the sentence of consumption and liquor, one bringing death, the other imitating it.

The woman watched. "Sorry," McCraw said, "he can't make it." She understood. She would sit awake in this dingy room, listening to the deep breathing, the sporadic fits of coughing, the moans of a man wrestling with life. The old radio wasn't repaired. Charlie could do it—maybe tomorrow. Then she could listen to some music or some voices, while his grave was being dug with a shot glass.

Room 306 was pretty full. The Reverend Dr. King was almost finished dressing. Hosea Williams was there. So was Abernathy, James Bevel, Jesse Jackson, and Andy Young had just arrived to report they had done nothing but argue all day at court. Dr. King was talking about his father as he patted cologne on his cheeks.

Abernathy said, "I don't want to bother you with this, but I can't go to Washington with you."

The leader frowned and said, "What do you mean, you can't go with me? You know I can't go without you."

"I told you I have a revival meeting at that time—it's only a preliminary meeting in Washington anyhow. I can't go, Michael, because the minister I asked to take my place can't make it."

"How about Neutral Long of the AME doing it for you? He's in New Orleans. Call him." Abernathy put in the call, but a secretary said that the minister of the African Methodist Episcopal Church was in conference. Dr. King asked the name of the secretary. He got on the phone. He had a way of asking, "Don't I know you?" rather than "Don't you know me?" He conversed pleasantly for a few minutes and then said: "Please ask the Reverend Long to come to Dr. Abernathy's revival and preach for him. Tell Neutral he must do this for Ralph. It's at the West Hunter Street Baptist Church. He knows."

He hung up the phone and buttoned his black silk jacket. "David," he said, "I know your people, and they're wonderful. If you hadn't been pastor there, I would have. Now, in case Neutral can't make it, you go to those people and tell them that you have a much greater revival that you must attend. Tell them you have a revival to revive the soul of America. Tell them your converts will not be limited to Atlanta, but from all over. They'll respond."

It was six o'clock. Billy Kyles, who had said five to ensure arrival at home by six, walked out of the room and stood a few steps down on the stairwell. The Reverend Andrew Young left and walked down the stairway to stand beside the big car and the chauffeur. Ben Branch, the leader of the Operation Breadbasket band, walked over to the car with Jesse Jackson.

Dr. King opened the door and started out. "Wait a minute," Abernathy said, "I forgot my after-shave lotion."

King walked to the railing and looked down. He grinned at Jesse Jackson, tieless and wearing a turtleneck sweater. "Jesse," he said, "I see you disobeyed me and didn't put on a tie." They all laughed because they knew that the Reverend Jesse Jackson wouldn't dress up for anyone.

"Dr. King," he said, "I'm not going to put on a tie. I don't need a tie to run with you all. A string around my neck has no relationship to my eatin'."

It was a relaxed moment for Martin Luther King. Billy Kyles was still waiting partway down the stairway. Some neighborhood blacks stood near the little office, looking up at the balcony to see, just once, the face of the man who fought in peace under the name of Christ. A.D. was still in his room. He was arranging a flight to Louisville, to home and church. Jesse Jackson glanced up at King again and said, "You remember Ben Branch?"

"Oh, yes," Dr. King said. "I remember him from Chicago. He played 'Precious Lord.' "

Bernard Lee cut in to tell Dr. King that it was chilly, that he ought to wear a topcoat. It was chilly. The sun was down behind the rooming house, and it had taken warmth with it. Dr. King made a move to go back into 306, then changed his mind. He had a thought, and he didn't want to forget it. "Ben" he said, "make sure you play 'Precious Lord, Take My Hand.' "

"I will," the musician said.

"Play it real pretty," King said, "for me."

"Hey, guys," said Billy Kyles, "come on." He looked at Chauncey Eskridge and said, "You can ride with me."

Abernathy was in the doorway, still patting his cheeks with cologne, when Jesse Jackson, looking up at King, said, "Oh, Doc . . ."

There was a cracking sound like two flat boards being slapped together. The bullet traveled at 2,600 feet per second. It hit its target before the sound ricocheted around the courtyard and off the walls of the rooming house and back again to the Lorraine. The Reverend Martin Luther King, Jr., neither heard anything nor felt anything. The heavy caliber bullet slammed him back from the rail with sufficient force to drop him flat on his back with his shoes almost against the railing.

In the doorway the Reverend Ralph Abernathy could see only the feet. He told himself, "That's no firecracker or Mike wouldn't be ducking like that." So he flattened himself inside the doorway, in case there were more shots. The bullet hit Dr. King a half inch below the right side of his lip, shattered his jaw, kept moving downward and to the left, hit the top of the trachea, and embedded itself in the spine at the bottom of the neckline, severing the spinal cord. Death, in such cases, is almost instantaneous; the heart may fight to continue its function, but a broken spinal cord, in addition to shock, is its own anesthetic.

Back from the open door, Abernathy was still on the floor, thinking that King was lying down only as a protective measure. The Reverend Billy Kyles, halfway down the stairway, was the first to realize that Dr. King had been shot. He hurried back up as others below automatically turned their heads toward the origin of the sound—the rooming houses behind the weedy backyard. The white man in 308, James Laue of the Justice Department, who was, in effect, the government's polite shadow, hurried out of his room and stared at the tarpaulin-covered swimming pool. He thought the shot had come from there.

Kyles bent over King. The right cheek was in two parts, with three inches between them. The brown eyes were wide open. In the courtyard, someone began to moan, "Lord, Lord!" Others picked it up as a dolorous chant. Dr. Abernathy heard it and got to his feet and rushed out, just as Kyles was rushing in, looking for a big turkish towel. Abernathy saw the hole in King's face and yelled: "Call an ambulance!"

Someone snatched a brown bedspread and wrapped it around the man's face. Men ran to various rooms and clicked the telephone receivers to call an ambulance; but Mrs. Lorraine Bailey had also heard the shot, and she was standing in the doorway, her fist against her mouth, looking upward at the porch in shock. No one was at the switchboard.

Abernathy unwound the blood-soaked bedspread and was surprised to find that the bleeding had stopped. He patted the left cheek. "Martin! Martin!" he moaned. "This is Ralph." Abernathy thought he saw the eyes move. He also thought he saw the lips move. "For God's sake," he yelled to Kyles. "Get an ambulance."

Andy Young and Bernard Lee were now at his side. "Oh, God, it's awful," Young said. "It's all over."

Anger replaced fright on Abernathy's face. "Don't you say that, don't you say that." Laue brought a big towel and double-folded it and placed it under Martin Luther King's head. Someone leaned down and listened to the chest and thought he heard a heartbeat. Solomon Jones, the chauffeur, asked a friend to go into the office and call the Lewis Funeral Home for an ambulance.

A group of uniformed men ran into the courtyard, and the men on the porch thought that they were policemen. They were firemen from a station a block away. In that station, they had a Memphis city ambulance. Everyone appeared to be too stunned by the sight on the porch to think of it. A policeman phoned headquarters that somebody at the Lorraine—maybe King himself—had just been shot.

The gold Nobel Prize watch on Dr. King's wrist felt the slam of the shot at 6:04 P.M. and survived, ticking off the seconds firmly and correctly, feeling the pulse of the man increase quickly and faintly, then stop. Black women, waitresses, maids, and guests were standing near the swimming pool screaming. Some of the black men up there on the porch were still lying flat. Four were standing, braving whatever dark danger there might be—Abernathy, Young, Kyles, and Lee. In a bathroom on the ground floor, A.D. was preparing to go home. He had not heard a shot.

An empty shell casing fell in the bathtub and rolled around the bottom. Surely, James Earl Ray must have been pleased. Once, just once, he had carried out an assignment correctly. Dr. Martin Luther King, Jr., had given him a minimum of three minutes standing in position on that porch. There was time, lots of time, to use the binoculars, to make certain that this was indeed the target, to set the rifle on the ledge of the window, to look through the cross hairs and see him close-up. It is probable that Ray took aim on the chest because the power and soft nose of the shell would have torn that chest wide open and tumbled as it traveled through lungs or heart or both. But at the last moment Jesse Jackson had said, "Oh, Doc . . ." and King had grasped the railing and bent forward.

If Ray felt any disappointment, he was quickly relieved because, as he squeezed the trigger, he saw King slam backward onto the porch and he did not move or twitch. This could be seen through the cross hairs or through the glasses. The shot made a tremendously explosive sound in the bathroom, and Ray was in no mood to linger. He picked up gun and binoculars and came out of the bathroom with both wrapped in a newspaper. The sound had awakened Mr. Stephens. He thought it sounded like a German 88. He went out into the hall in time to see a man, a silhouette of a man, walking up the dark hall. Willy Anchues came out of his bedroom just in time to confront the murderer. James Earl Ray had paused in his room for a moment. The Remington rifle was no longer inside a folded newspaper; it was inside a dirty green bedspread. In the same hand, he held a small blue travel bag. In it was his soiled underwear, a shaving kit, a cake of soap, and the binoculars.

Anchues said, "That sounded like a shot."

Ray was calm and smiling. "Yes," he said, "it was." He continued down the hall, selected the short stairway to the north of the manager's office, and walked down to the street.

He must have known that his fingerprints were on file in several places, including FBI headquarters, and he should have realized that his prints were all over the gun, the shaving cream jar, the binoculars. Still, he turned left, walked a few steps to a storefront with a recessed window, and dropped everything there. In this he was following the pattern of stupidity which had plagued his life of crime.

He had made his "big lick," and all that was lacking was the payoff. There was the possibility that his target might live, but Ray could afford the luxury of believing that his man would die. He dropped all the material which could be traced to him and did not notice that the store manager and two young black customers saw him drop the packages. The three saw a white man walk away from the store toward a white Mustang which was tightly parked at the curb.

Guy Canipe, the store manager, attached no significance to the package at that moment. Drunks on Main Street often discarded packages of empty bottles. The customers, Bernell Finley and Julius

Graham, returned to lifting long-playing records from the racks and reading the titles. Then something, a sense of something wrong, moved all three to go outside to find out what had been dropped. Canipe looked without touching and saw what he thought was a bedspread with the nose of a rifle sticking out and two cushions from a small boat. All of them saw the back of a man, in a white car, back up and pull out and move north on Main. He appeared to be in no hurry. James Ray drove north, thinking if he had been spotted, this would throw his pursuers off his trail. He planned to swing south as soon as he got lost in heavy traffic.

The small smile which was the trademark of James Earl Ray must have deepened a little as he passed the Butler Avenue firehouse. Three police squad cars had backed into it, blocking the fire engine and the ambulance. The six policemen had been detailed to cruise the area around the Lorraine Motel all day. They were assigned to watch for signs of riot, to control it while they called for help. As he passed, the fireman and policemen were racing in and out of the firehouse; one policeman was hopping over a fence. The police were there because this was their supper break; no superior officer had thought of ordering them to take a break one at a time. All three cars left the vicinity of the Lorraine at the same time—6 P.M.

The Mustang went by at the same pace as other cars. It is known that Ray turned his car radio on. Six P.M. is a radio news hour. The commentary made no mention of a shooting, except to say that the federal court had heard arguments from the city and the Southern Christian Leadership Conference about the injunction and an opinion was expected no later than tomorrow. There was hopeful news that Ho Chi Minh might be willing to discuss peace with the United States in a neutral area—somewhere in Europe perhaps, but that he was firm on one aspect, that the United States must agree to withdraw all troops before a settlement could be reached. This and some notable reactions from politicians about Lyndon Johnson's resolve not to seek another term of office dominated the newscast. The local news made no impression.

At 6:07 P.M. a Fire Department radio dispatcher sent a call over the air: "Shooting at four oh six Mulberry. Police are on scene. Four oh one respond." Four oh one was the ambulance in the firehouse around the corner from the Lorraine. It was behind police squad cars. The police had run off, at the first alarm, with guns drawn. The ambulance would have to wait.

A policeman, running back up Main Street from the south, passed the hilly lawn and stopped at Canipe's shop. His revolver was in his hand. Canipe and his customers pointed to the two bags. They pointed to the extruding muzzle of a rifle. The three men, excited, tumbling over one another in recounting what had happened, described the back of the white man who had dropped these things, and the Mustang. A few minutes later, Inspector N. E. Zachery, in charge of the Memphis Homicide Bureau, arrived. He borrowed a metal coat hanger and lifted the objects and turned them over. He ordered the patrolman to guard the packages until relieved. Then he began to disperse his men in the area to find out where the shooting had come from and—even more to the point—who had been shot.

At 6:06 P.M. someone from police headquarters phoned Robert G. Jensen, special agent in charge of the Federal Bureau of Investigation in Memphis, and was told that a man, probably Martin Luther King, had just been shot at the Lorraine. Jensen called Washington headquarters. The FBI was a bit slower than the Memphis Police Department. It wasn't until 6:30 P.M. that Jensen had orders to dispatch federal men to aid the local police.

The Lorraine was an enclosure of hysteria. Blue-helmeted policemen were running up and down stairs and in rooms. A lieutenant stood in the entranceway. Some blacks were on their knees in prayer. Others wept. An ambulance arrived from the Lewis Funeral Home at 6:08 P.M. A dignified middle-aged black, Ernest Merriwether, was at the wheel. A policeman told him to stop. Merriwether pointed up to the porch. "They sent for me," he said.

The policeman said, "Stay right where you are. A city ambulance is on its way." Merriwether kept the car parked outside the little switchboard office.

A man came running down from the porch with a mason jar half full of dark liquid. "Hey, Bailey," Merriwether shouted. "What you got there?"

The man held the jar up. "Dr. King's blood," he said.

"Yeah. What are you gonna do with that?"

"I don't know," the man said. "Maybe give it to a museum."

The city ambulance arrived, and two men took a stretcher from the back. Police on the porch helped them to place the body in a half-sitting position. A big towel was wrapped around the head; the mouth was pursed as if to murmur "Oh."

Policemen in the parking lot were asking which way the shot had come from. Abernathy and Jesse Jackson pointed to the rooming house on Main Street. Some police hurried around the block in squad cars. One hopped the back wall and ran through the weeds to enter the rooming house. Inspector Zachery ordered his men to inspect the rooming house from top to bottom.

The ambulance driver was ready. Several ministers suggested that Ralph Abernathy ride in back with his dead friend. The ambulance assistant helped him in. Andy Young hopped into the front seat. "Where are they taking him?" several men shouted. No one seemed to know. Merriwether backed his ambulance out into the street and followed. Solomon Jones took Bernard Lee in his car and drove out behind the two ambulances. In fire headquarters, a dispatcher yanked a switch, turning all lights on Main and Second streets green.

The nearest hospital was Gaston, a city hospital. The driver did not go there. He sped north to St. Joseph's Hospital, about twice as far away. At 6:10 P.M. Inspector Zachery's men had found two straps in Room 5-B which fitted the binoculars and case in front of Canipe's shop. They had also found shoe scuffs in the bathtub. At 6:11 P.M. a police dispatcher broadcast a *local* alert for "a young white male, well-dressed, believed to be in a late model white Mustang, going north on Main from the scene of a shooting." Properly, it should have been an all-points alarm, but Memphis police officials felt such an alarm would involve so many white Mustangs in surrounding states that traffic would be impeded. They must also have felt certain that the killer planned to remain inside the city, an incredible line of reasoning. In addition, the "north on Main" worked out exactly as James Ray had figured it would. Squad cars were concentrating north toward Kentucky when, in actuality, he was rolling south across the Mississippi border.

In the racing, screaming ambulance, Ralph held Dr. King's hand and pulled the towel away from his face. "Martin, this is Ralph," he litanized. "This is Ralph." He thought he saw King's eyes move and look at him. It is possible for life signs to be present for several minutes after the severing of the spinal cord, but they are meaningless and involuntary. King was dead before he hit the porch floor.

Behind them, Jones powered his Cadillac at top speed. Merriwether took his ambulance to the John Gaston Hospital by a shortcut, because it was the nearest and, if King died, an autopsy would be performed there. Bernard Lee, sitting beside Jones, told himself over and over: "He's dead. I know he's dead. I looked down at him right after it happened, and that man is dead. I saw his eyes roll once, but they didn't blink." Abernathy, still holding his friend's hand, recalled that he had run downstairs and told A.D. that his brother had been shot. A.D. did not leave his room. He collapsed in a chair. He did not go up to see his brother, nor did he go to the hospital. To Abernathy, so many things had happened so fast that it would take a long time to recall them. Had anybody phoned Coretta King?

The time in Atlanta was an hour later: 7:13 P.M. The phone rang. It was Jesse Jackson. "Coretta," he said "Doc's been shot."

Mrs. King was silent for a moment. This was the nighmare she had dreaded; these were the words she knew might be heard at any time. "Is he dead?" she whispered.

"No," Jesse Jackson said. "I don't know, but if I was you, I'd get the first flight out of Atlanta." The voice was almost under control.

"I'll check the next flight, Jesse."

"I think he was shot in the shoulder. Why don't you come to the motel and we'll take you to the hospital?"

Mrs. King put the phone back on its cradle. A few moments later it rang again. Another minister was on the phone from Memphis. "His condition is serious. He's not dead."

In the ambulance, the oxygen was flowing smoothly. The attendant regulated the valve, and Abernathy held the plastic mask over his friend's face. "How's he doing?"

"Very much alive," the attendant said. "Very conscious, good pulse, not even in shock, really." The ambulance was passing St. Jude Hospital at Winchester Avenue and was slowing for the turn into the emergency entrance of St. Joseph's.

A radio station interrupted a newscast to state that there was a report at police headquarters that the Reverend Martin Luther King had been shot at the Lorraine Motel. At the rooming house, the intoxicated and the sickly were aroused by noise of policemen with flashlights going through the corridors and rooms for clues. They questioned Bessie Brewer, Willy Anchues, and Charles Q. Stephens, and bit by bit, the mosaic of a stranger emerged. He had rented 5-B that very afternoon; the register was shown with the name "Willard"; one said he was "clean-cut"; another "well dressed," "had a sort of silly smile"; "he was in the bathroom several times"; "a drawl"; "paid with a new twenty-dollar bill."

Police took the bill, removed the bedclothes and pillows from the bed, dusted the room window and the bathroom window, confiscated the screen in the yard, found a dead cartridge case 30.06 in the bathroom, took photographs, and sent everything, including the package in front of Canipe's shop, to headquarters. There, Inspector Zachery examined the items in turn—a 30.06 rifle with telescopic sight; binoculars; five unused shells; a blue plastic bag containing two cans of Schlitz beer, a shaving kit, underwear, a hammer, pliers, a brush, and a copy of the April 4 Memphis Commercial Appeal, first section only.

At the Lorraine, the Reverend Dr. King's followers sat in desolation. A.D. did not leave his room. In 306, the Reverend Dr. Kyles and a few others sat in shock, sometimes speaking sporadically, aimlessly, trying to think of persons to call, turning up the radio for news, shutting it off, wondering if King would survive, watching police officers come and go, walking to the door to watch the crowd grow in twilight. Someone looked in King's bag and found a sheet of paper on which was written:

Ten Commandments on Vietnam:
1. Thou shalt not believe in a military victory.
2. Thou shalt not believe in a political victory.
3. Thou shalt not believe that they—the Vietnamese—love us.
4. Thou shalt not believe that the Saigon government has the support of the people.
5. Thou shalt not believe that the majority of the South Vietnamese look upon the Vietcong as terrorists.
6. Thou shalt not believe the figures of killed enemies or killed Americans.
7. Thou shalt not believe that the generals know best.
8. Thou shalt not believe that the enemy's victory means Communism.
9. Thou shalt not believe that the world supports the United States.
10. Thou shalt not kill.

This was to be read at an antiwar rally in New York on April 27.

The ambulance Ernest Merriwether was driving pulled slowly into the narrow alley leading to the John Gaston Hospital Morgue on Madison Avenue. The middle-aged man was certain that King had been taken here, not only because it was closer to the scene of the crime than St. Joseph's Hospital, but also because it was a city hospital, part of a two-block complex administered by the University of Tennessee.

Merriwether walked down the steps to the morgue. An attendant made a phone call and said that Dr. King had not been admitted to Gaston. The driver and assistant embalmer were perplexed. In cases like these, the Lewis Funeral Home made it a business practice to follow up severe accident cases to claim the bodies of blacks. Mr. Merriwether didn't know whether to go back to the funeral home or remain where he was. If King recovered, the ambulance would not be needed. If he died, the body would be shipped to Gaston at once for an autopsy. He drove back to the funeral home.

Mrs. King, in Atlanta, phoned her husband's secretary, Dora McDonald, and asked her to come over at once. She turned on the television, and by now regular programming had been preempted by the news about the shooting, although no one knew whether the wound was fatal or even serious. Coretta King was phoning Juanita Abernathy, explaining that she had tickets for the 8:25 P.M. flight to Memphis, in case Mrs. Abernathy wanted to join her.

She did not notice that her children had come into the room. They heard their father's name mentioned, and they crouched in front of the set. When she got off the phone, the boys asked, "What happened? What is it?"

Yoki, the eldest, ran weeping from the room, screaming, "Don't tell me! Don't tell me!"

Mrs. King called her back, took a deep breath, and assumed her controlled manner. "I'm getting ready to go to Memphis," she said, "because your daddy has been shot."

She said no more. The children accepted her calm attitude and assumed it as their own. Yolanda, who had never tried to do such chores, helped her mother to throw some clothes into a suitcase and lock it. The phone rang again, as it would all night long. This time it was Atlanta's Mayor Ivan Allen. "I called to ask if there is any help I can give you," he said. Mrs. King said she was leaving on an 8:25 P.M. flight. "Stay right where you are," the mayor said. "I'll be over in a few minutes to help." He got into a police car with a captain and moved fast.

The Memphis city ambulance backed up to the emergency entrance to St. Joseph's Hospital, and as Abernathy and Andy Young hurried out of the car, they were surprised to find that Bernard Lee and Solomon Jones were waiting in the Lewis funeral car. All three helped slide Dr. King from the ambulance. The only one who spoke to the toweled head was Dr. Abernathy. "Martin," he kept mumbling, "this is Ralph. Everything's going to be all right. You hear? Everything's going to be all right." The body was placed on a roller stretcher. Nursing nuns lined the corridor. They knew who the patient was. They prayed as he was turned into a room lined with light-green tile, and the door was closed.

A team of doctors and nurses was ready. The room was fairly small for such a large number of people and equipment—17 feet by 13. There was a heart-lung resuscitator, oxygen, a heart oscilloscope, a defibrillator, blood pressure gauge, a large overhead difusing spotlight, a sink, and fluorescent lights. On the far wall, as the towel was removed from the gashed face, the wide-open eyes did not see their original goal—Christ on a cross.

The team moved swiftly, whispering. One doctor examined the three-inch hole on the right side of the face; a nurse prepared an intravenous feeding of plasma and dextrose; a third nurse asked Abernathy and Lee to wait out in the hall. Lee, the one who resembled King in appearance and speech, said, "Don't you be concerned about us, miss. We're not going to leave, and we're not going to get in your way." She tried a second time as doctors lifted the body and began to cut his clothes off.

A surgeon pointed to the Nobel Prize watch and asked one of the ministers to remove it from the wrist. Bernard Lee did and put it in his pocket. Another doctor punched a hole in the bottom of Dr. King's throat and performed a tracheotomy. The electric monitor induced some wavy lines on the heart monitor, but Dr. King had been dead a half hour. "He's dead," Lee murmured to himself. "This is some kind of ritual they go through."

The clothes were removed. A sheet was placed caressingly on the body. A nurse carried the coat to a chair and draped it on the back. The Reverent Ralph Abernathy noticed that there was a hole in it. He permitted himself to think that this might be a serious matter. He listened to numbers as nurses repeated blood pressure findings and pulse. Man's scientific resistance to God's will continued for a half hour.

A doctor walked to the two men, peeling rubber gloves from his fingers, and said, "What they are doing now is what they do for important people—" He was caught by dead cold expressions and he amended the statement. "What they are trying to do, well, I doubt that they will be successful." The body had been turned facedown, and a doctor probed with his fingers and found the bullet, a colorless lump, sticking out between two vertebrae. It had lodged between them, severing the spinal cord, and had died there with Dr. King.

Somewhere the whirring of an exhaust duct stopped. A doctor pulled the sheet over Dr. King's face. A doctor glanced at Abernathy and Lee and said, "It's all over." The clock on the wall seemed to pause at 7:05. Bernard Lee walked to the clothing on the chair and removed a gold money clip and a checkbook.

"We will give the time of death to the press," one doctor said. "Any other announcement, we'll leave to you. They're waiting out in the reception room." In such cases of violent death, he explained, an autopsy was necessary, and either the ministers present or Mrs. King would have to grant permission because, if the killer were apprehended, the findings of the autopsy would become important.

"Will that be done here?" Abernathy said. The doctor said it would not but at a place called John Gaston Hospital. The body would be sent there at once. Lee and Abernathy remained in the emergency room for a moment or two, staring at the sheet.

By the time they walked out back the reporters and cameramen were present. The big lights went on, and the questions tumbled over one another. "How do you feel? . . . Is it true he died at seven oh five? . . . Who shot him? . . . The police are looking for a white man. Do you know anybody—"

The two men joined Andy Young and the driver in the limousine. "I don't want to answer any questions right now," Abernathy said. "I just want to go to the airport to meet Coretta. . . ."

Lee shook his head. "She can't get out of Atlanta this soon. Let's go back to the Lorraine and you tell A.D. Then we have to call Atlanta and get permission for an autopsy."

Police car 160, with Lieutenant Rufus Bradshaw at the wheel, was cruising the eastern section of Memphis on Route 14. At the corner of Jackson and Hollywood, Bradshaw was flagged down by a young man "who looked like a deacon." The driver was breathless with excitement. He said he had been listening to his citizens radio band, and a ham operator in a blue Pontiac had seen a white Mustang pass him by, had given chase, and begged "any available station" to relay details. The blue Pontiac was now behind the Mustang at high speed.

Bradshaw got out of his police car to listen. He heard the voice, the shrill sound, and he made notes. He called headquarters and relayed the information. In a moment, the police operator was on the air:

"Car One Sixty reported a white male driving a white Mustang on Summer from Highland." This would be a half mile east of Car 160's position, two streets north of the Chickasaw Country Club. "East on

Summer from Highland, white Mustang, responsible for this shooting. Cars thirty-six and forty-two, pull down. Subject is exceeding the speed limit east on Summer from Highland."

Bradshaw returned to the other car for more information. A minute later, the broadcaster said, "One sixty Repeat. One Sixty. You're being cut out. It's supposed to be a blue . . . all cars stand by . . . One Sixty repeat. One Sixty, you're still being cut out. Repeat. A blue Pontiac north on Mendenhall from Summer." This would be a mile farther east, indicating a turn north off Jackson, passing under Route 240 at the city limits. "One Sixty advises that this car is speeding over seventy-five miles per hour north on Mendenhall from Summer. There are three white males occupying a blue Pontiac, exceeding seventy-five miles per hour north on Mendenhall from Summer. Any location now, One Sixty?"

The police radio was silent for five minutes. The dispatcher came on: "The subject is on the way to Raleigh, north on Jackson toward Raleigh, a blue Pontiac occupied by three white males. These subjects are supposed to be wanted for the shooting." The police, bunched on the northern side of Memphis, sped eastward looking for a blue Pontiac. Winking red lights and sirens were seen and heard across the city. Car 160 was not reporting what Lieutenant Bradshaw saw, only what he heard from an excited voice on the citizens radio band.

The ham operator altered the streets: "speeding west on Macon . . . off Jackson onto Bayliss . . . down Homer to Macon . . . back west on Macon . . . at Jackson and Stage Road, running a red light at a hundred miles per hour." Shots were fired from the blue Pontiac to the Mustang. "Correction. The Mustang is firing on the Pontiac."

At 7 P.M. the radio reports stopped abruptly. Police began to wonder why, in a long and harrowing chase, the radio signal from the blue Pontiac didn't fade or gather strength.

It was a hoax perpetrated by an amateur radio operator. The badly needed police cars raced back to their emergency assignment.

In Atlanta the time was a little after eight. Lilie Hunter had moved into a new apartment. Her daughter Jackie, eighteen, was helping her unpack. Mrs. Hunter had been treasurer and bookkeeper of the Southern Christian Leadership Conference. Years earlier she had been Dr. King's secretary. Lilie Hunter was shoving end tables against the sides of a sofa. Jackie said, "Did you hear? Dr. King's been shot." Mrs. Hunter kept adjusting the end tables and polishing the tops. "Momma, the radio says he's dead." Mrs. Hunter started out the front door. "It's raining," her daughter said pathetically. "Momma, you have your bedroom slippers on."

The girl brought her mother a coat and shoes. The shocked woman got in her car and drove to the King home. Dora McDonald, who was Dr. King's current secretary, was present. Coretta King greeted Lilie with a dazed smile. The children were put in bed and soothed. Each woman assumed a task. Mrs. Hunter got Eastern Airlines on the phone and asked that two tickets be made out and ready for "Mrs. Martin Luther King, Jr., on the eight twenty-five flight to Memphis."

The clerk said, "Yes, ma'am. They'll be ready." Juanita Abernathy arrived breathless, wringing her hands.

Mayor Ivan Allen and his police captain hurried up the front porch and asked the women to hurry. Lilie Hunter and Dora McDonald got into the car with Mrs. King and Mrs. Abernathy. The car sped down the hill and across Atlanta to the airport. Someone remembered that Rachael Ward was with the children. Everyone assured everybody else that Dr. King's condition couldn't be serious. Mrs. King said she heard that it was a shoulder wound, that people seldom die of such injuries.

At the airport the police car was permitted to glide out onto the strip. Lilie Hunter ran back to the counter to get the tickets. A clerk said, "The Memphis manager just phoned. Dr. King died." There was disbelief on Mrs. Hunter's face.

Someone else said, "It just came over the radio."

At the gate, Lilie Hunter paused. Mayor Allen was speaking quietly to a policeman. "He's dead," the mayor said. "How are we going to tell Mrs. King?"

Lilie Hunter felt herself die a little. To Mrs. King, it was a husband. To Mrs. Hunter, it was a savior. She had grown up in Montgomery, Alabama, hating every white face she ever saw. She had husbanded this rancor until she started work for Dr. King. Slowly, over a long period of time, he had turned her thinking in the opposite direction. "Color," he had said many times, "has nothing to do with it. We have bad people. They have bad people. We got good ones; so have they."

Now the savior was gone, and it was more than a husband. It was a mentor, a Christian teacher of love, a hater of hate, a man who fought by keeping his hands down and accepting the blows of his enemies—the good man was gone. Lilie Hunter, dark and pert and blunt of speech, asked Mrs. King and Dora to step out of the car and accompany her to the airport ladies' room. The mayor followed them and stood inside the doorway. Mrs. King seemed apprehensive. The plane would be leaving any minute. Lilie looked at her beseechingly. "Your husband," she said firmly, then paused. "Your husband has passed on." Mrs. McDonald began to weep. Coretta King stood, head up, tilted a little back. A solitary tear rolled down her cheek, but she swept it away with her hand. She made no sound. Mrs. King walked out of the room.

The mayor said: "I'm sorry, Mrs. King. I'm very sorry."

Coretta King thanked him. "I don't think I'll go to Memphis," she said. "I'll go home to the children."

In the soft glow of the dashboard lights, James Earl Ray drove slowly and safely south, then east. He decided that he would go to Atlanta and figured he should make it by dawn. The car radio was on, and he heard the bulletins about the shooting, the excitement in Memphis, and then the pleasing announcement that Dr. Martin Luther King, Jr., had died at St. Joseph's Hospital shortly after seven o'clock. For once, the Smiler had achieved a "good lick," a successful job. He had drawn a bead on his victim and finished him with one shot.

From time to time, when headlights behind him approached at high speed, Ray expected to be stopped. The police were looking for a white Mustang. He wasn't afraid. There wasn't a bit of evidence in the car or on his person; his driver's license, made out in the name of Eric Galt, had a Birmingham address. Let them stop him and search everywhere. There was nothing to connect this man or this car to that crime. All he had to do was to get to Atlanta, ditch the car—a pity, because it was worth $1,000 on the open market—and meet his employer and get his plane tickets and his payoff.

It was going to be a slow, law-abiding ride, and he would stop somewhere on the road and buy a cup of coffee and gasoline. If he thought, even fleetingly, of all the convicts he knew and of how they said he was a born loser, they should see him now. He had pulled off the big job without a hitch, and here he was, free as a bird, watching the tawny concrete pass under his headlights.

Mayor Allen escorted Mrs. King up the walk to her home. If there was anything he could do. . . . She shook her head negatively. When she got inside, fatigued and sick, she found that little Dexter and Bunny were sleeping; Marty, the little man, was still awake; Yoki was answering phone calls. She followed her mother into the bedroom. The hat and bag were dropped on the bed, and Yoki said, "Momma, I'm not going to cry. I'm just not going to cry because my daddy's not really dead. Anyway, I'm going to see him again in heaven."

The child prattled on, tears inching down her soft cheeks. "Mommy," she said, "you're such a strong lady. Should I hate the man who killed my daddy?"

"No, darling. Your daddy wouldn't want you to do that." Mrs. King hugged her daughter. "You know, you're kind of brave and wonderful yourself. I'm proud of you. Your daddy would have been proud of you."

Marty and Dexter, now wide awake, sat waiting in their room. Their mother tried to speak to them. Marty wanted to say something, but the words stopped in his throat. Dexter, seven years old, said it for him: "Mommy, when is Daddy coming home?" This is a moment of trial.

"Dexter," Coretta King said softly, "do you know your daddy was shot?" The boy nodded. "He was hurt very badly. You go to sleep, and I'll tell you about it in the morning."

"All right," he said. Martin worked up a smile and a good-night kiss.

A phone call was waiting for Mrs. King. Memphis was calling. Would she permit an autopsy to be performed on the body? She asked if it was necessary. She was told that it was, and the findings would be important at any future trial. "All right," she said softly. "All right." The voice said that she would have to send a telegram to John Gaston Hospital agreeing to an autopsy. This would have to be done at once. It would have to be followed by a letter to the same place, with her true signature on it. "All right," she said. "I'll take care of it."

On the other side of Atlanta, Police Chief Herbert Jenkins stood inside the Ebenezer Baptist Church telling "Daddy" King the bad news. The old man displayed no shock. He wiped his glasses twice and asked a few questions. He pushed the cuticle up from a fingernail. This was news which was not news. This was a doom which could have been seen long ago. This was the deep toll of a requiem bell which he had heard many times. For this he had reared a bright boy, a brilliant boy, who had passed his father in depth of knowledge and natural leadership. It was a high price for the old man to pay, but he had known all along that he was going to have to pay it. The question was when, what city, what year, what day.

He would pay it now, and he could not afford the deep well of grief;

"Daddy" King required all the strength and calmness he exposed to the world to comfort his wife. For her there would be the release of wracking sobs—for him there was only the composed "Thank you, Chief" as Jenkins left.

Hundreds of millions of people had reacted in shock. Others shrugged; some rejoiced. Mayor Henry Loeb sat before the cameras and the bouquet of microphones and said, "After the tragedy which has happened in Memphis tonight, for the protection of all our citizens, we are putting the curfew back into effect. All movement will be restricted except for health or emergency reasons." Governor Buford Ellington, fearful of black rioting (as were many officials in many cities) called out the National Guard riot troops. "I can fully appreciate the feelings and emotions which this crime has aroused," he said, "but for the benefit of everyone, all of our citizens must exercise restraint, caution, and good judgment."

Some bottles were thrown at police cars, some windows were broken, a few fires were started; but the resentment was sporadic and sketchy. Most of the blacks remained at home, listening to the story on television. Police Chief Holloman issued an announcement: "I and all the citizens of Memphis deeply regret the murder of Dr. King today. Every resource of the Memphis Police Department, the Shelby County Sheriff's Office, and the Tennessee Highway Patrol is committed and dedicated to identifying and apprehending the person or persons responsible." Robert Jensen, special FBI agent in charge of the Memphis office, had his men out combing the city for clues. J. Edgar Hoover, at his office in Washington, phoned the news to the White House.

President Lyndon Johnson was in the middle of a meeting of diplomats and was irritated by the approach of an assistant with a note. He read it, said, "Martin Luther King's been shot in Memphis," and ordered Attorney General Ramsey Clark to take charge of the federal side of the investigation. Within a few hours, seventy-five special agents were on a Memphis plane.

Mrs. King phoned her father-in-law, and he said over and over, "I always felt I should go first." She phoned her mother and brother Obie, in Alabama, and asked them to come to Atlanta to be with her.

Memphis squad cars patrolled the streets slowly. The riotous chase was over. Policemen stared up and down Main Street and Beale and Second, looking for pedestrians and ordering them off the streets. The downtown shops were bright with lights, but customers were few. The city was faced with the irreversibility of a death it could not afford. The black sections of the city were patrolled with care, car windows rolled up and door locks on.

Off-duty policemen were called in. An hour passed, and Memphis was as quiet as King's heart. The Southern Christian Leadership Conference leaders, holed up at the Lorraine, moved freely up and down stairs, but only Abernathy was prepared to brave the Loeb edict. He went downstairs to A.D.'s room and walked in to find a man who was trying to insulate himself from truth. King's brother sat staring into space. He knew that Martin had been shot, but he was afraid to turn on the radio or the television. So he sat until Abernathy came in and put his arms around A.D.

Then the lively and sometimes irresponsible member of the family began to crack. "He's gone, A.D.," Abernathy said. "He's gone." The younger brother broke loose from the arms and the chair and walked the room sobbing. Abernathy could not cry. He said, "I'm going to the hospital where they've taken him. I got to be with him, A.D." He waited for the younger man to offer to go, but A.D. turned from reality.

He wiped his eyes. "I'll stay here, Ralph," he said.

There was a soft coolness in the night air as Abernathy trudged back up the outside stairs holding onto the railing like an old man. It seemed that everyone was in Room 306. They sat on the chairs, the beds, the floor. The black apostles had lost their messiah, and they were trying to face it, to admit it, to discuss it, but the shock was too fresh to be acknowledged.

All of them recalled the meeting in Birmingham when Dr. Martin Luther King, Jr., had requested the leadership of the Southern Christian Leadership Conference to amend the bylaws so that, in the event of his death or incapacitation, his place would be taken by the Reverend Ralph Abernathy and no one else. The convention had passed the measure unanimously. Everyone knew that Abernathy was the new head, but no one mentioned it. He knew it, too, but it would be indecent to bring it to the attention of this group.

Andy Young went into the bathroom and asked Ralph to come with him. He was troubled about some remark that he had made that day to King, something that could have been misinterpreted. He asked Abernathy if King had mentioned it, and Abernathy said that King had made no mention of it to him. When they emerged from the bathroom, Jim Bevel stood like a boy who has a set speech to make. "Martin is dead," he said. "Jesus died. In many respects, I loved Martin more than I did Jesus. Jesus hasn't come back"—he hung his head—"and Martin won't either." A few people nodded. There was no response. Abernathy was to fire three men from the hierarchy of the organization. Jim Bevel was to be the first.

"The course is clear," Bevel said. He stared at Abernathy. "We have our leader. Lead on until there is no hunger in this land; lead on until there is no poverty. Lead on . . ."

Abernathy left. He had to step on the place on the porch where his friend and mentor had been slain. He looked out into the darkness from which a rifle shell had split the air. Behind him, Andy Young and Hosea Williams and Bernard Lee followed. "If you're going to the autopsy," the Reverend Samuel Kyles said in the room, "count me out. I can't face it."

In the darkness, someone said, "There are a lot of reporters waiting down there for a statement."

"Not now," Abernathy said glumly. "Maybe in the morning, but not now."

When a group of Black Panthers in Los Angeles heard the flash on radio, they got together to discuss the apocalypse. The time to burn America to the ground had come. The young blacks could not help feeling glad that the "lamb" had been slain instead of themselves, the "lions."

"For two years," Earl Anthony said, "we had discussed taking it to this mad dog, racist America, and we knew our struggle would end in total victory or total defeat. We felt frustration because of Dr. King, that stumbling block. Sometimes we even said: 'If that man was dead, it would speed up time.' "

These Black Panthers met in a torture of delight. Each in turn said that he had waited for something to move King "out of our way." Now he was out of the way, and they were certain that a holocaust would envelop the city within twenty-four hours.

It didn't happen. Rioting occurred in 130 cities. The toll was $130,000,000 in damage—mostly in black sections—and 34 Negroes and 5 whites would be dead within the span of one day.

A former agent of the Federal Bureau of Investigation, Dan Smoot, spoke for the fearful white minority when he said that Dr. King "was closely associated with Communists and sex deviates. His program for America was the unadulterated Communist program."

Yes, there would be a summing up, by the right, the left, and the middle. By the faithful as well. Had a great Christian been cut down this night, or was he a janissary of personal ambition and private lusts, a man like any other, a stage manager and actor, a public paragon or a private pariah? Or perhaps all of them? He would be judged by his peers of press and pulpit now, and some would say that the hand of God had snatched from our presence a modern Jesus, and others would say that a divisive revolutionary had been slain, but not soon enough.

His public life had embraced a crusade of 13 years. It must be said that this is a short span in which to undo the racial injustices of 300 years. It wasn't even his goal or his announced dream until the bus boycott of 1955 in Montgomery, Alabama, had propelled him into a leadership he had not sought. The one day walk-to-work scheme had spread itself over a year. The fight begun by Martin Luther King in Alabama was won in Washington before the United States Supreme Court.

And yet, as a martyr on this night of April 4, 1968, he was closer to success than in life because, for the first time, he pinched the conscience of all. He was dead, gone, speechless for all eternity. He had been overtaken by the darkness he feared most, and now he would be sanctified—parks and boulevards and playgrounds would be named for him. The man who, in life, had been looked upon as a Satan of municipal trouble, had become the Black Christ.

In the dark, reporters and photographers sat on the big wall outside John Gaston Hospital like silent hawks. Merriwether had phoned before leaving the Lewis Funeral Home with his ambulance, and he knew that an autopsy was being performed by Dr. Jerry T. Francisco and his associates. He backed his ambulance up to the loading platform. Inside, Ralph Abernathy and Bernard Lee stared fascinated at a big sheet of brown wrapping paper covering the outlines of a body.

Gently, Dr. Francisco asked Abernathy to make a positive identification. Part of the paper was lifted, and he saw the gashed face of his dearest friend, the brown eyes still staring straight up. "That's him," his friend said, "that's Martin Luther King, Jr." Abernathy backed up against a wall to stand beside Lee. They had decided that they would stay with their friend through this last ordeal.

One doctor began the classic V incision from the two shoulders to a point below the sternum and then down to the pelvix. Another incised from one ear across the top of the head to the other, and pulled the scalp away as one might peel an orange. Saws were brought out and the entire top of the skull—called the calvarium—was removed. The work was orderly and unhurried; observations about heart, liver, lungs, and viscera were written on a pad; each was weighed and examined for grossness. They were then thrown down a deep and broad sink in the floor. The brain was lifted out carefully, examined, and weighed.

The two witnesses were sickened by the thought that there would be nothing left of their friend when this was over except skin and bones. The stomach was roughly sewn, and it caved in. The body was turned over. A probe removed the bullet in the spine, a mangled piece of metal. Ralph Abernathy had signed for permission to perform the autopsy because it was the only way he could get the body back from the city of Memphis. What was left was about a hundred pounds of disfigured clay. It looked like nothing, nobody.

Ralph Abernathy remembered Dr. King had brought one suit with him and that had been cut off by surgical scissors. He had to find a temporary suit; a temporary casket—until King got back to Atlanta where Coretta King could make the decisions.

One of the doctors called Ernest Merriwether in. He yanked a sheet from the nude body to show how little was left of Martin Luther King, Jr. "I'm afraid," he said, "you're going to have a closed casket ceremony. There will be no viewing of the remains." Merriwether knew that he and his embalmer, Charles Morris, could build up the stomach by fashioning a large ball of plaster of paris to place inside. A black man in Memphis, he made no charges, asked no favors.

He called his driver. "Help me wheel this out and put it on our stretcher," he said. Abernathy and Lee followed. The time was 10 P.M. The night sky was clear and cool; stars winked blue and white. From the high wall, flash bulbs popped like fire flies, and policemen could be seen crouching up there with rifles on their knees.

No matter what the condition of the body, Merriwether was content that the body was now "ours." It would require a lot of work to make the body presentable for viewing, but he and Mr. Morris would work all night, if necessary, to do the job. The ride back was only seven streets down Manassas to Beale Street to Vance, but the press waited on every other corner to take pictures of the passing ambulance.

Lee and Abernathy drove to the Lewis Funeral Home behind the ambulance in silence. Abernathy thought of Coretta King and what lay ahead in Atlanta. Lee was thinking of how Martin was about to take a long step forward—"go for broke" at the Poor People's March on Washington. Secretly, King was prepared to announce that Congress and the President should promulgate a bill which would eliminate poverty from the United States forever. He was planning to ask for a rock-bottom income of $3,600 a year for every family of four—black or white. Thirty-six hundred would not only eliminate ghettos, but it would create tremendous purchasing power which would filter up through the merchants with a good part of it being returned to the government as income tax.

He knew that a white Southern cry would be raised against it, that millions of black fathers would be called lazy and shiftless with no more energy than is required to get to a paymaster's window. King was to counter with the proposition that, whatever the black father earned, his wage would be supplemented by the government to reach $3,600 a year. It was a notion calculated to restore the prestige of Martin Luther King among his people. It was also calculated to place Lyndon Johnson and Congress on the defensive, a theme King could hammer again and again all over the South.

Lee thought of these things and knew that they were as dead as the man a half block ahead of them. No matter who followed in King's shoes, he was bound to lack the dynamism and the gift for making great masses of people hush and listen.

Merriwether turned into the driveway of the two-story funeral home and drove to the back. There was a small separate building which was used for embalming, and Charles Morris would be waiting. He backed the ambulance to the entrance. He and the driver carried the stretcher inside. Abernathy and Lee went through the side entrance of the funeral home to see Mr. Thomas, owner of the establishment. Again, the press hovered on the porch, ringing the bell, asking questions, getting few answers. Dr. Abernathy sent word that he would see them in the morning at the Lorraine Motel. Thomas asked what would be required. "Well," said Abernathy, "the man on the ambulance said that he would make Dr. King look like himself again." Lee looked around and noticed the good taste of the funeral home. There was good green carpeting, a large mirror adjacent to a stairwell, several large rooms with rows of metal camp chairs, and gray draped curtains in front where a casket would repose. The overhead lights could be sharpened or dulled by a rheostat.

"He is going to need a temporary suit of clothes, too," Abernathy added, "and all that goes with it—a shirt and matching tie—a temporary casket so that the remains may be viewed here before we take him back home." Thomas nodded. He understood. The two men asked if they could go out back and view the embalming. Thomas was reluctant. "It's not pretty to watch, but he was your friend. Come, follow me."

They walked out back and down a yellow concrete ramp and walked across the yard to the vague building which almost blended with the night. Inside were several bodies covered with sheets, a black arm or foot sticking out. The two men noticed the same tiled walls, the sloping floor, and the big open-throated sink in the middle. Morris talked little. He worked. Merriwether worked and talked. His natural dignity and graying hair lent itself to his attitude of speaking like a professor explaining science to a neophyte student.

"We figure to be finished with this job by about six A.M.," he said cheerfully. Morris cut the scalp stitches in the head and peeled it back again, exposing a deep pink and white cavity. The stomach sutures were ripped open. At 11 P.M. Merriwether was mixing plaster of paris into balls. He was working against time because he did not want the body to stiffen before the work was finished. He had two major tasks. One was to refashion a plump stomach; the other was to make a ball which would fit almost exactly inside the skull, so that when the scalp was pulled together, there would be no unnatural wrinkles on the forehead and the features would appear to be in repose. Morris had a difficult assignment, closing the ragged three-inch gash on the side of the face, but he had fifty-two skin tones from which to choose, and he matched and re-matched until even Abernathy could not tell where the wound had occurred.

It was late when an FBI agent arrived at police headquarters and asked Inspector Zachery if the Washington office could borrow all the evidence temporarily. There, in the most scientific laboratories, it would be examined and photographed and, within a few days, it would be back in Memphis police headquarters. At the time, no one knew what an easy case this was going to be. The murderer had left his fingerprints on the rifle, the bag he carried, the scope, the binoculars.

He had been in prison so often that his fingerprints were on file in Washington, and whether he assumed the name of Eric Galt or John Smith, the bureau would know within a few hours that the man they were looking for was James Earl Ray, the archfailure among thieves. Inspector Zachery told Jensen that his men had even sawed off the windowsill of the rooming-house bathroom, and he could have that, too.

All he asked was that each item be marked, and that the Federal Bureau of Investigation sign a receipt for it.

At Washington headquarters, the early guesses were that Dr. Martin Luther King, Jr., had been killed by a vengeful husband. For four years FBI agents had put a tap on King's phone no matter where he was. This had been executed on the order of Attorney General Robert F. Kennedy, who had proclaimed himself a friend of Martin Luther King. The FBI was tracking connections between King and known members of the Communist Party. What they were getting was anything else but.

Before the Memphis evidence arrived that night, the FBI was busy listening to tapes of Dr. King's conversations with women other than his wife, listening for clues. Around midnight, when a special plane arrived with Attorney General Ramsey Clark and seventy-five special agents, the evidence was carefully crated and sent to Washington. Then, and then only, did they realize that the quarry was not a jealous man, but an ignorant one, who would try anything if there was money in it.

Sleepless, Ralph Abernathy and Bernard Lee returned to the Lorraine. They were satisfied that the embalmers would make the remains look like Dr. King. It was after 11 P.M., and in a short while, this tragic day would be done. In Room 306, Billy Kyles, Jesse Jackson, and others of the ministerial group were answering phones, making calls, and trying to hold reporters off the porch. Ralph and Bernard moved between them and into the room. The door was locked. Abernathy told them the gruesome details of what he had seen and that everything was going to be "all right."

Someone had heard that Robert Kennedy was sending Coretta King on a special plane to pick up the body in the morning. It was thought that there would be a short viewing of the body in Memphis, a ministerial service over the remains, and they would get Merriwether or his driver to take the casket to the airport. The only piece of business not taken care of was that the Southern Christian Leadership Conference could not continue to exist without a head.

It was suggested that everyone remember that at last year's convention in Birmingham it was Dr. King himself who suggested that there should be a law of succession. He said that the members of the staff could vote for anyone they pleased, but he felt that because he and Ralph Abernathy had been so close for so many years, "he is best equipped to speak for me when I go." If there was objection, it was swallowed in silence. The board voted unanimously that Ralph Abernathy be known henceforth as executive vice-president of the Southern Christian Leadership Conference, with the right to succession as president.

A vote was taken in the room. It was unanimous for Abernathy. The jowly man with the mustache was now head of the organization. He too was pledged to nonviolence, and while this could scarcely have pleased some of the more militant members of the board, they did not fight his right to succession. The news was announced to the press at once. To some, Abernathy was a superficial joker, a man who would rather laugh than make momentous decisions; to others, he was as sincere as King, but a man who lacked the intellectual capacity to match his mentor. To still others, the Southern Christian Leadership Conference, without King, would lack impact and integrity; it would die slowly but surely no matter who led it now.

The lawyer, Chauncey Eskridge, wasn't dwelling on these things. He was thinking how ironic it was that in his public life, Dr. Martin Luther King, Jr., had raised $20,000,000 for his gallant fight, but that all he had to leave his family was $5,000 in cash. He had $15,000 in life insurance. Friends of the SCLC would, in time, raise the sum of $689,000 for Coretta King and her children, but on the night of his death, King was poor indeed.

At midnight, President Lyndon Baines Johnson ordered the flags at all military installations to be lowered to half-staff.

II. DAWN

3

ATLANTA IN THE SPRING is a granite boutonniere. Dogwood blooms everywhere; azalea lends it complementary colors to lawns and fields; redbud shivers in the cool breezes, and crab apple drops blossoms one at a time. Atlanta is also a miracle. It is one of the few cities in the world with a population of more than 1,000,000 not built on a navigable river. It was created by railroads, eight of which built their terminals within the city limits. Until World War II, Atlanta, Georgia, clung to its traditions of Southern gallantry and pink parasols.

Then big industry moved in, and with industry and industrial skyscrapers came the Northerners. The city, sprawled through two counties, became the true, if not the actual, capital of the South. By day it shone a thousand feet above sea level at the foot of the Blue Ridge Mountains. More than a hundred years ago it was one of the first Confederate States cities to reconcile itself with the North, even though it was the most ravaged of all—having been burned to ashes in a war between the states. Atlanta did more than extend a hand to the North; it cleared the charred wood, rebuilt the houses and farms, enticed business to use its warehouses as a distribution center, and invented Coca-Cola.

The man who made Coca-Cola was Asa G. Candler. He died the same year Martin Luther King, Jr., was born. Candler was an institution, a landmark, like Stone Mountain. King was a squalling infant born on a chill day in January, 1929. It would require four, close to five years, for him to understand that he was a black man, and even though the metropolis of the South was known to be tolerant, almost liberal with its blacks, there came a time in all families when little white boys were forbidden to play with little black boys.

The Kings were not poor. They lived in a two-story gingerbread house on Auburn Avenue, where a child could peek between the tall hedges and look down the hill at the ghetto. Martin Luther King, Sr., was a respected Baptist pastor. He was a stern preacher of the old school who boomed the words of promise and doom. His church was the Ebenezer Baptist Church, a brick edifice which seemed to acquire holiness with age. His father-in-law had been pastor of that church for thirty-seven years before him.

The oldest child was Christine, born a year before Martin Luther King, Jr., and two years before Alfred Daniel King, the stubborn independent member of the family. A.D. seldom accepted advice from anyone, except his father, who had swept his own mind clean of all influences except the tracts of the King James Bible. In downtown Atlanta, "Daddy" King drove his own car, refused to truckle to white tradesmen, and, on one occasion when he was buying shoes for son Martin, sat in the front of the store. When the shoe clerk asked, apologetically, that the pastor and boy sit in the rear, the minister intoned that the benches in the back were no more comfortable than those in the front, and, assuming that the shoes were the same, he would sit there or trade elsewhere.

On another occasion, a policeman stopped the Reverend Mr. King's car for a minor infraction and said, "Listen, boy—" Pastor King stopped him. He pointed to little Martin. "That," he said, "is a boy. I am a man." Nor was Pastor King's wife an "average" black. She was a school teacher with an abiding fear: that her husband's independence would bring trouble to the family.

The King children were ready for enrollment in a black school before the law required them to attend. School age began at six. Martin attended at the age of five, his mother standing beside him insisting that he was six. He proved his academic accomplishments by pointing to a sign across the street and reading it aloud: FOR WHITES ONLY. This was in the winter of 1934, and in April he told his classmates about his birthday party. "There were five candles," he said proudly. The teacher expelled him at once, and he spent a year at home playing games with white and black boys. At age six, he was again enrolled in the first grade, but his knowledge proved so superior to the childish textbooks that he was at once advanced a grade and sat in the second with his sister.

There comes a time in every child's life when "spending money" becomes important. Martin wanted a baseball. Martin wanted a kite to fly. Martin wanted a spinning top. The Reverend Mr. King handed down a neo-papal bull: "There will be no free spending money in the family. What you want, you work for." The boy was given a newspaper route and sold the Atlanta *Journal*. At the age of thirteen, he was assistant manager of a neighborhood station.

He enjoyed reading and rereading his father's books, and this bred discontent with public libraries. Those books had to be returned. Martin bought his books, kept them in his upstairs room, and read and reread them. He was young when he learned what it was to be black. He and A.D. shared a bicycle, and Martin had a white friend who rode the handlebars. They were the firmest of friends until the white boy's mother came to the door one afternoon and, with some hesitation, advised Martin to break up the friendship and "not come around here any-more."

The shock didn't bring tears. It stunned him. He had to find out what a Negro was and especially what was different about pigmentation. He always called Mrs. King "Mother dear" and referred to Grandma Jenny Williams as "Mama." He asked them what a Negro was and why he was one. He wanted to know whether blacks were special or unspecial. In either case, looking out from his dark eyes, he saw no skin color and could not understand its importance. The women told him the story of slavery as gently as possible and how the white man in Atlanta (there were two of him to every black) owned the businesses and resources and, because of the history of slavery, servitude and ignorance, looked down on the black as an inferior being whose existence could be suffered so long as he was not "uppity" and remembered "his place." None of it satisfied Martin's curiosity. He bought books detailing the history of slavery in Africa and the United States, the great war between the states, the freeing of the blacks, the story of Harriet Tubman, the skinny black woman of iron who plotted and engineered the underground escape routes to the North for runaway slaves.

There were black uprisings, doomed to failure and sudden death, by Nat Turner and Denmark Vesey, and there were prophetic preachings of George Washington Carver and Frederick Douglass. Martin was reading books about his race when he was twelve, and absorbing the things a youngster of fifteen might assimilate. Every book led to more questions, which led to more. Neither Chris nor A.D. displayed interest, pride, or shame in their blackness, and they spent carefree childhoods.

When he was eleven, Martin was transferred to a private laboratory school inaugurated by Atlanta University. The classes were small and the students exceptionally bright, but the school closed two years later. And yet Martin Luther King, Jr., had absorbed a great deal of knowledge, and he already had a budding credo which would never be altered: All a black man had to do to be an acceptable success in a white world was to be twice as smart as everyone else and twice as good a Christian.

It was simple.

"Daddy" King had a capacity for anger. The planes of his face were firm, and he was easily affronted. His reactions to people were almost a mirror of theirs to him. If they were considerate, the Reverend Mr. King could become courtly. When the voice and words were sharp (as in the case of a disagreement inside or outside the family), the thunderheads appeared on his brows and the deep bell toll of his speech dominated the scene. He was the one and only lion in his home and in his church. When the matter of racial tension arose, he looked down the table from one face to another and said, "You are as good as anybody else." It was a defensive credo used again and again. Of the family only Martin, Jr., accepted the dictum at face value. If his father said he was as good as anyone else, then he was as good as anyone else because his father would rather die than lie.

The Atlanta black comunity had dentists, doctors, teachers, lawyers, funeral directors, insurance companies, dignified churches, and a bank. Only the strong, the aggressive, the well endowed, and the well educated were successful. There were two black insurance companies and a chain of five black drugstores with qualified pharmacists. One industrialist was referred to as a millionaire, and he did not deny it; but he was a few hundred thousand short of deserving the name.

"Daddy" King was one of the strong ones. He grew up on a farm twenty miles outside of Atlanta. When he was fifteen, he dropped his hoe and went to Atlanta. He bent his back and carried freight in the railroad yards. At night, he washed himself and donned his one black suit and attended school. None of it was easy. Often, in class, he shook his head violently from side to side to remain awake.

He spent eleven years in high school. He studied five more in Morehouse College. By the time he had been ordained a Baptist minister, Father King was thirty-one years of age, married to Alberta Williams, and had a child. Life, he felt, was meant to be harsh, and he was prepared to accept it. That is why he wore dignity and found it impossible to forgive the chronic weakling. His children were told to sit straight in their chairs, and listen. A.D. could do it without absorbing the speech. Chris was polite and shy. Young Martin drank the words as gospel and asked questions.

As a high school junior, Martin was elated to find that his big words and the quality of his thoughts resulted in his being selected for the debating team. An arrangement was made with a black high school in Valdosta for three students from each of the two schools to engage in oratory. There would be prizes.

Martin Luther King, Jr., did not win. He was beaten soundly. His big words brought smiles to the faces of the parents and teachers sitting below the stage. On the way home by bus, a long trip, he sat in front and sulked beside a classmate. The bus made a village stop, and the driver ordered the blacks to go to the back of the bus.

Martin looked out the window. Older blacks got up and moved. The driver turned to stare hard at the boy. "Hey," he said, "I mean you. Get out of that seat and let those people sit down." Martin and his friend remained seated. The driver's voice lowered to a soft, ugly tone. "Nigger," he said, "I'm going to call the police. We'll see if you'll move."

His teacher, Miss Sarah Grace Bradley, walked from the back of the bus to Martin's side. She whispered to him. She asked him, for her sake, to move to the back of the bus. Slowly, he arose and, finding no seats in the rear, stood hanging onto a strap. His friend followed him.

He was not an average student by any standard. Morehouse College accepted Martin Luther King, Jr., as a freshman when he was fifteen years old. The black professors judged the stocky boy to be one of those rare students born with an old head. It was a deserved tribute because the King boy not only excelled in his studies, but was driven by curiosity to go beyond them.

While others tossed a ball on the campus after school hours, this one drained the library of every book he could find about American and black history. He was lukewarm about sports, and in disputes with his classmates, Martin Luther King, Jr., preferred words to fists. Late on sunny afternoons, the dark eyes darted across thousands of lines of type, and like most readers, King remembered the things important to him and forgot the rest.

By the time he was sixteen it was assumed by all except his mother that he would become an ordained minister and follow his father and his grandfather. Only "Mother dear" comprehended that Martin had not made a decision. For a while he thought of studying medicine. Law magnetized his mind at another time. Teaching—a full professorship somewhere—had attractions, too.

The more he read, the clearer it became that to be black was to be inferior. The whites had inflicted second-class citizenship on the black, and worse, many of the blacks subscribed to it. They refused to assert whatever legal rights they had, and they were apathetic about the future. The "poor white trash," who were hardly better off than the blacks, treated them like animals, beasts who could speak like humans.

This shocked young King more than those who lived down in the ghetto because they were aware of the situation at their first conscious moment and had learned to accept it. Martin came from a proud and affluent family; he never missed a meal; he had good clothing to wear; as long as he remained in his neighborhood, he was respected, respectful, and polite. On those occasions when he went downtown to buy something, he was a "nigger," one who would not be waited on in a store when his turn came, the butt of short tempers and acidulous tongues when he didn't make up his mind quickly or took too long reaching into his trouser pocket for money. And yet the money he placed on the counter was identical to that of the white people; his soft voice was more suppliant than the whites, and he was unafraid to say "please" and "thank you." He saw white farmhands whose skin was almost as dark as his own, and they were treated politely in the downtown stores. Thus skin tone could not be the explanation for this frightening situation which would remain with him for the rest of his life. It had to be more than color. The bones, the flesh, the anatomical structure were alike everywhere, but dark people were inferior and white people were superior.

In the heat of summer, he could not buy a Coca-Cola in a five-and-ten-cent store, nor could he use the sparkling water fountain in a white park. To get on a bus, he had to run to enter the front door, drop the coin into a clanking machine, and then run out to enter by the back door. Sometimes the white drivers accepted the fare, then slammed the back door before he could get aboard. When he complained at home, he was told that this was common practice and to expect more of it.

Friends who denied going through a red light in their cars to a policeman often came home with split scalps, the ruddy blood shining in rivulets through the black hair. Others were sent to hospitals unconscious and under arrest for "resisting an officer." A few never got home. Black men walked with their heads down; they dared not chance being caught looking at things they were not supposed to see. All of it seemed to be part of a world which had a desperate need for brutality.

He sat in the balcony of the local motion-picture house to see *Gone with the Wind* and was appalled to see that Hattie McDaniel, a stout black, won an Academy Award—an Oscar—for playing the loud-mouthed Mammy to the pretty white girls who talked incessantly of their beaux. Martin went back to the library and drew out a book on motion-picture history. He read that the greatest of all directors, David Wark Griffith, had, in 1915, produced a flickering silent picture called *The Birth of a Nation* in which blacks were depicted as amoral and thieves and the Ku Klux Klan was exalted as a strong force for justice and righteousness in the South.

Nor was this all. *The Octoroon* was an old picture which showed clearly that any person of mixed blood would be disinherited by both races. Pure blood lineage—extreme white or extreme black—was acceptable. Any mixture, however slight, on discovery meant instant disinheritance by the whites and a frigid attitude on the part of the blacks. So, he reasoned, it was blood that made the difference. It was like breeding a good setter with a German shepherd—the result was nothing.

He started to read the outline of an old motion picture of mockery— made in 1905—but King couldn't complete it. It was called *The Wooing and Wedding of a Coon.* Nor did he like to attend current pictures in which figures such as Stepin Fetchit were frightened by ghosts, stuttered, and ran in hysteria as the white audience laughed.

Other matters became apparent. Some blacks didn't like the word "Negro"; they preferred "colored." Others discounted both words in favor of "black." For a while, Martin King thought that the people of his race despised themselves. But he had figured out what kept most of them shuffling to and from work, accepting small wages for backbreaking labor: It was the church.

Nothing except food was more important to the Southern black than the church. He belonged to several denominations, but mainly, he was a Baptist. Church was his private and sacred sanctuary from the white man. There were three big churches within six blocks of Martin's house. The black man had to believe in Christ. Unless he did, there was no reason for continuing to suffer on earth.

Without Jesus Christ and a heaven after death, there was no hope at all. On Sundays the churches were crowded in the morning and they were jammed at night. Men like Martin Luther King, Sr., preached the word of Jesus and spoke of the serene beauty of heaven to lift the spirits of the black women in their big white hats and the black men in their black suits.

The church was the only place where a man with a message could draw the undivided attention of his people. It was the only place where, when the hymns were chanted, feet stomped the floor in rhythm and the mezzos mingled with the bassos, the faces shining with a rare and valid reason to smile, the hands clapping, and God listening. Escapism, yes. But it was also a reason to dress up and sit with the unseen God, no matter what his color, and know there was someone more powerful than the white man who loved and cared about you.

In his senior year at Morehouse, King decided to become a minister. It was not a final decision, but he felt that he could reach more of his people and preach more of his "uplift" creed from a pulpit than at a classroom chalkboard. He could teach the solemn dignity of his father to black people and make them conscious of their importance to the American economy. He might even be able to stop the happy and momentary shouts of "Amen!" and make the people think and talk of progress after they left the church.

The black students at Morehouse College, young men of intellect and learning, knew a "nigger" when they saw one. Their hope was: "Give us a generation or two to catch up and, percentage-wise, we will have as many lawyers, engineers and doctors as you."

Toward the end of World War II the blacks had good leaders—men like A. Philip Randolph, the tall, unsmiling head of the Pullman porters; Roy Wilkins of the National Association for the Advancement of Colored People (and William White, who preceded him); W. E. B. Du Bois, who begged all blacks to return to Africa; and strong local leaders such as the Reverend Martin Luther King, Sr., who not only was a clergyman of consequence in Atlanta, but was also a member of the board of the Citizens Trust Company, a member of the board of Morehouse College, a leader in the Atlanta NAACP, and an officer of the Negro Voters League.

There were strong men in the ranks, but the common man expected his leaders to accomplish advances without help. The 400 enrolled students at Morehouse College were constantly exhorted to act and think like "Morehouse" men, as though the college were the Harvard of the blacks. It had three classroom buildings, a dormitory, an administration building, and a small steeple. It was unimpressive except for its old magnolia trees, which lent a lofty dignity to what man had wrought.

In philosophy, Martin was a C student, and that tells the story of his first year at Morehouse. He was too young for the subjects which engrossed him. Also, he was slow to turn in papers required on certain dates. He was much more interested in his appearance. The greatness within the young man was masked by personal vanity.

Martin King had a massive ego, but he did not see himself as a leader of his people, a prophet of nonviolence. The most decisive thing about Martin Luther King, Jr., was his indecisiveness. He could talk "hot" on a subject one day and chill it with silence the next. He sought dates with pretty girls and, once they went out with him, moved abruptly to other girls. He set a high value on reason, and his assessment of his own intellectuality kept reminding him that nothing he had read had ever been settled by violence.

Bad men. Good men. White men. Black men. It was a complex and confusing world. There was much that young Martin wanted to learn about his race which could not be found on library shelves. A great deal of what he read was bloodied with bias, depending on the writer or the publisher. Some of it exalted him. Some of it was sickening. Of one thing he was now certain: He was a full-fledged member of an oppressed minority group. He knew he could not tolerate a white heel on the back of his neck, but he was also aware that he was not born to be a fighter. Nor did he envision himself as a Moses leading his people to freedom. If he had a youthful philosophy—and he did—it was to follow the mild legalistic line of the National Association for the Advancement of Colored People—progress could be made by resorting to the United States district courts. That was the way. The only way.

All his discussions with his classmates and with his teachers suggest that he did not subscribe to the feeling of many blacks that "we are a small nation inside a big one." King renounced that by pointing out that the original slaves, transported in chains to the original colonies, were Americans before there was an America, and, by unending toil, had helped beyond measure to make the new country a great one.

The absorption of so much knowledge in youth often leads to a cerebral complexity called confusion. Martin Luther King, Jr., had a large head with a protuberant forehead which was full of unassorted, undigested, unassessed facts. More and more frequently, he sought the counsel of Dr. Benjamin Mays of Morehouse College. The doctor was a scholar who, without pedantry or strain, could recite the pros and cons of current problems. Thus Martin had two anchors—his father and

Professor Mays. Their advice did not always agree, nor did they always complement each other, but King respected his father and his mentor.

The goal of Dr. Benjamin Mays was to turn this fertile young brain more and more toward God and church. In this, he had the support of Martin's father. It would not do to command the boy; there was a built-in resistance to direct orders. Subtly, he must be shown that the pulpit was his natural platform, that God was neither black nor white but without color and merciful, that a good middle-class Southern Baptist church attracted the best elements of the black community, the men with the most influence in the community.

King was approaching graduation, when there were thoughts he could not reconcile, whether he was articulating them at home or in school. Why must it be, he would inquire, that if the Baptists were Baptists and believed in the same Scriptures that there must be one Baptist church for whites and one for blacks? At what point did a professed Christian become a hypocrite? And why was it that the Roman Catholic Church, which was not a principal in the black question, had desegregated so many of its schools without being asked? Wasn't it true that Bishop John Fitzpatrick of Boston had invested a black priest, one James Augustus Healy, as the Bishop of Portland, Maine, away back in 1875? Did white priests bend the knee to kiss his episcopal ring? And wasn't it equally true that Bishop Healy's brother, Father Patrick Francis Healy, a black Jesuit, had been president of Georgetown University in 1873?

The wheels of black struggle seemed to be running forward and in reverse at the same time. One thing was beyond dispute: The majority was an inert mass. It suffered in silence because life for the black man had always been that way.

At times it seemed to Martin Luther King, Jr., that the more he learned, the less he knew. In addition, he recognized an introspective irrationality in his personal behavior. He was given to dark moods and moods of nonstop monologues. Once, when his younger and taller brother, A.D. slid down a banister at home, the boy collided with his maternal grandmother and knocked her unconscious. Martin, who was at home, blamed himself for the accident and, without a word, walked upstairs and tried to kill himself by jumping from a window. Less than a year later, when "Mama" Williams died, Martin was busy watching a parade. When he arrived home and heard the sad news, he trudged upstairs again and jumped from the same window.

On a later occasion, he altered his aversion to bodily contact by becoming quarterback of the Morehouse College football team. He literally flogged himself to do the things he knew he couldn't do and set for himself standards impossible to achieve. He was much too small and light to be a football quarterback; for the same reason he could not make a basketball player, but he took dead aim at it and made it. He was opposed to studying for the ministry on the grounds that the blacks had converted it to an emotional singing, stomping contest, but Dr. Mays swung the compass needle of King's thoughts until he could see the possibility of a new kind of black ministry, one which appealed more to intellect and rationality than to tears and shouts of "Amen!" Personally, the young man was pious and impious. In church, he could lead the singing of "I Want to Be Like Jesus," but when he had dates with girls, he was sexually aggressive.

As World War II ended, he went north to Connecticut with some fellow students to work in the tobacco fields. The purpose was twofold: The pay was better than in the South; it was also an opportunity to see what racial tensions, if any, there might be in the North. There he worked hard in the summer sun, but Martin King was elated to learn that he could sit anywhere in any restaurant and order food. To him, it was incredible, a miracle one read of in books, but never experienced.

In late August the youths boarded a train to return to the South. There too, they ate in the dining car with the white people. But when the train reached the Southern states, the black waiters politely asked them to use a table in the rear of the dining car. When they sat, the waiter pulled a shade down so that their presence would not be offensive to other diners.

The following spring Martin told his father, without dramatics, that he felt the call to the ministry. Father King felt a surge of fulfillment, a deep sense of satisfaction, but he masked it behind an attitude of doubt. What, he asked, made Martin so sure that he could preach effectively? The young man's knowledge of Scripture was good, but could he pass such food to souls hungry for spiritual nourishment?

Martin said he knew he could do it. His father suggested a trial church service in one of the small auditoriums in the big Ebenezer Baptist Church. If he failed, there would be no shame attached. The group was small. "Daddy" King told his son that many men felt the call to the service of God, but such a call was sometimes self-inspired; at other times the call was real enough, but the ability to preach, to hold the attention of hundreds of souls at one time, and to lift those souls so that they were more elevated leaving church than entering it was a factor.

Martin said he could do it. He didn't want to do it the way others did.

He would like to prepare his sermons as a balance between the soul and mind, the intellect and the emotions. The latter part was what he feared most, and it was the pit into which he fell first. In later years, Roy Wilkins of the NAACP was to say of speakers: "Put King on last. He's in charge of 'rousements.' "

Dr. Mays was the first man to say, "I'll be there." This young man spiritually, was as much his as he was "Daddy" King's. The word spread around Atlanta that a seventeen-year-old would conduct services, and Dr. George Kelsey, head of the theological department of the college, was delighted when "Daddy" King had to make an announcement that because so many people had sent word they would attend, the service would be held in the main church.

On Sunday, when the final hymnal notes of the organ fell to a whisper and then to silence, young Martin King, looking even more boyish than he was, stepped forward in a white surplice to the lectern, shuffled his papered notes carefully, and looked out at a field of expectant faces. His manner was softer, less flamboyant than his father's, but he preached the logical relationship between God and man, the suffering which man endured here to earn the serenity of heaven, and he could tick off the quotations of ancient prophets without recourse to notes.

It was not a timid first speech. The boy had assurance, and his phrasing was good; but it was delivered as though he realized that he was his father's son and his grandfather's grandson and that they had, in their time, made the very stones of the church weep while he was determined to make the stones think. When the services were over, "Daddy" King was so proud that he almost lost his dignity. He shook hands with old parishioners and accepted their congratulations at face value and nodded his head in wonderment.

Dr. Mays left the church just as pleased and proud. "The boy," he said, "is mature beyond his years. He spoke as a man who should have had at least ten more years of experience. He had balance . . . maturity . . . a grasp of life itself." That night "Daddy" King got down on his knees at his bedside to thank God for sending him such a son.

Martin accepted the compliments gracefully, almost with embarrassment. He had said he could do it. He did it. At once, he made another decision. He stopped dating girls and going to dances. This was the devil's path. He would not walk it. Instead, he would spend equal time alone in his upstairs room studying and restudying the Bible, milking the ancient words for the lessons of today. Some felt that he was purging himself of what he regarded as sin. He was rechanneling his energies from the flesh to the spirit.

He lapsed once and went to a dance. Baptist discipline is strict, and the word of God is not subject to symbolic interpretations. The things which Jesus said are taken in context and applied in context. The following Sunday "Daddy" King, at services, summoned Martin Luther King, Jr., to the pulpit and demanded a public apology. It was delivered contritely. And yet the lure of the flesh was so strong within him that years later, Martin Luther King, Jr., could preach fire and hell on the one hand and run off to a secluded place with a willing girl within the hour. Often he would have to fight the common conflict of sin versus virtue. The older he got, the less he resisted.

He was eighteen when he was ordained a minister and—honor of all honors—was made assistant to his father as pastor of Ebenezer Baptist Church. After his next birthday he was graduated from Morehouse and decided to enroll at Crozer Theological Seminary in Chester, Pennsylvania, to earn his master's degree in philosophy.

Crozer had advantages for young King. The first was not that it was held in such high regard, but rather that it was far from the domination of "Daddy" King. Christine was content to remain under the thumb of the unbending, unyielding father. A.D., who had surrendered to his personal whims and paid little attention to the voice of God's emissary in Atlanta, managed to enjoy himself. He too would become a minister in his own time and in his own way, but life to him was laughter, a whirling carousel, defiance, the easy way.

Martin was as far removed from his sister and brother in character and personality as if they had sprung from different loins. He loved his father, he respected his father, but he wanted to be bigger and better than his father. "Daddy" felt that his older son was trying to follow in his big footsteps, but this was never true. The young man was determined to make bigger and more permanent footprints, and he intended to combine the work of God with the injustices of man. He would be a preacher, but he would also be what some whites in the South referred to as an "uppity nigger."

He didn't fear appellation; it was part of the plan to combine the exaltation of soul, mind, and body. If he could make a handful of black men walk with their heads high, that would be a victory accorded to few ministers, most of whom were busy trying not to rock the racial boat, trying hard to maintain good homes and automobiles and bank accounts.

Martin had no desire to talk down to blacks in the idiom of the ghetto. He had heard his father, and other noted preachers, depart from their text to drop into the patois of the Southern black to make a point. Well, Martin was not going to fall into that trap. Let the people reach up toward his big words for comprehension. How could they ever equate with the whites of Atlanta if the two were speaking different tongues?

Nor did he appreciate communicants who "rocked with joy" when hymns were sung and who insisted on giving it a blues beat. The church was not intended for that. Grandpa Alfred Daniel Williams, who had founded the Ebenezer Baptist Church, never addressed his congregation in any way except in the manner of a shouting field hand. And yet he had enjoyed tremendous success. It was right for that time, that day, and maybe it was still attractive to some people who listened to "Daddy" King.

But the time was here to speak correct "white" English to middle-class blacks who employed blacks as their servants and in their businesses. There were other, smaller churches all over Atlanta where one could stomp and shout, where women could afford to faint from excitement and be carried out into the fresh air by ushers. One of the things the new Crozer student did not know was that Grandpa Williams was defensive about his "field Negro" speech. He liked to recall that at one Sunday service a precise parishioner who was rich stood to correct the pronunciation of the preacher. When the service was over, the Reverend Mr. Williams studied the collection plate and said, "I done give a hundred dollars, but the gentleman who corrected me gave nuthin'."

Martin's healthy youthful body was too full of juices and animal spirits to be forever engaged in a racial struggle. He played, he laughed, he had a needling wit which could make everyone laugh except his father. Martin was also gifted with healthy envy. He was hurt when young A.D. grew taller than he, but it did not lessen his affection for the playboy of the family.

He needed time, and yet time was the commodity he could not spare. He clawed his way through the academics of study, surging toward the top, and yet there were times when he would look at a half-finished thesis and shove it aside to go to a movie. Above all, he was conscious of his heritage, and he knew that he could not abide a life in which he was going to keep saying "yes, sir" to an insolent white clerk. His moods ran in sharply peaked mountains and precipitous valleys, and "Mother dear" sensed them and wondered what would happen to her bright and erratic son.

When he wasn't playing hard, with a philosophy that it is not how you play the game but whether you win, his conversations with his family sometimes made 180-degree turns from what the others knew of his racial feelings. Among his forebears were Irishmen and aboriginal Indians, but he showed no enthusiasm for them as suppressed minorities and seldom discussed them. Undoubtedly it was the fact that white Americans rated blacks lowest on the racial scale. Besides, he looked black. There was no place he could go to boast of the percentage of Irish or Indian blood in his veins. As far as Atlanta was concerned—that is, white Atlanta—he was a sullen and sometimes intractable black.

At times, the gentility of Martin's mother was triggered by a remark of bitterness, and then, unsmiling, addressing herself to her dinner, she would tell things that she did not want the children to know. "You had a great-uncle who was lynched," she said. "Some white woman accused him, and men came and took him out into the woods. There was no use following. No use crying. A kindly white woman came to your great-aunt's house that afternoon and told her where to find him. He was swinging from a tree." There was silence for a moment. "I guess the white men used him for target practice because his body was full of bullet holes."

"Mother dear" wasn't much of a conversationalist except when she was teaching. But the outbursts occurred sporadically, and they made deep impressions on Martin Luther King, Jr. "They tell you," she said once, "that after the Civil War the colored people were given the right to vote. And they were. It's called the Fourteenth and Fifteenth Amendments. But the white Northerners couldn't keep their troops down here forever, and near the turn of the century, they went home."

One of the prettiest and most talented girls in Alabama was Coretta Scott. She was black and aware of her gifts. Besides having a lovely face and medium dark skin, she had illuminated dark eyes, a natural singing voice, and a singular suspicion of most men. She was not an easy date. Like Martin Luther King, Jr., living in an adjoining state, Coretta Scott had a defiant pride in her blackness.

She and her sister Edythe were at school in Marion, Alabama, when they learned that their house had burned to the ground. They hurried home to find nothing left of all their father had worked for. It had taken backbreaking labor at logging for many years for Mr. Scott to build that house. He had displayed his contempt too often for the justice administered by the white man and was not surprised when the town officials told him that they could not investigate the blaze because the house had been situated slightly outside the municipal limits. Blacks seldom got into trouble with the local whites unless they spoke independently or owned something better than the white farmers. The Scotts had a cabinet victrola with recordings of spirituals.

Mrs. Scott was in tearful despair. Her mother had died recently, and crying had become a sporadic and irrational event. "Now," she said, weeping, "we have no place to go with Momma gone." The girls thought of all the beautiful furniture their father had bought and the work he had done on weekends to make the house more attractive and livable. He had also been able to send his children to school. The Scotts were middle-class blacks.

The house was gone, and they went to live with Grandpa McMurry. Coretta's father made no complaint about the burned house and returned to work the following morning. He, too, was beset by the conundrum of being black and industrious in a white country. He had no time for tears and worked doubly hard to earn quick money.

In the spring of 1943 he bought a small sawmill in the hills and refashioned it into something bigger and better with his hands. The sawmill was so attractive that a white man offered a considerable amount of money for it. Mr. Scott shook his head. "Sorry," he said. "I didn't build it to sell it. I'm going to work it."

The white man looked at him sadly. "Well," he said, "it ain't never going to do you no good." The Scotts attended church services on Sunday. On Monday, Mr. Scott drove to his sawmill. It lay in cold ashes.

Coretta's mother was married at sixteen. She often said that she had had no childhood, that she had been born a woman. She believed that the plight of the black man was permanent. She constantly said that no one could trust the white man, no matter what he said. Her husband dealt with white men and had learned to like a few but distrusted many.

The resentment Coretta Scott felt for the whites blossomed early. She and her sister had to walk to a black school, three miles in rain or shine. Every morning, as they clung to the shoulder of the road, the school bus for white children passed them, sometimes splashing mud. To balance this was the fact that Coretta was often called upon by the teachers to sing or recite. She never faltered or waited to be coaxed— Coretta felt that she belonged at stage center.

The little girl had a strong sense of injustice. She understood the inferior status of the black at a tender age, and Coretta wondered why so many of her people accepted it without a struggle. At the local drugstore, white children entered by the front door; black children who wanted to buy an ice-cream cone on a hot day had to stand at the side door. When the "man" finished servicing all other customers, he would pass out cones of whatever flavor pleased him and hold the other hand out for the money.

An echo from the King household filled the Scott kitchen when Coretta asked her mother why they had to live under the heels of the whites. "You are just as good as anybody else," Mrs. Scott said. "Get an education and be somebody. Then you won't have to be kicked around by anybody." Coretta's mother often pointed out that, although Edythe and Coretta needed new dresses, if they spent the money on education and books, someday they would be able to buy all the dresses they wanted.

The one surely happy day was Sunday. The Scotts were members of the Mount Tabor AME Zion Church, four miles from the farm. They made a ceremony of putting on their best clothes; all the faces were clean and shiny and smiling. If Mr. Scott's truck was working, they drove. If not, they walked, starting early so that they would not miss anything. The men's suits ran mostly to black, and many of them carried shiny shoes tied with laces over their shoulders so that the dust and mud of the unpaved roads would not mar their appearance.

The Mount Tabor Church looked older than some of its parishioners. Big slabs of congealed paint hung loosely from the walls like gossipy tongues flapping in the breeze. The pews were benches without backs. They were varnished every few years. On cold days, the congregation huddled close to the big stove up front as Coretta's grandfather and the others began to sing hymns. The preacher waved his arms from an elevated pulpit, and the singing became louder and more enthusiastic; feet began to beat; bodies swayed to the eternal promises of Jesus. High up in the rafters, kerosene lamps flickered yellow, and sooty smoke airbrushed the ceiling black.

The Mount Tabor Church had built in its opposition to sex and its symbols. The men sat on one side of the church; women on the other; the children in the middle. In the back were separate waiting rooms for men and women. When the collection plate was passed from pew to pew, a quarter was hoped for, but the people were poor and had large families, so there were more dimes than quarters dropped onto the plate.

Many of the men were unashamed to fold their arms and sleep through a dull sermon. If the preacher was a "rouser," the communicants became emotional. At every pause between sentences, they would shout "Amen! Amen!" or "Yeah, yeah!" or "Preach, man, preach!" All of them believed firmly in a God and a hereafter of rewards and punishment. Their faith in Him was unyielding, although they were surrounded by evidence that He did not believe in them.

It was in this atmosphere that the surge for equality with whites began. The church was a place which was owned, possessed and loved solely by the black man. It was the only place where all of them met and could look upon each other's faces. It was the only place of peace where ideals could be generated, where the weak clung to the strong, a place of mysterious promise from on high.

Few of them believed in the preacher, because he was often a semi-literate man who enunciated his words like a backwoods "nigger" and who was as full of fear of the white man as the rest of them—more so, because he had a well-paying position to protect. Angry whites often visited a black preacher to warn him to get his "uppity niggers" into line or there would be trouble.

On occasion, when a black man was beaten half to death or killed, the people waited for the following Sunday to hear the pastor denounce such inhumanity. He seldom, almost never, did. After one such beating Coretta Scott heard one say, "God loves us all, and we reap what we sow. Let us pray for our less fortunate brethren. . . ."

Crozer Theological Seminary in Pennsylvania was another planet to Martin Luther King, Jr. There were six blacks among ninety-four whites, and everyone appeared to be color-blind. The grinning boy studied almost endlessly.

King was the perfect student, the do-gooder, the debater; he read like a man possessed. He was first in his class and president of the student body.

But Martin was more reckless than prudent in his relationships with women. He had glanced at the attractive white daughter of Crozer's superintendent of buildings, and she had smiled at him. This led to a romance which bordered on the dangerous. On weekends, they sat in black cafés in Chester holding hands. Had the news spread, there isn't any doubt that King would have lost the friendship of many of his classmates, white and black; a full-blown scandal would have erupted on the campus.

The word reached the head of the school first, and he called Martin and the girl in. The young man had an engaging smile. "I'm glad you found out about it," he said, speaking for both, "because we decided that we wanted you to marry us!" The preacher groaned. He knew about the bare knuckles of racism all too well, and yet he sympathized with young romance. He talked and talked, pointing out all the reasons why such a marriage could not succeed—especially for a young man with a brilliant future.

When he concluded, Martin Luther King, Jr., hung his head and admitted that logic and reason were on the side of Mr. Barbour. He glanced sidewards at the girl, and she shrugged and admitted that marriage to a white girl could foreclose Martin's future and that they had better forget they had met. Within a year, the girl and her family left Crozer. Years later, when he was famous, he would tell and retell the story, especially after a public appearance when he felt in a mood to drop the mask of the winner and display the features of the loser.

The antidote to romantic depression, Martin found, was a common one. He immersed himself deeper and deeper into his schoolwork. For a time he dated no one. Once, on a walking trip in downtown Philadelphia, he learned that Dr. Mordecai Johnson, president of Howard University, was to lecture at Fellowship House regarding his findings on a recent tour of India. Martin bought a ticket and sat to listen to wisdom.

Dr. Johnson centered his talk not so much on the subcontinent as on the former South African lawyer named Gandhi. Martin King had heard and read about Gandhi before, but could find nothing in the little spectacled man's teachings which could be applied to the United States. Dr. Johnson, changed the negative feeling to positive within an hour. Passionately, he told how one small man of no particular standing had aroused an entire country. He had preached nonviolence in his battle to free his people from the British, had spent time in jail, had fasted for long periods of time, had forbidden his followers to raise a hand against the English or to fire a shot, but had not stopped them from lying across the main roads so that traffic could not pass. He fought the British salt tax by walking hundreds of miles to the sea to sift seawater and make his own salt. The British rulers were there, the Army was there, the Navy made "courtesy" visits to Indian ports, but none of them could withstand or fight the nonviolence that Gandhi offered his enemies.

Martin left the lecture in a frenzy of excitement. He went around Philadelphia all week buying books on Gandhi and Satyagraha, the nucleus of nonviolence.

Martin was no fool. He knew that the difference between the Hindus and the American blacks was that the entire country was unified behind Gandhi. In the United States, only one of every ten persons was black. Worse, even considering those insurmountable odds, not all blacks—not even 25 percent of them—would be willing to join a movement of nonviolence to gain what the law stated was rightfully theirs. They were a defeated, passive race.

As he left Crozer for Boston College, driving the new green Chevrolet his father had given him, the young man found himself in the awkward position of weighing Gandhi tactics against Marx militance. He could not subscribe to the philosophy of Karl Marx that there is no God, but he could believe and nourish the Marxist economic philosophy that the productivity and wealth of a people should be divided among all of them. He was inspired by Gandhi, who supported nonviolence and love of his oppressors with a certainty that money, in itself, was meaningless.

A man had to eat. He had to have a place to sleep, a place to work, but what good was money if his main goal was to save his immortal soul? To believe in God is to believe in a hereafter; ergo, an earth life is nothing but a harsh trial to prove worthiness to enter nirvana. Aggrandizement, beautiful homes, and servants and cars require money, and money led each supplicant farther and farther away from God.

In Boston, King and an old friend, Philip Lenud, rented a small apartment at 397 Massachusetts Avenue. The son of the pastor of the Ebenezer Baptist Church did not realize it, but he had been gifted with a brilliant mind with no brakes. It ran off the road, not once, but many times; but it was a superior mind. Often, in bull sessions with Lenud and other blacks, he was torn between being a pedant by explaining and sitting silently to avoid the animosity of young men who were trying to learn but lacked his gifts.

Boston was big and busy, a city smothering in the veins of tradition. Rows of houses melted one into another, and stout Irishwomen wore scarves over their heads and hurried in the cold, carrying milk pails to the grocery store. Intellectually, Boston was a top-and-bottom metropolis, a seat of learning and laborers; it was Harvard and Scollay Square; a port for Irish immigrants and high-stepping politicians; a place of brahmins, bulldozers, banks, and fresh lobster. In a cultural sense, it was ancient Athens and the back alleys of Skibbereen and Naples.

The Massachusetts Avenue apartment became the site of black forums. Students gathered to sip coffee and debate the political and academic problems of the times. It was a joy for Martin Luther King, Jr., to lounge on Saturdays and Sunday evenings, waiting for someone to offer an opinion so that he might oppose, not for the sake of inciting disagreement so much as to help himself and others to hone the edges of their mentality.

He wanted a doctorate from Boston College, and he was determined to get it with high marks. A world of problems and solutions entranced the student, and at Christmas, 1951, he was inundated with books. His friend Philip Lenud was a divinity student at Tufts College, and they crossed lingual swords without anger. These, for King, were the good old days. The only blot on his mind was that letters from home made him conscious of an old unwritten treaty. There was a neighborhood black girl with whom he had grown up. They had something that parents refer to as an "understanding." Letters from his father revived memories of that unwritten treaty and suggested that Martin "settle down."

King had outgrown his childhood sweetheart, and it is possible that she had outgrown him. The phrase "settle down" depressed him. Much better, King felt, to study hard and get out of school honorably than to assume an additional burden, no matter how sweet.

At the same time—Christmas, 1951—Coretta Scott was studying music at the New England Conservatory of Music in Boston. The number of blacks in Boston was sufficient to make it improbable that this boy and this girl would meet. The blacks of Boston were a sizable minority, and a gregarious boy and an introverted girl with a short temper could spend their lives in the same city without ever crossing paths.

Coretta, as a little girl, had worn jeans and had picked cotton. For a number of years, the pretty child erased from her mind the fact that she was black; her father had money and affluence, but the glittering dark eyes of Coretta—the tomboy, the tree climber, the shouter—never begged for equality, they demanded it as a God-given right.

At Antioch College, she had had white boyfriends. She could smile, hold hands, kiss, and listen to the lofty promises of marriage, but, as Coretta said of one, "He didn't have the guts." Although Coretta appeared to be the softest of feminine creatures, her brain was tough and often unforgiving. Her ambition to achieve "equality" almost dominated her life.

She understood and appreciated music; she had a fine voice, and she determined to be a concert singer. If she went home to Alabama, the best she could expect would be to sing in black churches. In the North, Coretta knew that she could be successful and appreciated. In the summer of 1951, after she left Antioch College and decided to go to Boston, she was out of funds. Her father had the money, but Coretta felt that she had leaned on his bankbook long enough and would not ask him.

A former teacher helped her try for a scholarship in Boston and a grant-in-aid from the Jessie Smith Noyes Foundation. It is a mark of Coretta Scott's iron will that she had left Alabama to go to Boston without any promises from anyone. Her father stood looking at her. "What are you going to do if you don't get that scholarship?" he said.

A small, cold smile came to Coretta's mouth. "I'll get a job," she said. "I'll work and go to school part time until I'm able to go full time."

The train trip to Boston was long, with varying landscapes of farms and towns racing past the window. The girl had lots of time to think, but thinking altered nothing. She would never again walk to school in a starched white dress and watch the laughing white faces as the school bus splashed mud. She would not be degraded by sitting in the backs of smelly Alabama buses, nor would she hoe cotton and truckle to the "white folks." That abrasive world had just passed behind the train, and Miss Scott was determined never to live in it again.

At New York, there was a wait of more than an hour before she could board the train to Boston. She phoned home. The news was good. Coretta Scott had been granted $650 from the Jessie Smith Noyes Foundation for study at the New England Conservatory of Music. At Antioch, an indulgent former teacher wrote to an alumnus living in a big old house on Beacon Hill. Mrs. Bartol told the new arrival that she could have a room and breakfast for $7 a week.

Coretta decided to enroll full time at the school, which left virtually nothing of the scholarship grant. She was gambling with money she didn't have, but once more the iron will won. After a week, the $15 Coretta had on arrival had dwindled to a few dollars. She bought graham crackers, peanut butter, and fruit for lonely dinners in her room. Before Coretta left home, her mother had told her not to worry, that she would send a little "spending money" from time to time. The mail had arrived with regularity, but there was nothing from Alabama in it.

The day before class enrollment Coretta received a phone call from

Bertha Wormley of the National Urban League. They had met in New York, and now the soft voice said, "How are you, Corrie? Is there anything I can do to help?" There was, but Miss Scott found the word "money" strangling in her throat. Pride is a banner difficult to lower and more difficult to raise anew. Coretta managed to say the word. She had only 25 cents left. Mrs. Wormley was one of those women who not only want to help, but try to make light of the problem.

"I work at the Statehouse around the corner," she said. "Now you just stop by here on your way to school, and I'll have it ready for you."

Coretta Scott felt that sinking, uplifting emotion which can come close to inducing tears. "I'll pay you back," she said. "I'll pay you back just as soon as I can."

Mrs. Wormley chuckled. "We'll let our grandchildren worry about that," she said, and hung up.

The following morning at the Statehouse there was a warm embrace and an envelope. Coretta opened it on the subway. It contained fifteen important dollars—important to Mrs. Wormley and vital to Coretta. For years afterward, the music student tried to repay the money, but it was always returned to Coretta as though Mrs. Wormley were afflicted with a bad memory and couldn't recall advancing the money.

Coretta Scott was not a weeper, but Mrs. Wormley caused tears to start down the smooth dark skin. She kept saying, "That woman barely knew me."

Mrs. Bartol helped, too. She was a mature woman, and she read the rebelliousness and the aching poverty in the young face. "From now on," she said, "I can give you some work and pay you for it. Clean your own room every day, clean two others on the fifth floor, clean the hall, and the two stairways." Coretta was also taught how to get down on her hands and knees and scrub floors properly. The pay consisted of a free room and breakfast.

Life is full of small crossroads, many of them perplexing no matter which turn is accepted. The more firmly convinced Coretta Scott became that the North was far more liberal and palatable to her, the more Martin Luther King, Jr., missed the South. He was almost ecstatic when he found a small Boston restaurant which served soul food: hog jowls, chitterlings, and collard greens. On another occasion, he said, "I wish I knew a few girls from down home to go out with. I tell you, these Boston girls are something else. The ones I meet are so reserved."

A married woman friend of his heard the despairing cry of the young

romantic and said she knew a pretty girl from Alabama who was studying music. Coretta Scott was a nice girl, she assured him, an intelligent
and independent girl—not one to be trifled with. At once, King asked
for her address but was refused it. Failing that, he supplied a description
of himself to be given to Coretta Scott. The woman listened agape. It
wasn't even close to what Martin Luther King, Jr., looked like or was.
What he gave her was his personal assessment of himself, physically,
mentally, and morally. In addition, he fancied himself to be an irresist-
ible Don Juan.

He was given Coretta's phone number and warned that she did not
particularly like ministers. When he called two days later, the two spoke
in guarded abstracts for a while. "I am like Napoleon at Waterloo
before your charms," he said. It was a country boy's notion of how to
smother resistance.

Coretta Scott said, "Why, that's absurd. You haven't seen me yet."

Afterward she confided to a friend: "I see him as an older man,
pious, narrow-minded, and not too well trained, like most of the
preachers I know from Alabama."

They dated on a tentative basis, his ardent warmth fighting the icicles
of her suspicions. Throughout a cold winter, they saw much of each
other, and King arrived at a swift and final conclusion: "This girl is for
me. I'm going to marry her."

His protestations of eternal love were received by Coretta as the usual
tactic of all males, most of whom would vow, "I love you and want to
marry you," without sincerity, merely to attain the age-old goal. When
summer arrived, Martin Luther King, Jr., couldn't wait to go home. His
wild brother, A.D., disregarding his father's advice, had married, and
became a country Baptist preacher. A.D. was willing to settle for this
type of life. He did not aspire to succeed his father at the big Ebenezer
Baptist Church, because he knew his brother, Martin, had better quali-
fications; also, he did not want to remain under his father's wrathful
thumb.

The person who did not want to go home was Coretta Scott. She
determined to remain in Boston, perhaps to continue her studies all
summer. By July, 1952, Coretta was convinced that her swain was
sincere and in love, and she was now certain that he was anything but a
down-home preacher. Normally, love is an emotion which overtakes a
romantic runner. In Corrie's case, she was one who would dwell upon
all the aspects of love and marriage as a banker might read an application for a loan.

When all the thinking was behind her, Coretta Scott found that she was in love with King but decided not to tell him. At this time, they were seeing each other almost constantly, and neither had any interest in anyone else. One summer day he told her he was going home to Atlanta. "When you go home to visit your family in Alabama," he said, "you pass through Atlanta. Why not stop off and visit me—meet my folks?"

"No," she said, "I don't think I will." It was not a truthful statement, but rather a test of wills.

Anger rose in his face. His eyes became glittering hard. "Okay," he said. "If you don't want to come, just forget everything. Forget it. Forget the whole thing." She tried to explain that her decision was not final, that she had additional work to do in Boston, that a doctor had advised her to have her tonsils removed at once, and that she couldn't get to Alabama before August.

This mollified the anger, but not the chill. He drove home alone in his green Chevrolet. Coretta still had reservations. She wanted to meet his parents; she wanted to see the church of his father; she had a desire to weigh what life would be like—even down to the type of living in a middle-class black community. She stopped in Atlanta the first week of August. Almost from the first, Coretta realized that her competitor was King's father. The young minister loved and admired the stern and righteous old man, but Coretta Scott wanted a marriage in which she would be the determinant, not a minister who might be inclined to make important decisions for her and her husband.

Then too, the whole family realized that "Daddy" King wanted his son to marry his childhood sweetheart; he saw no need for a sophisticated woman who would expose herself in a spotlight on a stage to sing songs. This excited a new emotion: jealousy. Coretta Scott did not want to be placed in the position of fighting for King; she wanted him to fight for her. She had no belief in dreams or their meaning, but she dreamed one night that the matter of the other girl and Coretta had come up before "Daddy" King, and he had turned a benevolent smile on Corrie.

She wanted to believe in that dream. Whether it meant anything tangible or not, the ever-present fighting spirit of Miss Scott helped her make up her mind. She would marry Martin Luther King, Jr. Definitely, definitely. She didn't know what it would do to her career, and she worried about it. She was going to earn that degree in music, and she was going to become a concert singer, marriage or no marriage. If he loved her, and she was sure he did, he could find a church in Boston just as easily as he could in Atlanta. Young Martin should realize that it would not be good for his future to remain in his father's shadow. In studies, in philosophy, in academic knowledge he had long surpassed his father. Why remain in the South where blacks were encapsulated by whites?

Corrie had thought out his future for him. So had "Daddy" King. So had Martin, Jr. None of them communicated with the others, but their notions were at variance with one another. Trouble always walks a stride or two ahead of happiness.

The wedding was fashionable. The bridegroom wore a white double-breasted tuxedo. The bride, in long veil, heavy drop earrings, and a gown of white organza and lace, held chrysanthemums and ferns. "Daddy" King performed the ceremony on June 18, 1953, at the home of the bride's parents in Heiberger, Alabama. Everybody who was anybody in black social life was present, and as an event, it had little in common with the crossroads blacks.

The bride had cast aspersions on the middle-class blacks of Atlanta, of which Martin, Sr., was an important member. She derided their heavy-handed economic security, their big showy homes, their "exclusive" clubs; but she was now Mrs. Martin Luther King, Jr., and she was expected to carry the name on a banner. It had led to terse table disagreements when she was in Atlanta, and the Kings had learned that the woman their son had selected had a mind of her own and a mind for changing the mind of their son, too.

Before Coretta would agree to the marriage, she wanted it understood that she was going back to Boston in the autumn of 1953 to continue her studies at the conservatory. Young King said that this was perfect because he wanted to return to Boston College; he had less than a year in which to qualify for his doctorate. The solitary schism between them, small as it was, would widen in time.

Coretta wanted a singing career in the North and nowhere else. She had worked hard to achieve it, and she had no intention of sitting in a Southern parsonage doing nothing but playing at the game of being poor and having babies. She wanted Martin to promise that he would seek a job as minister of a Northern church or one as a teacher of theology. He could afford to smile. "We'll see," he said. "We'll see."

The Reverend Martin Luther King, Jr., didn't know that he didn't understand the Northern black. He thought that blacks were blacks and that all his dark brothers endured the same humiliation and prayed for the same equality. King would never understand the Northern black and would never concede that he didn't. When, in later years, he boasted that he had lived among blacks in Boston, he omitted to state that these were young men who were in college, men who were studying to be engineers and doctors and lawyers. His contacts in Boston were as middle-class as those in Atlanta.

In Harlem, New York City, for example, there were, at the time of Martin's wedding, 400,000 blacks, many of whom slept on rooftops. Dope pushers rode bicycles selling colored balloons floating from the handlebars for 10 cents. Only the pusher and his slave knew that the red ones cost $5 and contained a diluted "fix" of heroin. Except in rare instances, a life of crime was not frowned upon in Harlem. It was reserved for the brave and the insane, and it was a better living than hauling garbage for "Whitey."

Preschool children, playing on the sidewalks, watched big-eyed as a neighbor sat on his stoop and bared his arm for a needle. They saw rats in hallways, police cars coasting down the side streets out of gear, the men inside watching. They saw black policewomen in ordinary dresses beg in hallways and vestibules for heroin and then, having bought it, flash a badge and arrest the pusher. They slept in the same rooms, in many cases, and saw and heard things which should have been denied their eyes and ears.

They did not have to sit in the back of any bus; they did not have to get off the sidewalk to permit the white man to use it; they did not have to play the supine "Uncle Tom" to win the favor of the boss. The women filled the churches, but many men wouldn't go near one except to rob it. In shopwindows, there were portraits of a black Christ, but the hard jade inside the black's breast made him smile because he could not imagine God saying, "Yassuh. My name Rastus," to anyone. The felony rate was high. In the lineup at downtown police headquarters, the bright shiny inspectors who conducted the interrogations despaired of ever getting truth from the men onstage, because most of them were addicts and would confess to murder, armed robbery, rape—anything to get to a hospital before those deep doubling cramps began and sweat dripped from eyebrows. "Yes, sir. I did it. I rang the bell, and when she came to the door, I asked her if she was alone and she said yes. I didn't mean no harm, just to get some money, but when that bathrobe began to fall open, I had another idea, and then I was afraid she could identify me—you understand?"

The inspector understood. The prisoner did not know the name of the girl, what color her hair was, the address, and whether she was stabbed, strangled, or shot. The numbers runners were small fry, but detectives and a group of black policemen called the King Cole Trio picked them up and helped send them away. They weren't gone a day when a new runner was begging the boss to appoint him to pick up the nickels, dimes, and quarters of citizens who lived on potatoes and bread, the fathers of rickety, retarded children, the husbands of sullen women who found jobs denied to their husbands.

Prostitution was so common—especially immediately above Central Park along Lenox and Seventh avenues—that pretty girls assigned themselves to cheap restaurants where they could sit and sip until a white John came in looking for action. "Action" ran on two levels: there were girls who had to resort to prostitution to make money and who played the game on the level and even had their fat and jolly once-a-week customers. The other group used the pretty black as a decoy and waited in the girl's apartment for her to show up with the John. He was promptly beaten, robbed, and stripped. If he was a married man—and this was customarily the case—he could be counted on not to complain to the police. The second group found the work more lucrative than the first, but the earnings had to be split three or four ways, and the decoy went home with about the same amount of money as her on-the-level sisters in sin.

Young blacks began to walk south at night and sit on tall rocks in Central Park waiting for a lone walker to appear. They worked in groups and spread themselves in such a way that no matter which way the quarry ran, he headed into a switchblade knife. From behind, a strong arm held his neck in the crook of the elbow. The police called it mugging. Central Park, once a place of curving drives amid greenery for carriages and matched horses, for figure skaters on icy lakes, for romanticists in slow-moving sports cars, was now a pit of silent vipers.

The reverend did not understand this behavior and could not read the heart of his Northern brother.

With the name "M. L. King, Jr." on the mailbox of an apartment near the conservatory in Boston, the young couple began a placid life. Coretta surprised and delighted Martin with her intelligent approach to personal problems, to a philosophy accommodating the dismal aspects of world affairs, to her self-assurance. His left-handed compliment to his bride was to shake his head in wonderment and repeat that he thought of women as homemakers, mothers, cooks, adjuncts to the careers of their husbands.

She attended school full time. King had practically completed all the studies for his degree, so he remained in the little apartment all day, cleaning, dusting, and sometimes cooking dinner. He was only twenty-four. Dr. L. Harold DeWolf, head of the Department of Systematic Theology at Boston University, already ranked him as one of the top five students he had taught.

Martin King believed in "personalism." Neither philosophy nor theology was an abstract in his mind. There was a personal God, one who could be addressd by a supplicant on a personal basis, and there was a man, a highly personal man named Martin King, who, like all other humans, had a direct relationship to his Maker. In philosophy, the same creed applied. Almost all true philosophers, in King's estimation, were great men, but one took from each the mature thinking which applied to "me" alone.

Hegel's *Phenomenology of Mind* and *Philosophy of Right* cut deeply into King's consciousness. The more he studied these works, the more he drew from them. At night, he sat in an easy chair, a floor lamp beside him, digging deeper and deeper into the conscious and unconscious aspirations of man and their attitudes toward one another. In another chair in another room Coretta studied music, from counterpoint to composition; from violin to trumpet. The remaining work King had was to write a thesis. He was permitted to select his subject, but the main qualification was that he not only had to research it down to the last detail, but also had to write it and submit it.

He chose a title obtuse to most people outside the realm of philosophy and theology—a difficult subject. It was called *A Comparison of the Conceptions of God in the Thinking of Paul Tillich and Henry Nelson Wieman.* To strengthen his intellectual muscles, King took special courses at Harvard University, and there, too, he impressed the professors with his quick and sure depth of thinking. And yet, as he began the work on his thesis, a gradual lassitude possessed him so that he required two years to complete 343 pages.

He would be back in Atlanta a long time before the work was done; before he could truly be called Doctor of Philosophy. As a "personal" philosopher, it is possible that Dr. King had, for some reason, picked a subject alien to his beliefs. Tillich, for example, contended that God stood outside the personal affairs of the world; he could not be solicited for personal help by a human suffering from a chronic toothache. Wieman contended that God was all-powerful and could penetrate all matters, but he would not concede, and could not conceive, that God was prepared to correct the evils He saw.

Sometimes King studied and wrote with several books open before him, trying to collate the depth of perception of the two men. At other times he surrendered early, clasped his hands behind his head, and sat dreaming. In knowledge, he was far ahead of most men of his age, no matter what their race. To have all the tools is one thing; to bring them properly to bear on a forest of ignorance is another skill.

The lovely bride could turn away from study at any time, but she had little time for dreaming. Coretta King was all woman, and even though she loved her husband to the fullest, she realized early in their relationship that the success of the marriage would not depend on rational compromise, but on her complete surrender.

She had come to Boston to study, and she had felt no need of a husband. Success on the concert stage was her concern. Nothing must stand in its way. On the first date, he said that she was everything he had been looking for in a wife, and Coretta did not like that because she was not an impulsive person.

At dinner, he had listened to something profound that she said, and remarked, "Oh, you can think, too." This, she had felt, was insufferable. The fact that he was a minister was another minus mark on his marital report card. Coretta did not like ministers. She had been thinking of giving up the Baptist Church and changing to a more liberal one or giving up attending church at all. And yet the deeper she had become involved with King on those freezing wintry nights of courtship, the more she had kept telling herself that she could not live without him. If this is the negativistic proof of true love, Martin Luther King, Jr., passed all the grades.

Now they were married, and when she wasn't studying, Mrs. King was working her way slowly and accurately to the conclusion that she was going to lose the last battle, too. He would not remain in the North, even though he had already received two good offers from churches. No, little by little, he would turn back home to the South, the land of black misery, and she would be a parson's wife, not only subordinating her career to his, but killing it. After all the years of study, she might be invited to sing solo in his church choir on Sundays or to sing at parties where something light and catchy would be the order of the day.

She remembered the night he had said, "I must have a wife who will be as dedicated as I am. I will be the pastor of a large church in the South. That is where I plan to live and work. I want the kind of wife who will fit into that kind of a situation. Can you adjust yourself to Aunt Jane?"

"Aunt Jane" was a generic black term for the ignorant parishioner who didn't know the difference, in a given situation, whether "You does" or "You don't." For Coretta, this was the night of artistic death, but she faced it and said she had grown up with Aunt Janes and would never look down upon them. This is what he wanted to hear. Each of them knew they had traveled a long way from all the Aunt Janes of their childhood.

Coretta had traded her head for a heart. She switched her studies from the performing arts to a music major. Her reasoning was that if she could not perform as a singer, she could teach voice in the South. Mrs. King was settling for less, far less than her pride could concede, but it was something. She could at least be a person in her own right, a person who could add to the culture of her people.

An offer from a church in New York was declined with thanks; one from Boston was turned down; a college in the North had offered a teaching post, another an administrative position; a deanship came from a third. Martin Luther King, Jr., thanked them and turned his dark eyes South.

The co-pastorship with his father at the Ebenezer Baptist Church in Atlanta seemed like the start of a dynasty. Everybody would know that he had got the post because of the power of his father, and Martin Luther King, Jr., wanted no gratuitous titles. He wanted to work, not with someone or under someone, but alone. A man can dream loftily. If he is both talented and stubborn, he may not have to lower his sights.

A letter came from the elders of the Dexter Avenue Baptist Church, in Montgomery, Alabama, explaining that, at this time, they had no pastor and would welcome King to preach when he was in that part of the country. The only way in which a small church in Montgomery could have heard of King, he realized, was through his father and perhaps some friendly members of the Ministerial Association.

The letter had another objective. The church needed a pastor. The elders, in their flattering letter, were auditioning. They undoubtedly had sent other letters to other ministers. King knew that. He had yet to finish his thesis and, at this point, felt mired down. He began to work more and more slowly—a forerunner of his average of thirteen hours to prepare a Sunday sermon—yet he found time to write a thank-you note to the Dexter Avenue Church and state that he would be happy to visit and to preach on a Sunday in January, 1954.

Since the Dexter Avenue Baptist Church was prepared to audition him, Martin Luther King decided to audition the church in turn by mail. He wrote to friends in Alabama and was pleasantly surprised to find that it was an "upper-income congregation" made up of doctors, teachers, lawyers, and professors of Alabama State College. This would mean that the parishioners were not be foot-stomping "Amen!" and "Preach, man, preach!" types.

The pastor who was leaving was the Reverend Vernon Johns, an eloquent orator. This was a good sign for Dr. King, because he saw himself in that particular light. Johns, however, had a talent which King did not possess: the ability to tell a story on himself. King had a narrow-spectrum sense of humor. Certain old-time Southern stories could make him laugh heartily, and he was an almost perpetual smiler, but although he did not seem to realize it, he could not laugh at himself.

His deepest concern was that he aspired to be an original philosopher and wasn't. His faith in nonviolence was borrowed from Gandhi and Jesus; his concept that all sin could be redemptive was taken from the Old Testament; he borrowed from Hegel, Nietzsche, Marx, even small sections of Tillich—and the young preacher did not feel proud of himself. What he failed to realize was that in the field of faith, belief, and credo, almost every possible thought had already been expressed and that his personal and careful culling from his peers would someday be packed together, and what would emerge would be the philosophy of Dr. Martin Luther King, Jr.

He could not envision this, nor could he look at himself with true objectivity. King did not see himself as a vain man with an overweening pride in himself—a sin unto itself—a man set apart from others. The critics among his confreres referred to King as "an actor," one whose eloquent hands, malleable features, and cathedral-belled voice pleased himself as much as it impressed congregations.

Arrogance and pride can also be interpreted as self-confidence, and King had a wealth of them. He could hardly wait to take Coretta back to Atlanta, finish his college work, and settle down to the business of saving souls.

The Dexter Avenue Church wasn't big. On a cold Saturday in January, 1954, Martin King and his wife stood across the street and studied the plain red-brick structure, the little white steeple, the side entrance to the vestry room, the polished old pews inside, and the stained-glass windows. The reverend hunched himself deep inside his topcoat and smiled. It was small, even uninspiring, but it could be his. Coretta King smiled because Montgomery was near her parents' home. She would much prefer that her husband be pastor of this nice church than to be under the domination of his father at Ebenezer Baptist in Atlanta.

It was not that she did not admire the senior King. To the contrary. He and his thin mustache and hard blunt voice appealed to her. This, Coretta told herself, was a man. And, as she had always promised herself: "If I can't find a real man, I'll wear the pants myself." She had a real man, but working in his father's church could reduce him to something less. Here, in Alabama, he could project his own notions of God and a philosophy for living. In his father's church, young King would mold his sermons to win his father's approval.

On Sunday, before a chilly crowd, Martin Luther King, in black cassock and white surplice, mounted the pulpit and looked down at the affluent, well-nourished blacks below. He had decided not to give them the fire and brimstone of Baptist Fundamentalism; the sermon would be called "Three Ways of Life" and would contain quotations and lessons drawn from better minds than his or theirs.

The people were skeptical; the people were interested; the people became enthused; the people began to admire; the people wished he would continue all day. He thanked them one and all and left without asking the elders of the church for the post of pastor.

It took the elders a month to send a telegram stating that he had been chosen unanimously to be their pastor. During that time he thought about various teaching positions, Northern churches, remaining in Atlanta, when all the while he must have known that Dexter was an ideal springboard for his lifework.

After he had kept them waiting a sufficient time, Martin King wrote a gracious note of acceptance, stating that as soon as he had placed his Atlanta work in order, so that too heavy a burden would not fall upon his father, he and his wife would report to Montgomery. "Daddy" King couldn't understand his son. Just as in the Bible, the prophet's son was turning away from him.

The boy had been ordained a minister before he left Morehouse College; he needed no further studies, but willfully, he had gone on to Crozer and from there to Boston University, and what had it done? It had given him so much to explore the mind of man that the soul was atrophying with neglect. He had also dishonored an old pledge between two fine black families and had spurned his childhood sweetheart for a high-flown sassy girl who wanted to sing and to think for herself. Even Mrs. King was slow to approve of Coretta. The boy was only twenty-four, and already he was co-pastor of a big Atlanta church with his father, and he was walking away from it to take a small church with a congregation of 300 in another state. A strange, strange son had been raised.

The Dexter elders were delighted that King had accepted the pastorate, but he placed a harsh condition upon accepting the post. He wrote that he had to complete his thesis for Boston University and would not be ready to move from Atlanta until September 1. This smacked of mouse-trapping the elders, but they agreed, and Martin Luther King, Jr., had won the leisure to write in his father's study or in Boston and to contemplate the city of Montgomery as a municipal personality.

A woman parishioner had said, "He looks lost up there without his mother." It wasn't intended as a compliment, but it was. King, small, pudgy, smooth-skinned, had a voice that rolled off all four walls of the church and echoed the truth off the gabled ceiling. And, because the elders had given him time to complete his doctorate, the young minister became generous and began to commute between Montgomery and Atlanta and Montgomery and Boston. He tried hard to be at his new church on Saturdays, preach Sundays, and fly back to work Sunday nights.

Coretta sat with him in Boston throughout the weeks that followed, and she concealed—at least tried to—her disagreement with his choice. She still had her dream of a parish in the North. And she knew all about Alabama. She had been born and reared seventy or eighty miles from Montgomery, the onetime capital of the Confederacy, a tidy city with an old Capitol Building near the Dexter Avenue Church to remind blacks to remain in "their place." Montgomery would not forgive a black a wrong, even a slight one, because to forgive would lower the racial barriers a hundredth of an inch, and Alabama, like Mississippi, inflicted its cruelty and injustice on the black man.

Dr. King was working on the final stages of his thesis in Boston when the radio intoned the news, on May 17, 1954, that the United States Supreme Court, in the case of *Brown v. Board of Education, Topeka,* had reversed an opinion of 1896 that separate but equal facilities for white and blacks were equitable for both. The marble walls of the chamber of the Supreme Court of the United States were, as always, cool and pale and neutral as Chief Justice Earl Warren read: "We conclude that in the field of public education the doctrine of 'separate but equal' has no place. Separate educational facilities are inherently unequal."

Twenty-four words. The rest of it was prelude, but the twenty-four words resulted in a lasting convulsion of the states—South and North. The twenty-four words would lead to suits about restaurants, trains, seats in buses, bathing at beaches, intermarriage, salaries and promotions in industry, even the use of lavatories. The twenty-four words, seemingly concerned with education, tore the scabs from old racial wounds, and blood was about to flow fresh and red from bodies black and white.

The press of the North, for a while, hailed it as a landmark decision. The South condemned it and reverted to its time-honored defense in cases where it disagreed with the federal government—states' rights. Long-haired, drawling members of Congress spoke seriously of impeaching Earl Warren, and millionaires of the South proclaimed the message on billboards.

The black sat in silence, watching and listening. He wasn't sure that the twenty-four words meant what they seemed to mean. Nor did he recognize immediately that if separate but equal facilities were unjust in school, they were unjust everywhere else. He was not as exhilarated as the NAACP attorneys who understood that the Supreme Court had applied an irreversible eraser to the skin of the black man and had made him white.

It would require another year before the Supreme Court recovered its composure and discovered that the law had no implementation, no penalty. Then they ordered the federal courts and marshals to ensure that the law would be obeyed "with all deliberate speed." The word "deliberate" may be referred to as the twenty-fifth in the dictum of the Warren Court, and the South interpreted it as meaning that the boards of education could drag their feet for decades. That word would be argued and defined in court many times over many years.

Martin Luther King realized that the Supreme Court decision meant that someone had opened the cell door a crack. He would wait to see if the white man would permit the black to kick it open all the way. A crack in a cell door might help the next generation, but King was still interested in his own. Coretta King was perhaps the most unbelieving of all. She simply did not trust the white man and was prone to question his motives if, individually or collectively, he became just or generous.

She had seen the booted heel on the neck of the black man; she had heard the stories of the lynchings; she had heard the phrase "uppity nigger" applied to anyone of her race who was caught reasoning. In growing to womanhood, with an increasing interest in men, she saw the manhood beaten out of blacks and became accustomed to the shuffling head-down black man in the presence of whites.

Twenty-four words and add one. Black robes had enunciated a black decision. It was as inarguable as a religious commandment. The United States of America, unknown to itself, was preparing for a revolution which had more in common with the Soviet street fights of 1917 than it did with the American Civil War.

When the Supreme Court handed down its decision on "separate but equal" rights, Americans took little notice of the seething rancor in the black breast; white America was ready to fight school integration, but made the mistake of thinking that the new law would appease the black man for another century.

The Kings stopped commuting between Boston and Montgomery in the summer of 1954. The little apartment, the home of two persons in love, two persons sharing notions of the future, was left for the final time with hot sunlight pouring through the windows on the packing of books, mementos and bric-a-brac. Coretta King had completed her work at the New England Conservatory of Music; Martin King had some final thoughts to imprison in his thesis. They moved to Atlanta.

At the age of twenty-five, King had completed nineteen years of formal study and looked the way he would for the rest of his life: a five-foot-seven-inch man with a slightly rolling gait, Oriental eyes, and a voice which seemed to hollow up from a deep well. His soon-to-be-acquired doctorate gave the young man a dignity which smothered his sense of humor. Life became grim. Souls were there to be saved, but bodies and minds must be fought for, claimed, and redeemed, too. He kept telling his wife that he was not going to be one of those Bible-whacking hallelujah ministers. He would appeal to intelligence, to reason, to raise the people of his small church to a higher level. He planned to be a black Moses.

The old red-brick church stood facing the main street in Montgomery. Opposite was the Supreme Court Building, a cold assembly of stones where blacks seldom won a battle. It was little more than half the size of Martin's father's Ebenezer Baptist Church in Atlanta, but perhaps even more elite in its choice of parishioners. Dexter was called by the poor blacks of Montgomery "the rich man's church." The new pastor met dignified silence when he proposed to the board of trustees that the doors be opened to the poorer blacks of Montgomery. He even proposed that he would go out on the streets, into the slums, and proselytize them. There was silence as the dark eyes around the table stared back at him. King had lost his first skirmish. He could not believe that blacks would actively cultivate a caste system within their ranks; but he saw it, and in his holy naïveté, he resented it.

Mrs. King had been opposed to living in the South. Although the parsonage, a big sagging white-framed building of seven rooms would need little money to make it habitable, she resented the fact that it stood in the middle of a black neighborhood. It was not that Mrs. King even desired to live in a white neighborhood. The irritation was that this was so typical of the South she knew. Blacks must live in black neighborhoods. Blacks, even in the heat of summer, must not drink from a department-store water fountain. Blacks must not ask to be served at a luncheon counter. Blacks must sit in the back of all public conveyances, and when those buses became filled, they must stand to make room for whites. Blacks must not defend themselves when accused of anything by white policemen in metal helmets. Here the lid of power was on the smoldering volcano, and no one was strong enough to lift an edge of it.

Martin Luther King, Jr., looked at the same things—the same church, the same Capitol, the same square, and the same ghetto—and being young and full of hope and logic, he found solace. He saw a church. A different one. This was not a temple in which he could walk casually, to sing, to look at familiar faces, to feel that he was, like Jesus, truly in his father's house. This one was his responsibility, a challenge to prove his leadership, a place where he would bend people toward God's will. He was a religious young man, but he had grown up in the Southern Baptist Church, and the awe of the Presence had left him.

Before he arrived in Montgomery, he had known that he was going to adopt his father's successful system of church operation. Plate collections would stop at once. There would be no money changers in the temple. Donations would be made directly to the pastor or to one of the elders, outside the sanctuary. Second, he would assert his rights as pastor at once, not to intimidate the elders, but to let them know that even though some of them were twice his age and more, his would be the decisive judgment about what would and would not be permitted in the Dexter Avenue Baptist Church. To them, some of his notions were startling. He expected social, as well as religious, action, and he expected fervor to go with it. For example, he organized committees of men to assist with various projects. Committees of women were formed, and not just for cake bakes. He expected all his 300 parishioners to be good Christians throughout the week as well as on Sunday; he demanded that all join the National Association for the Advancement of Colored People; he asked all over the age of twenty-one to go to the courthouse and register as voters.

After the first two weeks, his lounging parishioners began to sit up and listen. The young preacher was loud and politically conscious. He did not spend all his time speaking of the hereafter and redemption; often he coupled the spirit with the body politic and spoke of the great number of integrated workers at Maxwell Air Force Base as opposed to the nonintegration in the shops downtown. He endorsed the interracial Council on Human Relations, which sought equality for the black man.

In the dog days of August, when the red-brick walls of his church shimmered like a farm oven, he dissected the Supreme Court decision on integration in education and called it "a step," nothing more, just a step forward. The NAACP had used the courts to achieve this step, and this was God's way as He recited the law from the steps of the lawgivers, the steps of Solomon's Temple, long ago. One step must lead to another, and another until there were no social or industrial differences between the races.

The parsonage was redecorated and ready by September 1, 1954, and the Kings moved in. His new friends assured the reverend, in confidence, that he must watch his words because Montgomery still flew the stars and bars of the Confederacy. Everything worth touching was white and white-controlled. The races were at peace because the blacks remained supine. The population of Montgomery was 120,000—of which 48,000 were black and 72,000 were white. The average income of whites was $1,950; blacks, $970. The whites owned almost all the automobiles; 70 percent of all bus passengers were black. The municipal law stated that blacks must sit in the back of the bus, filling toward the front, but if a white boarded, a black sitting toward front must get up and give him his seat and go stand in the back. A black waiting in line at a supermarket checkout counter would not necessarily be waited on when his turn came; he stood quietly until the clerk crooked a finger at him.

None of it surprised the Reverend Dr. King. Although he had grown up in comparatively liberal Atlanta, he was aware, from the stories told by Coretta, that Alabama was racially vicious. The facts about buses were even worse than King thought: The first four rows of seats were always reserved for whites and must be kept empty even if blacks filled the rest of the vehicle to standing room status. As in most of the South, all blacks, including the aged and infirm, entered by the front door only to drop the fare in the box. They then left and entered the bus by the back door to be seated.

He learned much about Montgomery from a newfound friend, the young chunky Southern-drawling Ralph Abernathy, pastor of the First Baptist Church. Although the two men were different in many ways, Abernathy was magnetized by the learned young man; fortunately, their wives, Coretta and Juanita, also became friends. All of them felt that changes were coming, changes for the better racially, but they wondered whether it would happen in their time or in the time of the next generation.

No one had a plan to fight white oppression; there was no desire to attack and perhaps be killed in a lost struggle. Everyone told every one else: "Wait and see." It was the litany of the dead. Coretta King, who could have been a successful singer, had accepted marriage rather than a career. She worked as secretary to the pastor. She found solace in the fact that, at services, she could sing solo oratorios and gave a few local concerts. Her husband's life was tedious and repetitious. He got out of bed shortly after 5 A.M., worked three hours writing parts of his sermon; then he met with his church counselors or went to a luncheon meeting, reserving time for performing marriages, visits to the chronically ill and dying, and, each week, attending a half dozen committee meetings.

The spring of 1955 saw the Kings flying back to Atlanta to announce that Coretta was pregnant. This news was received ecstatically by the older Kings and their friends, particularly because the young reverend had had the "downs" when it came to being a father. Many times he had told Coretta, "Now, in case we can't have children . . ." as though, for some obscure and nonmedical reason, he thought himself sterile. He spoke of adoption as though it were a note to be met next year.

Mrs. King, Jr., typical of her confidence in most matters, understood more about menstrual cycles and the natural functions of the female than her husband. She had waited with patience, agreeing with her husband that "If we can't . . ." knowing that "We can." Now she was sure of it.

Nothing moves without a countermotion. As the blacks became a little bolder—"less timid" is a better phrase—the whites of the South were forced to think about a future of living with blacks as equals. Now even the moderates began supporting additional suppressions of civil rights in hope of keeping the black "in his place." White people who had never participated in a racial demonstration were ready to stand up and be counted; the White Citizens Councils threatened blacks from Delaware to Mississippi, from Ohio to the Florida Keys. But there were other white groups that worked courageously for equal rights in these dangerous times. One called the Association of Southern Women for the Prevention of Lynching sent representatives to any county where the white populace was about to take the law into its own hands. Mrs. Jesse D. Ames, a lordly lady in her eighties, led groups of women dressed in their Sunday best to stand on courthouse steps, looking down at the mobs of muscled, shirt-sleeved workers, crying, "You must harm us first. You are not doing this in the name of white womanhood. We don't want it."

The statement was shocking to men all over the South because it yanked one leg of the antiblack tripod loose. The cultivated and nurtured bitterness had been carefully predicated upon: (1) the protection of Southern white womanhood from the sexual aggression of the black "buck"; (2) the assertion that the black was halfway between a barnyard animal and a human being and therefore beyond reasoning or rationale; (3) the belief that he was undependable, shiftless.

The White Citizens Councils, activists prepared to fight the black man in each town of the South and to kill him if offered resistance, decided to ignore the courthouse ladies on the grounds that women did not understand the gravity of the situation.

The women, as always, proved to be more formidable than expected. They linked their antilynching drive with the minority of white liberal males throughout the South. By a secret underground route, informants used Associated Press offices and reporters to locate potential danger to the black man before it reached the explosive point, at which time the ladies appeared with their parasols, their gracious iron-clad defiance, and saved blacks from beatings and sudden death.

The counterforces, however, were stronger. The discredited and almost pathetic Ku Klux Klan began to appear again, night riding through ghettos and firing guns with intoxicated fingers. The statesmen in the halls of Georgia considered, for a brief, mad moment, asking the other states for help in abolishing the Supreme Court of the United States. Mississippi, slow-witted and perpetually angry, waited almost a year before voting into law: "It shall be unlawful for any member of the white or Caucasian race to attend any school of high school level or below wholly or partially supported by funds of the State of Mississippi which is also attended by a member or members of the colored or Negro Race."

Doors could be heard slamming shut everywhere. James F. Byrnes, from South Carolina and a former United States Secretary of State dug deep and far afield when he said: "If the age of our Constitution is to be held against the soundness of its fundamental principles, what about the age of our religion? If time invalidates the truth in one field, will it not do so in another?"

The Congress of the United States, by unspoken gentlemen's agreement, decided to do nothing to try to overturn the court decision. Through Statuary Hall and deep into the wells of both houses crept the litany: "Wait and see." In the White House, General Dwight D. Eisenhower, a man promoted by the people from the efficiency of military hero to the inefficiency of the office of Chief Executive, was irritated. He and most of the members of his Cabinet were disturbed. The racial situation, kept in delicate balance by walking the tightwire of deceit, had suddenly tumbled to earth, and it would be Eisenhower and his Attorney General, Herbert Brownell, who must get the act back up on the high wire without injuring blocs of votes.

He had to make a move. The President could not "wait and see." He desegregated the public schools of Washington, D.C., in the autumn of 1954, and to his way of thinking, this was compliance with the law and a gesture that would silence criticism. He lost the votes of some of his most trusted Republican members of Congress because they came from the North, and the North, not seeing the filth in its own house, expected him to clean up the South at once.

Someone in the President's group thought of the words which might extricate him, even momentarily, from trouble. He said he was "opposed to the concentration of further power in the ever-expanding federal government" and spoke sympathetically of states' rights, the hominy grits of the South. When he addressed himself to the "great emotional strains and the practical problems" of the South, President Eisenhower was being devious and wise. If the leash was to be snipped from the neck of the black in Mississippi, the whites knew that they would awaken to two black votes for every white one. The President was not opposed to school desegregation as a law, but it was obvious that he had decided on a policy of doing as little as possible to enforce that law.

The nine men of the Supreme Court, having set fire to the nation, were now confident that they could also extinguish the blaze. They invited a third hearing on *Brown v. Board of Education of Topeka* in April, 1955. Four states—Virginia, Kansas, Delaware, and South Carolina—were already determined to continue segregation. The alarm caused by the original decision induced the states of Arkansas, Florida, Oklahoma, North Carolina, Maryland, and Texas to join them. The opposition consisted almost soley of the NAACP, which represented no state, merely a loose national membership which kept lifting and falling as the blacks won a small victory or lost a big one.

The NAACP was unprepared for two surprises. The first was that the briefs filed by their powerful opponents did not try to overturn the law, but asked for an "unspecific" time in which to achieve desegregation. The second was that the Attorney General's office, representing the United States of America, filed an *amicus curiae* brief which, instead of demanding specific and timely implementation of the law, hid in the shadow of the drawling Southerners and requested a "flexible" course of action.

Six weeks later the Warren Court surrendered to pressure. With great dignity, the decision reaffirmed the principle of desegregation as a sop to the NAACP and its earlier decision, then acknowledged that there are "varied" local school problems upon which no court could set a time limit. Further, to keep the matter off the high federal docket in future, the Supreme Court ordered the lower federal courts, each in its own district, to measure compliance to the law. The judges in the Southern districts were almost all Southerners; the local appellate divisions of the South were composed of Southerners. The black, who saw a sunbeam of freedom for a moment, watched the ominous clouds close over the sun and wondered what he had won, if anything.

The comments of Martin Luther King, Jr., drew little attention. Something which he was sure was coming to a boil after centuries was simmering. His comments among his family and friends were less objective and ministerial than from the pulpit, and yet both had in common King's belief that desegregation could be accomplished without bloodshed or animosity if the white man could be shown that the black was not "different"; that he was just an oppressed and helpless man, someone not to be feared as white supremacists pretended; that the white man would never be truly free himself until his black brother was free. The last words endeared themselves to Martin Luther King, Jr., and he would use them again and again in public.

He did not, could not see himself as a great leader of a deserving people. King could tick off the names of the black giants of the past who had tried and failed. As the youngest and newest minister in Montgomery, Alabama, he had no intention of sticking his neck out on racial issues. He was willing to fight, but he had seen a local minister relieved of his post and church because white authorities called him a racial firebrand. To fight, a man needs more than intellect; he needs a weapon, and the best one is the backing of a lot of other people.

In the late summer, Claudette Colvin was yanked off a bus, handcuffed, taken to prison, and mugged, all because she had been slow to rise from her seat for a white man. She was fifteen years old. The news aroused the blacks of Montgomery, and a committee of protest was elected to go meet with Police Commissioner Dave Birmingham and the local manager of the bus lines, J. E. Bagley. Martin Luther King, Jr., was selected to serve on the committee, although he had not asked to be appointed.

The blacks met the whites in Bagley's office. Bagley opened the meeting by admitting that his bus driver was wrong and vowed to reprimand him. Commissioner Birmingham said that he would go further: He would issue a report to the city attorney and ask him to state a definite official Montgomery policy regarding seating arrangements on buses.

The black men hardly had time to speak; the two white men were talking "colored" talk, and no one could think of anything further to demand. Weeks later the young divine was shocked to find that the city attorney had no intention of clarifying a local statute, now or ever; that Claudette Colvin was convicted in court and given a suspended sentence; that the bus driver who called for police was still driving.

Nothing was as it seemed to be or ought to be. The difference was enormous, contradictory. The Supreme Court ruling in favor of the black served only to bring white hatred to the surface. In department stores, blacks appeared and sat at lunch counters: they sat a long time and outwaited the white adversary. They were served, and in the morning all the luncheon stools had been removed.

It must be emphasized that no one blew a bugle; no one heard one. King joined the Montgomery branch of the NAACP and was elected to the executive committee. He was proposed for president because he had a good attendance record, but at the request of his pregnant wife, he declined with thanks. She thought he had more than enough work, laboring over those lengthy Sunday sermons, visiting the sick, attending church committee meetings, and helping around the parsonage.

King was becoming more irritated with black ministers who told him that clerics should confine themselves to men's souls. "This view of religion," he said, "I feel is too confined." Montgomery was not a big city, but the black leadership was not only divided, Dr. King found, but actively fighting one another. The Progressive Democrats were headed by E. D. Nixon. The Citizens Committee, which had nothing in common with Nixon's group except pigment, fought its own political fights under Rufus Lewis. Mary Fair Burks and Jo Ann Robinson ran the Women's Political Council. R. L. Matthews held the reins to the NAACP.

In the autumn of 1955, Martin Luther King's hopes soared to the stars when he learned that all the groups, each remaining intact, would submit to a supervisory body to be called the Citizens Coordinating Committee. The boyish smile returned to the young chubby face. Reason, plain ordinary reason, should have told them that divided, they would dissipate their strength, that their only chance to be effective was to march in the same direction under the same banner of equality.

The Citizens Coordinating Committee fell apart amid shouted charges and countercharges. The boyish smile died. King did nothing to try to bind the wounds of the contending groups because there were too many of them and they were superficial. The world of the black was full of field marshals. Dr. King lost interest. He concentrated on convincing Coretta that the name of the baby, to be born in late autumn, should be Martin Luther King III. He liked the sound "the third" because it had a ring of tradition, like a grocer who could print under his name "est. 1798."

The infant was born on October 15, 1955. It was a girl, weighing nine pounds eleven and a half ounces. Coretta reminded him that this little girl was not to be the third anything. She reminded him that she liked unusual names, names often heard nowhere else. So the baby would be Yolanda Denise. The father did not think much of the name. Within a short time, everyone called her Yoki.

Almost all infants are warm and cuddly. Yoki was fat and warm and, as far as her father was concerned, would remain that way the rest of his life. It did not matter how many children the Kings were to be blessed with (he said it would be eight, Coretta said four; it would be four); there was a special something between Yoki and her father. She was the warmth on his lap against the icy winds of rebellion; she was the fervent warm kiss when all the learned lips were cold; she was the trusting, loving heart when even blacks would call him a "midget son of a bitch." Yoki, not understanding the issues, would place her little hand in his even when the time came that *his* father—almost in tears—turned his back on the dangerous political plans of his favorite son.

The evening was raw. The sun set early, and the twin eyes of cars and buses were a cold flame against the wind on Cleveland Avenue. The bus would be along any minute. The people, mostly black, waited along the curb at strategic places to be first aboard, first to get a seat. The slender middle-aged woman holding the bag in front of her with both hands was cold and irritable. She was Mrs. Rosa Parks, a seamstress, a neat person with glasses and a nice manner of speech, but that day had been a bit too much. Behind the rimless glasses, she watched for that bus.

Her feet ached. Ached like a sore tooth. She was not complaining, even to herself, but it seemed that life consisted of nothing more than crouching on her toes, with a mouth full of pins, before white women who thought that the hem was too long or too short, or it hadn't been sewn straight, or the neckline was too high, too low, too revealing, or not revealing enough. Besides, Mrs. Parks had done some Christmas shopping.

Had she been less intelligent, phlegmatic perhaps, she would have been more content. But she was intelligent, sensitive, a woman who devoured books and was politically conscious. This can be a dangerous combination when the feet hurt and the stomach doesn't have a hot dinner to look forward to. Just a seat on a bus.

Mrs. Parks followed the rule for "colored folks" and found a seat in the fifth row left, directly behind the first four rows for the "white folks." When she sat, the soreness of her feet eased a bit, and she looked out the window. She didn't care how long the bus took to get to her street.

Brakes sighed, and the bus started forward, fat and indolent, and then it stopped again. More people got on, mostly black. Rosa Parks could hardly bare to watch them run up the two steps, drop their coins, and run back down, bumping into others, to get to that rear door before it closed. The bus started, moved a little, and stopped. More blacks got aboard, plus a few whites. Mrs. Parks didn't look up to note that all the seats were now filled. Her interest was in her feet.

The driver looked. All the seats were filled. A few whites stood up front. "All right, all right," he said, looking at Mrs. Parks and two other blacks. "Come on. Get in the back." Rosa Parks looked up at the strong white man at her side, waiting. Three blacks got up and walked to the back. "Get out of that seat," the driver said, pointing at Mrs. Parks. All he saw was a small dark woman with a circlet of braids and a glint of light from her glasses.

"No," she said. "I won't."

Rosa Parks was not frightened. She had been secretary of the local NAACP chapter for years, and she was attuned to race relations and knew the difference between the loud and the ominous. This threat was ominous. Conversely, the bus driver seemed to understand that this black woman was one who was going to sit there just to defy him. So he yanked the ratchet on the emergency brake, ducked under the steel bar, and left to look for a policeman.

Suddenly, the chatter stopped. All the birds, dark and light, inside that bus, fell silent. They knew what he had said; they knew what she had said. There was seldom a confrontation except once in a while between an intoxicated Negro and a surly driver. This was different. An apparently gentle person, one who might wear gloves as a habit, had given the driver a flat no, and there was nothing he could do except call a policeman. If the word got around Montgomery that a small woman had successfully defied a big white brute of a man on the Cleveland Avenue bus, well, this would not be December 1, 1955, it would be hallelujah day all over the city.

The driver came back. The policeman walked up to Rosa Parks and took her under the arms. "What are you taking me for?" she said softly. "What did I do against the law?" He pushed her ahead of him.

Mrs. Parks was charged with violation of a Montgomery City ordinance governing racial accommodation on publicly owned vehicles. It was a proper complaint under municipal law, but Officer Day did not seem to know that these complaints were usually handled, and handled well for the whites, under the much broader and vaguer term "Disorderly conduct." He had written a racial complaint, and now, for better or for worse, the City of Montgomery had only one way out of the dilemma created by the "separate but equal facilities" dictum of the Supreme Court, and that was to acquit her. However, if that were done, it would spread through "Colored Town" like summer lightning and lead to more violations. "Disorderly conduct" had always been a grab bag for the police, especially when they desired to make an arrest but couldn't think of a violation.

The driver, J. F. Blake, felt that he had been forced to do the thing he did. Nothing in his record depicts him as a racist or even as a man accustomed to losing his temper. Blacks who remembered him said that Blake was not the kind of driver who cursed blacks or who took their money in the change box and closed the back door before they could get in. If Blake was angry about anything at all, it was that his bus was holding up downtown Christmas traffic while he looked for a policeman. That and the fact that Rosa Parks was such a gentle-looking person.

Within an hour of Mrs. Parks' imprisonment, the telephone wires caught fire. The news was traveling from person to person to person. The blacks phoned their friends, their pastors. The first call had been made by Mrs. Parks, who phoned Mrs. E. D. Nixon. For help, Mrs. Parks required the services of a black champion, and she could hardly have done better than E. D. Nixon. He was a burly Pullman porter, riding the plush cars out of the railroad station, and he had been a leader in almost every fight for black rights in Montgomery in the decade; further, he was a man who stood up, spoke up, and made himself heard.

Nixon phoned police headquarters, gave his name, and asked what the charge was. The policeman at the switchboard said it was "none of your goddamned business" and hung up. The next call went to Mrs. Jo Ann Robinson, president of the Women's Political Council; she said she had been apprized of the news and had heard it from attorney Fred Gray, another leader.

None of the male leaders discounted the worth of Mrs. Robinson. She and her 250 women members were militant, but not aggressively so. They represented no threat to the white males, and they were accorded more sympathetic treatment than their husbands. Someone said, "The only free people in the South are the black woman and the white man." Mrs. Robinson had persuaded the white merchants of downtown Montgomery to do two things the black males could not have achieved: desegregate the water fountains in the stores, and to send bills to blacks addressed as "Mr.," "Mrs.," or "Miss."

Three months earlier, Mrs. Robinson had begun to map plans to boycott the Montgomery Bus Line and had been looking for a suitable case. She thought she had one when the young black girl was evicted from a vehicle and arrested. However, when it was learned that she was pregnant and unmarried, Mrs. Robinson felt the girl was too vulnerable as far as public opinion was concerned, and so she has postponed her plans for the bus boycott. Now that none other than Rosa Parks, the epitome of respectability, had been arrested, and on a racial charge at that, Mrs. Robinson knew the time had come for the boycott.

Nixon went to police headquarters and bailed out Rosa Parks. "This," he said happily, "is what we've been waiting for." He asked her if she was willing to be the "symbolic case." She said yes. Nixon reminded her that she would lose her position as a seamstress, that she might not be able to find employment anywhere in Montgomery after the trial.

She nodded her birdlike head. "It's all right," she said.

The phone lines burned all night. E. D. Nixon wanted to prove to the white establishment that the blacks had tremendous power, especially when it came to buses. He called black leaders all night. Nixon was beyond fatigue. He was elated. Shortly after 5 A.M. he noticed among the list of clergy that there was no check mark against the name "M. L. King, Jr." Nixon was in a state where he had no time to persuade. He explained what had happened and asked King to be a member of the committee for a one-day boycott. There was silence on the phone. "Brother Nixon," said King, "let me think it out awhile. Call me back." Nixon knew that there was no indication of leadership in that kind of response. Still, the Reverend Dr. King represented 300 silk-stocking adherents, and they, too, would be important to the moral fiber of a boycott.

Later King said, "The apparent apathy of Negro ministers presented a special problem." Mrs. Robinson was more succinct: "They were busy preaching God and raising their salaries." Nixon might have declined to call back, but he took a chance on a refusal. He asked King if he had reached a decision. The pastor reminded Nixon that he had recently declined the presidency of the local NAACP because of his pastoral duties; now, in addition to his church work, he had a two-week-old daughter, but in spite of it all, he would serve on the committee.

Nixon thanked him and hung up. He now had a committee of respected blacks, and in Rosa Parks, he had the right prisoner. The Reverend Dr. King did not tell Nixon that, between phone calls, he had solicited the advice of his new friend, the Reverend Ralph David Abernathy. The stout mustachioed minister had virtues and graces different from those accorded to King, and yet the two complemented each other like hands laced in prayer. King had a head full of Nietzsche, Plato, and even Will Durant. Abernathy, who had come from the black backcountry around Marengo, where his father owned a ranch, was a black's black.

Abernathy said, "Join." King joined.

Nixon's group drew up a leaflet calling for a black bus boycott for Monday, December 5, the day of the trial. It was run off unsigned, and after school was out on Friday, boys were asked to distribute them to the blacks all over Montgomery. The Reverend Dr. King got out 7,000 additional leaflets—now that he was in, he was going to go all the way—and one of them got into the hands of a black domestic who could not read.

She handed it to her white mistress and asked her to read it. The woman was so shocked at the audacity of the blacks that she phoned it in to the Montgomery *Advertiser*. It is possible, but extremely doubtful, that they wished to help Nixon and his blacks. And yet, because it was news, they published the flyer on the front page of Sunday's paper, and now everybody knew that *der Tag* was Monday. Of course, the publication also had the effect of mobilizing the white community. It would have been in a better position to fight the blacks if the power company had been threatened, or a march on City Hall organized, but many of the white readers could see no future in a one-day bus boycott—and the bus company was owned by out-of-towners anyway.

Yet, in its very simplicity and limitations, it was a vigorous step. Mrs. Robinson seemed to be the only person who realized that history was taking place in Montgomery, Alabama. This small cloistered citadel of the Confederacy was about to be broken open, or the blacks were going down to a defeat which would set them back a half century. She wrote her own little leaflet, and purposely or not, it not only enlisted the aid of all blacks, but also forced all the black ministers to observe its commandments:

1. Don't ride the bus to work, to town, to school, or anyplace Monday December 5.
2. Another Negro woman has been arrested and put in jail because she refused to give up her bus seat.
3. Don't ride the bus to work, to town, to school, or anywhere on Monday. If you work, take a cab, or share a ride, or walk.
4. Come to a mass meeting Monday at 7 P.M. at the Holt Street Baptist Church for further instruction.

A split, not serious, began to develop. The ministers, in the habit of hedging their heavenly bets, had requested the sanction of the Reverend H. H. Hubbard to use his name as president of the Baptist Ministerial Alliance. He gave it. King and Abernathy also asked permission to hold a boycott meeting at the Dexter Avenue Baptist Church Saturday evening at 7 P.M. This was contrary to Mrs. Robinson's call for a meeting at the Holt Street Baptist Church, but Hubbard gave King his blessing.

Matters were moving so swiftly that efforts were duplicated and sometimes divided. King thought that the black Methodist ministers, holding a seminar in a local church, should be contacted, but he would not do it himself. Ralph Abernathy enlisted the aid of Mrs. A. W. West, whose husband, a prominent Methodist, had connections with the ministers. They agreed to help.

All the ministers pledged that they would preach the Monday boycott to their people on Sunday. They voted to amend Mrs. Robinson's proclamation slightly and to disseminate it. The Reverend W. J. Powell was voted to approach Montgomery's eighteen black taxicab companies and ask them if they could drive people—five to a cab—to and from work or to and from home and downtown Montgomery at a minimum fare.

In the ghetto, men in barbershops said that the ministers weren't going far enough: they vowed to beat the hell out of the white bus drivers. In its exuberance, the black community lost sight of the fact that they were only asking for the right to board a bus by the front door and take an empty seat; it was not a revolution.

The Sunday sermons were vigorous. The ministers spoke of persuasion rather than coercion. The flocks in their Sunday best fell silent; this, for them, was a time of test; it was a thing no longer confined to *Montgomery* but was chattering on Associated Press and United Press International keys to regional newspapers and on to shorter stories for consumption across the United States.

King spent the afternoon reading the paper. He was impressed, even fearful of the negative side of the boycott. He equated it with the actions of the White Citizens Councils, which had grown with the speed of poisoned mushrooms through the South. The whites used the local courts to preserve segregation, as the blacks used them to break it; the whites selected certain black businesses to bankrupt by boycott; the Montgomery blacks were doing this to the bus company. The White Citizens Councils threatened those among them who espoused a milder course; the blacks in the ghettos did the same over the fateful weekend.

The deadly parallels, King felt, would not bring the races together; it would polarize them. He sat in his easy chair, the newspaper open on his lap, his eyes closed, thinking. "The whole thing is immoral," his mind told him. "It is a negative, unchristian act." He could not lend his talent and his will to this, and there was only one way out. That would be to take the opposite tact and convince himself it was the only course to follow for positive, enlightened reasons. It required time; dinner was almost ready when the Reverend Dr. King found his answer: The boycott was not really a boycott; it was a group of blacks withdrawing their support from an evil system. He remembered reading Thoreau's essay on *Civil Disobedience* in college, and he even remembered a fitting quotation: "We can no longer lend our cooperation to an evil system."

That was it. The City of Montgomery had inaugurated the wrong and perpetuated the evil. The bus company was merely the external sign; the fight for the right must start there.

On Monday morning, Dr. and Mrs. King were up and dressed at five-thirty a half hour before Yoki's first feeding. They looked out across the front porch to see that the day was still as dark as the night. Coretta King made coffee; Dr. King said, "If we only get sixty percent cooperation; just sixty percent. . . ." His wife was more of an activist than that; her hope was to see no blacks on the buses at all; she could see no reason why, after all the publicity, after the sharp drawing of lines between merchants and police on one side and blacks on the other, that anyone should cross over.

On Highland Avenue there was a bus stop a few feet from the King house. The first bus was due at 6 A.M. Neither of them could keep away from the front windows. At 6, Dr. King was in the kitchen. He heard his wife call from the living room: "Martin! Martin! Come quickly!" He stood beside her and watched that first bus moving. Coretta's face was ecstatic as she pointed: "It's empty!"

The bus ran the South Jackson Line route, which carried more blacks to and from work than any other. It was truly empty. King was afraid to believe it, afraid to believe that a protest, organized over one weekend, could work that well. They waited at the front window for fifteen minutes. The next bus crept by. It was empty. There was no one aboard but the driver. The third bus went by. It held two white passengers.

It was a cold morning, and Dr. King might have enjoyed a second cup of coffee, but he was now in a fever of hope. He put on his heavy coat and ran to the garage and backed the family car out in a plume of steam. Slowly, almost in a majesty of meditation, Dr. King drove down one bus line street and up another, keeping close to the curb and watching and counting. He kept cruising during the peak morning hour and counted eight blacks in all the buses. He kept telling himself solemnly that a miracle—a real miracle—had occurred and he had been present to see it. He went home and made jubilant phone calls and listened to some; he embraced Coretta; he read some correspondence; he hugged Yoki; and, in the afternoon, in the late hours, he went out for another survey.

The South Jackson Line was used by black students at Alabama State College, and schoolboys rebel against rebellion. So King watched. The buses were still empty. He saw groups of black boys, books large and heavy under their sweatered arms, walking home or thumbing rides. A few men who worked nights were riding mules from the ghetto to their places of business. Some had cars and drove around picking up walking blacks, especially the infirm. Taxicabs staked out pickup points no more than three streets apart and took passengers aboard on a share-the-fare plan.

Police headquarters sent out a radio order that the blacks had organized "goon squads" to keep others from riding the buses and that two police motorcycles would fellow each bus to drive them away. In court, Mrs. Parks came up for trial. She was defended by Fred D. Gray, the black attorney. The prosecution argued that there was a municipal ordinance dividing the black race from the white on public conveyances and that the defendant did, in fact, violate that ordinance willfully and had publicly refused to correct the wrong when requested to by the bus driver.

"Ten dollars' fine," the judge said, hardly looking up from his desk blotter, "and four dollars' cost of court." Gray respectfully informed the judge that the decision would be appealed. "Duly noted," His Honor said. The lawyer and the woman left court with Abernathy, the Reverend E. N. French, minister of Hilliard Chapel of the AME Zion Church, and others. They weren't angry. They were elated. For a pittance, $14, it was possible that the white prosecution had made a $100 billion error. Besides, there was that glorious happy bus boycott.

Abernathy wanted to know at once whether the black people were going to abandon both the protest and the appeal through the courts, as they usually did, or whether they would seek guidance that night at the church meeting to elect a permanent leadership. Nixon made the decision for them. "Let's elect an *ad hoc* committee," he said. This would maintain the bus boycott beyond the one day. It might last only a few days, but it would hurt some bank accounts.

That afternoon the ministers, transformed into tigers, held a meeting with other leaders before the evening church meeting. The sweet sad façades of men dedicated more to the spiritual than to the material fell away, and they shouted for "real" leadership. They and others like Nixon and Gray voted to keep the boycott going until the company met certain minimal demands, including more courtesy to black people on buses.

The Reverend L. Roy Bennett, chairman of the boycott operation, opened the nominations for president. The entire assemblage, including Martin Luther King, Jr., was surprised to hear the dry voice of Professor

Rufus Lewis, from a dim corner of the church, say, "Mr. President, I would like to nominate Reverend M. L. King for president." Bennett, somewhat stunned, kept the floor open for other nominations, but there were none. Martin Luther King was elected unanimously. The new president later told friends that he was so astonished that he had no tongue to decline; that if he had had time to think it through, he would have declined the office.

This must be accepted on his word, but it is difficult to reconcile with his ambitions, his refusal to continue to serve in a big safe church second in command to his father, as well as his ability to single out the one thing among many that would benefit him. The church rang with applause, and King ⌄ose and took a modest bow. Elected with him were the reverends L. R. Bennett as vice president, U. J. Fields as recording secretary, and E. N. French as corresponding secretary and Mrs. Edna A. Dungee as financial secretary.

Names for the new organization were suggested and discarded. It was Ralph Abernathy who said, "How about the Montgomery Improvement Association?" This expressed precisely what the protesters were trying to achieve, so it was adopted. King took the podium and reminded everyone that there was a general meeting at 7 P.M. and they had better hurry home and prepare for it. Some warned that there might be newspaper spies at that meeting: "Maybe we ought to just sing and pray." Someone said that the names of the leaders should be kept secret.

At this point, the Pullman porter got to his feet. "We're acting like little boys," E. D. Nixon said. "Somebody's name will have to be known. If we're afraid, we might just as well fold up now. We must also be men enough to discuss our recommendations in the open; this idea of passing around papers secretly is bunk. The white folks are going to find it out anyway. We'd better decide now whether we are going to be men or boys."

It is possible—although there is no evidence to support it—that Nixon realized that once more the Ministerial Association had waited for a sure winner, then had come out of hiding to run it their own way—on tiptoe without hurting anyone's feelings. If there were two strong men at that afternoon meeting, they were Nixon and Abernathy. Contrary to the old proverb, they were learning from history that something can be learned from history.

On the evening of the Holt Street Church meeting, the new president of the Montgomery Improvement Association hurried home, washed, dressed, and, not finding time to put words on paper, knelt and prayed for guidance. He had fifteen minutes—no more—to allocate to God and, as is the case with all desperate supplicants, King was asking God to counsel and guide his steps and thoughts just this once.

The church was packed. Outside stood 4,000 people jammed in the streets. Church elders raced around Montgomery trying to find microphones and loudspeakers. Other ministers were introduced and spoke briefly on the racial crisis in Montgomery. Someone held a seat for Rosa Parks down front. She sat composed, as always, neither moving nor showing any tension or emotion. It was 8:30 P.M. before Dr. Martin Luther King, Jr., was introduced. Ordinarily, he spoke from a carefully prepared text. But this time, without the words being written down, without cue lines, he permitted his heart to dance on his tongue. This was a time for the yelled "Amens!" which he despised and the "Tell it to 'em, preacher!"

Calmly, slowly, he recited what had happened to Rosa Parks. Dr. King began to work himself up toward a shouting tirade. "There comes a time," he said, wagging an admonishing finger, "there comes a time when people get tired—tired of being segregated and humiliated, tired of being kicked about by the brutal feet of oppression!"

The waves of applause grew louder and longer. Some of the younger boys were whistling between their fingers. Outside, the crowd listened to the ripped sound of his voice emitted by old speakers.

"We had no alternative," he said, "but to protest. For many years, we have shown amazing patience. We have sometimes given our white brothers the feeling that we liked the way we were being treated. But we come here tonight to be saved from that patience that makes us patient with anything less than freedom and justice." Those who had heard of King but did not attend his church and knew little about him began to think that they had discovered an intelligent fighter. This man not only knew what he was talking about, but knew how to say it effectively.

"One of the great glories of democracy," he said, looking down between his hands holding the sides of the lectern, "is the right to protest for right." The head came up. The lips snapped shut and open enunciating an earthly gospel for the black. "The White Citizens Councils and the Ku Klux Klan are protesting for the perpetuation of injustice in the community. We are protesting for the birth of justice in the community.

"Their methods lead to violence and lawlessness. But in our protest there will be no cross burnings. No white person will be taken from his home by a hooded Negro mob and brutally murdered. There will be no threats and intimidation. We will be guided by the highest principles of law and order. Our method will be that of persuasion, not coercion. We will only say to the people: 'Let your conscience be your guide.' Our actions must be guided by the deepest principles of our Christian faith. Love must be our regulating ideal. Once again we must hear the words of Jesus echoing across the centuries: 'Love your enemies; bless them that curse you, and pray for them that despitefully use you.' "

The people were on their feet now, sounding like the roar of a jet engine as their shouts filled the hallowed places of the church. Dr. King kept waving them back down, shaking his head and holding both palms aloft to make them quiet. "If we fail to do this," he said, "our protest will end up as meaningless drama on the stage of history, and its memory will be shrouded with the ugly garments of shame. In spite of the mistreatment that we have confronted, we must not become bitter and end up by hating our white brothers. As Booker T. Washington said: 'Let no man pull you down so low as to make you hate him.' " This time, he was forced to turn away from the lectern, head bowed, before the crowd concluded the shouting and applause. "If you will protest courageously and yet with dignity and Christian love," he said slowly, almost pleadingly, "when the history books are written in future generations, the historians will have to pause and say: 'There lived a great people—a black people—who injected new meaning and dignity into the veins of civilization.' This," he concluded, "is our challenge and our overwhelming responsibility."

In a few minutes of time, Dr. King had become the Black Gandhi of America. He had introduced the nonviolent concept of battle; he had, by inference, informed his audience that the struggle, far from being over after a one-day bus strike, had barely begun; he had unfurled the banner of Christ as their unseen leader; he had warned the sheep they must band together; and he was unashamed to take a Churchillian quotation and invert it for his own use.

If there was a man at the Holt Street Church that night who did not feel a missed beat of the heart or look down at a palsied hand, he was highly unusual.

In his despair, Martin Luther King, Jr., wrenched immortal phrases from his soul: "We are tied together," he said of whites and blacks. "The Negro needs the white man to free him of his fear; the white man needs the Negro to free him of his guilt." Later, he would step beyond the battle lines and be mowed down by both sides for his outspokenness: "Three simple words can describe the nature of the social revolution that is taking place and what Negroes really want. The words are 'all,' 'now,' and 'here.' "

The White Citizens Councils would use King's words to frighten their constituencies. His language would lose friends for the cause. Nobody was willing to give the black man all, here and now.

As he returned to his seat among the pastors, he was told that the church had been jammed since 5 P.M.; that a report within the last half hour indicated that blacks filled an area four blocks around the church; that nearby white residents had protested the shouting coming from the loudspeakers and they had been disconnected, although the crowd outside remained where it was; and that police patrol cars were cruising quietly around the perimeter of the crowd.

Someone brought Rosa Parks to the rostrum and tried to introduce her. The crowd would not wait. It got to its feet to give her a standing ovation. If she was tired, it didn't show in her radiant face. She, no doubt, was as surprised to find herself in this position of Montgomery's Joan of Arc as King was to find himself the Moses of a movement.

Ralph Abernathy read the proclamation, doing it word by individual word and looking up from the text to make certain that all understood. It called upon all blacks not to use any Montgomery buses until: (1) courteous treatment by the bus operators was guaranteed; (2) passengers were served on a first-come-first-served basis—blacks sitting from the back of the bus toward the front; whites sitting from the front toward the back; (3) black bus operators were employed on black routes.

When Abernathy asked for the yeas, the rafters shook, and the asking for nays was a waste. The black people were prepared to hurt the white man's pocketbook as well as their own feet. The resolution had gone further than seating arrangements. It now involved employment of black drivers; it demanded guaranteed courtesy. The only section which could be called a retreat was the one dealing with blacks seating themselves starting in the back of the bus; whites starting in front. No one mentioned it, but this, of course, was a form of segregation.

III. HIGH NOON

4

THE STAID, prissy little world of Montgomery was thrust into a convulsive revolution. The bus boycott remained firm. Carl Rowan, a black reporter for the Minneapolis *Tribune,* flew to the city to see for himself. "The Negro ministers," he wrote sometime later, "had achieved the most unbelievable by pulling the hoodlums out of the craps games . . . and into the churches, where they sang hymns, gave money, shouted amen and wept over the powerful speeches." The strong as well as the weak joined hands, but all felt that they could not afford to risk hope. It was too much to expect, and yet the dark faces stared in wonderment when they saw rich white women in Cadillacs and Lincolns rolling into the ghetto to pick up their domestics for the day's work. And driving them home, too.

They saw affluent black women augment the taxicab service with their husband's cars, keeping everybody on wheels at less cost than that of the bus. Some whites tried the opposite tack and offered black employees the option of riding the buses or being discharged. More than 95 percent chose to quit. The Montgomery *Advertiser,* as Southern in character as to be expected, opened its columns to letters from readers, and they weighed five to one in sympathy with the boycott. One letter, from a white librarian named Juliette Morgan, compared the power of the movement to Gandhi's nonviolent fight against the British.

The police, on whom the heaviest impact had fallen, began to overreact. They arrested a black man named Fred Daniels for preventing a white woman from boarding a bus. The black community roared with laughter when the police had to release Daniels because the woman testified that he was only assisting her across the street. In the ghetto the police couldn't goad the young people into a fight. A silent staring passivity gripped the city, and the merchants were complaining to City

Hall that all the firings had hurt their Christmas business and to "get this damn nigger problem settled quick."

The bus company sent attorneys and officers from headquarters in Chicago to find out what the trouble was and to demand, under their franchise, that the officials of Montgomery straighten it out at once. The bus company carried 17,500 blacks each day each way. All these fares were lost, and the company was not in a financial position to hang on much longer. City Hall, certain that the American black did not have the will to fight, was sure he would soon abandon his bus fight. In fact, they would hurry the collapse by disrupting his taxicab pools and his share-the-ride plans by calling it hitchhiking, which was against the law.

The Reverend Dr. King was busy assembling committees. He organized a finance committee to pay drivers of secondhand automobiles to pick up blacks at certain stops at certain times. He also asked the finance committee to solicit donations for lawyers' fees and court battles. If the police became desperate, they might resort to mass arrests, in which case $25 to $50 would be needed to bail out each person from the city jail. If that sum of money was too great for the Montgomery Improvement Association, there was the problem of who would chose which ones should be set free and which left to languish in jail.

He already had an executive board, but Dr. King wanted a strategy committee to advise the executive board. For a while the pastor had so many committees dealing with so many contingencies that it was necessary for each member to serve on more than one commitee. All the while he had to be careful not to bruise any egos.

Nor had he forgotten that old goal of his, to get blacks registered as voters. At first, this did not appear to be related to the bus boycott, but when Tuesday passed and the report arrived that the boycott was now 99 percent effective, Martin Luther King, Jr., began to sense, with that cautious optimism of his, that this protest was bigger than buses.

By Tuesday night official Montgomery had still done nothing. The gentlemen of City Hall were surprised at the strength of the boycott, but not one of them, from mayor to patrolman, thought that the boycott could succeed or was intended to succeed. It was simply a display of black leadership intended to impress other blacks.

The time to act, the white community thought, was when the boycott began to hurt business, really hurt it. One white man, the Reverend Robert Graetz, joined King's boycott. He was a boyish-looking minister who preached at the black Trinity Luthern Church. The boycott committees didn't know whether to accept or decline Graetz as a member.

He was a friend of the black man. He was a minister of a black church. He understood black problems and tried to solve them. But he was white, and white was what they were fighting. All hands admired Graetz's courage because by joining the blacks, he became a leper in the white community of Montgomery.

The first crack in the cold white façade came on Wednesday. The Alabama Human Relations Council asked for a conference between the city and bus officials on one side and King and his executive committee on the other. Both sides were eager to accept while making doleful predictions about nothing would come of it. Secretly, the whites were hoping for heavy rain. Nature herself would then force the blacks back in the buses. The sky remained cobalt blue and the winds fresh and cold. When rain did come, it came hard and steady in the middle of the night.

The Reverend Dr. King's committee consisted of twelve, an almost Christ-like arrangement, and King was chosen as spokesman. He said he proposed to stick to the three original demands. Essentially, acceptance would cost Montgomery nothing, and each of the pledges could easily be violated a little at a time, until matters were back exactly where they had been.

The blacks arrived at the commission chamber fifteen minutes early. To ensure that no one might acquire a false notion of equality, the three commissioners had a table for themselves against the wall. The aluminum chairs facing them were for the blacks. J. E. Bagley and Jack Crenshaw of the bus company came in smiling weakly and sat at the end of the commissioners' table. At the stroke of eleven, Mayor W. A. Gayle, Police Commissioner Clyde Sellers, and Commissioner Frank A. Parks walked in, looking straight ahead, and sat at the middle of the table.

The mayor made no announcement of the purpose of the meeting. He merely called it to order and requested that the Reverend Thomas P. Thrasher, the white pastor of an Episcopal church and the man who had brought the contending parties together, make a statement. Thrasher stood and cleared his throat. The Reverend Dr. King, when nervous, always turned on a reassuring smile and kept it alive. He was smiling now. Thrasher said that the Council on Human Relations was conscious of the problem in Montgomery and had intervened because he and his fellow members had faith that both sides could and would deliberate "reasonably and unemotionally."

Mayor Gayle turned a stern judicious eye on the blacks and said, "Who's the spokesman?" The blacks were intimidated. They said nothing. The twelve, listening perhaps to the symbolic crowing of a cock, turned to stare at Martin Luther King. "All right," the mayor said, "come forward and make your statement." It was then that King noticed that the officials of Montgomery had made another monumental error: Two television cameras began to grind. The mayor must have known that he did not have a good case against Rosa Parks and the boycott; to permit King to state the case for the networks was to enlist sympathy and assistance from quarters he could never have reached.

King sat at the opposite end of the table from Bagley and Crenshaw. He folded his hands, studied them, rotated the thumbs together, and spoke softly. He said he wanted to make it clear at once that Rosa Parks was not the cause of the boycott; her arrest had merely precipitated the fight for human rights. "Our action," he said slowly, "is the culmination of a series of injustices and indignities that have existed over the years."

Although he was new to Montgomery, King was armed with names and dates and events of discourtesies, arrests, and abuses. It was a cruel mockery, he said, to force a black woman to stand over an empty front seat.

"Courtesy," he said, raising his head and almost dismissing the plea as something that should not be begged for, "is the least any business can grant to its patrons." So much money went from black pockets to the bus company that he thought it only fair that some of it be returned by hiring qualified black drivers. The minister was speaking well, and the cameras were whirring but there was no dynamite in the speech. King closed by assuring everyone that "we plan to conduct our protest on a high level of dignity and patience. Our aim is not to put the bus company out of business," he said, "but to achieve justice for ourselves, as well as for the white man."

King returned to his original seat. The mayor opened the meeting to general discussion. Police Commissioner Sellers said, in an aside, that the taxi companies had a license ruling that they could not charge less than forty-five cents per ride. King understood the threat. The cab-drivers were charging ten cents apiece—the same as the bus fare—to jam five or six persons into each vehicle and drive them downtown. If the city threatened to invalidate their licenses, the movement would be crippled.

The commissioners challenged the legality of altering the bus loading system because it was part of municipal law. "You are asking us," one said, "to violate the law." No one stood to say, "No, sir. We are asking you to change the law."

Crenshaw, attorney for the bus company, had listened quietly to the quacking. When everyone was talked out, he began his arguments and they were all straight, hard punches to the black's face. He implied that blacks didn't know what they were asking—the bus company, even if it wished, could not violate the Montgomery law, and wouldn't. The police commissioner interrupted to agree. So did Sellers. All of King's men could see that the other side had no intention of settling anything.

The Reverend Dr. King shook his head dolefully. The deck, as always, was stacked. The whites would not discuss hiring black drivers. Courtesy to riders was an arguable point, because the drivers were present to accept fares and drive a route safely; catering to passengers was not part of their work. King got to his feet and asked the mayor to adjourn the meeting. It was done quickly. As the blacks began to walk out, Gayle asked a couple of them, including King, to remain a few minutes more to see if both sides could reach an agreement informally. The young reverend from Atlanta had a working philosophy to refuse no offer of help, always to say yes to the opposition's offer to talk, no matter which side held the better cards. The press and the cameras were gone. Now, perhaps, both sides could afford to drop the self-serving speeches and get down to the business of compromise.

King's opening gambit, in a more relaxed atmosphere, was to restate the seating arrangements. Commissioner Parks, looking at the mayor, said, "I don't see why we can't arrange to accept this seating proposal. We can work it within our segregation laws." King and his friends began to smile, but the grins disappeared quickly.

Crenshaw, shaking his head, said, "But, Frank, I don't see how we can do it within the law. If it were legal, I would be the first to go along with it. It isn't legal. The only way it can be done is to change your segregation laws."

Parks retreated. The mayor rolled a pencil back and forth on the desk. Bus attorney Crenshaw had more to say: "If we grant these Negroes these demands," he said, "they will go about boasting of a victory that they won over the white people; and this we will not stand for." The words "this we will not stand for" seemed to imply that the bus company was in charge of the conference. Mayor Gayle did not assert his authority. He did not tell the bus company that the law would be changed by his commission; he sat in silence and did not refute the bus company's statement that "this we will not stand for."

King became angry. He spoke faster, though not louder. "I want it to be put on the record," he said, "that if our proposals are granted, we will make it our primary business to restrain our people from proclaiming any victory." Crenshaw smiled. King then asked Crenshaw directly what the bus company was willing to offer blacks.

The attorney shrugged. "We will certainly be willing to guarantee courtesy," he said. "But we cannot change the seating arrangement because such a change would violate the law. And as far as bus drivers are concerned, we have no intention now or in the foreseeable future of hiring nigras."

The word "nigras" closed the meeting. Everyone left depressed. The blacks felt that there was no ground for amicable dialogue. The whites felt that not only was the bus boycott costing a financially insecure company $7,000 a day, but Christmas sales in the downtown stores were dropping off alarmingly. The bus company owners—National City Lines, Inc., of Chicago—had profitable lines operating in thirty-four other cities, but the Montgomery Bus Line was running like a flat tire.

King reported on the conference to his executive committee and said that his demands had been mild. They certainly had. The executive committee suggested that King send a telegram to the president of National City Lines, state their grievances and demands, and ask him to come to Montgomery at once or to send a representative. Two days later a message arrived from the president stating that he was sending a vice-president to Montgomery. Everyone felt hopeful.

But this optimism, too, was dashed, because a week passed, and no one had heard from the vice-president. On December 15, King received an anonymous phone call stating that a C. K. Totten of National City Lines was in Montgomery. He had arrived two days earlier but had not got in touch with anyone on the black side. Late in the same day, King received a message from the mayor that he was calling a citizens committee to meet with the blacks and bus officials on Saturday, December 17. The executive board met quickly and agreed to make one more retreat in order to find some grounds for agreement with the bus company and the mayor. It was possible that there were no vacancies for drivers on the bus lines, so that condition number three would be softened to a demand that the bus company accept driver applications from blacks, assuming that some might be hired when vacancies occurred.

The meeting opened on a cordial note. The Reverend Henry E. Russell, brother of Senator Richard Russell of Georgia, was present and walked over to where Martin Luther King was standing and smilingly extended his hand. Other whites appeared friendly—almost too much so. At last a trio of men arrived: bus attorney Crenshaw, bus manager Bagley, and C. K. Totten, the vice-president from Chicago. Abernathy and King looked behind them and saw two blacks who were not members of their committee sitting with them. Abernathy made a face as though he had detected a bad odor.

Mayor Gayle presided, and somewhat wearily, he asked Dr. King to explain his side of the dispute. The pastor had uttered the words so often that by now he had cut the speech to the bone. Gayle then asked the bus company to respond. Totten got to his feet. King felt hope rise in his breast because this man, obviously a Northerner, would have a broader point of view, and his word as vice-president of the thirty-five bus lines could veto anything Crenshaw had said.

The shocking surprise was that Totten's rebuttal was exactly the same as that stated by Crenshaw. The difference was not in words, but in accent. There wasn't an original argument coming from his mouth.

When Totten sat down, Mayor Gayle looked from face to face to see if anyone had anything more to say. His calm eyes passed over King's, but there was no recognition and no request for recognition. The other blacks sat in silence. At last, unbidden, Pastor King jumped to his feet, the voice now loud and deep, as though in the pulpit: "Mr. Totten has not been fair in his assertions. He has made a statement that is completely biased. In spite of the fact that he was asked to come to Montgomery by the MIA, he has not done the Negro community the simple courtesy of hearing their grievances. The least that all of us can do in our deliberations is to be honest and fair."

The Negroes said amen. The whites were stunned. The next man to speak was Dr. Frazier, a segregationist from the Methodist Church. He was tall and dignified, the epitome of the statue of a statesman in a public park. Men, all men, he said, were weak and frail and prone to error. The blacks were wrong to boycott the buses, doubly wrong because they were being led by ministers whose proper place was in the pulpit. The work of the cleric was not to bring about confusion by becoming entangled in transitory social problems, but to do what they vowed to do—lead men's souls to God.

He spoke of Christmas, less than two weeks away, and of God's glorious gift of the Babe in the manger. With radiant face he admonished the black ministers to return to their flocks, call off the boycott, and lead their people to "a glorious experience in Christian faith." King was now beyond holding down. He shook off the friendly arms holding his elbows and stood. "We too know the Jesus the minister has just referred to," he said acidly. "We have had an experience with Him, and we firmly believe in the revelation of God in Jesus Christ." He drew a long angry breath. "I can see no conflict between our devotion to Jesus Christ and our present action. In fact, I see a necessary relationship. If one is truly devoted to the religion of Jesus, he will seek to rid the earth of social evils. The Gospel is social, as well as personal. We are only doing in a minor way what Gandhi did in India. Certainly no one referred to him as an unrepentant sinner; he is considered by many a saint.

"We have been talking a great deal this morning about changing customs," King said. "It has been affirmed that any change in present conditions would mean going against the 'cherished customs' of our community. But if the customs are wrong, we have every right in the world to change them. The decision which we must make now is whether we will give our allegiance to outmoded and unjust customs or to the ethical demands of the universe. As Christians we owe our ultimate allegiance to God and His will, rather than to man and his folkways."

Mrs. Jo Ann Robinson sat quietly, listening. King sat down. The mayor said that he would appoint a committee consisting of citizens to meet with the MIA and the bus company and work out a solution and bring it back to him in the form of a resolution for the city commission. He named three men from the MIA; eight "citizens," including the two strange blacks; and the men from the bus company.

The silent Mrs. Robinson got to her feet and said, "Mr. Mayor, you have stacked this committee. If you're going to have one, there must be as many Negroes on it as whites."

Gayle stared at her and said, "All right," with obvious reluctance. He appointed eight blacks to the committee. The Reverend Henry Parker became chairman.

In the first week, the Montgomery bus boycott was nothing more than a surprising and successful method of revenge. The whites were unified; the blacks were not. The whites controlled the government, the economic resources, the courts. The blacks had a brand-new organization called the Montgomery Improvement Association; it had thirty-six members. There had been racial unrest before—as was true of all cities with sizable black populations—but they expired quickly through boredom, through lack of cohesion, or at the end of police clubs.

Coverage in newspapers and on television made a success of the MIA and more especially of Dr. Martin Luther King, Jr. Ironically, neither medium was sympathetic to King's cause, but both disseminated the word. Nothing excites pity like helplessness, and for the next thirteen years, King would use the press and television to show the helplessness of his people as victims of prejudice and starvation, as martyred Christians with their bloodied heads.

It was cold, and the whites hoped it would become colder. A good hard rain would end the bus boycott. Blacks would never walk to work or to school. The buses were bright and dry.

Dr. King sat in his small pine-paneled office in the basement of the Dexter Avenue Church, worrying about the police threat to cancel taxi licenses for carrying five persons from shantytowns to downtown at ten cents apiece. He recalled that there had been a bus boycott in Baton Rouge a few years earlier. He called the Reverend Theodore Jeminsen in the Louisiana capital. The information that came to King's ear was invaluable. Jeminson remembered every step of the fight with the city authorities. The thing to do was to drop the taxicabs, except for those few who could afford the legal minimum fare, call a mass meeting, and draw up a private car pool. There was no law against driving people free; pickup points could be established every three blocks throughout Montgomery.

That night, King and his newfound friend, the Reverend Ralph Abernathy, signed up 150 car owners. Some could work the routes all day. Others could do it a few hours before or after a working day. Almost all the black ministers volunteered the use of their automobiles. The reverends divine also agreed to ask for more volunteers at their church services on Sunday. A transportation committee was organized, and these men and women worked all night to trace routes and cross routes through Montgomery. The system was divided into two parts. Dispatch stations, marked off to pick people up for work, would be operable from 6 A.M. until 10 A.M. Pickup stations, for taking people home from midtown areas, would be open from 3 P.M. until 7 P.M. Thousands of leaflets, with dispatch and pickup stations marked off, were given to the black communities by Monday. Most of the pickup stations were outside black churches, so that the boycotters could keep warm inside while waiting for cars.

The car pool worked so well that the White Citizens Council met and stated ominously that it had been executed with "military precision." It also lifted the spirits of the blacks, who were accustomed to defeat.

Day followed day, and each side expected a fissure to develop in the other side. Bagley, the manager of the line, said that 70 percent of all bus customers, under normal circumstances, were blacks. Of these, 85 percent remained off the buses. If the matter wasn't settled soon, he would have to remove buses from the line and fire some white drivers. Attorney Jack Crenshaw, who had been most intractable in dealing with blacks, began to make announcements about a meeting with them. "I think they ought to get their house cleaned first," he said. "There have been clear violations of civil rights of Negroes who have been kept from using buses because of fear and intimidation." One bus driver said the back of his bus was hit by a .22 rifle shell. Another said that bricks had been thrown at his bus in "Colored Town."

Black workers were told by their bosses that they were being fooled by their leaders, that the whole thing was a money-making scheme for a few ministers; they were told that Martin Luther King was a Georgian who had recently come to Montgomery to start trouble—why, everybody knew that he had just bought a new Cadillac for himself and a station wagon for his wife. Some white citizens visited black pastors and suggested that if there must be a boycott, they—not some alien like King—should lead it. Substantial white businessmen told black pastors: "If King was out of the picture and you took over the leadership, why, the picture would change overnight. We get along. We've been dealing with you for years. What do you need him for?"

Before Christmas Martin Luther King, Jr., offered his resignation to the MIA. The executive committee declined it unanimously. He promised them that he could work as well in the background as up front, but they would not hear of it.

The Montgomery *Advertiser* and Martin Luther King, Jr., had discovered each other. To the newspaper, King was firebrand copy, a new and dangerous type of racial troublemaker. To King, the paper was an outlet for his words, an outlet which spoke louder than all the churches in town. Each one, in superficial camaraderie, decided to use the other. When Dr. King saw a reporter, he stuck out the flat of his palm, shouted, "Hi, man!" and rubbed the skin across the journalist's. King was playing the "down-home colored preacher"; the *Advertiser* was playing the editorial umpire desirous of getting only the facts.

In a pre-Christmas editorial, the *Advertiser* noted that Bagley said that if the boycott did not end soon, he was going to drop 75 percent of his seventy-two city buses. "A negro spokesman, the Rev. M. L. King of the Dexter Avenue Methodist [*sic*] Church, apparently speaks with no little authority. He said 'We are not asking an end to segregation. We don't like the idea of Negroes having to stand when there are vacant seats. We are demanding justice on that point.'

"If the grievance is confined to that," the *Advertiser* stated, "then it should be heard promptly. Any other grievance should be fairly heard. Montgomery witnessed the dramatic event of the boycott with admirable and typical coolness. It is well, for protests of this kind are going to be a common thing in our state and community existence for a long time to come; ours being a time of evolution in old time custom and usage . . ."

The stumbling block to peace lay in dishonesty on both sides. The boycott was costing the bus company close to $2,500 per day. No one could estimate, except by the complaints of downtown department stores, how much it was costing in Christmas shopping. King told the *Advertiser* that his group would be satisfied with equitable seating arrangements. This was not true. The boycott was a stunning and unexpected success which had to lead to further assaults on the whites, assaults which would have less to do with desegregation in schools and more to do with the social acceptance of the black by the white. This was always the long-term goal, and the only way in which it could be achieved would be by chipping away, a bit at a time, at the marblelike resistance of the white community.

Neither side desired a long fight, but when the city notified the black taxi companies that mass riding was illegal, the flames were fanned. Donations from all over began to come in to the MIA. Television, radio, and the newspaper wire services started covering the story on a national basis. With the donations, the Montgomery Improvement Association bought ten station wagons for ten black churches. The commuters inside sang church hymns on their way to and from work.

Mayor Gayle and Commissioner Sellers suddenly joined the White Citizens Council as a lesson to the blacks. The net effect was that the battle lines were drawn honestly. A waterfall of threatening and obscene calls inundated the King household telephone. Soft Southern male voices seemed to end the monologues on one note: "King Coon has forty-eight hours to get his family out of Montgomery, or else. . . ." In the middle of the night, the Reverend Dr. King was awakened by the ringing telephone to hear an angry voice shout: "Listen, nigger. We've taken all we want from you. Before next week you'll be sorry you ever came to Montgomery."

It was then that Martin Luther King, Jr., began to think of death as something waiting in the wings. An understanding of death must have been with him—the irrevocable eternity of it—when he was a little boy and jumped from the window at the top of the stairs. But it is also possible that his comprehension then was of an elective sorrow—one that could be chosen. In childish joy, he could banish it from his presence; in anger or guilt he could summon it. Now it was with him when he did not seek it. He listened to a voice on the phone threaten him, and he went into the kitchen and made himself a cup of coffee.

Coretta King stood watching him, a man meditating over a wisp of steam, the great head down. She heard him say aloud, "Lord, I am taking a stand for what I believe is right. The people are looking to me for leadership, and if I stand before them without strength or courage, they will falter. I am at the end of my powers. I have nothing left. I've come to the point where I can't face it alone." He looked up and saw her standing in the doorway. He told her that he had just experienced the presence of the divine and a voice saying, "Stand up for righteousness; stand up for the truth; God will be at your side forever."

For the first time in his life, he was a public figure—admired and despised. People had a sharp ambivalence toward him, and he had an ambivalence toward himself. At public affairs, he was the outraged angel of justice; at home or among the men who supported him, he could be crushed easily and he was beset by the feeling that the wild horses of events were pulling him in opposite directions.

One evening he and Bob Williams, a Morehouse classmate, drove downtown to pick up Mrs. Lilie Thomas (treasurer and office manager of the Southern Christian Leadership Conference; later to be Mrs. Lilie Hunter). It was one of those nights when the rain is so light that it swirls in waving sheets of mist. Dr. King drove directly to the car pool. He picked Mrs. Thomas up and stopped for three more blacks awaiting a ride. On the way out a policeman stopped the car and asked to see Dr. King's license.

Another policeman peered through the wetness and said, "It's that damn King fellow." The minister showed his license, said nothing, and was permitted to go on. A motorcycle cop followed.

In the rearview mirror, King could see the headlight. "We're being followed," he said to the other passengers, "so we'd better be careful." He drove slowly, close to the curbside.

At the first stop, the cop pulled alongside and said, "Get out, King. You're under arrest for doing thirty in a twenty-five-mile zone." It might have been nearer the truth if King had been arrested for doing fifteen in a twenty-five-mile zone and thereby obstructing traffic.

Meekly, he got out. The cop frisked him and called headquarters. A patrol car arrived and took him to the Montgomery City Jail. At the desk where he was booked, King's arm was held up between his shoulder blades so that his head went down to the blotter to alleviate the pain. He answered the questions, signed a receipt for his watch and other valuables, and was thrown into a cell full of blacks. He looked around. They were all part of the boycott. Several of them, including a schoolteacher, begged him to get them out. He was Dr. King—the leader, the voice of power and righteousness, the man who spoke up to Whitey.

"Fellows," he said meekly, brushing the dust from his brown fedora hat, "before I can get you out, I've got to get out myself."

Williams and the others who had been in his car knew that there were five church protest meetings that night, and they went to all of them. The word spread through the city that King was in jail. Ralph Abernathy left the meeting with cash in his pocket and did the practical thing. He went to the jail and asked to bail King out. The officer in charge glanced at a clock and said, "You'll have to wait until tomorrow."

Abernathy was difficult to derail. "I am the pastor of the First Baptist Church of Montgomery," he said loftily. "Do you mean to tell me I can't sign bond?"

"No," the officer said absentmindedly, "you sure can't."

"Can I see Dr. King?"

The officer shook his head no. Abernathy went back to the churches and told the pastors, preachers, and deacons to assemble at once at the city jail. He was a black Paul Revere in a Pontiac. Again, the blacks responded to the call. Their presence attracted others. The steps and the sidewalks, far out into the street, were full of silent faces.

The warden became nervous. This situation ran contrary to all experience. Heretofore, for a hundred years, it had been a black in jail and white silent men outside, waiting to overwhelm the jailers and administer justice at once. Now it was a black inside and blacks outside. He phoned his superiors. Dr. King was hustled out of the cell, fingerprinted and mugged, and told, "All right, King. You're being released on your own recognizance. Now get out." He emerged on the steps, adjusting the snap brim of the hat and grinning. He heard the cheers. Later he told his wife that he had been frightened. He had not known where the jail was, and he didn't know what the white men might do to him inside. He had seen death unwanted, unbidden.

The house on Jackson Street was several blocks from the church, a two-story frame dwelling in an orderly row, each with its adolescent tree between the sidewalk and the curb. The porch had a red cement floor and white picket fencing. At night, a streetlight cast long shadows of the picket fence, making bars on the cement floor. These were the lonely nights. It was chilly enough, even inside, to wear a robe. Coretta King sat in the living room chatting with her friend Mary Lucy Williams. Dr. King was out, as usual, to meetings.

It seemed strange that in such a short time, no meeting was complete without him. He was here, there, everywhere. And yet he required thirteen hours to draw up one Sunday sermon for his parishioners. Often, he hurried in from the church vestry, ran upstairs, shaved quickly with that ugly-smelling powder, hurried down, gobbled food at the kitchen table, held his infant Yoki to his chest for a moment, kissed his women good-bye, and was gone.

It was like that on Monday, January 30, 1956. The time was early— 9:30 P.M.—but Coretta already had a robe on. Once or twice he had mentioned the possibility of an attack on the house with her and the baby alone in it—but Coretta was unimpressed. "I've seen things like that out in the country," she said, "but not in the city. Besides, who could pick this house out of all the other ones? I'll be all right."

The women were sitting in the front room when they heard a thump outside the windows, as though someone had tossed a rock on the porch. Mary Lucy Williams jumped to her feet in fright. Coretta King, calm but also aware of the possibilities, said, "It sounds as though someone hit the front of the house. Let's move to the back." They went straight through the guest bedroom toward the kitchen. They didn't reach it. They heard a clap of thunder and felt the floor shudder. Then there was the musical sound of breaking glass. A smoky sulfuric smell rushed through the rooms on the cold night wind.

Mrs. Williams grabbed Mrs. King and began to scream. Coretta King was frightened—one of the few times in her life she would admit to fright—but her mind was on Yoki, lying in a bassinet two rooms away. She broke away from her friend and hurried through the plain kitchen and then to the left to her bedroom. The baby was sleeping.

Mrs. King ran to the phone and looked at her shaking hands. Whom would she call? The police? What would they do? The doorbell rang. Mrs. King's panic increased. She was close to losing control. Who would ring the front doorbell? The bomber? Would he come in to finish the job? "Who is it?" she shouted.

She heard a "down-home" voice say, "Anybody hurt?"

The phone was replaced on its cradle. She went to the front door thinking they could have come in through the broken windows.

The porch was full of neighbors and vapors of bluish smoke. The faces Coretta King saw were as frightened as hers. The sound of the bomb explosion had torn through the entire middle-class black section around Jackson Street. People came running from all directions. She clutched the collar of the robe around her neck and said, "It's all right. Really, it's all right." But it wasn't. The living-room rug was covered with broken glass. The porch railing had been split, and the shadows of the wooden pickets were irregular on the red cement. A few inches to the right of the front door there was a small hollow, no bigger than a baby's head, in the cement.

People rushed all over the house trying to help. Outside, the street was jammed. Mrs. King phoned the First Baptist Church and asked Irene Grant to please tell the Reverend Mr. Abernathy or Dr. King that the King home had been bombed and to come as quickly as possible. She hung up, forgetting to explain that she and the baby were all right.

The news was like a swift-burning fuse. It ignited blacks all over the city, it coiled down to police headquarters, to the homes of the mayor and commissioners, to the office of Governor James Folsom. This was a bad situation. White opinion was that an inflamed red-neck had set up a stick of farm dynamite and a cap and had determined to use the time-honored method of putting the "head nigger" in his proper place.

Mrs. King didn't know many of the people wandering through her home, trying to be helpful, some getting angry and out of control. She phoned Abernathy's church a second time, to explain that she and the baby were uninjured. Dr. King was in the pulpit, in the middle of one of his sermons. Ralph Abernathy sat next to him.

King felt uneasy. People were tiptoeing from the back of the church to whisper to others in the pews. Twice he had noticed women whispering to Abernathy. Finally, in the middle of the peroration, King could stand it no longer. "Ralph," he asked, "what happened?" Ralph shrugged. Dr. King said, "Ralph, you must tell me. Something has happened, and I know it."

"Your house has been bombed, Doctor."

"Are Coretta and the baby all right?"

Ralph mumbled, "We're checking. We think so." It was poor news poorly delivered. But King did not panic. He said later that the religious experience he had had a few nights before sustained him.

He turned to the congregation. It was pointless to continue the talk. "Someone has tried to bomb my house," he said, and he could hear the collective intake of breath out front. "Everything is going to be all right. I urge you all to go straight home. Straight home—hear me? Don't get panicky and lose your heads. Let us keep moving with the faith that what we are doing is right and with even greater faith that God is with us in the struggle."

He hurried from the pulpit, pulling vestments over his head as he departed, and ran out to get into his car. By the time he reached Jackson Street the mob was enormous and police cars were parked askew in the area. Mayor Gayle and Commissioner Sellers were on King's front porch when he managed to force his way through. The house was full of people. He didn't want to talk to mayors or neighbors. In the kitchen, he saw his wife holding the baby. As always, she wore the subtle smile. He embraced them, losing his calm, and shouted, "Thank God you and the baby are all right." He asked her why she wasn't dressed. For a moment, this broke the tension, as though a woman should be properly dressed for a bombing.

The crowd out front began to sing "My Country, 'Tis of Thee," but the voices were roaring with rage. It was not their country, and it was anything but a sweet land of liberty. Some youngsters in the front ranks held broken bottles by the necks. White reporters on the porch told the mayor and police commissioner that they were afraid to leave. Sellers saw King come out, and he grabbed the pastor's hand and expressed regret that "this unfortunate incident" could have taken place in a great city like Montgomery. King said nothing. Mayor Gayle grabbed King's hand. The singers in the street sang louder. C. T. Smiley, principal of Booker T. Washington High School, was on the porch. He didn't think that a handshake could cover the so-called incident. "Regrets are all very well," he said to the mayor, "but you are responsible. It is you who created the climate for this."

The crowd began to shout insults at the police. The police did not respond, but their hands were on the butts of their guns. They were not looking for trouble, but if trouble started, they wanted to save themselves. No one could control a crowd this size. All it needed to erupt was a little more time to dwell upon the outrage. Just a little more time.

Martin Luther King stepped to the front of his porch. He held up both arms. The people stopped shouting and swaying. A few policemen inside the hedge were on one knee, looking up hopefully. In a loud slow voice, King said, "My wife and my baby are all right. I want you people to go home and put down your weapons. We cannot solve problems with violence." There was a pause. "We must meet violence with nonviolence." Before they could roar disapproval, he shouted, "Remember the words of Jesus: 'He who lives by the sword shall perish by the sword!' We must love our white brothers, no matter what they do to us. We must *make* them know that we love them. Jesus still cries out across the centuries: 'Love your enemies.' This is what we must live by. We must learn to meet hate with love."

Suddenly, there was a true silence. No one spoke. No one muttered. The shifting feet were still. Then King said: "Remember, if I am stopped, this movement will not stop because God is with this movement. Go home with this glowing faith and this radiant assurance." That was all. He looked down in the reflected light from the pole across the street, and he saw tears. They were stopped. Some shouted "amen!" others yelled: "God bless you, Reverend." They began to disperse.

Sympathy, as much as there was of it in Montgomery, was now with the blacks. They were truly the sore and afflicted, the subhumans who approached their masters on their knees. They offered love and begged for equality, and these were dangerous things. White sympathy was intellectual, not practical. There were places in Montgomery where it was agreed that the black should be able to lead a better life, to clothe, feed, and educate his young, but it was also agreed that it could not be permitted within the corporate limits of Montgomery.

Practical sympathy went to Mayor Gayle and his police commissioner, Sellers. For them, there was no correct course of action, certainly not one that would lead to peace. They were white, and they were responsible to their white brethren in the power structure. Blacks did not put them in office and couldn't keep them in power. They held the municipal reins tightly. If they loosened them, even slightly, even to guarantee such a simple thing as more courtesy from bus drivers to black passengers, the pale dome of the State Capitol would crumble, and the stars and bars of the Confederate flag, which hung *above* the American flag on Capitol Hill, would come down in tatters.

Nor could Gayle and Sellers treat the black ministers with the spitting contempt of other years. No one was sure what the Montgomery Improvement Association was, but it was a force. It had proved it was a force. No white man knew how many members it had, but the police knew that the black's ancient sanctuary, his church, was being used all over town for Monday and Thursday night meetings and that the blacks were united behind an "outsider." He was hitting the city in its pocketbook. The pain was acute; downtown business was demanding action but would not support the mayor if he made concessions to the blacks.

At the bombing of Dr. King's home, the mayor was frightened. So were his commissioner and his police. For a short time in darkness, they were at the mercy of the mob. One thrown bottle, one thrown punch, and Montgomery would have been in the throes of a race riot. City authority could not control the people; only Dr. King could do it. He had held his arms up, and there had been quiet. He had told them to go home peacefully, and they had gone home. There were five black sections in the city; King controlled them all. Ironically, he hardly knew his way from one section to another without a map or a guide.

Dr. King relished a short word like "cope." He could "cope" with this situation or that; someone else could be delegated to "cope" with uninteresting problems; the one thing the young pastor could not "cope" with were the phone calls from Atlanta. His father called two or three times a day and, whether by accident or by design, seldom to Martin's home. The phone was picked up in the study at the Dexter Avenue Church, and Lilie Thomas would hear an operator say, "Long distance—Atlanta, Georgia, for Dr. Martin Luther King, Jr."

The old man was perpetually worried. He had lived with "race" all his life, and he was not a weakling; he knew when he could stand up to the white man and defy him, and he knew when to walk away from sudden death. From what he read in the newspapers and from what he heard in the Ministerial Association, his favorite son, the living breathing phenomenon that God had placed in his hands, was so busy prodding the white man publicly that it had become a scandal in the South. Rumors had reached him that Coretta King, that pretty young singer, that stubborn independent mind, hardly ever saw her husband and had turned her affections toward her baby.

"You leave there!" his father commanded on the phone. "You come back here where you have a church. Listen to me, son. Just come on back home." There was parental demand, but there was forlorn entreaty, too.

"Daddy," Dr. King would say, "Daddy . . . just a minute, Daddy . . . Everything is going to be all right. *He's* going to take care of me. I don't like it when you worry and carry on so."

The father was unconvinced. He knew the white man better than his son did, and he had known him longer. "Everything is not all right from what I hear," he would say. "Your place is here." Sometimes he would fall back in abject retreat. "You know your mother's heart condition,

Martin. You know all this. I raised you to be the finest Baptist minister. You stay in the pulpit where you belong."

In the early part of 1956, young Dr. King was running ahead of his family. He was leaving them—Coretta, Yoki, his mother and father, and A.D.—behind. His affection had not lessened; his secret goals were bigger than preaching. Even the young editors at the Montgomery *Advertiser,* who saw him as good copy and a "regular guy" among black pastors, watched in fascination as the metamorphosis toward grandeur and leadership showed itself in the boldness of his gaze and the daring of his utterances. It is doubtful that King thought of himself as leaving his family behind, but as he worked longer and longer hours, each sixty minutes grew shorter. The doctor's work became his prime mission; his mission became his work. All other matters, including the leadership of his church, had to wait in line for spare moments. He felt guiltiest of all about his wife; he told his friends that she had given up a concert career for him, and now she had to spend long nights alone with the baby.

By the spring of 1956 Martin Luther King, Jr., began to believe that his leadership—so faint of heart at the start that he had thought of the boycott as lasting only one day—might be a momentous meeting of the man and the hour. There is no evidence that he accepted it as such, but King had an ego built like himself, short, broad, and strong. His heart's desire was to *lead*—not to be coequal with his father, but to be monarch of a good cause. For a black man of intellect, nothing could be more ennobling than to combine racism and Christianity, leading the snapping banners toward equality—thus ridding the black man of his inferiority while, at the same time, erasing guilt from the heart of the white man.

King read the newspapers and news magazines avidly, hunting for signs of America's awakening to a bloodless civil war. They were there. Racial pleas were piling up in the U.S. Court of Appeals and Supreme Court. Judicial inequity was the biggest gun the black man carried. In effect, the courts were now belatedly working for him.

These were signs of the times to King. He would not move into the desegregation of schools, because that battle was already led by the National Association for the Advancement of Colored People. He was a member, but Roy Wilkins and his battery of attorneys had it patented. There was no personal *Zeitgeist* there. His only worry was that the bus fight in Montgomery might die of apathy.

The reverend was properly pleased, on February 21, 1956, when the Montgomery County grand jury indicted him and eighty-nine other leaders of the boycott on the grounds that they were in violation of a

1921 statute prohibiting anyone from hindering a lawful business without "just or legal excuse." The trial lasted four days, and King's adherents showed up in court wearing cloth crosses on jackets and dresses inscribed FATHER, FORGIVE THEM.

On March 22 the jury convicted all of them, and once bail was posted prior to appeal, Dr. and Mrs. King left the courtroom to stand atop the courthouse steps, listening to the thunder of cheers from the blacks below. The race was again reunited; the danger of apathy was past; someone shouted, "Long live the King!" and others yelled, "No more buses!" The legal moves and countermoves were now on a judicial chessboard.

Dr. King decided that his people should raise their sights, fight for more. Bus desegregation, after all, was but a fragment of total desegregation. Why not fight for true brotherhood, a state in which whites and blacks would be equal politically, economically, and socially? Why not? The goal seemed far away, but it would never draw closer by fighting for a seat on a bus. The battle had already been joined in the courts; why not on the streets, in the stores where blacks could not drink from white fountains or use white rest rooms; or the restaurants where they could not buy a sandwich? Why not fight because blacks could not live in a house on white streets; or earn equal pay for equal skill or sit downstairs in a movie house or buy a ticket to a white dance? Why not fight for everything?

Four black women petitioned the federal court in Alabama to ban bus segregation. Within ninety days, the court stated that segregation in buses was illegal. The City of Montgomery appealed the decision and, in a desperate effort to crush the Montgomery Improvement Association, went into state courts to enjoin the Montgomery Improvement Association from operating an unlicensed transit system (the car pool). In a separate case, city attorneys asked state courts to freeze the assets of the MIA. By late spring the MIA had more than $100,000 in donations deposited in out-of-state banks. By the end of 1956 Dr. King was to have spent $225,000 and still have cash assets.

In retrospect, the White Establishment was stunned to find that it could not control blacks through fear. It was an old farm remedy which had worked before. Mayor Gayle even announced a false settlement to break up the opposition. One night King received a call from Minneapolis. The man on the phone was Carl T. Rowan, later in the USIA but at the time a black writer for the Minneapolis *Tribune*. He asked Dr. King to tell him the terms of the settlement of the bus boycott.

King's reaction was: "What settlement?" Rowan said news was coming over the wires of the Associated Press from Montgomery that three black ministers, representing the MIA, had come to terms with Mayor Gayle and that the boycott was over. The agreement, as announced by City Hall, was that the drivers would display uniform courtesy to all bus riders; ten seats in back would be reserved for blacks and ten seats in front for whites; extra buses would be assigned to black routes during so-called rush hours; the hiring of black bus drivers would have to be negotiated with the bus line, rather than the city. The Montgomery *Advertiser* was also preparing to publish the story. It was close enough to the scene to have made a verifying call to Martin Luther King or Ralph Abernathy, but the local paper did not.

King got off the phone and began to contact his committees and asked them to drive from black street to black street, notifying their people that any story of a settlement was false and the bus boycott was to be continued. King and a few other ministers went from tavern to pool hall asking for a moment of quiet to explain the danger. King then got in touch with the three ministers named in the story. They denied that they had anything to do with it and insisted that they were in favor of the boycott.

As the success of the boycott continued, Dr. King became more and more obsessed with the idea that the white police would arrest him and take him to a place where a "mob" would lynch him. He applied at police headquarters for a permit to carry a pistol. He was asked why he wanted it. "For self-defense," he said.

"Against whom?" he was asked.

He said he could name no specific person, but it was common knowledge that his home had been bombed, that he received threatening phone calls every day. The application was denied; but news of it spread all over Montgomery, and it was pointed out that the disciple of Mohandas Gandhi, the apostle of peace and brotherly love in the South, was trying to buy a revolver and shoot someone.

King was remorseful. Blacks who believed in nonviolence and Gandhism were ashamed of his act. Black leaders in Washington fell silent when asked what they thought of Martin Luther King. A. Philip Randolph, the tall, stern white-haired head of the Pullman porters, a man who had directed a national goodwill direct action campaign against white supremacy in 1942, and who had seen nonviolence transmuted into fire, riots, shooting and death, was silent. James Farmer, who had organized the Congress of Racial Equality in 1942, a man who believed that "relentless noncooperation" would redound to the welfare of the black, watched Montgomery in silence. Roy Wilkins of the NAACP had nothing to say. Thurgood Marshall, who led many of the court battles, was unavailable for comment. Adam Clayton Powell, black New York Congressman, was busy with other matters.

The anonymous bombings continued. The only real damage was to the feelings of the white community, which did not want to associate itself with archaic savagery, and, above all, was opposed to anything which would assist the black to play the martyr. The Reverend Ralph Abernathy's home was bombed; so was his First Baptist Church on the edge of Oakwood Cemetery. The Bell Street Baptist Church was bombed; the Mount Olive Baptist Church, the Hutchinson Street Baptist Church, the Reverend Mr. Graetz's home (he was the white minister of a black church). In most of the bombings, single sticks of dynamite detonated with a roar on front lawns or sidewalks. They were the calling cards of the lower strata of white society, a device designed to generate fear as the Ku Klux Klan once did.

None of these acts drew the public reaction of the King bombing; in each case, crowds of blacks assembled at the site of the explosion and left for home when the police so ordered. The leader of the MIA told a friend that he had had a "weapon" in his house but that, after discussing it with his wife, "we got rid of it." King had floodlights mounted inside the property line around his house. When his followers suggested he have a bodyguard, he chose his Morehouse College classmate Bob Williams. Mr. Williams taught music at Alabama State College, about three streets from the King home, but soon most of his days and nights were taken up driving Martin Luther King, Jr., to and from his appointments and also taking Coretta and Yoki on drives to Marion, Alabama, where she grew up.

King was never able to convince his family—or himself—that his life was not in daily danger. He knew it. They knew it. They talked it up; he talked it down. In the course of the boycott, white Montgomery reached for a "big gun" and drew Senator James O. Eastland of Mississippi as a speaker. Twelve thousand whites cheered under the waving flag of the Confederacy, and committee members solicited membership in the White Citizens Council, which now had 250,000 members throughout the South. As Eastland spoke, teen-age whites distributed leaflets to the crowd, leaflets which appealed to the lowest and most vulgar instincts:

> When in the course of human events it becomes necessary to abolish the Negro race, proper methods should be used. Among these are guns, bows and arrows, sling shots and knives. We hold these truths to be self-evident,

that all whites are created equal with certain rights, among these are life, liberty and the pursuit of dead niggers.

In every stage of the bus boycott, we have been oppressed and degraded because of black, slimy, juicy unbearably stinking niggers. Their conduct should not be dwelt upon because behind them they have an ancestral background of Pygmies, Head Hunters and snot suckers. My friends, it is time we wised up to these black devils. I tell you they are a group of two-legged agitators who persist in walking up and down our streets protruding their black lips. If we don't stop helping these African flesh eaters, we will soon wake up and find Reverend King in the white house.

LET'S GET ON THE BALL WHITE CITIZENS.

The weather became warm. The pale, unblinking stare of the sun was matched by unblinking eyes on sidewalks. Blacks and whites were out of temper. The bus boycott had become an endurance race, and neither side felt that it could suffer the strain much longer. People who were part of it—bus drivers and supervisors, city officials, black riders, car pool drivers, officials of the Montgomery Improvement Association—all were fatigued. Silently, men of many skin tones gave the whole battle one more week to be settled, then one more week, and one more. Martin Luther King, Jr., began to fall into silent moods. How much longer could his people hold out? They had been downtrodden before the battle began; now many walked to work or were out of work. The spirit in the hierarchy was dying.

How much longer? All of it was beyond the sincere understanding of the white people. Boycotting buses was a presumption on the part of the blacks. It was like a little boy sassing his daddy. They had no right to be unhappy, no right in the world to cause civic unrest. It was unthinkable that they had continued this struggle for so long. Deep in its heart, white Montgomery was certain it had always been good to its "niggers." Every fourth man boasted that he had been practically brought up by his black Mammy. Some had been wet-nursed by black women. Every "nigger" who understood his place and kept it was well treated. The police and the courts practically forgave him his Saturday night transgressions of getting drunk and knifing a man over a woman—everybody knew that "niggers" had no morals. The law looked away as long as what he did was done to his own in his own neighborhood. It was all right for a "colored girl" to wash white dishes with her black hands, but it would be out of place for her to eat from them with knife and fork.

How much longer? The disruption couldn't go on forever. It should have been stopped by the police long ago. They had always been able to stop anything that black rowdies started. The trouble with the "coon," they said, was that he was too stupid to know when he was licked. He could no more win this boycott that he could impeach Governor Jim Folsom and elect a black man. The propertied whites could not forgive the "white trash" for setting off sticks of dynamite which didn't do anything but make a big noise and get a lot of black folks out of bed. The "white trash" could not forgive their city administration for allowing all this folderol from one court to another with writs and injunctions which nobody understood. The city administration could not forgive itself for walking head first into a legal wall because some "colored" seamstress wouldn't move out of a bus seat because her feet hurt. Now all the black feet hurt from walking, and they were damned well going to continue to hurt until they came to their senses and got back on those buses.

For Dr. King, there were a few bright moments. Bayard Rustin came to Montgomery. He wanted to help the MIA. Coretta King rejoiced. She had heard Bayard Rustin speak in Marion and Antioch. He was a brilliant man, an executive of FOR (Fellowship of Reconciliation). Rustin was a Quaker with a real gift for public speaking. He was a mover. His organizing genius had launched the Congress of Racial Equality (CORE) as an adjunct of FOR. And with him came a white Texas minister, Glenn E. Smiley, a Methodist. He, too, had credentials and had served as field secretary of FOR. This was fresh blood, fresh ideas, sophistication.

Dr. King appointed Rustin as his executive secretary. Smiley became the pipeline between FOR and MIA and gave lectures and wrote brochures on nonviolence. He also arranged for FOR to make a film of the Montgomery boycott called *Walk to Freedom*. Suddenly, the Monday and Thursday church meetings became more lively and less repetitious. A veneer of élan suffused the dark faces of the executive committee, ministers all.

Invitations for Dr. King began to come in from black colleges and white service clubs. The mood began to rise again; a smile dimpled the good-looking face; he was wanted far beyond the borders of Montgomery. The press, the wire services, and television cameras kept him in the public eye and a degree of renown grew from what King regarded as his personal Gethsemane. He made speeches, accepted the sums from collections and donations, paid car pool drivers $25 a week, watched the mail pile up before volunteer girls writing notes of thanks.

Bayard Rustin urged King to enlarge the organization, the paid organization. Ten competent secretaries were hired. An office was found where letters and donations could be sorted, where responses could be typed promptly and properly. The Reverend R. J. Glasco was appointed executive assistant to Dr. King. Rufus Lewis, who owned a place called the Citizens Club, offered it to the transportation committee and threw in a banquet room free. Ralph Abernathy's First Baptist Church donated all the room it could spare for additional workers. No longer did the hundreds of small problems come to King's phone or desk; only the larger ones filtered slowly upward from a broad base. The Bricklayers' Union (black) built its own edifice and offered any or all of it to the MIA.

Operating expenses reached $5,000 a month. Deposits were going to a black bank in Atlanta. Cars in the pool were insured by a black insurance company in Atlanta. Roy Wilkins of the NAACP sent out a letter requesting all chapters throughout the nation to support the MIA with money. The United Auto Workers sent a check from Detroit for $35,000. King was humbled by a note from an unknown man in Switzerland: "Since I have no possibility to help you in an efficacious manner (this is such a bad feeling, believe me) and I burningly would like to do just something. I send you these 500 dollars . . . you would make me a very great pleasure if you accepted, because what else could I do?"

As a matter of routine procedure, the Police Department of Montgomery dispatched inquiries on all new faces in the MIA. They had been dismayed, months earlier, when the Atlanta chief of police had responded to their questions about Martin Luther King, Jr., by stating that he had no police record. They had queried other police departments, some with results favorable to their side, others not. The Montgomery Police Department announced, with gruff glee, that it had received a notice from the Police Department of Pasadena, California, that Bayard Rustin had been arrested in a parked car there on a charge of sodomy. The police sheet stated that there were three men in the car at the time. Suspects two and three were identified only by numbers and swore that they were passive participants to Rustin's aggression. The date was listed as "Police Report #66350, 1/21/53."

Dr. King paid little attention to the charge. This attitude of his would prevail over the years because: (1) there was no proof that the charge was true—an arrest sheet by itself has no conscience; (2) there would be a sporadic stream of charges, sexual in character, against many of his closest advisers in the years ahead: (3) he had a personal, well-concealed liberal attitude toward extracurricular sex; (4) there were ugly rumors about his own peccadilloes in both the black and white communities which might, if brought into public light, cause a scandal.

His enemies had more materialistic matters on which to dwell. Money was draining out of Montgomery. One of the influential white clubs, the Men of Montgomery, favored reaching a compromise settlement with the blacks, and were opposed by Mayor Gayle and the White Citizens Council. This led to a schism in white ranks, with the businessmen claiming that they had lost close to $1,000,000 in retail trade in the first three months of the boycott; the bus line asserted that it had lost $225,000 and could not pay the usual $20,000 franchise tax to the city. Slowly, inexorably, the white will was being crushed by the black.

The blacks who broke the boycott were not rewarded by the whites. Martha Walker was the wife of a blind black man whose leg was caught in a bus door. The driver put the vehicle in gear and dragged Mr. Walker, screaming in pain, before the victim was "discovered." Another black passenger who broke the boycott was threatened by the driver because he did not have the exact change. Mrs. Della Perkins boarded a bus and was called "an ugly ape." Mrs. Stella Brooks was in mourning because after her husband had deposited the change on a bus, the driver said the vehicle was too crowded, and he would have to get off. Brooks said he would get off if the driver would please give him his dime back. The driver said he would call a policeman and did. The policeman who responded heard the argument about the dime, lost his head in a frenzy, and shot Brooks dead.

Judge Eugene Carter found King and the eighty-nine co-defendants guilty of violating a state ordinance against conspiring against a private business. It was only a misdemeanor, but Southern states are notorious for permitting elastic jail sentences and fines in nonfelonious matters. The judge fined King $500 or 386 days at hard labor in the county road gang, and pointed out that he was passing a "minimal sentence because of the defendant's preachments of nonviolence." Dr. King's attorneys would appeal the decision again.

"No one can understand the feeling that comes to a Southern Negro on entering a federal court," King wrote, "unless he sees with his own eyes and feels with his own soul the tragic sabotage of justice in the city and state courts of the South." King and the lawyers moved into federal court to ask that bus segregation be declared unconstitutional and a violation of the Fourteenth Amendment of the Constitution of the United States. This time King was not the prime mover. The suit was filed by Robert Carter of the NAACP, using the MIA and King as plaintiffs. Fred Gray and others of the local boycott assisted in the suit, but the show was staged by the National Association for the Advancement of Colored People, which decided that this was a form of *Zeitgeist* for removing the boycott from a small city and, no matter what the decision, bringing it up to Washington and the Supreme Court for national adjudication.

Carter made a smart move. He knew that the last time the Supreme Court had ruled on the matter of national segregation was in 1896, when the Plessy doctrine was handed down. In that case, the High Court stated that separate but equal facilities for the races was valid. Mr. Carter reasoned that, in essence, the court decision of May, 1954, which ruled that separate but equal facilities in schools violated the spirit of the Fourteenth Amendment, set the stage for asking the court for a similar ruling on segregated facilities in general.

The Establishment in Montgomery underestimated the gravity of the situation by arguing, on a superficial plane, that if bus segregation were invalidated, Montgomery would become a bloody battleground between the races. Three federal judges sat listening to the monotony of the plea until Judge Richard Taylor Rives, in exasperation said, "Is it fair to command one man to surrender his constitutional rights—if they are his constitutional rights—in order to prevent another man from committing a crime?"

Listening, Dr. King nudged Ralph Abernathy and whispered, "It looks as though we might get a favorable verdict." He was right. Within a month, a favorable two-to-one decision came down, stating that the bus segregation laws of Alabama were unconstitutional. This was more than a triumph; it was a transfusion to struggling blacks everywhere. The City of Montgomery announced that it would file an appeal as quickly as possible and bring the matter before the Supreme Court. So the boycott went on.

White Montgomery was stunned. It stood not only to lose its own traditional right to keep the black man in his place in the back of the bus, but to lose it for all other Southern states. If the Supreme Court sustained the verdict, segregation was doomed in restaurants, on trains, buses and trolleys, in motion-picture houses, all public accommodations everywhere. The entire structure of racism was in peril. Rosa Parks' aching feet had walked a long, long way. King and his executive committee accepted the applause and took the bows, but the NAACP went quietly about the work of filing briefs for the higher court.

The benefits to the MIA were rich and tangible. The decision, not yet final, was explained to ignorant blacks who had no comprehension of law. The car pools kept in motion. Buses rolled up the hill from the square almost empty. There was no race riot. Martin Luther King, Jr., received an invitation to preach at the Cathedral of St. John the Divine in New York and delivered a sermon on May 17. A freedom rally was held in Madison Square Garden, New York, and among those in attendance to render a thunderous accolade to the MIA were A. Philip Randolph, Congressman Adam Clayton Powell, Mrs. Eleanor Roosevelt, Sammy Davis, Jr., and Tallulah Bankhead. When Rosa Parks was introduced, the blacks and whites at the Garden rally gave her a standing ovation. They did as much for E. D. Nixon, the Pullman porter who might have been the leader of the boycott fight except that he had had to work on a train leaving Montgomery on the morning the boycott started.

The Kings and the Abernathys drove to the West Coast for a vacation. There they enjoyed the fruits of a well-earned rest after a long period of tension.

It is an axiom that a lion cannot go hunting without leaving his lair unprotected. In Montgomery, there was trouble, black among blacks. On June 11, the Reverend U. J. Fields, who had been a member of the executive committee of the Montgomery Improvement Association, was shocked and surprised when he was not reelected to the board. The young man with the goatee, pastor of the Bell Street Baptist Church, said he was resigning immediately as recording secretary because the executive committee was "misusing money sent from all over the nation" and was using it "for their own purposes." The public charge was a morale boost for the white structure, which sensed the first split in the ranks of the MIA. Bitterly, Fields said that the leaders had assumed airs of "bigness" and were "egotistical and interested in perpetuating themselves."

A few minutes after the statement was in the hands of press and radio, the Reverend R. J. Glasco of the MIA phoned the news to Dr. King in California. The vacation was over. Dr. King persuaded Abernathy to remain in California for a few days with the women; he flew home at once. In Montgomery, he found that the Reverend Mr. Fields had little or no support and some were calling him a "Black Judas." His Baptist congregation met and voted him out as pastor, then, in remorse, voted him back in. On June 18, Fields phoned King. "I heard you were back in town," he said, "and I'd like to see you." He was invited to the pine-paneled study at the Dexter Avenue Church.

"I want you to know," he said, "that I was not referring to you in my accusations. I have always had the greatest respect for your integrity, and I still do. But there are some members of the MIA board that I don't care for at all. We never could get along."

King was a sharp debater. "You mean that your statements about the egotism of the leaders grew out of a personal conflict between you and one or two men on the board?"

"Yes," Fields said, "I guess that's true."

King took charge of the conversation. He had his man backing down, and he had no intention of relenting. He asked about the misappropriation of funds.

Fields' head drooped. "I don't know a single case of misappropriation," he said. "All those things I made up in a moment of anger. I felt that I had been mistreated by the board. This was my way of retaliating."

He was asked if he would make the same statements at a mass meeting that night. Fields didn't want to, but the Christian creed began to well up inside, and with some nervousness, he agreed that this was something he should do. A meeting was scheduled to take place at the Beulah Baptist Church at 7 P.M. The word was passed that the defector would speak. Some people were sitting in pews at 3 P.M. At 5 the church was filled. The faces were angry. In the June heat, sweat was a cheap commodity by 7 P.M. when the Reverend Dr. King walked out with the Reverend Mr. Fields and sat down in front of the altar.

Gauging the mood of the congregation, King decided to launch into his talk at once. As he saw it, he had two jobs to do: The first was to convince the people that there was no misappropriation of funds; the second was to listen respectfully to the Reverend Mr. Fields and to forgive him.

"I guess that I know as much about the MIA as anyone in Montgomery," he said, "and I can truthfully say that I do not know of a single instance of misappropriation of funds. The finance committee of our association is composed of honest men and women—persons whose integrity has been established over the year and whose character is above reproach." The people nodded, murmuring, "Amen. Amen." "I have implicit faith in the finance committee and the ministers who have spoken at fund-raising meetings all over the country."

He remembered that he also had to attack that accusation of "bigness." It might be construed as aiming at him. "Some of our leaders"— his voice moved up in volume and lower in key—"have received national and international publicity, but only the shallow-minded are excited over publicity. Publicity is evanescent; it is here today and gone tomorrow. . . . Whoever falls in love with publicity is not fit to have it and will end up in misery." He shrugged as though the point weren't worth the time he was giving to it. "The honors and privileges that often come as a result of leadership constitute only one side of the picture. The greater the privileges, the greater the responsibilities and sacrifices."

He moved on to the Reverend Mr. Fields. The mood of the people would not permit him to gloss over the charges, so he softened his tone, mentioned the blast uttered publicly by Fields, heard the boos, and said sadly, "Certainly it has created many unnecessary problems for us." Many jumped out of their seats to shout in agreement. "But," King continued, still using the tone of the forgiver, "we must meet this situation with the same dignity and discipline with which we have met so many difficult situations in the past. Let us never forget that we have committed ourselves to a way of nonviolence, and nonviolence means avoiding not only external physical violence but also internal violence of spirit.

"You not only refuse to shoot a man, but you refuse to hate him. Now in the spirit of our nonviolent movement I call upon you to forgive the Reverend Fields." He purposely paused here and then repeated the admonition of Jesus: "Let him who is without sin cast the first stone." The people understood the lesson; those who would judge Fields harshly began to surrender. Dr. King recalled the parable of the prodigal son who returned. "Will we be like the unforgiving elder brother, or will we, in the spirit of Christ, follow the example of the loving and forgiving father?"

The pastor turned away from the lectern. He adjusted his black robes and took Fields' hand to lead him to speak. The people, who used to equate apologies with servility, watched to see if Fields could apologize with dignity. They sat in silence. He hesitated; his goatee was quivering. "Lord," he finally said, "help us to live in such a way from day to day that even when we kneel to pray, our prayers will be for others." A loud amen came from the audience. Fields bluntly asked forgiveness for his mistake, and he held their hearts in his hand. He assured them that he had no evidence that money had been misused in any way by anybody. When he left, head bowed, the people burst into applause.

The applause belonged to King. He had done a masterful job of unrocking a boat. He told the people, and the news media, the things he wanted them to know and left unsaid everything else. He said nothing of the growling and grumbling in the MIA finance committee over top-heavy expense accounts in the hierarchy. Large sums were claimed for dinners, plane trips, gasoline, car usage, meetings, and other events which often seemed to be barely related to the MIA. Some of the ministers were leading lives which were exalted and expensive compared to their style of living before the boycott. Dr. King was aware of some of the protests; but the money kept coming in, the organization was solvent, and the car pool kept the lower-echelon members content. Besides, Dr. King had little experience in fiscal matters. He had learned from his father not to pass a collection plate, but to delegate a committee to be responsible for church tithing. He spent money for plane trips, suites at hotels, and rich food, but he could honestly claim that his speeches brought in more money than he disbursed. He did not live cheaply, but then, he never did. Some of the red-necks became bitter, seeing the little man in the expensive black silk suits with a tongue of a monogrammed kerchief peeping out of his breast pocket. His shoes gleamed; his shirts and ties were impeccable.

It was shortly after the Fields incident that a black man came from Maxwell Air Force Base to listen to Martin Luther King, Jr., preach. He was intelligent, short of stature, and had good features. His name was Bernard Lee, and he was painfully aware that orders on the base were strict: not to engage in any activity concerning the boycott in the nearby city of Montgomery. Lee was impressed, not only with the King's words and the cement of sense they made, but with the Palm Beach suit that bespoke affluence. This was no poor black preacher in a small church. This was a big man who might someday rock the nation.

On the way out, Bernard Lee paused to shake hands with the minister at the top of the steps. He went back to the base and did a great deal of thinking. On July 8 Bernard Lee was back in town, this time at a meeting in Ralph Abernathy's home. Again he was introduced to King. This time both men were struck by their resemblance to each other; not only did they look alike, but their voices were similar. Lee, after his Air Force discharge, became Dr. King's personal bodyguard, living with him, sleeping in the same bed when they were out of town, eating with him, protecting him from the "crazies," acting as his alter ego, and becoming the "man closest to Dr. King," even though King said many times that Ralph Abernathy was his best friend. Lee's wish to pledge his life and his energies to Martin Luther King had become a reality.

Summer was gone. School opened. Little black Alabama boys and girls went to black schools. Little white Alabama boys and girls went to white schools. The bus boycott went into its eleventh month, and tempers were short. The Supreme Court fight was still pending. The briefs—neatly typed with their "therefores," "whereases," "heretofores," and "be it knowns"—were in a big granite building in Washington. They had been studied by the law clerks. Notes had been added, questions had been raised on yellow foolscap, and all copies reposed on the desks of nine justices who were not in session.

In Montgomery, there was the monotony of watching near-empty buses climb the hills and come down again, almost empty. The blacks would hold out, it seemed to the whites, forever. Empty buses became a way of life. A young black in a pool hall could look out a flyspecked window, watch a bus go by, and try to remember how long ago it had been since he had been on one. A long time.

In late September, insurance companies canceled the liability insurance on the car pool's ten station wagons. The white companies had acted in concert. Collision insurance was another matter. It had been placed with black companies in Atlanta. The MIA had to go all the way to Lloyds in London to get liability insurance and pay a higher premium.

The City Commission ordered city attorneys, in late October, to press for a state injunction—already filed—against operating a car pool. Dr. King, who felt safe in federal court, asked U.S. Judge Frank M. Johnson for a restraining order. The judge refused. The car pool, the only transportation artery the blacks had, was in jeopardy. King and some members of his executive committee were served subpoenas. A hearing was ordered for Tuesday, November 13, 1956.

The city began to hope it could crush nonviolence. The Saturday before the hearing, the Ku Klux Klan decided to hood itself and hold a rally in Montgomery. Press photographers began to shoot pictures. The city sent police reserves and ordered the Ku Klux Klan out of town. The organization was told that it could not hold a rally in the city without a permit, and Mayor Gayle would not issue one. The onetime terrorist nightriders had fallen to low estate.

In the streets, the blacks were joyous. Mortal terror had been transformed into low comedy. That old devil boogeyman, the Klan, had been booted in the behind and run out of town. Blacks slapped their thighs and opened their mouths to shout laughter to the skies. It didn't affect Dr. King. He had no interest in the Klan.

On Tuesday, Circuit Court Judge Eugene Carter would—in effect—be asked to beat the federal courts to the draw in deciding the legality of that car pool.

The night before the Alabama court hearing, Dr. King, his voice solemn and loud, the tones reverberating through a crowded church like a deep bell, told the people the truth: that the injunction against the car pool was almost certain to be granted by Judge Carter. In the past year, he said, he had asked them for enormous sacrifices and he was no longer sure that he could beg them for greater ones. And yet, he warned, if the people did not submit to greater sacrifices, "all our months and months of protest will fail. This may well be the darkest hour before dawn. We have moved all these months with the daring faith that God is with us in our struggle. The many experiences of days gone by have vindicated that faith in a most unexpected manner. We must go on with that same faith. We must believe that a way will be made out of no way. . . ." The voice trailed off. The patient dark faces, the polished enduring planes of ebony, accepted the word of Martin Luther King as they accepted the word of the Almighty. The cause was lost. They had fought valiantly; they had sustained the best aimed blows of the tyrants, and they could still walk tall. They had been as obedient as good children. They had gloried in their leader and his victories, and he had won them all, except the last one. They would do as he said, even now, but they knew that the war had been lost. The people could not walk, day after day, from their peeling paint shacks to work downtown and then walk back in the evening.

When court convened on Tuesday, November 13, the City of Montgomery's lawyers opened the snaps of their briefcases, and black attorneys and white desegregated momentarily to ask each other the specifics of procedure. The judge was impassive above them, the bailiff at his desk, the stenographer waiting, and the people massed in the seats, with the blacks in back. Coretta King sat with Ralph Abernathy in the rear, where the proceedings did not sound like spoken words, but like the drone of bees around a hive. Up front, Dr. King sat looking disconsolate with the black lawyers.

The City of Montgomery opened its argument by specifying that the proceedings opposed the use of 300 automobiles and 20 station wagons operating as a private, unlicensed, unchartered means of public conveyance by a so-called organization calling itself the Montgomery Improvement Association. Because of this, the city had lost taxes from the licensed and properly chartered Montgomery Bus Line in excess of $15,000 and would like the court to note that it was asking compensation. The city attorney further contended that the so-called car pool was a public nuisance. The blacks asserted that the MIA car pool was nothing more than a neighborly share-the-ride plan designed temporarily to protest racial inequity on the Montgomery Bus Line. Mayor Gayle and Commissioner Sellers sat up front with impassive faces. This was their day, their day at long last—the day when the blacks were going to learn a hard and costly lesson. Ordinarily, neither the mayor nor the commissioner attended court sessions—leaving such matters to official attorneys —but they too had suffered the pressures of their people; they too had been derided and scorned for "inaction against the niggers"; this was a day to savor slowly, like a snifter of warming brandy.

The arguments were in tones of modulation, with exceptions duly noted for the record, and the court clock dragged its hands toward noon. Soon the judge would declare a luncheon recess. Dr. King lost the thread of argument and turned his mind within itself. The almond eyes looked sleepy. The hands were clasped on the table. There was a sudden stirring. He did not notice it at first. There was a scuffing of chairs as a reporter moved across the front of the court, bringing a frown from the judge. He handed a short sheet of paper to the mayor. Gayle and Sellers read it, stood abruptly, and left the court.

The judge expected decorum in his court. He watched the reporter tiptoe over to Martin Luther King. In the back of the court, Coretta King tried to stand to see what was going on. Rex Thomas, Associated Press reporter, handed a short sheet of teletype to the pastor. "Here," he said, "is the decision you have been waiting for. Read this release."

It read: "(AP) Washington D.C.—The United States Supreme Court today affirmed a decision of a special three-judge U.S. District Court in declaring Alabama's state and local laws requiring segregation on buses unconstitutional. The Supreme Court acted without listening to any argument; it simply said 'The motion to affirm is granted and the judgment is affirmed.' "

Dr. King read it twice. He couldn't seem to absorb the news. Fred Gray and others read it over his shoulder. There was a stirring among spectators. Local reporters ran from the court for the phones. The judge sat looking at the commotion and requested the city attorneys to proceed. They did. He rapped his gavel for order. Dr. King finally understood the teletype and sagged in his seat. He said later that he could hear his heart beat within his ears. Usually, his decorum in any situation was cool and mannerly. This time he lost it. He got up from his chair like an old man, still holding the paper which Rex Thomas expected to be returned, and walked back up the aisle to his wife.

The word was buzzed from pew to pew. Fred Gray, the MIA lawyer, asked the city attorneys what they proposed to do. The lawyers said that they would have to continue the local action and expected to get an injunction (which was granted later). They did not plan to implement the new law of the land until a copy arrived from Washington, and that might take weeks. It was the last stand of the modern Confederacy, but it didn't matter. The people who were seldom granted equity in law had been granted it. A miracle had occurred in the final hour, a miracle so perfect in its dramatic timing that it almost seemed contrived.

King literally dragged Coretta out of court to their home on Jackson Street. His happiness knew no bounds. He asked his followers to pass the word to the press, radio, television, all the media, that King was calling the blacks to meet tomorrow night in two churches on opposite sides of the town to decide whether the bus boycott should be called off. The speakers, he said, would have to travel from one meeting to the other. This, he reiterated, was not a victory of blacks over whites; it was a victory for justice and righteousness which would, in time, bring all men closer.

A big stone had dropped in a small pond. The word was everywhere. White Montgomery was disconsolate. Three hundred years of tradition had been ground into dust by nine strangers who didn't understand. The Montgomery Bus Line assembled its drivers, lined them up, and said that it would obey the new law. The bus drivers were among the most unrelenting of racists. The boss asked any drivers who felt that they could not obey the new law to step forward and quit. Six took a step forward. Some of the others, also racists, needed the job. They remained silent.

The blacks were cautiously jubilant. They believed the news and could not believe it. The radio announced that the Klan would ride that night, in spite of a Montgomery order to leave town. At 5 P.M. Judge Carter entered a restraining order against the car pool. It was anticlimactic, a feeble and almost comical protest of an inferior court to the Supreme Court, but Judge Carter, no matter what his juridical feelings, had to continue to live among the whites.

A reporter, almost out of breath, said he had called the Supreme Court clerk in Washington and learned that the order would not be mailed to Montgomery at once. It would be close to a month before the High Court would routinely mail it and demand compliance.

In the evening, forty automobiles loaded with white-hooded men in conical hats drove through the several black ghettos. In times past, the blacks extinguished their lights, and the hooded figures fired guns in the air or through windows. This time, the blacks turned their porch lights on and sat and watched the parade. They did not exult, and they drew no fire. They heard the derisive shouts, and some blacks walked their side-walks, not looking at the circus of cars; others waved to the hooded figures. In frustration, the lead car turned off into a side street, and the leaders announced that the night ride was over. Another tradition, a vicious one, died amid pity and smiles.

King called S. S. Seay, a friend who did not serve on any of the various MIA committees, and said that the MIA was going to have to remain off the buses until the Supreme Court order arrived, and yet it would have to obey the injunction of the local court against a car pool. He asked Seay to appoint a block captain on each ghetto street, who would be in charge of a neighborhood share-the-ride plan which would have no connection with the MIA. Seay agreed to organize it at once.

The following day was a busy one. King dressed in a gray suit at 6 A.M., found time for prayer and breakfast, and left his Jackson Street home with an unerasable smile on his face. He drove to the MIA build-ing and greeted the two secretaries who were already working. In his office, a small committee was working on plans and strategy for black people to register and vote—"no matter how long the white registrars take, no matter how they drag their feet, remain in line and do not leave it." The doctor was already broadening the field from boycott to polit-ical protest. He had also set up a credit union so that Montgomery blacks might own their own loan association for starting small busi-nesses and building homes.

At 9 A.M. all the clerks were present, and the girl at the switchboard channeled calls to the proper personnel. "Could Dr. King make an address in Minneapolis? In Syracuse? Cleveland? Sacramento?" Engage-ment pages were flipped. The girls were polite, but firm. "No. I'm sorry. He plans to be here in Montgomery on that day. A meeting is scheduled. No, he will be in Washington. Sorry, I can't give you another appoint-ment now." Martin Luther King, Jr., was a national figure. He was big. He was important. He was wanted.

He was bigger than his father now. It mattered not that the NAACP had taken the case to Washington; Fred Gray was the MIA lawyer, and Martin Luther King, Jr., was the symbol, the prophet, the man. "If my people had as much spirit and will in their hearts as they do in their feet," he said, "we could change the world." He would take no phone calls except from Abernathy, Seay, and the press. United Press phoned from New York and asked him if it was true that guards had been placed around the home and churches of the leaders of the movement. "Why, yes," King said, "but that's nothing new. We've had them for some time." Abernathy puffed into the room and worked out plans for the two meetings scheduled for tonight.

By sundown the mimeograph had run off thousands of leaflets designed by Dr. King. They were passed out before the double church meetings, and boys delivered them from house to house. It read:

This is a historic week, because segregation on buses has been declared unconstitutional. Within a few days, the Supreme Court Mandate will reach Montgomery and you will be re-boarding *integrated* buses. This places upon all of us a tremendous responsibility of maintaining, in the face of what could be some unpleasantness, a calm and loving dignity befitting good citizens and members of our race. If there is violence in word or deed it must not be our people who commit it.

For your help and convenience the following suggestions are made. Will you read, study and memorize them so that our non-violent determination may be not endangered.

First, some general suggestions:

1. Not all white people are opposed to integrated buses. Accept good will on the part of many.
2. The whole bus is not for the use of all people. Take a vacant seat.
3. Pray for guidance and commit yourself to complete non-violence in word and action as you enter the bus.
4. Demonstrate the calm dignity of our Montgomery people in your actions.
5. In all things observe ordinary rules of courtesy and good behavior.
6. Remember that this is not a victory for Negroes alone, but for all Montgomery and the South. Do not boast! Do not brag!
7. Be quiet but friendly; proud, but not arrogant; joyous, but not boisterous.
8. Be loving enough to absorb evil and understanding enough to turn an enemy into a friend.

For emphasis, some of the rules were repetitious. Above all, Dr. King did not want his people to strike the first blow, or the second. There would be provocation, but he wanted to ensure that it would come from the whites. "Now," he wrote "for some specific suggestions:"

1. The bus driver is in charge of the bus and has been instructed to obey the law. Assume that he will cooperate in helping you occupy any vacant seat.
2. Do not deliberately sit by a white person, unless there is no other seat.

3. In sitting down by a person, white or colored, say "May I" or "pardon me" as you sit. This is common courtesy.
4. If cursed, do not curse back. If pushed, do not push back. If struck, do not strike back, but evidence love and good will at all times.
5. In case of an incident, talk as little as possible, and always in a quiet tone. Do not get up from your seat! Report all serious incidents to the bus driver.
6. For the first few days, try to get on the bus with a friend in whose non-violence you have confidence. You can uphold one another by a glance or a prayer.
7. If another person is being molested, do not arise to go to his defense, but pray for the oppressor and use moral and spiritual force to carry on the struggle for justice.
8. According to your own ability and personality, do not be afraid to experiment with new and creative techniques for achieving reconciliation and social change.
9. If you feel you cannot take it, walk for another week or two. We have confidence in our people.
God Bless you all.

The matter of buses was now in its delicate and dangerous phase. Abernathy and King called upon the white Ministerial Association of Montgomery, in the name of Jesus Christ, to step forward and preach conciliation and courtesy at their churches. The majority answered that they did not dare speak of such matters from the pulpit. A few said that they would dare to try on Sunday. An officer of the White Citizens Council stated: "Any attempt to enforce this decision will lead to riot and bloodshed." Another white group proposed the establishment of a car pool for those who did not want to ride the buses with blacks. King did not bother to remind them that among their members were those who had sought an injunction against a black car pool. The Men of Montgomery, the club which had, in the past, tried to bring white and black together, asked if a joint statement, with the MIA, could be issued, asking both sides to be tolerant and courteous and to obey the highest court in the nation. Two club members blackballed the suggestion, and since the bylaws required unanimity, the joint plea was not written.

King and his closest advisers appeared from behind the altar of the first church they would speak at that night promptly at 7 P.M. The applause was deafening. He had hoped, after suitable hymns, to announce the court decisions, but the people already knew. Four thousand people jammed each of the two churches. The Reverend Bob Graetz opened the proceedings with Paul's Letter to the Corinthians: ". . . when I was a child, I spake as a child, I understood as a child, I thought as a child; but when I became a man, I put away childish things. . . ." At that moment, the 4,000 throats opened in a deafening roar of sound, standing, stomping, shouting. King spoke softly, whispering the good news as though he wanted the people to emulate his attitude that a quiet, respectful demeanor would carry the day.

Abernathy arose to speak and said that a journalist had approached him and reproached him about the interruption of the Scriptures by the congregation. The fat reverend could play the buffoon and elicit hearty laughter when whole congregations were depressed, but he was wily, and he understood the innermost hearts of blacks better than his statesman-like friend.

"Yes," said Abernathy, "I told him it is peculiar for people to interrupt Scripture, just as it is peculiar for people to walk in the snow and rain when there are empty buses available, just as it is peculiar for people to pray for those who persecute them; just as it is peculiar for the Southern Negro to stand up and look a white man in the face as an equal." It had the desired effect. The audience was in a frenzy of joy. The important business of each meeting was dispatched quickly. The people were asked to endorse a decision by the executive board of the MIA to call off the boycott, but to refrain from boarding buses until the decree was served on the officials of the city. The people agreed.

In the following few weeks, the blacks assembled in churches to be taught how to practice restraint in buses. Chairs were lined up at altars to resemble bus seats. From the parishioners, a dozen "actors" were asked to take seats. Some were playing the parts of racist white men; others were suppliant blacks. Some whites were courteous. Some were not. The blacks were taught how to respond to each. The "acting" required a few minutes, and the group would return to the pews, and another dozen summoned forward. King and his committee were anxious to find out how much insulting behavior his people could absorb without retaliating.

He learned. Some "white" actors made remarks which elicited pushing and shoving from those acting as the bus-riding blacks. On a few occasions, a black cracked a "white" with his fist. These were the dangers, and the people were rehearsed over and over again to avoid them. The executive board, including King, was now reconciled to the time it would take to desegregate the buses. It could be well used to instruct their people how to react. Some of the people were not ready for fresh humiliation. Many of them equated desegregation with total equality and were confused. It was painful to learn that the white man would still be the "boss man"; it was a hurt to learn that the only thing which had been won was an empty front seat. Those who thought that conditions would change for the better in Montgomery were stunned to find that the South was going to remain the solid superior South. The MIA could feel a letdown in morale—a year of walking in hot sun and stinging snow had achieved no more than what Rosa Parks had originally insisted was her right: to sit where she pleased.

Preachers went to local high schools and colleges to teach black students how to behave on buses. This was a difficult lesson because it was being taught to strong young hearts and sensitive minds which had, in the process of educating thmselves, lost faith in the supine credo of their fathers. The elders would be tractable, but the young believed in striking back. It was hard for them to understand that even a small step is still a step forward.

On December 18, 1956, the City of Montgomery issued a civic pronouncement: "The decision in this bus case has had a tremendous impact on the customs of our people here in Montgomery. It is not an easy thing to live under a law recognized as constitutional for these many years and then have it suddenly overturned on the basis of psychology. . . . The City Commission, and we know our people are with us in this determination, will not yield one inch, but will do all in its power to oppose the integration of the Negro race with the White race in Montgomery, and will forever stand like a rock against social equality, inter-marriage, and mixing of the races under God's creation and plan."

The statement had nothing to do with the issue. It was obviously a palliative for the whites, and it stirred up old white fears of black sexual aggression and the "mongrelizing" of the races. The ineptness of Gayle and Sellers and their legal counsel closed on an undignified whimper. Two days after the city edict, on December 20, the Supreme Court decree arrived in Montgomery and was served on the city.

Martin Luther King, Jr., stood at the lectern of St. John A.M.E. Church and said at the end of his sermon, "Now our faith seems to be vindicated. This morning the long awaited mandate from the United States Supreme Court concerning bus segregation came to Montgomery. This mandate expresses in terms that are crystal clear that segregation in public transportation is both legally and socially invalid. In the light of this mandate and the unanimous vote tendered by the Montgomery Improvement Association about a month ago, the year-old protest against city buses is officially called off, and the Negro citizens of Montgomery are urged to return to the buses tomorrow morning on a nonsegregated basis.

". . . We must act in such a way as to make possible a coming together of white people and colored people on the basis of a real harmony of interests and understanding. We seek an integregation based on mutual respect."

These words, uttered so soon after the defeat of the white structure in Montgomery cost the blacks the sympathy and understanding they may have received from a minority of Southerners. As the face and the words were broadcast on networks, they also lost the sympathy and understanding of a part of the racially sophisticated North. Across the nation, the last two sentences were freely interpreted as a bid for—and a threat of—"social equality," which, in spite of protests to the contrary, was no more palatable in the United States than in South Africa.

Dr. King was, figuratively speaking, out of work. He was not content with being pastor of the Dexter Avenue Church or co-pastor of Ebenezer. He had, by his perseverance and, more poignantly, by the perseverance of his 30,000 poor blacks, become a national celebrity. Photos of Martin Luther King were appearing on walls from Salem to San Diego, and his father's plea that it might be wise for him to return to church fell on ears still ringing with the sound of hosannas. The winner of any battle must look for a stronger adversary. King displayed political acumen in hoping to harness the economic and voting power of blacks for the welfare of his people but misfired in timing it for the night after beating the bus company. The black haters said, "I told you so." Editors asked, in big type, what Dr. King meant by "a coming together of white people and colored people."

The threats in Montgomery started at once. A brick was thrown through a bus window. The small number of whites who rode the buses began to boycott them. United States Senator Lister Hill of Alabama "greatly deplored" the Supreme Court order and promised to use "every lawful means" to set the ruling aside, knowing that there was no "lawful" means of reversing the Supreme Court. The man who led the Montgomery White Citizens Council, Luther Ingalls, stated that "any attempt to enforce this decision will inevitably lead to riot and bloodshed." These were words abused so frequently that they elicited no comment. Leaders of other Southern states felt Alabama had waged a poor fight which resulted in the Supreme Court order being imposed upon them, as well as on Montgomery. Some banded their legal talent together in an attempt to nullify the order—but again the whites were not acting, they were reacting. Always, it seemed, they sat in legal lassitude until after the courts made a decision and then bounded to their feet firing blank cartridges.

A night bomb exploded in Montgomery; a shotgun blast tore through a door in Martin Luther King's home; black heads were cracked; some blood flowed; but the power structure had been tumbled, and that was the ultimate determinant. C. C. Owen, president of the Alabama Public Service Commission, sounded the last lingering note of taps over the old South and its obnoxious traditions by pledging to "urge all public transportation companies to make every effort to keep harmony among passengers by assigning seats in such a manner that the races will be kept separate." It was as though the officials could not, or would not, read. King said it more succinctly: "The law cannot make a man love me—religion and education must do that—but it can control his desire to lynch me."

All the comments pro and con, like summer thunder, were loud and unproductive. Governor James "Kissin' Jim" Folsom sat in regal silence for a year within one city block of the battle. Then he pontificated: "The only way I know to defeat the Supreme Court decision regarding segregation is to keep such cases out of the courts. That is what I have been preaching for the past two years, and I'm going to continue to do so by working with men of good will of all races." This, beyond argument, was the supreme *non sequitur* of the struggle, even in humorless Alabama.

On the shortest day of the year, December 21, 1956, Martin Luther King, Jr., assembled a few friends at 5 A.M. in his home on Jackson Street. Mrs. King made coffee, and Bernard Lee stood on the porch to watch the first bus come by. Ralph Abernathy was present; so was the white minister—a Southerner born—Dr. Glenn Smiley. On the sidewalk, television cameras had been set up, and lights focused on the sign that said BUS STOP. Reporters huddled in heavy coats; still cameras were ready. Lee knocked on the door.

At 5:55 A.M. King, Smiley, and Abernathy stepped out onto the porch, saw the empty bus coming, headlights on full, and walked down to the corner. The bus sighed to a stop, the front doors flipped open, and King deposited three dimes as the small crowd gaped.

The white driver, sounding like a gentle satire on the Dr. Livingstone and Stanley dialogue in deepest Africa, said, "I believe you are the Reverend King, aren't you?"

King saw the broad smile and, nonplussed, said, "Yes, I am."

The driver snapped the doors shut and said, "We are glad to have you this morning."

Smiley and King sat in front. There was no incident. Downtown the little party transferred to a white district bus. Most whites got aboard, saw the blacks up front, and took empty seats. An old white man stood beside the bus operator, although there were empty seats in back. Someone suggested that he sit. In a low voice he said, "I would rather die and go to hell than sit behind a nigger." A few other blacks got aboard. A white woman absentmindedly sat beside one, then, realizing what she had done, jumped to her feet. "What are these niggers gonna do next?" she asked. A few whites, seeing empty seats in back, ignored them and sat beside blacks. One said facetiously, "It sure looks like we ain't gonna have a white Christmas." The black in front turned and grinned. "It sure don't," he said.

One black woman was slapped as she got off the bus by the front door, but she neither retaliated nor uttered a word. A reporter asked her why, and she said, "I could have broken that little fellow's neck all by myself, but I left the mass meeting last night determined to do what Reverend King asked." A week later, when bus integration was a fact, white hoodlums waited for the dark quiet of night to fire shotgun blasts into buses. A young black girl was beaten by four white men as she left a bus in a poorly lighted section. A pregnant woman was shot in the leg.

Whites boycotted public vehicles as the blacks had done. The Montgomery Bus Line became a black line on which any passenger could occupy any seat without offense. Attendance at the MIA meetings fell off sharply. Dr. King's organization began to die. Always subject to fits of depression, he was extremely despondent now. All the terrifying things he had read as a boy about the persecution and exploitation of blacks was still fresh in his mind. Could it be true that his destiny was only to win one boycott in a small town?

It couldn't. The ultimate good of his people was as much in his heart as his insatiable personal ambitions. The two were fused. He must leave God while using His name for other work; he must find larger dragons to slay. He talked to Louis Lomax, a black writer who had already made a name in letters, and it required few words to find that they were in agreement. They both felt that like Paul, the preacher had to go out into the world of the pagans and the Philistines—this time to achieve racial harmony.

It is a diamond-hard truth that as the year 1957 arrived, one man profited hugely from the Montgomery boycott. Dr. King was a national figure, a dark comet arching high and alone in the heavens. There were offers of full professorships at $50,000 to $75,000 per year; a lecture tour at $1,000 to $1,500 per talk; a cover story by *Time* magazine; a bid from Harper & Row to write a book.

In Montgomery, Alabama, the black was back in "his place." He mowed the white man's lawn, ran his errands, polished his car, lived in the same kindling wood shacks, was called "boy," and took silent solace in his victory over the White Establishment. Often, around the family table, he referred to King as L.L.J., which meant Little Lord Jesus. This was his hero, and more than his hero. This was his people's leader, come on earth to deliver the indentured from Egypt. The Promised Land was out there in the white world. Even the unlettered black knew that he would not attain that world without a series of confrontations, but he was patient in the knowledge that between Egypt and Judea, the Jews had been lost in the desert for a long period of time. He had waited; he could wait.

Perhaps King's greatest accomplishment was that for the first time the white people of the United States were being forced to study the black man and his problems. For the first time, scores of millions of Americans who had seen blacks without ever noticing or caring, began to feel the pangs of conscience. They had seen—truly seen—this young man on television, and they had heard his words of Christianity and brotherhood. The people did not appreciate the black man and did not want him in their midst, but Dr. King brought him to their attention as a human being with few rights, no assets, a forlorn figure without a friend. He too had feelings and sensitivities; he had children who would be forced to learn that they are inferior. King pricked the white sense of honor and justice North as well as South. In one year the young doctor had achieved something vague, shapeless, and constant—something which he did not yet see: He had brought the black before the whites and placed the whites on trial.

E. D. Nixon resigned from the Montgomery Improvement Association, and King could not persuade the Pullman porter to reconsider. Nixon was no Brutus. He had complained that the MIA used loose and dangerous bookkeeping procedures. Too much of the $225,000 which had poured into the association was being spent by members of the executive committee in unsupportable and unaccountable telephone calls, travels, and meals. As he saw it, the MIA should correct its accounting and force everyone, including Dr. King, to itemize all expenditures down to the penny and to present signed receipts from airlines, restaurants, and railroads. Dr. King refused to back Nixon and lost a good man.

Time magazine's stringer in Montgomery was Bill McDonald of the *Advertiser*. As he worked on the cover story, digging, probing, interviewing, sifting facts from superlatives, he was surprised to see the MIA fall apart. Meetings were called, but the blacks were exhausted. They could not tolerate one more exhortation to sacrifice their freedom or their feet. Attendance fell off; the receipt of funds declined; King knew that the spirit of the people was flagging. He lost Nixon; he lost money; he lost the people. Author Lomax had been right in counseling a broader front and a higher goal, but Dr. King was surrounded by men of narrow vision, some of whom could not see over the next hill. "Frankly," he said, "I'm worried to death. A man who hits the peak at twenty-seven has a tough job ahead. People will be expecting me to pull rabbits out of the hat for the rest of my life."

Another minister found the higher goal for King. In Tallahassee, Florida, the Reverend C. K. Steele issued a round-robin call for a conference of Southern civil rights ministers to be held on January 10 and 11 in Atlanta, Georgia. Steele was moving—and moving fast. King and Abernathy heard the call and decided to attend. It was awkward to know that the initial impetus came from a source outside the MIA, but once the call was issued, both men had to join or be content to sit outside the action, watching.

Nor did it help to know that the first meeting of the nearly sixty black ministers would be held in "Daddy" King's Ebenezer Baptist Church. King and Abernathy hastened to join.

Steele and his friends were prepared to aim high, no matter what the consequences. They were given an affirmative vote to: (1) request President Dwight D. Eisenhower to journey South and make a major policy speech demanding that Southern white officials abide by the law, as enunciated by the Supreme Court; (2) ask Vice President Richard Nixon to tour the South and confer with white and black leaders; (3) demand that Attorney General Herbert Brownell, as chief law enforcement officer of the nation, visit the Southern states to urge local authorities to comply with the law.

The assembled ministers did not expect action. The Eisenhower administration had "leaked" information that it would not pursue racial problems; it believed that each state was conscious of court decisions,

and each in its own good time would obey. The value of the appeal to
the national administration lay in the public relations field. Eisenhower,
Nixon, and Brownell could juggle invitations with sympathetic refusals,
but the Reverend Mr. Steele and his new organization would be placing
the administration in a racially defensive posture.

The Reverend Mr. Steele's own bus boycott in Tallahassee had
reached an impasse because Governor LeRoy Collins had suspended all
bus service in Florida's capital city. The winds were not favorable for
desegregation anywhere. In the North, as well as in the South, the antiblack elements were more articulate than those who proclaimed a
checkerboard brotherhood. Boards of education disagreed, resigned,
regrouped, and found themselves fighting parents who vowed to withdraw children from classes where black students represented anything
more than tokenism. Twenty million blacks who had moved freely
among whites watched in fear as battle lines were being drawn. Slowly,
inexorably, the nation began to convulse. If there were any neutrals,
they were the millions of blacks who chose to "mind our own business"
and figuratively speaking, remain indoors. Black youth and white power
were the true antagonists, and as the struggle began, the races grew
farther and farther apart until, in time, communication was almost
impossible.

Dr. King and the Reverend Mr. Abernathy were sleeping in Atlanta
when a phone call stirred both. Juanita Abernathy told them that the
Abernathy home had been bombed and that bombs wre exploding in
several parts of Montgomery. Both men dressed and left at first light.
Three Baptist churches had been shattered by explosives. The front of
Bob Graetz's home was in ruins. Blacks stood silently at each bomb site,
and Dr. King marveled at the restraint of his people. White Montgomery
also deplored the vandalism. The editor of the *Advertiser,* Grover Hall,
took to his typewriter and wrote a scathing editorial entitled: "Is It Safe
to Live in Montgomery?" A white minister, the Reverend Merle Patterson, stood before television cameras and denounced the bombings as
"unchristian." Influential citizens pitched in with public statements
expressing horror and demanding that the police locate and punish the
offenders.

Once they had both seen that their families were well and taken care
of, King and Abernathy took the next plane back to Atlanta. The new
organization of ministers adjourned to meet again in New Orleans, this
time to elect Martin Luther King, Jr., president and also to name the
group to the Southern Christian Leadership Conference. Once more,

King had been projected into "the picture" and was standing front and center, a place he desired and deserved. Beaming, he promised to abide by the bylaws and to do all in his power—with the help of the other members—to bring racial justice to the South.

When he got back to Montgomery, he was told that the mayor and commissioner used the bombings as an excuse to cancel all bus service—a belated imitation of Governor Collins' solution to racial strife. As always, Dr. King called a church mass meeting at once. His mood was low; the little gains he had achieved were wiped out. People were walking to work. City officials maintained that the reason they stopped all bus service was their fears that buses loaded with blacks might be bombed.

At the meeting, King broke down. He had asked the people to join him in a prayer asking for divine guidance. Suddenly, all the frustrations choked him, and he burst into tears. "Lord," he shouted, "I hope no one will have to die as a result of our struggle for freedom in Montgomery. Certainly, I don't want to die. But if anyone has to die, let it be me, Lord." The audience leaped to its feet. The passive faces were alive. "No! No!" the people shouted. Men moved out of pews and strode toward the pulpit. Two ministers grabbed King around the middle to keep him from falling. They half carried him to a chair and begged him to sit. Others got to the lectern with hands raised and begged for quiet. In five minutes, order was restored, but the white press, sitting down front, had a fearful, though only momentary, glance at what could happen if the blacks lost control. The newspapers reported tersely that Martin Luther King had "collapsed" at a meeting.

Officially, the City of Montgomery continued to apply pressure. Ordinances were passed making it a crime for whites and blacks to play together or even to share the same playgrounds. Montgomery's Class C baseball team had two blacks on its roster; they were dismissed. A black man was arrested for permitting his children to pause at a white zoo to glance at caged animals. Segregationists issued public statements warning against the dangers of "race mixing."

The only substantive result of this appeal was to stir up the "poor whites." On the night of January 28, the People's Service and Cab Stand was bombed; the home of a sixty-year-old man was bombed—although no one could figure why. Fourteen sticks of dynamite, sufficient to demolish several homes, were found smoking on the front porch of Martin Luther King's home on Jackson Street. They were tossed into the street, where they fizzled out. The terrorism ended by the next morning. Rewards were offered for the capture of the bombers. Two white men were arrested. They were acquitted in county court. The buses began to run again. White Montgomery stopped moving backward. Black Montgomery stopped moving forward.

"L.L.J.," the leader who had proclaimed the honor of going to jail rather than obey "unjust laws," paid a $500 fine to the Montgomery court on his earlier conviction for violating the antiboycott law. Some of the other members of the MIA, who had remained in jail for months, were released in a tactical "amnesty," which also freed five whites held on charges of bombing. By unspoken agreement, both sides began to retreat from further confrontations.

Nor did the President of the United States want to get into the struggle. He chilled King's hopes by not responding to the invitation to go South and make a major speech. The reply came from the high priest of the White House, Sherman Adams. The President's schedule prohibited a Southern journey. Vice President Nixon could not be roused to visit the South either. The Attorney General found the invitation "inopportune." The highly placed whites seemed to know when to look away from an "unjust law." Dr. King told his intimates that he had expected this. However, he pointed to all the publicity the Southern Christian Leadership Conference had received, and this, he felt, was payment of a kind.

As though to revenge himself on Eisenhower, Dr. King, through the SCLC, sent a second letter to the President asking for a White House conference on civil rights or, "if some effective remedial steps are not taken, we will be compelled to initiate a mighty Prayer Pilgrimage to Washington." It was meant as a threat. The character of the President, whose most prominent trait was perpetual self-righteous indignation, made him the least likely person to respond to this sort of action. Nor had threats ever affected him. In addition, his temper had a low boiling point. The response, from a Presidential aide, was that the "moment is unpropitious." Plans for the Prayer Pilgrimage were begun.

The Southern Christian Leadership Conference earned its way in the press by mimeographing all challenges and favorable news. The White House remained silent. Public relations, properly exploited, is a powerful weapon. Dr. King was unimpressed by the power of the press, and, when *Time* magazine's issue of February 18, 1957, put King's face on its cover and published a long favorable story, the pastor was flattered. The story referred to him as "the scholarly Negro Baptist minister who in little more than a year has risen from nowhere to become one of the nation's remarkable leaders of men. . . ." It was heady wine designed not only to please the recipient, but to excite the envy of leaders of the NAACP, CORE, the Urban League, and the Black Muslims.

The story was sufficient to alter King's attitude. Bill McDonald of the *Advertiser,* who had researched the facts with Lee Graves, saw King change from a "jivey-speaking pastor (Hi ya doon, man!)" to one of awesome dignity, who no longer sat on a desk in the city room of a newspaper to chat with reporters; instead, King called "press conferences" at certain hours on certain days. Even his enemies did not doubt that the *new* Martin Luther King had sufficient educational background, plus a fine command of rhetorical English, to sustain the cool, fresh elegance of his manner. In spite of youth and inexperience, he was prepared to lift his people to a station equal to that of the whites. His fellow pastors in the SCLC reminded King that the Southern Christian group meant Southern only. The young president shrugged and said that the name was poorly chosen because there were blacks in the North and West who needed organizational assistance and he would not be confined by geography.

Calmly, Mrs. King told her husband that she was pregnant. He was overjoyed and said he would pray for a boy. He wanted a Martin Luther King III. Except for Coretta's good news, everything else seemed to have come to a standstill. King needed a crusade badly—a big one. None was forthcoming, and officers of the SCLC counseled patience. His frustration was obvious to the congregation of the Dexter Avenue Church. The committee members quietly solicited funds to enable the Kings to make their first trip abroad.

On February 24, the congregation, barely able to conceal its pleasure, handed King a generous purse of $2,500 and told him to take his wife on a trip to Europe. The MIA, almost bankrupt on receipts of $225,000 in a year, gave the Kings an additional $1,000. Mrs. King's physician felt that her pregnancy was still in a sufficiently early stage so that there would be no danger in traveling.

The problem was where to go. Dr. King read that the Gold Coast of Africa would soon achieve national independence and that prominent blacks were being invited from all over the world for the hauling down of British colors and the raising of the new flag of Ghana. The Kings joined Ralph Bunche, A. Philip Randolph, and Adam Clayton Powell in New York to fly to Africa. During the first leg of their flight to Lisbon, the captain invited Dr. King to join him on the flight deck. There, in the dark of night, he saw the soft red glow of instruments and, as he sat in the jump seat, speeds, altitudes, throttle settings, and radio navigation were explained to him. When he returned to his seat, he told his friends that he had sat at the controls. "If I had a few more lessons," he said, "I think I could fly us to Accra by myself."

There was a short stopover at Lisbon, then the plane came down at Monrovia, Liberia, and finally landed at the capital city of Accra. The Kings were told that lodging had been arranged for them with a local English family. The ceremony of independence took place at a British polo field outside town, where a crowd of 50,000 blacks sat in colorful robes. Scattered among them was a small number of whites. It was an exhilarating experience to see ebony-black Africans dominate the scene. And yet it was obvious—perhaps for the first time—to King that the American black was no longer African in any sense. Hundreds of years of subjugation and interracial sex had robbed him of his complete blackness and his African character.

At the stroke of midnight on March 5, Prime Minister Kwame Nkrumah ordered the British flag hauled down as 50,000 cheered. It fluttered to the bottom of the staff, was properly folded by black soldiers in white helmets and red uniforms. When quiet was restored, Nkrumah said: "The battle is ended. Our beloved country, our new country, Ghana, is free forever." No one yelled: "Amen, brother!" No one gloated. The people were content that they were their own masters now. For the first time in their lives the Kings walked among blacks who owned all the land, all the shops, and administered the government. Nor was that all. They were summoned to a private audience with Nkrumah, who surprised the American pastor by being acquainted with the story of the Montgomery bus boycott. He could not believe—even when Nkrumah told him so—that he was known and respected in many lands. The pastor came away from the audience feeling more certain than ever that his destiny was to be leader of his people.

He came away with another feeling—a painful one. The man who enjoyed soul food had partaken of African fare—sometimes served on leaves of sea grape—and he had dysentery. Mrs. King was ill of food poisoning. Her husband was wracked with pain. Father Michael Scott, who heard of it, told Lord Hemingsford, who sent a British naval physician to him. Later in the day Nkrumah heard and sent his doctor. The following morning Dr. King felt so weak that he was barely able to leave his bed, but there were public functions on the calendar. The Kings attended. At one they met Vice President Richard Nixon, who said cordially, "Stop by and see me when you are in Washington."

The reverend was in Washington, completely well, on March 25, but the White House doors remained closed to him. Roy Wilkins and A. Philip Randolph counseled patience, but Dr. King was tiring of the word. He was irritated and said that the gathering of massed blacks in Washington might move the President, Vice President, and Congress to action.

At home, King worked on his book, found time for domestic life and his church, sermonized about his trip to Africa, and tried, by sheer will, to hold the MIA together. It was not possible. However, he was able to transfer the membership nucleus to the SCLC.

The plans for the Prayer Pilgrimage moved forward slowly. When King flew to Washington for the first committee meetings, he learned that he would not be called upon to lead the Prayer Pilgrimage. He was asked only to participate and to speak. The National Association for the Advancement of Colored People—through Wilkins—suavely announced that it would sponsor the mass meeting. The date had already been agreed upon: May 17, the third anniversary of the notable Supreme Court decision abolishing desegregation in schools. Dr. King had a passive interest in schools but felt that it was not his field. His real interest was in civic rights, equality for all, and mass nonviolence as the appropriate weapon.

The NAACP underwrote the expenses, and appointed the Reverend Thomas as national director of the meeting. At noon on May 17, more than 30,000 people—10 percent of them white—stood in a warm Washington haze between the Lincoln Memorial and the Mall. Television and newsreel cameras stared like electronic cranes. King sensed that he was on trial before the old leaders of his people, and he had decided to combine an intelligent plea for justice with the repetitive phrase which always had impact in the South.

A. Philip Randolph, the true elder of the group, spoke first. Roy Wilkins, dispassionate and cool, was introduced. Then came Congressman Adam Powell and two massed choruses which intoned hymns. Stout Mahalia Jackson drew applause from the crowd as she sang. There were short addresses by the reverends C. K. Steele, Shuttlesworth, Borders, and Davis. Dr. King's watch ticked on, and he feared that the people would be tired of standing, tired of listening, before he was introduced.

Not so. They were waiting for the newcomer. When he was introduced, a roar was heard all the way to the Washington Monument. Mrs. King heard it on her radio at home in Alabama. Out front, such successful blacks as baseball star Jackie Robinson, actress Ruby Dee, movie star Sidney Poitier, nightclub entertainer Sammy Davis, Jr., and singer Harry Belafonte applauded the man who had had the courage to fight the white racists in their own territory. He had fought with little, and no one cared how little he had won—the fact was that he had achieved victory.

King slid his sheets of paper onto the lectern. He began by indicting both the Democrats and Republicans for their treatment of the black man. It was not one, but both parties, which could share the blame, he said. He was sorrowed by the "silent and apathetic" treatment of black people at the White House—he pointed over the trees to the Executive Mansion, and the crowd roared approval. The federal government, he pointed out, had no choice but to obey the law; next, he entreated the "quasi-liberal" whites, many of whom were in the crowd before him, to move from a position of benevolence toward the black man to one of positive commitment to the cause. Nor did he spare the white moderates of the South. They would have to make themselves heard above the din of hysterical racism, he said. They would have to face their fellow legislators and civic officials and speak out firmly. Last, he demanded that black leaders—no names were mentioned—start to provide moderate but positive leadership for the vast mass of blacks who were waiting to hear the voices of truth. "It is always difficult," he said in that deep baritone voice, "to get out of Egypt."

Dr. King lowered his head, lifted it, and, enunciating each word slowly, set them rolling down over the crowd to the Capitol and the White House said:

"Give us the ballot, and we will no longer plead—we will write the proper laws on the books." The crowd screamed "Amen!" "Give us the ballot, and we will fill the legislatures with men of goodwill." The crowd shouted in unison, "Give us the ballot!" King went on in his extraordinary voice: "Give us the ballot, and we will get the people judges who love mercy. Give us the ballot, and we will quietly, lawfully implement the May 17, 1954, decision of the Supreme Court." The crowd stood. Once more: "Give us the ballot, and we will transform the salient misdeeds of the bloodthirsty mobs into the calculated good deeds of orderly citizens."

He was, by any test, the man of the hour. The crowd did not want Dr. King to leave the lectern. The people yelled, cheered, and begged him to go on. The young man held both arms aloft in a black cassock—his sign of peace, his benediction. This was his first speech—except for sermons—in the North, and his charm, his positive approach, his moderate and just goals won approval in many parts of America.

In the crowd, his father bowed his head—pleased to bursting, but crushed with worry. He loved his son, but he had lost him to history—a long narrow road without room to turn back. In a manner of speaking, the whole family had lost the man with a mission. No one asked Coretta King what she thought; the gilded honors accruing to a husband are supposed to brighten a wife's face, too.

Truly, he was now a national figure. Truly, he was a new leader—a Christian following the bare feet of Jesus and Gandhi. He won the Spingarn Medal, awarded by the NAACP for contributions to race relations; he shared the annual award of the National Religion and Labor Foundation with a Roman Catholic priest, Father John LaFarge, SJ, and a Jew, Senator Herbert Lehman of New York. In May, King was awarded honorary degrees by the Chicago Theological Seminary, Howard University, and his alma mater, Morehouse College.

West of Montgomery, Highway 80 doesn't go anywhere. It wanders a crooked line between steamy, bottomland farms, sometimes in four lanes with a grassy island between opposing lines of traffic, often narrowing abruptly to two. Fifty miles west, there is a humpback bridge over the chocolate snake of the Alabama River. On the far side a main street of shops flashes by the windshield. In a moment, the town of Selma is diminishing in the rearview mirror. The road continues to a crossing with the north-south Highway 43 at Demopolis. It sags a little, then moves into the sovereign State of Mississippi to collapse at Meridian.

East of Montgomery, Highway 80 goes south first and then turns north around dozens of hopeful salesmen standing in used-car lots, and goes to Tuskegee and Phenix City and Columbus, Georgia. To the citizens of Selma, seat of Dallas County and the home of Sheriff Jim Clark, Highway 80 was a ribbon to the rest of the world. Clark was a stout, strong man who didn't want any trouble, never went looking for it, and respected blacks who remained in the eastern section of town near the railroad yards. He enjoyed the confidence of the whites, who elected him to keep the peace in Dallas County, apprehend malefactors, if any, and to keep his deputies out of "Colored Town" when the "nigras" staged razor fights over a woman.

The sheriff enjoyed a successful, somewhat dull tenure in office until the spring of 1957. Fifteen miles south of Selma was Dallas Lake. When warmth seeped into the hummocks and brambles and fat-headed catfish swam near the surface with long whiskers trailing, Dallas Lake staged an opening ceremony. Clark didn't attend. He was perspiring over paper work in his county office. Some of the leading citizens of Selma and other nearby towns made a picnic of it. Some blacks also made the trip. For the whites, fishing the lake was fun. For the blacks, it was dinner. Slowly, the dark ones filtered away and, bamboo poles in hand, inched through the bushes around the far side of the 100-acre lake. It was a good day for everyone. The sun was a cool bronze when starter buttons were depressed. Shiny cars and rusty ones backed away from the shore. The old automobiles gave the right of way to the shiny ones. It was dark in Selma when the picnickers returned.

One black family began to fret. There was an old man missing. He was eighty, and the family thought he had returned in another car. He was missing, and it was unlike the old man to wander off by himself. He was no longer firm of foot, and sometimes the teen-agers took his arm and helped him across the main street of Selma. Excitement mounted. It would not do to phone the Police Department of Selma, because it had no jurisdiction at Dallas Lake. The county sheriff's office was the proper body, but the blacks did not believe that Clark would send his deputies fifteen miles south, with hound dogs, to find a crotchety black.

The family drove to Montgomery instead. There they contacted Martin Luther King, Jr., leader of their race, the man unafraid to approach the White Establishment and demand justice. King phoned the newspapers and wire services with a story that the old man was mysteriously missing in a place where hate racism was a deep tradition. If foul play was not involved, why was the helpless old man missing? The story made the newspapers, and in the morning, an aide of Governor Folsom phoned the sheriff and said, "What are you going to do about that old man?" Word was spreading that the old man had been killed.

Clark sent deputies out with rowboats and grappling hooks to find the old man. They didn't find him. That night Dr. King phoned Sheriff Clark and asked what he had done about the man. The sheriff didn't like the tone of voice and said, "What man?"

"The old man who is missing at Dallas Lake."

"Oh," said Clark, "that man. Well, in the first place, no one reported him missing to this office. In the second place, I am sending all available forces out to find him in the morning. You might be interested to know that I had to read about it in the papers before I knew anybody was missing." The sheriff had read about Dr. King and didn't like him. King had heard a lot about Clark and didn't like him.

In the morning, county authorities tried to enlist additional help from the blacks. One and all, they declined on the grounds that it would be a bad sign if he were found dead. The sheriff found the old man on the far side of the lake with a fishing pole in his hand. He was dead. The soft drizzling rain shone on his face. A deputy phoned Dr. Rehling, a toxicologist, and an anatomical expert named Van Pruitt, who was not a physician. They arrived in an hour. Rehling had the instruments. They removed the pole from the stiff black hand, laid the body back on the edge of the lake, and performed an autopsy. They said the old man had died of a heart attack. He had trudged through too many sticky bushes. The finding was official.

The eviscerated body was returned to the family. Black Selma would not believe that this was a natural death. White folks had done the old man in. No doubt about it. The word spread like a seeping stain. It reached Montgomery. Responsible ministers asked Dr. King if something shouldn't be done about Selma. He agreed that the town was seething with racism, but he had so many commitments in so many parts of the country that Selma would have to wait. He knew that he would get around to it, if for no other reason than Jim Clark's cool contemptuous attitude. The sheriff would have to be shown that this was a new world, a progressive world which could reach into little Selma and frighten it with nonviolence.

Selma was on a list of cities.

The Vice President, Richard Nixon, had a capacity for enduring and executing ugly chores. He performed odious errands all over the globe for his President, and he managed to go and to do, without committing Eisenhower. Now he had a new one. A letter from Dr. Martin Luther King, Jr., had arrived on his desk on May 16, 1957. It reminded Nixon of the cordial meeting in Accra and the invitation to the White House. Nixon knew—as did Eisenhower and Sherman Adams—that failure to respond favorably would give the blacks an additional publicity weapon. It was up to the Vice President to find a way of conferring with the blacks, listening sympathetically, and promising nothing more than understanding.

When King received an invitation to meet Nixon in the White House, he called a council of Bayard Rustin and Ralph Abernathy to draw up a list of "requests" to place before the second man in the nation. The pastor did not want to attend his first White House conference unprepared. When the three men got to the "nitty-gritty," it was Rustin who drew up a list of six pertinent points:

Dr. King was to begin by reciting the daily injustices suffered by 11,000,000 Southern blacks who were now possessed of a firm resolve to do something to achieve equality with the whites. They intended to do this either with the help of Washington, which should implement the new laws, or without the help of Washington, by a series of nonviolent confrontations. This statement of policy was to be followed by six points:

1. Convey the idea that neither political party had done much to advance the cause of civil rights.

2. Make it clear that the South could not solve all its problems without positive federal action.

3. Impress upon the Vice President that the great majority of white Southerners were ready for change, but required federal urging.

4. Ask the Vice President to convey to President Eisenhower that the latter should take the civil rights issue to the nation as he had his struggle for the foreign aid bill.

5. Call on Nixon to do the following: Make a trip South and speak in moral terms for civil rights in general and voting rights in particular; urge Southerners, black and white, to obey the laws and uphold the Constitution; call together all Republican Representatives and Senators and impress on them the importance of passing the civil rights bill now in committee before the Congress.

6. Indicate to Vice President Nixon and Secretary of Labor James Mitchell that something beyond logic and mind was needed at this point.

On the afternoon of June 13, 1957, King and Abernathy stopped at the west gate of the White House, presented their identification at the sentry box, and were admitted for the first time to the majestic and serene beauty of the Executive Mansion. Both carried briefcases. An usher led them to Nixon's office. The Vice President shook hands heartily, and invited both men to sit. The Secretary of Labor was admitted, and the four men began a pleasant discussion. Mr. Nixon tried to keep the conversation on his recollections of Ghana and the racial calm of America, but Dr. King waited politely until the theme was exhausted, then proceeded with his "preamble" and his six points. Abernathy was silent most of the time, listening to the political fencing of two men. Labor Secretary Mitchell spoke only when he was addressed.

It would have been unacceptable if the Vice President declined all of the points, and he searched for one he could accept, perhaps "in principle." He found it in point five, which asked him to make a trip South urging black and white compliance with civic rights laws. Nixon, who enjoys one of the brightest political memories in the United States, knew that any tinkering with the power of the Southern white structure could induce the reaction of a rattlesnake. In 1948, Strom Thurmond had formed a States' Rights Democratic Party and had become its nominee, taking electoral college votes away from the major parties. Southern Congressmen and Senators were known to filibuster for weeks against legislation tending to liberalize the South. Mr. Nixon also knew that his boss, Dwight D. Eisenhower, was serving his second term as President and could not succeed himself. If Nixon aspired to the office— and he did—he would need all the votes north and south, east and west, he could muster. In addition, there was the stark fact that the 11,000,-000 Southern blacks had practically no vote, no power.

The suggestion to visit the South, Nixon said, was a sound one. It was worth consideration. However, he said to Dr. King, such a trip could not be made if it became public knowledge that he was being induced to make the trip by the black leaders. No, that would not do. It would require thinking to find a way of doing it in a "spontaneous manner." He was sure it could be done—but not at the present time, of course. Besides, every reporter in the West Wing knew that King and Abernathy were in the White House to promote civil rights. A certain amount of time would have to elapse, therefore, before the trip could be taken.

After two hours, King and Abernathy left. King was meditative. Abernathy thought that King had been too deferential to the Vice President. The president of the SCLC shrugged: "After all, he is the Vice President of the United States." Abernathy made a grimace. He was an earthy man, and he disdained the subtleties of circumlocution. The conference had borne no fruit; nothing had been promised, nothing could be expected. Nixon could announce that he had promised in Ghana to meet Martin Luther King in the White House; he had honored it. King, who had arrived with a list of requests, left with none honored. For public consumption, he would say that the meeting had been friendly, that the U.S. government was conscious of its responsibilities in the field of human rights and proposed to do something about it.

Back home, the pastor applied himself to another task. Black newspapers and magazines had been publishing a blizzard of editorials and articles comparing the forthright leadership of King with the slow legal

manner of Roy Wilkins. This was followed by stories that there was
personal enmity between Wilkins and King.

The leader of the NAACP ignored the stories. Dr. King was distressed by them. A press conference was called in Montgomery, and Dr.
King denied that there was anything but the closest of collaboration
between the two organizations. His respect for Wilkins was unbounded.
Besides, the SCLC was a "supplement" to the court-oriented action of
the NAACP. The statement, instead of restoring peace between the
organizations, began to polarize them. King flew to New York, posed for
pictures with Wilkins, and bought two $500 life memberships in the
NAACP—one for himself; one for the MIA. Wilkins turned on his
restrained smile for the cameras, but the two men knew that there were
other voices within their organizations sowing discord. The National
Urban League got into the dispute. Many, who watched King's star arc
higher in the political sky, demanded fresh and stronger goals for the
NAACP and the Urban League. One group left the Urban League,
called itself the Disturbed Committee of the Executive Secretaries
Council, and demanded a bolder approach to racial equity.

All this was embarrassing to Dr. King. He had begun a new Crusade
for Citizenship, a drive to register millions of Southern blacks as voters.
The SCLC could not do it alone; it had a small membership and little
money. Roy Wilkins had approved the crusade and promised to help
SCLC with Southern NAACP chapters and money. Without that NAACP
help, the Crusade for Citizenship could be consigned to the junk heap.
And Martin Luther King would have to find another cause and another
platform.

The worrisome, frustrating and hot summer was almost over when
Ranganath Diwakar, a Hindu disciple of Mohandas Gandhi, flew to
Montgomery for private talks with Dr. King. The bony ascetic face
studied the well-nourished one and discerned at once the weakness in
Martin Luther King's adherence to the Gandhian principles. He wasn't
suffering. He was living well; he had a house, a church, money in the
bank, an automobile, a television set, and rugs on the floor. The poor
suffered physical privation, but King rode the skies in splendor, accepting awards and degrees at black tie dinners.

A cool waterfall of British words fell from the lips of Diwakar. He
reminded King that Gandhi had suffered *personally*. Gandhi had engaged in long, self-imposed fasts which wracked his body and reduced
his frame to a drumlike skin on a skeleton of bones. The Mahatma had
actively sought to be jailed by the British. He deliberately broke his

body as an example to his followers, to prove that the mighty British lion could not break his spirit. To become a bigger man, King was going to have to become a smaller one, Ranganath Diwakar seemed to be saying.

Later King told his wife that he had to reevaluate his position. He said he now understood how "superficial and shallow" his knowledge of nonviolence was. His followers could be aroused to action only if their leader accepted personal punishment. The lesson about starving publicly was lost on King. He enjoyed food, as his figure attested. For him, food was designed for a greater joy than stilling the pangs of hunger. It was a pleasure unto itself, and he could not bring himself to fast as Gandhi had. Sooner or later, he was sure, Montgomery would open an opportunity for him to go to prison, and this time he would not be bailed out or pay a $500 fine.

As school opened late that summer, Congress passed the first civil rights bill since 1875. The Democratic and Republican leaders of both houses warned the Southern Congressmen and Senators that some measure would have to be placed on the books, and the Southerners warned that it had better be an idealistic and toothless measure, or they would filibuster against it all year. Had it been a just and proper act, it would have ordered United States marshals into the South to supervise the registration of blacks as voters. Instead, it created a Civil Rights Commission to *probe* voting irregularities—the South was not mentioned, nor were Negroes—and it "authorized," but did not order, the Department of Justice to send out federal court injunctions to Southern states where poll taxes had to be paid—some retroactively—and literacy tests asked such questions as "What is the capital of Madagascar?" and "Name the Fourth Amendment to the Constitution." Congress had not given the black man its hand in friendship; it had mailed him a fingernail paring.

The South remained peaceful. Blacks, through habit, moved toward the sidewalk curbs to make room for whites; the black man still entered a white house by the back door, hat in hand, giggling before anyone greeted him. He had played the witless "darky" so long that he could do nothing else. The Southern Christian Leadership Conference realized that it was fighting the acquiescent black as much as it was the arrogant white. Civil rights ministers, among them Dr. King, were possessed of a helpless feeling that they were braving new worlds in many cities and states but that once they departed, the wave of the past would wash away the progress.

The Reverend Dr. King arranged for twenty-one mass meetings in twenty-one Southern cities on the birthday of Abraham Lincoln, February 12, 1958. The SCLC did not warm to "Give us the ballot now," because it would require a decade of registration before the black vote would be able to tip the balance in Southern elections. The ministerial alliance was in favor of something with more immediate and dramatic results but couldn't say what that something was. King insisted that he would double the black vote in a year. Experienced people shook their heads over that assertion, knowing that white registrars could delay a line of black registrants with interminable questions, lunch breaks, coffee breaks, rigged telephone calls, patience-trying devices which would tire feet and weaken the will.

On the twelfth, King addressed a rally with the opening gun of what he hoped would be continuing pressure on the United States government to send marshals to the South to ensure more black registration.

"America must begin the struggle for democracy at home," he said. "The advocacy of free elections in Europe by American officials is hypocrisy when free elections are not held in great sections of America. To Negro Americans it is ironic to be governed, to be taxed, to be given orders, but to have no representation in a nation that would defend the right to vote abroad. . . .

"Let us make our intentions crystal clear. We must and we will be free. We want freedom now. We want the right to vote now. We do not want freedom fed to us in teaspoons over another hundred and fifty years. . . . Today, because the Negro cannot vote, Congress is dominated by Southern Senators and Representatives who are not elected in a fair or legal manner. . . . We Southerners, Negro and white, must no longer permit our heritage to be dishonored before the world. . . ."

Admirable sentiments, and fruitless. The black masses watching Dr. King, loving him and listening to words understood only that he was pointing to long rocky roads, and they had no heart for bleeding feet.

The militants understood. The educated understood. They were willing to brave the long wait at the county registrar's office for the right to cast a ballot, but the rich blacks and the poor blacks, for separate reasons, were not resolute. The rich quietly contributed to the SCLC, and the poor quietly listened to Dr. King; but the fervor was lacking. The drive for voting rights made small ripples in the political seas, and the white structure was irritated rather than alarmed. In some states, the white women registrars said, "How old are you?"

"Forty-two."

"If you haven't voted since you were twenty-one, you can vote now, but you will have to pay a poll tax of two dollars a year. The arrears come to forty-two dollars."

"What?"

"Sam, you can hear as plain as I can. You owe forty-two dollars. If you haven't got it, forget it." Hundreds who had waited all day forgot it. Behind Dr. King, a following wave of assistants was needed to help these people establish their rights. There was no wave, no counsel.

Far off, a man listening could hear the first rumblings of summer thunder. Here and there, a few policemen were attacked. Now and then, young black people rebelled and smashed store windows. Law enforcement officers were shooting black malefactors to kill. It wasn't more than a sporadic sound. A disturbing sound, a slight vibration under the feet. It was as though a well-run machine had misfired. Martin Luther King heard it. He visited Los Angeles in February and the black *Herald-Dispatch* did not genuflect in the presence: "This paper submits that Reverend King's philosophy reflects neither the long and stubborn struggle of Montgomery Negroes to end bus segregation nor the flaming heroism of Negro children braving hostile and jeering racist mobs."

In the Congress, Representative Charles Diggs shook his head in sorrow: "Rallies and speeches are fine for inspirational purposes, but—"

On Easter Sunday, King was back in Montgomery leading an orderly rally of 2,000 from his Dexter Avenue Church up the hill to the Capitol Building. There, within 15 feet of where Jefferson Davis had once proclaimed a new nation, a confederacy of Southern states, King protested the execution of Jeremiah Reeves for the rape of a white woman. The police and the Alabama state troopers stood around the perimeter of the Capitol, revolvers swinging losely at their hips. King led fifteen ministers in a public Service of Repentance. Reeves had died at the age of sixteen after exhausting court appeals for mercy.

In the early summer of 1958, the White House decided to teach Martin Luther King the art of the possible. It was time for a White House conference—his public "demands" irritated President Eisenhower because they left the press and the blacks with the impression that until now, the White House had not listened or tried to ameliorate race conflict. A. Philip Randolph, Roy Wilkins, Adam Powell, and others were old hands at accepting Presidential invitations from the White House. The Reverend Dr. King received his first one in June.

The conference was held in the big Oval Office, on a rug embossed with the seal of the President of the United States. King was ushered in by a Secret Service man. The President, pink and hearty, extended his hand and grinned. So did Dr. King. Neither felt comfortable: Eisenhower because he had been publicly dragooned into calling the conference; King because he had to share the stage with Randolph, Wilkins and Lester B. Granger, the executive director of the Urban League.

The President, in the middle of serving his second term, displayed increasing stubbornness to party dictates and, when asked what Richard Nixon had achieved as Vice President, told a startled press conference: "Give me a week and I'll think of something." This independence and tactlessness permeated the conference with the blacks.

The President sat the gentlemen on facing sofas and listened to Randolph read a nine-point proposal. Mr. Randolph said that copies of the plea would be left at the White House. Mr. Eisenhower sat with his hands clasped over a crossed knee. Granger, Wilkins, and King smiled as the points were enunciated. Eisenhower noted that each one was listed as a "proposal," not a "demand."

In brief, the black leaders asked that: (1) the President of the United States take a personal lead by making a public announcement that the civil rights law would be vigorously upheld and implemented by him; (2) Eisenhower also convoke a conference of white and black Southern leaders to find a way to bring the races together peaceably; (3) government information on problems of integregation be made available to both races in all communities; (4) Eisenhower request both parties in Congress to promote a civil rights bill with teeth in it; (5) the Department of Justice be ordered to give legal assistance in embattled communities; (6) the same department assist citizens to register and vote; (7) the FBI interest itself in the wave of bombing and "murderous brutality" directed against defenseless blacks; (8) the life of the Civil Rights Commission be extended for an additional year; and (9) Eisenhower make it clear that federal money would be withheld from Southern communities which encouraged segregation in housing, hospitals, and education.

The proposals were reasonable and lawful. When Randolph concluded reading them, the President unclasped his hands, shook his head sadly, and said: "There are so many problems—Lebanon, Algeria . . ." His words stopped. The black leaders knew at once that either the President did not comprehend the nine points or, more likely, did not want to honor them. He spoke vaguely about the complexities of race versus race, of the difficulty in changing men's hearts. His visitors knew now that they were going to leave the White House emptyhanded. He would not speak out on obeying the new civil rights law because he would not alienate the Southern white vote; nor would he command the Department of Justice and the FBI to move into the Southern states to enforce compliance. It was beyond his abilities to ask Congress to forgo party policy and unite to help the blacks.

The President posed congenially with the leaders for a White House photograph. They left crestfallen. At a meeting later in the day, King proposed that the blacks move ahead without the White House by staging student study-ins. Thurgood Marshall pointed out that it would hardly be considered brave to send young students to do the work of men. Later King wrote of the Eisenhower conference: "His conservatism was fixed and rigid. Any evil facing the nation had to be extracted bit by bit with a tweezer because the surgeon's knife was an instrument too radical to touch this best of all possible societies."

That summer Montgomery was hot and silent. King completed the final corrections on his book early, and his publishers told him that it would be in the bookstalls in September. He was asked if he would travel to stores for autograph parties, and Dr. King agreed. One more year was dragging toward autumn with no mission in sight. The city of Montgomery remained aloof from its blacks. The MIA was not much more than a listing in the telephone directory. Men of all hues sat waiting for something to happen. Nothing came from the White House; the lawyers of the NAACP took leisurely vacations because the courts across the land were in recess.

But summer was not over—and soon to explode into violence. On August 29, the Reverend Ralph Abernathy was sitting in his church office when, at dinner hour, an irate black, Edward Davis, charged into his office swinging a baseball bat. Mr. Davis accused the reverend of having "unnatural" sexual acts with Mrs. Davis, a communicant of the church. Davis shouted he was going to kill Abernathy with the bat.

The reverend ran out of his office, yelling to his secretary, "Get the police! This man is trying to kill me!" Abernathy made the street door ahead of his assailant and ran in darkness shouting for help. Davis ran behind him, swinging the bat. The police grabbed Davis and, at Abernathy's insistence, took him into custody.

A baseball bat and a pistol were found on Davis. Abernathy pressed charges, even though he must have realized that, regardless of the verdict, it would be his reputation that would be damaged—not Davis'—

and in spite of the fact that he knew that Mrs. Davis, when questioned, said she and he had had sexual relations.

The first hearing in the matter was held in recorder's court. The Kings and the Abernathys arrived together. A police guard held King and his wife outside the door. Dr. King said he had a right, as a citizen, to be admitted. The guard shoved him back. "May I speak to lawyer Fred Gray?" he said softly. "He's inside, and I think he can straighten this out."

The guard smiled. "Boy," he drawled, "if you don't get the hell out of here, *you'll* need a lawyer."

Another guard, standing behind the Kings, said, "Boy, you done it now—let's go." Coretta King was stunned as both men grabbed her husband, forcing his head down. His gray hat fell to the floor. In tears, she followed.

On the courthouse steps, one of the guards nodded at her. "You want to go too, gal?" he shouted. "Just nod your head."

Martin Luther King twisted in the arms of his captors and begged: "Don't say anything, darling. Go away." At police headquarters the two policemen shoved King past the desk, saying, "Book him for loitering," and took him to a cell full of blacks. They unlocked the door, said, "Everybody out," and pushed the minister in. He was slammed against a wall. The policeman behind King crooked his elbow around the pastor's throat; the one in front kicked him and tried to knee King in the groin. After roughing him up for several minutes, they left to alter the charge to "resisting an officer" and to report to the desk sergeant. In the street, the word was already passing among the blacks that Dr. King had again been arrested on a false charge, and streams of people were moving toward the Dexter Avenue Baptist Church. They knew that this time he would remain in jail, because he had promised he would never again pay a fine.

At 1:43 P.M. a disheveled Dr. King walked down the aisle of his church to the front, dark hands touching his. He had spent a total of ten minutes in jail. The errant policemen had returned, chastened, and said that the pastor was being released on his recognizance.

It was then that King learned that the Reverend Mr. Abernathy's assailant had been bound over to a grand jury. The all-white jury was to spend little time on what they considered to be a case involving two black men in a ghetto fight over a woman. However, when King's case came up in court, the reverend was found guilty of "resisting an officer" and fined $10, plus $4 in court costs. King refused to pay and was ready

HIGH NOON **209**

to serve fourteen days, but the fine was paid for him. Commissioner Sellers said that he would not permit King to use the city jail for a "publicity stunt."

"When I go to jail," Dr. King proclaimed to his followers, "the whole world knows about it. When you go to jail, no one knows about it. . . . We must go out and no longer be afraid of going to jail. I pledge that I will never pay a fine on any charge arising from our fight for freedom." At home, the Kings had a serious discussion. He said that he did not want to go to jail unless his wife agreed that he should, because he felt that she would suffer the most by being alone. No matter what her personal feelings or sacrifices, Coretta King felt that the most effective thing would be to go to prison and serve the time inflicted by the law—following the tradition of Gandhi. Suffering by the leader was important to the movement.

"If anybody had told me a couple of years ago, when I accepted the presidency of the MIA," he said earnestly, "that I would be in this position, I would have avoided it with all my strength. This is not the life I expected to lead. . . ."

The man who aspired to mold events was being molded. The leader was being led. He knew neither the road nor the obstacles; Martin Luther King was more an innocent than a sophisticate. Perhaps his most serious mistake was in thinking that black people, because they were black, were unified. His inability to understand the Northern blacks became obvious when he arrived in New York for an autographing party at Blumstein's department store in Harlem. His book had just been published, and on the night before the party, he drove through Harlem nodding and waving from the plush back seat of a limousine. Blacks pelted his car with eggs. He had no comprehension of what it meant to live on those filthy streets, crowded into a ghetto of 450,000. His lofty words induced no applause in Harlem; he was just one more black preacher from the South who told his race to lie down so that the white policemen could walk over them.

The following morning, September 20, 1958, King emerged from his car still smiling and waving. Black nationalists heckled him and booed. Shocked and puzzled, he went into Blumstein's for the autographing party. Inside, he sat alone at a desk, smiling at a line of women—mostly black—who held copies of his book. There was a kind word to say to each one as he signed his name with a flourish. One woman, however, ignored the line. She walked to the desk and said softly, "Are you Dr. King?"

He looked up from a book and grinned. "Yes, I am."

The expression on the woman's face changed swiftly. "You son of a bitch!" she screamed, and took a long Japanese letter opener from her purse. "Luther King," she shouted, "I've been after you for years!" The blade came down hard, tore through the white shirt and into his ribs until only the handle was sticking from his chest.

Martin Luther King sat quietly, knowing what danger there was in moving. The others, waiting in line, began to scream. His attacker ran for the front door but was stopped by employees. Another woman, shrieking hysterically, tried to pull the letter opener from Dr. King's chest. He turned pleading eyes on her, motioning her not to do it. A store employee slowly removed the woman's hand from the blade. Someone phoned Harlem Hospital for an ambulance. A black photographer snapped in a flash bulb and caught a shot of King with the letter opener buried deep in his chest.

At the hospital, Dr. Emil A. Naclerio and two other surgeons noted that the wound was deep and in a dangerous area of the chest. They did not touch the letter opener. The shirt and underwear were cut by surgical scissors around the weapon. King was conscious, but in shock. If this was to be the end of his life—and he must have weighed the possibility—he did not cringe from it. Breathing was difficult, but he obeyed the doctor's injunction to "take little ones."

Naclerio and his assistants were, in all likelihood, more frightened than Dr. King. They realized that since the point of the dagger had missed the heart, if he sneezed, it would mean sudden death. An operating room was prepared. The mere taking of X rays required caution. Naclerio examined the wet plates. His fear became fact. The point of the blade was leaning against the outer wall of the aorta, the huge vessel which carries blood from the heart to the rest of the body. A cough, a sudden movement, could kill the pastor.

The operation required three hours of delicate work. When the patient was anesthetized, Naclerio removed a rib section to give himself room. Next, he had to watch the pulsing of the aorta so that he could grasp the blade and begin to withdraw it as the aorta contracted. Nurses mopped perspiration from medical brows. The shiny tip came away easily and was carefully drawn from the chest. The little dent in the aorta was clear. King was examined for lung puncture. Under the diffusing beams of an overhead light, he was sutured and sent to a private room. He would live.

Police had taken the would-be assassin to Harlem headquarters. She had a small Italian revolver in her purse. Her name, she said with mustered dignity, was Mrs. Izola Curry. She was forty-two years of age and lived in New York. A captain asked her why she attacked Dr. King.

"People are torturing me," she said.

"But why King?" the captain said.

"Him? He's trying to convert me from being Roman Catholic." Under gentle coaxing, the woman rambled. Everybody knew, she said, that King was head of the NAACP. "Me, I'm opposed to integration." Photographers and newspaper reporters asked questions, but what Mrs. Curry had to say made no sense. The police captain notified a deputy chief inspector that the woman was definitely "deranged," and she was taken downtown for a hearing and possible commitment to an institution.

Coretta King was home in Montgomery, waiting to meet her husband's plane, when the phone rang. It was Dr. O. Clay Maxwell, pastor of Mount Olivet Church in Harlem. He said, "How are you, Mrs. King?"

"Fine, thank you," she answered and the terrifying carousel of thoughts began. Was he dead? Dying? Hurt? The voice on the phone took an eternity or two to respond. "Now, Mrs. King," it said, "I want you to prepare yourself. I have some bad news for you."

She was determined to be brave. Coretta King could hear her heart beat. "Dr. King was stabbed by a woman as he was autographing books, Mrs. King. I can tell you that he is alive, but it is serious, very serious."

Mrs. King hung up the phone and began to cry. Her brother was a house guest and did his best to comfort her. The airport was called, and Coretta King was booked on the first plane to New York. A few minutes later Abernathy telephoned to ask if what he had heard on the radio was true. He said he would join her on the trip to New York. The news flash brought people running to the house, and the ringing of the phone became insistent and unremitting.

The following morning Mrs. King and a group of relatives and friends arrived in New York and drove immediately to Harlem Hospital. Dr. Aubré D. Maynard, a native of Jamaica, explained the operation to Mrs. King. She remarked that the bizarre incident reminded her of Palm Sunday: "First they glorified him; then they crucified him." Mrs. King concealed her shock when she saw her husband with plastic intravenous tubes in his arms and nostrils. He was sedated, but he smiled and could speak a little. His first utterance was the thought of the true Christian:

"Coretta, this woman needs help. She is not responsible for the violence. Don't do anything to her; don't prosecute; get her healed."

In magistrate's court, Mrs. Izola Curry stood before Judge Vincent Rao. Newspaper reporters were present in numbers. "I understand," the judge said, "that this is the woman accused of stabbing the Reverend King with a knife."

"No," snapped Mrs. Curry, "it was a letter opener." Howard Jones, assistant district attorney, knew better than Mrs. Curry that the hearing was a short formality; it was not a trial or even an indictment. "I'm charging him as well as he's charging me," she said.

The magistrate looked up from the charge sheet. "What have you got against him?"

"I'm charging him with being mixed up with the Communists," she said. "I've reported the case to the FBI and it's being looked into—"

"This woman is ill," Rao said. It lay within his discretion to commit the woman to Bellevue Hospital for psychiatric examination, and this was done. Later Bellevue sent Mrs. Curry to Matteawan State Hospital for the Criminally Insane.

Ten days later Dr. King was well enough to leave the hospital. For him it had been a stunning trauma, a touch of the wings of death. His attitude had been courageous. Hundreds of blacks had stood outside Harlem Hospital day and night, behind police rails, singing hymns and praying for his recovery. Certainly many were the same people who had thrown eggs at him and jeered and heckled him. Beyond doubt, the attack won more sympathy in the North for Dr. King than his speeches and rhetoric. Both whites and blacks felt drawn to his cause because he had displayed courage and a capacity to suffer. He was indeed the black Gandhi. But it was Coretta King who would remind her husband that Gandhi was assassinated by one of his own people.

There are times, in the slow eastward spin of the earth, when a fiery comet in the dark skies appears to stand still. The reverse is also true; to the comet, the earth appears to be inert. The world was in a balance of good and evil as the year 1959 opened with sessions of the state and national legislative bodies, the crowing of Moscow over the superior feats of its astronautical sciences, a terse State of the Union message from Dwight D. Eisenhower, the emergence of the junior Senator from Massachusetts, a mop-haired realist-*cum*-idealist named John Fitzgerald Kennedy as a Democratic aspirant for the Presidency, and a climbing national crime rate. These were the heralds of dawn that year, and none of them represented a challenge to Martin Luther King, who remained a meteor in the limbo of the heavens.

The Dexter Avenue Baptist Church plucked at his conscience but not his enthusiasm. There was time, and time to spare, to work for his church, and there was time to sit at home with his wife and the baby; time to explore broader goals with Ralph Abernathy, Lawrence Reddick, and Bernard Lee. But the SCLC appeared to be indifferent, and the MIA was moribund.

He reminded his wife that they had received an invitation to visit India a year earlier, but since Chester Bowles had been unable to arrange a meeting with Pandit Nehru, the trip had been postponed. Perhaps this would be a good time. As always, the matter of expenses arose. King calculated that such a trip would come close to $6,000. He did not have enough money of his own, and he would not ask his father for it. The MIA, which had cheerfully permitted the leader to spend thousands of dollars on many trips, could no longer contribute. Quietly, Dr. King made phone calls to various organizations. All declined to help, on the grounds that the trip would serve no productive purpose. The American Society of Friends took an opposite stance; they would pay for the Kings to make the trip to India if the black community gave $500 as an evidence of endorsement.

The money was easily raised, and the little party left Montgomery in the first week of February. The preacher, who had studied more about Mohandas Gandhi than millions of Hindus, thought he might learn even more by walking in the Indian lawyer's bare footsteps. When the plane landed in New Delhi the press duly noted Dr. King's observation: "To other countries I may go as a tourist; to India I come as a pilgrim."

Prime Minister Nehru found time for an informal dinner with the Kings. The young man from Georgia was flattered to find that a chief of state was so well acquainted with his struggles for racial equality. Nehru spoke of his country's suffering and its determination to eradicate caste.

Gandhi had removed the British lion, claws and all, from the backs of 400,000,000 suffering subjects, but freedom from England left India starving alone. Sixty million untouchables were still not permitted to enter the pink, gaily designed temples. What freedom meant was a succession of laws enacted by the national Parliament and designed to help the helpless. Sadly, there was no implementation of the measures, and life in the great subcontinent consisted of too many people, too little food, too little education, too much patience in the face of disease and slow death.

The Kings placed a wreath of flowers on the ghat where Gandhi's emaciated body had been burned. The pastor made speeches at universities and before the Society of Friends; Coretta King, wrapped in a sari, sang spirituals for the natives. Dr. King's efforts to observe the progress which followed in the wake of Gandhi was a shocking experience. For the first time, he saw filthy beggars dying in village streets, children racing around the bodies playing games. He saw the well-fed pallbearers of India, the vultures, sitting high in trees in their shiny black cutaways.

Dr. King flew south to Madras and perspired under the slowly turning ceiling fans. He chatted with older men who had known Gandhi and who could tell him more about his spiritual mentor. In spite of the intense suffering he saw everywhere, pain, filth, and degradation which, in comparison, made the poorest Southern farm black seem affluent and secure, Martin Luther King felt elation. He told a friend that it was like having lunch with George Washington, tea with John Adams, supper with Thomas Jefferson, and a nighttime discussion with Tom Paine.

Martin Luther King refused to see that the revolution of Mohandas Gandhi had died with him. Hindus starved to death by the millions, and the central government fought over caste and sect seats in the Parliament. The Indian birthrate continued to grow and now equaled the population of Australia. Even the rajahs, whose vast holdings had been nationalized and redistributed by the democratic government, were given lucrative allowances in return for their land.

King could not or would not see that discrimination was a vast and tragic fact in India. At Trivandrum, on the edge of the Indian Ocean, the doctor addressed a big crowd. Gandhi, he said, had led the way to equality and freedom for all people. His way led to enduring justice and peace. "The choice is no longer between violence and nonviolence," he said, "but between nonviolence and nonexistence." A reporter later asked King what tangible gains had come of the Montgomery bus boycott. The doctor stated: "Our real victory is not so much the desegregation of the buses," he said, "as it is a new sense of dignity and destiny." He said that thirty-five Southern cities in the United States had abolished bus segregation since the Montgomery boycott.

If Dr. King was looking for something he might use in the struggle at home, he found it in the Mahatma's original army of peace volunteers. It was an army without weapons, an army which abhorred violence, but an army. The army was inbued with *Satyagraha*—soul force. The credo of such an army fitted with Dr. King's notions of massive protest, the peaceful appeal of thousands of suffering faces.

There had been, however, miscalculations in its use. The British arrested Gandhi in 1919, and while he sustained imprisonment in silence, his followers issued a call for *shanti sena* to demonstrate against the British oppressors with nonviolent marches. English soldiers attacked the peace army, which responded with a general strike and deadly ambushes against the British. The country was in a state of revolution when the viceroy decided to liberate Gandhi. At once, he denounced the lack of discipline of his followers and demanded an end to the national strike. The true leader of his people brought peace to the nation. "Victory is impossible," the bespectacled Hindu stated, "until we are able to keep our tempers under the gravest provocation." But tempers had been lost. And nonviolence had been superseded by violence.

If Pastor King proposed to emulate Gandhi in America, he must have known that he would first of all have to make himself undisputed leader of his people; he would require unity of purpose in his people; he could not afford "loss of temper" in the face of violent white reaction to his designs. Granted those necessities, he could make the presence of racial discrimination in the United States unbearable to the government and the citizenry. Without undisputed leadership, unity, and perpetual nonviolence, the dice of history would roll against him and he would be assessed as irresponsible and dangerous. He would be denounced as "a Communist."

When American crusaders of any political persuasion become powerful enough, the opposition begins asking, "Is he a Communist?" As the crusader and his crusade become even more powerful, the word is passed: "He *is* a Communist." As he was about to leave India, King thrust aside the narrow shielding cloak of the cleric for the broad and vulnerable one of the politician. Now the question was asked: "Is he a Communist?" Martin Luther King was not. There were radicals among his followers—at least one of whom had been a party Communist. The pastor was as aware of them as they were of him. Ironically, as this group worked on plans to use King to further their ends, he told close friends that he would bend the radicals to do his work.

A week after the Kings returned from India, a young black named Mack Parker was lynched by a white mob in Poplarville, Mississippi. All the demands for arrest and punishment of his murderers were reduced to a murmur in a few days. Malcolm X fired an oral cannon at Dr. King, damning him for advocating nonviolence in the face of violence from the "blue-eyed devils."

The dilemma of Dr. King was that he was a hero among liberal whites and conservative blacks, but he could not attract the activists of either race. He hurried north to appear on a television program, *Meet the Press.* Afterward Governor Nelson Rockefeller, of New York, dispatched his private plane to pick up Dr. King and fly him to Albany. Whatever was discussed was not revealed, but the publicity for both men was enormous. King was to be honored many times by "Whitey"; in the eyes of many blacks, this was his personal sin; this made his movement suspect. He dressed like "Whitey"; he talked like "Whitey"; he consorted with "Whitey." Maybe King was trying to be "Whitey."

The criticism was unjust, but Martin Luther King could not resist a private plane, an honorary degree, an award for Americanism. Intellectually, as Dr. Benjamin Mays had stated, he was old beyond his thirty years, but emotionally, he was the small-town youngster bedazzled by the bright lights. He saw himself, in an age of social unrest, as the only refuge for the white liberal. He was right. But "Whitey" was using him, as King thought he was using the radicals on his staff. He was moved to ask his white friends to state their unconditional commitment to the goals of the SCLC, but few of them did. They cheered him on, counseled him, heaped honors on him, and contributed to his coffers, but they would not risk being ostracized.

King would. And did.

It is possible that if a man finds that he has never done anything right, he might, with effort, learn to do something wrong right. The Smiler made valiant efforts, but the results, as befits a man of low intelligence and less knowledge, always seemed to end in low comedy. In the autumn of 1959, James Earl Ray planned another armed robbery. Had he studied his criminal record, practically all arrests and quick convictions, he might have felt like a despairing suicide who keeps trying to hang himself with a shoelace.

This time, it was a Kroger market at 3417 Ohio Street in St. Louis, Missouri. As always, when he required an accomplice, Ray chose a loser. James Owens was forty years of age and had been paroled after serving time for both burglary and larceny. He was a slow-witted man whose idea of disguise was to wear blue sunglasses. Ray told Owens that he had "cased" the Kroger store. Robbing it would be as easy as hitting the floor after falling out of bed.

The two men arrived at 8:45 A.M. with exposed revolvers. They walked into the store. The Smiler wore the small grin of confidence; Owens stood next to the checkout counter, waving the gun nervously. Ray confronted the manager, Donald Schaefer, in his office. Schaefer, a tall man and perhaps nearsighted, tried to shake hands with the gun. He thought that Ray was a pal from the Army.

"Get a paper bag. Fill it with money," James Earl Ray said.

Schaefer took another, and very detailed look, at the holdup man. There was $18,000 in cash in the store safe. "I need another key," he pleaded.

The Smiler began to feel nervous. "Get it," he said.

Schaefer tried the incredible. He summoned a clerk on the public address system. Ray shifted from one foot to the other. He kept looking over his shoulder toward the front of the store. James Owens was still there, waving the gun at customers and cashiers. The clerk was taking a long time getting to the manager's office. Schaefer had, in fact, summoned a clerk he knew was too busy to respond. Ray, however, was willing to compromise. If he could not make the "big lick," he was prepared to accept the little one.

He backed out of Schaefer's office and hurried to the front of the store. It was not yet 9 A.M., but there must be some cash in those registers. He pointed his gun at Hazel Meyer, checkout clerk. She opened the drawer, withdrew a fistful of bills, and pressed them into the Smiler's left hand. Robert Culis, who was waiting to be checked out with groceries, watched the Ray transaction and committed his features to memory. So did Miss Meyer.

"Hurry," said Owens. The two backed out of the store and jumped into a black Ford. As Ray stepped on the accelerator, Schaefer stepped boldly onto the sidewalk and jotted the license number: Missouri A 13-331. Customer Culis bravely hopped into his automobile and followed the Ford. A third car joined the chase. Apparently, James Earl Ray had been reading crime magazines. He turned the Ford into a side street, divided the $120 in his hand ($80 for himself; $40 for Owens), and ran over to a parked Plymouth. If Owens felt like whimpering over the prospect of facing twenty years in the penitentiary for $40, he did not get the opportunity to protest as he and Ray drove off in the Plymouth. By changing cars, the Smiler was certain that he was safe, even though he must have felt chagrined about the booty. The courageous Mr. Culis, however, was at the head of the street and jotted down the license of the stolen car: Missouri M-83-671.

Schaefer, standing on the sidewalk waiting for police, saw Culis return. The customer gave the manager the new license number. The police took down both numbers and issued an all points bulletin. Less than fifteen minutes after the robbery, Patrolman Ralph King cruised down Park Street and saw the Plymouth parked before a rooming house. The cop radioed for help. Detective Harry Connors arrived in an unmarked car in time to see Owens leave the rooming house and start the Plymouth. Connors pulled up alongside so that Owens could not move. He was arrested, and no one could blame him for thinking that the police were magicians.

Ray was in a back room when he heard heavy feet coming up the staircase. This was a familiar sound, which he interpreted properly. He emerged from his room at speed, turned to the back, looked off the sun porch, and saw a policeman below. Obviously, that was not the way to freedom. An old roomer stuck his head out to identify the commotion, and a cop at the head of the stairs yelled, "Freeze!" The old man didn't. In fright, he slammed the door. A shot splintered the paneling and, when the fracas was over, the old roomer left and was never seen again.

Detective Connors saw James Earl Ray come out of a hall bathroom. He yelled, "Hold it!" but Ray didn't. The thief ran back down a corridor, with Connors behind him. There was no escape, so Ray grabbed the detective around the waist and tried to hug him to death. Since Ray was skinny and Connors was stout, this turned out to be another impossibility. The cop pushed Ray away, but the convict lunged back for one more hug. Connors fired a shot into a wall, reversed his revolver, and brought the butt down on the Smiler's head. Ray staggered back into his room and sat.

His forehead was bleeding in rivulets down his face. "I guess you want me for the Kroger job," he said. Two policemen searched Ray and found a total of $81.63. "That's my share," he said. Two revolvers were found in the room. The police took Ray to the St. Louis City Hospital, where his head was stitched. At police headquarters, little prodding was required to get a confession from the prisoner. Ray's rationale appeared to be that his admission of a crime meant nothing because he was clever enough to escape from any prison. He spent some of the best years of his life planning to get out of jail, just as he spent a few of the finest moments of his life planning to get in.

Bail was $10,000. The prisoner did not have it, so he spent two months in jail. The prison physician, Dr. Dowd, is said to have treated Ray for a venereal disease, but Ray said it was a kidney strain. On the morning of the trial, Ray was still thinking of escape. He had been convicted three times of felonies, and the fourth one could mean a life sentence. An elderly deputy sheriff, Earl Riley, handcuffed Ray to his wrist. They marched from prison through tunnel to municipal building, up an elevator, out across the corridor to the court cages reserved for prisoners.

Riley bent over the lock on James Earl Ray's wrist, twisted the key, and was kicked in the stomach. He fell. Ray ran. The felon ran to the wrong elevator, one with two screen doors and two locks. Riley overtook his man and grappled. Ray ran down a corridor toward Officer Bright, who waited for him with gun drawn. Ray stopped. The old deputy sheriff wanted to kill him. The word of the attempted escape seeped through the building and reached the ears of John C. Casey, Jr., trial judge.

When the prisoner stood before the bar, he demanded counsel and a jury. Attorney Richard Schreiber became his lawyer and learned two things in two days: (1) His client insisted on conducting his own trial; (2) the prisoner said he would be his own best witness, even though Schreiber pointed out to him that once he took the witness stand, the door would be open for the prosecutor to ask details about Ray's criminal history. The judge called all parties into his chambers. There Ray spurned the advise of the lawyer and the judge. He repudiated his confession and claimed "the cops beat it out of me." When the parties returned to the presence of the jury, Casey admitted the confession as evidence. Ray conceded that he had nothing to repudiate it. His defense seemed to rest on what he called illegal entry. "I think my constitutional rights was violated," he said from the witness stand, "when they come in the house like that. They didn't know who they was after; everybody was shooting and grabbing me, and they didn't know if I was paying for a room or anything."

The police may have had a problem proving that the two revolvers had been found in Ray's room, but the prisoner gave them the evidence they needed. He said he had heard that Detective Connors had been offered a bribe to keep the two guns out of the case. "Now I deny the charge that anyone offered him money," the prisoner testified, "due to the fact I don't think any of my relatives has two hundred dollars. I know none of my friends has and I haven't."

The jury deliberated for twenty minutes. The verdict was guilty. Judge Casey ordered James Earl Ray to be confined in the state penitentiary for twenty years.

No year is a good year, if only because it adds its weight to preceding years. Nineteen fifty-nine was no exception. It was the year of riots for independence in the Belgian Congo, with disciplined black troops firing rifles into their people. It was the year that Virginia's Governor J. Lindsay Almond told the citizens that he was "helpless" to prevent desegregation.

The President was moved to send a special message to Congress on civil rights, citing seven points, among which was "support and encouragement of school integration." Fidel Castro responded to an invitation by making an eleven-day speaking tour of the United States and Canada, seeking aid for what he referred to as a "democratic Cuba." Little Rock transferred a few token blacks to a second school, and rioting broke out at the old Central High School. The Police and Fire Departments were able to control the disturbance.

The United States Civil Rights Commission asked President Eisenhower to appoint federal registrars in areas where blacks were finding it difficult to register. This had not been among the seven points the President had recommended. He had no intention of making it the eighth.

Another autumn had come to Montgomery. Chill winds whistled mockingly at preachments of love and nonviolence. It was a time for saving the souls of church communicants. For one who has savored the kind words of the world, a pulpit sermon is dull. The Southern Christian Leadership Conference had set up headquarters in Atlanta. Ella Baker, dark and attractive, worked out of that office. So did Bayard Rustin. Dr. Martin Luther King, Jr., all but commuted between Atlanta and Montgomery, and each time he returned to the provincialism of Montgomery with the conviction that he could no longer divide his time between big things and small things—the small ones would have to give way. There was no doubt that the SCLC promised a bigger role in life than the Dexter Avenue Baptist Church—not that King would deprecate church work; the fact was that he required a larger stage for his talent.

If there was a reason for not making the move at once, it was that he would again work part time in his father's Ebenezer Baptist Church. It would also mean that he would again face the fusillades of "Daddy's" pleas to give up this dangerous nonsense and get in the pulpit and stay there. If he moved to Atlanta, Dr. King would have to fight his father's brand of love with his own stubborn unyielding variety. Martin was glad that, at last, A.D. and "Daddy" had patched up their mutual rancor. A.D. now served as assistant pastor at Ebenezer.

Mrs. King stated that she was reluctant to make the move, but this may have been in deference to the generous Montgomery churchgoers. The pastor was not as gentle. On Sunday, November 29, he stood before the Dexter Avenue congregation and announced that he was "unprepared to preach" and would turn the matter over to an assistant pastor. After the sermon, the people remained in the pews, awaiting King's benediction. He stepped up to the pulpit and asked everyone to remain seated for a moment. A letter had been received, he said, from his father's church in Atlanta, offering him a co-pastorship. He had responded formally by stating that he would give the offer "my most prayerful and serious consideration."

The people out front watched the serious chubby face, and they knew what was coming. He said that in four years in their behalf, he had done the work of six men. He recalled the dangerous and dramatic days of the Montgomery bus boycott. After an agony of soul-searching, he found that he had no choice but to combat injustice on a broad scale.

There was a real danger, he said, of "losing my creative resources." There was an additional peril of "becoming a physical and psychological wreck." He continued solemnly, "I cannot stop now. History has thrust something upon me which I cannot turn away. I should free you now." There was a clear analytical question of who was being freed, but the people felt affection as well as admiration for Dr. King, and they wept. He asked them to sing, and they sang with pale furrows of tears staggering down dark cheeks. Their love was intact. When the last singing note died, Dr. King said, "I would like to submit my resignation as pastor of the Dexter Avenue Baptist Church, to become effective on the fourth Sunday of January, 1960."

A woman with a deep contralto voice began to sing "Blest Be the Tie That Binds," and the congregation followed her. King, ready to turn and leave the pulpit, broke down. He, too, cried.

The New Year arrived and, with it came new hope, broader goals. Nineteen hundred sixty could, in the opinion of the Reverend Dr. King, be an outstanding one because both the Democratic and Republican parties would have summer national conventions, and this would give him an opportunity to bargain with each and place the increased black voter registration squarely behind the party offering the blacks the most.

However, the black vote, if it had importance, would be in the Northern factory towns, where many blacks were already registered. In the South, the white vote would still dominate, and the eleven states would swing their electoral college weight this way or that, depending on which party, which nominee, favored placating the traditional South. Neither party was prepared to join the struggle for racial equality except in principle. There was also the hard practical question of whether Dr. King or anyone else could encourage the blacks to vote as a mass for one candidate.

Still, King believed that he, as the new leader of his people, could move political mountains. His was optimistic as he flew back and forth between Montgomery and Atlanta. On one of the afternoon flights to Atlanta, he struck up a vigorous and friendly conversation with a white man. Both exchanged views on race and were in agreement. The white man asked Dr. King if he could stop at the restaurant in the Atlanta Airport and continue the conversation. The pastor said yes. At the restaurant, a woman with an armful of menus smiled at the white man and said, "Follow me, please." To Dr. King, she said, "I can seat you behind the curtain over there." The white stranger was astonished. Dr. King was furious, although he must have known this would happen in segregated Georgia. Perhaps he had simply forgotten. He was very used, by now, to being the guest of honor at "mixed" banquets.

"We want to have dinner together," the white man said.

The woman remained cool. "He knows," she said, pointing to King, "that the food behind the curtain is the same, the tableware is the same. Nothing is different—even the view out the window is the same."

"I won't do it," Dr. King said. "I won't go back there." He said good-bye to his newfound friend and left, a black man in the segregated South.

The same evening Ezell Blair was reading a black "comic book" which explained racial inequities. A black freshman at the Agricultural and Technical College of North Carolina, in Greensboro, he was concerned and militant about segregation. He showed the book to his roommate and said they should do something. They decided to go to the local bus terminal restaurant and sit at the same counter as the whites. They got nowhere. The word from management was blunt: "We don't serve Negroes." They left, conferred in their room, and said, "Let's have a boycott."

The next day the two young men and two of their friends sat at the lunch counter of a local Woolworth five-and-ten-cent store. They arrived at 10 A.M. The man behind the counter said that they would not be served. Unlike Dr. King, who left in anger, they sat in peace. No one called the police. No one tried to remove them bodily. They sat until 12:30 P.M. and departed. The next day they were back at the same place. And the next. By the fourth day they had been joined by white students from the Woman's College of the University of North Carolina, who occupied counter stools and refused to order food unless the blacks were also served.

A news reporter heard about it and referred to it as a sit-in. The story was read in Durham, North Carolina. Students from the black North Carolina College joined with whites from Duke University and started a sit-in at a local restaurant. It spread to Winston-Salem, with blacks from Teachers College and whites from Wake Forest joining. Within two weeks after Blair and his roommate started the peaceable sitting, many Southern lunch counter owners protested the black action by closing down. The sit-ins had spread to colleges in Virginia, Tennessee, South Carolina, and Florida.

The Kings were moving into a rented house near the Ebenezer Baptist Church. They read about the sporadic sit-ins, but the students had no leadership; the movement was spontaneous. King had an ambivalent feeling about college students: they would work feverishly for several days and then collapse in apathy. The police and the press kept this movement alive. The police arrested forty-one students at Shaw University and St. Augustine College. The photographs in the newspapers of blacks hauled off by the scruff of their necks aroused more black and white students.

At Florida A & M College in Tallahassee, the local police barely waited for blacks to sit. They were arrested at once. Within forty days the sit-ins had spread to ten states. Only in Houston and San Antonio did the authorities confer with restaurateurs before sit-ins began. In both cities, eating places were desegregated at once. In the North, where Woolworth stores had been desegregated years earlier, blacks picketed the stores because of segregation at their Southern stores.

Dr. King marveled that the students managed to keep the movement in motion. He sat in his office, near the rear of the church, reading about it and wondering if the SCLC should give it direction and assistance. The students were achieving something with his spirit of nonviolence. They could be a powerful force for good. He would call Ralph Abernathy and ask him to move to Atlanta. He'd talk to Ella Baker, the attractive woman who was the beating heart of the SCLC. If the student demonstrations could be encouraged to spread. . . . If they would pledge to be non-violent. . . . If they required assistance from such as Bayard Rustin and Ella Baker and Bernard Lee—people of purpose and enthusiasm. . . . If. . . . If. . . .

Two tall deputy sheriffs walked in. They had a paper. It called for the arrest of one Martin Luther King, Jr., at the request of the State of Alabama. An indictment had been handed down by the Montgomery County grand jury on two counts of perjury against Dr. King. He had willfully lied, the indictment stated, in filing his 1956 and 1958 income tax returns. Dr. King called his father. "I have no pretense to absolute goodness," he told the deputies, "but if I have one virtue—just one—it's honesty."

His father arrived, sputtering and frowning at the deputies. They said that they had nothing to do with the order. They were sheriffs from Georgia complying with a request from Alabama. They would have to take King into custody. "But who," the doctor said, as he was led outside, "who will believe me?" His father arranged for an immediate hearing before Fulton Superior Court Judge Jeptha Tanksley, who saw it as a small case and set bail at $2,000. When King returned home, he told his wife: "You know I don't have the money to fight such a charge in the courts." There was another aspect: Such a trial would encompass the use of a white jury. A white jury can be an obstacle to a black looking for justice, but an Alabama white jury can be insurmountable. The case had more emotional aspects than legal.

One friend said, "It's the country's duty to see that you are properly defended." King said that many people would believe he had stolen money from the MIA or the SCLC because they wanted to believe such things. Later his wife reported: ". . . he agonized to the point that he even experienced a feeling of guilt." King had a speaking engagement in Chicago, and he canceled it. Then he thought better of it and re-scheduled the speech. He was greeted with a standing ovation.

The people opposed to him, King felt, were politically motivated. He visited Dr. Ralph Bunche at the United Nations, even though none of his associates could understand what Bunche could do about a state trial in Alabama. "Look, Martin," Dr. Bunche said calmly, "it's the word of the State of Alabama against the word of Martin Luther King. There is no question in my mind which the country will accept."

Fred Gray, who had helped in the legal problems at Montgomery, was

King's attorney of record for this trial. But an array of volunteer legal talent also attended: Arthur Shores, Orzell Billingsley, Peter Hall, Chauncey Eskridge, Robert Ming, and Judge Herbert Delaney. King's friend and disciple Bayard Rustin organized a Committee to Defend Martin Luther King. None of this gave the doctor what he needed most—peace of mind. He fretted over a finding of guilty and the prospect of serving time in jail for this kind of offense.

Alabama charged that, in 1956, King claimed his total income was $9,150 when it was $16,162; in 1958, he accounted for $25,248, although Alabama computed that year's income at $45,421. It seems hardly possibly that Dr. King at any time tried to enrich himself from his public works. Often he received $1,000, sometimes $1,500, for making a speech and, when he got home, tossed it into the funds of the Movement. He was a creature of comfort and enjoyed traveling first class in every respect. He enjoyed good clothes and the services of a secretary and, whenever possible, a personal staff. But his habit with cash was to take what he needed and deposit back in the fund a large part of his earnings, and he managed to be careless about both.

At the first hearing in Montgomery Courthouse, the prosecution stated that the 1958 tax had been disputed before and, rather than fight the charge, Dr. King had made out his personal check for the disputed amount. King's lawyers asked why, then, was 1958 a part of the bill of particulars? The state replied smugly that it had never cashed Dr. King's check, that King was aware of it by consulting the balance in his bank account, and that his reparations did not alter the charges.

The defendant was released on bail and ordered to return for trial in May, 1960. King's adversary was an old and respected antagonist, Montgomery solicitor William Thetford.

If Atlanta, the hub of the South, had a cherished friend, it was the well-fed black. The black money hierarchy wanted no demonstrations, no protests, nobody rocking the boat. Some blacks called them Black Brahmins. They owned the Citizen Trust Bank; the black press; black politics; black insurance companies. They, like Martin Luther King, Jr., grew up "on the hill." They overlooked the black ghetto like benevolent wardens. Their power was so great that, in 1959, when young militants of Albany, Georgia, decided to desegregate their town with sit-ins, they first sent a committee to Atlanta to consult with the Brahmins. They were told, in effect:

"You see, kids, we've been in this a long time. We want the same things you do, but we know by now they can't be gotten overnight. It's our experience that you have to work slowly to get lasting results. We'd hate to see your movement backfire and spoil things we've worked so hard for. You need guidance, and we hope you'll have the vision to accept it."

The young people went home discouraged. What did "overnight" mean? How long was "overnight" for the fat black cats of Atlanta? No one knew. Everyone knew that they had power; they could apply pressure, unseen and crushing. "Overnight?" Even Martin Luther King, Jr., was not about to foul his father's nest with protest marches and boycotts. He was refused service at the airport restaurant, and he accepted the rebuff. He was willing to fight in any other city, but not Atlanta.

There were others, cast in limbo somewhere between the Brahmins and the poor, who thought that Atlanta should not be spared the public spotlight. There were 4,000 black students in Spelman College and Morehouse. There were white students in other colleges who wanted to help. They read about sit-ins all over the South. Roslyn Pope, Julian Bond, Lonnie King, and Professor Sam Williams of Morehouse drew up a manifesto of freedom and equality. They plotted the Atlanta sit-ins as they had once plotted debates. No one was hurt. Few were offended. Everything in Atlanta was gentlemanly. They asked the great Dr. Martin Luther King, Jr., to support them, but he declined. He felt that the SCLC, which had its headquarters in Atlanta, was vulnerable to counterattack.

In the same week, King went to Montgomery to participate at a sit-in rally at Alabama State College. The governor of the state had expelled ten students. Fifteen hundred students attended the rally. Ralph Abernathy introduced Dr. King. The pastor was enthused about the Montgomery sit-ins; he said that they should be continued, bearing in mind always that the important aspect was "nonviolence." The students were young, impressionable and impressed. It did not occur to them to organize, and it did not occur to Dr. King to suggest that they seek a name for their movement and elect officers.

The sit-ins, disparate and spontaneous, continued to spread. Almost all the Southern towns fought the new nonviolent aggression, but Orangeburg, South Carolina, decided to fight fire with gasoline. The Reverend Matthew McCollum brought the militant students of Claflin College and South Carolina State together. He stressed two points to the young people. Point one: Walk in separate small groups by different routes to the stores chosen for sit-ins. That way the police could not arrest them for staging a public demonstration. Clock the exact time required by each group to reach the store so that all would arrive at the same time. Point two: Anyone who felt that he might strike back if "kicked, slapped or spat upon" was to leave the group. Nonviolence meant nonviolence.

Two big sit-ins were staged. The first, on February 25, 1960, was over before the police had been alerted to it. At the second, on March 15, the police and firemen were waiting. It was a cold clear day in Orangeburg, and about 750 students were involved. On command, the police tossed tear gas bombs, and students began to shout, writhe, and run. The firemen turned on their heavy-duty hoses, and the cold stream spun students against walls, knocked many to the sidewalk, and caused scores to fall to their knees weeping. Violence won over nonviolence. Drenched students shivered in the cold as they were herded into groups by policemen with clubs. Five hundred were apprehended. One hundred and fifty were booked on charges and tossed into cells. A solitary wry laugh sounded through the city jail when a bruised, trembling student assumed a high-pitched "down-home" tone and asked, "You sure Martin Luther King started like this?" The SCLC was doing nothing about the sit-ins or advising the students in any way until Dr. King found the Reverend Wyatt Tee Walker. He was not, and would not be, the closest man to Dr. King. That place was reserved for the Reverend Ralph Abernathy. But the out-spoken Walker was an efficiency expert. He was hired as executive director of the SCLC, and overnight the organization came alive and was a factor in the racial struggle.

Walker made enemies at once, but the criticism within the organization was muted: "Walker's throwing Dr. King's weight around." It was the only weight Walker had. The edifice of the SCLC was being built around King; without his leadership, it would be an aggregation of Southern amen preachers. The Reverend Mr. Walker was a thin man with an abrasive ability to say no whether it was the opportune time or not. He quickly became the buffer between King and the world. He accepted the blame for whatever went wrong with the SCLC and gave the credit to King for whatever it accomplished. He worked earnestly with Fred Shuttlesworth, James Lawson, James Bevel, and Andrew Young.

The SCLC soon became a taut and efficient organization. Paid workers and volunteers were expected to do a day's work. Coffee breaks, desk chats, and excuses were discouraged. An invitation arrived from Malcolm X for Dr. King to address a Black Muslim educational rally in a New York City armory. Dr. King knew that the Muslims would hoot him down; he knew that Malcolm knew it. And yet he worried about a polite way to decline. Wyatt Tee Walker's office staff found it. They did to Malcolm what Eisenhower had done to King: "His schedule will not permit an appearance in New York in June. Sorry. . . ."

The SCLC sent invitations to sit-in leaders of ten Southern states to attend an organizational rally on April 15 at Shaw University in Raleigh, North Carolina. Ella Baker took charge of the project. There was a degree of delicacy involved, because the SCLC had neither originated nor supported the sit-ins and Dr. King now hoped to organize the students. The Reverend James Lawson, who had led some of the sit-ins, was also affiliated with the Southern Christian Leadership Conference. He became the bridge between King and the students. Ella Baker, who had graduated from Shaw University, asked for the use of a meeting room from Good Friday until Easter Sunday. About 200 student leaders accepted the invitation; 147 actually attended.

It was decided, for the sake of peace, that Martin Luther King *and* James Lawson would be keynote speakers. King spoke first. The students listened with respect. They knew that this was the man who had fought so valiantly in Montgomery for bus desegregation. They honored him for it. But the Movement had spread far beyond the supine Christian ethic of "tired feet." They had expected a monumental man; what they saw was a rotund man of boyish enthusiasm.

He suggested "some type of continuing organization," as well as a "nationwide campaign of selective buying," which, in effect, would boycott stores which did not cooperate; third, he asked for "volunteers who will willingly go to jail rather than pay bail or fines." He asked them to take the freedom struggle into every city, town, and hamlet in the South, a large order indeed. Last, he begged the students to "delve deeply into the philosophy of nonviolence." He spoke too of reconciliation with the white man. "Our ultimate end must be the creation of the beloved community."

The applause was ringing and respectful. Those who had already braved police clubs and fire hoses fell silent. The "beloved community" seemed to be a long way off. Some no longer wanted it, even if the white man offered it. The young had scores to settle with him; it was high-flown philosophy indeed that conceived of a "reconciliation" with the man they had been fighting. And if they were not expected to fight further and more stubbornly, then what were they doing at this meeting?

Lawson, more militant than King, but yet a man committed to nonviolence, leaned his hands on the podium and opened with an attack on the hypocrisy of the white power structure and the black middle class. He recalled his experiences as a missionary in India and could expound the

strengths and the weaknesses of nonviolence. Politics, to his way of thinking, was the transmission of power, and power was what the Movement
needed. One of the most rebellious of the students began to listen. He
was Stokely Carmichael, a native of Trinidad, British West Indies, and a
student at Howard University. Carmichael had told his friends many
times what his attitude toward the white man was: "I never take the
approach that we've got to teach them to love us. I have thought that's
nonsense right from the start."

The three-day series of meetings closed with no action. Dr. King was
trying desperately to adopt the sit-in students; he wanted to make them an
integral part of the SCLC. He could not see that the students were
divorced from his philosophy. And yet, in their intellectual poverty, they
were willing to use his words: "We affirm the philosophical or religious
ideal of nonviolence as the foundation of our purpose, the presupposi-
tion of our faith and the manner of our action. Nonviolence, as it grows
from Judaic-Christian tradition, seeks a social order of justice permeated
by love. Integration of human endeavor represents the first step toward
such a society. . . ."

Dr. King was pleased. He promised support from the SCLC. The
students closed the Sunday meeting with an old hymn sung spontane-
ously to the rhythmic clapping of hands: "We shall overcome. . . ."

At a later meeting the students called themselves the Student Nonviolent Coordinating Committee, a topheavy title which was reduced to
SNCC. It was natural and predictable that the students would ask King to
be a SNCC adviser and that he would accept. It was equally predictable
that, as the young people became more organized and felt their growing
strength, that they would move to the left of the SCLC, split away from
it and Dr. King, and eventually renounce the ethic of love and reconciliation for something called Black Power.

The guards on the towers around Jefferson City Penitentiary had an
excellent view of the ant trap below. The insects, each clad in green
denim with a black stripe on the trousers, used their exercise period to
gather in groups. Some tossed a ball back and forth; others walked, hands
in pockets against the chill breeze curling down inside the walls; some sat
at checkerboards with kibitzers around the perimeter; the so-called shit-
house lawyers argued legal precedents for new trials, appeals and the
filing of briefs. One man walked alone.

James Earl Ray led an uncomplicated life. When he was free, he was
plotting one "big lick," the sum result of which always got him back in

prison. When he was in prison, he spent practically all his time plotting to get out. Jefferson City Prison was a hard place to do time. The prisoners had their own hierarchy, and these men were respected and courted by the prison keepers. There was traffic in narcotics and homosexuality and the cruder forms of sadism. Among 2,000 jailbirds, there were only eight attempts to break out each year, and these, with rare exceptions, were failures.

Ray was a loner because he wanted to be alone and because he hated the fact the other prisoners referred to him as a hillbilly. He spent his spare time lifting weights and reading spy stories. The prison librarian has a record of 400 suspense stories lent to the Smiler. He may have read them for entertainment, but more probably he devoured them for an idea—a workable idea—for getting on the other side of those grim walls.

He did odd jobs for money and saved every penny of it. If a prisoner was broke and needed a few dollars, he could contact the loner, but the interest rates were high. Also, if Ray did not get the money back on time, he hounded his man, never fighting for it, always whining, begging, demanding what was "rightfully" his. After the first year, the word around the prison was that James Earl Ray had plenty of money. He had slyly set up an underground pipeline to get it out of jail and to get it back in. Some thought that he was trafficking in drugs, but this is doubtful.

Except in his cell block, Ray was unknown. Once, the warden refreshed his memory and said: "Penny ante. Innocuous. He couldn't join the team." James Earl Ray, still assessing himself as clever and sly, examined everything including the laundry chutes to find a way out. He made little scratch notes of where the guards on the walls stood and what angle of vision they had. Convicts who were in his debt called him a tightwad, a penny pincher. It may have been Ray's virtue that he was never known to do something for nothing.

Lillian Smith, a hospital worker, was being driven to work at Emory University by Martin Luther King. The month was May; the farmland of De Kalb County was loamy; dogwood lifted brightly colored faces to the sun. A policeman flagged the car down. King knew he hadn't been speeding. He presented his license and registration to the officer. "How long you been back in Atlanta?" he was asked. A little over three months, King replied. "You a permanent resident in Georgia now?" The doctor nodded. "How come you still have Alabama plates on this car?" Dr. King said he hadn't got around to changing them. He was under arrest.

It was a violation which could have happened to any careless car owner. But whether the arrest was politically motivated or not, Dr. King posted bond. He was tried later and found guilty. Judge Oscar Mitchell imposed a fine of $25 and placed King on probation for one year. The fine was paid at once, and Dr. King left De Kalb County forgetting one thing—probation. He was thinking of something far more serious, the trial on two counts of income tax evasion.

"Daddy" King said that he would be at Martin's side at the trial. So too would Coretta King and Dr. Ralph Abernathy. Others wanted to make a show of solidarity, but King didn't want it. There was bound to be an all-white jury, and they would surely find him guilty, he felt, because the black could not get justice at the hands of the whites. There would be no point in further alienating the jury, the judge, and the prosecutor by filling the court with blacks.

On May 6, 1960, the office personnel at the SCLC cheered when the radio announced that President Eisenhower had signed a civil rights bill. Dr. King did not cheer. The document was proclaimed as a milestone in human progress—the second such bill to be signed since the Civil War—but King and his staff knew better. The only muscle built into it was a paragraph stating that the Department of Justice *could* take action on behalf of any person denied the right to register as a voter, provided that the voter proved "a pattern or practice" of discrimination. It would be a difficult, almost impossible thing to prove. Nor was there any part of the bill which made it mandatory for the Department of Justice to take action against Southern white registrars. Three months earlier, Southern legislators had filibustered against the civil rights bill until it had been diluted sufficiently to make it palatable. Besides, they wanted Title II kept in the bill. This provided federal prison sentences for persons crossing state lines "to foment violence." Title II was aimed at Martin Luther King and all other black leaders who might cross state lines to help the Movement.

Instead of broadening civil rights, the bill narrowed them. Dr. King publicly counseled patience, but a black backlash began to hurt him. *Student Voice,* a black news sheet, sounded a warning note: "There is a time for all things. A time for thought, a time for speculation, a time for investigation, but most assuredly this is not a time for straddling the fence. The American Negro is engaged in a gigantic life-or-death struggle with the foes of human decency. Is it possible that some of us occupying positions of leadership are trying to stay the hand of fate?"

On Monday, May 23, 1960, Dr. King and his family swept into the Montgomery court. He counted himself lost. The right or wrong of the matter was not at issue; the City of Montgomery had an excellent chance of finding Martin Luther King guilty of something which would put him in jail for a long time. It did not take long to seat a jury of twelve men, all white. They were busy watching the judge and stealing quick side glances at King, who sat at his counsel table. As always, he was impeccably dressed, the dark silk suit shining, the corners of a white kerchief showing in the breast pocket, shoes gleaming. He was smiling, and his hands were clasped on the table.

It was a lawyer's fight all the way. Fred Gray and his array of assistant counsels contended that the figures presented by the prosecution as Dr. King's true income were exaggerated. Auditor after auditor was questioned about how he arrived at total income for 1956 (the trial involved the first count only), and the defense attorneys tried to prove that certain sums had been added which truly should have been subtracted— for example, those occasions when Dr. King traveled and paid his own plane fare, his own car rental, his hotel bills and food. These had been added to totals as income, and it was manifest carelessness on the part of state tax auditors.

Day followed day. Witness followed witness. The star witness, state tax agent Lloyd Hale, did well under direct examination by the prosecutor. However, when the defense got him, one of the first questions asked was "what evidence of fraud did you find in Dr. King's tax return for 1956?" The court was stunned to hear the witness mumble: "No evidence of fraud." The defense attorney asked the witness if it was not true that after the matter first came up, that Hale had told Dr. King personally that he saw no fraud at all in the tax returns. Hale said yes. He also admitted an error in computing the tax for 1956.

By Saturday the trial was over. Evidence was of small consequence. Dr. King's mood sank as both sides summed up. His lawyer told the jury that the State of Alabama had erred by contending that a taxpayer's income is the total of all the bank deposits he might make in any one year. The judge charged the jury. It was out almost four hours. Dr. King was in a silent funk.

The jury came in, and the defendant stood. The white foreman said, "Not guilty." Dr. King stood straight; he could hear his wife sobbing behind him. A white jury had broken tradition—defense attorney Delaney burst into tears. The judge dismissed the defendant, and the prosecution decided to drop the other indictment. The Kings returned to Atlanta reminding each other that "something happened to that jury.

Something really happened." This time God had spoken from Montgomery.

Summer arrived early in Atlanta and stayed late. The SCLC was involved in a mammoth drive to register black voters. It did not go well in spite of exhortations from Dr. King, Wyatt Tee Walker, and Ralph Abernathy. This was a year of national elections. A strong and unified black vote would draw attention to civil rights. The small number of willing registrants in Mississippi and Alabama was harassed, but the other Southern states were reluctantly signing blacks to full citizenship. The blacks were apathetic. Even in Atlanta, which proclaimed itself "too busy to hate," the King volunteers failed. Church ministers refused to mention it in Sunday sermons. Blacks in ghettos saw no honor in being appointed precinct captains to drive neighbors to polling places.

Nor was Dr. King doing well with SNCC. The more militant students were passing the word from campus to campus that King and his nonviolence betrayed the organization. A few said that he was a person who bubbled with enthusiasm and then went home to forget SNCC. Others said he had had "his day," as though Montgomery were in the dusty files of history. Others said that they had got the word from Atlanta that Dr. King couldn't stand the domination of his old man and that was why he didn't want any strong men around him. If SNCC achieved anything, they warned, it would be Dr. King who would bask in the spotlight.

The bushy-haired, bespectacled Bayard Rustin was thinking politics. When King had gone to the White House to meet Nixon, Rustin had drawn up the unanswered proposals. Now the Democrats and Republicans would be holding their national conventions, and Rustin wanted King to ask for hearings before each platform committee and to make the following demands:

1. Both parties should repudiate segregationists within their own ranks and make a forthright declaration that any form of discrimination is unconstitutional, un-American and immoral.
2. Both parties should endorse the spirit and tactics of the sit-ins as having the same validity as labor strikes.
3. In accordance with the Fourteenth Amendment of the Constitution, congressional representation must and should be reduced in areas where Negroes are denied the right to vote.
4. Both parties should explicitly endorse the 1954 Supreme Court decision as morally right and the law of the land.

Rustin and King must have known that the proposals were foredoomed. It amounted to a forthright rejection of support from the entire tier of

Southern states. Politically and realistically, each proposal was more punitive than the preceding one. The rule of Congressional representation by population blocs could not be altered in one area without changing all areas. Rustin had a subtle point in the fourth demand because politicians North and South had remained silent when the order to desegregate had been handed down by the Warren Court. And yet the response of most public figures to this proposal was: "It *is* the law of the land, and everyone knows it. Compliance is another matter."

This time, it seemed that Rustin was bereft of workable ideas. For example, his final proposal—that both political parties take a clear moral stand against colonialism and racism in all its forms, especially in Africa—was at best impractical.

Although he was rarely seen, Rustin was the strongest and most effective follower to have Dr. King's ear. He was a radical accustomed to the charge of being a Communist or a Socialist. At all times, Rustin placed the cause, the Movement, ahead of his personal ambitions. In the summer of 1960, when he wrote his proposals for the conventions, he asked Dr. King not to discuss the points with Chester Bowles before they had a chance to talk together. No reason was given, but he began to act like a man who felt that powerful forces had singled him out for liquidation.

Adam Clayton Powell was opposed to Rustin and seemed ready to support the SCLC if the doctor would dump his aide. Congressman Powell, the most powerful black officeholder in the country, had all but convinced King that Rustin was dangerous. The doctor mentioned the Powell conversations to Rustin and said he would stand by him no matter whose support it cost. "You can't do that, Martin," said Rustin. He seemed agitated, and his spectacles were halfway down his nose. "I won't let you do it. The Movement has got to take priority over personal considerations. I'll resign; there's no alternative." Dr. King begged him to reconsider, but in begging he betrayed the truth that the resignation would be accepted. The close, confidential affiliation of the two men, with Rustin as the idea man and King the voice, was about to be strangled because of an ultimatum based on inference.

Bayard Rustin resigned. King accepted. James Baldwin wrote in *Harper's Magazine*: "He [King] lost much moral credit . . . especially in the eyes of the young when he allowed Adam Clayton Powell to force Rustin's resignation. . . . King was faced with the choice of defending his organizer, who was also his friend, or agreeing with Powell; he chose the latter course." For the moment, the slick, sophisticated Congressman and the naïve Georgia boy were political allies. Ironically, one of the few discernible things they had in common was Jesus Christ. Both were church pastors.

Powell, King, and Randolph staged a loud civil rights rally in Los Angeles in July, as the Democratic Party was convening in the same city. Dr. King invited all the leading candidates to address the blacks. They miscalculated. The leaders could not or would not risk taking a stand on civil rights. John F. Kennedy was busy corraling votes until 4 P.M. of the evening on which balloting would begin. Lyndon Johnson of Texas had a bloc of Southern votes and the endorsement of almost all the Democratic Senate and House. Stuart Symington, one-time Secretary of the Air Force and protégé of former President Harry Truman, had a scattering of votes which could decide the nomination if thrown in a block to one of the leaders. Hubert Humphrey of Minnesota was hoping that Kennedy and Johnson would fight each other to the death and the convention would then select him as a compromise candidate. To espouse civil rights or to oppose it would lose, not gain, votes.

Powell, King, and Randolph waited for the "next President of the United States" to come to the rally hat in hand for black endorsement. Lyndon Johnson sent Oscar L. Chapman to speak for him, and Chapman was cautious and friendly. Eleanor Roosevelt sent a telegram asking support for Adlai Stevenson, the 1956 nominee. Symington spoke for himself, without cracking any political eggs; Humphrey surprised everybody by taking the dais and shouting that he would rather be right about civil rights than be President. The word was sent to Senator Kennedy's headquarters that Symington and Humphrey had spoken.

Kennedy found time. He arrived, right hand in jacket pocket, thumb out, beaming the smile which made him famous. As he walked toward stage center, the blacks booed. It was rude, but the young man from Massachusetts maintained the smile and held both hands up. The presiding officer of the rally, Clarence Mitchell, pounded the lectern for quiet. He got it. Kennedy spoke seriously but generally about civil rights, being careful not to say anything explosive which might make headlines in the morning papers. When he finished, instead of boos, applause rang through the hall.

Many had spoken, but few had said anything. The standing ovation was reserved for Powell, when he told the audience, "Our demands for civil rights are a revolution—a revolution of passive, massive resistance." Martin King followed and said, "We have a determination to be free in this day and age. This is an idea whose day has come. We want to be free everywhere"—he waved both arms over his head—"free at last, free at last."

The rally was far from a milestone in civil rights. The only people who spoke plainly and fervently for civil rights were blacks. The rally failed also as a publicity device. It swayed no votes in the big smoky convention. John F. Kennedy was nominated on the first ballot. He owed nothing to blacks and was prepared to give them nothing until it was politically advantageous.

Kennedy was leaving the ballroom when Dr. King met him near an exit and shook hands. For a moment, two doomed men smiled at each other. King said, jokingly, "You know, we need a civil rights bill for the disadvantaged. A real civil rights bill. A sort of second emancipation proclamation."

Kennedy nodded, as he permitted an aide to take him by the elbow. "Maybe you're right," he said. "Maybe you're right."

Bernard Lee had aligned himself not only with the SCLC, but also with SNCC. In common with other King apostles, young Lee felt that King was losing control of the Movement—"things are happening right here in Atlanta and he isn't in them." The local SNCC group planned two sit-ins, and Lee thought that Dr. King should be asked to participate. He arranged a meeting at the pastor's home. A.D. was present. So were Fred Bennett and Lonnie King.

Softly, patiently, Bernard Lee explained that the date had been set and the group referred to it as D Day. They were going to hit Rich's department store and Walgreen's drugstore on Cain and Peachtree. Lee said he had enough "troops" for both stores, but they thought that the presence of Dr. King—right here in his home city—would make it an important sit-in. The pastor looked at A.D. Both had the same father and the same problem. The iron old man had tried to keep his boys out of trouble and in the pulpit. A.D. was rebellious and did as he pleased. Martin tried to convince his father that he was not making trouble for the white man, or looking for it. He had even adopted his nonviolence theories from the teachings of Jesus Christ, as well as Gandhi.

A.D. was going to be in Walgreen's on D Day. The newspapers would say that Martin Luther King's brother was at the sit-in, but where would Martin the leader, Martin the martyr, be? Dr. King nodded. He would attend the sit-in. He would go to Rich's store and carry a sign, just like everyone else. The young people were happy. Dr. King remarked it was unfortunate that Rich's had been picked, because Dick Rich, a white man, had done as much as anyone in Atlanta for the black man. He even contributed large sums of money to black colleges.

Lee shook his head negatively. True, Rich did help the blacks in many ways. All the more reason why his store should be picked for a sit-in. Rich still adhered to the old ways: A black couldn't get a drink of water in his big store. A black could get killed trying to go into the Magnolia Room to ask for a sandwich. When a black woman tried a hat on in Rich's, the clerks put a tissue lining in the hat. When black men or women sat to buy shoes, they had to wear "footlets" before putting anything on their feet. If, Lee said, all of this is humiliating to the black man, then Rich isn't the friend he pretends to be. Money isn't everything. So it was Rich's. And Walgreen's.

D Day arrived. Dr. King was driven to Rich's store, grinned at the young pickets and sit-ins, waved to one and all, and slipped a sandwich sign over his head and shoulders. It read: MAKE DEMOCRACY WORK IN OUR COMMUNITY. Behind him strode the Reverend Samuel Williams, president of the Atlanta NAACP, who wore a sign reading: IF YOU CAN'T WORK HERE WHY TRADE HERE? SNCC's, boys and girls, hurried through the "In" door to the store. Some sat at the lunch counter. Others went into the Magnolia Room and sat reading menus and giggling.

King shed the sign and walked in behind them. He too sat in the Magnolia Room. Someone phoned for the police. White women customers looked horrified and hurried for the "Out" door. King looked up and saw Dick Rich, sitting at a corner table in the restaurant, his eyes brimming with tears. "Why me?" he said, but no one responded. Police arrived in squad cars within minutes. The word was phoned to the sit-ins at Walgreen's. Bernard Lee led his "troops" to Rich's store in time to see Dr. King being led to a squad car by Sergeant Little. A few moments later Lee was arrested. Scores of sit-ins were dragged from the store. All were booked on a charge of violating the City of Atlanta's segregation ordinance.

Atlanta was not Montgomery. The metropolis did not intend to help the Movement with publicity. It held the students and Dr. King for a few days and released them on their recognizance for future trial. The trial was postponed to death. "Daddy" King was scandalized. He felt that Martin and A.D. were going too far. They had been born and brought up in this city; further, "Daddy" King was a respected figure among whites and blacks, and he could not afford to have revolutionaries in the family.

Martin, as a peace gesture, agreed to meet Dick Rich at a lawyer's office. He brought Bernard Lee with him. Nothing was accomplished, except that King was embarrassed when Rich began to cry. The merchant said he had tried to be generous with blacks. The pastor nodded but pointed out that the store was still segregated. Rich's lawyer said that the store was segregated, as King very well knew, because it was the law of the city—it was not Rich's law. Bernard Lee shrugged the situation off. Talking with the white man was like talking through a wall of glass; both sides could see skin color but could hear nothing.

Mayor William Hartsfield proposed a sixty-day truce so that the case for desegregation could be fairly reviewed, but both sides understood that this was a palliative which, after sixty days, would have to be renewed. If not, no one, not even Martin Luther King, Jr., could stop the SNCC members from staging more demonstrations, any one of which could cause an accidental death or a public abuse resulting in race riots.

Dr. King had a lapse of memory about his own situation in relation to the law. On October 20, 1960, De Kalb County asked Fulton County to apprehend King for violation of the twelve months' probation imposed by De Kalb in the vehicular registration arrest. De Kalb County maintained that he had been released, after paying a fine, on condition that he remain out of "trouble" for the next year. Since he had just been arrested by Fulton County for demonstrating at Rich's store, he was in violation of the probation.

Donald Hollowell, attorney for King, worked for five days to prevent the transfer, but he lost. Two detectives, one with a cigarette in his face, the other smoking a cigar, handcuffed Dr. King and led him away. Judge Oscar Mitchell, who had been relatively lenient with Dr. King in the summer hearing, was now severe. Hollowell tried to convince the judge that one could hardly say that there had been a violation of probation unless the prisoner was tried in Atlanta and found guilty. King had been picked up by police in a department store in a neighboring county. Anyone, including his honor, might be apprehended on a false charge. Hollowell's client was merely charged with violating an ordinance. Suppose he was found not guilty?

Mitchell said that he would "construe" Dr. King's behavior in Atlanta as "trespassing," and as this was a violation of law, he was now adjudged guilty of violating his probationary period. The sentence was pronounced abruptly: ". . . to serve a term of four months at hard labor in Reidsville State Prison," the prisoner to be taken thereto by the sheriff's office in the morning. Hollowell rushed back to Atlanta to prepare and file an appeal for a stay of sentence. King certainly had no intention of serving four months at hard labor for a vehicular registration violation, if legal talent could free him.

The lawyer was back at the De Kalb County Courthouse with his appeal at 7:30 A.M. The sheriff's deputies were grinning. "Sorry," they said. "Your nigger was taken to Reidsville early." Hollowell passed the word to King's family and friends; the SCLC called the press to raise a hue and cry against Georgia justice. Some papers stated that the deputies, driving over the red clay roads to Reidsville, could, if they chose, set up an ambush for Dr. King and pretend that they could not protect him. Others complained of the treatment which would be accorded to Dr. King behind the great penitentiary walls. Hollowell realized that the legalities were not insurmountable—the vehicular charge and the trespassing charge were both misdemeanors—but he was too worried about his client's life. He appeared before Mitchell and announced that he was appealing the sentence and reminded the judge that bail could be set. Should Judge Mitchell be so vindictive as to deny bail, a confrere of Hollowell's was prepared to file an appeal before the State Supreme Court. Before a decision could be reached, the news was humming on wires all over the country. Telegrams reached the White House begging President Eisenhower to intervene. The Chief Executive, of course, had no jurisdiction in a local violation of law. He could not free King or request that he be freed unless he was willing to sustain an inundation of such requests from the kin of offenders all over the United States.

Unofficially, John F. Kennedy, Democratic nominee, phoned Georgia authorities and asked that Martin Luther King, Jr., be released. This too was fruitless. His office at the time was that of junior Senator from the State of Massachusetts, and he had no power in Georgia except the prestige of being the Democratic nominee for President. Kennedy also phoned Coretta King to tell her of his concern.

Within two hours, King's imprisonment became a political ploy. Eisenhower's Vice President, Richard Nixon, was the Republican nominee to succeed him, and some of the White House thought that it would help Nixon if he did something or said something. Aides drew up a statement: "It seems to be fundamentally unjust that a man who has peacefully attempted to establish his right to equal treatment, free from racial discrimination, should be imprisoned on an unrelated charge, in itself insignificant. Accordingly, I have asked the Attorney General to take proper steps to join with Dr. Martin Luther King in an appropriate application for his release."

The statement was read aloud by phone to the Nixon camp, which was busy campaigning. The word came back from the Nixon camp to the White House that such a statement might do more electoral harm than good; it could alienate the white South and, even though the Republican Party did not expect much assistance from the South in the election, it would be better to permit the idealistic Kennedy camp to rush to the rescue of King. Richard Nixon, when asked about the detention of Dr. King, had nothing to say.

The second move by the Kennedy group occurred when Robert F. Kennedy, the nominee's younger brother, phoned Judge Mitchell to ask why bail was not permitted in the King case.

Mitchell was too shocked for words. Young Kennedy had no official standing at all, did not hold elective office, and, by phoning, was trying to influence a judge in the execution of his duties. However, Mitchell had a good comprehension of law as it applied to his court, and he knew that this case would allow bail. After one day in jail, Martin Luther King, Jr., was freed on bond. The moment Hollowell won his point, on October 27, he brought in four small planes full of reporters and photographers from Atlanta to Reidsville. A press conference was held by Dr. King at the gates of the prison. As King and Hollowell boarded one of the little planes, the apprehensions of the blacks began to show when the engine sputtered, smoked, and died. People standing by shouted, "Sabotage!" A black inmate of the jail yelled, "Long live the King!" After a second attempt, the engine started, and the plane rolled off the short runway and into the sky.

Some of the credit for getting King out belonged to Hollowell, but he got none. The press and the King family gave it solely to John F. Kennedy who certainly had more to lose in alienating the South than Nixon. On Sunday, "Daddy" King stood up in his pulpit and told his black congregation, "It took courage to call my daughter-in-law at a time like this. Kennedy has the moral courage to stand up for what he knows is right." The elder King knew that his congregation was Republican; he also knew that most Protestant groups distrusted any Roman Catholic running for high office. But because one Kennedy brother had phoned Coretta King and the other Judge Mitchell, "Daddy" King, in an emotional bath, proclaimed, "I've got a suitcase full of votes and I'm going to take them to Mr. Kennedy and dump them in his lap." The congregation roared approval. His son, however, refused to endorse Kennedy's aspirations. "There are moments when the politically expedient is the morally wise," he said.

In Atlanta, Mayor Hartsfield ordered the charges of trespassing filed against fifty-one persons, including King, be dropped at once. This was done in municipal court. If there were no charges against King in Atlanta, then De Kalb County had no case. That too was quietly nol-prossed. Roy Wilkins said, "I understand that everybody but the lawyers got Martin King out of jail." There would be no phone calls from the Kennedys to the Kings for two years.

Black leaders watched the Presidential campaign move down to its final days and were prepared, in the event that John F. Kennedy won, to claim that the black vote had tipped the scales. However, Kennedy and Nixon had appeared in a series of television debates, and these were the determinant.

On the other hand, the publicity attendant on Kennedy's phone call to Mrs. King alienated many white votes in the North, as well as the South. Fear of the black race caused many to vote, not for Nixon, but against Kennedy. And there was the Roman Catholic issue as well. The result was such a close contest that it was not until 3 A.M. New York time that Kennedy, sitting with his family at Hyannis Port, Massachusetts, claimed the election. He won by 112,881 votes, a plurality so small that the victory was a disappointment.

Martin Luther King, Jr., and other black leaders claimed that the black vote had made Kennedy President. The President-elect did not acknowledge this and refused to comment on it. In fact, he did not thank Dr. King or his father for their support. Only Vice President-elect Lyndon Baines Johnson sat to write a gracious note to the Kings. "I want to let you know," he wrote, "how much I particularly appreciate having had your support."

The Nobel Committee decided that no one deserved the Peace Prize for the year 1960.

IV. THE WANING LIGHT

5

IN THE EARLY DAYS OF 1961, Dexter Scott was born to Coretta and Martin King, and James Earl Ray's mother died of cirrhosis. The events were not related, and this may be said of the rising tide of black belligerence. The young people were better educated than their parents, and their horizons were broader. To them, whatever was worth having was worth fighting for, and it was here that those who would do battle and those who would resort to rhetoric and persuasion lost each other. Wisdom, which can be attributed to Roy Wilkins, Martin Luther King, and black publishers, was opposed by SNCC and other fragmented groups of young people who wanted everything at once. The young also husbanded an inbred suspicion of their elders and put their trust in each other and such militant leaders as they could find.

A student of such matters would search a long time before finding a more unlikely place for racial unrest than Albany, Georgia. It was the fifth largest city in the state, but that gave it no status. Albany consisted of 38,000 whites and 18,000 blacks, all living directly or indirectly off the peanut which grew in southwest Georgia. It was a city of quiet streets and predictable habits; it was Spanish moss hanging from elms on the edge of a pretty lake. The soil was as black and spongy as devil's food cake. A society of sorts had matured in Albany; it consisted of rich whites who sold hogs or nuts or ran banks and granaries and who knew one another on sight or glancing over the top of a cocktail glass. There was a second echelon, municipal servants—state representatives, city commissioners, police officers, and tax collectors. The third were rednecks who worked the menial jobs, hauling garbage, driving trucks, feeding animals and fowl, most of whom aspired, by obedience and subservience, to escalate to the second echelon.

There was a separate society, as apart from the first as one magnetic pole is from the other. These were the 150 rich blacks, powerful under the same rules as the whites. There were 1,200 blacks on the second branch of the social tree, and they owned filling stations and small farms and had a little money in the bank. The rest, possibly 16,000, were poor blacks who were often called "niggers" by rich blacks. All these either worked for the white man in the fields or on the streets in town or were labeled "shiftless."

All explosives require a detonating cap, and the role fell to James Gray, editor of the Albany *Herald*. Gray lived in a city where news of progress in the outside world was often distasteful. His paper published news calculated to enhance white supremacy, and he used stories about blacks which made them appear to be inferior and ignorant. The Albany *Herald* was so sure of its position that it reacted like a rattlesnake to any talk of equal rights for blacks. No black was going to be allowed to talk "uppity" while Gray and the *Herald* were in business.

The Reverend Benjamin Gay, pastor of Bethel AME Church, was a most unlikely person to hit the detonator with a hammer. He and his fellow black ministers had read about progress in racial relations in outside publications, and they thought that the white man in Albany should be gentled forward. They met and devised a polite note addressed to James Gray asking him to stop printing stories which hurt the black race. Editor Gray could not believe that the scum of conflict had at last reached Albany. The races had lived in peace for a hundred years. The editor and the white power structure behind him were old believers in the truism that if you surrender an inch to the black man, he will ask for a yard.

Gray published an editorial in which he counseled the ministers to tend to their flocks, mind their business, and remain outside the affairs of the *Herald*. The white clergymen, who also saved souls from sin in the name of Jesus Christ, were silent. They knew better than to buck the local newspaper, assuming that they had a desire to stand beside the black lambs. A few nights later a car moved slowly past the home of Pastor Benjamin Gay, which was subject to a rain of rocks. The homes of two other black signers of the letter were stoned.

The police did not pretend even to try to identify the rock throwers. No one made a presentment to the grand jury to investigate the matter. No one reproved editor Gray for being a firebrand. A black letter sent to Mayor Asa D. Kelley asking him to appoint a biracial committee to discuss and correct grievances was filed without a response. The Criterion Club, the epitome of black society in Albany, ignored the complaining ministers. The local chapter of the NAACP pretended that nothing happened. The professors at the local black college, Albany State, would not permit a discussion by students of the actions of the militant ministers or the white editor. Albany State was endowed by rich blacks who believed that a third-rate curriculum was better than no curriculum, and the faculty was employed to isolate the students from intemperate aspirations. The garbage dump and the cemetery between the college and the main street of Albany were literally and figuratively obstacles, and anyone who tried to bridge them could die in either one. The teachers taught that a successful life consisted of a good car, a roof, and meat in a refrigerator. In church, the students at Albany State heard the round bell tones of "Amen!" and learned that Jesus was watching their every move and making up His mind what kind of hereafter they deserved. The "here" could be pretty palatable for a student who behaved and knew his place; the "hereafter" could be an eternity of unlimited joy.

The young scholars, caught between the cautious teaching of their peers and the racial struggle burgeoning in the outside world, joined the NAACP's Youth Council. Two weeks after the stoning of the homes of the ministers, the young people wrote a letter to the city commissioners demanding that public facilities be desegregated at once, to conform with the law of the nation. The commissioners did not answer the demand, but they knew that the letter was an unprecedented step, something so reprehensible that, if unchecked, would lead to greater demands. Gray responded publicly in his paper. He advised the commissioners to reject the demands. Quietly, steadily, the White Establishment moved into action.

Two bold moves had been made to start "trouble" in Albany in one month. They required strong, steady punitive action. Black cooks and maids were fired if, on questioning, they did not denounce the ministers and the students. Store janitors, drivers of dump trucks were laid off, and whites were employed to replace them. The benign benevolence of the community toward black cultural projects and charities stopped. Blacks in automobiles were stopped by policemen and hauled off to the city jail. The "Colored Town" area of Albany was effectively sealed off at night by patrol cars. The attitude of the older generation to the young blacks was: "Now see what you've done." Red-necks pointed to old trees on the main streets and reminded blacks that "niggers" had once swung from those branches.

A few of the affluent blacks tried to make peace by reminding the white politicians that very few blacks had ever registered to vote, and those few were "housebroken." The whites did not want peace; they wanted the supine, shuffling, giggling black men of their youth. Two brothers named King (Chevene and Slater), in concert with Dr. William G. Anderson, and Mrs. Irene Wright, decided to write another letter. This one would ask outside black assistance. The letter did not go to Dr. Martin Luther King, Jr. It was addressed to SNCC. In response, two field workers, Cordell Reagan and Charles Sherrod, both in their early twenties, made the journey to Albany to assess the situation. Both had experience with sit-ins, and they decided that the first thing Albany ought to do would be to open a voter education center. Later, massive outside assistance could be requested, and black Albany would force the whites to accept them. Sherrod and Reagan said that it would require time, and time was all Albany could afford.

In the same state, up Route 75, Dr. King was pursuing an unrelated action. He had been cordially received by prime ministers and presidents, and he was sure that more could be accomplished by going directly "to the top" than by shivering in a picket line. Kennedy was now his man, and Dr. King offered public reminders that without black support, Kennedy wouldn't be sitting in the White House. In addition, King asked the President to enlarge his Cabinet and appoint a "Secretary of Integration." To this there was no more response than that the ministers of Albany received after sending their letter to the editor.

Second, he called for a "Marshall Plan for America." No echoes ricocheted under the dome of the Capitol. If his proposals were not acceptable, his speeches became less so. King began to needle President Kennedy. "The President has proposed a ten-year plan to put a man on the moon," he said. "We do not yet have a plan to put a Negro in the state legislature of Alabama." He denounced Kennedy for "critical indecisiveness." And went on to say, "The administration too often retreats from a battlefield which it has proclaimed a field of honor." Scorn and contempt crept into the words. "It is a melancholy fact that the administration is aggressively driving only toward the limited goal of token integration." He went one step further to mock Kennedy's cry for a New Frontier: ". . . the New Frontier is unfortunately not new enough; and the Frontier is set too close to the rear." If Dr. King's hope was that he would be invited to the White House for a meeting or if he expected a government appointment in the field of race relations, his speeches would certainly not help him. Kennedy would discuss race relations with Roy Wilkins, with Adam Clayton Powell, with A. Philip Randolph, but not with Dr. King.

While the pastor kept his sights high, aimed at the source of power, the Congress of Racial Equality, SNCC, and the SCLC held a meeting in April, 1961, a communal discussion by dissident elements of the Movement regarding sit-ins. Belatedly, CORE and the SCLC realized that the youthful SNCC had become an organization that accomplished things. The students had taken the headlines from the older organizations, had forced many stores to desegregate lunch counters and other facilities through boycott and harassment, and CORE proposed to "mobilize" the students. This is translated as "control." The SCLC directors felt that a promise of financial support and moral support in "the field" would win the cooperation of SNCC.

It did. The blending of the three organizations was bound to be an asset for all. The SCLC and CORE would supply the money, the lawyers, the direction; SNCC would supply the personnel and the courage. The students said that the program could go further than sit-ins; they would tour the South in buses, calling them Freedom Rides. This too seemed to be a stroke of genius because it would be nonviolent, and because the young people had the courage and stamina to brave rocks and beatings in the cities where they would travel to assert the full rights of the black under the law.

To show solidarity, the three organizations appointed Dr. Martin Luther King chairman of the Freedom Ride Coordinating Committee. However, CORE took the lead without conferring with Dr. King. At the start, the closest King came to participation was the arrest of his men, Ralph Abernathy and Wyatt Tee Walker. The actual leader and director of the Freedom Rides was James Farmer, director of CORE. He laid out a map of cities to be visited by the Freedom Riders and sent a copy of the map to the President with a timetable of arrivals and departures. It was hoped that Mr. Kennedy would order his brother Attorney General Robert F. Kennedy to send federal marshals to each city for the purpose of restraining local police from violence, but either the President did not fully comprehend the situation, or he decided to sit on the sidelines and see what happened. The President brought the matter up at his "bangboard hour,"* an informal discussion group of intimates held in the Oval Room between 6 and 7 P.M. every evening when he was at home. At these meetings, the President invited open criticism from such men as Lawrence O'Brien, Kenneth O'Donnell, Robert Kennedy, Pierre Salinger, and David Powers.

They could discuss any or all topical subjects. They could tell the President his course was wrong or right; they could counsel, suggest, analyze, and, when the hour was done, President Kennedy made his decision and expected his friends to work toward that goal whether they subscribed to it or not. In the sphere of racial unrest, the policy was "hands off." Kennedy was enjoying a short honeymoon with his Congress, and he did not want to incur the displeasure of the Southern wing of his party. No matter what his personal feelings were, his political attitude was sound: If he lost the Southern wing of the legislative bodies, he would not only lose whatever slim chance he had for a civil rights bill, but he would risk the loss of a large part of the New Frontier goals in other quarters. In the larger scope of politics, the President's reasoning was understandable; however, he was placing himself and his administration in the rear guard of the fight for racial equality with too little help too late. He proposed to extend federal assistance only when it was obvious that violence had been committed.

Two buses—a Trailways and a Greyhound—left Washington on May 4 with the first Freedom Riders. White and black volunteers, numbering no more than a dozen, started on a trip through Virginia, North and South Carolina, Georgia, Alabama, and Mississippi. At each stop, the groups got off the buses, ignored the "For Colored Only" signs on the rest rooms, and desegregated the lunch counters. The advance publicity had been plentiful. Southern municipal authorities knew when to expect the buses and what to do about the mixed couples. Whites tried black toilets; blacks tried white ones. In some cities, they were greeted with sullen silence; at lunch counters, service was so slow that no one was served before the bus was ready to leave. In other places, small groups of whites waited to hoot the "nigger lovers."

The riders knew that the chances of violence would increase as the buses throbbed into the Deep South. Alabama and Mississippi would be the worst. They were surprised when the bus stopped at Rock Hill,

* In October, 1963, President Kennedy invited the author to write a book about him—a dual portrait as a chief executive and a family man—to be called *A Day in the Life of President Kennedy.* At that time the writer became acquainted with the "bangboard hour."

South Carolina, and they saw a group of white hoodlums waiting for them to get off. Policemen stood behind the hoodlums. The riders got off, and the hoodlums grabbed black John Lewis as he walked toward a "White" waiting room and beat him to the ground. Albert Bigelow, a white retired U.S. Navy commander, was the next to feel the wrath of the crowd. He was punched and kicked. A white girl, Genevieve Hughes, next off the bus, was pushed to the ground. The police then stopped the violence.

The two buses moved onward through South Carolina and Georgia. They crossed the state line into Alabama north of a town called Abernathy and westward along Route 78 to Anniston, Alabama. The buses were about fifteen minutes apart, the occupants singing, reading, chatting, studying farmland rolling past the bus windows. Outside Anniston, a group of white men blocked the road. The first bus stopped. Men with two-by-four pine boards stepped forward and knocked the windows out of the bus roaring vile epithets. A fire bomb was tossed inside, and everyone, including the driver, ran for the exits. The bus tires were punctured; the riders were beaten.

The second bus, owned by Trailways, moved past the scene of carnage without stopping. Freedom Riders inside looked back, stunned at the flames and flogging. White men with movie cameras made clips of the "action" for television. Later, police squads arrived and brusquely dispersed the mob. The news reached Atlanta. Pastor Fred Shuttlesworth of the SCLC sent automobiles to take the Freedom Riders to Birmingham. Their bus had been burned out.

The Trailways bus, momentarily safe from attack, turned north into Anniston. There trouble waited. Eight hoodlums boarded the bus, armed with sticks and tire irons, and beat all the Freedom Riders, white and black. They ordered the driver to start at once for Birmingham. By this time private cars with reporters and photographers flanked the bus. Some drove ahead; others followed. At Birmingham, another white mob was waiting. The eight hoodlums snickered and ordered "everybody out." Black James Person and white James Peck were the first off. Person was hustled into an alley by part of the mob, some of whom yelled "Now you're gonna git it, nigger!" He got it. Peck was beaten by six men who called him "nigger lover." Again, the local police were too late to prevent mayhem. Person's dark face was lopsided when he was found, and he could not talk through it. Peck's face and head required fifty-three stitches.

Both bus drivers quit. Trailways and Greyhound stated that they could sustain no more loss of equipment and that none of their drivers would be permitted to man the buses. Nobody wanted to go on to the next stop, Montgomery. The beaten, the frightened were stranded in Birmingham. They hurried to the airport in time to catch a plane for New Orleans and were threatened by a white mob at the ticket counter. The day was May 14, and Martin Luther King was on a lecture tour. That evening he saw the carnage on television and heard a report that a second Freedom Ride of young militants was preparing to leave Nashville, Tennessee, for Montgomery, Alabama. King knew better than most what these young people could expect there.

He phoned Washington, trying to get federal assistance, but he was told "We are keeping abreast of the matter." He could not contact the President or the Attorney General. The Kennedys kept "abreast" by sending a young editor, John Seigenthaler, on one of the Freedom Rides to watch for the White House. In Montgomery a new governor sat, but he sounded like the old one. John Patterson indirectly opened the gates for the mob action when he announced, "The people of Alabama are so enraged that I cannot guarantee protection for this bunch of rabble-rousers." That was the moment when the Kennedy administration faced the same choice as the one which had confronted Dwight D. Eisenhower in Little Rock: federalize the state National Guard and use it to keep the peace, or inundate Montgomery with federal marshals. The President vacillated.

The disreputable Ku Klux Klan waited at the Montgomery bus terminal. White women surrounded the mob, hoping out loud that their men would be real men and show the "niggers" that Montgomery wasn't going to stand for any nonsense. The bus pulled in on the morning of the twentieth. A crowd of 300 waited. The motion-picture cameras were poised and ready; white people hung out of windows across the street. There was not a policeman in sight.

The first young man off the bus was James Zwerg, a white student from Wisconsin. "Kill the nigger-loving son of a bitch!" the women screamed. Zwerg was knocked down by the mob; he staggered to his feet and was knocked down again. A white workman took careful aim and kicked Zwerg's front teeth out. A group of Klansmen armed with baseball bats picked black William Barbee as their target. It would be three weeks before Barbee remembered anything, and then it would be in a hospital bed. President Kennedy's on-the-spot observer, John Seigenthaler, was next. He was smashed and rolled out onto the soft tar road.

The women kept screaming for more. John Lewis, who had already been beaten once, was mauled again. Norman Ritter, who was observing and taking notes for *Time-Life,* was picked up by the mob and tossed to the ground. The violence continued for almost twenty minutes before the police arrived, under the direction of a new commissioner, L. B. Sullivan. The 30 venomous whites were ordered to "go home." Victims were lying on the ground, but no arrests were ordered, no witnesses interrogated. The white James Zwerg was semiconscious. He was on the ground moaning. A Southern white reporter asked Commissioner Sullivan if he had called for an ambulance.

"No," said Sullivan. "Every white ambulance in town reports their vehicles have broken down."

The reporter shook his head in disbelief. "He needs medical attention," he said.

The commissioner was bland and terse. "He hasn't requested it," he said.

In Washington, the Kennedys now moved swiftly. The Attorney General announced that 400 federal marshals would be in Montgomery by sundown, and an additional 200 by morning. Governor Patterson, who had expressed his helplessness in the face of the mob, now took the opposite tack and said that the State of Alabama could solve its own internal problems. He blustered that he might even have his state troopers "arrest" the federal marshals. Martin Luther King announced that he would be in Montgomery "in the morning" and would stage a massive rally at Ralph Abernathy's old First Baptist Church at night.

This provoked some of the militant blacks, who saw King as one whose heart was in the right place, but whose lack of personal courage betrayed him. Robert Williams, part of the NAACP group, sent an ultimatum to King in Atlanta:

"The cause of human decency and black liberation demands that you physically ride the buses with our gallant Freedom Riders. No sincere leader asks his followers to make sacrifices that he himself will not endure. You are a phony. Gandhi was always in the forefront, suffering with his people. If you are the leader of this nonviolent movement, lead the way by example."

Six hundred marshals were not enough. The sun was setting when a white mob began to gather outside the First Baptist Church. Twelve hundred blacks and a few whites braved the taunts and threats of the crowd to go inside. Local policemen were on the sidewalks and in the streets, exchanging pleasantries with the mob. The crowd grew, until somewhere between 3,000 and 4,000 angry people surrounded the church. At that point, when darkness fell, there was no way to get in or out of the building.

The marshals phoned Washington that they could not control the situation. Inside, Martin Luther King got on the phone and called the Attorney General's office for more assistance at once. The Attorney General phoned Governor Patterson and told him he had a choice. Either protect the lives and persons of the people inside the church, or assume the risk that President Kennedy would federalize the state National Guard and do the job himself. Patterson said he needed no help. He called a few hundred troops and ordered them to the First Baptist Church to keep order. By 8 P.M., Southerners all, they were fraternizing with the local police and the mob.

Dr. King, among old friends inside, assumed the leadership role again. "The ultimate responsibility for the hideous action in Alabama," he thundered, "must be placed at the doorstep of the governor of the state. We hear the familiar cry that morals cannot be legislated. This may be true, but behavior can be regulated. The law may not be able to make a man love me, but it can keep him from lynching me."

Outside in the darkness, a voice yelled, "We want to integrate too." This may have been a signal. At once, rocks and bottles spun in the air and crashed through stained-glass windows. Women inside the church screamed. Dr. King begged everyone to be calm. Broken glass tinkled; rocks rolled between pews. One man was injured. "Let us join hands and sing," said Dr. King. In the chancel, the beaten and battered Freedom Riders opened their mouths and led the long slow choruses of "We Shall Overcome."

In the mob, federal marshals tossed tear gas bombs. The crowd turned its attention to the federal men and chased some. The action did not alter the mood of the crowd. It waited like a vicious watchdog. An hour later, in a lull, Martin Luther King emerged in the doorway with Ralph Abernathy and the Reverend Fred C. Bennette. He was about to plead with the white crowd to permit the blacks to go home in peace. As he opened his mouth, a tear gas bomb whizzed by. Bennette picked it up before it exploded and tossed it back into the mob. He pushed King inside. A voice yelled from the darkness: "We'll get you, nigger." It cannot be disputed that the black people in the light of the church had more courage than the light people in the dark outside. The black prisoners did not panic. They sang. They prayed. They listened to speeches and sermons. Most of all, they waited. As it grew later, the crowd outside tired of standing. Groups of people drifted away. The National Guardsmen urged the rest to go home. In the early light, Martin Luther King and 1,200 others were free to leave.

Montgomery became a national scandal. Robert Kennedy asked the Interstate Commerce Commission to order desegregation of all buses, trucks, trains, planes, any commercial vehicle which moved across state lines. The commission, whose members had read the Supreme Court bus decision, was goaded into lethargic action. It decreed that all such interstate transportation must be desegregated by November 1, 1961. This, in effect, gave the South a reprieve from the Supreme Court decision. It had five additional months in which to obey a law which dated back to 1956.

In Washington, Attorney General Kennedy proposed a "cooling-off period" for the Freedom Riders and the South. This would benefit the white South, which asked nothing more than a succession of cooling-off periods in which they could return to the status quo. The proposal met with approval from many black ministers in the South who feared violence. King conferred with SCLC leaders in Atlanta, and they decided to reject Kennedy's "cooling-off period" in favor of a "temporary lull." The response of the students was raucous laughter.

Lerone Bennett, Jr., a student and later a biographer of Martin Luther King, felt that King's "following was unraveling at the seams. Nor could he deny the charge that he was following, not leading; reacting, not acting—rushing from fire to fire blowing on other men's flames."* The doctor was being forced, against his will, into a more militant posture. His four-step plan, which had seemed so workable and so right a short time earlier, was imperiled by the boldness of the young. King had reasoned that each campaign should have four steps: (1) propaganda to expose the evil; (2) mobilization of the people; (3) nonviolent public protest; and (4) negotiation with the white adversary. The SNCC group believed that the age of municipal confrontation had arrived. Mobilize those willing to sacrifice themselves and face an entire community. When the municipality tired of the fight and became reasonable, select another city for a similar confrontation.

At dawn on May 24, friendly reporters were awakened by a telephone message: "Seven come eleven the dogs don't run to Jackson." It meant that the Freedom Riders would leave Montgomery for Jackson, Mississippi, at 7 and 11 A.M. Why a code was used is mystifying, because when

---

* Lerone Bennett, Jr., *What Manner of Man* (Chicago, Johnson Publishing Co., Inc., 1968).

the newsmen reached the Montgomery bus terminal, 400 troops with rifles formed a double line around the buses; overhead, two helicopters reported the progress of the ride. In Washington, Robert Kennedy sat with earphones on, connected to a special hookup which enabled him to listen to police radio reports as they came over the air from Montgomery.

The first bus had twelve riders, seventeen newsmen, and a squad of armed soldiers peering out of windows. On the highway in front of the bus were twenty-two police squad cars and two battalions of National Guard. Martin Luther King, Jr., watched the small group of gallants leave, marveling at the soldiers and the squad cars, the helicopters and planes overhead. The Freedom Riders were singing, but Dr. King wasn't. The fight for racial equality was at a standstill if so few riders required so much protection. He must have thought of those many churchgoers a few nights earlier who had so little protection. He knew also, as he watched that first bus pull out, that there would be more and more Freedom Rides staged by SNCC and that the SCLC and SNCC must, by the separate nature of their ideologies, part and pursue individual goals. When that time came, and it would be soon, he would remain with the SCLC and give SNCC the blessing a father bestows on a wayward son.

The attempts of James Earl Ray to escape prison were seldom more successful than his attempts to stay out of prison. He selected a balmy day to try again, and he was caught before he got out of the gate. His attempt didn't even raise the conversational level in the prison yard. James Earl Ray was thirty-one years of age and had spent sixteen of them under arrest. The escape attempt added more time to his sentence and canceled whatever time off he may have accumulated for good behavior.

The warden complimented Ray on his good work in the prison bakery but noted on a progress report that his antisocial behavior "seems to be pretty well established." Freedom had drawn farther and farther away from Ray because of the numerous attempts to escape. Prison, he learned, was one institution which will not tolerate failure.

The onyx edifice of black solidarity began to crack. Many leaders produce many schisms and, as the year 1961 began to slip off the calendar, it became obvious that black militants and nonmilitants were as far apart as the blacks and the whites. Everyone in the Movement had two adversaries: the white man and some black people. No one could deny that there was merciless logic in the harsh preachments of Elijah Muhammed; no one could deny that there were strengths in the Gandhian approach of Martin Luther King; all looked up to the NAACP lawyers to win new rights by law; CORE and SNCC preferred action to speeches; some of the leftist groups favored complete disunity—revolution and gun battles. The grin of contempt was reserved for Martin Luther King's negativistic hope: "The law may not be able to force the white man to love me, but it can stop him from lynching me."

None of the various factions had lost sight of the fact that few of America's 22,000,000 blacks would involve themselves in the Movement; their combined memberships did not total 1,000,000. The passive majority waited patiently for better times, more equitable laws, and silently aligned itself with the struggle—but only from the safety of its home.

In Albany, Georgia, the two SNCC members, Charles Sherrod, twenty-two, and Cordell Reagan, eighteen years of age, had spent most of the year assessing and selecting student leaders, turning away from the frightened ministers and the affluent blacks, organizing, organizing, organizing. They were intelligent young men on a mission. The staid blacks feared them both, but especially Sherrod. He wore cheap cotton shirts, wrinkled loud slacks, and floppy sandals. He seldom spoke, and then only in a dreamy tone. Some of the ministers suspected that Sherrod was a Communist; the basis for suspicion was his attire. As a member of SNCC, Sherrod worked carefully within the Albany NAACP Youth Council to undermine it and bring the membership into the hands of SNCC. When the Youth Council fell into line in October, Sherrod and Reagan returned to Atlanta and reported to both the SCLC and SNCC that Albany was ready for phase two. Wyatt Tee Walker, who had contributed money to the education of Sherrod, said that Dr. King would allocate some SCLC funds to help.

On the morning of November 1, phase two began. Sherrod, Reagan, James Forman, and two others got aboard a Trailways bus bound south to Albany. The police in Atlanta phoned their confreres in Albany and said that trouble was on the road. When the vehicle arrived in Albany, ten policemen were waiting. The SNCC tactic was to try to desegregate the facilities of the bus terminal first, but they saw the policemen and decided to postpone it. In the late afternoon they were back at the terminal with some local students. The police had left, and the students sat at the white lunch counter, used the white men's room, and waited for the white reaction.

The white police of Albany did not club the blacks from the premises. They had read of the loss of white prerogatives in other cities and decided to act formally. The blacks were requested to leave—or face arrest. Apparently, the police did not realize that on that day the Interstate Commerce Commission ruling on desegregation had gone into effect on interstate vehicles and public facilities. In fact, the ruling stated that all such vehicles had to post signs reading: "Seating aboard this vehicle without regard to race, color, creed or national origin, by order of the Interstate Commerce Commission." Similar signs were ordered posted in terminals. A white member of SNCC, Salynn McCollum, phoned the Justice Department in Washington to cite the violation of the new law. SNCC hoped to pit the Southern city against the Washington Establishment. It didn't work. Miss McCollum was thanked for being a good citizen.

The blacks went into seclusion. The Albany fight appeared to be over before it had started. SNCC found that its organization of militants was strong on words, short on deeds. Sherrod and Reagan began building all over again. In two weeks they had organized the Albany Movement, and had voted Dr. William G. Anderson as president. They had persuaded the conservative Ministerial Alliance to join the group, as well as the aloof Criterion Club and the NAACP. By the twentieth plans had been formed to challenge Albany's racist laws. On November 22 three members of the Youth Council invaded the bus depot dining room. They were arrested at once by Police Chief Laurie Pritchett. Later in the day a young woman and a man asked for service in the same dining room. They were arrested. The formal charge was more clever than the crude "city ordinance" violations of Montgomery. This time, racism was left out of the matter, and "disorderly conduct," "failure to obey an officer," and "tending to create public disorder" were substituted.

Albany had a list of black voters, and as elections came up on December 4, the whites turned out en masse to overwhelm the black vote. Asa Kelley was elected mayor, and, under local law, would take office on January 11, 1962. Buford Ellington was elected to serve as mayor pro tem; the whites were shoring their Establishment with strong men. Freedom Riders arrived in Albany on trains from Atlanta. Bernard Lee was in the first group, with James Forman. The tactic would be pointless if the riders were not arrested. Newspapers and other media had been told that SNCC would test the new ICC ruling at the Albany,

Georgia, railroad station at 3:30 P.M. on December 10. When Chief Pritchett arrived, he found 300 local students shouting and some "outside agitators." There are few phrases which can surpass that one for arousing white Southern tension.

The passengers disembarked to cheers—four were black; five were white—and moved at once to the "White Only" waiting room. Pritchett had summoned extra police. He ordered the nine persons out of the waiting room. They picked up their luggage and prepared to leave. At this point, the chief lost his head. "You are all under arrest," he shouted. "All of you." The SNCC leaders relaxed. Pritchett's action ensured that their efforts would receive plenty of publicity. Cameras snapped and whirled; so did pencils on pads as police moved among the blacks hauling them off to jail. By nightfall Albany had become the focus of the nation. The police action also brought the uncertain blacks into the Albany Movement.

Once embarked on a course of prosecution, Pritchett lost all avenues of retreat. Two days later, hundreds of black high school students paraded to City Hall, singing and chanting. By December 15, 500 people had been jammed into the small jail. Albany had been taxed beyond its limits. The mayor pro tem announced that the city would hold "unofficial talks." Three whites and three blacks were named to a committee. The Albany *Herald* trumpeted that the group had "no authority." This broke the spine of the committee before it could negotiate. Mayor Kelley, who had yet to assume office, was irritated because he had had a good look at SNCC demands, and they were mild: integration of bus and railroad facilities in compliance with the law; formation of a permanent biracial committee; dismissal of charges against all members of the Albany Movement.

The irony of all the movements was that once a confrontation had begun, neither side could retreat because of the militancy of its supporters. Another tactic was used. A hundred demonstrators were freed without charge, and Georgia's Governor Ernest Vandiver sent the National Guard to Albany.

On the sixteenth Dr. Anderson phoned Martin Luther King, Jr., and asked him to come at once to Albany. This outraged the militant SNCC's. "We plant the seed," they said. "Dr. King reaps the harvest."

King was not enthused about Albany. The ordeal of Montgomery was five years behind him, and he knew that little municipal fights would not free the black man in this century. A much bigger stage was required. He was ready for a national battle for civil rights, but his Southern

Christian Leadership Conference wasn't strong enough to undertake it. In spite of his lack of enthusiasm for the project, when the phone call from Dr. Anderson came in, King told Abernathy that he thought they should go to Albany.

They left the same day. Dr. King thought that he was there to lift morale and to pledge SCLC support of the Albany Movement. At a mass meeting in the Shiloh Baptist Church that night, Dr. Anderson—to the amazement of Dr. King—shouted fervently, "Reverend King will lead us, won't you, Reverend King?" The Albany blacks cheered and gave Dr. King a standing ovation.

For some reason, King reverted to his Southern preacher style of sermon. "Don't stop now!" he said in that fine baritone voice. "Keep moving. Don't even get weary, children. We will wear them down by our capacity to suffer!"

A morning march of all hands was scheduled for City Hall. "Eat a good breakfast," Dr. Anderson admonished the people. "Wear your walking shoes and warm clothes." The time of the march was 7 A.M. Dr. King, Ralph Abernathy, Dr. Anderson, Bernard Lee, and the SNCC students stood outside the Shiloh Church in the cold early light. The black family men were not there. Cadres of students were sent through Albany to round them up. The response at most front doors was a shy no. The men and their wives had been brought to a high emotional pitch at the church meeting, but most of them worked for "white folks" and they were afraid to be seen in the line of march. Before the day was over, the students saw their parents as so many whites had already seen theirs—afraid to risk whatever they had for any cause, no matter how noble.

It was sundown before Dr. King was summoned to lead the march. There were 260 persons—about 1 percent of the black population— standing in shivering ranks. It was a pitiful showing. Dr. King led and began to sing "We Shall Overcome." The tune was taken up by the marchers. The farther they got into the main part of town, the louder they sang. Whites in cars pulled to the curbs to watch, some to jeer. Pedestrians stopped to look. Shop owners emerged on sidewalks to watch. Some thought that Dr. Anderson was overwrought. He chanted to the whites: "God bless you. God bless each of you. Strike me first. God bless you." Men in the front rank stared at him with concern. At Oglethorpe Avenue and Jackson Street, Chief Pritchett waited, arms folded. Behind him stood a hundred policemen. Pritchett ordered the marchers to disband. He reminded them that they did not have a city permit to march, that they could not obstruct traffic and disturb the peace.

Dr. King waited passively for the inevitable, and it came. The marchers were arrested. The number of persons in the local jail now exceeded 600. Journalists from many parts of America concentrated on the small once-isolated city. "I have refused to post bond," Martin Luther King stated. "If I am convicted of this charge, I will refuse to pay the fine. I expect to spend Christmas in jail, and I hope that thousands will join me." From the jail, Abernathy issued a call to blacks from all parts of the country to make an immediate pilgrimage to Albany. Governor Vandiver was called for help. Vandiver phoned Attorney General Robert F. Kennedy begging the Department of Justice to stop "outside agitators" from visiting Albany. Kennedy's position was that the governor had to be aware that no one could restrict any American from traveling to any part of the country at any time. Pritchett began to transfer scores of prisoners (including King) to jails scattered over three counties.

As it was in Montgomery, so it was in Albany. White businessmen began to force the politicians to become more conciliatory. Some suggested that the bus station and the railroad depot would have to be integrated anyway under law. Why not offer Dr. King this little bone, in addition to freedom for the imprisoned marchers? What would it cost Albany? Very little. Just a bus stop and a depot. The schools in town would remain segregated, the stores and businesses could keep their "White only" signs in restaurants and drinking fountains, and Albany could be rid of all its "outsiders" and persuade its local people to behave. James Gray, editor of the Albany *Herald,* vented his wrath on those who favored conciliation. His editorial was: "Keep on Fighting for Albany."

On Monday, December 18, the City of Albany and the SCLC announced a truce. Martin Luther King was released from jail on $400 bail. The leaders had agreed to instant desegregation of the bus station and the railroad depot. Local buses remained segregated. So did parks, libraries, and motion-picture houses. Dr. King advised the local black leaders to boycott the *Herald* and to boycott certain racist stores. The SNCC group were dissatisfied. They announced that they had not agreed to any truce because their demands had not been met. They could not disown Dr. King, but they felt he had betrayed their larger purpose of making Albany a model desegregated city. On the steps of City Hall, King told a large group of newspaper reporters that he had high hopes for the future of race relations in Albany. He complimented the Albany police on their restraint and pointed out that Chief Pritchett had removed his uniform cap and "prayed with us" before ordering everyone arrested. "This city's problems," he announced, "can best be settled on a local level." Some of the reporters appeared bewildered. They said they felt that everything King was saying was at variance with what he had demanded when he had come into town two days earlier. One reporter did not attempt to keep the acid from his question. "Are Albany's blacks oppressed amid hopeless conditions," he asked, "or are they not?"

Someone took Martin Luther King by the arm. "We have to leave now, Dr. King," he said.

Chief Pritchett was no less generous. He pointed out that his men had not used police dogs, hoses, or clubs. "I realize that I'm living in a changing world," he intoned. "You've got to adapt yourself to the situation." He smiled. "We are not in the old school." Attorney General Robert Kennedy gratuitously telephoned Kelley to compliment him on the "orderly manner" in which the City of Albany had handled a sensitive situation. Kelley was no less courteous. The White Establishment and the Black Establishment were pleased and somewhat smug.

The New York *Herald Tribune* jarred the hierarchy of the SCLC by calling Dr. King's attention to "one of the most stunning defeats of his career." One of the original Albany missionaries from SNCC was asked what he thought. "You curse first," he said, "then I will." A black newspaper in Pittsburgh, the *Courier,* counseled blacks not to believe that a truce indicated peace in Albany. Everyone wanted to know what had happened to "Christmas in jail."

At home, King read the adverse reports and changed his mind about his victory. "There was friction between Albany leaders," he said. That would account for the resounding defeat. "We made a mistake in attacking the political power structure instead of the economic power structure," he said, and in this he had a valid point. "You don't win against a political power structure where you don't have the votes. But you can win against an economic structure when you have the economic power to make the difference between profit and loss."

Some asked bluntly about his loss of leadership among the young— the militant, agitated, marching students were threatening to expel their elders from the movement and take leadership away from those who pledged nonviolence. Sherrod, when asked to comment on King and the

SCLC, said, "There was constant war between us as to strategy." The students were angered by the devotion of the press to Martin Luther King. SNCC spokesmen said, "We were working here long before De Lawd showed up to pull his miracles." They laughed at Ralph Abernathy's appeal to blacks all over the country to make a pilgrimage to Albany when they knew all too well it was almost impossible to get the local blacks to demonstrate.

SNCC and the Albany leadership tried to salvage something out of the debacle. The truce between the blacks and City Hall had been guaranteed until January 11, 1962, when Asa Kelley would become mayor. He had promised, at that time, to meet with local people and try to redress grievances. By that time, King, Abernathy and SCLC, and the NAACP were long gone. The mood of the whites was jubilant. They didn't know how to deal with "outside niggers" but they could easily frighten their own.

Dr. Anderson and his committee asked the City Council to hire black policemen, to arrange a system of interracial hiring for jobs throughout Albany, and to desegregate the local bus lines. The City Council, with Mayor Kelley disagreeing, rejected the demands at once. The seven-man board advised the Albany Movement to "earn acceptance for your people by encouraging the improvement of their moral standards." A bus boycott began. It lasted five weeks. The bus lines shut down. Albany, Georgia, returned to its traditional Southern ways.

James Earl Ray celebrated the coming of Christmas with another attempt to escape from prison. Secretly, he had assembled bits of metal and wood and made a ladder. The rungs were held together with string. He had carefully chosen a section of the eastern wall of the Jefferson City Penitentiary, a wall only fourteen feet high and out of range of the guards in the watchtowers. Darkness came early, so he tried to get out before evening roll call and supper.

With the ladder under his arm, he slinked through the empty laundry room and went to the wall. He propped his ladder up and began to climb. He was four feet from the top when the contraption collapsed under his weight, and he fell to the ground. A metal pipe fell, too, on his head. He was not present at the 7 P.M. check, so guards went looking for him. Ray was found in the laundry room, bleeding profusely. The guards thought he might have been injured by equipment and took him to the infirmary. Later the bits of string, wood, and metal were found, but Warden Swensen decreed that no prisoner in his right mind would try to fly out into the world on that flimsy structure, so a second "attempt to escape" was not placed on Ray's record.

Still, Swensen felt impelled to do something about the incident, so he sentenced the meek Smiler to six months "in the basement." There, James Earl Ray was granted one full meal every three days and was isolated, with plenty of time to assess one more failure.

Then came the year of the hypocrite, 1962. It was not a vintage year for anyone. The United States sent Lieutenant Colonel John H. Glenn into a successful orbit of the earth . . . The United Nations continued to expiate on the subject of the brotherhood of nations but voted to deny membership to China, which represented one of every four human faces in the world. The Supreme Court decreed that racial segregation in intrastate as well as interstate transportation was illegal. The Southern states and cities continued to practice it by intimidating the black. Two Roman Catholic bishops, Rummel of New Orleans and Hallinan of Atlanta, announced that their diocesan schools would be desegregated at once. The Supreme Court outlawed the reading of prayer in school by a vote of six to one. The Eighty-seventh Congress sent to the states an amendment (Article XXIV) to the Constitution denying any state the right to assess voters with a poll tax. At the same time, some Senators tried to prevent President Kennedy from sending United States marshals into the South to help the black register as a voter.

It was not a good time to be a prophet, but it was a good time for a prophet to earn a living. Dr. King made $6,000 a year as co-pastor of Ebenezer Baptist Church; he requisitioned whatever he pleased from the SCLC for travel; he wrote a newspaper column for black weeklies; he cited the Psalms and God's Good Word in *Ebony* magazine; on invitation he made florid speeches and raised funds.

Basically, Martin Luther King was a creature of the flesh. He fought his desires and was defeated by the devil of temptation on many battlefields. From babyhood onward, he was short and heavyset, one who enjoyed food as a special pleasure. As he grew, he developed an appetite for wine, but rarely did he drink too much of it. Women were a challenge to his virility, and black or white, when they came too close, they were singed. A Chicago reporter referred to King as "what jazz musicians call loose," though the reporter was not assailing King's morals.

The doctor was, in sum, a short man with a tall ego. He cast a long shadow, and he knew it. Underneath the engaging smile was a mind confident of its superiority to others. His ego was such that he dealt solely with presidents and premiers, avoiding second- and third-echelon politicians. His heart's desire was to play Gandhi or Christ, or a combination of both, but the modesty and self-denial required by those roles were foreign to him, so he tried to play statesman instead. Dr. King was absolutely correct about one thing—he was not part of a civil rights movement; he *was* the movement. Not just a figurehead, a personality— he was all there was within the Southern Christian Leadership Conference. Nor did he want a strong man to stand behind him. Dr. King never beckoned Wyatt Tee Walker toward the throne, or Bayard Rustin, or even Andrew Young.

It was Ralph Abernathy whom he selected to follow him. Abernathy could be trusted not to play the part of Dr. King if he died early; Abernathy could be depended on to canonize him. Abernathy would also keep King's secrets: the errors of judgment; the times when his courage flagged; the insurmountable temptations of the flesh; the jolly private evenings when educated blacks could sit and mimic the "Aunt Janes" and other amusing and ignorant blacks.

When he was home, his habit was to arise early and read for thirty minutes before breakfast. He had a bookmark in scores of volumes and a good habit of being able to pick up the story where he had dropped it. At breakfast or after, he placed several records of opera music on the record player, shuffling around the rooms in overly large carpet slippers, humming and searching. At Coretta King's piano, he would sometimes sit and roll out the opening cadenzas of the *Moonlight Sonata* as though he would project his soul through the sweet sad strains. After twelve or sixteen bars, he would stop because he knew no more.

He loved his children but lost them to his wife. He could indulge in childish play for only short periods of time. A phone call would interrupt, he had an appointment or someone with whom he had to confer. He would hold Yoki and say, "Bet you don't know where Yoki's sweet spot is," and she would kiss him on a dimple. "Bet you don't know where Mommy's sweet spot is," and the child, giggling in her father's arms, would kiss him on the lips. "Bet you don't know where Dexter's sweet spot is. . . ."

If one can measure human beings in terms of values, as opposed to leadership abilities, the accolade would have to go to Coretta King. She was a stronger personality, a more militant and radical person than her husband, an intelligent wife and mother, a woman whose counsel was sought in a field where few women trod.

Deep in her breast, she was aware that she was married to a dead man except that she did not know the hour or the place of death. His mission, to "walk among mine enemies naked" was to beg for the gleaming sword on the bowed neck. Mrs. King would not transmit her fears to her husband, nor would she beg him—as his father did so often—to leave the great war for freedom and return to the safety and sanctity of the chancel. No. She thought that her husband might be overtaken by the gray wings of the bird of death at any time, and yet it might not happen for years and years. She did not want it, but she could not be suppliantly feminine and weep while waiting. As she dressed the children and ordered them out to play in the yard, she felt that she too might lose her life. Now and then, when she addressed audiences, Coretta King would hold her bony chin a little higher, the dark eyes glittering with lights, and murmur, "If I perish, I perish." Esther had once said those words, and Coretta King meant them as sincerely.

When her Martin became a public figure, Coretta was as surprised as he was. Her elation was soon diluted because the new calling intruded on their marriage. She knew the dangers of defying the white man, and the higher he rose, the more accustomed she became to sitting in the evenings, waiting for that phone call. The counterweight to fear was the knowledge that her man was making a long-term effort to right an old wrong. She was bitter about what it meant to be a black person in a white world. And her husband's great calling was balm spreading warmth and tenderness on a hard heart.

There was laughter in their lives, too. The two could tell "down-home" stories which were amusing with philosophical point. Coretta King had to smile when her husband insisted that he was a great cook, "only I don't have much time." He was despotic about her clothing, insisting on accompanying her on shopping sprees, always favoring the broad full skirts with the gathered waist and tucked-in blouse. He was opposed to anything as figure-revealing as a sheath. "That dress is one thing in front," he would mutter ominously. "It's another thing in back."

On the increasingly rare occasions when he had a few days at home, Dr. King was a contented man. He saw nothing but adoring faces. He could lounge; he could chat freely without guile; he could watch television; he could think about a subject for a sermon and work it out in lavishly brocaded phrases; he could partake of soul food in gluttony; he could visit the campus, swap small talk with professors and students; he could drive to the scenes of his childhood; hold his mother's big homely face in his hands; feel the warmth and admiration of "Daddy," the man who boomed and expostulated with joy when his favorite son was at his side; he could project an SCLC budget with Wyatt Tee Walker and say, "Ask the foundations, man. We going to need a lot of money this year [$200,000 for the year 1962]." Dr. King accepted one dollar a year as salary.

Atlanta had a special place in his heart. It was exempt from his cruel mission. He had picketed Rich's department store with reluctance, but when he tried to enroll his children in a white Episcopal school in Atlanta and they were rejected on racial grounds, Dr. King remained silent. No thunder of "another Little Rock" poured from his throat, no threat of a sit-in, no suit in the courts—just defeat.

The SCLC rented a new headquarters in the black Masonic Temple, a block from Dr. King's father's church. It was on the opposite side of the street, and he could walk briskly from one office to the other. In the SCLC office he had shelves of books with imposing titles, a few framed photos of Coretta King and the children, and a square desk with two telephones. One was the SCLC number; the other had no number. He functioned in either office, although his preference was for the study in the back of his father's church.

If he had a choice, Dr. King might have spent his life on the black voter registration problem because he understood that this was where the black in America would find the power to achieve equality. But he could not arouse his people. They preferred him to make dramatic appearances before white mayors and chiefs of police and thereby act out their collective dreams of successful confrontation.

The most powerful of King's enemies was Dr. Joseph H. Jackson, ministerial president of the National Baptist Convention. Dr. Jackson represented 5,000,000 churchgoing blacks. He stated that the place of a man of God was in his church, interpreting the words of Jesus Christ to his flock and saving their souls. He opposed Martin Luther King in the North and South. A schism developed within the big body—the older sedate and sedentary ministers allying themselves with Jackson; the younger activist group siding with King. The previous September, an open fight had developed at a National Baptist Convention, and one of the ministers had died of a heart attack. Jackson blamed the "crime" on Dr. King, though he was not at the convention when the fight developed. A retraction was demanded from Dr. Jackson. If it was given to Dr.

King, it was tendered privately. When King was arrested in Albany, Georgia, Dr. Jackson's contempt congealed on his tongue. He had no comment in February when King and Abernathy journeyed to Albany to be swiftly tried and convicted of disorderly conduct and parading without a permit. Sentence was postponed until July 10. Perhaps, in the fight with Dr. Jackson, King had the last word. He led a young group of ministers from the Jackson organization and formed another, the Progressive Baptist Alliance. This weakened the original organization by one-third.

The fratricidal battles among the blacks hurt all groups. The movement toward equal civil rights was bleeding to death from self-inflicted wounds. Someone had to bind them, and Dr. King thought he could by uniting all factions with his SCLC. He offered his hand in brotherhood, but it was declined by the other leaders because they felt that they could dispense with King's nonviolent approach and his ability to draw the light of publicity to himself.

Abernathy and Walker set about to find a goal worthy of King's talent, but they failed. The pastor said that he, personally, would like to desegregate Birmingham, Alabama, because it was the most racist big city in the South. Montgomery, he assured his personal staff, was small potatoes compared to Birmingham. But they could not go into Birmingham uninvited because the Reverend Fred Lee Shuttlesworth had organized his own group inside the city; it was called the Alabama Christian Movement for Human Rights (ACMHR).

Birmingham, with a municipal population of 340,000 and a suburban population of equal size, was a big industrial complex squeezed in a narrow area between mountains called Jones Valley. Natives called it "Bummingem." It was less than a hundred years old, but the mountains around it held 66 billion of tons of coal and about 30 billions of tons of iron. The blast furnaces of Bessemer cast a bronze pall of smoke across Birmingham, but the city rose above its grime with fine art museums, parks, lakes, good schools, and elaborate Southern manners.

In the late spring the Reverend Fred Shuttlesworth left his beloved Birmingham for Chattanooga, where Dr. King and his SCLC was holding a meeting of members of the board. Shuttlesworth was slender, a handsome dandy, and he asked the SCLC to consider Birmingham as its next target. This was what King had hoped for, and he endorsed the proposal and referred to Shuttlesworth as "the most courageous civil rights fighter in the South." The board concurred without dispute and publicized its decision to hold its annual SCLC convention in Birming-ham in September. White Birmingham knew that this meant that the city would be host to a large body of "outside agitators" in the early autumn.

Shuttlesworth reported that his group, supported by black students from Miles College, had initiated a selective boycott of downtown Birmingham stores two months earlier, and it was 95 percent effective. A few of the stores were already negotiating to remove the "White" and "Colored" signs from lunch counters and drinking fountains. The big stores were being hurt economically by the boycott, but, said Shuttles-worth, the mayor and councilmen were more racist than the ordinary citizens and were demanding that the signs be restored. This was especially true of the director of public safety, Eugene Connor, known to his friends as Bull. Dr. King listened carefully as Shuttlesworth in-sisted that any campaign in Birmingham would not be easy. Even white moderates had become targets of Commissioner Connor and his Police Department. Birmingham was determined—stubbornly determined—to remain racially apart no matter what the laws of the nation proclaimed.

Dr. King was so impressed by the report that he called a special meeting of the board and his personal staff. The meeting lasted three days and was exploratory. The doctor was conscious of the weaknesses and failures at Montgomery and Selma; now that he had a big and truly formidable target, he demanded the best strategic thinking of all hands. His personal feeling was that he now had sufficient experience to know what *not* to do. Lesson number one was not to attack the political structure of a city, except in reprisal or self-defense. Lesson number two was not to try to desegregate "everything"; it was tactically smarter to pick a few targets, vulnerable targets, and stick to narrow goals. Lesson number three was not to depend on local unorganized blacks, because they lived with the situation and were frightened by it. Lesson number four was to hurt the white man economically until he could no longer stand the squeeze without facing bankruptcy. From Bayard Rustin he had learned philosopher George Santayana's observation that those who do not learn from their mistakes are condemned to repeat them.

Board and staff made notes of King's remarks. He enumerated all the don'ts but knew none of the do's. Someone suggested that it was not going to be an easy or even a quick fight, so the Battle of Birmingham was given a code name: Project C, meaning confrontation. All leaders within both groups were given code names, so that, if an informer gained access to the files, little could be deciphered. Other code words were assigned to various types of demonstrations, marches, sit-ins, and boycotts.

King's image needed a big fight and a big victory. He was tiring of being called "Little Lord Jesus" and "Uncle Tom." The citadel of Birmingham must crumble before him.

King was aware that the SCLC would have to use the President of the United States in order to win in Birmingham, and Dr. King proposed to use President Kennedy early, months before Project C would start. He now mailed a letter to the White House asking for assistance before it was required. It is possible that he was aware that the Kennedy brothers were trying to use him and his movement to political advantage. If so, he was playing the same game he played with Communists—two scorpions in a bottle and no one daring to sleep.

King did not tell President Kennedy that there was an impending confrontation in another city in the South. The letter, dated May 17, 1962, asked the President to place the power of his high executive office behind compliance to the new laws and measures which ordered desegregation in education, housing, and transportation. In drawing up the letter, King had the services of attorney William Kunstler and others on the SCLC staff. "We believe we need not and should not struggle unaided," he wrote. "Our efforts to achieve human decency and human rights by eliminating the unlawful restrictions upon the exercise of our civil and constitutional rights seek to uplift and enrich our entire country." Lofty words; statesmanlike phrasing.

"In short, Mr. President, we are firmly convinced that there exist sufficient constitutional and statutory sources of power to enable you to use creatively the authority and moral prestige of your office to dramatically advance human rights in America. As the 100th anniversary of the Proclamation of Emancipation draws near we, along with millions of our fellow citizens and the peoples throughout the world, are watching and waiting to see whether America has at long last fulfilled the hopes and dreams arising from the abolition of slavery. We appeal to you in order that we may now have to wait no longer. We appeal to you because we love so dearly this great land of ours. We appeal to you because we yearn for the time when we can stand in the full sunlight of human decency and join hands with our white brethren, north and south, east and west, and sing in joyous hallelujah

"Jehovah hath triumphed—

"His people are free!"

President Kennedy was aware that, if he responded in an agreeable tone to this letter, King would release both letters to the press, and the result would be a political storm of gale force. The subject of the letter may have been discussed at the evening "bangboard hour," but if so, none of the participants has acknowledged it. The President's confreres realized that morally he was being shoved into a corner, a corner from which there would be no escape, and they counseled that it would be wise not to respond to the letter. Phoning was suggested, but President Kennedy did not want to phone and give King the chance to start a dialogue, so it was decided to have an assistant phone the SCLC and tell whoever was there that President Kennedy had received the letter, appreciated Dr. King's efforts, and would weigh the contents carefully. He would, in sum, do nothing, say nothing. Both men were trying to outwit each other, but so far, neither had been able to use the other.

The bright firebrand Stokely Carmichael felt himself drawing away from SNCC. The student organization had offered something, a striking force for blacks, but Carmichael now saw it as a weaker instrument than it had appeared to be, though not as weak as the SCLC. He was sure that race riots would descend upon the cities of America; there would be blood and fire in the streets. His feelings about the black community, especially the younger side of it, were correct. Carmichael watched television, and he felt that the medium was covering the demonstrations too well. When black women were knocked down by police, or children herded off in vans, or someone slapped the face of Martin Luther King, Stokely Carmichael reasoned that millions of passive blacks were angered beyond reason.

Time and television eventually controlled him and his ability to reason. "I've had so much law and order," he howled, "I swear before God I want some chaos! I want some chaos so bad I can taste it on the tip of my lips, because all I see is law and order, everywhere I go, law and order . . . nothing but law and order." The second initial of SNCC stood for "nonviolent." Stokely Carmichael could not countenance that word. There were hordes of well-educated blacks to whom the word had become anathema. "Nonviolent" was the white pig's pacifier, while the white man was anything but nonviolent. The Christian ethic was reserved for only the black man. Heaven had two dismal entrances: "White Only" and "Colored Only."

Carmichael had followed King with reluctance. They parted after

Selma and before Watts. The young man stoked his ideology with shovelsful of hate.

Judge Durden's court was hot. The voices of lawyers rose and fell like mirages of sound. Ralph Abernathy mopped his brow and mustache. Martin Luther King tried to tuck a white kerchief inside his shirt collar. The tall doors of the court were kept open onto the cool dark corridors. The windows were open. Fans whispered their prayers to the dead air of Albany, Georgia, in July. The weather was a far cry from that cold December day of the march. The judge had determined the degree of guilt of the leaders of that march. He could punish the defendants with jail sentences, but Albany had no appetite for recrimination. The city would like to be done with racial antagonism. A few weeks earlier, a black café manager had been shot by police for resisting arrest. Teenagers had been arrested for standing before City Hall. Cordell Reagan, still the worker in the vineyard, had been sentenced to two months in prison for sitting at a white lunch counter.

The judge said, "A fine of one hundred and seventy-eight dollars or forty-five days in prison at hard labor." The fine was deliberately small. Durden looked shocked when King stood and said, "I elect to purge myself in prison." Abernathy nodded. The situation was back where it had been last year. The two men would go to jail, and the blacks would spread the fire all over town and start marching on City Hall, on the jail, and soon Albany would have a first-class riot. Durden was left with no choice. The men went to jail, and the word was flashed on the teletypes across the nation. Nelson Rockefeller suggested that the Department of Justice open an investigation of Albany. Assistant Attorney General Burke Marshall was ordered to prepare a detailed report on the matter for the President of the United States. Marshall was also requested to phone Mrs. King and tell her that the department was doing all it could to free Dr. King.

Albany blacks began to mobilize. Young children stood near the jail and sang "We Shall Overcome." They were arrested for singing. It was hot in Albany and getting hotter. After two days in jail, someone paid the fines. The best guess is that it was an attorney for the SCLC. However, when Martin Luther King was freed on the morning of July 13, he looked surprised. "I've been thrown out of a lot of places," he told a mass meeting, "but never before have I been thrown out of jail." Dr. King held a press conference. He had to hurry back to Atlanta on business, he said, but he would be back on Monday, the sixteenth. His desire, he said, was simply to force the city commissioners to hold a hearing on black demands.

The battle of Albany, like an old volcano, was hot again. Sparks flew and blood ran. Parson C. K. Steele of Tallahassee arrived in Albany and led a group of demonstrators, all of whom went to jail. A thousand blacks jammed Shiloh Church cheering Dr. King on the sixteenth as he outlined a "nonviolent protest which will turn Albany upside down." Few could understand why, having lost the fight against the political structure of a city, the pastor had returned to renew the fight. The boycott of stores on the main streets was renewed. Some owners talked of selling out and leaving Albany. One man tried to sell his business at half what it had cost him. He had no bidders.

Young male blacks barred the streets of the ghetto one night. No white tried to enter, but they stood with arms folded, as though waiting for an attack. Someone phoned the police. Chief Pritchett responded with his men and, for the first time, was met with an avalanche of broken bottles and heavy stones. The chief showed great courage; he walked through the lines alone, got to Shiloh Church, and told the blacks assembled: "We're here to plead with you and to solicit your cooperation, and we know that we will get it." No one laid a hand on the chief. He walked out as tall and alone as he had walked in. Mayor Kelley was certain that matters had gone far enough. He asked Federal Judge J. Robert Elliott for an injunction against the SCLC, SNCC, and, specifically, several black leaders, including Martin Luther King, Jr., of Atlanta. The court was requested to enjoin those parties from starting, planning, joining, or endorsing any parades, demonstrations or meetings in public places. Judge Elliott granted a temporary injunction. Dr. King agreed, through counsel, to abide by the decision. "Out of respect for the leadership the federal judiciary has given, the enjoined parties and organizations have agreed to the order . . . and will work vigorously in higher courts to have said order dissolved."

King called for a "Day of Penitence" to atone for the rock throwing at Chief Pritchett. He led the public prayer meeting in a downtown area. Pritchett was not grateful. He removed his uniform cap while the praying was going on, then arrested King and others for violating the federal restraining order. The sly side of the pastor was beginning to show. He asked other preachers, who had not been named specifically in the injunction, to start demonstrations. The Reverend Samuel Wells took the hint. "I've heard about an injunction," he shouted to 150 followers, "but I haven't seen one. I've heard a few named, but my name hasn't been called. My name is being called on the road to freedom. . . . When shall we go? Not tomorrow! Not at high noon! Now!" They marched downtown singing "Ain't Gonna Let Nobody Turn Me Aroun'," and Pritchett, now weary beyond fatigue, met them and arrested them.

Three thousand members of the Ku Klux Klan massed outside Albany waiting to move in and fight the blacks. A sheriff's deputy kicked a pregnant black woman who was bringing food to jail. She had a miscarriage. By sundown the news was that she had been kicked to death. Judge Elbert P. Tuttle of the federal circuit court of appeals set aside the injunction of the lower court. Dr. King's followers were again permitted to demonstrate. But Albany—white Albany—had no feeling or respect for injunctions or law unless it inhibited the blacks while granting freedom of action to the whites.

SNCC became further alienated from the SCLC. Sherrod and others, including most of the student demonstrators, objected to Dr. King's "Day of Penitence." They felt he had no right to state that they had committed a wrong by throwing bottles. Also, his man Wyatt Tee Walker was issuing commands as though the Albany Movement were the private domain of the SCLC when everyone knew it was a SNCC venture from the start.

In the evening, a SCLC rally was held at Shiloh Church. The leaders knew that the blacks would be aroused by the jailing of King, and they proposed a massive demonstration downtown. All who were ready to march were invited to approach the altar rail. No one moved from the pews. Andy Young was stunned. "Now, friends," he said, "we have the names and addresses of those who have signed their names as being ready to go. Now is the time to get our affairs in order." The people sat. Young turned to Pastor Wells, who hurried forward.

"You cannot fail," he begged. "If we do, we will lose our brothers and sisters now in jail." Then, slowly: "We would like to have you get off your seats and come down front."

The blacks remained in the pews. SNCC's Sherrod, dismayed, stepped into the breach. "You ought to be ashamed of yourselves for sitting on your chairs while our leaders are sitting in a filthy jail," he shouted. "What's more important—to suffer now and be free later or be a slave for the rest of our lives?" The tired men and women moved to the altar rail.

More than a thousand people were in jail. Those outside were as weary as the whites. Pritchett kept herding demonstrators into a fourteen-foot-wide alley beside City Hall and asking names and addresses, handing out citations, and sending people off to other jails. Ten Senators requested the Department of Justice to free King and his demonstrators. A cordon of ministers, priests, and rabbis motored to the White House to ask President Kennedy to secure Dr. King's release. The best the President could do was to declare that he could not understand why the officials of Albany refused to confer with black leaders.

In a cell, equipped with a radio and desk, Dr. King wrote his "People in Action" column for black newspapers. In it, he noted that black women in Albany were paid $15 a week as housemaids; that few black heads of family could persuade white employers to grant them the federal minimum wage of $1.15 per hour. Economically, the blacks of Albany were less well off than in the days of slavery; in that era, they lived in cottages, paid no rent, got free medical and dental care and clothing. King went on to state his personal goal in the battle: "Albany will serve as a guidepost for other communities to grapple with the dilemma of accelerating the painfully slow process of desegregation. . . ." Albany—and what happened there—was to be the model for future "negotiations" in all other Southern cities.

Mrs. King brought the children to visit Dr. King. He was upset because he had appealed to Attorney General Robert Kennedy for assistance and also Burke Marshall. Both had suggested that King "give up" in Albany. Obviously, they had little appreciation of his personal position—he could not lose Albany in 1961 and lose it again in 1962. Somehow, someway, Dr. King must climb out of this small cul-de-sac and reappear in the sunlight as a winner. It had to be done, and no one but he could do it.

Dr. and Mrs. King talked of these matters as Yoki and Marty ran up and down the prison corridor. Coretta King was calm. Much of the time she stood close to her husband whispering. On one occasion, she made him laugh. Yoki said she had heard, in school and on television, that her father was in prison, and she was hurt. She wanted to know why. Her mother explained that her daddy was in jail so that other people might be free to go wherever they chose. The child's attitude switched from one of sorrow to ecstasy: "Oh, good," she said. "Tell him to stay in jail until I can go to Fun Town [a white amusement park in Atlanta]."

The Klan remained outside Albany. So did the 12,000 national guardsmen alerted by the State of Georgia. Those who came in were 75 priests, rabbis, and ministers who stood in front of City Hall to pray for Dr. King. "The Yankee preachers are here," a policeman said.

Chief Pritchett emerged. "All right, reverends," he said softly, "I want to know what your purpose is."

Dr. Norman Eddy of New York said, "Our purpose is to offer our prayers to God."

Rabbi Richard Israel of Yale University began to read aloud from the Old Testament. "All right," Pritchett shouted to his men. "Take them to jail."

This time King remained in jail for thirteen days. When his second trial began, he appeared in court looking well rested. The determinant in this case was not whether King was guilty or innocent; his guilt in parading and demonstrating was easily proved; the city and the judge was aware that the Department of Justice had filed an *amicus curiae* brief in federal court asking that the permanent injunction against black demonstrations be held in abeyance until Albany complied with the national laws against segregation. Legally, Albany was boxed so that it could not move in any direction without a violation of law higher than its municipal ordinances.

The trial was brief. King and his people were found guilty. The judge suspended sentence. On the steps of the court, Dr. King stood free in the hot sun. Journalists pressed around him, asking for a statement and especially desiring to know what the next move in Albany would be. Leaders of SNCC tried to interpose and explain that the fight in Albany was just beginning, that there was much to do in the city, but Martin Luther King made it clear that he now felt that he was a hindrance to peace in Albany. He announced that with his departure, the city would feel free to open negotiations with local black groups; his absence would give both sides a chance to "get together."

King and his staff had hardly left the city limits when Mayor Kelley announced that he was unaware of any plans to negotiate with blacks. Within the week, the City Council underwent the formality of meeting with SNCC leaders and pastors. They listened to demands that Albany desegregate interstate buses and trains under the ICC ruling; that cash bail be refunded to prisoners at large on their own recognizance; that the city stop interfering with local bus desegregation; and that peaceful protest marches be permitted. The officials listened and quickly voted no to all demands. Many of the clerics who were still in jail vowed to fast until death; some lasted thirty-six hours; two could not go beyond twenty-four. At the end of the week the men of God accepted bail and hurried homeward.

September 3 was Labor Day, and Albany's schools were to open in the morning. Three thousand hooded Klansmen held a meeting in a pasture outside Albany. They burned crosses and made loud speeches demanding a parade through the city to teach the "damn niggers a lesson." When they had concluded their threats, Chief Laurie Pritchett sent word to their leaders that a parade permit had been denied and, if any of them showed up in town, they would be sent to jail with the "niggers." The Klan disbanded. No one would be permitted to disturb the status quo, which was once more suitable to the whites. Dr. Anderson led some black children to segregated schools in the morning, but he was turned back by teachers, principals, and the school superintendent.

Night riders set fire to Mount Olive Baptist Church, then burned Mount Mary Church five miles away. The I Hope Baptist Church was next. In each case, the arsonists arrived at 2 A.M. and the Fire Department at 2:30. A year and a half after the struggle the New York *Times* reported that Albany, Georgia, was exactly the way it had been since Reconstruction days. In sum: no progress and an increase in racial bitterness.

The four black churches lay in pale ashes. The communicants did not have the means to rebuild them. Dr. King asked a former baseball player, Jackie Robinson, to head the fund drive to restore them. Who cared about four black churches? Almost everyone, it seemed. While Robinson was trying to raise funds in one area, readers of the Atlanta *Constitution* contributed $10,000; Governor Nelson Rockefeller of New York sent $10,000; the United Church of Christ solicited $5,000; the Episcopal Church sent $4,000; the blacks of Albany itself contributed $4,000; the National Council of Churches donated $1,000. Trappist monks of the Roman Catholic Church said that they would fashion twenty-four stained-glass windows. Segregationist Mayor Carl Rountree of Dawson, a suburb of Albany, issued a statement: "We feel that since this particular church was burned by people who live in Dawson and Terrell County, it is our job to do this." Residents responded with funds and skilled labor to rebuild one of the churches so that it would be stronger than ever.

In Atlanta, Martin Luther King III reached the third grade of elementary school before his parents could find an integrated school. Mrs. King drove Marty and Yoki to the school grounds and home again. There would be some problems—minor to adults, catastrophic to children—she knew. Mrs. King had to maintain a ready wit to answer questions. First and most formidable, was the continual problem of reassuring the children that although they were black, they were not inferior to others. Coretta King knew that television and motion pictures, two main avenues of childhood enjoyment, pandered to white skin, Caucasian features, straight or wavy hair, narrow nostrils, and thin lips.

At proper times, she discussed black versus white and tried to indoctrinate a natural pride in being dark.

She told the children that God had made all his creatures equal, each unto the other, but the wounds in the children were bleeding. "Don't cry," the mother said. "This is what your daddy is trying to change. He is trying to make it possible for you to go any place you want to go, do anything you want to do."

The days were cool again, and the winds of contention were momentarily stilled. Across the muddy Alabama River, Sheriff Jim Clark, big and pink and bulky, sat in his office in a sweater. A man was in the outer office waiting to see the sheriff. He was Arthur Lewis, a Jew who owned the Selma Buick agency. Lewis was known as a substantial citizen. The sheriff called him in and was handed a sheet published by B'nai Brith, an organization which promotes brotherhood. One of the stories said that Martin Luther King was planning "a swing through the South." Jim Clark asked why this should interest him. Lewis said that King was coming to Selma, and there had been threats against the preacher's life.

Clark said he had no knowledge that King was coming to Selma and, even if he did, the sheriff had no interest in the matter unless lawlessness was involved. When Lewis left with his paper, the sheriff contacted the nearest Federal Bureau of Investigation office. The agents knew nothing about King's projected visit and less about threats. The sheriff, who had informers among the blacks, asked for information and learned that few blacks knew anything about the visit. So the sheriff contacted Atlanta to find out when it would occur.

Two carloads of blacks came along Route 80, close together. At the county line, Clark was waiting with eight deputy sheriffs and eight members of what he called "the posse." The two cars were told to pull off the highway, and the big sheriff approached the first one and caught Dr. King's disarming smile. There was a little conversation. The sheriff learned that, besides King, there was someone named Wyatt Walker and a woman, Dorothy Cotton. "King," the sheriff said, "we heard you were coming to Selma, and I don't want any trouble. My men are here to protect you and your group. So follow us."

The visit was mysterious. The first person Dr. King visited was Arthur Lewis. Next, he chatted with the school superintendent, Joe Pickett. In the evening, King went to the Green Street Chapel in "Colored Town." He addressed a good crowd, but informers reported to Clark that he "said nothing, very mild." The doctor and his group had supper in a black restaurant. As they left, the black owner ran to the sheriff and said, "I want you to understand. I had nothing to do with them coming here." It was understood. The sheriff and his men formed a phalanx of squad cars to lead Dr. King back across the high humpbacked bridge and out of the county.

A few days later the doctor flew to Washington for a meeting with President Kennedy. The Chief Executive had agreed to the meeting because he wanted to discuss something called the American Negro Leadership Conference on Africa. Dr. King did not attend the meeting to discuss Africa; he was there to corner the President and discuss America.

They talked for an hour. King said that the black man was rapidly reaching the exploding point. The President, handsome in a brown suit with gleaming shoes, said that his staff had spent considerable time studying the Movement and always arrived at the same answer: register more black voters. This, Kennedy insisted, would achieve real power. It would take time, of course, but it would obviate the necessity of bloody confrontations.

King did not want to discuss black voters. The Department of Justice had already counseled him and the Movement to drop all demonstrations and channel energies into registering black voters North and South. King told the President that he could see no reason why the SCLC, SNCC, the NAACP, and other groups should drop all public protest in favor of the voter drive. "The Negro does not want to neglect all other rights," he said, "while concentrating on one."

The private chat broke up with cordial smiles and handshakes. "The President," King said ruefully, "must change the trend from saying 'Something must be done,' to coming up with a strong, specific program. It does no good to apply vaseline to a cancer." Neither man admired the other. Kennedy saw King as a demagogue preaching nonviolence but ready to appeal to the television screen to help him and the Movement. King saw the President as a man not committed to correct racial injustice.

"If tokenism were our goal," he said, after the conference, "this administration has adroitly moved us toward its accomplishment. But tokenism can now be seen not only as a useless goal, but as a genuine menace. . . . It tends to demobilize and relax the militant spirit which alone drives us forward to real change."

In any case, it was time for SCLC to get back into action. Project C had benefited from staff work. Wyatt Walker set up headquarters in Room 30 of the A. G. Gaston Motel at Birmingham. It was called "the command post." The Reverend Shuttlesworth and his stalwarts of Birmingham's ACMHR were called to endless conferences about the mood of the city, its strengths, its weaknesses, its public personalities. D-Day was pinpointed at a week before Easter, so that a boycott of stores along Third Avenue and North Twenty-sixth Street would affect the merchants quickly. Something unforeseen occurred—the mayoralty race had turned out to be indecisive. There would be a runoff on Tuesday April 2, 1963. The two candidates, Albert Boutwell and Bull Connor, were engaged in a final campaign. The SCLC could not begin demonstrations in Birmingham until the election was decided. If either candidate knew about it in advance, each would try to "outseg" the other, to the detriment of the Movement. Wyatt Walker used the delay to take a notebook and canvass the shops in downtown Birmingham, noting the number of entrances and exits, number of seats at each lunch counter, and the attitudes of managers and clerks toward blacks.

Dr. King decided that now was the time to tell both Kennedys that a gigantic civil rights battle was projected for Birmingham. If the Kennedys had any prior intelligence about it, they pretended to be surprised. King said that if the "confrontation in Birmingham" descended into violence, the government would be forced to act to restore peace. His strategy was that if he could win alone, he did not need the assistance of the government; if he lost and heads were bleeding in riots, he would put the President "on the spot" by calling upon him for help publicly. The threat did not move the Kennedys from their passive position. King said that he wanted merely to give the President advance notice of his plans. The Chief Executive no longer pressed his point that the road to power lay in the ballot box. It represented tedious undramatic work on the part of blacks, and Dr. King saw voting rights as a long-term side issue to the main battle.

Slowly, inexorably—and perhaps subconsciously—the word "violence" began to creep into Dr. King's vocabulary. He was a sincere Christian, a disciple of Gandhi, but his repetitious plea for nonviolence seemed further and further removed from the tide of the Movement. Wyatt Tee Walker, the ascerbic martinet, told it to King directly: "We have got to have a crisis to bargain with. To take a moderate approach, hoping to get help from the whites, doesn't work. They nail you to the cross." King was being shoved to the radical left. He went to Birmingham to help conduct workshops for confrontation. Shuttlesworth and the SCLC found 200 blacks who were willing to pledge themselves to go to jail for the cause. It wasn't many.

Between meetings at the A. G. Gaston Motel, in black Birmingham, King flew all over the United States soliciting "cash bail money" for the hundreds who were bound to be arrested by Bull Connor's policemen. He reminded sympathetic audiences: "As Birmingham goes, so goes the South." In New York, singer Harry Belafonte was host to seventy-five black and white liberals to raise bail money. Advice and counsel are always gratuitous, and at this meeting it was seriously suggested that the Movement drape the Statue of Liberty in black. The pastor flew on to Chicago, still firm in his resolve not to warn white Birmingham of the pending action. There was a reporter present at the meeting, representing the Chicago *Sun-Times*, and the following day there was a story about King stating that he was preparing for "the most difficult campaign he had undertaken," a fight against segregation in Birmingham, Alabama. He was attending meetings all over the country, he said, to recruit a "volunteer force" which would be notified to join the fight "several weeks before D day."

The secret was out, assuming that it had ever been a secret from the politicians of Birmingham. A tour of sixteen Southern cities was begun, with Dr. King pleading for "cash bail" much more earnestly than he asked for volunteers willing to journey to Birmingham to risk cracked heads and jail. In Los Angeles, affiliated black organizations raised $75,000. Enthusiasm for the struggle was building in many states. King's pleas for money did not fall on deaf ears. It was coming in faster than ever before. If there was a negative community, it was black Birmingham. The more the local blacks learned about the impending crisis, the more they worried about it. Some of the ministers begged Dr. King and Fred Shuttlesworth to postpone or cancel the confrontation. Plans were too far advanced for retreat. Not only the future of Birmingham but the future of Dr. Martin Luther King as well hung in the balance. If he lost the fight in Birmingham, after his defeat in Albany, he knew that he would be a small figure on the perimeter of the Movement, a man who had fathered the fight and lost his touch. All the power King could command or persuade would be brought to bear on Birmingham, and he would have to bring the city to its knees or lose himself in a maelstrom of militancy.

Those committed to go to prison signed Dr. King's pledge card:

I hearby pledge myself—my person and my body—to the nonviolent movement. Therefore, I will keep the following ten commandments:

1. Meditate daily on the teachings and life of Jesus.
2. Remember always that the nonviolent movement in Birmingham seeks justice and reconciliation—not victory.
3. Walk and talk in the manner of love; for God is love.
4. Pray daily to be used by God in order that all men might be free.
5. Sacrifice personal wishes that all men might be free.
6. Observe with both friend and foe the ordinary rules of courtesy.
7. Seek to perform regular service for others and for the world.
8. Refrain from the violence of fist, tongue and heart.
9. Strive to be in good spiritual and bodily health.
10. Follow the directions of the movement and of the captains on a demonstration.

The SCLC command post in Birmingham was busy every hour of every day. Headquarters in Atlanta corraled all the outside assistance it could. It solicited assistance from NAACP, CORE, SNCC, and the Southern Regional Council, not neglecting the seventy-five clergymen who had been arrested in Albany while praying. There were small and sometimes elite organizations from distant places which sent money and promised help. Birmingham was a coalition of many forces, many units, under the direction of Dr. King. In addition to great contributions of money and volunteers from other cities, Dr. King had intellectual help from civil rights leaders, too. He had alerted the President of the United States to a cry for help, worked out the goals he had set, and even issued what King was pleased to call his Birmingham Manifesto.

The goals were: (1) the desegregation of lunch counters, rest rooms, fitting rooms, and drinking fountains in stores and shops; (2) the upgrading and hiring of blacks on a nondiscriminatory basis throughout the business and industrial community of Birmingham; (3) the dropping of all charges against jailed demonstrators; and (4) the creation of a biracial committee to work out a timetable for desegregation in other areas of Birmingham life.

To keep peace in the city, Birmingham had only to grant numbers one and three—desegregation of shops and facilities and to free those in jail. Neither would work a hardship on the life of the community, no matter how racist its views. Two and four could easily be promised, without intent to comply with them. The hiring of blacks could be defeated by hiding behind such words as "level of education, efficiency, competence." Number four, the biracial committee, could be ordered into being by the mayor, with the white members prepared to hesitate, procrastinate, and postpone.

The manifesto, on the other hand, was a pretrial verdict. Dr. King designed it and had refined it endlessly. "The patience of an oppressed people cannot endure forever," it said. "The Negro citizens of Birmingham for the last several years have hoped in vain for some evidence of good faith and resolution of our just grievances. . . . We have been segregated racially, exploited economically, and dominated politically. Under the leadership of the Alabama Christian Movement for Human Rights, we sought relief by petition for the repeal of city ordinances requiring segregation and the institution of a merit hiring policy in city employment. Twice since September we have deferred our direct action thrust in order that a change in city government would not be made in the hysteria of community crisis. We act today in full concert with our Hebraic-Christian tradition, the law of morality and the Constitution of our nation. The absence of justice and progress in Birmingham demands that we make a moral witness to give our community a chance to survive."

Attorney General Robert Kennedy permitted himself to be quoted as saying that the "Battle of Birmingham" was "ill-timed." In this, one must feel sympathetic to King's cry that any time for a fight is a bad time. The Reverend Billy Graham asked for a "cooling-off" period. Among Birmingham's black affluent society, King felt hostility. As always, these were the people who stood to lose the most in defeat, gain the least in victory.

Roy Wilkins, whose NAACP was an integral part of King's armament, felt a growing alarm as D day approached. He said that the blacks of Birmingham are "some of the roughest in the United States. If there is an incident there, I shudder to think what will happen, because they will not—the great rank and file of the hundred and forty thousand Negroes will not—accede to the fine discipline of Dr. King."

It was too late for anyone, even King, to stop the battle. He had been caught up in the fiery vortex. His subordinates were soliciting elementary schools for little children to join the street demonstrations. Later, he would write that: ". . . it is clear that the introduction of Birmingham's children into the campaign was one of the wisest moves we made." Martin Luther King had altered direction. In Montgomery, he had been an apostle of Christ crying in the wilderness; in Atlanta, he was the lamb sleeping among wolves; in Albany, he had been politician and publican; in Birmingham, he was a warrior.

Bernice Albertine, his third child, had just been born, but King, for the first time, was too busy to spend time with his wife. The battle was joined, and he would go to Birmingham.

White Birmingham felt invincible. It was ready for marches, sit-ins, demonstrations, even riots. If red blood had to flow, it would flow down black faces. The Northern owners of the steel mills and the mines agreed with their plant managers and the Southern politicians that the city was secure in its resolve to resist Martin Luther King and that conciliation would be misinterpreted as weakness. Birmingham would have to stand fast, as it once did when white men from the North had tried to unionize the mills.

The mayoralty election between Eugene "Bull" Connor and Albert Boutwell (both were segregationists) was won by Boutwell. The city—staid and stiff, politically—was in political chaos. C. B. Hanson, Jr., publisher of the Birmingham *News,* and James E. Mills, president of the Birmingham *Post-Herald,* had urged their readers to rid themselves of the tight three-man form of commission government in favor of a mayor and nine councilmen. The people, in a referendum, endorsed the views of their newspapers. Nine minds, instead of three, would interpret Birmingham's archaic political credos. When Boutwell won, Connor contested the matter in court. Until there was a decision, confusion reigned. The old three-man government insisted that it was still in power until the term of office expired in 1965. The new government was to win the court fight, but the old, defeated one hung onto City Hall throughout April and May, six of the most crucial weeks in Birmingham's history.

The day after the mayoralty election had been settled or, more properly, unsettled, Dr. King announced that he was present in the city to lead black demonstrations until "Pharaoh lets God's people go." This was the starting cry. In Washington, President Kennedy had partly capitulated by sending a civil rights message to Congress asking an end to discrimination in voting rights. He signed an open housing act which prohibited discrimination but failed to provide for banking and building-and-loan penalties, thus permitting the holders of first mortgages to continue to grant loans to whites and deny them to blacks.

On April 3 the first few groups of young blacks walked through the business section, without ostentation, and sat at lunch counters. They were asked to leave. They didn't. They were arrested. Thirty-five blacks were in jail on the first day of the Battle of Birmingham but there was no excitement. At night, the black churches were crowded, and visiting ministers preached the power of the movement for civil rights; they prayed; they exhorted; they demanded volunteers; they worked the crowds up to a pitch of tension. Martin Luther King renounced, momentarily, his elite white man's diction and appealed to the crowd to respond to each thing that he said. They did.

There were no plans for King to participate in any of the demonstrations of the first week. The postponement of D-Day between the first municipal election and the second had left the local blacks drifting sullenly back to defeatism. Before he could risk jail, the pastor had to shore the will and confidence of his Birmingham followers. To do this, it was necessary that he address afternoon meetings and evening meetings; it was doubly important to counteract the influence of the local preachers, who counseled their elders and their parishioners to remain off the streets and away from the SCLC movement. "Dr. King deserves the respect of all for what he has done for our people," they said, "but he came to Birmingham uninvited by any of us; he sat in Atlanta and selected Birmingham by himself. He is not acquainted with conditions here, and he has been staying out at the Gaston Motel planning demonstrations and asking our people to pledge themselves to go to prison— and he has done this in secrecy, not even telling us his plans or even the day when he plans to strike."

And yet, as Dr. King pointed out to his silent audiences, secrecy was necessary. A public pronouncement of plans would have influenced the runoff election, and Police Commissioner Connor might have won on a pledge to keep the Birmingham black "in his place." The early political history of George Wallace, King pointed out, was not one of a rabid racist, but he had been defeated once on that issue. Now he was the newly elected governor of the State of Alabama, and George Wallace was preaching "Segregation now, segregation tomorrow, segregation forever!" The more the black man came out into the open to fight for what was rightfully his, the more he tended to polarize the whites into a frenzied opposition. There would be no easy way to win, he said, but if the black could win a few rights and community respectability in Birmingham, King felt that the entire nation might fall into line. Over and over, he stressed Birmingham as the keystone in the fight. He was still preaching nonviolence, but King referred to the arrest of thirty-five sit-ins as a "probing action."

Commissioner Connor, big, steely-eyed, expressionless, a man with a straw hat worn forward to shield his eyes, had two choices. The first was to do what his nature and experience told him to do: bring his police reserves to every black demonstration, show no mercy, and beat the participants back into their ghettos. This method would result in bad publicity, but it would also take the edge from local black courage and, in effect, remove local blacks from the scene of battle in downtown streets. In that event, Connor would be fighting only the SCLC and other "outside" organizations. The second choice was to order his policemen not to use violence, but rather to herd the protesters into groups and take them off to jail quietly. He chose the second method, and for the White Establishment, this was a mistake of enormous proportions.

On Saturday, the first marchers formed ranks in front of the Sixteenth Street Baptist Church. It was a bright morning, and the marchers sang hymns as they headed toward City Hall. A policeman outside the church stepped into a phone booth and called police headquarters. When the marchers were three blocks from City Hall, Bull Connor was waiting with double lines of policemen. Blacks who were not in the march also heard the news and hurried to the center of Birmingham to watch the action from the sidewalks. There wasn't any. The police moved quietly among the marchers, asking them to display permits for parading. When none was shown, forty-two were arrested and taken in police vans to jail. The blacks on the sidewalks cheered. In their judgment, the white man, for the first time in Birmingham history, had shown that he was afraid to club a black man. This brought a host of fresh volunteers to the SCLC.

On Sunday there were more paraders, more polite arrests. On Tuesday, Commissioner Connor had 400 singing blacks in the Birmingham jail. Blacks from outlying farm areas heard about the peaceful demonstrations and the peaceful arrests, and they got into cars and hurried to Birmingham. On the way in, large signs erected by the Chamber of Commerce greeted them: IT'S SO NICE TO HAVE YOU IN BIRMINGHAM. Attorneys for the Southern Christian Leadership Conference were busy posting cash for bailing prisoners from jail. Commissioner Connor was facing the same marching blacks over and over. In addition, the glad tidings that blacks were not remaining in jail reached the weak and worried, and additional recruits for marching stepped forward. On Wednesday, Birmingham did two things to stop the tide. The first was to swear out an injunction against King, the SCLC, and the marchers. This was accomplished in the Supreme Court of Alabama and forbade all demonstrations until both sides could be heard. The second was to demand cash in future for bailing out prisoners, and this was impossible, because the SCLC had all its cash tied up in bail already posted.

Once again, Dr. King was faced with a "good law" versus a "bad" one, and he proposed to be the judge of which was which. He called a meeting of leaders at the Gaston Motel for Good Friday morning, April 12. This time, even "Daddy" King showed up. It was not merely because he worried; this was the Easter season, and he would have liked to have had his son return to Atlanta to join him on the altar at the Ebenezer Baptist Church. As a law-abiding citizen, the young pastor realized that he could take the Alabama injunction to a federal court and have it reversed or, failing that, to the court of appeals. Instead, he chose to regard the injunction as a "bad" law. "It will be disobeyed," he announced. "Negroes are not anarchists advocating lawlessness." If anyone was wrong, it was the Alabama court, he said.

King's apostles were glum when he told the secret meeting that Good Friday was a special day to be arrested. It had significance, he insisted. Ralph Abernathy, who supported King even when he did not agree with him, said that he was the only minister in his new Atlanta church and he would have to be present for Easter services. The movement could hold still for one weekend. A.D., who had a church in Birmingham, felt no enthusiasm for going to prison. Some ministers stated that Easter was secondary to the main issue: They felt that the injunction should be obeyed. Their argument was that if the SCLC expected the whites to obey injunctions, then blacks would have to learn to obey rulings which favored the whites. Otherwise, both sides would be engulfed by anarchy.

"I want to meditate about this decision," Dr. King told his confreres. He said that he would go into another room and pray for guidance. He returned in workman's overalls. "I have decided to take the leap of faith," he said. "I have decided to go to jail. I don't know what's going to happen; I don't know whether this Movement will continue to build up or whether it will collapse. If enough people are willing to go to jail, I believe it will force the city officials to act or force the federal government to act." He turned a frowning gaze on the faces again. "I'm going to jail today."

His real fear was slowing of the battle. Black Birmingham had been dragging its feet. Once in motion, it must be kept moving, faster and faster until the government was ready for a reconciliation. His fear was well founded, and the antidote was a proper prescription. The men in the room began to sing "We Shall Overcome," but neither what King said nor what they sang changed many minds. Martin said, "Ralph, I know you want to be in your pulpit on Easter Sunday, but I am asking you to go with me." These requests were always in the form of friendly ultimatums—"Either you are with me, or against me"—and Abernathy always did his friend's bidding.

"You know, Martin," he said, "I have always been in jail with you and I can't leave you at this point." Others could. And did.

Dr. King embraced his father as Abernathy donned a pair of overalls and a cheap shirt. They rode in a group of automobiles to Zion Hill Church, and it became obvious that Dr. King had decided on this course of action the night before, because the marchers were waiting in ranks. He went into the church, where the women and old men sat, and he announced from the pulpit that he wanted to be a good servant to his Lord and Master, who was crucified on this day. As he left, some women cried, "There he goes, just like Jesus!"

Policemen on foot, policemen in squad cars, a mobile communications center—all were in operation as the march started. King and Abernathy led the way, walking through the streets under the studied silence of many, the cheers of a few. When the marchers sang, pedestrians sang with them. The sun was bright and warm. Forsythia spread its buttery lace against walls. Azaleas were budding, intricate colors on many branches. Near the downtown area, Commissioner Bull Connor ordered a halt. He told the marchers to disperse. They stared at him. "Okay," he said. "Arrest those men." Two policemen grabbed King and Abernathy by the backs of their shirts and almost lifted them off the pavement. Policemen closed in from all sides and declared the marchers under arrest; among them was Al Hibbler, a blind singer.

Two reporters moved in on King as he and Abernathy were waiting for police vans. The pastor could have played the Black Jesus by linking again his arrest with that of Christ. Instead, he lashed out at the black ministers of Birmingham who would be preaching in quiet, safe pulpits on Easter Sunday. "There are some preachers in Birmingham who are not with this Movement," he said. "I'm tired of preachers riding around in big cars, living in fine homes, but not willing to take their part in the fight. He is the freest man in the Negro community. The white community can't cut off his check. If you cannot stand up with your people, you are not fit to be a leader!" Among those not in the march and not risking imprisonment were almost all of influential black Birmingham society: including A. G. Gaston, a millionaire; Arthur Shores, a well-known attorney; John Drew, an affluent insurance broker; and Lucius Pitts, the president of Miles College. (All were supporters of the SCLC.)

"We want all of our rights here and now!" shouted Dr. King. "Negroes are not afraid any more!" His words were becoming increasingly inflammatory and exaggerated. Connor, lounging nearby, said nothing. He stared silently out from under his hat. Dr. King saw the commissioner. Each might have said of the other: "There is the enemy." If either one could break the will of the other, it could have profound repercussions on the Movement. At the moment, the commissioner had the law on his side. He was arresting King, Abernathy, Hibbler, Shuttlesworth, and the marchers for violating a state injunction. Connor had permitted them to march seven blocks so that he would have enough witnesses and enough photographs to prove a violation in court. The police vans arrived, the nonsense was over, and he ordered King and Abernathy to be placed in solitary confinement, a calculated act of cruelty.

Abernathy was King's security blanket. Ralph could be lighthearted and amusing, even in jail. The two had always shared a cell. Now each was alone. Dr. King made two requests: a phone call to his wife, who was convalescing from the birth of Bernice Albertine, and an opportunity to consult with his lawyers. Both were denied. When the door clanged, he was alone and lonely; there was no light in the cell ceiling, no one to talk to, and, so far as he knew, no help on the way. Again the terrors of prison were upon him, and he sustained the carousel of dismal thoughts about being beaten and brutalized. If Bull Connor wanted to kill King, that too could be arranged. They could say he tried to escape; a ring of cell keys would be clenched in his dead hand. Dr. King had had the same thoughts before, but this time they were in sharper focus. Pacing back and forth did not relieve the sensation of impending doom. He asked for some paper and a pencil. It was brought to him, and he wrote eagerly as the little patch of light crept across the damp floor and up a wall toward twilight and darkness.

In the morning, the SCLC attorneys asked to see Dr. King. Permission was denied. Apparently they did not fear for his safety, for if they had, they could have sworn out a writ of habeas corpus and forced Connor to bring King to court. They could strike a greater blow for civil rights, the leaders felt, if they could tell the press, tell the world that Bull Connor was keeping King in solitary confinement for the crime of marching peaceably on Good Friday. They were right.

Actually, the danger to Martin Luther King was not personal, but political. Assistant Attorney General Burke Marshall, who had tossed the protective mantle of the United States government over the person of Dr. King on several occasions, was angered when he heard that King had deliberately violated a state court injunction. He realized that the pastor was forcing the hand of the White House. Marshall was also aware that his superior, Attorney General Robert F. Kennedy, had personally advised Dr. King not to proceed in Birmingham until the Boutwell government assumed the reins of office. He knew too that only a handful of Birmingham's 150,000 blacks had taken part in the confrontation. When reporters put the question to Burke Marshall, his mouth was grimly set. "The federal government," he snapped, "has no authority to take legal action or to intervene in Birmingham as the situation now stands."

In addition, eight leading white churchmen had signed a public plea asking Dr. King to stop his battle. Among the signers were Episcopal Bishop C. C. J. Carpenter, Rabbi Milton L. Grafman, and Auxiliary Bishop Joseph A. Durick of the Roman Catholic Church. The posture of the white clergymen puzzled and angered King. Part of their open letter to their flocks said: ". . . we urge our own Negro community to withdraw support from these demonstrations and to unite locally in working peacefully for a better Birmingham. . . . When rights are consistently denied, a cause should be pressed in the courts and in negotiations among local leaders, not in the streets. We appeal to both our white and Negro citizens to observe the principles of law and order and common sense."

At best, the letter was pitiable piety; at worst, it was an eleventh hour plea to maintain the status quo—Connor in his seat of power; the blacks on the floor licking shoes. The clergymen had not been moved to do something for the poor Birmingham black before Martin Luther King arrived. In substance, an out-of-town preacher was doing for the black man what a sense of social justice should have prompted the white clergy to do years before.

When the first early rays of sun tossed a square of light into his cell, Dr. King enriched his solitude by writing an answer to the white clergymen. He did not hurry; there was time to dream up awesome phrases, time to rebut the well-fed gentlemen who had, by circumlocution, judged

King and had found him wanting. He wrote the draft between Saturday and Tuesday, and revised it again after he had regained his liberty:

MY DEAR FELLOW CLERGYMEN,

While confined here in the Birmingham city jail, I came across your recent statement calling my present activities "unwise and untimely." Seldom do I pause to answer criticism of my work and ideas. If I sought to answer all the criticisms that cross my desk, my secretaries would have little time for anything other than such correspondence in the course of the day, and I would have no time for constructive work. But since I feel that you are men of genuine good will and that your criticisms are sincerely set forth, I want to try to answer your statement in what I hope will be patient and reasonable terms.

I think I should indicate why I am here in Birmingham, since you have been influenced by the view which argues against "outsiders coming in." I have the honor of serving as president of the Southern Christian Leadership Conference, an organization operating in every southern state, with headquarters in Atlanta, Georgia. We have some eighty-five affiliated organizations across the South, and one of them is the Alabama Christian Movement for Civil Rights. Frequently, we share staff, educational and financial resources with our affiliates. Several months ago, the affiliate here in Birmingham asked us to be on call to engage in a nonviolent direct-action program if such were deemed necessary. We readily consented, and when the hour came we lived up to our promise. So I, along with several members of my staff, am here because I was invited here. I am here because I have organizational ties here.

But more basically, I am in Birmingham because injustice is here. Just as the prophets of the Eighth Century B.C. left their villages and carried their "thus saith the Lord" far beyond the boundaries of their home towns, and just as the Apostle Paul left his village of Tarsus and carried the gospel of Jesus Christ to the far corners of the Greco-Roman world, so am I compelled to carry the gospel of freedom beyond my own home town. Like Paul, I must constantly respond to the Macedonian call for aid.

Moreover, I am cognizant of the interrelatedness of all communities and states. I cannot sit idly by in Atlanta and not be concerned about what happens in Birmingham. Injustice anywhere is a threat to justice everywhere. We are caught in an inescapable network of mutuality, tied in a single garment of destiny. Whatever affects one directly, affects all indirectly. Never again can we afford to live with the narrow, provincial "outside agitator" idea. Anyone who lives inside the United States can never be considered an outsider anywhere within its bounds.

You deplore the demonstrations taking place in Birmingham. But your statement, I am sorry to say, fails to express a similar concern for the conditions that brought about the demonstrations. I am sure that none of you would want to rest content with the superficial kind of social analysis that deals merely with effects and does not grapple with underlying causes. It is unfortunate that demonstrations are taking place in Birmingham, but it is even more unfortunate that the city's white power structure left the Negro community with no alternative.

In any nonviolent campaign there are four basic steps: collection of the facts to determine whether injustices exist; negotiation; self-purification; and direct action. We have gone through all these steps in Birmingham. There can be no gainsaying the fact that racial injustice engulfs this community. Birmingham is probably the most thoroughly segregated city in the United States. Its ugly record of brutality is widely known. Negroes have experienced grossly unjust treatment in the courts. There have been more unsolved bombings of Negro homes and churches in Birmingham than in any other city in the nation. These are the hard, brutal facts of the case. On the basis of these conditions, Negro leaders sought to negotiate with the city fathers. But the latter consistently refused to engage in good-faith negotiation.

Then, last September, came the opportunity to talk with leaders of Birmingham's economic community. In the course of the negotiations, certain promises were made by the merchants—for example, to remove the stores' humiliating racial signs. On the basis of these promises, the Reverend Fred Shuttlesworth and the leaders of the Alabama Christian Movement for Human Rights agreed to a moratorium on all demonstrations. As the weeks and months went by, we realized that we were the victims of a broken promise. A few signs, briefly removed, returned; the others remained.

As in so many past experiences, our hopes had been blasted, and the shadow of deep disappointment settled upon us. We had no alternative except to prepare for direct action, whereby we would present our very bodies as a means of laying our case before the conscience of the local and the national community. Mindful of the difficulties involved, we decided to undertake a process of self-purification. We began a series of workshops on nonviolence, and we repeatedly asked ourselves: "Are you able to accept blows without retaliating?" "Are you able to endure the ordeal of jail?" We decided to schedule our direct-action program for the Easter season, realizing that except for Christmas, this is the main shopping period of the year. Knowing that a strong economic-withdrawal program would be the by-product of direct action, we felt that this would be the best time to bring pressure to bear on the merchants for the needed change.

Then it occurred to us that Birmingham's mayoralty election was coming up in March, and we speedily decided to postpone action until after election day. When we discovered that the Commissioner of Public Safety,

Eugene "Bull" Connor, had piled up enough votes to be in the run-off, we decided again to postpone action until the day after the run-off so that the demonstrations could not be used to cloud the issues. Like many others, we waited to see Mr. Connor defeated, and to this end we endured post-ponement after postponement. Having aided in this community need, we felt that our direct-action program could be delayed no longer.

You may well ask: "Why direct action? Why sit-ins, marches and so forth? Isn't negotiation a better path?" You are quite right in calling for negotiation. Indeed, this is the very purpose of direct action. Nonviolent direct action seeks to create such a crisis and foster such a tension that a community which has consistently refused to negotiate is forced to con-front the issue. It seeks so to dramatize the issue that it can no longer be ignored. My citing the creation of tension as part of the work of the nonviolent-resister may sound rather shocking. But I must confess that I am not afraid of the word "tension." I have earnestly opposed violent tension, but there is a type of constructive nonviolent tension which is necessary for growth. Just as Socrates felt that it was necessary to create a tension in the mind so that individuals could rise from the bondage of myths and half-truths to the unfettered realm of creative analysis and ob-jective appraisal, so we must see the need for nonviolent gadflies to create the kind of tension in society that will help men rise from the dark depths of prejudice and racism to the majestic heights of understanding and brotherhood.

The purpose of our direct-action program is to create a situation so crisis-packed that it will inevitably open the door to negotiation. I there-fore concur with you in your call for negotiation. Too long has our beloved Southland been bogged down in a tragic effort to live in monologue rather than dialogue. . . . I must make two honest confessions to you, my Chris-tian and Jewish brothers. First, I must confess that over the past few years I have been gravely disappointed with the white moderate. I have almost reached the regrettable conclusion that the Negro's great stumbling block in his stride toward freedom is not the White Citizens Counciler or the Ku Klux Klanner, but the white moderate, who is more devoted to "order" than to justice; who prefers a negative peace which is an absence of ten-sion to a positive peace which is the presence of justice; who constantly says: "I agree with you in the goal you seek, but I cannot agree with your methods of direct action"; who paternalistically believes he can set the timetable for another man's freedom; who lives by a mythical concept of time and who constantly advises the Negro to wait for "a more convenient season." Shallow understanding from people of good will is more frustrat-ing than absolute misunderstanding from people of ill will. . . .

Oppressed people cannot remain oppressed forever. The yearning for freedom eventually manifests itself, and that is what is happening to the

American Negro. Something within has reminded him of his birthright of freedom, and something without has reminded him that it can be gained. Consciously or unconsciously, he has been caught up by the *zeitgeist*, and with his black brothers of Africa and his brown and yellow brothers of Asia, South America and the Caribbean, the United States Negro is moving with a sense of great urgency toward the promised land of racial justice. . . . Never before have I written so long a letter. I'm afraid it is much too long to take your precious time. I can assure you that it would have been much shorter if I had been writing from a comfortable desk, but what else can one do when he is alone in a narrow jail cell, other than write long letters, think long thoughts and pray long prayers? . . .

Yours for the cause of Peace and Brotherhood,
MARTIN LUTHER KING, JR.

The letter, which King called "Letter from Birmingham Jail," totaled 6,400 words. Part of it was written on newspaper margins, part on a pad smuggled to Dr. King by a black jail trustee, all of it written leaning against a wall. Although King painted himself as an abject servant of Jesus and had "two honest confessions to make," he was the avenging angel. He had sustained a blow from his Christian and Jewish confreres in their original letter, and he husbanded his time, patience, and intellect to expose them as men with pretensions to having one foot in heaven, but who really had one sensitive ear to political winds.

Having indicted the indicters, it is a pity that Dr. King did not include a series of notes he had written about the time of the birth of Bernice, called Bunny. Gazing at the infant, the pastor reflected on what it is like to be born black. The following constitutes part of his written notes:

"You would be born in a jim-crow hospital to parents who probably lived in a ghetto. You would attend a jim-crow school. You would spend your childhood playing mainly in the streets because the 'colored' parks were abysmally inadequate. If you went shopping with your mother or father, you would trudge along as they purchased at every counter, except one, in the large or small stores. If you were hungry or thirsty you would have to forget about it until you got back to the Negro section of town, for in your city it is a violation of the law to serve food to Negroes at the same counter with whites.

"If your family attended church, you would go to a Negro church. If you wanted to visit a church attended by white people, you would not be welcome. For although your white fellow citizens would insist that they were Christians, they practiced segregation as rigidly in the house of God as they did in the theatre. If you loved music and yearned to hear the Metropolitan Opera on its tour of the South, you could not enjoy this privilege.

"If you wanted a job in the city, you had better settle on doing menial work as a porter or laborer. If you were fortunate enough to get a job, you could expect that promotions to a better status or more pay would come, not to you, but to a white employee regardless of your comparative talents. On your job, you would eat in a separate place and use a water fountain and lavatory labeled 'Colored' in conformity to city-wide ordinances.

"If you believed your history books and thought of America as a country whose governing officials are selected by the governed, you would be swiftly disillusioned when you tried to exercise your right to register and vote. You would be confronted with every conceivable obstacle to taking that most important walk a Negro American can take today—the walk to the ballot box. The ultimate tragedy is not the brutality of the bad people, but the silence of the good people. . . ."

At noon on Easter Sunday, Martin Luther King had been in jail for forty-eight hours. He missed the hopeful, soothing attitude of Ralph Abernathy; he was not permitted to send out for food; he ate prison fare. He heard no voices except the dim and garbled mumbling of guards at the end of the cell block. He was not allowed to phone his wife or summon his lawyers. And yet he had been told one thing by his jailors: Bail was $300. It was a small sum; the SCLC lawyers, bailing out other prisoners, could have freed Dr. King. But King would not be freed so quickly. The longer he stayed in jail, the more national pressure would be put on the White Establishment in Birmingham.

A. D. King held Easter services in his church and led his people downtown, intending to lead a prayer meeting in front of the jail. The police arrested all of them. Shortly after noon, two of King's attorneys, Arthur Shores and Orzell Billingsley, were permitted to visit their client. They saw a sleepless man in overalls alone in a cell. He had not been abused or hurt. No one had visited him or interrogated him. They were concerned that the Movement in Birmingham was slowing to a stop. The huge reserves of cash had gone for bail. The federal government had not interposed on behalf of Dr. King, and in spite of phone calls to various federal officials, no response had come from Washington. They told the pastor they now felt that he could accomplish no further good by playing the martyr. He was vital to the cause, directing the Movement, organizing the protests, and, most important of all, injecting hope in the heart of the black man. The visit with the lawyers was over almost before it began, and King was left with the difficult decision of what course to follow.

Mrs. King had been in constant touch with Birmingham by phone from Atlanta. It was Wyatt Walker who struck the first note of real fear. "Coretta, I haven't been able to get a phone message through to Martin. . . . They're holding him incommunicado."

Mrs. King said, "Do you think if I made a statement to the press about this situation it would help?"

"Do you know what I think you should do?" Walker replied, "I think you ought to call the President." It seems likely that Walker was availing himself of the services of the worried wife, the new mother, to do what the SCLC leaders had failed to achieve—bring the President of the United States into the action at Birmingham.

"I will try if you think I should," she said, "but first I wish you would try to check with Martin to see if it's all right with him, because I don't want to do it if he doesn't approve." If Walker could reach King for permission and learned that he was alive and well, then he was no longer being held incommunicado and there would be no need to phone the President.

Later on Easter afternoon, Walker phoned Atlanta and said, "It's no use, Coretta. I can't get through to Martin. You have no alternative but to call the President." Mrs. King phoned the White House several times, explaining patiently who she was and asking to speak to Mr. Kennedy. The White House switchboard always has a direct "patch" to wherever the President might be—in this case at the winter home of his parents in Palm Beach. However, the operator in each case told Mrs. King that she had "no number for the President or members of his family at Palm Beach."

On that Easter Sunday afternoon, the President and his father had boarded the fifty-foot family launch, *Honey Fitz,* and, encircled by Coast Guard cutters and small Secret Service craft, had left Palm Beach inlet for a short cruise in the warm Atlantic. Mr. Kennedy had a special ship-to-shore telephone, hooked to the power of the Coast Guard cutter, and, with his "bagman" aboard carrying secret codes for dialing instantaneous retaliation in the event of attack by a foreign power, could reach the White House switchboard with ease or receive a phone call if he was so disposed. Mrs. King tried to reach Vice President Lyndon Johnson, but he too was unavailable. "There must be someone I could call who would be able to help me get to the President," she said.

The operator said, "What about Pierre Salinger?" The President's press secretary, a rotund and jolly cigar smoker, was taking his ease at the old Kennedy Palm Beach mansion facing the sea. It was a big Spanish-style home, with poinsettias and mimosas, a blue-tiled swimming pool, beamed ceilings, and silver-framed photos of kings and queens and prime ministers on pianos and coffee tables. Yes, Mrs. King said. Yes, she would speak to Mr. Salinger. While she was waiting to be called back, Harry Belafonte, the singer, phoned. He said he didn't want her to be worried about her husband. She said that she was worried, so worried that she was trying to reach President Kennedy to tell him how anxious she was about her husband's safety. She was seeking some intercession so that her husband could speak to her. Mrs. King felt depressed, and she told Belafonte that the phone was ringing all the time; she had to take care of her children and a new baby; she wished she could be in Birmingham to be with her husband. The singer advised her to hire a secretary and a nurse and to send the bills to him.

The second phone rang, and Mrs. King heard a voice say, "Mrs. King, this is Attorney General Robert Kennedy. I am returning your call to my brother. The President isn't able to speak to you because he's with my father, who is quite ill. He asked me to call and find out what we can do for you."

She poured out her worriment: "I was calling because I am concerned about my husband. . . . At this point, no one is able to see him. Usually, they let him telephone me, but I have heard nothing from him directly. I understand that he and Reverend Abernathy are being held incommunicado, and I am awfully worried. I wondered if the President could check into the situation and see if he is all right." She said she understood that her husband was sleeping on bare steel springs without blankets or a pillow. The Attorney General did not seem to be touched by this. The creature comforts in jail are minuscule, and many prisoners sleep on concrete floors. Robert Kennedy told Mrs. King of the difficulties federal officials faced when dealing with local officials such as Bull Connor and added that it was his hope that after the new city government took over, something could be done in Birmingham. He promised to look into the situation and let her know.

A day later, little Dexter answered the ringing phone and babbled into it. Mrs. King picked up an extension and heard an operator say, "Will you get your child off the phone, please?" Then she heard a familiar voice: "Hello, Mrs. King. I'm sorry I wasn't able to talk to you yesterday. I understand my brother called. I just wanted you to know that I was with my father. He's ill, and I couldn't leave him." Mrs. King recognized the voice of the President. He asked how Mrs. King felt and said he understood that she had just had a baby.

"I'm all right," she said, "but I'm terribly worried about my husband."

"I know you'll be interested in knowing that we sent the FBI into Birmingham last night. We checked on your husband and he's all right." There was a silence. Then he said, "Of course, Birmingham is a very difficult place.

"I want you to know we are doing everything we can," the President continued. "I have just talked to Birmingham, and your husband will be calling you shortly. If you have any further worries about your husband or about Birmingham in the next few days, I want you to feel free to call me. You can get me or my brother or Mr. Salinger. You know how to get me now."

He did not mention that it required considerable prodding by the FBI and the Attorney General's office to move the Birmingham officials. In Birmingham's view, the arrest was a local matter ordered when King disobeyed an injunction, and the federal government was not a party to the action and should, legally, remain aloof.

Within fifteen minutes, Dr. King was on the phone with his wife. She thought his voice sounded fatigued. He told her he was all right. When she described her conversation with the President, he said, "So that's why everybody is suddenly polite. This is good to know." The doctor spoke softly, almost whisperingly, as though jail guards might be nearby, listening. He asked her to get word to Wyatt Walker about her conversation with Kennedy "so that a statement can be released to the press."

It became comparatively easy for interested parties to see King after Easter Sunday. On Monday morning, King's New York attorney, Clarence Jones, arrived at the cell to tell him that overnight Harry Belafonte had raised $50,000 for bail money. The pastor grinned. "You have lifted a thousand pounds from my heart," he said. It was good to know that someone "out there" cared. The sum would temporarily free 166 blacks of the 400 in jail. All would be free by Wednesday even without bail. Practically all the 400 had been arrested on "criminal contempt of court" charges, a wrong automatically righted by serving five days in jail. Only King, Abernathy, Shuttlesworth, and a few leaders were booked on "civil contempt" charges, a state law under which the crime can be expiated only by admitting the contempt in court. The penalty was usually a suspended sentence or small fine. If convicted on the civil charge, a stubborn prisoner may, theoretically, spend his life in jail if he chooses not to apologize to the court.

The 400 had been booked on Friday. Attorney Clarence Jones and Dr. King knew that legally they had to be freed on Wednesday, and this was Monday. The "civil contempt" trial of the leaders had been set for April 20. Dr. King would serve eight days before being brought to court. The movement had already achieved national—and sympathetic—treatment, and he was determined not to admit contempt and apologize for it if he were found guilty. In a sense, he was playing into the hands of Bull Connor and the white structure, which could keep him in jail until he was ready to recant. On the other hand, King was certain, now that he had the President of the United States *and* public opinion behind him, that Birmingham would be anxious to relieve itself of his presence in jail, and, to achieve it, King was prepared to make the Establishment truckle to him.

Mayor Boutwell was sworn in, and even though the black community saw him as a "moderate segregationist," Bull Connor still directed the Police and Fire Departments and remained the prime adversary. Some said that, before the demonstrations began, he had phoned Police Chief Pritchett in Albany and had learned the lesson of "nonviolence in police duty." He had tried it, but gentility in the case of fractious blacks was not in his nature and ran against the grain of his policemen. Connor's patience with King was running thin.

On the day that Boutwell was sworn in, Coretta King had recruited enough domestic help to enable her and Juanita Abernathy to visit their husbands in Birmingham. Both were admitted to jail. The four had much to talk about, including the fact that the time had arrived for both men to return to the Movement. It had all but ground to a halt. King, Abernathy, and a few others paid $300 bail and left for Room 30 in the Gaston Motel. On the thirteenth arrest of his life, Dr. King remained in prison eight days. He left telling the press that he desired to remain behind bars, but "as the situation is now developing in Birmingham, I must meet with the strategy committee." The topic of the meeting was how to use children in the demonstrations. In the opinion of such leaders as James Bevel, Andy Young, Bernard Lee, and Dorothy Cotton, the children could be sent to public libraries and parks to desegregate them. It would be an exasperating embarrassment to Bull Connor, who would hardly dare to arrest such young offenders. Some could be sent to white schools just to stand or sit in the classrooms.

Whatever was done would have to be done quickly, because the Movement had lost much of its fascination for the press and was off the front page. The pastor urged the leaders to visit schools, enlist students, invite them to after-school meetings, and explain that "we talk of bringing freedom to Birmingham, not in some distant time, but right now." One of the first group of "recruits" turned out to be what King called "six tiny youngsters." They were not turned away. Andy Young told them to go to the white library. "You won't get arrested there," he said, "but you might learn something." They went to the children's room of the library and sat and read, not lifting their eyes to watch the shocked librarians watching them.

The trial of the SCLC leaders was perfunctory. The Birmingham prosecutors asked permission to approach the bench and changed the charge from civil contempt to criminal contempt. A five-day sentence and a fine of $50 was levied against each of the ten men as they were found guilty. The judge announced that he would give the defendants until May 26 to appeal. Bail of $300 was continued. Martin Luther King reached the sunshine bubbling with triumph. The White Establishment, he was sure, had a big crack in its edifice. It had been *afraid* to send him back to jail. On the other hand, the Birmingham press saw it as a shrewd move on the part of the city to keep King out of jail and thus rob him of his martyr image. It also bought time for Birmingham in which to think out its next move, without having to face wave after wave of blacks singing in front of the jail.

Attorney General Robert Kennedy phoned Dr. King and tried to persuade him to moderate his campaign. He was declined. King did not need counsel or assistance from the Kennedys now. The pastor pointed out that the oppressed condition of the black man had been going on for 300 years and that he must make his move for complete freedom now, under law, or remain content to be eternally inferior to the white. Kennedy was frustrated. He and the President had helped this man, but the pastor refused to temper his attitude toward direct confrontation. Next, Kennedy called Governor George Wallace of Alabama. He tried to persuade Wallace that the University of Alabama would eventually be desegregated, so why not do it now? The governor gave the impression that it would not occur while he was alive.

The Attorney General looked haggard when he reported to the President. "There's no communication," he said. "It's like a foreign country. What do you do?" Nothing. Nothing at all. The contending forces had been committed since the Supreme Court decision on school desegregation in May, 1954. Nine years later, both sides were prepared for one battle, a final battle.

Six days after King's trial, the pastor assembled about 1,000 children at the Sixteenth Street Baptist Church, bordering Kelly Ingram Park. This was the heart of the Black Belt, and it is one of the ironies of ideological warfare that both sides preferred this battleground. The blacks wanted it because their strength was here. Bull Connor liked it because he saw himself as an iron cork in a dark bottle. His men did better fighting blacks around Kelly Ingram Park than in white downtown. If damage was done, it didn't matter. There would be no white outcry at brutality. The night before each demonstration Commissioner Connor cordoned the area with carpenters' horses, and behind them stood policemen in helmets carrying nightsticks. King felt the risk in involving children on a riot-provoking march would be borne by Connor. The police felt that the onus for even one death would rest on King for sending "boys and girls to do a man's work."

Dr. King reveled in the situation. He complimented Jim Bevel for originating it and referred to it as "inspiration." Later he wrote: "At one school, the principal gave orders to lock the gates to keep the students in. The youngsters climbed over the fence and ran toward freedom." It was 1 P.M. on a schoolday when King sent the students on their way to demonstrate in the downtown section. They were brighter, more clever, than their parents because they left the exits of the Sixteenth Street Baptist Church in small groups of ten to fifty.

The police were slow-thinking. They permitted the singing prancing children to curl around the barricades and disappear. The white officers did not realize that these groups planned to meet at a designated place to form one huge dark wave of children. By the time the cops tried to stop them the blacks were pouring out of all the church doors at top speed. Policemen began to chase them, yelling, "Halt! Stop in the name of the law!" but the children fanned out, dodging in and out of alleys and over fences in diverse directions. It was like spilling an apron full of fresh-picked peas. No hands could hold them.

They re-formed ranks downtown, still dancing, still singing. They harmed no one; they disturbed no trade; they impeded traffic a little. Police reserves were called. When they arrived, the children stopped running. They walked silently, heads down, for this was the serious part of the business. They had been asked if they were willing to face prison in the name of freedom, and the response had been a unanimous yes.

Scores of boys and girls were taken from the marching ranks and arrested. By nightfall Dr. King announced that about 500 students were in Birmingham Jail. Almost all of it had been filmed by news photographers; the zoom lens close-ups showed the police crouched before girls no more than seven or eight years of age, demanding name, address, age, and writing these on a court summons before yanking them to patrol vans. Clubs swung at big boys trying to run away. The pictures showed masses of children, big-eyed and a little afraid, looking small and helpless before the police with their helmets and billy clubs.

The SCLC called for another—and larger—demonstration for the next day, Friday, May 3. The law may have been on Commissioner Connor's side, but public opinion was contemptuous of him and his police, in some cases, horror-stricken. The spectacle, seen on television sets in black homes throughout the country, was bound to set teeth on edge and start riots in trouble spots. Nonviolence, as many officers on Dr. King's staff had hoped, was being overtaken by violence. It was still sound strategy for the doctor to preach the philosophy of passivity so long as it goaded the white man to violence, which united the American blacks as nonviolence never could. It did more than that; it moved liberal white sentiment further toward an active role on the side of the blacks.

The commissioner had run out of police vans on Thursday; on Friday he supplemented them with school buses. From the sanctity of the church, Dr. King addressed the biggest mass of children he had ever seen. "Yesterday was D-Day," he said. "Today will be double D-Day. Thousands of you may be arrested." Five hundred children got out on the streets before the police, in squads, manned the church exits. Behind the barricades, the commissioner and his men stood waiting; this time the police were accompanied by firemen, who connected heavy hoses to nearby hydrants.

Children inside the church formed groups trying to break out of an exit. The police around the church ran to that exit while larger groups escaped from another one. This was repeated several times. The children were manhandled by the furious police. Those free ran to the barricades. "Turn those hoses on," Connor said. Firemen manned the heavy nozzles, and high-pressure streams of water crossed the carpenters' horses on a flat trajectory. It caught dozens of groups of running students and spun them across sidewalks, slamming some into storefronts, spinning others across sidewalks. A stream of water ripped a cotton shirt from a boy's back. Girls screamed as they held hands and fell, clothing drenched and awry, hair plastered in their eyes as the relentless water moved them like autumn leaves in a gutter.

A second group of policemen stepped into the front line. Each held a German shepherd on a leash. At a command, the leashes were unsnapped, and the dogs, running and snarling between the lines of water, attacked and bit demonstrators and pedestrians, many of whom had paused to watch the drama. Commissioner Connor had predicted that the demonstrations would run out of control and had called Governor George Wallace for help. Wallace sent a state investigator to sit, watch, and report. This man became so enraged by the blacks that he drove his automobile into the crowd of demonstrators. From nearby rooftops, other blacks loosed a cascade of bricks and bottles at the police and firemen. Again, violence was being met by violence. Hundreds more went to jail on Friday. Clerks required most of the day to book them for unlawful assembly and inciting to riot.

On Saturday, James Bevel, the young minister who had thought up the children's demonstrations, was at the Sixteenth Street Church and saw crowds of angry black adults join the students at the start of a new march. He saw switchblade knives and revolvers in the hands of men. Stones and bricks were raining from roofs. The Reverend Mr. Bevel became frightened. He grabbed a bullhorn from a policeman and hollered through it, "Everybody get off this corner. If you're not going to demonstrate in a nonviolent manner, than leave. Everybody off this corner. . . ." The crowd listened. The demonstration broke up. Bevel had barely averted what might have been the first catastrophe of the Movement.

On Sunday, peaceful black couples entered twenty-one white churches. They were admitted to four, turned away at the others. At one church door, a pious white elder tried to explain his position: "This church was built by white people with white people's money, and only white people can worship here." No one heard the voice of the Jew echoing down the rocky slide of centuries: "Love ye one another." Praise and criticism poured in on Dr. King from black leaders. Roy Wilkins said that the photos of children being spun across sidewalks by water from fire hoses had converted him from his legalistic posture to that of an angry activist. Others stated that the use of children was cynical and contemptible. "Where were they," King asked scornfully, "with their protective words when down through the years, Negro infants were born in ghettos, taking their first breath of life in a social atmosphere where the fresh air of freedom was crowded out by the stench of discrimination?" Children had been used; King proposed to use them again.

Birmingham became an international scandal. Photos of snarling dogs with fangs exposed as black children cowered; pictures of black children skidding and tumbling under high-powered water hoses, were published all over the world. Wayne Morse stood in the United States Senate to state that what was happening in Birmingham "would disgrace a Union of South Africa or a Portuguese Angola." The New York *Times* thundered that the barbarities were reminiscent of "totalitarian excesses." Attorney General Robert Kennedy called for a truce. Cautiously, he said that Birmingham was at fault in not granting rights to blacks; on the other hand, he thought that Martin Luther King's timing represented poor judgment. He said that Mayor Boutwell stated that he proposed to "resolve the difficulties facing the community." Mr. Kennedy wished that a peace plan could be agreed upon at a table, "not in the streets."

Bull Connor's personal assessment of the black was encapsulated in one sentence: "If you'd ask half of them what freedom means, they couldn't tell you." His opinion was shared by most of his policemen and firemen and a segment of the white electorate. Jefferson County Sheriff Melvin Bailey, who toured jails bulging with 2,000 blacks, told a group of business and civic leaders that if the race war did not stop, it would be necessary to impose martial law. This would mean asking Governor Wallace for national guardsmen to patrol the streets, and no one doubted that Wallace was eager to get into the fight.

The governor, realizing that Commissioner Connor was about to be inundated by a passive black wave, anticipated the call. Secretly, he phoned Sheriff Jim Clark in Selma and asked if he could take his "posse" up to Birmingham and furnish some assistance. The sheriff agreed. He had organized an unofficial posse of substantial citizens five years earlier ostensibly as a water patrol, but actually to augment the force of deputies in Dallas County in case of "trouble." Clark took part of his regular force of eight deputies and about a hundred members of the posse to Birmingham, where, at the governor's request, they remained for three weeks to help Connor's men. Colonel Albert J. Lingo of the state troopers was also ordered into Birmingham with a few hundred additional men. Birmingham became a city under siege.

Sheriff Clark hadn't been overly anxious to go to Birmingham. "Trouble," which always means the black, had already started in Selma. No public demonstrations had begun, but the sheriff could see the pattern of events. He swore out a restraining injunction against black church meetings, and Judge James A. Hare granted it on the grounds that the "outside" blacks who were calling the meetings were, in effect, advocating the overthrow of the government of the United States. Sheriff Clark knew the court injunction against Selma's blacks would keep peace for only a while.

All Dr. King could do was to boost morale by passing the word that he would get "around to Selma" soon, that he was very busy "up in Birmingham." He kept his word. The SCLC lawyers knew that they could break the injunction by appealing to any federal court. In time, that would be their first move.

The demonstrations in Birmingham grew in size and frequency. What Dr. King had not been able to achieve—the mobilization of the local adults—Connor did for him. The barricades had placed the blacks in an enclave; the apartheid which the Birmingham black man had felt for hundreds of years was now a physical reality. He was told that he could leave his ghetto one by one, but not in groups. He had seen the pictures of black children swept away by high-powered water hoses, policemen cracking running blacks with clubs, savage biting dogs. The adult black had been lifted out of his apathetic hopelessness to a dangerous anger. Those who had not been inside a church for years were in pews now, walking up to the altar rail eagerly when the question was asked: "Who will pledge to participate in a nonviolent demonstration?"

The jails were full for miles around. Two thousand black faces were behind bars and sleeping in prison corridors on concrete. Dr. King said, "Keep pouring it on," and the people did. He did not participate in any marches, but there were plenty of local ministers who were, in effect, the penitents of the Movement, men of God who had once begged their people to remain outside the Movement and who now wanted to lead. They knew they would face hoses, dogs, and imprisonment, but they swallowed their fears. The Reverend Charles Billups stepped out of New Pilgrim Baptist Church on a day dull with clouds, a chill breeze brushing the multitude of faces.

"March on in the name of the Lord!" he shouted, and they marched. This time, there were no dragging feet. Crowds of blacks stood on the sidewalks, cheering. Ahead stood Commissioner Connor, with his policemen, his dogs, his firemen and hoses, all tense behind the carpenters' horses.

Police lieutenants and captains yelled to Billups, "Stop in the name of the law!"

The reverend began to tremble. "Move on in the name of the Lord!" The police tried once more. The blacks kept moving toward the barricades. The commissioner nodded to the firemen. "Turn on the hoses," he said.

Billups dropped to his knees. The crowd behind him knelt. A babble of sound echoed off the walls of the surrounding buildings. "Turn on the hoses, dammit!" The firemen looked at one another. The blacks, on their knees in the street, wailing a discordant assortment of prayers, were too much to face. One fireman burst into tears and dropped a nozzle. The others dropped hoses. The dogs were snarling on their leashes, but the policemen held them close. The reverend finished his prayer and stood. His followers got to their feet slowly. They had braced themselves for physical horror, and it had not come. Billups began to sob. A small cheer went up from the pedestrians, and it died in their throats. White policemen were crying.

"We just want to march to that park," the clergyman said. He pointed. The words were almost apologetic. He walked ahead "in the name of the Lord," and the law stepped aside to permit him and his marchers to pass. For the first time, white men and black men blinked at each other through the distortion of tears and, for a brief moment almost understood each other. The Reverend Mr. Billups went to the park, stood under the trees, and tried to say something. His heart was too full; his mind gave his tongue words which he would never again recall. Then he said, "Go home. Please go home. God bless you." It was the first crack in a white marble façade.

In this campaign, Dr. King had twenty-five assistants who left the Gaston Motel every morning to work their way through the black districts, announcing fresh and larger demonstrations, devising ways of bedeviling the community. The first sweet taste of triumph was in the mouths of the conferees, and it was difficult to contain. In the press and television, the blacks were white; the whites were black. King was a gentle Jesus; Connor was a sadistic Satan. Dr. King no longer worried about victory; he worried about continued pressure.

King had made no attempt to discuss matters with the White Establishment. It was Deputy Attorney General Burke Marshall who requested a meeting between black and white leaders on Tuesday, May 27, at the Birmingham Chamber of Commerce. The sense of alarm felt by President Kennedy over events caused him to alert federal troops and ask the Attorney General to "settle that thing." Robert Kennedy was on the phone day and night with Marshall, asking what progress could be reported. The answer was none. Marshall required three hours of conversation with Dr. King and his staff to convince them that he had not been sent down to Birmingham to ask for a one-sided cooling-off period. King was eventually convinced that Marshall was willing to mediate the matter without asking the black community to stop its demonstrations.

If the pastor was intransigent at the start, Marshall found that 125 white leaders were even less eager to commit themselves to any form of reconciliation. Their spokesmen gave Marshall the same argument he had heard in so many Southern communities: "You people up there in Washington don't understand our problems, and you don't really give a damn." And: "This was a good, law-abiding city until that black son of a bitch came in. Everywhere he goes, there's trouble. One of these days he'll take his mob to Washington and then the Kennedys will see what it's like." And: "We can't deal with him under any circumstances. He'll strut and crow that we knuckled under to him, and we don't propose to do that under any circumstances."

The meeting adjourned for lunch. The 125 white men stepped out onto the sidewalk and stopped in shock. There were black faces everywhere. They were marching up and down sidewalks, sitting on curbsides, lying down in front of department stores, forcing their way into white restaurants to sit and wait. The civic and business leaders were shaken. This meant that Commissioner Connor's barricades had been breached. Policemen in helmets arrested a handful of leaders, but there was no place to herd the crowds. The black was everywhere, singing, dancing, sitting glumly, shouting greetings—it was as though the part of Birmingham that really mattered had suddenly become all black.

Some men were in favor of cancelling lunch. Others insisted that they knew a place which was still segregated. The group pushed and shoved through the yelling mob to find a restaurant. The dialogue of indignation stopped. Some men were learning. Others were maturing in one day. Still others were sure it would be better to die than to surrender. After lunch, Burke Marshall conferred with the whites again. He brought about an agreement whereby a few of them would meet *secretly* with King and some of his aides that night. As Marshall pointed out, nothing could be lost by listening.

At the meeting, the whites said that dialogue would be pointless under the threat of race riots; the blacks said that stopping the marches would look like failure of the Movement. Marshall and an Assistant Attorney General conferred with one side, then the other, then both. For more than two hours, it appeared that the only thing they could agree on was that the meeting was to remain secret. In the third hour, a slight break came. Dr. King said that he would not call off the demonstrations, but he was willing to call a pause in them from Wednesday morning until Thursday morning. If, in the interim, both sides could reach a meaningful agreement, demonstrations would be canceled, but he asked for some evidence of good faith.

As King and Abernathy left the meeting for the Gaston Motel, they were rearrested on the earlier charge of violating a court injunction. It appeared to be white treachery, and aides sped through Birmingham spreading the word that Dr. King was again in jail. The two men were released before the blacks could assemble. The Movement had attained a highly sensitive trigger finger, and the precept of nonviolence was dying in King's presence. He needed a settlement of sorts as a control over his people; the whites required a saving of face. Birmingham was just about due for a bath of blood in the downtown streets. Policemen were overworked, and their tempers were short. The new motto seemed to be: If you can't arrest any more of them, crack some heads. That'll make 'em think.

Forces outside the city sought peace. The Secretary of the Treasury, Douglas Dillon, phoned the heads of big businesses in Birmingham. Edward Norton, chairman of Royal Crown Cola, received a telephone plea to help the cause. So did Frank Plummer, president of the Birmingham Trust National Bank, and William H. Hulsey, chairman of the board of the Realty Mortgage Company. This kind of pressure influenced the white structure from the top down. Secretary of Defense Robert McNamara was asked to phone men of influence whom he knew from his days as president of Ford Motor Company. Roger Blough, chairman of United States Steel, was requested to phone his Birmingham subsidiary, Tennessee Coal and Iron Company. Louis H. Pollack, professor of law at Yale University, was asked to notify Roy Wilkins and the NAACP that peace had to be made possible. President Kennedy made Birmingham the opening statement in a White House press conference and emphasized the administration's hope that both sides could be reconciled.

Riots were sporadic through the city on Wednesday. The request of Dr. King to pause for twenty-four hours was honored by many, ignored by a few. Hoses were turned on; dogs were unleashed. Paving stones and broken bottles were hurled. Three policemen were injured; fifty blacks were treated for wounds. But the Battle of Birmingham had moved beyond Commissioner Eugene Connor; beyond Dr. Martin Luther King, too. Dick Gregory, a television comedian who had led one children's march, had been beaten three times for protesting the treatment accorded children under arrest. The New York *Times,* trumpeting from a distance, stated "Doctor King and his lieutenants appear to have little control of the demonstrations. . . ." The New York *Herald Tribune,* assessing the escalation of tension in Birmingham, said that nonviolence had gone beyond the bounds of peaceful assembly. The threat of sudden death was "made especially ominous by the Negroes' use of school children as front line troops."

On Wednesday and Thursday, while the secret negotiations continued, 1,200 police officers patrolled Kelly Ingram Park, near the Sixteenth Street Baptist Church. The SCLC issued a national appeal for bail money so that more blacks could be freed to participate in planned demonstrations. Almost at once $200,000 arrived from the United Automobile Workers Union and the National Maritime Union. Within a few hours, the SCLC lawyers were at the jail and were surprised to find that at least 1,200 persons had already been released, leaving 790 still inside. Once more, the forlorn Ku Klux Klan announced that it was ready to march on Birmingham to protect the purity of the whites from the degradation of the "nigras." It was hollow comedy, but it pointed up a somber fact: As Dr. King could no longer control the blacks, so too the responsible citizens of Birmingham could not control the red-necks.

By Thursday no agreement had been reached, but Dr. King maintained the "pause" because both sides were close to accord. On Friday morning Burke Marshall found both sides ready to agree to four points. A statement was dictated, typed, revised by both sides, retyped, and became a morally binding document. It provided for : (1) desegregation of lunch counters, rest rooms, fitting rooms and drinking fountains in all downtown Birmingham stores within ninety days; (2) placement of blacks in clerical and sales jobs in stores within sixty days; (3) release of prisoners still in jail on low bail; and (4) the establishment of permanent communication between white and black leaders.

The agreement was announced by Dr. King. The dimples in his cheeks deepened as he faced the press. He looked like the winner, although he had often preached that blacks cannot refer to civil rights victories as victories or triumphs, because it angers the white man, who is prone to begin the discrimination and harassment all over again. "This is the most significant victory for justice we've ever seen in the deep South," he said. "This is the time that we must evince calm, dignity and wise restraint. Violence must not come from any of us. . . . As we stand on the verge of using public facilities heretofore closed to us, we must not be overbearing and haughty in spirit. We must move now from protest to reconciliation." There was room in King's heart for an accolade to certain of his enemies. He praised the "white persons of this community who worked so diligently for a just solution to our mutual problem. They must also be given credit. They are men of goodwill."

He could not explain why he did not mention the white men of goodwill by name. They had requested that their names not be made public. They were satisfied to be referred to as the Senior Citizens Committee. It would take white reporters a week to dig up the individual names. It was the Kennedy administration which had coerced the business leaders into acting as a committee of conciliation, but having done it, the men dreaded being identified. Dr. King left Birmingham at once and was in Atlanta that Friday night, May 10, to celebrate his victory with his family. Blacks, North and South, rejoiced with King because they believed he had cracked the racist façade of the most racist city in America. It was *the* story in newspapers, on radio and television. The gentle preacher of nonviolence had won his greatest fight. After this, all other municipalities would topple with less struggle.

But surely Dr. King must have known the agreement was almost worthless. When he was negotiating the few demands, among the white faces on the other side of the table he saw neither Mayor Boutwell nor Commissioner Connor. In fact, there were no Birmingham officials present. His agreement was with a group of private businessmen; the City of Birmingham was not a party to it and could not be dragooned into sending a representative to the meetings. Either Dr. King was lying to himself, or he was lying to the world. Later, when he committed his thoughts to paper, he wrote: "Birmingham was to emerge with a delicately poised peace, but without awaiting its implementation, the Negro had seized the weapon that had won that dangerous peace and swept across the land with it." King must have known that the peace had not been honored by "implementation" even when he wrote those words.

The blacks would witness some desegregation in stores, here and there, an intelligent and compliant black would be promoted to a "white" job, but any biracial committee formed would have no official sanction, no authority to do anything but discuss and dissemble. The white man would settle back into his traditional ways—except in such instances as when federal law intervened—and the black would return to the squalor of his ghetto.

Birmingham was now left to Pastor Fred Shuttlesworth, the man who had borne its weighty cross before the advent of Dr. King. He was the man who had to live in the city, who had to ask that the four simple provisions of the agreement be observed, who had to pick up the scattered fragments of hate, the crumbs of rancor from both tables. It was Shuttlesworth who would also have to explain the great victory to the communicants of his church and his organization, so that they could anticipate the good times to come.

The white community felt a sense of pleasant exhaustion. A terrible trial had been visited on Birmingham, and it left as quickly as it came. No one, not even the mayor, could tell any white man the manner in which he had to treat blacks. In racial matters, each man was his own master. The more substantial citizens were willing to act peaceably, willing even to accord more respect to the wishes of the black. If there was a problem left, it was vengeance, and this is always the preserve of the ignorant.

On Saturday night, A. D. King was sitting in his suburban home with his wife, Naomi. The reverend heard a tremendous roar. By reflex, he grabbed Naomi and dragged her toward the back of the house. A bomb had exploded on the lawn. Naomi King was screaming as a second bomb went off on the little porch, tearing part of the front of the house and causing the building to lean on its foundations. There was smoke and the acrid smell of dynamite. Over at the A. G. Gaston Motel, someone tossed some sticks of dynamite at Room 30 and missed. The bomb went off in the ground-floor office. Frightened black faces began to appear from behind curtain windows. No one was out front. Shattered glass sparkled in the saffron light.

By midnight in Birmingham the militant blacks were on the streets with guns, knives, and clubs. This time they had been truly provoked, and this time they would get "Whitey." Bands of men ran through white sections of town. When they met policemen who challenged them, they stabbed one and beat others. Police reserves were called. A few state troopers poured into the city from camps on the outskirts. Suddenly, there were no men of "goodwill," white or black. White cars in driveways were set afire. Two stores were in flames. And still the black bands raced through alleys and down side streets. A white taxicab driver was stabbed. Groups of cops caught up with blacks and beat them senseless. A. D. King stood on the sagging remains of his porch and pleaded with the blacks to forget it, to go home—hadn't they learned that they could not correct wrongs with violence?

The race riot petered out before dawn. Two apartment houses were in flames. Fifty persons, mostly blacks, were being treated in hospital emergency rooms. A man from Kentucky drove into Birmingham, took a wrong turn, and passed the Gaston Motel as 4,000 blacks stood outside chanting. He drove over broken glass, and all four tires blew out. He sat in terror as bricks and bottles rained on his car. Sheriff Jim Clark of Selma and Colonel Al Lingo of the troopers saw an old armored car, requisitioned by Commissioner Bull Connor, turn into the street and rescue the stranger from Kentucky. Men fighting the flames in apartment houses were fired on by people hiding in darkness. Toward the end, the police became merciless. When they saw a black male on the street, they pointed to the nearest black home and yelled, "Get in that house!"

"I don't live here."

"Yes, you do, nigger. You just moved in."

When the sun rose, the city was quiet. Martin Luther King hurried back to Birmingham and, assured that his SCLC members had not been part of the riot, visited A.D., checked on the damage to his house, and spent the rest of Sunday with Ralph Abernathy and Wyatt Walker going through the ghetto begging the men to give up violence. A few became so convinced that they handed over revolvers and knives to the pastor, who, at nightfall, brought them back to Atlanta. King displayed them at SCLC headquarters and marveled at the power of nonviolence over violence.

The complete assessment of the Birmingham campaign would require time and staff effort. On the surface, it appeared to Dr. King to have been a resounding victory for civil rights, and he did not propose to analyze it in public as anything less. He was fatigued by his tensions of Birmingham and it was good to be home with his wife and the children, good to be out of the "front line." Fatigue in Martin Luther King never implied lassitude. He could be worn down by long hours of work and nervousness, but seldom to the point where he did not want to put his time to use.

The time was ripe, he felt, for another book. His first one, *Stride Toward Freedom,* had done well and, in time, was to sell 200,000 copies. The second, called *Strength to Love,* was a failure; it consisted of a set of sermons. He phoned his agent and asked what kind of market there would be for a third book. She called on Victor Weybright, of New American Library. Weybright turned out to be a devotee of Martin Luther King and had contributed funds to the Southern Christian Leadership Conference. So King had a plus factor in the publishing world—a sound editor, as well as a follower of the Movement. Wey-bright made an offer for a book, provided that Dr. King would work at it and have the manuscript ready in a few months. There was a ready-made title for it: *Why We Can't Wait.*

Contracts were signed and promises made. The editor knew that the name of King would guarantee a certain sale. The fact that he had been in newspaper headlines made him an obvious candidate for television talk shows. This, in turn, would mean more sales. Unremitting work was the requirement; Birmingham should not be permitted to cool too long in the public mind. King said he would get to work on it at once and have it ready for autumn, 1963, publication. But Dr. King's enthusiasm for any project followed the same pattern: start in high gear; remain on a plateau of enthusiasm for several weeks; postpone the work in favor of matters that had become more and more pressing. And so it was with the new book: He began work at once on *Why We Can't Wait* and worked on it steadily for six weeks. Then the speaking engagements began to pile up, and he was urged more and more by his associates to settle on his next goal, on the next city to feel his wrath. It was impossible to finish the book until the following year.

White Birmingham felt that its city had been restored to its owners. In the third week of May the Board of Education expelled 1,000 black students from schools on the premise that they had participated in unlawful demonstrations. In itself, the action was witless. It did nothing to enhance the fortunes of the city; it opened the old racial wounds, and it tossed 1,000 children onto the streets. Whatever the reason for expelling the students, the Board of Education could not keep the young out of school permanently, depriving them of the right to a free education. In Atlanta, Martin Luther King feared that the Birmingham blacks would again be driven to excesses. He hurried to the city to calm the leaders, begging them not to fall into a trap.

This, he insisted, was a court matter. He was right. The doctor phoned the NAACP in Washington and asked for legal assistance. It was given at once. The weakness in the white Southern thinking was that properly constituted authorities could inflict any hardship on blacks without fear of recrimination. It had been the rule of thumb for a century, so deeply ingrained that it was difficult for Southern judges to equate the black man to what was regarded as white law. On May 22, in federal court, the action of the Birmingham Board of Education was upheld. In the afternoon Judge Elbert P. Tuttle of the Fifth Circuit

Court of Appeals ruled that the decision of the lower court was in error and ordered it reversed; Tuttle also condemned the Birmingham board for expelling the students.

Within three days, all the black children were back in school. The Supreme Court of the United States dealt Birmingham an additional blow when it handed down a decision that blacks could not be prosecuted for demanding service in privately owned stores. The Court stated that refusal to serve a customer of any color or group could not be taken as the policy of the store owner; it had to be interpreted as the policy of the city and the state in which it happens and is therefore unconstitutional. While Birmingham reeled under these blows, the Alabama Supreme Court ruled that Mayor Boutwell and his nine new councilmen were the duly elected officials of Birmingham, and Commissioner Connor and former Mayor Haynes were to leave City Hall and turn over the government of the city to Boutwell. The new mayor tried to restore order in the city by declaring that he favored the racial peace pact signed by business leaders and black leaders. However, he did not propose to sign it and make it a city ordinance.

In Washington, President John F. Kennedy devoted an entire "bang-board hour" to a discussion of civil rights—more particularly to the public position of the President. The others talked and Kennedy listened, then said he proposed within ten days or two weeks to send a civil rights bill to Congress, a bill with some teeth. The black man, he pointed out, was now pressing violently for rights which had been guaranteed to him a century ago. Kennedy saw it as more than a matter of law; it was a moral issue which could no longer be ignored.

On the evening of June 11, the President preempted the television network shows to speak to the nation. Ten hours earlier Governor George Wallace of Alabama, having made sure the press and TV cameras were focused on him, had blocked a University of Alabama doorway to two black students, then had stood aside when United States marshals ordered him to. The students had been registered and admitted.

"One hundred years of delay have passed since President Lincoln freed the slaves," Kennedy said, "yet their heirs, their grandsons, are not fully free. They are not yet freed from the bonds of injustice; they are not yet freed from social and economic oppression. And this nation, for all its hopes and its boasts, will not be fully free until all its citizens are free.

"We preach freedom around the world," the President said, "and we mean it. And we cherish our freedom here at home. But are we to say to the world—and much more importantly to each other—that this is the land of the free, except for the Negroes; that we have no second-class citizens, except for Negroes; that we have no class or caste system, no ghettos, no master race, except with respect to Negroes? Now the time has come for this nation to fulfill its promise. The events in Birmingham and elsewhere have so increased the cries for equality that no city or state or legislative body can prudently choose to ignore them.

"The fires of frustration and discord are burning in every city, North and South. . . . We face, therefore, a moral crisis as a country and a people. It cannot be met by repressive police action. It cannot be left to increased demonstrations in the streets. It cannot be quieted by token moves or talk. It is a time to act in the Congress, in your state and local legislative body, and, above all, in all of our daily lives."

It was a bolder commitment than Abraham Lincoln had uttered in January, 1863. The A. Philip Randolphs, the Roy Wilkins, those who had worked interminably and tirelessly for civil rights found it difficult to believe that a President, at long last, had placed his administration firmly behind the Movement. It moved millions of liberal whites closer to the black man's aspirations and polarized the segregationists and those who feared the black into an opposite camp. Except for the South, newspaper reception to the speech ranged from enthusiastic to cordial. Within the week, the White House sent a bill called the Civil Rights Act of 1963 to Capitol Hill. It was not a strong act, but it had sufficient teeth to set the segregationists in Congress on edge and to fuse them into a single body with the power to challenge the bill's passage.

Two days after Kennedy's forthright speech, Medgar Evers, the thin, taciturn head of the NAACP in Jackson, Mississippi, was shot to death at the doorway to his home. Federal agents went into Jackson and prodded the local police into action. A man named Byron De La Beckwith was charged with the murder and, within two weeks, was freed when a white jury could not arrive at a verdict.

For more than twenty years, A. Philip Randolph had been dreaming of an orderly, dignified march on Washington to display the power of the black man to Northern and Southern legislators. After Birmingham, he again spoke of it as a logical step, a means of maintaining pressure and keeping the Movement in motion. Martin Luther King was interested. So was Roy Wilkins, John Lewis of SNCC, James Farmer of CORE, Whitney Young of the Urban League, and Dorothy Height of the National Council of Negro Women. The idea of a monumental demonstration in the capital appealed to all, and each leader realized that it was too big a project for his organization alone. The dignified Randolph said that the march would be for "Jobs and Freedom." King suggested that it would put pressure on Congress to pass the Civil Rights Act of 1963.

Randolph did not respond to that idea. He was determined to be the leader of the leaders, and none disputed him. The date he suggested for the march was Wednesday, August 28, 1963. He formed a Unity Council for Civil Rights to organize the march, to arrange for arrival times and means of feeding several hundred thousand blacks in a city which was Southern in character, and to set up a timetable for speeches. He selected Dr. King's onetime assistant, Bayard Rustin, to "coordinate" the march, to be assisted by Cleveland Robinson and Walter Fauntroy of the SCLC. In mid-June they began to work.

Dr. King was here, there, and everywhere, speaking, lifting morale, admonishing. He and other black leaders were preaching that a great civil rights victory had been won in Birmingham, and the officials of Birmingham were, by now, too wise to deny it. On June 16, King spoke in Keuka Park, New York. He saw the faces in the dark audience as the suspicious jades one could expect in the North; they saw him as a pompous preacher addicted to endless figures of speech. This time, he surprised them. The audience became more attentive as they caught a hint of violence in his words. If the civil rights bill was not enacted by Congress, he said, he could see a "season of terror and violence. . . . Certain elements will work violence if the people of the nation do not recognize the desperate plight of the Negro. . . . The brutality they are experiencing as a result of their quest for equality may call for retaliation."

When reporters asked him if he had changed his attitude and favored violence, Dr. King said no. And yet one speech after another warned of impending violence, and the blacks who heard the speeches knew that if there was violence, it would come from them. King addressed 25,000 people in Los Angeles, 10,000 in Chicago. Toward the end of June, King led 125,000 people in a Freedom Walk in Detroit. He made a speech in Cobo Hall, related each of the goals of the black, and appended the paragraphs by saying solemnly: "I have a dream. . . ." He drew prolonged applause, but he drew a standing ovation when he concluded with the sentence: "I submit to you that if a man hasn't discovered something he will die for, he isn't fit to live."

At this time, King was king of the Movement. He was at stage center, and more than that, his personality dominated the field of civil rights. He was loved, he was revered, he was respected, he was despised, feared, mistrusted, but he was not ignored. He preached, he exulted, he entreated, and his speeches seemed to become more and more radical. He condemned the word "moderate" before 10,000 people in Kentucky. "If moderation means slowing up in our fight," he said, "then moderation is a tragic vice which members of our race must condemn."

His closest strategic collaborator, Wyatt Tee Walker, asked a group of blacks "Whether we want to continue local guerrilla battles against discrimination and segregation or go to all-out war." At the SCLC convention, in the presence of King, Walker asked the delegates to dwell upon the possibility that the slow response of whites to civil rights might make it necessary to "immobilize the nation."

News of the March on Washington reached the President, and he reacted antagonistically. He called a meeting of civil rights leaders at the White House for Saturday, June 22. The writing of his civil rights bill and his speech to the nation were positive efforts to make the unnecessary mass demonstrations, with their possibility of violence, and he did not want one in his backyard. He called in Randolph, Wilkins, Farmer, King, and Young. On the white side, he had Robert Kennedy, Lyndon Johnson, and Stephen Currier, president of the Taconic Foundation and actively interested in promoting civil rights and soliciting pledges of money from his friends.

The dialogue at the meeting was largely between A. Philip Randolph and John Kennedy. This is not to say that the others did not contribute thoughts and ideas, but it was dominated by two men. The amenities did not last long. The President was fairly blunt. The August march had been planned and publicized without anyone's notifying the government, a government which had gone on record as aligning itself with the Movement. The black leaders said that no one thought of consulting the President because this was to be an exercise in peace; it was not to be a demonstration in the usual sense. There would be a mass of people, singing, some speeches.

"We want success in Congress," Kennedy said, punching the air with an index finger, "not just a big show at the Capitol. Some of these people are looking for an excuse to be against us. I don't want to give any of them a chance to say: 'Yes, I'm for the bill, but I'm damned if I will vote for it at the point of a gun.' " The march or demonstration was poorly timed; the net effect would be to arouse the animosity and fears of the opponents of civil rights and perhaps adversely affect those who hadn't made up their minds about the bill.

The civil rights leaders could not see the danger. From their side, they were certain that the white man could give them nothing without being forced to give it—and force meant continuing pressure. Randolph had permitted one President—Franklin Delano Roosevelt—to talk him out of a black march on Washington by promising nondiscrimination in wartime jobs. He would not be persuaded again. Martin Luther King said the march "could also serve as a means of dramatizing the issue and mobilizing support in parts of the country which did not know the problem at first hand." He saw nothing friendly or affirmative in Kennedy's glance. "I think it will serve a purpose," Dr. King said. "It may seem ill-timed. Frankly, I have never engaged in any direct action movement which did not seem ill-timed." He turned his eyes blandly on the Attorney General. "Some people," he said, "thought Birmingham ill-timed."

The President laughed. "Including the Attorney General," he said. Kennedy lost the gamble. The blacks were going to hold the rally. No one could stop them. When the meeting adjourned, Lyndon Johnson and Stephen Currier counseled the President that he had a third choice: He could *own* the march, claim it as his by participating in its planning, taking it over, copyrighting it. He said he would think about it.

The President was worried. He had confidential reports from the Department of Justice, and they ran counter to what the black leaders had told him. Black men from all parts of the United States were talking openly about choking the corridors of public buildings in Washington by sitting in them; they proposed to force their way into the Senate and House of Representatives and sit. There would be so many scores of thousands of blacks that no police or military strength could dislodge them. Some local black leaders spoke happily about bringing the "whole United States" to a halt.

Kennedy knew that when the final hymn had been sung at the rally, no assortment of nonviolent leaders could prevent the militant cadres within the Movement from staging violent confrontations with the government. King and Randolph could not prevent the city of Washington from becoming a bloody battleground if the crowd were influenced by the militants. Control and restraint were lacking within the Movement. Besides, a new note of suspicion had been sounded. The President no longer trusted Martin Luther King. Reports from the Federal Bureau of Investigation, sent to Robert Kennedy, indicated that King had

Communists on his staff; there was also an oral FBI report to Robert Kennedy which stated that although it could shadow King, the FBI no longer felt it could protect him from a would-be assassin. The report said that the reverend displayed an unusual interest in women in many cities; some were black, some white. "We can't protect him from an irate husband," the report stated.

Robert Kennedy had a private talk with Martin Luther King and accused him of having Communists in his entourage. The doctor was surprised at the charge and asked the Attorney General to give him the names. The only person Kennedy would name was Jack O'Dell, an editor of *Freedomways* magazine, and the Attorney General was careful to say that O'Dell was not a Communist, but that he had "Communist connections." The pastor promised to look into the matter. As in the case of Bayard Rustin, King spoke to his friend, told him he trusted him but permitted O'Dell to resign from the SCLC. He was out of the organization on June 26.

The alliance between the administration and the Southern Christian Leadership Conference was, on the surface, firm and binding. In speeches, Dr. King crowed about the "new Kennedy," a phrase which grated the President's sensitivities. A complete dossier on Dr. King, his personal habits, and his organization was being gathered by the Federal Bureau of Investigation and sent to the Attorney General, who routed it directly to the President.

The order to tap King's phones came in early July. The FBI, unleashed, does a thorough job. It tapped the pastor's private phones and the phones of the SCLC. It also alerted its Atlanta office to shadow King. The tap was not installed until October, 1963, and from that time onward, there was little that King did or said, or that his staff did or said, that the FBI did not know and report on.

The President was on a state visit to Germany, saying, in Frankfurt, that "our cities will defend your cities." Many of the American cities could not, at the time, defend themselves from racial convulsion. The City of Birmingham was attempting to organize an "unofficial" biracial committee to resolve its problems; Placquemine Parish, in Louisiana, was in a convulsion of protest; the murder of Medgar Evers brought timid blacks in Jackson, Mississippi, into the open; Albany, Georgia, was seeking a formula which would placate the blacks without surrendering white prerogatives; New York policemen learned that it was dangerous to try to arrest a black man on any charge in a black neighborhood; Rome, Georgia, was the setting for black demonstrations against white power; Cambridge, Maryland, was embroiled in mass arrests and gunfire in the streets; Danville, Virginia, was bracing itself against black threats to reform the town or wreck it; Chicago blacks were mobilizing under a banner called Operation Breadbasket; SNCC assumed a more militant posture as part of a political divorce from Martin Luther King; white students joined black on college campuses across the nation to fight discrimination; in Chicago, a reporter coined a phrase to open a story on racial unrest: "This is a long, hot summer. . . ."

The Movement had reached a plateau. Outbreaks were occurring in many cities, without asking help or advice from the SCLC, SNCC, the Urban League, the NAACP, or CORE. Tempers were hot and short. The fearful black had learned at last that he was feared.

Dr. King could not afford to permit his personal leadership to lapse, so he selected Danville, Virginia, near the North Carolina border, as his next goal when the Reverend L. V. Chase of that city pleaded for assistance. King sent Fred Shuttlesworth, of Birmingham, and Jack O'Dell, who had just resigned from the SCLC, to Danville, where there had already been a bloody confrontation between its blacks and its police.

The weakness in the civil rights battle lay in its strength—the person of Dr. Martin Luther King. In the minds of millions of the disenfranchised he was truly the Little Lord Jesus now. Hundreds of local organizations felt that their troubles could be resolved by a personal appearance of the doctor. His presence, standing at a lectern in defiance of official white authority, was sufficient to calm the troubled waters and to bring new rights to replace old wrongs. King, in the minds of many, became *the* key.

On Thursday, July 11, Dr. King and his staff, including Ralph Abernathy, drove into Danville. Authorities had sworn out injunctions against demonstrations on July 3, then on July 10, thinking that one or the other day would be the dates of King's arrival. So his appearance in Danville on the eleventh was "legal." An enormous crowd of blacks waited in the hot sun for the pastor. They knew that he would lead them to victory no matter how long it might take, and when he stepped up to the podium, his forehead shiny with sweat, the roar of approval carommed from the helmets of tense white policemen and troopers.

"I have so many injunctions," Dr. King said, "that I don't even look at them anymore. I was enjoined January 15, 1929, when I was born in the United States, a Negro." This was what they wanted to hear—defiance of the Establishment. If he could ignore an injunction not to march, they could and would. At his side, preachers Dunlap, Campbell, and Chase and taxicab owner Julius Adams led the applause. After the speech Dr. King ordered Ralph Abernathy to lead the protest. King left Danville before the march began—so much to do, so many speeches to make, so little time. . . . Abernathy led the march only a short distance before policemen began surrounding the demonstrators. He left, managing to avoid arrest this time.

Dr. King returned for a visit or two. He knew that Danville was split in a bitter fight between SNCC and the SCLC, but he could do nothing to bridge the schism. When demonstration subsided, he knew it was a defeat—the schools were not desegregated, and the dismal image of the black working as a janitor was unchanged. "Walk together, children," he told the poor of Danville. "Do not get weary. We will be with you until this problem is solved."

The time had come for Southern cities to move into the twentieth century, and Mayor Boutwell of Birmingham made it obvious that no one on either side was going to push him toward racial progress or away from it. Every move would require time and that is what he proposed to take. But move he did. The biracial committee which was to have formed two weeks after Dr. King left Birmingham, was now convened, two months later. Each progressive step taken by Boutwell was executed quietly as though the white government feared giving King grounds for claiming success.

On July 15 the mayor called together 200 white and black leaders of Birmingham's businesses, professions, and churches. He told them that they had the official endorsement of the Birmingham City Council. "This," he said solemnly, "can well be the beginning of our finest hours." Moderate black leaders who had opposed King's campaign moved into positions of power. They, in turn, formed a smaller committee to maintain the peaceful status quo and prevent young hotheads from staging sit-ins or parades. The first test of the new organization occurred when a black man was shot by a white policeman. The black community protested and was permitted to demand an explanation from City Hall. Mayor Boutwell ordered the chief inspector of the Police Department to give it.

In August, Boutwell led the new City Council in repealing all ordinances covering segregation of the races on the grounds that none could be enforced. Closed white parks were opened to all. A few blacks, who protested that this wasn't putting any bread into the mouths of their children, were told that the white community would back Boutwell so long as it felt it wasn't being "pushed." Birmingham was doing more and more for its disenfranchised, little by little. The white structure kept crying that it was progressing because "men of reason" had met, but no student of the racial movement in America can deny that it was Martin Luther King who triggered the change.

The President returned from Europe knowing that his wife would soon give birth to their third child. In early August, a boy was born and christened Patrick Bouvier Kennedy. He died within a few days of lung edema and, for the first time since Kennedy's advent to the Presidency, an aura of youthful exuberance and beauty was transmuted into a veil of sorrow. Kennedy, in unremitting pain from a crushed spinal disk, canceled appointments after the funeral. Mrs. Kennedy departed for an extended rest on a yacht cruising around the Greek islands.

The Attorney General informed his brother that, since the Presidential trip to Europe, the March on Washington had grown in size and momentum. Fourteen major organizations had joined Randolph's group. By the first week of August $100,000 had been contributed to the effort. A New York City police organization of black officers had volunteered to send 2,000 members to Washington to act as marshals.

The President and his staff were beset with a worried feeling that they were "outside" the demonstration, that the participants could become riotous after the rally. Kennedy came to a decision. He invited the black leaders back to the White House and, after an amiable conference, publicly endorsed the March on Washington. Pointedly, he told these men that he would expect them back at the White House immediately after the rally. He planned a little "stag" reception, he said. This meant no wives. It also meant that he had corraled the leaders for a "command" appearance the moment the final curtain went down. In accepting, the leaders robbed themselves of any opportunity to criticize the Kennedy administration. It would be crudeness personified to vilify the President of the United States and accept his hospitality. It was a clever stroke; the March on Washington became an almost official event. Kennedy announced that he, in conjunction with civil rights leaders, had decided to have a peaceful camp meeting in Washington to promote racial understanding. The notion that a mass of blacks would be in the capital on August 28 to pressure Congress was softened.

Truly, it was A. Philip Randolph's show and his dream. He worked hard with Bayard Rustin and Cleveland Robinson to place every detail in proper order. He wanted no long-winded speakers. "Eight minutes is enough time for anybody to say what he wants to say and get off," he said. The word went out to Wilkins, King, a young man named Floyd McKissick, who was to substitute for James Farmer, Whitney Young, and all the others. The Washington archbishop of the Roman Catholic Church, Patrick O'Boyle, was to deliver the invocation. It was not considered necessary to remind him to come in under eight minutes.

Volunteer assistants were recruited by the thousands. They would be at the Washington and Baltimore airports, Union Station, the bus terminals, in front of the White House and the Capitol, to direct the pilgrims to the base of the Washington Monument at 9 A.M. The combined groups expected 125,000 blacks and about 25,000 whites. The television networks and the national press were given badges and were told that the crowd would be treated to some high-class entertainment for ninety minutes. Then all would be asked to walk leisurely to the nearby Lincoln Memorial, there to stand near the great reflecting pool for the speeches. The opening remarks would be given by Randolph, and as Martin Luther King was the hero of the hour, he would be presented last. The benediction would be uttered by Benjamin Mays, Dr. King's revered teacher.

Rustin forgot one thing: topics. It was assumed that each speaker would choose his own and digest it within the allotted time. Some say that it was agreed that no one would attack the Kennedy administration; the black had found a new and powerful friend. So it was *tacitly* understood. On the night before the march, John Lewis of SNCC released his talk to the press. When a copy reached Archbishop O'Boyle, he phoned Randolph's office and said that if Lewis delivered that speech, he would not be present. This started a last-minute rush to locate copies of the speech and retrieve them. John Lewis was told that his speech had to be revised. One sentence of the original read: "In good conscience we cannot support the administration's civil rights bill for it is too little and too late." Overnight, this was altered to read: "True, we support the administration's civil rights bill, but this bill will not protect young children and old women from police dogs and fire hoses. . . ." He refused to revise another section and read it verbatim: "This nation is still a cheap place for political leaders allying themselves with open forms of political, economic and social exploitation . . . I want to know—which side is the government on?"

It was a belligerent piece of craftsmanship. Another part of the talk originally read: "The next time we march, we won't march on Washington, but we will march through the South, through the heart of Dixie—the way Sherman did." This was changed to: "We will march through the South, through the streets of Danville, through the streets of Cambridge, through the streets of Birmingham. But we will march with the spirit of love and the spirit of dignity that we have shown here today."

The first small groups in the March on Washington were in the city at the base of Washington Monument at 1 A.M. It was hot, and they sat on the grass, murmuring, dozing, dreaming. The sun came up early, a buttery blob of heat beyond the Maryland shore, and thousands came. They came in cars, trucks and buses. Some walked from the Washington ghetto, one of the largest in America. Others arrived by plane. Some brought sandwiches; others carried suitcases. Some teen-agers from Wilmington, North Carolina, began to dance and sing "We Shall Overcome." Some parents carried babies. Others carried banners of many colors declaring FREEDOM NOW!

In a cool hotel suite, Martin Luther King sat with Mrs. King and made one final revision of his speech. He had worked on it, silently and alone, almost all night. It had to be condensed within eight minutes of time, but it had to say something important. King's habit was that he could say something important ad lib much more forcefully than he could write it. His problem was that he always got involved in figures of speech which were worthless unless carried out to an imaginative conclusion. Before Coretta King retired, he said he had considered using the "I have a dream" which he had tried in Detroit but decided against it. He chose instead to use a figure of speech, enunciating and reenunciating that America had given the black man a bad check. The check had been issued a hundred years before, in this city, by Abraham Lincoln, and it had never been redeemed.

In the morning, Dr. King was near collapse. Dead-eyed, he looked out the hotel window at the mobs of blacks walking toward the Washington Monument. Typists were getting out copies of the speech for the press. As he watched, he was listening to reports on television. "A small number of Negroes have assembled," a commentator said. This was discouraging. But Dr. King had been told that his speech would be carried live on television and radio, and he hoped that scores of millions of people would hear his words.

It was close to noon when the Kings left for the Washington Monument. After a short ride, they became enmeshed in a tide of happy people which swirled around the car. The mood was akin to that of a massive picnic; no one hurried; the streets were jammed with people on foot. More than 200,000 had gathered at the meeting place, and one of every four faces was white. There was an aura of joyous chaos. The leaders lost their leadership. Crowds were directed to move to this side or that side, and they paid no attention. Randolph and Rustin tried to round up the people for the march on the Lincoln Memorial, but more than half of them were already there, some sitting on the sides of the reflecting pool with bare feet in the water. Randolph tried to find the leaders, so that they could form ranks and start some sort of march, but they too had been swallowed by scores of thousands of faces. When Rustin found Dr. King, he said that the wives would have to stand out front with the crowd—there were no seats for them. Rustin drew several leaders together, but there was no march to lead; they fell in somewhere in the middle of the masses of people and made the "march" lost in the crowd.

The mood of the people infected the speakers. There was no doomsday defiance in it; it was like Christmas Morning, with everyone anticipating a gift, but no one demanding a great deal. There was no order, just friendly chaos. Many of the entertainers promised for the morning found no way of leaving the air terminal. All the taxicabs had been spoken for; all the private cars of the organizations were in use. Burt Lancaster, movie star, stood with Robert Ryan, Marlon Brando, Sidney Poitier, and Charlton Heston and read a short speech on civil rights with the shriek of jet planes outside the windows. Black school bands decided to "play it loose and loud" and drowned one another with marching songs and hymns.

At the Memorial, Joan Baez had already sung "We Shall Overcome" and Peter, Paul, and Mary rendered "How Many Times Must a Man Look Up Before He Can See the Sky?" The big crowd grew bigger. Silvery microphones lifted each voice on electrical crutches and expanded the songs to the hot August sky. The people clapped in rhythm; they chanted the songs; they swayed like a sea of grass in a windy meadow. There was no control, and none was required. The people had taken over the March on Washington. Between songs, the ascetic face of Norman Thomas, perennial Socialist candidate, was seen at a microphone, and tears slipped down the old face as he whispered, "I am glad I lived long enough to see this day." Stout, serene Mahalia Jackson came to the microphone and brought tears to the faces of thousands of listeners as she sang "I Been 'Buked and I Been Scorned."

Faces moved to the front of the stand and faded back again, and the crowd stomped and whistled when it recognized the famous. There was Sammy Davis, Jr., Dr. Ralph Bunche, Jackie Robinson, Bob Dylan, and Lena Horne.

A. Philip Randolph, who had also lived to see this day, kept his eyes dry and his tongue moist. He hushed the crowd, introduced the speakers, listened, and got them off. The day became a form of musical lobbying for civil rights, and Randolph could not have met a finer moment in time to drop his dignity. But he didn't. His hands shook a little as he introduced each notable; but there was no quaver in his voice, and his bearing was ramrod straight. Walter Reuther, a proved friend of civil rights and president of the United Automobile Workers, spoke.

On the rostrum, Dr. King had his speech on his thigh and was crossing out certain phrases and substituting others. He was disturbed because the program, starting at 9 A.M., was going on too long, and he doubted that the crowd would hold, or even be in a mood to listen to him as the final speaker. Besides, there was little left to say. The other speakers had asked for a comprehensive civil rights law including black access to all public accommodations; protection of voting rights; penalties for discrimination in public housing; withdrawal of federal money from projects which did not guarantee blacks a fair share of all jobs; education to be integrated within a year; a national minimum wage of not less than $2 an hour; a massive program, to be financed by the government, to train blacks for better jobs and find the jobs for them; more power given to the Attorney General to implement these matters and to furnish attorneys to those denied their constitutional rights; a reduction in Congressional representation to those states which, in effect, disenfranchised minority group voters.

Dr. King was right. At 3 P.M. the fringes of the crowd began to walk away. Collars had wilted in the humidity. Damp blouses were plastered against backs. Branches of big trees hung motionless. The dome of the Capitol faded in bluish haze. It was thirty minutes past three when Randolph held his bony hands up for silence, and introduced Dr. Martin Luther King, Jr., as a "man who personifies moral leadership." It was not a stirring introduction for the new hero from Atlanta; it was restrained, as though Randolph felt that King had a place among the leaders but was not to be considered *the* leader.

King approached the microphones wearing a deeply solemn expression. A roar of approval came from 200,000 throats before he uttered a word, and it was the thunder of surf on a rocky coast. For a moment, he placed his sheets of paper on the lectern and permitted the crowd to pay him tribute. Then he smiled, and the boyishness bubbled to the top and he waved both hands to the people. It would require time to start his speech. However, once the round, deep tones emerged from his throat and the slow cadence hit the ears of the people, there was silence except for the words which excited them to a frenzy of approval.

"Five score years ago," he said, "a great American, in whose symbolic shadow we stand, signed the Emancipation Proclamation. This momentous decree came as a great beacon light of hope to millions of Negro slaves who had been seared in the flames of withering injustice. It came as a joyous daybreak to end the long night of captivity.

"But one hundred years later, we must face the tragic fact that the Negro is still not free. One hundred years later, the life of the Negro is still sadly crippled by the manacles of segregation and the chains of discrimination. . . . One hundred years later, the Negro is still languished in the corners of American society and finds himself an exile in his own land. . . .

". . . There will be neither rest nor tranquillity in America until the Negro is granted his citizenship rights. The whirlwinds of revolt will continue to shake the foundations of our nation until the bright day of justice emerges."

Once more, he was using the repetition of a single word or phrase for emphasis. He had said that he would not use the Detroit phrase about a dream, but at this point, Dr. King reversed himself and strode boldly into a historic speech.

"I say to you today, my friends, that in spite of the difficulties and frustrations of the moment I still have a dream. It is a dream deeply rooted in the American dream.

"I have a dream that one day this nation will rise up and live out the true meaning of its creed: 'We hold these truths to be self-evident; that all men are created equal.'

"I have a dream that one day on the red hills of Georgia the sons of former slaves and the sons of former slaveowners will be able to sit down together at the table of brotherhood."

The dense crowd came alive. It caught the cadence. It whooped and hollered as though Moses himself had come down from the Mount to tell them what life was going to be like. "I have a dream"—the swell of noise from throats engulfed everything, and Dr. King had to stop. Behind him, almost lost in the crowd, Coretta King found her eyes misting. She had desired, with all her heart, to be at his side on this day, at this hour. It was not that she wanted to share his glory; she had sensed that this would be a great moment in his life, and she had only wanted to be nearby.

"I have a dream that one day even the state of Mississippi, a desert state sweltering with the heat of injustice and oppression, will be transformed into an oasis of freedom and justice.

"I have a dream that my four little children will one day live in a nation where they will not be judged by the color of their skin but by the content of their character.

"I have a dream today.

"I have a dream that one day the state of Alabama, whose governor's lips are presently dripping with the words of interposition and nullification, will be transformed into a situation where little black boys and black girls will be able to join hands with little white boys and white girls and walk together as sisters and brothers.

"I have a dream today.

"I have a dream that one day every valley shall be exalted, every hill and mountain shall be made low, the rough places will be made plains, and the crooked places will be made straight, and the glory of the Lord shall be revealed, and all flesh shall see it together. . . .

"And if America is to be a great nation this must become true. So let freedom ring from the prodigious hilltops of New Hampshire. Let freedom ring from the mighty mountains of New York. Let freedom ring from the heightening Alleghenies of Pennsylvania!

"Let freedom ring from the snowcapped Rockies of Colorado! . . .

"Let freedom ring from every hill and mole hill of Mississippi. From every mountainside, let freedom ring." His voice softened, became almost meditative, as he reached the conclusion.

"When we let freedom ring, when we let it ring from every village and every hamlet, from every state and every city, we will be able to speed up that day when all of God's children, black men and white men, Jews an Gentiles, Protestants and Catholics, will be able to join hands and sing in the words of the old Negro spiritual, 'Free at last! free at last! thank God Almighty, we are free at last!' "

Martin Luther King picked up his notes and stepped back to his seat. The crowd was silent. It was stunned. Then, as Randolph stood to announce the closing benediction, the people went wild, screaming, waving placards by the hundreds, smashing them to the ground, knowing in its collective heart that "I Have a Dream" would stand as one of the most moving speeches of modern times. Only the speaker knew that their enthusiasm had lifted him free of himself and soared him to a height he had never known where the heart speaks for itself. Many wept. On the rostrum, some of the leaders regarded the speech as emotional poetry. Emotional or not, Dr. King's speech pricked the conscience of a nation. Millions of whites who were aware of a racial revolution in the South heard it on their television sets and caught the personal passionate plea of the unwanted brother to be wanted. The dream for his four children had a solid impact on many who had children. The fearful Southern red-neck, committed to the credo that the black man is a bridge between the animal kingdom and the human, derided the speech as typical "coon shouting."

At the White House, John F. Kennedy greeted the leaders with a firm grip and a pleased smile. He had canceled all appointments to sit with a few advisers and watch the march on the three television screens set in a white cabinet to the left of his desk. It had been peaceful, much more peaceful than he had expected; a few of the speechs had been critical and acrimonious, but most of them were conciliatory; the turnout, which the President had privately predicted would be small and therefore dangerous to his legislation, was bigger than anyone had expected. In fact, between the end of the march and the arrival of the black leaders, Presidential enthusiasm had caused him to issue a 400-word press release, in which he stated: "We have witnessed today in Washington tens of thousands of Americans—both Negro and white—exercising their right to assemble peacefully and direct the widest possible attention to a great national issue."

As the soft drinks and cocktail sandwiches were served, the President became serious. He said he was not optimistic about the passage of the civil rights bill. It would require strong bipartisan support to squeak through, and he doubted that it would even be taken out of committee to the floor of the House. He was giving them the word gently, sprinkled with wit and laughter. Nor was it any fault of his that the bill would die on polished desks in the Capitol; he had had the courage to ask for its passage, but he could not risk Congressional veto of the remainder of his domestic and foreign program to force civil rights to a vote.

The President bade a cordial farewell to each of the black leaders, and as they walked out through the West reception room, reporters were waiting for Martin Luther King. He had made his statement for the day, but the press corps knew that he was always good for one more metaphor. "The march," he said, "subpoenaed the conscience of the nation before the judgment seat of morality." Then he hurried out into the late sunshine.

Schools opened in September, and nine years had elapsed since the United States Supreme Court had ordered desegregation of all institutions of learning from kindergarten to college. The order contained the phrase "with deliberate speed" and boards of education, North and South, chose to focus on the word "deliberate" and ignore the word "speed." No educator, no matter what his prejudices, could deny that nine years was a long time. Prior to the summer recess in 1963, the federal courts had admonished the boards of education to draft plans "at once" for orderly desegregation. This resulted in reluctant tokenism, where a few acceptable and preselected black students had been transferred to white schools. In Alabama, a handful of black children were to be admitted to the lower grades in white elementary schools located in Tuskegee, Mobile, and Birmingham. The ambitious and vituperative George Wallace, governor of the state, saw an advantage in opposing the tokenism. He requested the Board of Education of Birmingham to close three schools involved in a small amount of integration. The board complied. This aroused the Reverend Fred Shuttlesworth and the black community.

It also aroused the white community, which had carefully worked out its plan of minuscule mixing of very young whites and very young blacks. The Birmingham *News* was outraged: "Wallace now not only defies federal courts, he defies the wishes of legally constituted local authorities. . . . What federal court orders make inescapable still will come. But in the interval, a governor so enthralled with his own sense of power will have created near-havoc. . . ." The effect of the governor's action was to split the whites. Those who favored a little step at a time in black progress opposed Wallace at the tops of their voices. Those who believed in segregation were encouraged to fight the Birmingham Board of Education and to open hostilities anew with the blacks.

The United States Department of Justice went to court at once and swore out a restraining order against the governor. The schools were reopened, and a few children were admitted to the chants of hate from white students. The South's major problem was always the same: the lower strata of whites. The poorly paid, mean-living families needed something or someone to which they could feel superior, and the black was ideal. In his ignorance, the so-called red-neck was also prone to violence. He felt that he could injure, maim, even kill a black man, and "any white jury will give me a medal." Rational white society had no control over this kind of hatred because, unlike the black, the red-neck could not be identified by color or speech. As a person, he was seldom a courageous man; his violence was perpetrated in lynch groups, the Ku Klux Klan, White Citizens Councils. By himself or with one or two others in an automobile, he often terrorized black communities with fire bombs, explosives, and shotguns, almost always at night.

On Sunday, September 15, the day was hot; the windows of the Sixteenth Street Baptist Church in Birmingham were tilted open. On the main floor, ushers in their Sunday best placed hymnals in the pews; two women gossiped in the pastor's office. In the basement, there was the indistinct burbling noise of many children talking. This was a Sunday school class. A teacher was explaining the lesson "The Love That Forgives," from the fifth chapter of Matthew. The little faces, freshly scrubbed, boys uncomfortable in jackets and ties, girls in cotton prints, many with black shiny pigtails festooned with pink and yellow ribbons, grimaced; the bodies squirmed. Some paid more attention to each other than to the teacher.

The teacher was reading: "You have heard that it hath been said 'Thou shalt love thy neighbor, and hate thine enemy! But I say to you, love your enemies: do good to them that hate you: and pray for them that persecute and calumniate you. That you may be the children of your Father who is in heaven, who maketh—"

A package came through the side window. The children turned to watch it bound between chairs. Outside, a car was heard moving away. There was a blinding light. The children heard no sound. The chairs, the desk, the bodies lifted away from the source of the great light, some floating end over end, others being smashed against the walls of the church. No one cried. People blocks away heard a tremendous roar. Shards of colored window glass from the basement and the main church spun outward across the street. The noise stopped; falling glass in the neighborhood made its own music. Cars slammed to a stop. Men ran toward the church.

Then came the first small whimpers from the basement. They did not sound like sobs or childish crying. When the first men arrived in the basement, the room was fogged with bluish smoke. Some youngsters, bleeding profusely, crawled on the floor. Some were still unconcious, with broken limbs. Four girls were dead. The floor became slippery with blood as women screamed and men lifted children out of the building.

Some were fathers who had brought their daughters and sons to Sunday school. They panicked and, in the bluish gloom, called out their names. The hoarse shouting further confused and frightened the conscious.

Within a few minutes police cars and fire engines surrounded the church. This time black men became savage. They shoved assisting policemen away and yelled, "Don't you touch that kid. Don't you lay a finger on her—get the hell out of here!" The news siphoned up the echelons of command quickly. Mayor Boutwell heard about it, heard that there was "some dead kids, don't know how many," and held his hand over his eyes. An hour later black men and boys were rioting through the streets. Policemen, menaced by mobs armed with clubs and knives, drew guns. By afternoon two black boys were lying dead of bullet wounds.

The mayor appeared on television and begged for an end to "this senseless reign of terror." To the blacks, it was no longer senseless. Some insane and unknown person had driven by in a slow-moving car, tossed a bundle of sticks of dynamite through an open basement window, and moved away serenely. One of the signers of the unofficial Birmingham pact said, "There wouldn't have been any trouble if Wallace had stayed out. Why did he do it? Why didn't he let us alone?" In Washington, the President expressed a similar thought: "It is regrettable that public disparagement of law and order has encouraged violence which has fallen on the innocent." No word of condolence to the bereaved families came from Governor George Wallace. A few White Suprematists said that there was no doubt that the bombing was the work of an *agent provocateur,* a militant black who wanted to incite his people to riot. The first edition of the Birmingham *News* to reach the street hit the target of the problem: ". . . Negroes of Birmingham have a hard right to ask why the bombings of the past have not been solved, for it is their flesh and blood, their property, which has been the target of the dynamite planters. Every white man certainly should be asking himself how he would feel if for years the unidentified had made his wife, his children, his home, his church, the object of such hatred." By sundown three ghetto areas were in flames.

In Atlanta, Dr. King preached his sermon at the Ebenezer Baptist Church and hurried to Atlanta Airport to catch a plane to Birmingham. He visited each of the families and tried to console the parents. He wanted a single funeral for the four girls, but the parents of one were beyond the rhetoric of salvation. They said they would hold a private ceremony. A writer, John Killens, announced that the slaughter of the innocents closed the nonviolent phase of the movement. "Negroes must be prepared to protect themselves with guns," he said.

The father of Denise McNair, dead in her coffin in his living room, heard the words and shook his head sadly. "I'm not for that," he said. "What good would Denise have done with a machine gun in her hand?"

Standing near three small caskets in the church, touching their polished surfaces with his hands, Martin Luther King sorrowed. "They did not die in vain," he said. "God still has a way of wringing good out of evil. History has proved again and again that unmerited suffering is redemptive. The innocent blood of these little girls may well serve as the redemptive force that will bring new light to this dark city." He scanned the faces in the church. All black. Not one white person had attended to say a prayer for the murdered little girls.

As he spoke, a black civil rights dentist, R. N. Hayling, was abducted in Florida by the Ku Klux Klan. The whites took three other blacks with them and, in a lonely place near St. Augustine, joined 250 raging whites. One was sent to fetch five gallons of gasoline. Others heaped piles of brush and logs. A man yelled "Work on his right hand first. He's a dentist." The shrill voice of a woman kept screaming monotonously, "Castrate 'em! Castrate 'em!" In the crowd, a white minister, Irvin Cheney, sneaked off and went for the sheriff. By the time the authorities arrived the four blacks had been beaten unconscious and the brush fire was blazing. When the sheriff drew his gun, the whites dispersed. The dentist went home and resigned from all civil rights activities. Four Klansmen were arrested and acquitted.

If good was to be wrung from evil, a lot of people were waiting to see the miracle. In Gadsden, Alabama, electric cattle prods were used on blacks. The upright white citizens of Danville, Virginia, began to wear guns in their belts, even though it was against the law. The downtown streets of Cambridge, Maryland, smelled of blood from broken heads. Malcolm X announced that the civil rights struggle in America "has reached its lowest point." In New York, black writers asked for a nationwide campaign against Christmas shopping in honor of the dead girls. James Baldwin said that Americans "have no right to celebrate Christmas this year."

Many civil rights leaders felt that the nation should be punished for what had happened in Birmingham. In Atlanta, Dr. King's SCLC drew up a campaign of national civil disobedience. A meeting of leaders was called to endorse it. Wyatt Tee Walker saw it as a nonviolent blockage of airports, railroad depots, bus terminals, streets, and commerce. He could see America grinding to a halt. He had the advocacy of Martin Luther King, who felt certain that millions of blacks would lie in doorways and across highways on command. The plan was detailed by Diane Bevel and sent to all major civil rights leaders for endorsement and cooperation. One of the men most effected, Reverend Fred Shuttlesworth of Birmingham, looked at the plan and declined to participate.

"I submit," Walker said, "that a nationwide work stoppage might attract enough attention to persuade someone to get this monkey of segregation off our backs, once, now and forever." The SCLC endorsed the plan. A week later, word reached Atlanta that the NAACP wanted nothing to do with it; neither did CORE, SNCC, the Urban League, and others. Dr. King ordered his people to drop the campaign. The appeal to boycott Christmas was also turned down. King then publicly demanded that the President order Birmingham to be occupied by federal troops. The soldiers, he said, "should take over the city and run it."

Assistant Attorney General Burke Marshall was given the task of responding to it. "No federal statute can cure the crisis in Birmingham," he said. "There isn't any magic piece of legislation. The city of Birmingham must continue to be run by the people of Birmingham. . . ." King then placed four SCLC demands before the City Council, threatening to begin mass demonstrations anew. Black leaders in Birmingham said they would hold no demonstrations, and Mayor Boutwell and the City Council ignored King's four-point ultimatum.

The town of Selma, Alabama, was acting like an old volcano; the main street had been quiet for months; the *Times-Journal* seldom had an occasion to break out a banner headline. Then Dr. King would arrive in a car, or the SNCC missionaries would start making civil rights speeches in black churches, or an old black would be found dead beside a lake, and suddenly little flashes of fire would light Selma, and black lava would trickle through the white areas.

There were some good summery days in October, and Sheriff Jim Clark worked near an open window in shirt sleeves. One day, without warning, "they" began to show up. The blacks arrived in their good clothes and good manners and asked where to go to register for voting. Elmer Peterson had the books; he was on the voting board. Normally, he wouldn't see more than a dozen blacks in a year, and most of them would be disqualified from voting for one reason or another.

Peterson saw them coming, and he went into the sheriff's office and asked what the hell was going on. Clark took a look. There was menace in the softness of his voice as he said he figured that King and all those outside "niggers" had come in and stirred these people up. Elmer said he might need some help holding them off. The sheriff didn't think there would be any trouble, but his deputies would help keep the blacks in a proper line.

The registrar said that potential voters would have to prove that they could vote; they would also have to answer a list of questions to prove their knowledge of their country's history. "Like what?" Clark said. Elmer Peterson took a paper from his pocket and began to read the questions: "Where was the first capital of the United States? What is an excise tax? Name the three main branches of the United States government and their functions."

The blacks came. They stood in line. They were turned down as voters or discouraged from pursuing the matter. Some came from Selma. Others came in farm wagons and trucks from Massillon, Beloit, Cahaba, Orrville, Browns, and Safford. One day 700 of them stood in a long queue stretching from county headquarters down the block and around the corner. More came. Policemen sent them to the sheriff's office, where they were handed numbers and told to come back another day.

Those in line were told that they must stand in place. Peterson took his time with the questioning, and the line barely moved. The police kept reminding the prospective voters that if anyone stepped out of line, he would have to go to the back of it. The Board of Registrars placed an advertisement in the Selma *Times-Journal* stating that anyone wishing to register for voting in Dallas County would have to be prepared to respond to a list of questions about the history of the United States of America. This was fashioned to stop blacks from coming to the courthouse. It kept thousands from coming into Selma on a fruitless mission. They knew the electoral deck of cards had been stacked, and they couldn't fight it.

But the young kept coming in. They complained that they stood all day long and couldn't use a bathroom or even leave the line. "Those are the rules," a policeman said. The sheriff sat in his office thinking, wondering how much longer he would have to wait in line himself before that old volcano blew the lid off the town.

It was a sunny autumn day in Dallas, Texas, and the President of the United States had five and a quarter inches of his head blown off by an assassin. The news of the murder of John F. Kennedy spread around the world like a colossal nuclear shock wave. The graceful charmer was gone, and two hours later, in a jet plane, Lyndon Baines Johnson, Texan and Southerner by family tradition, was sworn in as President. For billions of people on several continents, the news was an emotional wrench because the Kennedy family—John, Jacqueline, Caroline, and John-John—were the handsomest in history and easily the most publicized. Mr. Kennedy was also the most powerful man in the most powerful country in the world, and the ease with which he had been killed turned the minds of all toward violence.

The long-legged strides of science in the twentieth century, in addition to the veneer of gentility which it wore, fooled Americans into thinking that they were too civilized to be violent. It required mourning, examination of conscience, and a laboriously planned tableau of tragedy called a state funeral to bring the nation to admit that it was still a conglomeration of frontier rancor and bigotry—quick to draw the gun, slow to dwell upon consequences. The shock was greatest among the elite of big and small towns, because they had honestly believed in the American dream. It had less of an impact on the chronically underprivileged, those who lived on the edge of violence—the blacks. In the ghettos, black people wept that day, but they were also weeping for themselves because they could not believe that what happened to them could happen to him. Still, the news was not a shock because ghettos trade in daily death: knifings, street fights, gunfire, and, of course, the common sight of a running black and a white policeman with a drawn revolver.

In Atlanta, Dr. King and his wife sat magnetized to the television set all day. After the thirty-fifth President had been pronounced dead in Parkland Memorial Hospital, King bowed his head. "That's the way I'm going to go," he said. "I told you this is a sick society." His wife did not answer. On some far-off day, at a certain hour, a given minute, some misguided malcontent—white or black—would aim a gun at her husband and gently squeeze a trigger. He might miss; he might hit. Either way, the phone would ring and she would say, "Hello. Mrs. King speaking," as she always did, and she would hold her breath for the news. In her heart, she had lived with that hour, that minute, for a long time but she did not complain, did not beg him to turn homeward from his mission, because it was her mission, too. She had lived with the possibility of his death so long that she cherished even more the few hours they had together, the rare times they spent with the children.

"That's the way I'm going to go," he said. His life was a demand note in payment for his boldness. Too well he knew that wherever he went preaching nonviolence, his critics were right when they said that violence followed his wake. Sometimes, when he traveled with his look-alike, Bernard Lee, and they stopped overnight in a motel and shared the same bed, the same thoughts, Dr. King would say, "I'll never live to see my fortieth birthday. I'll never, never make it." And Lee, who was his bodyguard and his friend, fretted, wondering how he could recognize the danger and stop it, how he could place himself between the doctor and death. If the time came . . . if there was a moment of warning . . . if he could knock King to the ground and safety . . . if. . . .

In the penitentiary at Jefferson City, Missouri, a group of prisoners were talking about the assassination, paying little attention to James Earl Ray. He walked up and down alone, but he could hear the opinions. The men were all losers, all jades. One said, "Someone made a million dollars." Someone else said, "The man who murders King will make another million." A prisoner recalls that James Earl Ray paused, smiled, and said, "That's the million I want to collect."

The White House was outlined in lights day and night. Everyone, from President Lyndon Johnson down to the newest secretary, worked long hours, departed exhausted, and had to leave word with phone operators where they could be reached. The few who felt like relaxing at a movie had to tell which movie. The new President worked himself harder than his staff; the big shambling man had deep furrows in a tough face, and they became deeper and deeper as the days went by. The President had asked the Kennedy assistants to stay on with him. He had said, "I need you more than you need me." There were domestic and foreign problems, an escalating war in Vietnam, and a hundred or more administrations and bureaus which were responsible solely to the President for their activity and welfare.

Seven days after Johnson assumed office, he summoned Roy Wilkins to talk about civil rights and, more pointedly, the Kennedy bill which was dying in the House. Two days later, he found time to chat with Whitney Young of the Urban League; forty-eight hours later, on December 3, he called Martin Luther King in for a fifty-minute conference. The blacks in Washington now realized that Lyndon Johnson might be a better man for the cause than John Kennedy. Martin Luther King believed the contrary: Johnson was a Southerner; his forebears had fought for the Confederacy. In that short conference, Johnson won over King; he convinced the minister that civil rights was probably the most important domestic item, and he proposed to keep goading Congress until strong bills were passed. King was struck by how much the new President knew about the civil rights movement.

He departed, as always, through the West Wing press room, and King told the reporters that he was "very impressed by the President's awareness of the needs of civil rights and the depth of his concern." He went further. "As a Southerner," he said, "I am happy to know that a fellow Southerner is in the White House and is concerned with civil rights." And yet, he told the press, he had warned Johnson that demonstrations had been called off only during the Kennedy mourning period and would be quickly resumed.

Two weeks later, a mass of marching blacks gathered in Joel Hurt Park in Atlanta, and Dr. King said, "Negroes are disappointed with Atlanta." His native town should, he said, become a "model city." Black comedian Dick Gregory arrived with twenty-five members of SNCC. Dr. King could express disappointment in Atlanta, but SNCC felt that the message was not reaching Mayor Ivan Allen. The young militants did not march to a park; they asked no speeches; they sat in the Dobbs Restaurant on Peachtree Street. They sat in others. Wyatt Tee Walker joined them. "Outside" blacks joined their protests. Three hundred were arrested. Result: The Dobbs chain desegregated its restaurants, and two local Holiday Inns followed. It wasn't great or even far-reaching, but it was progress.

There were more than 900 public demonstrations in 1963; there was racial strife in more than 100 cities and towns in the South; police arrested 20,000 people; the fires, bombings, rock throwing, and gang fights are innumerable. Collectively, they caused the white man to retreat from his position of impervious domination of the black; he was worried, and he wanted to know just how little he would have to concede to make the black content and keep the dark-skinned man out of his home. The races were bargaining with each other in bad faith. In Birmingham, the biracial committee was in being, and both sides agreed on one thing in 1963: Hire some blacks for the police force to patrol black areas. It wasn't much, but the committee agreed that it would be a good thing for Birmingham. The first black was to wear a uniform and a badge in the city three years later.

The trappings of equality may fill the ego, but they leave the stomach empty. Without a good breakfast, a student cannot concentrate on schoolwork. At the close of 1963, 12 percent of white families were regarded by the United States government as "poor." This corresponded to 40 percent of black families. White mothers represented 9 percent of those listed as "head of family"; this corresponded to 23 percent of black families. In the North, the employable black earned 56 percent as much as the white equivalent with the same skills. In the South, the black earned only 40 percent as much as his white brother. Houses in black ghettos paid 25 percent more rent to their white landlords; even insurance premiums were higher for blacks because they were poorer risks and more prone to disease.

The year closed well for Martin Luther King. Edward T. Clayton, his publicity agent, received a phone call from James Keogh, one of the editors of *Time* magazine. "We're getting ready to do a kind of end-of-the-year story on civil rights," he said, "and we want to use Dr. King on the cover." Keogh said that the problem was that the magazine preferred to have King pose for one of their artists than to paint a portrait from a photograph. This was not a problem. Clayton was delighted. So was Dr. King and the entire SCLC organization. It was an accolade of magnitude: national recognition and the usual in-depth story inside the magazine.

Happily, Dr. King gave an artist two three-hour posing sessions and answered a multitude of questions from *Time* magazine researchers and reporters. The editors had more than a cover story in mind. They were making Martin Luther King their Man of the Year. King issued a modest statement: "I consider this to be a tribute to the Negro's great and gallant struggle," he said. "I would like to think that my selection is not a personal tribute, but a tribute to the whole freedom movement."

The House of Representatives passed a civil rights bill under the prodding of President Lyndon Johnson. Southerners sent word to the White House that Johnson had an election coming up in November, and he was going to be "damned sorry" for pushing that bill through. Southerners in the House, however, had no misgivings, because the bill now went to the United States Senate, where Senators from the South could be depended upon to talk it to death.

Spring came early to St. Augustine, Florida, the oldest city in the United States. There was a thriving business in displaying the artifacts of Ponce de Leon's Spaniards, and tourists paused with cameras to photograph the restored slave market. No one photographed Dr. R. N. Hayling, the black dentist who, with three others, had almost been burned to death by the Ku Klux Klan in 1963. He was still working on white teeth in black faces. He had resigned from the NAACP after his ordeal but now had the extraordinary courage to join the Reverend C. T. Vivian in trying to shake St. Augustine's 15,000 whites loose from their intense prejudice. He didn't want to do it but felt he had to. Now his home had been bombed and, on another occasion, shotgun blasts had blown out the windows.

Martin Luther King, in early March, was in Orlando. When he was told of the racial situation in St. Augustine and that blacks had no protection in the local courts, he sent Dorothy Cotton, of the SCLC Atlanta office, and Hosea Williams, one of the more militant men on his staff, to consult with Hayling and Vivian. A marching demonstration was organized to integrate one black church and one white motel. The result was instantaneous and merciless. Among those arrested and placed in jail was Mrs. Malcolm Peabody, the mother of the governor of Massachusetts, and Mrs. John Burgess, wife of the black bishop of the Episcopal Church. To show firmness of purpose, other whites waited while two black homeowners tried to enroll their children in white schools. Late at night, both houses were burned to the ground.

St. Augustine was a small town compared to Birmingham, but it maintained a much more intense flame of racial hatred. The power structure in this old seacoast town did not lie in the hands of the mayor and the Police Department. The power was H. E. Wolf, banker and bigwig in the Democratic Party; it was the St. Augustine *Record,* a mirror for white faces; it was an organization called the Ancient City Hunting Club, composed of rifle experts who sometimes made a sport of hunting two-legged "coons." Politics was divided between two political groups: the far right and the ultra-far right. Anyone who was plain right risked being called a Communist. The black was one-fourth of the population and 1 percent of the power.

Martin Luther King drove into St. Augustine on May 28. The press corps followed him, and sitting with Abernathy, he urged "all men of conscience" to come to St. Augustine and take part in the demonstration. Banker Wolf and the power structure braced for the battle. They knew that other Southern cities, some larger and stronger than theirs, had fought the pastor from Atlanta and, after a great deal of bloodletting, peace had come only when the whites had agreed to certain black demands. St. Augustine was prepared to die on its feet rather than truckle to King. The SCLC called a strategy meeting with Hayling and Vivian at a cottage fronting on a black beach. King opened the meeting and spoke of touching white hearts with Christian nonviolence. The local blacks wondered if King knew the town. He urged leaders to solicit marchers from Florida Memorial College, because the young people had the zest and the courage required for the opening of the struggle. He spoke of the slave market: It was a symbol of the persecution of the black man. Dr. King asked that blacks be told that the marches would take place after supper, that they would meet at black churches in the section southeast of Constitution Place and, in solid ranks, march on the old slave market, there to stand and sing "We Shall Overcome."

The march was staged. Nothing happened, except that one white man yelled, "You niggers have had it!" If the people of St. Augustine turned away from the demonstrations, ignored them, black support for the movement might wither in a week. But the white segregationist, without realizing it, was working for Dr. King. The Klan was determined not to permit a second march to take place. Its members and its fringe of rednecks waited at the slave market for the demonstration on Wednesday, May 27. They carried pieces of pipe and bicycle chains. The marching blacks took a look and wisely marched by. On the third night they were ordered to march to the slave market, there to stop and kneel and pray. They did. A white mob was held behind police lines. "Niggers ain't got no God!" a man shouted, and the police parted ranks and permitted the whites to go through. The blacks did not move. The whites waded through the kneeling men, shoving them aside, and fought the newsmen on the edge of the crowd. Cameras and tape recorders were grabbed and smashed; pens and pads were tossed in air. White men and women got into automobiles and drove to the beach headquarters of the SCLC. Rifle and shotgun blasts tore through the cottage from all sides. The men fired and roared off.

The campaign in St. Augustine would follow a now-familiar pattern. The blacks would act; the whites would overreact; the blacks would seek redress in court; the whites would intimidate; exhausted, both sides would reach some form of tacit agreement which would form a perpetual truce; and the SCLC would move on to the next target city. Sheriff L. O. Davis rose predictably to the bait: he forbade night marches. The SCLC went to federal court in Jacksonville. Judge Bryan Simpson listened to the arguments, the charges and countercharges. The SCLC claimed that Sheriff Davis, not satisfied with the normal strength of his deputies, had recruited 100 "specials," among whom were Ku Klux Klansmen. Thus the black was forced to fight two white forces, one which had sworn to uphold the law and the white mob, led by Holsted Manucy, a hot headed racist known to his friends as Hoss. The

SCLC attorney, William Kunstler, requested an injunction against the sheriff's ban and, a week later, got it.

King returned from a speaking engagement in Los Angeles and called a press conference. He called St. Augustine "the most lawless community that we've ever worked in in the whole struggle. . . ." In the evening, Dr. King addressed a hot crowd in an airless church. Each time he paused, the crowd roared its approval. "I want to commend you for the beauty and the dignity and the courage with which you carried out demonstrations. . . . You confronted the brutality of individuals who feel they can block our righteous efforts toward a free and just society by beating Negroes—and not only Negroes, but by beating white people who are here to give objective coverage to what is taking place in this community. But amid all this, you stood up. . . . So I want to commend you, the heroes of St. Augustine. Soon the Klan will see that all of their violence will not stop us. For we are on our way to Freedom Land, and we don't mean to stop till we get there. Now they do other things too. You know they threaten us occasionally with more than beatings here and there. They threaten us with actual physical death. They think that this will stop the Movement. I got word way out in California that a plan was under way to take my life in St. Augustine, Florida. Well, if physical death is the price that I must pay to free my white brother and all of my brothers and sisters from a permanent death of the spirit, then nothing can be more redemptive. We have long since learned to sing anew with our foreparents of old: 'Before I'll be a slave I'll be buried in my grave and go home to my Father and be saved.' "

When Federal Judge Simpson handed down his decision, he did more than warn Sheriff Davis not to impose injunctions against black marchers. He listened to a lot of related testimony. The authorities of St. Augustine were told to stop asking excessive bail from people arrested at the demonstrations. If it was true, he said, that the sheriff's men jammed ten prisoners into an eight-foot sweat box, this constituted cruel and unusual punishment under the Constitution and must be stopped. He also noted that twenty-one women had been forced into a small padded cell where there wasn't room to move or to fall. Simpson's ruling enraged the White Suprematists and Klansmen. They swore to confront nonviolence with violence.

Harry Boyte, a white representative of the SCLC, was in St. Augustine with his son. At noon, the elder Boyte was beaten unconscious; by evening the windshield of his car had been shattered by shotguns. A hundred state troopers were sent from Tallahassee, but it wasn't certain whose side they were on; earlier in the week, the State of Florida had elected a new governor, Hayden Burns, a Jacksonville segregationist.

At noontime, Dr. King, Ralph Abernathy, and a group of workers stepped to the door of the Monson Motor Lodge. The manager, James Brock, stood in the doorway. TV cameramen set up their tripods for the action. Dr. King said, "We want to have lunch—five of us."

Brock shook his head. "We can't serve you here. We're not integrated."

The pastor said, "We'll just wait around."

Brock frowned. "What's your name?"

"Martin Luther King."

"My name is Brock. I'm the manager here. As you probably know, you're on private property. I ask you on behalf of myself, my wife, and my children to leave."

Dr. King would not leave. Nor did he try to force his way inside. An old white man strode in from the parking lot, shoved King aside and said, "Get the hell out of my way!"

The black man and the white man stood for twenty minutes. "If we integrate now," Brock said, "it will hurt our business." The motel stood with its back to the town and overlooked beautiful Matanzas Bay.

Abernathy thrust his head forward. He pointed to a sign. "Does your invitation to serve tourists include Negroes?"

Brock gave him the Southern white man's response: "We serve Negro servants of white guests in the service area back there."

King pointed to his friends. "Do you understand what that does to our dignity?"

Brock was losing his temper. "Will you take your nonviolent army somewhere else?" he said. "I have already had eighty-five people arrested here."

"We'll wait in the hope that the conscience of someone will be aroused."

Obviously, someone was aroused. The police arrived with sirens wailing, dome lights flashing. King and Abernathy were taken to the St. Augustine Jail. A few members of the press were admitted. Both prisoners were sitting at a small table. "This is the nicest jail I've been in," Dr. King said. Three days later he and Abernathy left the jail after paying $900 bail. Dr. King then flew to New Haven to accept an honorary degree from Yale University.

He underestimated St. Augustine. When Dr. Hayling asked the doctor to leave Orlando and come to the oldest city in the country, King thought of it as one more small hate-filled town, a structure bound to topple under the unremitting pressure of 3,800 Negroes. He miscalculated.

The police, except in emergencies, had withdrawn from action. The white answer to the black thrust was being delivered by hundreds of violent rowdies. The movement was not fighting law enforcement officials this time. Hoss Manucy and hundreds of white citizens who hated blacks were the enemy. These were the men who waited in silence for the black marchers to arrive near the slave market and raced through the ranks swinging chains and pipes. Sixteen rabbis left a Jewish convention in Atlantic City to march with the blacks. They were not assaulted, but a wave of anti-Semitism swept through St. Augustine. Young blacks sent to white beaches had been beaten. Others staged a "dive-in" at the Monson Motor Lodge swimming pool, and a white man emptied the contents of a bottle marked "muriatic acid" on them. They fled screaming.

When Dr. King returned, he was appalled. He appealed to the President. Mr. Johnson replied it was impossible to send federal marshals to St. Augustine. The "best friend" the Movement ever had in the White House was unable to help. King, who knew that St. Augustine was depending on the tourist dollar to celebrate its soon-due four hundredth birthday, announced that "St. Augustine is not going to celebrate its quadri-centennial segregated." The city had been promised $350,000 of federal money to dress up for the occasion. The SCLC tried to stop the grant on the grounds that the community was deliberately in disobedience of a federal injunction not to interfere with night marches. The federal government told the city that the money would be given on time.

The first peace move came from the white side. Bankers H. E. Wolf and Frank Harold joined with Florida State Senator Verne Pope to proclaim that a committee was about to come into being to bring racial peace to St. Augustine. The gentlemen did not mention appointing black members. The oversight was called to their attention, and they said that local blacks would be on the committee with whites. The stumbling block lay in the word "local." The whites did not intend to negotiate with the Reverends Martin Luther King or Ralph Abernathy. King told the "local" black leaders that they had fought white viciousness for a long time and lost. No peace offer had been made until the SCLC had come into town. And, assuming that the bankers and the senator were sincere, what did they propose to do to stop Hoss Manucy and his brutes, and Sheriff Davis and his deputies? Dr. King suggested that the local black leaders think these questions over before rejecting the SCLC demand to be represented on the committee.

The first surrepitious peace offerings had been made, but the SCLC sent to Savannah, Georgia, to bring Hosea Williams to the scene to lead a rally. Williams belonged to the militant wing, and on occasion, his words could fire a crowd to a pitch of rage. He spoke to blacks on Friday afternoon at the slave market. St. Augustine's unofficial vigilantes leaned against posts and walls, watching, listening, snickering. "Negroes have shed their blood here," Hosea Williams shouted, "that Jack Kennedy shall not have died in vain. And Medgar Evers and the children of Birmingham too!" The applause was boisterous. "Yes," he shouted, "they died and we may die, but we will die with this in our mind—if the black man loses his freedom, no man may be free!" When he concluded, the black bodies linked arms, swaying, and sang "We Love Everybody."

That evening, the whites held a rally in the same place. The speaker was J. B. Stoner, a lawyer from Atlanta. Part of his practice had been the defense of Klansmen. "We whites," he said sonorously, "are due for more rights, not less. When the Constitution said all men are created equal, it wasn't talking about niggers." When Stoner concluded his inflammatory talk, he and 200 whites marched through the black section of town. They were flanked by armed state troopers walking police dogs on leashes. The bias of the law enforcement men was now out in the open. A sign unsettled the white marchers; it read: WELCOME. PEACE AND BROTHERHOOD TO YOU. When Stoner led his well-protected group back to the slave market, he signaled for silence and said, "Let's give a hand to our law enforcement officers for protecting us from those black savages."

The racial convulsions of St. Augustine began in March; in June they were still going on. Martin Luther King was worried because the desegregation of the little city had required so much time and had met with such iron resistance. He was a man with a carefully planned schedule and the calendar of coming events was becoming crowded. He had promised to devote himself to a summertime drive for Southern black voter registration; there was to be a big People-to-People March in the state of Mississippi to honor Medgar Evers; the Democratic National Convention was to be held in Atlantic City in August—and King wanted to be there to make his presence felt; the little town of Selma had been in the planning stage for more than a year, and the people there were waiting for Martin Luther King. Wyatt Walker, who usually helped with much of the administrative details, was working on a project involving the writing of a twenty-volume compendium of black history. That meant that almost all the decisions at the SCLC were left to Dr. King. King's presence was the black man's strength and weakness. He felt that if he made an appearance at each city where the struggle for equality was going on, as he had at Danville, Virginia, he would create the momentum for the blacks to work out their salvation and "reconciliation" with the whites. King made the difference between a chance for victory and certain defeat. The whites knew that he brought with him nation-wide publicity of a type they didn't want. When he preached nonvio-lence, he became a Christian hero; when he was jailed, he was a martyr; when the tides of fortune went against his organization, he appealed to the President of the United States. King appreciated his importance, but even if his continual presence had not been required, his zest for round after round of battles was seeping his spirit. He had given too much of himself; fatigue was in his face. His choice would have been to take charge of the strategy from a seat in Washington, to command an army of unarmed blacks from afar, but he knew that was impossible. The people wanted to see him in their midst, alive and talking, aligning them with God in all that they did. He was a very young man to be a father image.

The St. Augustine bankers and the state senator continued their secret meetings with the blacks, pointing out that the United States Senate would soon be passing President Johnson's civil rights law. Couldn't the demonstrations wait a week or so? The President was certain to sign it, and the whites would then have a face-saving device for granting addi-tional freedoms to blacks: the new law. Dr. King said that he could see the logic of this approach, but he was still waiting for the formation of a biracial committee, and by biracial he made it plain that he meant the inclusion of Dr. Hayling. The whites weren't sure. They had asked for "law-abiding" citizens, and Hayling, they said, had been arrested in the demonstrations. The pastor smiled and waved everyone away. There was no point in talking if the negotiators were not prepared to act in good faith. He said he would prefer to continue the nonviolent demon-strations.

A group of blacks invaded the Monson Motel again and went swimming in the pool. Whites were told that this is what would happen if additional rights were granted to blacks. King talked nonviolence, but his followers asked for violence. A county grand jury made up of whites demanded a thirty-day suspension of hostilities and the "immediate" departure of Dr. Martin Luther King. Peace became remote.

On Sunday a priest named Father Seymour invited blacks to Trinity Church for the first time. Some knelt in the aisles; some sat in rear pews. King saw a ray of hope in this gesture. At the same time, he received word that the Mississippi Summer Project had begun: Two whites named Andrew Goodman and Michael Schwerner were the first to go there. They were accompanied by James Chaney, a Mississippi civil rights worker, who had volunteered to be their guide. This was the beginning of a new and important campaign, and King wished with all his heart that he could leave St. Augustine. "We have no alternative now," he told Ralph Abernathy, "except to sink deeper in *this* struggle."

The whites in St. Augustine seemed to have lost power over Hoss Manucy and the police. They continued to harass black demonstrators. In one melee, a policeman offered his club to a white man. "Here," he said, "want to use this for a few minutes?" On the beach, a white man collared a black boy, smiled over his shoulder at a grinning policeman, and said, "Don't be too rough when you take us in," and drove his fist into the face of the boy. A white minister from California proclaimed piously: "Jesus Christ belongs to the white man." In an aside to the congregation, he said, "Go get the niggers." Nineteen blacks were injured on one day. A teen-age black girl was physically unhurt, but white men tore every shred of clothing from her. A *Newsweek* reporter was savagely mauled.

Clearly, matters were going beyond what St. Augustine could afford. Florida's Governor Farris Bryant, who could have stopped all of it at the start with his troopers and the National Guard, risked contempt of court by banning night marches near the end of June. The blacks, momentarily, could not march. Hoss Manucy and his men melted into the darkness of the quiet streets. For a few nights, those who wanted to listen could hear crickets. Dr. King could wait no longer. He had no victory, no biracial committee, no promises that the black man of St. Augustine would be any better off than before. If anything might improve the lot of the local black, it would be President Johnson signing a civil rights bill. On Tuesday, June 30, Dr. King disbanded his beach headquarters and left for Atlanta. Someone asked what had been accomplished. "I am hoping for the best," he said.

Thirty days later, Dr. Hayling went to court and sued the city of St. Augustine for denying blacks their civil rights. This time he won. The white bankers and the state senator were spared their pride by reminding their critics that "everybody must abide by the law, whether we like it or not." Dr. King proclaimed St. Augustine a victory.

President Lyndon Johnson, sitting in the Cabinet Room of the White House, took the first of an assortment of pens to sign the civil rights bill. On the opposite side of the table, the photographers were ready. The press gave the bulk of the credit to Martin Luther King, as the President gave him one of the pens. This was not entirely so. It would be correct to state that Dr. King had brought the plight of the black to public attention through his personal sacrifices and public confrontations. But it was the consummate politician, Southerner Lyndon Johnson, who had forced the bill through both houses at the possible cost of losing eleven or more states in his campaign in November.

During the summer of 1964, winds of heat and hate seared the corn and baked the bricks of old tenements. It was a time when a million blacks in a hundred towns stopped the obsequious shuffle to the white man's tune and spat with contempt and called him "Whitey" to his face. Slowly, steadily, the racial volcano began to erupt; the boiling black lava seeped into Fifth Avenue and Lakeshore Drive and Walnut Street and Sunset Boulevard and Nob Hill. It was the summer white men bought rifles and revolvers. After dinner, lights began to go out; police cars skirted the perimeter of black sections; night mobs walked the streets with clubs, broomsticks, guns, and knives; for the first time, black men bolted their doors in fear of blacks. Black-owned storekeepers hung out signs: SOUL BROTHER.

It was the summer the black leaders lost control of the Movement.

It began with the arrest of two white men and a black in Philadelphia, Mississippi, for speeding. They were Andrew Goodman and Michael Schwerner, the young white members of CORE, and their guide, James Chaney, a Mississippi civil rights worker. The young men were in Mississippi to survey the area and test the racial climate before the main body of blacks, including Martin Luther King, arrived for the People-to-People March honoring Medgar Evers. Philadelphia, in Neshoba County, Mississippi, is noplace going nowhere. Sheriff Lawrence Rainey's deputies pulled the car to a stop, and the three men were taken to headquarters. It was a small arrest in a small town, hardly worth the trouble of gossip in a Southern town of 5,160 persons.

The three men were never seen again. It required a little time for anxiety to show. The sheriff said he did not know where the men were;

they had been held for six hours on a charge of speeding and released. No one could disprove it. Rainey and his deputy, Cecil Price, lounged in the shade and, for the moment, did not feel the hot wrath sweeping the country. Neshoba was a law-abiding county. There was a Choctaw Indian reservation near the Tallahaga River, and a young brave might get out of order now and then; but most of the time was spent watching out-of-state cars go by. Rainey began to see some "foreign" license plates. They belonged to newsmen sent from Memphis and Birmingham and New York and New Orleans, all pulling up in front of his office to inquire, "What happened to those CORE men?" The sheriff explained that it was a matter of exceeding the speed limit, holding the two whites and the black, and letting them go.

Four days later, President Johson sent 200 unarmed men of the United States Navy to comb the brush and woods of Neshoba County to find the missing. He directed the FBI to send men to Philadelphia, Mississippi, because it looked as though Rainey was not sufficiently alarmed to have his deputies do any searching. A week later the Navy men left. They had found no bodies. The Federal Bureau of Investigation kept special agents in the county. Rainey couldn't understand all the fuss, but the mouths of men around little Philadelphia began to slam shut. The harder they slammed, the more certain the FBI men became that the three had been killed. It was impossible to turn over every boulder, go through every field of brush with a fine comb, so they turned their attention to locating an informer. This requires intelligence and patience in an area of hate. They had it. They worked through the hottest weeks of the summer, knowing that someone knew something. They gave up looking for the dead; they needed one live man.

A burned-out station wagon was found. It had been used by the three "speeding" civil rights workers. Black leaders planning the People-to-People March to dramatize their drive to register black voters knew that time was running out. If black delegates were to sit in Southern delegations at the national conventions, Mississippi blacks had to register. If it were possible in Mississippi, then it was possible anywhere. The white population of the state was 1,257,000 against a black population of 921,000. The strength of both sides was more evenly matched than the numbers would indicate because, in many counties, the blacks outnumbered the whites two to one. Registration under the Johnson civil rights law was possible, if the local people could brave the long queues, the insolence, and take a chance on losing the white man's goodwill and jobs.

The leaders had formed one more organization, this one called the Council of Federated Organizations (COFO), a loosely knit alliance of the NAACP, SCLC, SNCC, and CORE. However, the disappearance of the three men frightened more than Mississippians. It scared COFO, too. One of the young men of SNCC, Bob Moses, stated the aims of the People-to-People March succinctly: "Our goals are limited. If we can go and come back alive, that is something." Moses had done some of the preliminary work by going into Mississippi secretly and making plans with NAACP leaders. Charles Evers, brother of the murdered Medgar, assumed the presidency of the state NAACP. Dr. Aaron Henry had organized a political party of blacks to rival the completely white Democratic Party. It was called the Mississippi Freedom Democratic Party, and it proposed to buck the political establishment. Hundreds of white students (and few blacks) began their college summer vacations by placing themselves at the call of SNCC. Stokely Carmichael proposed to play a leading part in the march and, at organizational meetings, referred to the SNCC students as "sweets."

The march began under a broiling sun and a dozen disparate philosophies. Crowds of blacks and whites walked along the edge of a highway, singing "We Shall Overcome." Some glanced across shimmering fields of corn to see blacks on the rickety porches of tenant farmers, watching the blacks watch the blacks. The Mississippi Highway Patrol sped up and down the line, squeezing it toward the ditches, urging everyone to "keep it moving." At each town or city line, more police cars joined and told Dr. King and Stokely Carmichael and Dr. Henry, "We don't want trouble. You just keep marching right through our town and out the other side." The camera crews rode on the backs of trucks taking random shots when the people in the front line linked arms and sang, waiting for the violence without which the march held little interest for television. The White Establishment of Mississippi husbanded a sustained hostility and fear toward the black because, in the course of time, the black population would outnumber the white, and the whites frightened each other by talking of the day when Mississippi would have a black governor, two black Senators, and the law would be black, too.

The march was twenty miles north of the capital city of Jackson when the leaders called a halt. The sun was going down; the people were tired. The town was Canton, a junction between Routes 51 and 16. The marching plan laid out by Stokely Carmichael called for pitching tents on the playground of the black McNeil elementary school. Madison

County police said that the marchers could not use the school grounds overnight. It was a black school, but it was also a public school and therefore Canton City property. Stokely Carmichael went into Canton's "Colored Town," asking people to join him at McNeil School. The people poured out of houses, not understanding the issue, but glad to display silent strength for the Movement. Carmichael led a crowd of them onto the school grounds, ordered the trucks to back up and start disgorging the tents, and joined hands with Dr. King and Floyd McKissick. "They said we couldn't pitch our tents on a black school! Well, we're going to do it now."

As the trucks were unloaded, blacks formed a huge circle and sang "We Shall Overcome." Canton police and Madison County police put in a radio call for help from the state highway patrol. Reinforcements arrived quickly. Dusk had hardly laid a finger on church steeples when the augmented police force donned gas masks, tossed tear gas into the dancing crowd, and moved in holding guns by their barrels. Someone had told them "No shooting," so they clubbed every black they could catch. A local black woman, on the ground, tried to stand, and a policeman kicked her in the spine. "You wanted your freedom, nigger!" the cop shouted. "Well, here it is!" Blood began to flow. Piercing screams tore the fabric of a soft evening breeze. A white premedical student fell with two broken ribs and a partially collapsed lung. Dr. King was surrounded by members of his staff and hustled off to an automobile. Floyd McKissick got away. Stokely Carmichael shouted, "They're going to shoot. Get the people out of here." They got. They walked on tired, sore feet. The local people watched them go; it would require more than Stokely Carmichael to get them out of their homes again.

Mississippi's senior Senator, James Eastland, got on the air to announce that his state "never had fiction—uh—friction, with our Negroes."

The group slept in the open on a black farm. In the morning, after buying such food as they could, they started toward the capital city of Jackson. They were weary, abused, wary of ambush at every turn in the road. If the white man was going to stop them, he would do it soon. On Saturday night, COFO held its final encampment. Whitney Young arrived from the North. James Meredith, who had braved the University of Mississippi, to enroll as the first black student, was there. The leaders held a meeting. Dr. King reminded everyone that tomorrow was the big day. They would stage a mass rally in front of the staid old Capitol

Building, and King nominated Charles Evers to make the main speech. After all, he *was* the brother of the slain Medgar Evers; he *was* the leader of the Movement in the state—this would keep the White Establishment from calling attention to "outsiders" like himself. King was voted down so quickly that he was stunned. SNCC said it was opposed; so was CORE; the Mississippi Freedom Democratic Party said no: Dr. King should be the one to address the rally; the doctor sat on the grounds of the Negro Tougaloo College and nodded his head. He would speak.

Long marches seem to attract the bulk of the people on the first day and again on the last. Few will brave the hot sun and burning feet and the fury of the police in the remote places between. So it was with the People-to-People March. On the last day, a great number of blacks drove out from Jackson and came in from surrounding towns to stand in the ranks for the final walk into Jackson. They were enthused, and they sang their way into the outskirts of the city. But when they reached the square where the Capitol Building stood, they saw the lines of helmeted policemen; they also saw frightened blacks standing quietly on sidewalks around the square watching and waiting. Dr. King and his leaders were 500 feet from the Capitol Building when the police said, "Stop!"

The leaders wavered a moment, then came to a halt. Martin Luther King spoke of his old dream of a free America and talked of the "nightmare" he had experienced in Mississippi. "One day," he said, "right here in this state of Mississippi, justice will become a reality for all." The marchers huddled around him, as sheep to a shepherd. Beyond them were the helmets, the clubs, the tear gas. The march broke up quietly, and the caravan of cars drove east on Route 80, tossing talcum of dust on a necklace of little towns.

It was not a victory, and King did not call it one. He returned to Atlanta dejected. He was tired. He was an old young man. Mrs. King suggested that they take the children to New York and see the World's Fair. The doctor agreed—it would be a fine opportunity to spend part of the summer with his family. A New York friend offered the Kings the use of their apartment in August and they were there, on West Seventy-second Street, when the Federal Bureau of Investigation announced that it had found the bodies of James Chaney, Michael Schwerner, and Andrew Goodman. A mud dam had been built across a branch of the Tallahaga River near Philadelphia to provide water for cattle. The three bodies had been found inside the dam. They had been there for forty-four days, and the news sickened the nation.

The FBI had its informer. He recited twenty-one names of the lynch party which had killed the black and the two whites after they had been detained on a charge of speeding. The cattle dam was just going up, and it seemed a safe place to bury the victims. Among the twenty-one named as conspirators were the sheriff and his chief deputy. The State of Mississippi could not be prodded into trying the malefactors. The federal government, sorting its file of old laws, was surprised to find that murder, including the assassination of a president, was not a federal offense. The twenty-one could only be indicted and tried on charges of conspiracy to violate the Civil Rights Code and conspiring to impede the freedom of citizens under an 1870 penal code. Conviction would bring a penalty of ten years in federal prison and $5,000 fine. FBI Special Agent Henry Rask testified in court that he had a signed confession from one of the men indicating that it was a Ku Klux Klan lynching party. U.S. Commissioner Esther Carter, hearing the charges, refused to admit the confession as evidence, and charges against the men were dismissed.

The Democratic National Convention opened in Atlantic City on August 24. No one doubted that the party would nominate President Lyndon Johnson by acclamation. He would chose his Vice Presidential running mate, and the gathering would break up in a chorus of huzzahs and waving of American flags. There was more excitement for the delegates in being wheeled up and down the boardwalk or drinking in striptease nightclubs.

Two days before the convention, the black civil rights group stood before the credentials committee. Martin Luther King, Aaron Henry, and Bayard Rustin asked, in the case of the State of Mississippi, that the regular Democratic Party delegates be ruled off the convention floor and, in their place, Dr. Henry's Mississippi Freedom Democratic Party be seated. It was a source of embarrassment to the National Committee because, for the first time since the Civil War, a white group was pitted against a black one. The Johnson administration was committed more deeply to civil rights than the Kennedy government which preceded it, but, if the white Mississippians were to be unseated, the party could lose all eleven states in the Southern tier, with a total of 111 votes out of a national total of 301. The November winner would require a minimum of 151 votes. Southern politicians, normally voting Democratic, are quick to anger and slow to make peace. By seating the black rump delegation, President Johnson could be making a gift of 111 electoral

votes to his opponent, Senator Barry Goldwater, who would then require only 40 more additional votes to reach the minimum number of
needed votes.

The credentials committee reported directly to Johnson as did the
platform committee. The President was running the convention from the
White House by telephone. Dr. Henry's MFDP testified before the
credentials committee that it was the duly elected delegation from
Mississippi because the whites, in excluding blacks from polls and party
counsels, had forfeited its right to represent the state. Dr. King was
impressed with the zeal and fighting spirit of Henry's group. They would
settle for nothing less than that all the blacks be seated and all the
whites ousted.

The committee said it would prefer to seat some blacks, some whites.
Aaron Henry, Mrs. Fannie Lou Hamer, and Ed King, the Mississippians, decided that they wanted all or nothing. Dr. King applauded their
stand and endorsed them at a press conference. Later, at a meeting,
Bayard Rustin persuaded Dr. King that he was wrong. If the credentials
committee were pressed too hard, it would have no choice but to seat
the white delegation and write the civil rights group off as a loss. This
would not affect the fortunes of the Johnson administration much
because the blacks did not have enough registered voters to represent a
balance of power.

King understood. He shifted his position and urged Aaron Henry to
accept half a loaf. The MFDP delegation sat *in camera* listening to him
in stony silence. The will of Dr. King did not prevail. The Mississippians
respected him and felt a deep gratitude for what he had done for the
Movement, but sixty-eight of them voted to follow the impossible path
of righteousness. They would sit in all the seats or none. The white
delegates could not be half right, while the black was half wrong. They
pressed the issue before the credentials committee and lost. They left the
convention with their heads up. Their departure widened the split between the militant, direct action attitude of SNCC, which applauded the
stand of Dr. Henry's little group, and the SCLC, which had pleaded for
compromise and lost. The enmity between the two organizations was
now in the open; nonviolence became a bad word.

King had a program of his own which he brought to the attention of
the convention. It was called a Bill of Rights for the Disadvantaged,
taking away some of the limelight from President Johnson's recently
inaugurated project called the Poverty Program. Johnson's notion was to
lift the lower-third income group of the nation to a level of subsistence

which would create new jobs, higher levels of median income, and, idealistically, place almost 200,000,000 people on a footing where no one would starve, and every family would have a roof over its head and an opportunity for economic improvement. Dr. King's document concerned only the blacks. It was here that two projects crossed wires, causing sparks which, in time, would doom both programs.

The SCLC plan opened on the premise that the worker is worthy of his hire. Throughout two centuries of slavery, the black had not been paid for his toil. "Not all the wealth of this affluent society could meet the bill," King stated. "Yet a price can be placed on unpaid wages. . . . The payment should be in the form of a massive program by the government of special, compensatory measures which could be regarded as a settlement in accordance with the accepted practice of common law. Such measures would certainly be less expensive than any computation based on two centuries of unpaid wages and accumulated interest.

"I am proposing, therefore, that just as we granted a GI Bill of Rights to war veterans, Americans launch a broad-based and gigantic Bill of Rights for the Disadvantaged, our veterans of the long siege of denial. I am specifically proposing that the platform of [this] party include an endorsement and support for the broad plan of such a bill."

Both the platform committee, which heard the proposal, and the convention were opposed to giving the matter consideration. It sounded to the politicians as though only the blacks would benefit. In the White House, President Lyndon Johnson and his advisers already knew that they had the black vote. Martin Luther King and all thinking blacks, South and North, would have to vote Democratic or possibly lose all they had gained under the reactionary administration of Barry Goldwater. "They have nowhere else to go," the Democrats said, and they were right. Boldly, the party had turned down Dr. King on two matters and, at the same time, stripped him of alternatives.

On August 25, President Johnson was nominated by acclamation. All that was left was his choice of a Vice President. He telephoned Senator Thomas Dodd of Connecticut at the convention and asked him to hurry to the White House with Senator Hubert Humphrey of Minnesota. The President, who enjoyed keeping his own secrets and springing his own surprises, hung up. When the two men arrived at the Executive Mansion, both were perspiring. Dodd thought that there was a good chance that Johnson was tapping him for the number two post; Humphrey thought he too had a chance. The President went about his routine business and kept both Senators waiting. When he called them in, he said he wanted Humphrey to be his Vice President. His wish was that Dodd would go back to the convention at once and spread the word. By nightfall, Humphrey's name was in headlines. Ten days later Robert F. Kennedy announced his resignation as Attorney General of the United States. He said he would transfer his family to a residence in New York State so that he could campaign for a seat in the United States Senate. Now Kennedy followers felt no need to keep up the pretense of loyalty to President Johnson. The big team which John F. Kennedy had brought to Washington when he was sworn in as President left Johnson en masse and rallied to support "Bobby" for the Senate, certain that he would run for the Presidency and win in 1968.

In the field of education, dishonesty begins at the top. Superintendents of boards of education are, in the main, frustrated politicians. In principle, the ladies and gentlemen are entrusted with the care of thousands of young and formative minds for five hours each weekday. In actuality, many of the members see themselves as omnipotent judges of principals, teachers, and students, watchdogs with a keener knowledge of books to be banned from the system than those which might broaden the stream of information intended to slake the thirst of the young.

In the United States the practice of electing or appointing members of a city or county board of education is a political matter, and the results are largely political. Seldom are seats on boards of education filled by those best qualified to do the work—retired teachers and educators. Thus, when desegregation became a law from on high, Southern boards of education spent a disproportionate amount of time working to subvert the law. In the years between May, 1954, and September, 1964, the Southern high schools had fallen academically to a point where applicants for Ivy League colleges were being declined in large groups, and most graduates had to settle for smaller and less exacting colleges.

The black man, in all parts of the United States, was faced with an insuperable problem: In mathematics, in history, English, geography, and the sciences, his black school was behind the teaching in comparable white schools by eighteen months to two years. When he was transferred to an integrated school, he was lost in a maze of facts which were beyond him. To catch up, it would be necessary, in most cases, to drop him back two grades. This was a humiliation. In addition, he often had to learn to get along without friends, without anyone to play with at recess, to submit to the acid comments of white children, and to eat lunch by himself. Often a sweet and smiling teacher was laden with racial hatred: The black child would always fail in her class. Economic reprisals were often used against the parents of a black child enrolled in a once-white school. Jobs were lost by the fathers; mothers were dismissed as cooks and housekeepers.

When Dr. King returned from a September visit to Berlin and Rome, he complained that he felt "tired, tired, tired." He seemed to be drained of strength, ideas, and initiative, and the sense of deep fatigue persisted. Dr. King had been marching, preaching, protesting for eight years, and the American black man was still almost as far from freedom and equality as when Mrs. Parks sat in the front of a bus with tired feet.

Mrs. King finally persuaded her husband to go to St. Joseph's Hospital in Atlanta for a complete checkup. On October 13, in the middle of the Presidential campaign between Lyndon Johnson and Barry Goldwater, the doctor packed his pajamas and checked in. The tests proved nothing more than that the patient was tense and needed rest. On the following morning, the phone rang in the King home, and Coretta King answered. The caller identified himself as representing the Associated Press and asked to speak to Dr. King. Mrs. King replied that her husband was not at home.

"Mrs. King," the Associated Press man said excitedly, "we have just received word from Norway that your husband has been awarded the Nobel Peace Prize."

Among those who knew her, Coretta King kept her emotions corked at all times. If she wept, she wept alone. If she laughed, she never did so loudly or uncontrollably. If she was angry, her speaking voice became more remote. She said quietly that she would get in touch with her husband and that either he or she would call back the AP with a statement.

"This year the prize is worth fifty-four thousand dollars," the reporter said. "What do you suppose Dr. King will do with all that money?"

"Knowing him," Mrs. King replied, "I expect he will give it all to the Freedom Movement."

Coretta King phoned her husband at St. Joseph's, hardly able to restrain her pride. "How is the Nobel Peace Prize winner for 1964 feeling this morning?"

There was no response. Then Dr. King seemed to awaken. "I'd better check to see if this is true," he said. It was. Eight members of the Norwegian Parliment had convened as a committee to consider nominees for the annual Nobel Peace Prize. They felt Dr. Martin Luther

King, as the black leader who struggled with White America for equality in a nonviolent manner, was the greatest advocate of peace in 1964.

King had little rest after the matter became public. Phones seemed to be ringing everywhere; the preacher no longer needed rest. He felt strong and well. The award, one of the most prestigious in the world, was in his hand. Archbishop Paul J. Hallinan of the Roman Catholic archdiocese of Atlanta visited the hospital room and offered his congratulations. That and the felicitations of Mayor Ivan Allen of Atlanta would be the only accolades King would get from the South. The archbishop said, "May I give you my blessing?"

"Of course," said the smiling face on the pillow. Hallinan made the sign of the cross. Then he dropped to his knees and asked the Reverend Dr. King for his blessing. It was one of the few times that Dr. King was humbled by a gesture. He gave the archbishop his blessing, and long afterward he could not discuss the Nobel Prize without thinking of the archbishop on his knees. Later in the day there was a press conference in the solarium of the hospital, and Dr. King stated that the money would go to six organizations in the Movement. Afterward, as he sat alone with his wife, he told her, "For a while when you phoned me I thought it was a dream."

When the Norwegian Parliament considered the nominees for the peace award, they bandied big names about before sifting them down to Martin Luther King. Although the names of those considered are not made public, the other men were: Dwight D. Eisenhower, Konrad Adenauer of Germany, Anthony Eden of Great Britain, and Charles de Gaulle of France. Only two blacks had been awarded a Nobel Prize prior to King. One was Ralph J. Bunche of the United Nations, an American; the other was Albert Luthuli, leader of the African National Congress.

Telegrams of congratulations arrived at the King home from men of stature in almost every field of endeavor. Robert Kennedy wired that "the prize is richly deserved" and noted that the Baptist preacher's life symbolized "the struggle of mankind for justice and equality through nonviolent means." Someone in Birmingham asked Bull Connor for his opinion of the award. "They're scraping the bottom of the barrel," he said.

Director J. Edgar Hoover of the FBI knew better than anyone else that there is more than one skeleton in every closet. He had begun to inquire into the activities of King when the pastor first became involved in the civil rights movement. His men had reported there were leftists and former Communists in the pastor's entourage, and this had led to the order for wiretapping. The trouble with sophisticated eavesdropping is that not only does it capture and parrot the desired material, but it also bags everything, including the whispered mouthings in a motel room. The private life of King, licentious or not, was not proper material for the electronic bugs, but they picked up his most personal words and deeds. Had Director Hoover been selective, he might have eliminated all except pertinent material from his top secret reports; but Hoover chose not to be selective, and highly personal material was included with political digests which were sent to Attorney General Nicholas Katzenbach, President Lyndon B. Johnson, and Speaker of the House John McCormack.

On November 18 the pastor was on Bimini, an island thirty-five miles southeast of Miami, enjoying the hospitality of his sometime friend Adam Clayton Powell. Dr. King was working on rough drafts of two speeches—a short one of gratitude for the night he received the Nobel Prize and a longer, more philosophical one for the following day in Oslo. On November 18 J. Edgar Hoover was in Washington in the middle of an unusual (for him) dissertation. He was holding a press conference for women journalists. The pad pages were flipping on knees, the ball-point pens were dancing, when someone mentioned civil rights and Martin Luther King. The man with the ruddy bulldog face took a breath and referred to King as "the most notorious liar in the country." It was hardly a diplomatic statement; reflex anger had coughed an explosion. The women wanted more, but J. Edgar Hoover wasn't going to tell what he knew. All he would say was that King had once stated that Southern FBI agents had failed in their duty because they were Southerners.

The explosion hit the White House and rocked it. The newly announced winner of the Nobel Peace Prize had been attacked by the Holy of Holies of Justice. No one can doubt that the Johnson administration tried to get Hoover to retract, or restate, or dilute the seven words, but Mr. Hoover was an immovable force. The words reached Dr. King, who dropped his Nobel speeches to devise a statement in rebuttal. In all likelihood, he sought counsel from Congressman Adam Clayton Powell; that would account for the conciliatory tone of the release given to the press. "I am appalled and surprised," the pastor said to reporters standing near the beach. "What motivated such an irresponsible accusation is a mystery to me."

In Washington the press begged Director Hoover to give them more details about King's "lying." His laconic response was: "I haven't even begun to say all I could about that subject." Hoover left for a trip to Chicago, where he made an address at Loyola University. In it, while enunciating his views on law enforcement, Hoover took an oratorical swing at the civil rights groups as being led by "zealots or pressure groups" and "spearheaded at times by Communists and moral degenerates." The indictment was severe and blunt; no one doubted the name of the person he had in mind.

Black leaders began to issue statements defending Dr. King; so did white leaders. On the other hand, Senator Thomas Dodd of Connecticut, formerly a special agent of the FBI, said, "I'm very certain that Hoover knows what he's talking about." One thing was certain: The freshly gilded statue of Martin Luther King, Jr., had been tarnished. Something had to be done to stop it.

Presidents from the time of Calvin Coolidge in 1924 could have told the black leader that the worst course to follow would be a public brawl with J. Edgar Hoover. Some Presidents were powerless in Hoover's presence; Attorneys General gave Hoover as much power and latitude as he asked for. Those who tried to fight him or just to edge Hoover toward retirement and replacement had learned from the incoming mail that Hoover was a living saint, not to be touched by human hands. King did two wrong things: First, he told the press that Hoover's statement, sadly must be the result of "extreme pressure. He has apparently faltered under the awesome burdens, complexities and responsibilities of his office. Therefore, I cannot engage in a public debate with him." Then he asked for an appointment with Hoover to discuss the matter.

The telegram was on Hoover's desk. It was datelined New York. The director studied it and told subordinates that he did not want to see King; on the other hand, if he refused, the pastor might assume the role of the martyr. So a message went out that Hoover would meet King in his Washington office on December 4. King thought that the FBI director was irritated solely because of what he had said in Georgia concerning the fact that Southern FBI agents were Southern in sentiment. He did not know about the wiretapping. King arrived at the big granite building on Pennsylvania Avenue with Ralph Abernathy, Andrew Young, and the head of the SCLC in Washington, Walter Fauntroy. These men were not permitted to the private part of the conference.

The talk lasted for only a short while—the director imperious and mysterious, the doctor puzzled and ill at ease. King left without a fare-well handshake. In the marble corridor, he chatted with reporters, put on his best smile as though all had gone well, and said he was not at liberty to discuss the conversation he had had with the FBI director. He then discussed with the reporters the fact that FBI agents in Mississippi had arrested twenty-one men in connection with the murders of the three civil rights workers.

The animosity of J. Edgar Hoover directed itself more to the personal life of Dr. King than to his public existence. The assignment given to FBI agents was to probe for Communist elements within the ranks of the Southern Christian Leadership Conference, as well as to check on King and his confreres' political ideologies. Evidence was uncovered that within the inner group were a few persons sympathetic to the Communist cause. The two times that such matters were drawn to the attention of Dr. King, he publicly asked the man to resign. However, he continued to consult the men in question either by telephone or in person, thus continuing the relationship. Unknown to King, all this was on tapes. At one time, officers of the SCLC told him that they had never seen so many "telephone repairmen" at the office day after day, and he was warned of the possibility of telephone taps. But the doctor pooh-poohed such notions. In sum, they wouldn't "dare." *Au contraire,* the government, like a mad scorpion, was stinging itself to death with tele-phone taps. This was the reason why the President of the United States, in order to protect himself from secret agencies, within and outside his government, installed a scrambler phone, a transmitter which dis-oriented syllables and words and could be reassembled into comprehen-sive words only by a similar instrument at the other end of the line.

The director of the Federal Bureau of Investigation, whose men manned the King taps, learned nothing which could threaten the internal security of the nation, but the old bachelor found some of King's other activities distasteful. The major question is whether this was the proper business of the FBI in the first place.

Thirty blacks in two planes took off from Atlanta early in December. King had his closest friends with him in one plane. Mrs. King, "Daddy" King, and the women and children were on the second plane. There was a bubbling joy on both aircraft, because the prize, in a real sense, belonged to all of them and the honor itself represented a Christmas beyond all happy Christmases. It was a tour of triumph. The parties stopped in New York where Dr. Ralph Bunche had arranged for informal meetings with representatives of Sweden, England, and Norway and the tall, dashiki-clad representatives of Africa.

The highest honor magnetized lesser ones. Wherever the Kings stopped, ranking officials greeted them at the airport, customs inspections were circumvented, limousines and guides provided, and sometimes hotel suites. On Sunday, Martin Luther King was guest preacher within the long, narrow bands of sunlight which pierce St. Paul's Cathedral in London. The church was crowded. The surpliced Anglican priests made their solemn procession from behind the main altar. King appeared small, almost boyish, in the ornate elevated pulpit. His father did not weep but only because he couldn't. His shiny rimless glasses swept the grandeur of a house of God he never dreamed existed, and he saw his boy up there, commanding the attention—nay, the admiration—of many of the great of Great Britain. He listened, as the microphones picked up the voice and lifted it and magnified it to crash its repetitive Southern cadences against the old stone walls, the holy amphitheater where kings and queens had prayed for generations.

Coretta King sat, with hands folded, listening. After the first few words, she recognized the topic. It was the "Three Dimensions of a Complete Life." Strange, he had saved this one for important occasions. The first time she heard it was when he was still in school and he preached a sermon at a small church in Roxbury, Massachusetts. The second time was his first sermon in his first church, the Dexter Avenue Baptist Church in Montgomery. Now, at the zenith of his pastorate, he had chosen it once more.

The party arrived at the old-fashioned city of Oslo on December 8. It was midafternoon, but at the sixtieth parallel, the sun arose late and set early. As the plane doors opened, the American Southerners stepped out into intense cold. Off the ramp, a crowd of young Norwegians waited, setting up a cheer before the plane engines were cut. Officials of the Nobel Peace Prize Committee, headed by Gunnar Jahn, had warm smiles and handshakes for frozen visitors. A group of little girls stepped forward, yellow hair flying in the cold wind, to present bouquets to the shivering Kings.

There is an old-world charm to Oslo, staid, still, and white in winter. The Kings and their friends stared at the equestrienne statues, the open markets with fruits and codfish and herring sold from boxes, the hotels with their tiny attic windows where maids and kitchen help slept, the police in shiny black helmets, and, in the midst of nineteenth-century leisure, the sleek ultramodern Rådguset—City Hall—with its severe

planes, modern glass, and twin towers. They drove down the broad Karl
Johans Gate and saw, high on a rocky eminence, Akershus Castle, built
in the year 1300, before there was a Christopher Columbus or an
American slave. When the visitors asked about parks and playgrounds,
the Norwegians smiled. The architects of Oslo had long ago used every
excuse to create additional parks, and, in 1950 the Oslo Corporation
(town council) secured in perpetuity the ninety-seven square miles of
woodland surrounding the city as a "playground." After all, one of
every seven Norwegians lived in Oslo.

The King party occupied a wing of one floor in the hotel. Whenever
they were in those rooms, away from the public eye, they could relax,
revert to "down-home" dialect and horseplay. Young bellboys in pillbox
hats carried silver trays of ice and liquor, sandwiches and cookies, and
candies. The rooms in that wing had big beds and old-fashioned plush
chairs and sofas, lace curtains underlaid with heavy draperies. These
rooms, too, had been tapped by electronic devices.

On the second night, there was a private birthday party for Marian
Logan, a member of the group. There were champagne toasts. Afterward the party gathered in the lounge. The man who best saw all the
shiny greatness and the deepest shadows had been almost silent since the
trip began. "Daddy" King interrupted a toast, patted his wife's hand,
and got to his feet. The gay chatter up and down the tables stopped. The
faces turned slowly from young King to old King. He raised a pointed
finger, a gesture his son recalled from his boyhood. It was a preface
meaning: This is important. "I want to say something to all of you
now," "Daddy" King said slowly, almost pontifically, "and I want you
to listen. I want to try to tell you how I feel. I guess most of you know
this, but I just have to say it now anyway." He paused. He drew in a
long breath, as he often did in the pulpit. The words were coming so
slowly, so solemnly, that Bayard Rustin sensed the heavy pride in the
old man's heart and bowed his head. "I guess most of you know this,
but I just have to say it now anyway. I came from nowhere." Coretta
King began to cry. "My father was a sharecropper, and I didn't get the
opportunity to get much formal training when I was growing up." Some
of the women began to weep; tears came to some men's eyes. A.D.
tasted salt tears on his lips. The old lion was about to concede that there
was a young, stronger, far better lion in the family.

"It wasn't until I left the farm and went to Atlanta that I was able to
get any real education. I was a man when I finished college, a grown
man with my wife and three children." The old man waved his hands

futilely. "I wanted my children to have all the things I had not had. I prayed for the Lord to let them do the things I could not do. This young man here became a minister, and I wanted him to have the best training available, so he would be able to get his PhD." He did not want tears and had not expected them. "Daddy" King was reciting facts.

"I always wanted to make a contribution, and all you got to do if you want to contribute, you got to ask the Lord, and let Him know, and the Lord heard me and in some kind of way I don't even know, He came down through Georgia, and He laid His hand on me and my wife, and He gave us Martin Luther King, and our prayers were answered." He expiated on his boy's growing mission in life, the leadership of a great race of people, and the sinister aspects of brothers, black and white, facing each other with hatred. The older pastor laid a large hand on his wife's shoulder. He shook his head in sorrow. "You don't know how it feels when some stranger calls you on the phone and he tells you he wants to kill you—or kill your son."

The son was weeping, too. "I have to talk about this, because even though I feel so proud tonight about what is happening here in Oslo, I also must be humble. I don't want to get puffed up with pride. I am not that kind of person. So I have to continue to pray so that the Lord will keep me humble. The devil is busy out there, and we have to pray that God will keep my son safe." It was obvious that he wanted to close, to say something appropriate; he didn't realize that he had said all the things and thought all the thoughts of which a father is capable. "The King family will go down not only in American history," he said, staring at Martin, "but in world history as well because Martin King is a Nobel Prize winner." Then he sat. No one applauded. The faces staring mutely were the faces of children. He had unlocked his heart, swung the rusty gate wide on its creaky hinges, and, for a rare moment, permitted his family and his friends to look inside. It was enough.

In the morning, Martin Luther King looked down with dismay at his clothes in neat array on the bed. Coretta King laughed. "I'll never wear this stuff again," the pastor said. He slid into the pinstriped trousers, wiggled his feet into the patent-leather shoes, and tried manfully to fit the stiff wing collar into the brass collar buttons fore and aft. The harder he worked to dress, the louder he made a comedy of the formal attire. There was a broad, black-and-white striped cravat which had to flow in a narrow band around the stiff collar, then flower into a knot and slide broadly down the shirtfront. King surrendered, Mrs. King helped him. "Now the frock coat," she said, and the black man from Georgia stared into the pier mirror and didn't believe his eyes. He looked handsome, but he didn't think so.

When he and his wife were ready, they were driven in state to the University of Oslo. The ceremony was to be held in Festival Hall, a narrow auditorium with rows of curve-backed chairs for the 800 guests. Up front was a shallow stage, about eighteen inches off the floor. Nearest the edge was a broad ornate lectern with a vase of white flowers on the floor before it. Behind it was a group of musicians—27 of them—mostly strings. Dr. King's family and friends were seated down front. King Olaf V and Crown Prince Harald emerged from the rear of Festival Hall. Gunner Jahn took Martin Luther King by the arm and presented him in deferential whispers. The king and prince and two aides moved up the center aisle and sat in special cane-backed chairs. In the crowd was Queen Louise of Sweden, who sat quietly in a cloth coat with a plain fur collar, topped by a navy blue beret, waiting for the ceremonies. The Nobel Committee sat in front.

There was music, and that too was solemn. Dr. Jahn went to the lectern and began to read the citation which was part of the award. "Dr. King has succeeded in keeping his followers to the principle of nonviolence," he said. ". . . an undaunted champion of peace . . . the first person in the western world to have shown us that a struggle can be waged without violence . . . without Dr. King's confirmed effectiveness of this principle, demonstrations and marches could easily have been violent and ended with the spilling of blood." Jahn motioned for King to approach. There was a handshake, and the pastor was presented with a gold medal lying on plush with a striped neckband and the scroll.

He was not expected to make a speech; that was scheduled for the following day. King was to limit himself to a few remarks: "Your Majesty, Your Royal Highness, Mr. President, Excellencies, ladies and gentlemen," he said. "I accept the Nobel Prize for Peace at a moment when twenty-two million Negroes of the United States are engaged in a creative battle to end the long night of racial injustice. . . . I am mindful that only yesterday in Birmingham, Alabama, our children, crying out for brotherhood, were answered with fire hoses, snarling dogs and even death. I am mindful that only yesterday in Philadelphia, Mississippi, young people seeking to secure the right to vote were brutalized and murdered.

"Therefore I must ask why this prize is awarded to a movement which is beleaguered and committed to unrelenting struggle; to a movement which has not won the very peace and brotherhood which is the essence of the Nobel Prize. After contemplation I conclude that this award, which I receive on behalf of the movement, is a profound recognition that nonviolence is the answer to the crucial political and racial questions of our time—the need for man to overcome oppression without resorting to violence. I accept this award today with an abiding faith in America and an audacious faith in mankind. I refuse to accept the idea that man is mere flotsam and jetsam in the river of life which surrounds him. I refuse to accept the view that mankind is so tragically bound to the starless midnight of racism and war that the bright daylight of peace and brotherhood can never become a reality."

Dr. King stepped away from the lectern, smiling and bowing to the thunder of applause. The orchestra played a selection from Gershwin's *Porgy and Bess*. The blacks thought it was in poor taste. When the party returned to the hotel, the jubilation became emotional. There were drinks and cries of joy, hugs and kisses. One member of the party—no one seems to remember who—said the proper words at the proper moment. "Martin, you have said that this prize really belongs to all the people in the civil rights movement. Now we want to tell you who it belongs to. It belongs to you, because we would not have come so far without your leadership. We want you to know this."

It was his. The rules governing the Nobel awards were specific in stating that prizes are to be awarded annually to one, two, or at most, three persons; the selection, as stated in *Encyclopedia Britannica,* is based on "professional competence and international range." Criticism of Dr. King's selection was largely inspired by racism and envy. Among academicians, some surprise was expressed because King's work had no "international range." It wasn't even Pan-American and, at the time the award was made, was narrowly confined by the name of the organization he led: the *Southern* Christian Leadership Conference. The technical rights or wrongs were of no consequence: Dr. King had won a Nobel Prize and it belonged to him and him alone.

The day after receiving the award, the doctor delivered his Nobel lecture, a somewhat lengthy polemic, which, had anyone noticed, moved Martin Luther King from the American stage to the world stage, as once he had moved from the confines of Montgomery to the southern tier of states. He had worked on the phrasing of this speech at Bimini in the Bahamas, at Atlanta, and stopped refining it only when the clock ran out in Oslo.

He made it clear at the outset that he was speaking, not solely for the American black man, but for mankind. "Oppressed people cannot remain oppressed forever. Something within has reminded the Negro of his birthright of freedom, and something without has reminded him that it can be gained. Consciously or unconsciously, he has been caught up by the *Zeitgeist,* and with his black brothers of Africa and his brown and yellow brothers in Asia, South America and the Caribbean, the United States Negro is moving with a sense of great urgency toward the promised land of racial justice." This paragraph caused a number of frowns. For eight years, Dr. King had proclaimed that his mission was "brotherhood" between the Southern black and the sons of former slaveowners. His aspirations were poetic in his "I Had a Dream" speech, and in many others, he rightfully stated that the white man would not be free until the black man was free. But in Oslo, for the first time, he embraced the Orientals. His reference to the Caribbean and South America was also another first.

"What the main sections of the civil rights movement in the United States are saying," he continued, "is that the demand for dignity, equality, jobs and citizenship will not be abandoned or diluted or postponed. If that means resistance and conflict we shall not flinch. We shall not be cowed. We are no longer afraid." The words were challenging, threatening, and warlike. King moved closest to his own noble motives by making a sharp turn in the speech. "Nonviolence has also meant that my people in the agonizing struggles of recent years have taken suffering upon themselves instead of inflicting it on others. . . . It seeks no victory over anyone. It seeks to liberate American society and to share in the self-liberation of all the people. . . ."

The trip home was triumphal. New York City placed fireboats in the bay to arc streams of iridescent water into the sky. Mayor Robert Wagner asked Dr. King to address the City Council. There was a reception for him at the Waldorf-Astoria Hotel. At night there was a mass salute to Dr. Martin Luther King at Harlem's 369th Armory. Eight thousand blacks stirred up a din of enthusiasm as King appeared onstage with Governor Nelson Rockefeller and Vice President-elect Hubert Humphrey. "For the last several days," King said solemnly, "I have been on a mountaintop, and I really wish I could just stay on the mountain; but I must go back to the valley. I must go back, because my brothers and sisters down in Mississippi and Alabama are sweltering under the heat of injustice. There are people starving in the valley, and people who don't have jobs, and people who can't vote."

From New York, King journeyed to Washington and the White House to be congratulated by President Johnson. Back home in Atlanta, a great crowd greeted the hero and one must contrast this with the evening when a waitress would not serve dinner to him and a white friend. In fact, Atlanta was split in its reaction to the Nobel laureate. He was too big to ignore, too controversial to applaud. White Atlanta fought itself for a month over whether to have a testimonial dinner to Dr. King or to ignore him. At last, ashamed of the adverse publicity the subject drew in the press, Atlanta staged the dinner at the Dinkler Plaza Hotel, where whites were grouped at their tables and blacks sat at others. One is impelled to suggest that relaxed on the dais, spooning a fruit cup, Martin Luther King kept his thoughts to himself as he studied the human checkerboard below.

This was a cold rain on a cold wind. It came down out of the north in ragged marching sheets and slammed against the bright windows of Swift's drugstore. A few people on Broad Street were huddled deep in heavy collars. The sky was solid Confederate gray. A hundred years before, the northern wind had been blue. General James H. Wilson's Union infantry had come across the fields ragged and wandering, had forded the muddy Alabama River, and had taken Selma, the iron foundry of the Confederacy. Selma did not want to be taken again. It was damned if it would be taken again. Twenty-eight thousand people were silent in the rain. They knew that Selma was under a black siege. The people were hushed, like birds deep in tree branches waiting for the first roll of thunder.

It was due. Some wondered why Selma; why not Tuscaloosa or Anniston or Decatur or Mobile? They were big and vigorous—worthy targets. Selma was something that happened suddenly on Route 80 and was gone before a driver had a chance to study it in a rearview mirror. If there was excitement, it was that the small local Police Department did not get along well with the county sheriff's department; Selma was a prissy Southern belle hiding behind a fan waiting for a lover who died. The Albert Hotel told the story on its face. It was a long four-story redstone building with ancient arches and cathedral windows. The people were told that it was a copy of a doge's palace in Venice, and they lived off that grandeur. It had a big lobby with potted palms and ancient tables and old-fashioned rooms.

Coming west from the capital city of Montgomery on Route 80, the driver passed Craig Air Force Base, where pilots trained in shrieking aluminum birds, shattering the silence of Selma, only two or three miles away. To get into Selma, the man on foot or in an automobile had to cross the cocoa snake of the Alabama River, using the humpbacked Edmund Pettus Bridge. On the west side of Route 80 was Broad Street, altitude 130 feet, and then nothing again. If anyone made a right turn off Broad, he would be in "Colored Town," and after a few blocks of small houses, a few government development houses, and some churches, he would be bounding across the tracks of the L & N, where diesels backed into strings of freight cars all night, made their little journeys to other tracks, and coupled one set of toys with another.

The Student Nonviolent Coordinating Committee had been in that part of Selma for eighteen months. Slowly, steadily, inexorably, they had worked the blacks upward from passivity to activity. They were slow to respond—they had seen what the sheriff and his men had done to people who wanted to register to vote. They saw Jim Clark as a soft-spoken man who could break your head in half. He was bad trouble smiling.

SNCC was in Marion, too, a small town twenty-five miles northwest of Selma. It is difficult to work with frightened people; they listen to the speeches and then go home saying, "Let's wait and see." The field secretaries for SNCC found the ground rocky for tilling, but they were young and indefatigable and certain that a year and a half had produced some shoots and plants. The best they could do was to average eighteen blacks a day to register for voting. On a day of cold rain, the County Courthouse was as quiet as a museum on Sunday.

The rain stopped. January 2, 1965, was cold and clear. Saturday afternoon, no one was working. Two cars came in from Montgomery, passed the automobile dealers shops, and lifted over the Edmund Pettus Bridge. Near the Albert Hotel, they turned right and went to Brown's Chapel AME Church and stopped. Martin Luther King got out. He already had a report from his chief aide in Selma, Frederick D. Reese, who predicted violence. He had similar reports from a sounding group he sent ahead as advance men: Harry Boyte, Rachel Dubois, Mew Soon Li. They were called the Operation Dialogue Department. It was not going to be easy, they counseled, to get past Sheriff Jim Clark. One item they did not mention was that it was not going to be easy to get past SNCC.

Dr. King and his party hurried inside the church to the standing applause of 700 blacks. Selma's time had come. The pastor was unhappy with the voter registration drive. He told the people that many more must register to vote. This indeed was the Black Belt of Alabama, and it would remain supine and powerless without the vote. "We are going to start a march on the ballot boxes by the thousands," he said. "We must be willing to go to jail by the thousands." The people sat in silence. "We are not asking," he intoned slowly, shaking his head negatively, "we are demanding the ballot." He was finished and gone before midnight. King had promised to make a speech in Lincoln, Nebraska, the following day. The first spark was sputtering in a vacuum.

The dangerous division in Selma was not just black versus white; it was black versus black and white versus white. SNCC was determined not to permit Dr. King to walk into town at whim, order "thousands" to be prepared to go to jail, and then, having lit the fuse, hurry out over the Pettus Bridge. SNCC had done the spadework, and SNCC was going to lead the demonstrations. On the white side, Mayor Joe Smitherman did not like the provocative tactics of the sheriff, so he appointed a moderate man, Wilson Baker, as chief of police. This put the white structure in the position of having Baker, as chief of police of Selma, willing to discuss matters with the blacks, and Jim Clark, as sheriff of Dallas County, with Selma as the county seat, prepared to herd the blacks back into "Colored Town" every time they appeared in groups on Broad Street.

When the first large group of demonstrators appeared on the courthouse steps, Clark stood on the top step, held his hands out for silence, and barked: "You are here to cause trouble. That's what you are doing." He stared at Hosea Williams in front. "You are an agitator, and that is the lowest form of humanity. If you do not disperse or go in as I direct you, you will be under arrest for unlawful assembly." He pointed to a side door in an alley. "The line forms there," he said. No one moved. Jim Clark went down the County Courthouse steps alone, thrashing and hitting with his nightstick. The demonstrators left.

Inside the courthouse, Clark said that if that side door was good enough for white voters, it was more than good enough for blacks. He wasn't going to permit anyone to walk up those front steps unless that person had business in court. On January 18, Martin Luther King was back in Selma. He was to learn that it was easier to break the will of a big city than a small town. He heard that white Selma was ready to fight under the sheriff and ready to be reasonable under the police chief. He also heard the bitter recriminations of SNCC, and he chose to ignore them. He felt confident that black Selma could attain its rights in one massive show of force. The population consisted of 13,000 whites, 14,500 blacks. The whites knew the population figures. If blacks were permitted to vote in large enough numbers, there would be a black mayor, a black chief of police, and a black municipal judge. As the blacks seeped out of "Colored Town," the whites knew that then they would not only be a minority in numbers but in power as well. Therefore, white Selma looked upon the presence of Dr. Martin Luther King as a threat to its existence, a final battle presaging extinction, as their forebears thought when they saw General Wilson's bluecoats coming across those same fields in 1865.

The blacks left "Colored Town" in smaller groups on Monday, the eighteenth. Most of them were young. In groups of twelve, they began to run slowly toward the center of town. Some went to the movies and sat in the orchestra seats, joshing each other in loud whispers and laughing as the usher came down the aisle and flashed his light in their faces. He left. They went to the drugstore and sat and asked for ice cream. Some hailed a bus, not anxious to go anywhere, but wanting to see the startled face of the driver when they occupied all the front seats. Others went into white restaurants, sat down, and asked politely for menus. They were given them. Martin Luther King and a half dozen of his lieutenants walked into the Albert Hotel, the decaying sanctum sanctorum. "We want to register," Dr. King said to the startled manager. "Then we want lunch before we go to our rooms."

A young white man came up behind King and said, "I've been trying to talk to you." The pastor turned, pen in hand. He was smashed on the head twice and kicked in the thigh. He fell against the desk, his head ringing. Blacks grabbed the white man and held him until police arrived in the lobby. He went to jail. King ate his lunch, the first black since Reconstruction days to eat in a white restaurant in Selma. He complained of a bad headache. Some urged him to see a doctor, but he said he was going to lead 400 adults to the courthouse. The weather was freezing. King led the march down Broad Street toward the Pettus Bridge, stopped a block short of it, and turned right to the County Courthouse.

The day was Monday. Waiting on the top step, backed by armed deputies, stood Jim Clark, 220 pounds of barely controlled fury. "You come here to register these people?" he said softly. Dr. King nodded. "No registrars working today. Bring them some other time." The pastor said that he would like to go inside and see if there were any registrars in the election office.

"You just take my word for it," the sheriff said. "Nobody's here." King hesitated. The blacks waited. King shook his head and turned away. The crowd began to march back.

"Don't worry," King shouted to them. "We'll be back." A young black woman broke from the crowd, ran down the alley, and through the door. The sheriff caught her in the office of the registrar. It was empty. He grabbed the back of her dress. She pulled. Clark let go quickly. He knew what would happen if a story got into "Colored Town" that he had ripped the clothes from a girl. She turned to him and displayed the venom so many of the blacks had repressed for so long. "You white son of a bitch!" she said and spat in his face. Deputies took her to jail on a charge of resisting a peace officer.

The press arrived in Selma. The gentlemen spent considerable time running to Dr. King to find out what the next move would be, and then to Jim Clark to ask what he was going to do about it. Someone asked Circuit Judge James Hare his opinion, and he assumed the grave dispassionate air of the man on the bench. "You see," he said, "most of your Selma Negroes are descended from the Ibo and Angola tribes of Africa. You could never teach or trust an Ibo back in slave days, and even today I can spot their tribal characteristics. They had protruding heels, for instance." Regardless of their ancestry, 62 blacks were in jail on that day, and 150 more were arrested the following morning. The mayor, Joseph Smitherman, wasn't talking. He was a bright young man of thirty-five who had aligned himself with the business community. They were segregationist in character, but they wanted to make peace with Dr. King and his followers. Selma had been withering in economic solitude, and it hoped to attract Northern industry to a place where labor was cheap and the word "union" had been an epithet for more than a hundred years. If the Smitherman credo could be capsulized, it might be "modernized racism." They were opposed to the sheriff and his clubbing of blacks, and they were willing to desegregate the movies and the old hotel, too. Of course, voting was another matter. After World War II, although a great number of blacks had died under the American banner, only 6,000 blacks were allowed to vote in the State of Alabama. Now, according to the whites, the black man had gone a little too far—100,000 of them were registered voters, and Martin Luther King was trying to register 370,000 more.

Dr. King listened to the plans laid out by Andrew Young, Hosea Williams, and Ralph Abernathy. The SNCC group had a campaign, too, and both sides were recruiting the same blacks for widely variant goals. One morning, 105 qualified black schoolteachers marched to the Dallas County Courthouse in Selma to be registered. The chairman of the school board waited at the courthouse and, in his most unctuous manner, said, "You cannot come in here and register now. The board is not open." The teachers stood listening. They didn't move. So Jim Clark emerged from the courthouse with his nightstick in his hands. He went down the steps swinging. The teachers left.

That evening King addressed his people and in the speech warned Clark: "If they refuse to register us, we will appeal to Governor George Wallace. If he doesn't listen, we will appeal to the legislature. If the legislature doesn't listen, we will dramatize the situation to arouse the federal government by marching by the thousands to the places of registration. We must be willing to go to jail by the thousands." The formula was familiar. The militants of SNCC snorted. They had supported King and his nonviolent marches and his appeals to the President of the United States. They knew that if the 14,000 blacks of Selma were lifted off their prayerful knees and onto their feet and marched in a solid mass to the County Courthouse, there was no county or state power that could stop them from rioting and tearing Selma apart and, if necessary, burning it to the ground, courthouse, Jim Clark, and all. But philosophies are nothing more than aspirated hopes, and sometimes there is more satisfaction in knowing that one can do something violent, and not doing it, than in doing it and smelling guilt in the ashes.

The county authorities announced that the voting registrars met once every two weeks, but that when they met, no blacks were waiting outside the courthouse. The blacks responded by demanding that the registrars meet more frequently. The authorities announced that the bimonthly meetings were a matter of tradition in Selma, not something devised to thwart blacks. On January 30, a Saturday, Martin Luther King let it be known to the National Association for the Advancement of Colored People in Washington that he planned to march to the courthouse on Monday; this, in turn, would probably mean arrest and jailing. It was time to start swearing out injunctions and restraining orders against the White Establishment.

The march started late on Monday morning. King and Abernathy led 770 marchers. The majority were schoolchildren. They danced in rhythm down Broad Street, singing, "Ain't Gonna Let Jim Clark Turn Me 'Round" and "I Love Jim Clark in My Heart." As they passed Gentry's Chevrolet shop, mechanics came out from under cars and greasing racks, wiping their hands as they watched in amazement. "Some niggers going to be killed before this is over," one said. "Be killed like flies." It was Police Chief Wilson Baker who herded the blacks into jail. An additional 700, including King and Abernathy, were arrested that day. The next day 500 more were jailed. Dr. King was getting the white man to play the King gambit: stuff the jails until they were unstuffable.

But Chief Baker was not Clark. He went through the jail after six hours and released all adults who were residents of Selma; they were told to come to court for trial at a later date. Nonresidents were told that they could have their freedom on $200 bail. Dr. King and Ralph Abernathy scorned the offer. Among other things there was an advertisement due to appear in the New York *Times* the next morning entitled A LETTER FROM MARTIN LUTHER KING FROM A SELMA, ALABAMA, JAIL. To meet the *Times* deadline, it had had to be written on the weekend prior to the march. The ad told about the hundreds of arrests of blacks in Selma, blacks whose sole ambition was to be good citizens and vote. The ad closed by asking for cash contributions to the cause.

While King was in jail, another "outsider" arrived in Selma. The tall, cavernous figure of Malcolm X walked Broad Street. He was a lonely, sinister-seeming man. The word passed that "Malcolm is here, right here in Selma," and it frightened more blacks than whites. Uninvited, he walked to a lunchtime meeting at Brown's Chapel. Casually, he asked to be introduced, and the SCLC men told the crowded church the name of the man. He spoke, as always, courageously and defiantly. His point of view was miles away from Martin Luther King's. The white men had been talking about some "bloodletting," he said, holding long arms and huge hands out to the crowd. If the black people feared this, he said, they were wrong. Nothing could be gained by continuous marching to the courthouse and marching back again. Either the black man was every bit as good as the white man, or it would be better to drop the campaign and go home. The trouble with the black man was that he didn't know how tall and strong he was. Prayer and church are all right for God's kingdom, but the black man did not have to convince God. He had to convince that sheriff, and the only way to do that was to walk right up to him and trade him blow for blow.

Malcolm X spoke of violence as though it were inevitable and good. His blunt eloquence moved the people, aroused them to shouting chants. The fearful hostility they felt deep inside was being put into words by this tough man from New York. He was their suppressed fury speaking: to go out and maim the white man for what he was doing to the blacks. The Southern Christian Leadership Conference officials did not appreciate the speech. The talk was almost over when Coretta King and Juanita Abernathy reached the chapel. They had come to Selma to see their husbands, to ensure that they were not being mistreated, and to carry messages back to the SCLC leadership. "You're going to have to come inside and greet the people," Andy Young said dolorously, "because Malcolm X is here, and he's really roused them. They want to hear from you."

The women went inside. Mrs. Abernathy spoke first. Mrs. King understood what she had to do: She emphasized and reemphasized nonviolence, the people must understand that it was the gospel of the Movement. The entire Movement had been lifted from lifeless cause to one which occupied the primary attention of the nation because the black man, in pleading for what was rightfully his, was the nonviolent hero. It was the white man who was violent. It was an inspiring speech, and listening from the sidelines, Malcolm X crossed and recrossed his long legs.

Afterward he was introduced to Mrs. King. He was impressed by the gentle manner in which she had undermined his speech. She was impressed to find, not a crude, rowdy man, but an intelligent human being. "Mrs. King," he said, "will you tell Dr. King that I planned to visit with him in jail? I won't get a chance now because I have to leave for New York in time to catch a plane for London. I'm going to address the African Students Conference." She nodded, looking up to study the planes of the face which had pulled itself from the depths to search for truth and preach it. "I want Dr. King to know that I didn't come to Selma to make his job difficult. I really did come thinking that I could make it easier. If the white people realize what the alternative is, perhaps they will be more willing to hear Dr. King."

The NAACP lawyers flew to Alabama and appeared in federal court before Judge Daniel Thomas. They requested an order to Sheriff Clark to stop interfering with black voter registrants. The judge was willing to issue such an order, but he wanted to state his judicial opinion about behavior on both sides first. He said he would not tolerate violence. "Unnecessary arrests have been made provoked by unnecessary assemblage by people at improper places." His order directed that the sheriff's office issue to voter applicants numbers from 1 to 100 and that the line be formed in front of the courthouse, not in the alley. He was certain that both sides were at fault in the matter at hand. He said to the NAACP lawyers that "no sufficient reason has come to this court why some of them could not have appeared on registration days, days on which the registrars have practically no applicants to process." The order was handed down, and both sides misinterpreted it. The sheriff's office said that numbers from 1 to 100 would be handed out each day at the front of the courthouse, but that no more than 100 blacks would be permitted in the waiting line. The blacks said that the numbers should run from 1 to 100 and be marked for consecutive days of registration and that the process of handing out these numbers could go on all day, even if 1,000 were in line. The registration board, to show compliance with a federal order, met for three consecutive days, but asked each applicant so many difficult and confusing questions that only 70 persons were processed. Each citizen was told that he would be notified, in about three weeks, whether he had "passed." Judge Thomas, angered, clarified his ruling by stating that no one could arrest civil rights workers who "peacefully" encouraged the waiting blacks to secure the right to vote. He further ordered the registrars to stop asking involved questions of registrants and to "speed" the work.

Judge Thomas' decision did not please Martin Luther King. After four days in jail, he and Abernathy bailed themselves out for $200 apiece and returned to rekindle the militant spirits of blacks who thought that because of the court decision, no more demonstrations would be required. The caldron required a brighter fire. High school students appeared in front of the courthouse and smiled at the sheriff standing on the top step. "You don't want to arrest us," they taunted. "We'll make you arrest us." The sheriff began to crack. He and his deputies and his posse stood almost alone in their savagery, except for the secret endorsement of Governor Wallace.

It is certain that the sheriff did not know that, in his brutal anger, he scored more for the cause of civil rights than most workers for the Movement. Clark had aroused the wait-and-see blacks. He moved them off their rockers to the roaring rage of the downtown protest. On February 10, the sheriff and his deputies encircled 165 demonstrating children and marched and trotted them out of town into the farm country. Some, who could not keep the pace, were prodded from behind by chuckling deputies. "You kids want to march," one said, "we'll give you a good march." Youngsters trotted and ran inside a corral of trucks and cars, some sobbing.

The sheriff was executing the will of the people, the red-necks of Dallas County. What he didn't realize was that he was also working for Martin Luther King. The children's march brought maddened parents into the streets. The sheriff saw the whole campaign as a last-ditch struggle for the whites; the choice to him was simple—overrun or be overrun. Early in February he and his deputies had arrested 3,400 people, and there was no place left to put them. State officials phoned Clark to cut down on arrests, to permit peaceful demonstrations. The jails were glutted; law enforcement officers were exhausted; local courts, trying schoolchildren for marching and taunting, were embarrassed in the presence of NAACP attorneys, who made notes and knew that if those arrested were found guilty, the decision would be reversed on appeal. The structure of Selma was in collapse.

Fifteen Congressmen, led by Charles Diggs, a black man, flew to Selma to investigate the horrors they had been watching on television. Dr. King demanded that the registrars meet "daily" to enroll voters. He flew off to Washington to confer with Vice President Hubert Humphrey and Attorney General Nicholas Katzenbach. King could expect strong support from the fifteen Congressmen who had visited Selma. They would return to Washington and what they would have to say would ensure a national audience. The pastor did not seem to be aware that he commanded a far larger and more sympathetic audience than the Congressional delegation. All America and most of Europe were repelled by what they were seeing daily on television: helmeted deputies chasing black children with clubs and electric cattle prods; the screams of running women; the sight of brutal law confronting mass passivity. The presence of the Congressional delegation did not force Sheriff Jim Clark to retreat. On the contrary, the sheriff looked upon Congress as a far-off body of "outsiders" who did not "understand our problems." Clark's solitary goal was to shove the blacks back to "Colored Town" and keep them there.

Dr. King was in Washington to ask the administration for a strong voting rights law. He was sick of the cheap tricks. He didn't request a strong voting rights law; he demanded one. Humphrey and Katzenback assured him that President Johnson already had one "in the works." It was about to be submitted to Congress. If this seemed another polite evasion to King, he was wrong. Lyndon Johnson had set his staff to work on a voting law which would eliminate requirements involving education, questionnaires, and poll taxes. To make it enforceable, the Justice Department would have the authority to send officials to any state, any voting precinct, to ensure that voters could properly register if the local authorities dragged their feet. Johnson was prepared to address a night session of both houses about the bill, and he was prepared to be belligerent about it—to give the legislators no more than six or eight weeks to "do the job." King left Washington, not completely mollified, but more hopeful than he had been for a long time.

King came back from Washington to say something which, if it had come from the lips of Malcolm X, would not have surprised anyone. "Selma will never get right and Dallas County will never get right," he shouted, "until we get rid of Jim Clark." "Rid" held a connotation of death. He did not say "until we defeat Jim Clark." One of Dr. King's aides stood in front of the sheriff and called him "brute," "fascist," and "Hitler." The sheriff doubled his fist and smashed the Reverend C. T. Vivian in the mouth, then arrested him for "criminal provocation." When the news reached Brown's Chapel, an SCLC worker lifted his head from paper work and said, "Every time it appears that the Movement is dying out Sheriff Clark comes to our rescue."

The lavish ground-floor office under the Capitol dome at Montgomery was a busy place. Aides were in and out with reports to Governor Wallace. His small dark face, which alternated between broad smiles and lip-curling snarls, faced a telephone most of the day. He had remained offstage at Birmingham except in the closing of schools, but he had felt no compunction in calling Jim Clark and his posse to leave Dallas County to fight blacks up in Birmingham. Currently, he was in touch with Clark in Selma, and since Clark's public action remained oppressive, one must assume that he had the endorsement of his governor. Late in February Wallace decided that it was time to reverse his posture of august silence. He ordered Colonel Al Lingo and his state troopers to stop all night marches in Dallas County. At first Dr. King said that he had no intention of abiding by the governor's order. But his lawyers asked him to abide by it until they could upset the order in federal court.

Clark collapsed and was taken to a hospital. One doctor said, "A mild coronary." Another said, "Total exhaustion." The sheriff had proved he was as dedicated to his work as Martin Luther King was to his. Clark in a hospital was an object of pity; the archetypical enemy had been carried offstage. The SCLC did what it could. It sent 200 schoolchildren to kneel in front of the courthouse and pray for the recovery of the sheriff "in mind and body." Deputies watched helplessly, disbelieving. The SCLC did not ask the children to say a prayer for James Bevel. He had been beaten insensible by sheriff's deputies and had sustained a concussion of the brain. He was in one bed; Clark was in another. Bevel was chained to his.

Dr. King drove in from Atlanta. It was a long drive, and he had a head cold. "My voice is gone," he croaked to the people, "but my feet are in step." He led the people to the courthouse again, and again he turned away when the order came from a bullhorn. Then he drove to Camden, Alabama, a place where no black had ever voted. Blacks collected around Dr. King's automobile. "You all want to vote, don't you?" he asked the people. They nodded timidly.

One jeaned farmer said, "I filled out the form, but I can't get anybody to vouch for me." The rule of Wilcox County was that a registered voter must vouch for an applicant. The whites vouched for one another cheerfully. As long as Wilcox County kept all blacks off the rolls, no black could vouch for a black.

Sheriff P. C. Jenkins, who had served Wilcox County for twenty-six years, put it succinctly: "I'm in politics myself and it wouldn't look right. Maybe some other white can vouch for them." He knew better. Dr. King got back in his car and drove to Marion, where his wife had been born and reared. The Movement was as timid in Perry County as in Wilcox. Black merchants who traded with whites were seldom militant and, except in rare instances, were never seen in a public demonstration. In Marion there had been no marches, but the police arrested a civil rights activist and put him in jail. The frightened blacks remained sullen and fearful until Dr. Martin Luther King stopped for a few moments. That night, inspired by his attitude of "do something," 400 young people marched in protest to the one arrest. State troopers were called, and they ran through the ranks savagely. A young man, Jimmy Lee Jackson, was shot in the stomach. It was a bad wound because he remained conscious and required several days to die.

When the news of Malcolm X's killing reached Selma, it chilled Dr. King to the marrow. He had never admired Malcolm X, or Elijah, or any of the other militants whom he called "the crazies," but violent death frightens the living. Two days before, Jimmy Lee Jackson had died for civil rights; Medgar Evers was gone, the idol, John F. Kennedy, never knew what hit him; three civil rights workers were part of an earthen dam; a week before, the government had uncovered a black plot to dynamite the Statue of Liberty, the Washington Monument, and the Liberty Bell. Black teachers were refusing to pledge allegiance to the American flag. Now the tough man, the courageous man—he too was gone. Who would be next? Dr. King felt depressed. He was the biggest target in the country. He had been tipped off that the Ku Klux Klan was trying to hire a man to kill him. It might be true. It might not, but it was wiser always to believe the worst. It was not just the Klan. There were other racists who were willing to pay to have him killed. There were rich whites all over the South who sat in their lavish homes and seethed as the image of Martin Luther King came on their home screens. They would be willing to pay. Glad to pay. King knew it. All they needed was a reliable intermediary who would be paid to find a killer to do the job. The name of the rich man need never be known. Martin Luther King, in the middle of his latest campaign, felt depression seep through his mind and possess him.

Who is next? Maybe I am next.

Stalemate. In most conflicts, the word means that no one wins. In Selma, stalemate meant victory for the whites, defeat for the blacks. Wave after wave of blacks had crashed against the courthouse walls and receded in disorder to "Colored Town." An enormous amount of missionary work could be checked off as a total loss. SNCC field secretaries had lived and worked in Selma for a year and a half before the first black voter appeared to be registered. Martin Luther King had visited sporadically, conferring secretly with ministers, weighing Selma, assessing it, going away to other towns in other states, always coming back, waiting for the proper moment. The proper moment had arrived immediately after New Year's Day, 1965, and the long, cold nights of January had crept into the barren days of February. Calendars everywhere were being flipped to March, and there was no victory. Jim Clark was recovering; he was allowed to confer with his deputies; soon he would be back in uniform, a hard man on granite steps roaring orders through a bullhorn. More and more outsiders were coming to Selma —liberal politicians, white ministers, Roman Catholic nuns fluttering like dark swans on Broad Street, white students—but Selma stood firmly on its racial bitterness and would not be moved.

On Friday, March 5, Dr. King flew to Washington to confer with President Johnson. He needed that voting rights bill now, this moment. He needed federal registrars to go to Selma and sign up thousands of blacks. Johnson was sympathetic. He sat in a rocker between sofas, legs crossed, listening and interrupting. The talk, which was on the Presidential appointment calendar for thirty minutes, went on for two and a half hours. The President knew what King wanted; the President wanted what King wanted. But what could anyone do with Congress? The Southerners who carried the weight on the committees could be prodded gently, only gently. Would it not be in their best interests to stop action on the voting rights bill as long as Selma remained in the nation's headlines? Would this be a proper time for a Southern Congressman to betray white Alabama? No, it would have been better politics to pass the voting rights bill first, then stage a civil rights fight in Selma. The SCLC action had tied the President's hands; now that King was demanding quick assistance, help was impossible to grant.

There was but one avenue open for the blacks—expand the action. Make it bigger, broader, more horrendous. Dr. King was back in Brown's Chapel on Friday night. He announced that on Sunday the people would march from Selma to Alabama's capital city of Montgomery—fifty-four miles. They would bring their case before Governor George Wallace. Everyone who understood the gravity of the situation knew that Wallace would revile the marchers or turn his back on them. The march had no goal except to keep anguished Selma in the public eye. If Jim Clark did nothing to stop the people, if the state troopers assisted the blacks on their long walk, if Wallace met them on the steps of the State Capitol and agreed to expedite the registration of black voters, then all was lost. Selma, like old coffee grounds, would be flushed into oblivion.

Dr. King told his people, "I can't promise that you won't get beaten. I can't promise you won't get your house bombed. I can't promise that you won't get scarred up a bit, but we must stand up for what is right." The SCLC announced that Martin Luther King had been persuaded not to go, that his personal leadership was needed for the welfare of his army. Hosea Williams and John Lewis would lead the march.

Governor Wallace, on Saturday, issued a state order prohibiting the march. The order gave official sanction to the presence of Sheriff Clark and all his deputies, in addition to Colonel Al Lingo, Major John Cloud, and their state troopers. Lingo, Cloud, and Clark understood the governor's prohibition to mean that it was their collective duty to stop the blacks at any cost. Wallace intended it to mean to block their progress at the Edmund Pettus Bridge until they tired and turned back. On Saturday evening, the governor left Montomery and was "away" for the weekend. The ranking state officer in the capital was Seymour Tramel, finance director.

The stage was set. White Selma vowed to be standing on the curbsides early Sunday morning to jeer the blacks. None of the natives had forgotten the stories told by their grandparents about General Wilson and his Union troops sacking the city in 1865 and leaving a regiment of blacks to occupy and rule. The whites, parents and Christians, would be on the sidelines hoping for the worst. The national and international press poured into Selma on every plane, train, bus, and automobile. The Albert Hotel ran out of rooms. Small homeowners were taking in temporary boarders at outrageous prices. Confederate flags were hawked and sold on Broad Street. A few shopowners boarded up windows. Martin Luther King had made his speech to the gallant martyrs and left for SCLC headquarters in Atlanta.

King receive last-minute intelligence from his field generals. One stated that in the morning the state troopers would be equipped with tear gas. To counteract this, it was decided that the marchers would form at Brown's Chapel, march to the bridge, confront the sheriff and the troopers, and turn back in orderly fashion. At the proper moment, Hosea Williams would give the order. The poor, the disenfranchised, the friendless, the unarmed, the peaceful would be photographed facing the might of the State of Alabama and turning back, not in cowardice, but in the spirit of nonviolence. One disheartening phone call stated that Selma's 14,000 blacks had lost their esprit; they didn't want to march; they didn't want to be hurt; they didn't want to die. Of 14,000 blacks, the SCLC would do well if it got 750. As white Selma prepared to go to Sunday services and hurry to the bridge to watch the "fun," black Selma prepared itself to remain indoors.

Late Sunday morning, King and Abernathy preached sermons in their respective Atlanta churches as SNCC and SCLC field officers in Selma rapped on doors and entreated people to assemble for the march at Brown's Chapel. At last, there were 500 persons standing on Sylvan Street. Some were silent, disconsolate. Others made small jokes which induced hysterical laughter. Some looked for Dr. King. Others saw Hosea Williams of the SCLC and John Lewis of SNCC and nodded good morning. The march began.

A policeman in a car left the scene and drove to the bridge. "They're on their way!" he shouted. Men mounted their horses. Troopers on the far side of the bridge adjusted gas masks. Major Cloud stood before them. On the near side of the bridge, Sheriff Clark and his deputies, equipped with clubs and electric cattle prods, stood aside to let the marchers pass. White Selma, men, women, and little children, fringed both ends of the bridge, waiting with suppressed excitement as crowds once had waited at hangings in England.

The desultory little band marched up Sylvan Street four blocks to Water Avenue, made a right turn and walked five more streets, and found itself at the base of the bridge. The marchers heard the rising roar of the crowds and saw the sheriff and his men stand aside to let them pass. The marchers turned left onto the bridge, climbing up the span slowly, listening to the venemous epithets of the white citizens, wishing it didn't have to happen, hoping it would all pass peacefully. At the top of the span, the marchers saw the state troopers ahead. They were spread all the way across the far end of the bridge, two ranks deep. The masked faces with the big glass eyes were people from another world; clubs were held with two hands across thighs. The white people marching with the blacks began to understand the terror in the black heart, and they marveled at his bravery and questioned their own. Slowly, the little band started down the far side of the bridge. Major John Cloud brought a bullhorn to his lips. "Turn about," he said loudly and slowly, "turn about and go back to your church." The people kept marching. "You will not be allowed to march any further." Williams and Lewis stopped. The people behind them stopped. The bullhorn shouted: "You have two minutes to disperse!" The marchers stood. "This is an unlawful assembly" Cloud shouted. Stalemate. Stalemate again.

Hosea Williams was indecisive. He wanted to salvage something from the situation. "May we have a word with the major?" he shouted.

A minute passed, then more than a minute. "There is no word to be had," Cloud said. "You have two minutes. . . ."

Williams and Lewis stood as though nailed to the bridge. They could not move forward; they could not live with themselves if they went backward. Suddenly, the roar of the crowd stopped. In the silence, the pleasant sound of horses could be heard moving into place. Behind the marchers, Clark and his deputies moved onto the bridge, closing the avenue to retreat. Cloud turned his bullhorn to his state troopers. "Troopers, forward!" he yelled. The state police came forward in a solid line. The blacks shouted for mercy; some fell to the ground; some knelt and prayed loud. Clubs flailed left and right, like old-time farmers with sickles chopping a tall field of rye. Heads were split; bodies were broken. Shrieks were heard up and down the slow muddy stream called the Alabama. White pedestrians were in a frenzy of joy; women screamed for the troopers to kill. Clark's deputies came up behind as the marchers turned to run. "Get those niggers!" he shouted above the bedlam. "And get those white niggers!" Horsemen came onto the bridge screaming the shrill rebel cry of long, long ago.

Tear gas canisters rolled among the fallen marchers, and milky clouds stained the cold blue air. The horsemen were armed with long bullwhips. Holding the reins in one hand, the men slashed left, then right, then left at the fleeing falling people. "Kill them!" a pedestrian hollered. "Get those black sons of bitches!" A trooper curled a bullwhip across the back of a black and shouted: "March, nigger! You wanted to march! I'm gonna help you!" Some of the older marchers fell on the bridge and did not move as the horses jumped across bodies and the curling white gas nauseated some back to consciousness.

It was over in five minutes. So was the atom bomb at Hiroshima. The minuscule eternity had clearly demonstrated to civil rights people that there were no civil rights. Major Cloud's troopers stopped at the Selma side of the Pettus Bridge, and Clark's men drove the blacks back into "Colored Town." There blacks paused and picked up rocks and hurled them at the deputies. Some blacks fled into houses where they didn't reside. Some stood at Brown's Chapel, weeping. The sheriff's men chased the blacks through their own section, beating those they caught. Chief Wilson Baker and his men were on Sylvan Street, too. In formal tones, he ordered the sheriff and his men to get out of "Colored Town." "This is our territory," he said. "It's not county. Now get out." Clark and his men left and quickly returned with carpenter's horses and ropes. They sealed "Colored Town" and posted deputy sheriffs at all roadblocks.

Baker saw the tragic black faces, the bright-red blood. He sent some cars to the bridge and had other blacks taken to a black hospital. John Lewis had a fractured skull. Hosea Williams escaped with minor injuries. Sixteen blacks were seriously injured. Forty others were given emergency treatment at the hospital. A hundred more limped home and bound their wounds. A rock caught Sheriff Jim Clark on the forehead. John Lewis, brain reeling and afflicted with double vision, stood before the nonmarchers in Brown's Chapel livid with anger. "I don't see how President Johnson can send troops to Vietnam," he shouted. He stood up close to the altar, looking like a man who will stifle tears with roaring rage. "I don't see how he can send troops to the Congo. And yet he can't send troops to Selma, Alabama." He paused, holding a long deep breath. "Next time we march," he said, "we may have to keep going when we get to Montgomery. We may have to go on to Washington."

Public reaction was instantaneous. Selma was the most publicized town on the globe. Momentarily, the world was in shock. It could not believe the things it saw on film. The gleefully vicious expressions on the faces of law enforcement officers, the swinging clubs and long whips, the fright on the faces of kneeling blacks, the streaming blood, the hand-clapping white pedestrians appeared in homes from the White House to the ghettos. The sound of clubs on heads echoed all around the world and returned to Selma within a few hours. Governor George Wallace, who had not expected his proud Alabama to be depicted as a climate of hate and viciousness, spoke too quickly and delivered the *non sequitur* of the time: The troopers, he said, had undoubtedly saved many lives by stopping the blacks at the bridge because, beyond it, they would be without protection. On the Pacific coast, Coretta King was preparing for a concert. The news plunged her into despair. In Detroit, Governor George Romney and Mayor Jerome Cavanagh called for a march to protest what had happened in Selma. Night riots broke out in several cities, and fire bombs were rolled into tenement hallways.

Martin Luther King, almost inarticulate, phoned his wife in California and told her that he had not led the march because he had been warned that there was a plot to kill him in the melee. To the press, he said: "When I made a last-minute agreement not to lead the march, I had no idea that the kind of brutality and tragic expression of man's inhumanity to man as existed today would take place." He announced that he and the Reverend Ralph Abernathy would lead the march from Selma to Montgomery within forty-eight hours. The announcement alarmed Lyndon Johnson, who sent an emissary to dissuade King from marching or from staging one. The secret talk was pointless. Martin Luther King would lead his people on Tuesday.

The *Alabama Journal,* anguished over what had happened, stated: "By dumb, cruel and vastly excessive force, we have made new civil rights legislation almost a dead certainty: we have stained the state and put the lie to its claims of peace and harmony: given enough rope, as if they haven't already been supplied it, our strategists will hang the state in vainglorious self-immolation." Other newspapers noted that Wallace excused the brutal scene on the grounds that troopers were saving "unprotected" blacks' lives. The papers, in editorials and cartoons, wondered whether the blacks preferred to be clubbed by white racists on the open highway or friendly troopers. Others, equally partisan, pointed out that the blacks were in violation of a court order not to march, and the troopers were upholding the law in stopping the march. Nor can the SCLC leadership be held blameless: It was not until after the riot that it was learned that the organization had ordered four black ambulances, three white doctors, and a group of nurses to follow behind the line of march to the bridge. It must be reasoned that they expected blood to flow. This, in turn, makes it difficult to believe that Martin Luther King was speaking the whole truth when he said, "When I made a last-minute agreement not to lead the march, I had no idea. . . ."

Neither side could retreat. In a small way, it was like two nations

after blood has been spilled. The March on Montgomery had no significance other than publicity; it would not alter Governor Wallace's
racist position; it would not bring to life new laws or expunge old ones.
On Monday, the United States federal court issued a temporary injunction against the Tuesday march, and President Johnson asked publicly
that Dr. King postpone it.

In Selma, white and black liberals from thirty states were assembling
for the second showdown. Once again, the doctor was at an impasse. He
felt that the courts were being used for trickery. At the Albert Hotel,
King sat until 4 A.M. arguing, reversing himself, pleading. To those who
sat disconsolately listening, offering ideas, he made a telling point:
James Forman of SNCC would go ahead and march no matter what the
court said. He conceded that this didn't make it legal, but it made them
more militant than he. Finally, he waved his arms in dismissal. "It's
better to die on the highway than make a butchery of my conscience,"
he said. "I'd better go through with it."

He went to bed. But at 5 A.M. the phone rang. He had two callers.
One was Attorney General Nicholas Katzenbach; the other was LeRoy
Collins, head of the Federal Community Relations Service. Collins, the
urbane graying former governor of Florida, had been to Selma seeking a
formula for peace and reciting a litanous refrain: "I'm not on either
side, but. . . ." They asked King to cancel the march. The doctor said
he couldn't. He was very sorry, but it was too late. Within a few hours,
people would begin to assemble. Governor Collins said that he would
call on Colonel Al Lingo and Sheriff Jim Clark and try to work out an
agreement. King wished him luck.

Across the Pettus Bridge the darkness was deep. Troopers and
deputies got what sleep they could where they could. An automobile
dealer had donated a small office to Lingo and Clark. They dozed. They
talked. A small light remained on, and without comment, they checked a
map showing the tedious route to Montgomery, fifty-four miles east. A
couple of troopers stood at the bridge. The tide of incoming automobiles
had almost stopped. Looking down the side of the bridge, a policeman
could see Broad Street, Selma, sound asleep.

Governor Collins drove up and went into the little shack. To Lingo
and Clark, he was a highly polished gentleman, but it wasn't easy to
equate that soft drawl with the cause of civil rights. Both sides looked
on him with suspicion. As he had said, he was not on either side,
but. . . . His function was not to judge who was right and who was

wrong, but to keep each side from the other's throat. The three men sat. Collins said, "King is determined to march."

Jim Clark rolled a pencil on the desk and replied softly, "We're not gonna let him." He ticked off two points on his fingers: One was that, if King marched, he was in deliberate violation of an injunction and the state troopers were going to uphold the law; the second point was the order from Montgomery (Governor Wallace) was that the state government didn't want those blacks on Route 80. The colonel and the sheriff kept restating Governor Wallace's official position: that the blacks couldn't march fifty-four miles without getting hurt, without impeding traffic, and that white racists would be waiting around every bend in the road.

Collins smiled it off. He saw the map and pulled it to him, asking Clark to show him where his men would be stationed. Clark took the map and drew a line across the highway. Collins studied it. The line was a hundred yards off the Pettus Bridge on the Montgomery side. It bisected Kings Inn Road and William Rufus Road. Collins pointed to the line. "If King marches his people out of Selma, across the bridge, and stops here"—he pointed—"then we can expect no trouble?" Lingo and Clark nodded. No trouble. But no march on Montgomery either. The blacks would have to stop before reaching Kings Inn Road and turn back. Both officers would consider that simply a march within the city limits of Selma and not a violation of a court order prohibiting a march on Route 80.

Collins thanked "you gentlemen" and went back to the Albert Hotel. He still had the map with the pencil line. He showed it to Dr. King and said, "You must stop here or there will be trouble. This time you can cross the bridge unmolested. Stop your people on the far side until we can get this thing straightened out in court." The pastor began to smile. Incredibly, there was a way out of this mess. Incredibly. . . .

The day was a perfumed atomizer of spring to come. The people were late in arriving at Brown's Chapel; SNCC and SCLC men were busy herding people, white and black, into line. Mrs. Paul Douglas, wife of the United States Senator, fell into line. As the people were marshaling their courage, Governor Collins was back conferring with Clark and Lingo. "Now let us get this straight," he said. "They are going to march this far, no further. They are coming across this bridge, and they will stop before the line of troopers. I expect you fellows to keep your men under control. The Negroes will stop, then turn around. I have the agreement of Martin Luther King, and I don't want any violence." The officers shrugged. It was all right with them.

Early in the afternoon, Dr. King led 900 persons in prayer. Then, shouting defiantly, he said, "We have gone too far to turn back now. We must let them know that nothing can stop us. Not even death itself. We must be ready for a season of suffering." When the march began, there were 1,500 people in the ranks. Dr. King was up front with James Farmer, James Forman, Fred Shuttlesworth, and John Wesley Lord, bishop of the Methodist Church.

They followed the same route—up Sylvan Street to the old Confederate naval foundry, turned right on Water past the old St. James Motel, by the Lafayette memorial, then left onto the bridge. By the time they got to the top of it, the marchers were shouting, "We're on our way to Montgomery! We're on our way! Ain't gonna let nobody turn me 'round." Up front, some of the leaders began to sing "We Shall Overcome." On the far side of the bridge, an old lady pinned a large button on Clark's uniform. It read: "Never." The marchers continued down the bridge without opposition.

They got the bridge behind them. Straight ahead, carpenter's horses were stretched across the road. Behind them stood troopers and sheriff's deputies. No one reached for a club or a canister of tear gas. All of them had been advised that Martin Luther King would approach the wooden horses, stop his people, and turn back. Lingo stood on the side with Clark. "John," he said to a trooper, "open up that damn barricade and see how far they'll go." The road to Montgomery was open. Dr. King stopped, then started a prayer. Many fell to their knees. The road was wide open and seductive. The people in the rear ranks were moving up on the front. Dr. King turned toward his people. "Go back," he shouted. "Turn around and go back."

None seemed to understand the order, but they obeyed. There was some faltering; the lines began to merge into a homogeneous mass. Others took up the shout: "Back! Back!" Lingo watched the blacks cross back over the bridge. Clark smiled and shook his head. When the marchers returned to the church, reporters pressed around Martin Luther King. "We have had the greatest demonstration for freedom today that we have ever had in the South," he said. The words were duly quoted and sent over the teletypes to the nation. Some reporters drove to the far side of the bridge and spoke to Colonel Lingo and Jim Clark. There they heard the story which purported that Martin Luther King had agreed not to pass the barricades, knew all along that his people were not marching to Montgomery that day. In the first demonstration, the bloodied ones got halfway across the bridge; King was proclaiming a victory because he had crossed the entire bridge. Clark kept reminding the reporters that he had no agreement with King, had not spoken to him. LeRoy Collins had done all the talking, and it had been explained to him that any march within the city limits of Selma could not be considered a violation of the court order, and those barricades were standing at the city limits.

The men of the press returned to King with the fresh news. "In all frankness," he said sadly, "we knew we would not get to Montgomery." The marchers disbanded as the sun was setting. In Washington, Lyndon Johnson was relieved at the news but so worried that he was preparing an address to both houses of Congress.

Three Unitarian ministers strolled down the Selma streets and turned into a black restaurant. As they ate, they talked about the march. James Reeb, who had a wife and three children and was pastor of a large church in Boston, was doubtful that the march had achieved much. He was glad that he could stand up for the things in which he believed, but here he was still in Selma and not marching toward Montgomery. The three ministers paid their bills and walked out into the chill night air. Four white men in windbreakers were waiting on the sidewalk. One held a five-foot two-by-four board in his hand. "White niggers!" he screamed. "Where's your hammer and sickle?" The fighting started before the ministers understood the gravity of the situation. The two-by-four board lifted high, then crashed into the skull of the Reverend James Reeb. He fell unconscious. The four men fled into the night. Chief Wilson Baker arrived on the scene and quickly commandeered an ambulance to drive all night to Birmingham, where there were hospitals where brain surgery could be performed. Reeb died. His final conscious vision had been of white men with their features contorted with hate.

In the morning, there was a street riot. The rioters were seventy priests and nuns who had flown from Chicago to protest the murder of a Protestant minister. It was a shouting, shoving melee and police didn't know whether to use their clubs on the nuns or not. To further confuse the scene, Archbishop Thomas J. Toolen of Mobile-Birmingham made a speech in which he condemned the action of Northern clergy flying to Selma to fight law enforcement officers. They "are out of place in these demonstrations. Their place is at home doing God's work." The archbishop delivered himself of one more opinion: "Martin Luther King is dividing the people." The bishop was fighting a rearguard battle; the priests and nuns of other dioceses not only remained in Selma, but recruited more by telephone. In addition, the archbishop was risking dividing his own clergy, many of whom felt that blacks are people and entitled to all the rights granted to others. "Souls," one said, "are colorless." And yet, as if to drop irony upon irony, the seventy-nine-year-old archbishop was a desegregationist. He had ordered all Catholic schools in his archdiocese to be completely desegregated within six months.

The gentlemen's agreement at the bridge hurt Dr. King. Disenchantment with his leadership spread from SNCC to NAACP to CORE and part of the SCLC. In a church speech, he tried to justify what he had done. "At least," he said, "we had to get to the point where the brutality took place. And we made it clear when we got there that we were going to have some form of protest and worship. I can assure you that something happened in Alabama that's never happened before. When Negroes and whites can stand on Highway Eighty and have a mass meeting, things aren't that bad."

Chief Baker was tired of all of it, all sides of it. Laconically, he announced the arrest of three men on charges of murdering the Reverend Mr. Reeb. He had searched for them. He had found them. "I'm still looking for a fourth man," he said. Sheriff Clark had taken no part whatsoever in the manhunt.

Texas is Western; Texas is Southern. Lyndon Johnson was a Southerner wearing a big Stetson. The New York *Times* editorialized, with its customary restraint, that Johnson had made "what is probably the deepest commitment to the Negro cause of any American President." Any student of American history knows that the word "probably" could have been dropped. The Southern chief executive, facing the vengeful and bitter South, addressed Congress. "What happened in Selma," he said, "is part of a far larger movement which reaches into every section and state of America. It is the effort of American Negroes to secure for themselves the full blessings of American life. Their cause must be our cause too." He was interrupted by prolonged applause thirty-six times. "Because it's not just Negroes, but really it's all of us who must overcome the crippling legacy of bigotry and injustice.

"And . . . we . . . shall . . . overcome! . . ."

The President described the voting rights bill he was submitting to the ladies and gentlemen in his audience. His words lashed almost as a whip. This was not a bill to be delayed behind other legislation, he said. It was to be given top priority. He reminded them that he had waited patiently for eight months for an earlier civil rights bill to be considered and passed; this time, he said, he would give them eight weeks. He wasn't requesting; he wasn't begging; he was demanding.

Johnson took a long chance; it paid off. The nation examined its conscience the following day and found itself guilty. Martin Luther King was surprised. He had begged Johnson for help when the SCLC got itself into trouble, and the President had said no. When the pastor heard the speech and read it in the newspapers, he said that the President "revealed great and amazing understanding of the depth of the problem of racial injustice."

While King was praising Johnson, the sullen handsome James Forman led a march to the County Courthouse in Montgomery. He was putting President Johnson on trial and, in a subtle manner, Martin Luther King too. Five troopers and ten mounted sheriff's deputies met the marchers and charged through them. Eight were injured. Forman and his SNCC were now in Montgomery, King's old backyard. They were testing his civil rights victory of almost nine years before. That night Forman addressed a crowd at the Beulah Baptist Church, and he spoke in anger.

"Did President Johnson mean what he said?" he asked. He asked the people to join him in testing the new doctrine of equality. He proposed that the black community of Montgomery "tie up every bus, every street and commit every act of civil disobedience ever seen because I'm tired of seeing people get hit." Dr. King had flown to Montgomery to thwart SNCC reaction. He asked to speak after Forman, and even though the words he used to persuade were peaceful words and lacked the fire of militancy, his mood prevailed. He cleverly moved from voicing the outrage which his audience felt to moderation and pacification. Why not an "all-out" peaceful march on the courthouse? Get everybody out; walk with God. Then let us see what the white man will do. When the speech was over, Forman shook King's hand. He had calmed. He was willing to try an all-out peaceful march. King, in this small matter, had won a more potent victory than many others which he had proclaimed as triumphs.

They marched. It was a big orderly crowd. Ralph Abernathy went to the front line, linked his arm with Martin Luther King, and murmured, "Here we go again, Martin." King, remembering the Montgomery of so long ago, when Forman and Lewis were teen-agers, said, "Ye-e-e-s." The white structure of Montgomery had also had a meeting, and no one wanted to start that Rosa Parks situation all over again. They furnished a hundred policemen to flank the marchers and protect them. At each intersection, black policemen directed traffic, grinned, and waved the marchers on.

Martin Luther King stood on the steps of the courthouse. There was no microphone; the rain was falling in a cold slant, and the people pulled rain capes over their heads. Dr. King used an old-fashioned megaphone. "We are here today," he said, swinging the megaphone slowly from side to side, "to say to the white men that we will no longer let them use their clubs on us in dark corners. We are going to make them do it in the glaring light of television." Afterward the black leaders went into the courthouse to confer with Sheriff Mac Butler and with John Doar, head of the Civil Rights Division of the Justice Department.

Governor Wallace suddenly reversed himself and said that all eligible citizens of Alabama should be permitted to vote. The racial deck was being reshuffled so rapidly that it was difficult to detect the clubs from the spades. Then the governor took another step forward. He said that he would permit a march from Selma to Montgomery if the federal courts so directed.

The case was heard in federal court at once. At issue was the temporary injunction of Judge Frank M. Johnson against a march on Montgomery. The judge ordered King and his leaders and the state troopers and Jim Clark to appear. To the judge, it was a matter of adjudicating contempt proceedings, but everyone knew that this was mainly for the record; the larger issue was whether any group of people was entitled to stage a long protest march without harassment from law enforcement officers. In law, are the marchers entitled, instead, to protection?

Judge Johnson was not going to let Dr. King off the hook easily. "Is it correct to say that when you started across the bridge, you knew at that time that you did not intend to march to Montgomery?"

King said, "Yes it is. There was a tacit agreement at the bridge that we would go no further." Thus, under oath, he revealed that when he told the marchers that day that nothing could stop them, that they were marching on Montgomery, he had no intention of marching beyond the city limits of Selma. The confession saved him from being cited for contempt, but the news media hanged him. Metropolitan papers stated that there was "open contempt" for Martin Luther King's leadership and that civil rights spokesmen "charged that King had betrayed them by his behind-the-scenes bargaining."

Judge Johnson called state troopers to the stand, and under oath, they testified that a march on Montgomery would present a "hazard" to the blacks. The speed limit was sixty miles an hour; the road was filled with curves, with four lanes narrowing suddenly to two and there were high embankments which would conceal people on foot from drivers of automobiles. According to their testimony, the troopers were doing the blacks a favor by clubbing and gassing them on the Pettus Bridge.

The judge asked to hear the other side of the story, and the black lawyers submitted a brief called "Proposed Plan for March from Selma, Ala. to Montgomery, Ala." It proclaimed the march peaceful in intent; it would require five days; marchers would hug the side of the road and not impede traffic nor endanger themselves; on a map were designated fields where black farmers had agreed in writing to permit the marchers to rest overnight; in addition, there were street maps of Selma and Montgomery, with heavy crayon lines showing the precise route the marchers proposed to take.

Judge Johnson read it, item by item. There were paragraphs dealing with the preparation and delivery of food for the marchers, trucks equipped with washing machines and others with toilet facilities, a rearguard detail to pick up litter, ambulance service in transit, transportation to bring the marchers back to Selma. The document, in sum, was a lawyer's dream. Johnson recessed court and, the following morning, authorized the march. He went further. He ordered Governor Wallace and officials of the State of Alabama not to "harass or threaten" the marchers but, on the contrary, to provide protection from hostile whites. It also extended to the President of the United States a right he already had, to use federal troops to protect the marchers. The judge brought into sharp focus an old constitutional right when he wrote that law enforcement men had "stepped across the constitutional boundary line that lies between the interests of the public to use the highway . . . and the right of American citizens to use it for the purpose . . . of protesting their grievances."

Wallace reversed himself. He assumed his helpless posture. An appeal went to President Johnson to send U.S. marshals to Alabama at once to "provide for the safety and welfare" of the marchers. The governor addressed a joint session of the Alabama legislature. In the ancient offwhite well, with the shallow gallery filled with the ladies and the relatives of legislators, Wallace had to look good. These were segregationists. Before he opened his mouth, they knew he had lost the war.

The short man with black hair and dark eyes told the legislators that Alabama didn't have sufficient manpower to protect a "colossal demonstration" sanctioned by a "mock court." The use of the latter phrase might have brought a contempt citation if Judge Johnson wished. Most observers, however, saw it for what it was: the mewling of a partisan politician who had painted himself into a corner. According to the governor's figures, proper protection of the marchers would require the services of no fewer than 6,171 officers on eight-hour shifts. The cost to the state would come to $360,000. He did not mention that the salaries of the officers would have been paid anyhow, even if they lounged in the corridors of the Capitol.

Lyndon Johnson had no time for diplomacy. He signed a document placing the Alabama National Guard under federal jurisdiction. He signed a second one ordering the Secretary of Defense to send as many units of the United States Army as necessary to protect the marchers. Wallace was not only helpless, but powerless. He drew applause by referring to the civil rights leaders as "Communist-trained anarchists" who were specialists in "street warfare." He asked the racists along the march route to remain away from the scene. "I do not ask you for cowardice," he said. "I ask you not to play into the hands of the enemies of our nation and our freedom." The governor was asking the red-neck farmers not to do what he had done—try to stop the marchers with violence. Had he practiced what he now preached, the original pitifully small group of blacks would have walked to Montgomery in stages, stood in front of the Capitol to hear Martin Luther King talk and pray, and disbanded and gone home. Instead, Wallace, Lingo, and Clark had transformed a small incident into an international scandal.

March day was Sunday, March 21. It was windy and sunny and joyous in "Colored Town," Selma. Huge military jets landed at Craig Air Force Base across the river. Helmeted soldiers with rifles debarked. Ranking officers were driven to the Selma National Guard Armory. There a direct hot line was established with the Pentagon in Washington. In Montgomery, other officers had a similar telephone line; both parties were connected to officers along the line of march by two-way radio. All 30,000 Alabama National Guard troops were posted in their armories, but because the federal government did not trust them, 1,800 Regular Army military policemen were brought in to walk with the marchers. Two helicopters quivered overhead. A shop owner on Broad Street stood on the sidewalk and said, "Wouldn't surprise me if they sailed a battleship down the Alabama River."

Sylvan Street was jammed. So was the Albert Hotel. A. Philip Randolph, tall and stately, watched the scene. Ralph Bunche was present. Richard Millard, Episcopal bishop, flew in from California. Walter Reuther of the United Automobile Workers was ready. Rabbi

Abraham Heschel of the American Jewish Theological Seminary stood in line. Paul Screvane, president of the New York City Council; Constance Motley, black president of the Borough of Manhattan; John H. Franklin, historian, and a personal representative of Governor Nelson Rockefeller were there. Notables who had taken no part in the bloody mess were being ushered to the front by SCLC field secretaries, while local blacks remained in back.

SNCC threatened to boycott the march. They said that although their people had done all the work, Dr. Martin Luther King was proclaimed the hero of the hour. Both sides spent three days in secret caucus prior to the march. Dr. King sent Hosea Williams, Andrew Young, and James Bevel to indulge a shouting match with John Lewis and James Forman. When the men calmed down, they all agreed that the march was going to be held and they might as well participate together.

It was almost 1 P.M. when Martin Luther King arrived with Ralph Abernathy. There were 2,800 people jammed between Brown's Chapel and the newish George Washington Carver apartments. "Walk together, children," Dr. King shouted. "Don't you get weary, and it will lead us to the promised land. And Alabama will be a new Alabama, and America will be a new America." The local people cheered hoarsely, but many of Selma's 14,000 blacks remained home. They desired with all their hearts for something good and decent and equitable to happen, but they were not going to walk fifty-four miles to get it. In addition, Dr. King had agreed to abide by Judge Johnson's ruling within a ruling that no matter how many persons started to march, after eight miles on Route 80, Doctor King would reduce the number to 300.

At 12:50, blacks in the rear were shouting "March!" and the rear ranks began to telescope with the front. Those up forward were pushed into walking; then an old truck with a television camera on the back burst into loud backfires and bluish smoke which choked the first half dozen ranks. This time the marchers turned directly onto Broad Street. Whites in their Sunday best dotted the curbsides, staring cold and unblinking at the marchers. A few children held hate placards: "Martin Luther Coon"; "Bye Bye Blackbird."

The marchers began to sing "We Shall Overcome," and the wave of sound competed with the whirring helicopters overhead. They walked up the hump of the Pettus Bridge and down the other side. The only sign of force that could be seen were United States Army units walking along the sides of the road. By the time they passed Craig Air Force Base the singing had stopped; the trudging had begun. The people had seven more miles to go. A few whites on farms paused to watch them go by. The military squeezed the marchers toward the right edge of the road so that traffic could pass. The soldiers walked on the outside so that a racist automobile owner could not "accidentally" hit any black marchers without first hitting the military. Squad cars were a half mile ahead and a half mile behind.

The sun was down when they reached the big open farm owned by David Hall, a black man. Military messages flashed back and forth on the hot line. Nothing untoward had happened. The first day was over; the marchers had achieved 7.3 miles. A car picked the Kings up and returned them to Selma. Chartered buses arrived to take the bulk of the marchers back, too. Sleek cars paused for sleek people. Some returned to Selma; others moved on to Montgomery Airport. Three hundred remained to pitch tents, fetch kindling, and start cooking food. Army troops stood guard all night around the perimeter of the farm.

On the second day, the marchers started at 8 A.M. They were in Lowndes County, more firmly racist than Dallas. There were no incidents. There were fewer than 300 marchers; they were outnumbered by the soldiers, who were four paces apart far ahead and far behind. Dr. King traversed the march from back to front in a car, the window rolled down, smiling and talking to the people. A military message crackled to the Pentagon. It said: "The possibility that snipers are hiding in the trees worries army troops." There were no snipers. The people of Alabama were doing their best to ignore the marchers.

On the third day, Martin Luther King flew to Cleveland to make a speech, and on Wednesday he and his wife flew to Montgomery to rejoin the marchers. They were a little more than ten miles from the city. It was night, and a group of well-known entertainment stars, including Leonard Bernstein, Billy Eckstine, Harry Belafonte, and Sammy Davis, Jr., were entertaining the marchers on an improvised stage under bare temporary lights.

In the morning, there were 20,000 people ready to march. It was difficult to locate the few who had walked from Selma to Montgomery. They were lost in rows of people stretching two miles down the highway. It was decided not to start the march so far from Montgomery but rather to move the starting point to St. Jude's Hospital, two miles outside Montgomery. The Kings, leading the big parade, started up Oak Street to Jefferson Davis Street. They walked through the black section of town where the residents stood on porches and curbs laughing, waving, weeping. Dr. King had a strong happy stride. He went up Mobile Street to Dexter Avenue, and, as Mrs. King said, "Oh, it was good. Very good." There were troops flanking the long deep ranks; there were soldiers with rifles on rooftops; military planes roared overhead.

They walked up the hill past the old red brick of the Dexter Avenue Baptist Church; it was like a homecoming. Then on up to the big plaza before the State Capitol. There a wooden platform had been raised. On the upper steps of the Capitol state troopers were posted. Dr. King and his friends were to be permitted into the plaza, allowed to speak, but not to touch foot on the Capitol steps. Mrs. King, eyes dancing with tears, saw her mother and father in the crowd. They had come all the way from Marion for the great moment. "Daddy" King was there, too; he wasn't strong enough to march, but he was assertive enough to want to be up there on the stand with his son.

There were speeches and speeches. Someone asked about seeing Governor Wallace, and a boy in the crowd held up a big placard which caused the crowd to break with laughter. It showed a group of blacks before the Capitol. A balloon over the top asked: "Have you an appointment?" Mrs. King saw Rosa Parks sitting nearby and wondered what she was thinking. Her tired feet were ten years older, but her face wasn't. When Martin Luther King was introduced, the crowd went wild. He said he wanted to present a petition to Governor Wallace, but the governor's executive secretary said that the governor was busy, and he would take it to him. Dr. King said he put the petition back in his pocket. The crowd boomed approval.

"Last Sunday," he said, "more than eight thousand of us started on a mighty walk from Selma, Alabama. We have walked on meandering highways and rested our bodies on rocky byways. Some of our faces are burned from the outpourings of the sweltering sun. Some have literally slept in the mud. We have been literally drenched by the rains. . . . They told us we wouldn't get here. And there were those who said that we would get here only over their dead bodies, but all the world together knows that we are here and that we are standing before the forces of power in the State of Alabama saying: 'We Ain't Gonna Let Nobody Turn Us 'Round.' . . ."

He was, in every good sense, the uplifting Southern preacher. Again, the repeated phrase, the calling of God to witness the righteousness of the black's cause, had brought the huge crowd to a high pitch of enthusiasm. But he didn't tell them what the march had achieved, except the freedom to march, and he did not mention the President who pressed for voting legislation and who, with Federal Judge Johnson, made the march possible and safe. Martin Luther King had won another victory, and he left town for Atlanta within a few hours. The litter of old polemics would be swept up by others.

Mrs. Viola Liuzzo was one of the sweepers. She was a small volatile brunette from Detroit, wife of a Teamsters Union local official, and mother of five children. She had become concerned about the plight of blacks in the South and had asked her husband for permission to help in Selma. He had said yes on the understanding that she would not march, not demonstrate. She had driven to Selma in a two-door Oldsmobile and offered her assistance to the transportation section. She would be needed—as would other women volunteers—on the night the march concluded in Montgomery. Everyone was told to get plenty of rest because there would be Selma blacks who would have to be driven home. Each round trip on Route 80 amounted to 108 miles and each volunteer was expected to make at least two of them.

A nineteen-year-old black, Leroy Moton, was assigned to Viola Liuzzo's car as guide. He knew the pickup points in Montgomery, and he knew where Route 80 narrowed and curved in the darkness, pierced only by headlights. He was a quiet boy, a kid half-ashamed of his "down-home" accent. The SCLC put him in the transportation section because of his timidity. On the night that Dr. King made the big speech in Montgomery, the young man seemed determined to do everything that was expected of him because, when the first trip was completed, he said, "Everybody all out. Have to go right back to Montgomery."

Mrs. Liuzzo swung the car out of Selma, across the dark bridge, and straight down Route 80. She had a heavy foot on the gas pedal. The Oldsmobile was going so fast it was swaying. Behind them, another car kept pace; Mrs. Liuzzo could see the glare of the headlights in her rearview mirror. Three times the car behind them pulled up close but found no room to pass. The road leveled, lifted up in blackness to a rise, fell away again in a turn to the right, came back. She watched the headlights stab the blackness of the countryside.

The car behind pulled up again, and this time it drew alongside. There were four men in it: There were members of the Ku Klux Klan; one, unknown to the others, was a paid informant of the FBI. A man in the back said, "All right, men. Shoot the hell out of them." Mrs. Liuzzo, with her window rolled up against the roar of night air, looked briefly at the men in the other car. One of the men rolled down a rear window, aimed a .38 revolver, and fired two shots through the driver's window. The others began to fire their guns into the car. Leroy may have been timid in some matters, but not in this. He crouched on the floorboards as the glass shattered. The Liuzzo car began to slow down, wobbling on the road as the Klan car sped by into the darkness.

The FBI informant said, "I don't think you hit them."

The man in the rear rolled up his window. "Baby brother," he said sweetly, "don't worry about it. That bitch and that bastard are dead and in hell. I don't miss."

He was half right. Mrs. Liuzzo was dead. Leroy Moton was alive, praying that the carful of Klansmen would not come back.

When the news reached Atlanta, Coretta King felt all her elation sink into despair at the thought of five motherless children. She assessed the situation succinctly: "The sight of a white woman in a car with a black man on a dark Alabama road. How much farther we still have to go."

Her husband had a different reaction. He appeared on nationwide television and said, "I hope to call on all Americans to refuse to buy Alabama products. I hope to call on the Secretary of the Treasury of the United States to withdraw all federal funds that it has on deposit in Alabama banks. And finally, I think it is necessary to call on all federal agencies, in line with the 1964 civil rights bill, to withdraw support from a society that has refused to protect life and the right to vote." This statement was deplored by civil rights leaders from all parts of the country. They felt that the first to suffer an Alabama boycott would be the blacks. If such a boycott gained impetus, white employers would discharge black workers first. Whitney Young, Jr., of the Urban League told reporters that he was opposed to any plan which "makes no distinction between the good guys and the bad guys."

The news media barely mentioned the boycott; they were still mourning Mrs. Liuzzo and in shock again at America's violence. It was still in editorial ecstasy over the March on Montgomery. Here, the white press and the black press split. The whites saw the march as a long step forward in civil rights. The black press and black leaders tossed oratorical darts at the march. Dr. Cobbs wrote in the *Negro Digest:* "While the purpose of the march was ostensibly to dramatize the plight of the Negro, there have been few benefits in terms of lasting gains." SNCC announced publicly that Dr. King had done nothing more than take his place in front when the march started. One big gain was that the SCLC, which had been in debt for $95,845, was inundated with a blizzard of checks and money orders from people wanting to help the cause. Ralph Abernathy beamed happily when he announced, "We're going to have our first million-dollar year."

Sheriff Jim Clark, riding leisurely through quiet Selma, noticed that the blacks were still black, the whites were still white, and that racial relations in Dallas County were exactly where they had been before the march. Most of the blacks were back in the balcony of the movies, not because anyone forced them to sit there, but because the price was only fifteen cents.

The Klansmen who killed Mrs. Liuzzo were caught. Mr. Liuzzo still owed payments on the Oldsmobile, but he could not bear to look at it. He asked General Motors Acceptance Corporation to sell it for whatever sum he still owed. Sometime later, the following advertisement appeared in the Birmingham *News:*

> NOTICE—Do you need a crowd-getter? I have a 1963 Oldsmobile two-door in which Mrs. Viola Liuzzo was killed. Bullet holes and everything intact. Ideal to bring in crowds. $3,500.

In the spring of 1965 Dr. King had decided to break the sectional bonds of the Southern Christian Leadership Conference, with or without the consent of the board members. A meeting was scheduled in the early part of April in Baltimore, and the pastor felt that he was ready for a larger stage, a bigger, more militant theater. The South remained his first love, but he now saw the word "Southern" in the SCLC as a geographical prison. In the manner of most missionaries, he was zealous to spread the good word to the whole country, to the world.

There was some mutterings of disagreement at the annual meeting, but the board members realized that the SCLC *was* Martin Luther King and only Martin Luther King. Others did valiant work in the racial vineyard; in recent years some men, such as Hosea Williams and Wyatt Tee Walker, had done more than King. The staff in Atlanta was overworked, recruiting new members, soliciting new affiliates, settling internal disputes, asking for funds, responding to cries for help from many cities. But King was king; if the SCLC lost him as a figurehead, the SCLC would lose momentum and power as a civil rights organization.

The board members felt that, as soon as President Johnson's voting rights bill became law, the SCLC should concentrate its energies and substance on a registration drive to encompass 120 rural counties stretching from Virginia south to Louisiana. There would be little glamor and practically no drama in this if the federal government sent registrars to supersede the Southerners. However, SCLC leaders saw the President's act as the true key to black power, and they proposed to put field workers into every one of those counties to cajole the apathetic black into an automobile ride "downtown" to become a voter.

Dr. King agreed. However, he rejected the notion that he lead the drive. He proposed Hosea Williams as the field general. The board concurred. King then brought up his idea for boycotting the products of the State of Alabama. The board members could not subscribe to it and felt that the nation's 22,000,000 blacks were not sufficiently unified to sort the corn, the beans, the Bessemer steel of Alabama from that of the rest of the nation. Dr. King made a strong issue of it, and the board voted for the boycott. His next proposal was to start a personal campaign in the Northern ghettos, where the plight of the blacks was often worse than in the South. Again, the board opposed him and pointed out that the North had its own organizations and its own leaders—its problems were "different." Dr. King insisted. He had, in fact, already agreed to campaign in Chicago with the Reverend Jesse Jackson, who was doing a handsome job creating jobs for blacks. Some members felt that the South needed more leadership, not less; more marches, more demonstrations. The pastor was tiring of those confrontations; he had been through so many and had stood to speak in so many public squares where, in bright sunlight, he could not tell which window might have a rifle leaning on the ledge. Nine years of danger were behind him, and at the age of thirty-six, he was an elder statesman. That is the role he wanted to play.

They could not stop him. He was a black man living on borrowed time, and there wasn't a white man in the South who would have bet that Dr. King would have lived this long. Further, he told the board that he felt strongly about world affairs, and he intended to speak out on the war in Vietnam. It was here that the apostles openly opposed him. They could not stop him, so they proposed a resolution that if Dr. Martin Luther King, Jr., spoke out on foreign affairs, he would do so as a private American citizen, not as president of the SCLC. The resolution was passed, but the men knew that when Martin Luther King spoke, the nation and the world would see him as voicing the attitude of the American black, the figurehead of 11 percent of the American population.

King had wanted to enlarge the scope of his mission as long ago as 1959. It was then that an Italian editor asked him a question about world peace. King had responded, with some asperity, that peace and nonviolence were not philosophies to be applied to neighborhoods, but to nations as well. But there were men on his personal staff who reminded him that the world, with the Nobel Prize, had heaped high honors on him as a man of peace, and the world was waiting for commandments for peace. Besides, his wife was a political activist with sharper, more finely honed opinions than his; she would be willing, perhaps even eager, for him to speak out on world affairs.

Immediately after the conclusion of the March on Montgomery, the tenor of King's talks changed. He made speeches in Demopolis, Greensboro, and Eutaw, Alabama on May 11, and while he gave lip service to voter registration, he began to relate the plight of the American black to what he called the worldwide class struggle. "I'm not going to sit by and see war escalated without saying anything about it," he said. "It is worthless to talk about integrating if there is no world to integrate in." At this point, he sunk the shaft deep into his strongest political ally, Lyndon Johnson. "The war in Vietnam must be stopped," he said. "There must be a negotiated settlement even with the Vietcong."

The statement made headlines. There was a reverberating roll of political thunder. Overnight, Martin Luther King lost support among middle-of-the road Congressmen. They said he wasn't competent to make such observations; Southern legislators were delighted that Dr. King was at last revealing himself as a "Communist sympathizer." In Petersburg, Virginia, Dr. King took another international step. If the Johnson administration could not find a way to negotiate peace in Vietnam, he said, he would mass his followers in teach-ins and peace rallies. In August, he told a cheering crowd that he planned to appeal directly to President Johnson, Ho Chi Minh of North Vietnam, the Vietcong, and the South Vietnamese government. He also advocated a seat in the United Nations for the People's Republic of China.

The doctor traveled to Chicago to test the muddied waters of the North. He and the SCLC led eighteen rallies in three days, marched with 20,000 followers to Chicago City Hall to protest de facto school segregation, and delivered thirty speeches. He expended a great deal of energy in a short span, and when he left, one black leader said, "Chicago will never be the same."

All of Dr. King's men could not breach the schism between him and SNCC. It grew wider with time, and it must have hurt Dr. King because he had adopted SNCC at its birth. It was one of the poorest civil rights groups, but it was young, stubborn, and militant. In the summer of 1965 Stokely Carmichael was emerging as the leader, and he was a more formidable gutter fighter than John Lewis. SNCC was poor financially, but it had friends. There were 150 chapters of Friends of SNCC on college campuses. These white and black men and women worked for the common cause, staging benefit dances, selling booklets, soliciting small donations, staging lotteries. In August, the hierarchy of SNCC had a fund-raising drive at a Hollywood discothèque and invited motion-picture stars to attend, to listen, to donate. Marlon Brando gave $5,000; so did Richard Burton and Sidney Poitier. James Garner and Harry Belafonte parted with $3,500 each; Burt Lancaster and Paul Newman tendered checks for $1,000. But SNCC was neither as big nor as potent as its potential. In the summer of 1965 it had 225 paid-up members.

The big news that summer was the signing of the Voting Rights Act. Usually, such bills are signed in the Cabinet Room at the White House, but this time, Lyndon Johnson sat at a gleaming mahogany desk in the President's Room in the Capitol. He had invited so many white and black leaders for the event that it was difficult for the big man to break through the crowd to shake hands. "Today," he said, "is a triumph for freedom as huge as any victory that has ever been won on any battle-field . . . today we strike away the last major shackle of fierce and ancient bonds." The bill, without equivocation or loopholes, gave the right to vote to the black man. It did more than that. It placed the Department of Justice and its legal talent at the side of the voter, a formidable team to oppose the white registrar. No state, no county, no crossroads community in the South could stop the black from voting, and he was not reqired to respond to obtuse historical questions. It was the longest, firmest step the United States had taken to grant full citizen-ship and the power implied within it to the black. Even Rosa Parks, now a secretary to Michigan Congressman John Conyers, stood on tiptoe in the room to see history made.

The President was ebullient, and he had a right to be. He had shamed Congress into passing the bill. Martin Luther King was equally certain that his March on Montgomery had pressured Congress into passing it.

This made him bold. When the ceremonies were over, he approached the President for a private word. Johnson's beaming smile drooped to the solemn linear wrinkles of a hound dog. He bent his six feet four down to listen to the five feet seven. Dr. King asked the President to make a formal statement that he would eradicate the economic isolation of the Northern black. The President said this was not the time or place for such an assertion. Dr. King, still smiling, asked if the President would do something to assist the City of Washington to establish home rule, considering that it was more than 65 percent black. Johnson shook his head no and walked away.

Later King's friends told him bluntly that he had made a tactical error. They reminded him that Johnson had responded to the black man's cry for political power more quickly, more surely, more positively, than any President in history. This was not the day to plague him with additional problems.

That day, August 6, King lost whatever rapport he had had with Johnson. Both continued to work for civil rights, but Johnson was permanently disenchanted. Civil rights leaders told King, "Martin, lay off Vietnam. It's his problem, not ours. Civil rights is as big a domestic issue as Vietnam is a foreign issue. Stick to civil rights." The mail arriving in bundles at the SCLC headquarters in Atlanta showed that Martin Luther King had lost some popular support. Bayard Rustin cautioned him to remain silent on the Vietnam problem. His father begged him to stay out of it. King's main support in continuing to speak out against the war came from his wife. She thought he was a big enough international figure to speak out for peace and cause big men to pause. The only time Lyndon Johnson permitted himself to discuss Vietnam with Martin Luther King was in a telephone conversation. The President asked the pastor to stop talking about the war until King had time to confer with United Nations Ambassador Arthur Goldberg. Johnson was willing to set up a "briefing" conference between the two men. King consented.

The big aluminum jet planes are on "final" when they pass over Watts. They shriek in pain, trailing long black plumes, as they come in low for Los Angeles International Airport. The people who can afford to be inside the big aircraft can't hear the noise. The people who can't afford to be on the planes hear the noise day and night. They are black, living in old houses and cold-water flats seven miles inland from Manhattan Beach, a small blackhead on the broad face of Los Angeles. From Broadway to Compton Avenue, there is nothing for the eyes but sleazy shops and bars, a square of green called Will Rogers Memorial Park, railroad tracks. A couple of hundred acres of resentment.

Watts is a cemetery for the living buried between the Harbor Freeway and the Santa Ana Freeway, both of which make it possible for travelers to pass the area without seeing. August was hot in the flatland, and black children played stickball on 116th Street and 102d. Women leaned on pillows at front windows, watching the moving faces below. The area is three miles long, three miles wide if the surveyor ignores the encroachments on the sides. On Wednesday, August 11, at suppertime, Marquette Frye was driving to his mother's house in Watts. He lived there. So did the stepbrother Ronald, who sat beside him in the car. Marquette was an infrequent drinker because he had little tolerance for alcohol. He had been drinking on August 11. "There's a cop behind you," Ronald said. Marquette heard the siren, saw the motorcycle in his rearview mirror. He wasn't looking for trouble, so he pulled to the curb.

Blacks came running, rolling out of hallways like so many marbles. Some came from a block west, the 11600 block of Towne Street, where Wallace and Rena Frye rented an apartment. Officer Lee W. Minikus pulled his cycle to the curb, set the kick stand, and walked back to the car. Marquette Frye was already out from behind the wheel. The officer took him by the arm and led him to the sidewalk. About three dozen men and women were around them, listening and laughing. Some were sipping cans of beer. They were amused because the police officer was so polite with his questions, and the black man was so confused that he was funny. Somebody pointed at Marquette and said, "He's a comedian," and everyone laughed. The policeman asked Marquette if he had been drinking. Young Mr. Frye looked at his feet and said he'd had a few screwdrivers. "Where's your license?" Minikus asked. "You were doing fifty in a thirty-five mile zone."

Ronald got out of the car. Both young men looked properly shocked at the notion that anyone in his right mind would speed at fifty miles per hour in a thirty-five mile zone. Marquette fanned his pockets. He said he guessed he had lost his license. In a furry, faraway tone he guessed maybe he either left it home or lost it. Maybe it was lost. A sense of fear began to override the screwdrivers. He remembered that he had been arrested five years before on a charge of petty theft. The cops had spoken to him like a bunch of uncles and let him go. A year later he was in court on a charge of robbing a grocery store. He remembered. He remembered. While he was out on bail, he had been arrested again for stealing $18.

Rena Frye was in her kitchen, cooking a rabbit. A woman knocked on the door and told her that a policeman had her sons around the corner on Avalon. The mother turned the gas down under the rabbit and ran down the stairs in a loose housecoat. Policeman Minikus asked Marquette to walk a straight line on the sidewalk and to hold his hand far out in front of his face and then touch his nose. Young Frye couldn't do either. The crowd laughed. It was growing larger. "Man," someone said, "that kid is loaded." The policeman smiled in spite of his attitude of detached efficiency.

Marquette began to see the amusing side of the dilemma. He laughed when the people laughed. He liked Minikus because the policeman was not overbearing. Minikus turned on his two-way radio and asked for a motorcycle officer to respond to a Driving While Intoxicated charge at Avalon and 116th Street, and a sheriff's car to take a prisoner to the county station.

Officer Robert Lewis, on a patrol motorcycle, was nearby, and he responded at once. A moment later Officer Larry Bennett was at the scene with a county car. The convergence of police vehicles brought more people outdoors. The time was 7 P.M. There was plenty of daylight. Rena Frye ran toward the crowd, the big housecoat ballooning around her little body. She pushed her way through. County Officer Joe Gabel arrived with a tow truck and chain and had trouble backing toward the parked Buick. Mrs. Frye saw it and shouted, "That's my car!" Mrs. Frye ran to Officer Minikus. He said the car would be released to her.

It was an average dull arrest except for the laughter. Rena Frye was not laughing. She pushed her way to Marquette's side and stood looking up at his face. "Are you drunk?" she said. Marquette tried to hug Rena. She pulled away from his arm. He stopped laughing. "I can smell it," Mrs. Frye said. "You better go with them."

Officer Lewis tossed handcuffs to Minikus. The policemen approached Marquette Frye, and the prisoner turned away. The officers could hear shouts in the distance and the sound of running feet. Lewis sensed a chilling change in the crowd. He reached his motorcycle and put in an "eleven ninety-nine"—officer requires assistance. The people, in silence, began to press inward. Lewis got his nightstick. So did Minikus. Bennett struggled to his car and got a riot gun. After he held it in the crook of his elbow, he remembered that it was not loaded.

A distant wail of sirens was heard. The sound grew from several directions. Ronald came to his brother's assistance and was warned to "stay out of it." Marquette seemed to be in a frenzy. He lunged at the man with the shotgun and screamed, "Go ahead. Kill me!" He backed away when Lewis tried to hit him with the stock of the gun. Squad cars were pulling to a stop with squealing rubber. Policemen were running. A sergeant tried to take charge. No one could hear his commands. A policeman, Wayne N. Wilson, made the first contact between white and black. He jabbed his nightstick into Marquette's belly. Frye struck out with his fists. Wilson whacked him on the forehead with the stick, and blood streamed down the side of Frye's face. The boy began to sag down the side of the wall.

The crowd heard the crack of wood on skull. "You don't have to do that," someone shouted. The silent people began to roar. Black faces contorted with anger. From where they stood, it appeared that an intoxicated youth was being overpowered and beaten by too many policemen. From the law's side, it appeared as though they had better get Frye out of there before the crowd became a riotous mob. Minikus was still the arresting officer, so he took his weakened prisoner and dragged him by the back of the neck to the transportation car, opened the front door, and pushed him facedown on the seat. Then he handcuffed him.

Ronald Frye, excited by brutality, swung at a policeman. Rena Frye jumped on the back of Minikus and ripped his uniform shirt. Another policeman grabbed Mrs. Frye, pulled her loose, and bent her over the fender of a police car. She was screaming, "Help me! Help me!" A policeman put in a second call for help, and red lights were flashing and sirens wailing all over the Watts area. The lights and sounds, in turn, brought more people outdoors, running to see what was going on. Two policemen handcuffed Mrs. Frye and shoved her into a back seat. Ronald saw his mother struggling and attacked the officers. He too was handcuffed and pushed into the car.

Bennett got behind the wheel of the police car with the Fryes inside and moved it through the crowd and down Avalon. There were close to thirty squad cars parked up and down the street. Superior officers in the group knew that the prisoners had been taken away; the next move was to leave the area as fast as possible. The crowd would jeer; it would dissipate. The policemen got to their cars and motorcycles. They appeared to be retreating. This gave the crowd courage to transform itself into a mob. As the police cars scrambled out of Watts, the match had been struck, the fire lighted. Squad car radios crackled with the warning: "Police cars—stay out of Watts. Repeat. Remain out of Watts."

Watts had an outside friend. No one knew what he looked like, but he talked Watts talk. He called himself Magnificent Montague, and Watts turned him on on its radios at seven every morning and shut him off at ten. He was a disc jockey, a player of recordings, who sandwiched his swift rhythms with KGFJ chatter. "Ya-ahhhh!" he breathed. "Burn, baby, burn!" It was the way he said it. The teen-agers in Watts who walked with a girl, passed their friends leaning against store windows and gave perfect imitations of Magnificent Montague: "Ya-ahhhh! Burn, baby, burn!" Quickly, it became a catchphrase. No one pretended to know what it meant; the words had a defiant ring to them. Burn, baby, burn!

By 9 P.M. that Wednesday night, darkness was on Watts. Reports were coming into the huge skyscraper called Los Angeles police headquarters that unruly crowds were forming in Watts. Headquarters sent in eighty-two officers. They established a command post at a main intersection—Avalon and Imperial. Superior police officers patrolled the area and estimated that several mobs aggregated 1,500 youths and men. A report went to headquarters: "Insufficient manpower for a sweep of the area."

Still, squads were sent down Avalon to seal the biggest crowds off. For the angry blacks there was no way out, no way in. From the darkness, bottles were thrown by the neck to twirl end over end at the police.

At 10 P.M., two hours and fifty minutes after the arrest of Marquette Frye, the police lost control of Watts. Watts lost control of itself. An elderly white couple, traveling through Watts in a car southbound toward Compton, was hidden under a cloud of black youths, who climbed the hood, the roof, swung the doors open, and dragged the people to the street. They were beaten. One of the teen-agers unscrewed the gasoline tank cover, lit a piece of paper, stood away from the car, and tossed it with accuracy. Watts began to light up. Sergeant Richard Rankin, at the command post, ordered a second retreat. "Let's get out. See if they'll go about their business." The police did not require urging. They fled.

The people were the law. Not the people, properly, because most of them were inside their homes behind bolted doors. The mob was the law. A young man stood on top of a parked car with arms outstretched, and preached in almost holy tones: "Burn, baby, burn!" The street temperature was ninety-two degrees. For the first time, Watts belonged to them. Rumors spread rapidly. "The cops beat a pregnant girl to death. Saw it myself. . . . The fuzz took a little old lady wasn't doin' nothin' and beat her bad and handcuffed her. . . . Cops took a boy out of a car, pushed him against a wall, and busted his head this wide open." Soon closed doors were opening. The restrained anger of the black man was bursting outdoors. This, everyone knew, was going to be a night where anything was possible, where nothing was punishable.

Sergeant Rankin requested, by radio, that Los Angeles police units reassemble at 108th Street and Clovis Avenue. The retreat was north and east. The state highway patrolmen remained in their cars off the edge of Watts, which was not in their district. They waited almost an hour for a call for help from Los Angeles. It did not come, so they disbanded and resumed their separate highway patrols. Automobile drivers and passengers were coming out of Watts with mouths mashed, teeth out and huge dents in their cars. Bus drivers made it at top speed with stones, bottles and two-by-four planks slamming into the sides of vehicles, smashing windows, and injuring passengers with flying glass.

The onus of misjudging the situation falls on the hierarchy of Los Angeles—Police Chief William H. Parker and Mayor Sam Yorty. The moment the local police were forced to leave the scene of the riots, both men should have been informed of the violence potential. Local police lieutenants and captains were sure that if Watts were left to itself with no police to fight, it would "simmer down."

Bands of young blacks, followed by women and children, hurried through the streets. One group passed a gasoline station. "Burn, baby, burn!" someone shouted. Someone else said, "No. Blood owns it." There was a grocery store with a night light over the cash register. The windows tinkled inward. Then the women trailed in, warning the children who followed to watch out for glass, and walked up and down the darkened aisles, picking out the foods they needed. They stole carts and walked out the broken front doors, little ones hanging onto the handles. A police car slowed, but no one got out to stop the looters. No police ordered the people to return the groceries. On the same street, men found a liquor store. The windows went in, and they ransacked the shelves for the most expensive whiskeys and stole cartons of cigarettes. Others were interested in food, but many congregated in front of pawnshops. They took rifles, shotguns, revolvers, pistols, binoculars, watches, and rings. They no longer needed rocks. They were armed.

Three police cars moved up and down 103d Street. They saw the looting, spotted the rifles and guns, and kept moving.

At 2 A.M. Watts was quiet. By 4 A.M. the few fires had been extinguished, and Watts slept. The newspaper presses were spewing a shocking story to the world. In San Juan, Dr. Martin Luther King, attending a convention of the World Disciples of Christ, heard the name "Watts" for the first time. He had no affiliates there, and he had little understanding of the metropolitan black, but he booked himself out on the first plane. He intended to drive slowly through the section, with a few aides, telling people his name and urging them to practice nonviolence.

By 5 P.M. on Thursday, Police Chief Parker was on the telephone with

Lieutenant General Roderic Hill of the California National Guard. Parker conceded that the riot had not burned itself out and he might require help from the National Guard. The general dispatched Colonel Robert Quick to Los Angeles to act as liaison between the police and the military. No one could appeal for help to Governor Edmund "Pat" Brown. He was in Greece on vacation. Lieutenant Governor Glenn Anderson was in charge. General Hill conferred with him. Both were reluctant to send the Fortieth Armored Division into Watts unless Parker's policemen lost control of the situation. It was barely dark at 8:30 P.M. when the first bands started out. Without leadership, without conferring, they concentrated on automobiles first. They stopped them, beat the occupants, turned the cars over in the street, and set fire to them. It was a muggy evening, with clouds low over the area, and the flames tipped them with crimson and apostrophes of smoke. Fire alarms were turned in; it became a game. When the pumpers and hook and ladders arrived at a burning car, rifle fire broke out from rooftops. The firemen dashed out of Watts. One gray-haired veteran took his helmet off, pushed his matted hair back, and said, "If they want that slum to burn down, who are we to stop them?"

Wednesday's games did not satisfy Thursday's crowds. The first big fire was set in a store one block from where Marquette Frye had been arrested. Looting began in earnest; cars were borrowed and made repeated trips to carry heavy merchandise from stores, and once empty, they were then set to the torch. When the mobs learned that the police on the perimeter of Watts would not stand their ground when challenged, the looters spread outside Watts.

Dick Gregory, a black comic, drove in from Ontario, California, and walked into the Seventy-seventh Precinct to tell the captain that he might be able to help. He was given a letter endorsing his presence to policemen and a bullhorn for addressing mobs. He drove into Watts with two young members of CORE. At Imperial and Central, the streetlights were out, but the flaming, crackling wooden buildings brightened the thoroughfare. Gregory identified himself; the people knew he was blood; they also knew that he was one of the hardest workers for black equality. He picked up the bullhorn and said, "Get your wives and kids off the street." There was something special in the tone. He was imploring the burners and looters to do something about their families which should have occurred to them. The crowd wasn't friendly. It was hostile and ashamed. "Get your wives and children off the street!" He hung the horn at his side. The crowd began to taunt him. He listened. The situation was more hopeless than he had thought possible. He spoke through the horn. "I didn't come here to tell you what to do and what not to do," he said, almost angrily. "I came here to tell you to get the women and kids in the house. If anything happens, they're going to be the first ones hit." The crowd taunted him again. Dick Gregory paid no attention now. He walked up and down the streets, begging people to go home. Somewhere a single shot was fired. "I'm hit!" Gregory said. His thigh had been grazed. Gregory limped toward the mob, holding the blood on his trouser leg. It was a form of bravery difficult to define. He went up to the people, speaking to one or two separately. He even located the man who had shot him. The rifleman apologized. Gregory said it didn't matter. "The important thing is to get home, get in before somebody gets killed." The crowd began to move away, began to break up. As he walked away, heading for a hospital, he heard a voice say, "We're gonna burn again tonight."

The cry remained "Burn, baby, burn!" but the action cry was "Beat that bastard. Teach him to keep his ass out of Watts." Street lights were shot out one by one. The Los Angeles police asked the county highway patrol for assistance. That group came into Watts in cars in single file. The youths on the rooftops could not miss. They hurled bricks, rocks, and Molotov cocktails. Within three minutes, five cars were in flames. At 111th Street and Avalon, the county police found 10 city policemen under attack by a crowd of 1,000. Blacks laughed. The police did not fire. The blacks knew they wouldn't. Sergeant Nicholson said his mouth was dry as his county group tried to rescue the handful of city policemen. "We were walking targets in the middle of the street," he said.

A peace meeting between Deputy Chief Roger Murdock and John Buggs, a black leader, proved worthless. Attending was the Reverend H. H. Brookins, a black peacemaker. Murdock wanted to know what would bring peace to Watts. The two men stated twin demands: (1) Pull all police out of Watts and allow black community leaders to restore law and order; (2) if the first proposal was unacceptable, send black officers only, and put them in civilian clothes and in unmarked cars. Murdock said no. He shrugged off the suggestion about black policemen with what Buggs and Brookins considered an affront: ". . . they don't make a conspicuous target at night."

Friday was another quiet and pretty day. Parts of Watts looked like a town passed in the tide of war. Governor Brown was flying home from

Athens. The White House was telephoning, demanding to know what had happened, what triggered it, and why it had not been stopped. Parts of the Fortieth Armored Division were ordered into Watts. In addition, 900 policemen and deputy sheriffs were ordered in. Too late, much too late, 2,900 lawmen were about to saturate the section. Besides, the presence of the troops and armored vehicles would amost certainly fan to life the graying embers of hatred.

As the curtain of night rose slowly, the action began. Rioters charged Oak Park Hospital, considered holy ground by both sides until the third evening. In another part of Watts, a three-block area was in flames and residents were screaming, dragging children and bedding down in the streets in the hot sucking wind. A small mob of young blacks took over two streets and set fires in fifteen buildings. There were more than a hundred streets in Watts, and all of them, on this night, became no-man's-land. Many residents phoned police and begged to have their families "evacuated," but the switchboard operators couldn't detect the authentic calls from the dangerous decoys.

The fury of the mob was underestimated. Early on Friday a phone call from the governor's office in Sacramento to a police sergeant at the Seventy-seventh Precinct brought this assessment: "Everything is pretty much under control now." By 10 P.M. Fire Department units were refusing to go into Watts, and ambulance drivers left their vehicles and refused to pick up the injured. There were fewer small crowds. Police radios reported: "Manchester and Broadway, crowd of one thousand. . . . Avalon and 114th, crowd of eight hundred. . . . 103rd and Clovis, fifteen hundred people." The crowds began to spread beyond Watts. Many were heading north, smashing stores in the direction of the Colosseum; others were raging south in Willowbrook and Compton. About 3,000 deadly weapons were stolen from sporting goods stores in one night.

"Burn, baby, burn!" Watts created its own shroud, hanging gray-black a thousand feet over the streets. "Whitey! Whitey! We got Whitey!" a mob roared as they caught thirty employees in a large department store. Police and Guard units closed in and rescued most of them.

At 4 A.M. on Saturday morning, the mobs scattered and went home to sleep. At dawn, protected ambulances began the search for the injured and the dead. Firemen fought to save whole blocks of buildings. An 8 P.M. curfew was placed on Watts. Like so many other official actions, this too was late. So was Governor Brown; so was Martin Luther King;

so was the military. Watts had an appointment with death, and everybody was late for it.

More national guardsmen were called in Saturday. The alerts for additional units continued. The biggest race riot in American history was going to require more than 13,000 soldiers, more than 1,000 policemen, and clanking monsters akin to tanks. Until evening, Saturday was almost as quiet as other days. Then a whole block of stores went up in flames on Broadway. The people of Watts were paying no attention to the curfew. Watts was a battle area, and the soldiers began to sweep the streets of people. There were 8,500 soldiers in there, with 5,000 working the perimeter of Watts. It was such a heavy array of firepower that officials wondered how the young mobs could continue to loot, to set fire, to run through alleys. After midnight, Watts became a charred ghost town. The only sounds were heavy military boots clopping slowly on sidewalks, rifles at the ready, looking into dark empty windows for dark empty faces.

On Sunday, Watts began to become sick of itself. The crowds were smaller, more furtive. Some contented themselves with standing on street corners to shout insults at police and soldiers. Governor Brown was in the State Building, listening to many sides of a many-sided story.

In the afternoon, Dr. Martin Luther King arrived in a car. With him were Andrew Young and Bayard Rustin. The pastor was well protected and was driven up and down the dismal sunny streets with brick walls lying in streets, past houses with hollow black eyes, streets of stores gutted of merchandise, and small knots of growing boys. The car stopped several times and he walked through ruins to get to a small group of boys. "I'm Dr. Martin Luther King," he said.

One boy grinned. "We won," he said.

"How can you say you won?" asked the pastor, pointing to a burned-out town.

"We won," the boy explained, "because we made them pay attention to us." King rode up and down the littered streets, talking and counseling, assuring the people he would try to mediate for them. The violence and destruction shocked him, and his words of love and brotherhood fell on deaf ears.

On Monday the people of Watts heard the dread words "hunger" and "disease." There were few places where 80,000 people could shop, buy food or medication, and doctors would not make house calls. Black leaders, who had remained in hiding throughout the rioting, now appealed for government assistance in feeding and treating the rioters. On Tuesday Governor Edmund G. Brown ended the curfew. The troops began to pull out of the area. Funerals became the order of the day.

The State of California and the City of Los Angeles began to add the cost of Watts:

> Dead: 35
> Injured: 883
> In jail: 3,598
> ———
>   4,516

Damage by fire: $175,000,000. Damage to property: $46,000,000. Merchandise looted: $1,000,000. Total: $222,000,000. Watts, in its wrath, had disemboweled itself. The final fires had been wetted down when the governor announced the formation of a biracial committee of seven members; Lyndon Johnson sent LeRoy Collins to "consult"; within a week, the federal government agreed to send $20,000,000 to clean Watts' face.

Overnight, many tons of food were shipped into Watts. Anyone who lacked food needed only to wait in line and take emergency rations. One black man opened the package of food and dropped it to the floor: "Look what they're giving us," he said in disgust. "TV dinners."

In Washington the Johnson administration was conscious of the deep and desperate struggle of the black man to be accepted as an equal, and Lyndon Johnson was trying to resolve the struggle in favor of the black. But who was his leader? Whom could Johnson deal with? Race riots were erupting in many parts of the country, and they polarized the blacks from the whites. The black militant wanted revenge while Martin Luther King wanted peace. Floyd McKissick, the new director of CORE, made excessive and immediate demands on the White Establishment, with the threat of violence as a "persuader." Elijah Muhammad asked the Muslims to live separately from the "White Devils"; Roy Wilkins of the NAACP worked for the end of ghettos and the beginning of fair housing integration. A new unit in Oakland, California, calling itself the Panthers, was armed to the teeth and was ready to establish a separate nation of blacks.

The blacks never had a leader. There was no man who could represent 22,000,000 people of varying degrees of militancy and apathy. The black graduating *summa cum laude* from Harvard University couldn't understand what the Alabama farm black was talking about. Who in Watts was a leader? Jesse Jackson was a Chicago leader, but he had the support of less than half his blacks. Adam Clayton Powell was a Harlem leader, but if a riot started, he too would have to run for cover. The Nobel Prize winner preached peace, love, and nonviolence, but war and hate were in his wake.

The President remembered his promise to Dr. King to arrange a meeting with United Nations Ambassador Arthur Goldberg to be "briefed" about Vietnam. The meeting took place on September 10, President Johnson was trying to stop King from making more anti-Vietnam statements. Only the President, the Cabinet, the National Security Council, and a few leaders in Congress were aware of the under-the-table moves being negotiated between the United States and North Vietnam. Dr. King was about to be made privy to whatever the Chief Executive and the UN ambassador thought they could divulge without violating national security.

Dr. King brought with him Bayard Rustin, Bernard Lee, and Andrew Young. The ambassador made it a cordial visit, as well as an informative one. Dr. King was told that Mr. Goldberg and the President, dealing through neutral embassies, had hopes that Ho Chi Minh was about ready to start peace talks. Any public utterances by Dr. King or any other imposing American figure which called for a laying down of arms would give aid and comfort to the enemy and would stiffen his position. The United States must be unified on this question, or it would be bogged in Southeast Asia for years to come.

King listened and asked questions. Bayard Rustin, the politically conscious member of the team, also had questions to ask. King was mollified but would not commit himself on future policy. President Johnson got a digest of the talk, and asked Vice President Hubert Humphrey to invite a few black leaders for a short cruise on the Potomac. On September 15, the Presidential yacht slipped its moorings in the basin at eventide and started downriver to Mount Vernon, where the home of George Washington could be seen on the southern shore. There, a military band played "The Star-Spangled Banner," the captain of the yacht swung to port, and the yacht was turned back toward Washington.

Humphrey was acknowledged, by blacks, to be the best friend they had in Washington. He did not fake his enthusiasm for the black man's aspirations. This made him the best man to soften the black leaders in their attitude toward the Johnson administration's policy in Vietnam. Aboard the yacht, recipients of the "royal treatment" were Dr. King; Whitney Young, of the Urban League; Clarence Mitchell, leader of the Washington chapter of the NAACP; Andrew Young, of the SCLC; and Floyd McKissick, of CORE.

The party sat aft in wicker chairs, discussing black problems. The Vice President could talk faster than any of them—and did. He ticked off the accomplishments of the current administration for the black and promised more to come. The breeze became strong, and the party moved inside to the old-fashioned paneled main cabin. They sipped drinks and talked more. It was a pleasant sail but did not lead to a solution of the plight of the American black or of the white men who tried to help him.

Collie Leroy Wilkins, one of the men in the back of the car which had pulled up beside Viola Liuzzo's car on that dark night in Alabama, was on trial for his life. He had been a member of the Ku Klux Klan. The FBI informant who had infiltrated the Klan and sat in the car with Collie Wilkins was prepared to testify that it was Wilkins who shot Mrs. Liuzzo. If Wilkins was afraid, he concealed it well. The first trial ended with a hung jury—no verdict. The second, prosecuted by State Attorney General Richmond Flowers, was another matter. Mr. Flowers was taking dead aim at the Klansman. "The blood of this man's sins," he said to the jury, "if you do not find him guilty, will stain the very soul of our county for an eternity."

The attorney general was trying, but he too was bucking a tradition as old as the harvesting of cotton. Some members of the jury admitted that they felt that civil rights workers were inferior human beings. The court ruled that they were qualified to be jurors. Flowers appealed to the Alabama Supreme Court. The lower court ruling was upheld. On the jury were six men who admitted that they were White Supremacists. Wilkins was acquitted of murder in a storm of applause in the courtroom.

Sixty days later, a jury in Selma acquitted three white men of beating the Reverend James J. Reeb to death.

And yet man made one small step forward. In September, when the schools were ready to open, Atlanta would be desegregating a few schools. Coretta King took the children and enrolled them in one. It was something.

6

Time, for Martin Luther King, became a prison. The hour, the minute became the bars from which he struggled to free himself. The waking time seemed to shrink. So did sleeping time. He was the highly respected international gentleman of note he had aspired to be; but the bigness chafed, the demands impaired his church work, the flights to faraway cities irritated the husband and father. In addition, there was the question of which specific goal was to be tackled next. The Movement dared not stand still; like a corporation, it thrived on expansion and successful ventures. Big, bigger, biggest.

His shadow, his bodyguard, his double in appearance, Bernard Lee, was young but worn out. The two men averaged 20,000 miles a month in travel. Often there was no time at home. The flight plan would be to Canada to a dinner, to Los Angeles for a fund-raising speech, to Miami for a ministerial conference, a school in Wisconsin, a seminar with leaders in Washington, on to New York, then maybe, just maybe, a plane to Atlanta, hurry-up kisses from Coretta King and the children, dictation of letters in the den, a swift visit to the SCLC headquarters and a conference with Ralph Abernathy, then back to the airport.

There was a book to be written and no time to write it. There was a love of reading and no time to read. Dr. King dozed in a window seat on planes, and Bernard Lee read *Time* magazine, *Newsweek,* The New York *Times,* and the Atlanta *Constitution.* The shadow had to digest all the important stories and remember them, then repeat them to the substance. When the jet landed—wherever it landed—the local press was waiting. Dr. King had to compose thoughts and phrases while the plane was in flight so that he would have something to say when he landed. Sometimes, in a strange hotel in a strange city, King would awaken with the phone ringing. Often, it was Harry Belafonte. "You need a rest. You're killing yourself. Come to Aruba and spend a week." This would bring a fatigued smile, and the pastor would tell his friend how he would love to go, love to sit in the sand and think of nothing, love to forget time. But he didn't have the time to forget time.

In the late hours, there were knocks on the hotel room door. Lee answered all of them. Often, there were strange women in the corridor. Young or old, black or white, their notions of the best way of expressing admiration were questionable and beyond realization.

Lee screened male visitors, too. Business executives, municipal officials appeared at hotels and asked to see King. Bernard Lee could do no better than postpone. He would ask for a telephone number and say he hoped that the doctor would have time to call back. He seldom did. The time for the morning shower, at six thirty, became shorter and shorter. Shaving lotions and razors gave way to odoriferous creams. Ties were often left on chairs knotted, so that they could be slipped over the neck in the morning.

The year 1966 started by staring coldly at Martin Luther King. The bus boycott was a decade behind him and Dr. King was laden with honors, but a missionary is no better than his most recent convert.

"Chicago," Dr. King said. The SCLC had made timid forays into the North before, but this would be a full-scale campaign. The directors were reluctant, but the indomitable president had pointed to a map and said, "Chicago." So that would be the next target. "If we can break the backbone of discrimination in Chicago, we can do it in all the cities of this country," King stated.

Chicago was a complex and contradictory city when it came to race relations. It had no segregation laws; it had a huge and politically potent black population; Chicago had a black Congressman; it had black aldermen and black ward leaders; it had black banks; black insurance companies; black policemen; not least, it had the Reverend Jesse Jackson browbeating white shop owners into hiring more and more blacks; it had an old-line Democratic mayor, Richard J. Daley, who had the black vote in his hip pocket. On the other hand, most of Chicago's more than 900,000 blacks lived in ghettos, working at inferior jobs for less pay. Their housing, their schools, their stores, and their public utilities were substandard. A large part of the black ghetto population was on welfare, receiving checks from the government while not working, and paying the price of public charity by being unable to own automobiles or property. Beyond the ghettos were the Chicago suburbs, some of the most racist areas in the United States.

Martin Luther King could find but one black enemy in Chicago. He was Dr. Joseph Harrison Jackson, president of the 5,000,000-member National Baptist Convention, the man who had literally read Dr. King out of the black Baptist organization. Dr. Jackson was a figure of such prestige that Pope John XXIII had invited him to attend the Second Ecumenical Conference in 1962. There is no indication that Dr. Jackson approved of anything that Dr. King did or said.

"If we can break the backbone" was a poorly chosen phrase for the man who preached nonviolence. The SCLC staff told Dr. King that the "groundwork" for Chicago was running to $10,000 a month, and in spite of all the natural allies he could find there, more and more field secretaries would have to be paid to go North to work. Icy winds and blinding snow swept downtown Chicago in January, and no one on the SCLC staff enjoyed the prospect of working there in the winter.

King decided that he could understand Chicago's problems better if he lived in the ghetto along with the black man he was trying to help. His advance agents rented four rooms for him in an old tenement in the Lawndale section, a slum abutted on the east by a house of correction; on the south by an isolation hospital for communicable diseases; and on the west by one of the most racist little towns in America—Cicero. The landlord hastily had the rooms freshly repainted, had the heating system fixed, and fumigated the apartment.

About 200 people were in the street when the doctor drove up to accept occupancy. They cheered. He looked around at the old buildings, and he was muffled against the cold as he told reporters that President Johnson's two billion three hundred million dollar outlay for rebuilding cities was "encouraging, but we are going to need billions and billions." At City Hall the pastor walked up the front steps; no one stopped him. Two policemen saluted as he went in to be welcomed to the city of Chicago by Mayor Daley. The mayor was a large man with pink skin and a built-in scowl.

Daley was not effusive; he was polite. All city departments, he said, had been ordered to cooperate with King. The mayor was telling the pastor that there would be no reason for riots and fire; Chicago was standing at his side. King also met Police Superintendent O. W. Wilson and his staff. "I believe," the mayor said dryly, "that this is the first police department in the country that he has met with." The newspapers quoted Dr. King as stating that in Chicago he was ready to "break any law for the cause of civil rights."

"I am confident," the mayor told the press of City Hall, "that there will not be any reason for breaking the law."

Next, King drove out to the big Tudor house in which Elijah Muhammad lived and made peace with him. It is possible that Dr. King feared the Muslims of Chicago and what they might do to him, but this is doubtful. Whatever the reason, Muhammad did not come to him; he went to Muhammad. When the meeting was over, Elijah made no announcement. King did. "The time has come when we, the Negroes, must see our mutual problems. It is not the time for us to be fighting each other." He spoke of the Muslims and the SCLC forming "a common front."

The reaction was bewilderment. The Muslim fundamental principle was to separate the races; the SCLC's was to bring them together. One was violent; one nonviolent. The first believed that Allah was God; the second proclaimed Jesus Christ. The "common front" was perhaps that both men agreed not to intrude on the other's work. One thing was certain: The press could not get a comment from a leader of any black organization on the meeting.

The doctor conferred frequently with Chicago civic leaders and civil rights leaders. These people each had certain local knowledge and some municipal power. They were ready to recognize King's greatness, but they wanted to know what kind of campaign he proposed. They asked for the specifics: What are the goals? Point out the enemy. How many people do you have? How many do you want? Where and when will public demonstrations be held? But whenever concrete plans were mentioned, Dr. King could not bring the dissident groups together.

The Reverend James Orange, one of his staff, tried to solicit sympathy for Dr. King in the ghetto areas and sustained eighteen beatings by black gangs. He and James Bevel had been in Chicago since October, and they learned that "blood" was insufficient for insuring a man against getting killed by gangs like the Cobras and the Vice Lords.

There were 3,500,000 residents in Chicago, and more than 900,000 were black. "More Negroes here," King said, "than in the whole State of Mississippi." But they were not tenant farmers. The vision of Christ on the cross could not move them, as it did in the South. Hosea Williams, a strong militant, felt depressed. "We're used to working with people who want to be freed," he said. Chicago, hog butcher to the world, butchered its people. Greed was the credo; the poor black paid $100 a month for an apartment which, in another area, would go to whites for $80. The corner grocery charged from two to eight cents more for a can of tomato soup or a quart of milk. The time payment plan was the best device the slum merchant had; he didn't want cash. Interest averaged from 25 to 40 percent.

SNCC and CORE had strength and tried to overthrow the system in the ghettos, but could not agree on a policy. Dick Gregory said he would run for mayor of Chicago against Richard Daley, and some said that was the funniest line the comic uttered. Dr. King placed trust in the word and the leadership of an independent, the Reverend Albert A. Raby, but he could not bring the dissident groups together.

Charles Sherrod, solemn and friendly, told Martin Luther King that this time he was "out of your depth." The weakness of the King campaign was that the staff, working inside Chicago for ninety days, had not done its task. It had practically no rapport with the Urban League, with CORE, with SNCC, the NAACP, each of which had worked Chicago so long that their officers regarded it as a second home. A director of the Urban League, Bill Berry, who admired Dr. King, stated with sorrow that "the field workers and the young people did not understand that the methods of Selma are not transferable intact to Chicago."

The Chicago *Sun-Times,* which, like the Chicago *Tribune* and other papers, had reporters accompanying Dr. King all day every day, found one great good coming from his campaign. Slum landlords who heard that King had been walking up and down their street sent painters and plumbers at once. They could not afford citations for building code violations and sanitary code violations. None of them had previously feared the Chicago building inspectors, who remained friendly to landlords and overlooked unworkable toilets and sinks, plaster falling from ceilings, lack of heat, and infestation of rats so dangerous that couples with infants took turns sitting up all night. The *Sun-Times* said that if Dr. King kept walking, his presence might stimulate a "healthful and helpful shock wave in every street." Eight of every ten buildings in Lawndale were sixty years of age or more; the unemployment rate among blacks was 7.6 percent at a time when the national average was 3.4 percent. Many who did part-time work were classified as "underemployed." Welfare families could not easily seek employment outside Lawndale because that would require an automobile, and a car would automatically make them ineligible for relief.

The campaign was almost a month in being and had not moved. Downtown, the rich and powerful business community awaited the explosion which would burst the seams of Chicago, but there was no explosion. Dr. King was feeling his way around a big tough city. But he was in the wrong place. There were 300,000 blacks on the West Side where he lived. There were more than 600,000 living on the South Side, where he was seldom seen.

However, neither he nor James Bevel worried about the inactivity. In Atlanta, they had worked up a chart which allowed eighteen months for the SCLC to achieve success in Chicago. Bevel wanted permission to organize a slum union of tenants on the West Side and South Side, people who would pledge not to pay any rent unless conditions were bettered. If enough agreed to the plan, the city could not make them comply. But King advised thinking about it awhile. Bevel also counseled what he called "Cold Cut Weekends," during which residents would use neither gas nor electricity. By cutting their revenue, he reasoned, the utility companies would be forced to improve service. King was cautious about this, too.

Mayor Daley had friends inside the Movement, and he was advised of each new plan. The rent strike idea caused him to prod the Building Department into sending inspectors through the slums west and south looking for violations. They found them. One of the first landlords to feel the wrath of the city was Claude M. Lightfoot, leader of the Communist Party in Illinois. This rocked Chicago with laughter. No one had known that the topmost comrade owned a slum dwelling at 3443 West Twelfth Place. Eleven violations were charged against Lightfoot. He was embarrassed. "I made no profit on the building," he said, "and my income taxes will show it."

Warily, Richard Daley watched the hiatus spread peaceably over January and part of February. His intelligence units were working inside the SCLC, and wonderment grew in City Hall that the nonviolent preacher was still spending three days of each week in Chicago and no violence followed him. The spell was broken in the middle of February. It began with street fights and shouting. By the third night, roving gangs, looters, and snipers to the number of 5,000 were working the West Side. A thousand policemen were ordered into the area. Shopwindows were smashed; looters stole; fire bombs rolled into empty shops.

Governor Kerner sent 1,500 national guardsmen, with carbines and bayonets, into the area. Dr. King drove from one area to the next in a car, preaching nonviolence through a rolled-down window, but the people paused only long enough to point with wonderment and shout,

"Look! Martin Luther King!" before they returned to their work. A bottling plant and packing company plant tossed millions of bright fire-flies into the night sky as they burned. Bands of blacks were found in the slums testing revolvers. Police vans picked up looters by the hundreds. Young boys with fire bombs were interrogated by police to find out who had instructed them in their use. As a result, Mayor Daley issued a statement in which he accused black leaders of planning the riots. There was nothing spontaneous about them, he insisted. He refrained from accusing Dr. King but said that King's staff was in Chicago "for no other purpose than to bring disorder to the city." He added that Dr. King's assistants had shown still photos and motion pictures of the riots in Watts to young blacks.

The politicians were surprised when the pastor said yes, that the Reverend James Bevel of his staff had been showing pictures of the Los Angeles riots. They were shown, he maintained, to display the "nega-tive" aspect of rioting. He and Bevel had called the violent gang leaders in to see "how rioters destroy their own neighborhoods and accomplish nothing." Neither King nor Bevel had thought of the possibility that the motion pictures would have the opposite effect on black gangs, that the vision of blacks running amok through white stores and apartments, rifling, looting, burning, and clips showing dazed policemen cruising by slowly, afraid to make an arrest, would embolden Chicago hoodlums to emulate Watts.

The three-day riots did enormous damage and broke the solid image of black leadership into fragments, so that some favored Daley and others favored King. The riots stopped when the national guardsmen were told, "If you are fired on, shoot to kill." When the ghetto was quiet, Dr. King went to City Hall for a conference with Daley and came out with a four-point agreement: (1) Sprinklers would be installed on fire hydrants so that black children could splash and play in the summer-time; (2) Daley would request federal funds for swimming pools; (3) a racially mixed committee would be appointed to counsel the Police Department on improving its relationship with minority groups; (4) put two workers in each police precinct in the riot zone to help the people keep the peace.

By any standard, it was a small piece of cake to be cut for 900,000 mouths. On his part, Dr. King requested the leaders of the three biggest gangs—Cobras, Roman Saints, and Vice Lords—to come to his apart-ment at 1550 South Hanlin Street for a conference. He heard their grievances, separated the lies from the truth, and counseled that more could be accomplished in dealing with "Whitey" peacefully than by starting a war.

Stokely Carmichael, the fiery star of SNCC, arrived in Chicago and made a speech to the young which, to them, made more sense: "The only nonviolence we need," he said, "is nonviolence among ourselves. We've been shooting and cutting the wrong people." His audience cheered.

Daley invited twenty-five black ministers to City Hall for a full afternoon conference on black needs and how to satisfy them. Dr. King was invited but would not attend. The mayor passed out fact sheets to the clergy showing what Chicago had already done, what Chicago was committed to do this year, and asked the men to spend time conferring with their parishioners on what ought to be done. The mayor was in a smiling mood on a gusty March afternoon. He said that neither he nor his assistants had a monopoly on which measures were best for the common good and which were not. That is why he solicited their collective knowledge. He wanted each man to feel free to strike off the list any of the proposals which, for practical purposes, would be a waste of funds and to tack on whatever each thought were "primary" needs.

The next conference was in two weeks. Dr. King was again invited, and again he did not attend. He was in Europe with Harry Belafonte raising money for the SCLC. The entertainer was probably the largest single donor of money to the SCLC. A percentage of his earnings on his singing tour through Europe went to Dr. King.

Attorney Stanley Levison, who supervised the SCLC funds and investments, warned King that if he made more public pronouncements on Vietnam, he would bankrupt his organization. To Martin Luther King, this was a tender nerve. "I don't care if we don't get five cents in the mail," he said, outraged. "I am going to keep on preaching my message." He was back in Chicago on March 25 to lead a peace march to the Coliseum. He spoke the truth as he saw it when he told the crowd: "We must combine the fervor of the civil rights movement with the peace movement." The people applauded politely. They had little interest in wars far away. Until the roar of cannon fire rattled the windows of their homes, they could feel no interest in Vietnam or the problems of Israel, China, and the Soviet Union. And yet King felt that he was winning the people to his point of view.

The following month he addressed a fund-raising banquet in Great

Neck, New York. As King glanced, nodding and smiling, at the faces along the dais, he could not help being impressed by the absence of many civil rights leaders. Wilkins wasn't present. Forman wasn't. Lewis, Carmichael, Randolph—the list was endless. The man who was there was Whitney Young. The half-white half-black face stared at Martin Luther King without expression. When the two men met at the conclusion of the speeches, an argument broke out. Dr. King wanted to talk about Vietnam. Young's tongue was bitter and rude. Dr. King lost his composure. He began to shout. "Whitney," he said, "what you're saying may get you a foundation grant, but it won't get you into the kingdom of truth."

Young stood back and studied Dr. King's expensive suit and alligator shoes. The crusher was accompanied by a sarcastic smile. "Martin, you're eating well." Friends of both men kept saying "Hush!" and "Please be quiet!" At last, several men stepped between the two.

Frustration is common enough among all men, but to James Earl Ray it was a full-time career. On the night of March 10, 1966, he made his third escape attempt. Ray bunched up his blankets to make a contour dummy in his bunk, precisely as seen in the movies, and climbed a metal pole to a window twelve feet above his cell floor. He had stolen a pair of wire cutters, and these were used to make a hole slightly larger than a square yard in heavy mesh covering a window. Slowly, he snaked through the hole and found himself on top of an interior prison wall. Quietly, he crept along the wall until he came to a fan ventilator. He crept inside and curled up.

The idea was to wait until the penitentiary was quiet, then to crawl to the three-story administration building, an acrobatic feat of note, scale the roof, and climb to the outer wall, then to drop down into the street. Ray began his escape at 9 P.M., when the lights went out. By 9:30 a guard passing the cell decided that the form in James Earl Ray's bunk didn't look like him. So he unlocked the cell door and found he was right. Within a few minutes, the alarm was sounded, and guards in pairs searched the prison.

Some had no more intelligence than he. They couldn't find out how he had got out of the cell. No one thought of looking up. The guards kept searching for twenty-seven hours. The following night, exhausted, James Earl Ray crept out of the fan and gave himself up. He was frisked and found to have a few dollars, two razor blades, a cracked mirror, and a small package of pills. This time the warden was not in a forgiving mood. Ignorance and stupidity are afflictions, and no man is entirely free of either of them; but Ray seemed to have no other qualities.

McCormick V. Wilson was appointed by the Jefferson City Circuit Court to represent James Earl Ray, but the best suggestion he got from his client was to request a mental examination. It was granted, and Ray was taken in handcuffs from Jefferson City to the Fulton State Hospital. The doctors required thirty-nine days to work up a mental and emotional evaluation of the prisoner. The superintendent, Dr. Donald B. Peterson, said the findings were negative. "He showed no more nervousness than the average person facing trial," he said. "He was rather reserved, but we just didn't find anything unusual. There was nothing in his mental makeup or background to indicate anything but a recidivistic criminal whose crimes were all associated with money."

With money. The biography of James Earl Ray is a story of a slow mentality in search of money. Money was God; money was all. If he had escaped, it is certain that Ray would have spent his time devising a crime which he called "one big lick" and, with his proclivity for poor planning, would probably have been back in a few months. The only other obsession the doctors could find was that James Earl Ray was a hypochondriac. He read as many medical books as possible, used Latin terms for body organs, and, in one burst of illnesses, assured the physicians "I have all of these." He also had a suspicion that he had cancer and heart disease.

The court gave him additional time to dwell on money and sickness.

The civil rights movement, from its inception, was akin to a giant flywheel on a generator. When the Movement reached top speed, no one pulled back on the power. More and more was applied by more and more radical leaders. King was losing control of the flywheel; so were the usurpers. The Movement was racing eccentrically, and soon the wheel must smash itself.

The whites, even the liberal whites, said the blacks were moving ahead too fast. The United States was trying to undo, overnight, what it had done to the black man for 200 years. Whereas formerly a black could not get a job in a big white establishment, corporations made it a matter of company policy to bring more and more blacks into their organizations. The government, the states, the counties, and the municipalities were doing the same thing. It became a good thing to be a black. On radio and television, he suddenly appeared in white dramas and commercial advertising. Always, he was cast in a good light; the day of Stepin Fetchet and Amos and Andy was dead. There were many who did not want to oppose a black in a lawsuit because he was a black.

Black leaders were demanding so many demands, promising so many promises, that the flywheel spun faster. In Hollywood, California, Dr. King was addressing a huge church assembly, saying, "The Negro is freer today than he was ten years ago, but he is not yet free. The Negro enjoys more dignity than ever before in our history, but he is not equal." He envisioned a peaceful revolution, he said, but revolutions cost money—"money now being spent on war."

John Lewis convened SNCC at Nashville, Tennessee, and said that he was opposed to excluding whites from policy-making within the organization. This cost him his job as president. He was replaced by Stokely Carmichael. One of Carmichael's first official acts was to decline an invitation extended by President Johnson for a civil rights conference in Washington. In the next breath, Carmichael said he was opposed to integration as an "insidious subterfuge for white supremacy. . . ."

In the middle of May, white and black peace groups met in Washington to protest continuance of the war in Vietnam. Fifteen thousand people were present, led by a psychologist-pediatrician, Dr. Benjamin Spock, and the chaplain of Yale University, William Sloane Coffin. Martin Luther King wasn't present, but he sent a message, which was read by Coffin: "The pursuit of widened war has narrowed domestic welfare programs, making the poor, white and Negro, bear the heaviest burdens at the front and at home." In addition, he accepted the post of co-chairman of a group called Clergy and Laymen Concerned About Vietnam. Roy Wilkins of the NAACP, who tried to remain above the politics of the Movement, was moved to criticize King publicly for mixing the issues of war and racial struggle. But as SNCC paid no attention to King, King paid no attention to the NAACP.

The White House conference on civil rights was held the first week of June. President Lyndon Johnson, reader of newspapers and watcher of television, realized that the Movement was dangerously askew and insisted that he go over the list of 2,400 invitations one by one. Stokely Carmichael had already spurned attendance. Johnson didn't want Martin Luther King to hold any office but was willing to invite him as a guest. King's subordinate in the SCLC, Walter Fauntroy of Washington, was designated vice-chairman of the conference. Ben Heineman, president of the Chicago and Northwestern Railroad, was named chairman.

A. Philip Randolph was honorary chairman. The sensitive Vietnam question was placed in the hands of Howard University's president, James Nabrit, Jr.

The convention was barely in session when President Johnson, who carefully staged his surprises, appeared and said that he would like to indulge himself in the unprecedented act of a President of the United States: introducing someone who was not a chief of state. He introduced Thurgood Marshall, whom he had appointed the first black Solicitor General. The two-day conference had been planned to the minute. Marshall spoke glowingly of civil rights gains made under the Johnson administration. Floyd McKissick handed an anti-Vietnam War resolution to Dr. Nabrit, who called for a committee vote, which killed it. Whitney Young told the White House press corps, "The Negro is more concerned about the rat at night and the job in the morning than he is about the war in Vietnam."

Dr. King's advisers met with him at a hotel after the opening day and advised him to withdraw from the conference. He was being snubbed by the President. The pastor didn't reflect before making a decision. He said he would attend the second and closing session. He did, and he spoke briefly in support of Randolph's plan for helping the American black. Mrs. King came closer to stage center. The convention asked her to sing.

There was Chicago. There was always Chicago; but summer was close, and the old refrigerator in the smelly kitchen could melt ice into water much better than it could reverse the process. Lawndale was depressing: it was not Martin Luther King's town. He had never known a Lawndale. There had to be another place, a place that needed him.

There was. In June, James Meredith began walking south on Route 51 in Mississippi. Once he had braved the violence of the white man to enter the halls of the University of Mississippi. He had read that freedom had come for the black man. He would see. With three friends, he began a lonely 210-mile trek from the Tennessee border to the state capital at Jackson. It is a long empty highway, unless Meredith counted such places as Hernando and Senatobia and Batesville and Grenada as exciting. The June days were hot with a big brass sun standing still in the sky and the poplars and elms on the sides of Route 51 holding their breath for a breeze. The nights were black as the four companions in dry grass listening to the pond frogs belch and the crickets chirp and the rising sound of an automobile coming hard and fast, the sound diminishing to a whimper over the next hill.

Meredith had to make this walk. If no white man stopped him, if no highway patrol car stopped and a voice said, "Hey, boy!," if no cell door clanked open for no reason, if no pale fist smashed his mouth, then he and his frightened friends would reach Jackson and they could say that truly freedom had come to Mississippi. He walked down through Hernando, and he kept to the side of the road, hands in pockets, head down, the feet replacing each other in front of his gaze. Soon the big reservoir would be on his right, trees near the edge drinking freely and bending over the edge to indulge their narcissism. A shot fractured the still air, and James Meredith fell. The three friends ran.

The shotgun blast came from wild shrubs behind him. The shell was filled with small birdshot. James Meredith had sixty pellets in the head, neck, back, and legs. Cars stopped. Police were called. Meredith was not dead. He was conscious. The patrol cars fanned out and picked up the white man with the shotgun. He was not a Mississippian. "Then why did you do it?" an officer asked.

The man shrugged. His brows wrinkled in a frown. "I don't know," he said. "I just don't know."

The wounded man said he didn't want to go to a Mississippi hospital. "Where you want to go, boy?" He said Memphis. They drove him north and put him in a hospital bed. Meredith was in no danger. The first radio news flashes had announced that James Meredith, the "Mississippi loner" had been ambushed in Mississippi and shot dead. The news electrified most civil rights leaders. Stinging sweat was running down hot cheeks, and the long, long summer had barely begun. There is no cause like a dead crusader; nothing matches it for stomping apathy to death. There *was* a place other than dreary Lawndale.

Memphis was the place to be. So said Martin Luther King. So said Floyd McKissick; so said Stokely Carmichael and Jim Lawson of the Memphis SCLC and Bernard Lee and the black reverends. Everybody who was anybody in civil rights headed for Memphis.

When Dr. Martin Luther King and Floyd McKissick of CORE arrived at the bedside, Meredith told them that he planned to check out. His wounds, though painful, were superficial. King and McKissick paced the room advising the new martyr to stay right where he was—at least for several days. No one could evict him from a hospital if he was still in pain. He could remain there, and they proposed to start a new, bigger

Mississippi march to Jackson. They would start from the spot where he had been shot. His name was on the lips of America as an innocent student felled by a white racist's bullet.

Meredith's doctor had told him he could check out when he wished, and the young man was determined to leave the hospital. He got dressed and took the next plane to New York. There he held a press conference and, in the middle of it, fainted. This was recorded by television, radio, and newspapers and made it appear that Meredith was more grievously wounded than he realized. The Meredith March was on.

In Washington, Representative Emanuel Celler of Brooklyn said, "There are times when the civil rights movement has no greater friend than its enemy." Officials of Mississippi agreed. There had been a degree of racial peace in the state since the last march, since the burial of three civil rights workers in an earthen dam near Philadelphia. Official Mississippi was banging its fists against walls. Mississippians no longer wanted blacks lynched, shot at, or maimed. The result, in the past few years, was an agony of marching chanting blacks baiting the whites. Mississippi stood a faint chance of settling back into its antebellum attitude of paternalism toward the "nigger," if outsiders would remain out of Mississippi and leave the "niggers" to the state. This was the new philosophy. An outsider, unknown, had come in and, with one blast, spoiled it. There would be all hell to pay, and Mississippi knew it.

On June 8, the marchers assembled at the spot on Route 51 where the shooting had occurred, and Governor Paul Johnson announced testily that this time he would provide police protection "to see that these demonstrators get all the marching they want." King, McKissick, Carmichael, Roy Wilkins, and Fannie Lou Hamer of the Mississippi Freedom Democratic Party led the little army. Women dressed in their Sunday best, with dark dresses, white hats, and sunglasses. The men, bareheaded, wore T-shirts and slacks; some wore open-neck sports shirts. They chanted and sang, and there were long silences, too. They walked slowly, in no hurry to finish the 200 miles, a dark slender hatpin striking into the white heart of Mississippi. It could have been turned back by tear gas and guns, but this would have led to bigger, more purposeful marches. The overall vision was one of many people on an afternoon walk, loosely knit and not in ranks, the sun hot and hard, the spinached hummocks of cool trees tempting their eyes.

Highway patrol cars moved up and down the outer flank of the marchers, squeezing them toward the side. This was the "protection." The police said that their fenders came close to stragglers because they were wandering out on 51 and someone was going to be killed by a passing car. In the evening the marchers, without suitcases and changes of clothes, without motels or roofs, sat on the open roadside and kicked shoes off and rubbed tender feet.

Automobiles arrived and took the leaders back to Memphis. They stayed at the Reverend James Lawson's Centenary Methodist Church. They had dinner and then conferred. The weakness in the situation was that they had a "spontaneous march" on their hands, with no means of considering the welfare and daily needs of the marchers. Martin Luther King wanted to discuss that problem. Young Stokely Carmichael had other ideas. He had been on a collision course with Martin Luther King for a long time, and he wanted a showdown now. "I'm not going to beg the white man for anything I deserve," he said flatly. "I'm going to take it." The argument began about the importance of violence. King became acidulous. He said he favored nonviolence because it was the only *practical* means of attaining rights. "I can't imagine anything more impractical and disastrous for any of us, through misguided judgment, to precipitate a violent confrontation in Mississippi. We have neither the resources nor the techniques to win."

They talked in a Memphis motel until the early hours. Although the leaders were aware that the march could be a bloody one, Dr. King's eloquence prevailed. He won the votes of Roy Wilkins and Whitney Young for nonviolence. Floyd McKissick agreed to go along with them this one time. The group drew up a march manifesto urging everybody to suffer in silence. President Johnson was asked to send federal voting registrars to Mississippi at once. In the morning there was a new enemy. Charles Evers, director of the Mississippi NAACP, complained that his signature was on the manifesto and he had not been consulted. He was brutally candid. "I don't want this to turn into another Selma," he said, "where everyone goes home with the cameramen and leaves us holding the bag."

Martin Luther King was all but commuting between Chicago and the march. He flew to Chicago that morning and would be back soon on Route 51 to march again.

The people marched. In the morning, the leaders walked behind the sound trucks with lively step and smiling faces. The trucks left. A car pulled up, and Dr. King said farewell. Evers marched, but he didn't like it. "I don't see how walking up and down a hot highway helps," he said. "I'm for walking house to house and fence to fence to get Negroes registered." He had to be mollified. The leaders stopped in the town of

Panola and showed fifty blacks the way to the courthouse to be registered. Grenada, which was trying to register blacks, became inundated with work when the marchers stopped there. Of a black population numbering 8,000, only 700 had been registered. The march stopped long enough to lead 1,300 more to the courthouse.

Once the marchers passed by, the black registrars were fired. No more blacks approached the courthouse. Dr. King returned to the march, and Charles Evers criticized him and his stand on Vietnam to the press. Some of the marchers changed the lyrics of "We Shall Overcome" to "We Shall Overrun." Others sang: "Jingle bells/ Shotgun shells/ Freedom all the way/ Oh, what fun it is to blast/ A trooper man away." Carmichael insisted on stopping the march in Greenwood, where he had once been arrested. Dr. King was opposed to the idea, but the militants won the day and the march stopped.

Stokely Carmichael stood up before 600 patient walkers. He saw the metal helmets of the police around the perimeter and, beyond them, the frightened local people. Although no police were attempting to rescue him, he shouted, "This is the twenty-seventh time I have been arrested, and I ain't going to jail no more. What we need is Black Power!" It wasn't a new term. Carmichael had used it before. About 1920, Marcus Garvey had used it. In 1954, Richard Wright wrote a book about Ghana called *Black Power*. From Carmichael's lips, it projected hatred and insurrection. Hosea Williams grabbed the microphone and shouted "Black Power!" A subdued roar came from many throats. "Get that vote and pin that badge on a black chest!" he roared. "Whip the policeman across the head!" Martin Luther King could endure it no longer. He grabbed the microphone. "He means with the vote," he said. Stokely Carmichael wrestled the microphone from King and said slowly and sarcastically, "They know what he means."

The march continued. While King was back in Chicago, it was decided to turn off Route 51, when they were only twenty-five miles from Jackson, and march to the east on Route 16 to Philadelphia, where three civil rights workers had disappeared. "We're going to have a memorial service," the marchers told reporters. Martin Luther King flew back to Mississippi and found his place in the ranks. This, he knew, was not part of the original Meredith March, but it was good politics because it was dangerous. Little Philadelphia had not forgotten that earthen dam; Sheriff Lawrence Rainey had not forgotten the furor. Hatred of the black man was so intense in Philadelphia that the whites had little interest in the state government's strategy of permitting the marchers to get to Jackson, make their fiery speeches, and go home. In Philadelphia, white faces were crimson with rage. No governor, no state police would tell these people how to behave.

Outside the town, the lead trucks set up a small camp on a black farmer's property. The group headed into Philadelphia, and the whites stood on their porches and lawns, watching the tired, straggling army file by. The crowd asked Martin Luther King to speak. As he stood on a small truck, he noticed the local policemen around the edge of the crowd. Everything was normal until a white mob came running around a corner, broke through the black ranks, and tossed cherry bombs. King kept talking, begging for quiet, but the bombs made a shattering racket and women ran screaming from the group.

The policemen, almost on signal, turned their backs on the blacks. They saw nothing; they heard nothing. The second wave came. These were white teen-age boys. They attacked with shrieking rebel yells and flying fists. Blacks, old and young, began to fall. Dr. King looked down at the scene in shock. The time was 8 P.M., and darkness was overtaking Philadelphia. Some black men, tired of the old custom of permitting whites to strike without retaliation, hit back and hit hard. Other blacks took it up. Soon white youths were stumbling and falling all over the road. Suddenly, the policemen saw and heard. They waded through the two-toned skins, beating blacks and yanking whites loose from the melee.

The marchers walked back to their campsite. They would leave in the morning on the long walk back to Route 51, then south to Jackson. Tired, some bleeding, they slept on the ground. In the dead of night, there were three rifle attacks on the campsite. A few armed blacks fired back into the darkness. Dr. King told the television cameras that within a few days, he would lead a second march, a much bigger one, on Philadelphia.

When the march reached Route 51 again, white mobs were waiting. More blood flowed; tear gas dispersed the marchers. They fled to a black church. There King spoke angrily about the lack of protection from the state police. He said that FBI men had followed the march all the way, not to help, but merely to observe and report. He knew that John Doar, chief of the Department of Justice's Civil Right Division, was present, and King wanted to know what good did it do for Doar to run around with a handkerchief against his nose begging whites to "take it easy." A telegram was fired off to President Johnson. There was no response.

King's strength was being undermined from several directions. The

White Establishment was tired of long hot summers. The government was alienated from Martin Luther King because of his stand on Vietnam. The civil rights leadership had carved itself into so many political segments that it was rare for any two groups to agree. Charles Evers made a violent speech in the next small town, and Dr. King lost his temper. "Look here, Charles," he said, "I don't appreciate your talking like that. If you're that violent, why don't you just go up the highway to Greenwood and kill the man who killed your own brother?"

In Washington, the President held a press conference. He said, "We are not interested in Black Power. We are not interested in White Power. But we are interested in American democratic power with a small 'd.' "

The last day of the march, between Tougaloo and Jackson, James Meredith, all but recovered from his wounds, joined the group in an automobile. ". . . the Mississippi highway patrol chief has accepted all responsibility for security," he said. "He has given me his word." Bumper stickers were licked and slapped onto the rear of black cars. They depicted a springing black panther with the words "We're the Greatest."

As always in the long marches, this one had begun with a large crowd, diminished to a small one after the first day, then built up to 15,000 marchers on the last day.

This time the marchers were permitted closer to the State Capitol. The drawing cards were such actors as Marlon Brando, Burt Lancaster, Sammy Davis, Jr., Anthony Franciosa, and Dick Gregory. Outside the square, hundreds of National Guard soldiers stood with rifles. The scene was set for a disciplined intelligent appeal to grant to the black man the fulfillment of a promise made 100 years before—equality. But this was not to be. Charles Evers had paid to have a speaking platform erected, and in the first order of business, the militant leaders voted not to permit him to speak. "This applies," they said, "to all NAACP leaders." Whitney Young was told in icy candor that he would not be permitted on the stand unless he signed the original march manifesto drawn up in Memphis. He signed.

SNCC workers handed out big placards reading: "Move Over or We'll Move On Over You!" Someone chanted: "What do you want?" The crowd chanted: "Black Power!" The speaker crouched and cupped his ear. "Can't hear you. What do you want?" The roar was intensified: "Black Power!" and it ricocheted around the old Confederate square. Dr. King was not permitted to lead; he was cordially invited to a backstage meeting of the militants. There he heard that his SCLC was to be tolerated and nothing more. SNCC was now in charge. The crowd chanted: "Black Power!"; the SCLC group countered with "Freedom Now!" NAACP men handed out American flags; SNCC Field Secretary Willie Ricks ran into the crowd, demanding, "Give me those flags. That flag does not represent you."

Carmichael was running the show. On cue, when the name of Martin Luther King was mentioned, part of the crowd booed. There was no intelligence involved in the final demonstration. No one made a dispassionate appeal. The young people swayed to the songs, chanting slogans of hate. The great Hollywood actors were introduced. The voice of reason was silenced. When evening arrived and the first scented breeze anointed the old buildings, the crowd left. A few blacks with hammers dismantled a wooden stand. Two policemen watched them load the lumber onto a truck. The march had lasted from June 6 to June 26, and its main significance seemed to be the phrase "Black Power!"

The press was left with that phrase to dissect, to juggle, to bandy. To the white racist, it meant that the blacks were about to start a bloody revolution and take over the country. To the moderate white, it was defined as voting strength. To the millions of politically ignorant and passive whites, the phrase meant nothing. To Dr. King, it meant "black supremacy" which, he felt, was as evil a prospect as "white supremacy." Roy Wilkins said that Black Power was black racism which could lead only to black death. "The whole business," he said, "showed the NAACP again how difficult it is to have genuine cooperation on an equal responsibility basis with groups that do not have the same commitments and which may very well be pursuing certain goals that have nothing to do with civil rights at all."

In Atlanta, Dr. King couldn't sleep. He was thinking of "Black Power!" versus his own slogan "Freedom Now!" The only way he could resolve the conflicts in his mind was to get out of bed and write them: "I went home that night with an ugly feeling. Selfishly, I thought of my sufferings and sacrifices over the last twelve years. . . . But, as I lay awake thinking, I finally came to myself, and I could not for the life of me have less than patience and understanding for those young people. For twelve years, I and others like me had held out radiant promises of progress. I had preached to them about my dream. Their hopes had soared. They were now booing because they felt we were unable to deliver on our promises."

Within three days, CORE voted to accept the slogan of "Black

Power!" National Director Floyd McKissick said, "As long as the white man has all the power and money, nothing will happen because we have nothing. The only way to achieve meaningful change is to take power." Two days later, the NAACP divorced itself from "Black Power!" What the white racist had not been able to do, the blacks did to themselves: They had fragmented the Movement.

Chicago had moved serenely through the seasons—autumn, winter, spring, and now summer—and Dr. King was no closer to breaking the city's spine than Daley was King's. There was no enemy anywhere. The mayor chose to play the role of competitor to Pastor King. One can but marvel at the shrewdness of the old-line politician, especially as a counterpuncher. No matter what King preached, Daley followed with a similar speech. No matter what was proposed, Daley said it was already being planned and executed. No matter what the doctor promised 900,000 blacks, the mayor was in a firmer position to fulfill the promise: money; jobs; housing; relief. The Southern Christian Leadership Conference showed a loss of $200,000, so far, on Chicago.

At the end of June, when Dr. King left Mississippi after the James Meredith March, he stopped at Atlanta to pick up his wife and four children for a summer in Chicago. When the youngsters saw the cracking sagging appearance of the neighborhood, they were not happy. The parents explained that this was how the poor black lived, and that their father's lifework was to change neighborhoods like this for the better. In the dark hallway, a small light in the ceiling fought dirt and grime and lost. Chicago was so hot that all windows had to be left open. The screens did not filter the roar of the big city, or the street calls of children at play, or the sirens of police cars and fire engines, or the laughing, the shouting, the brawling going on in other apartments.

The doctor had brought secondhand furniture. The rest of it had been donated. There was a linoleum tile floor in the living room, bare floors in two bedrooms running straight back to the kitchen which had been painted over so many times that it hung in lumps and cavities. Marty and Yoki were especially puzzled. They were used to a nice house with a nice lawn in a nice neighborhood with a nice housekeeper and nice friends of their parents who were especially nice to them. Out front in Chicago, there was a little black dirt between sidewalk and curb, a mass of children who ran, shouted, played, and fought. The gentle upbringing to which they were accustomed was no source of insulation against depression and meanness.

Within thirty days the personalities of the children were changed. Martin Luther King, who seldom had time for his family, noticed that they were becoming sullen. They refused to obey. They displayed hostility, even to one another. Swiftly, they were absorbing the credos of the ghetto. In July, King sent them home to Atlanta.

Several times King brought his workers together and admitted that the campaign was lagging. His desire, he said, was to weld all the blacks of Chicago together in a protest movement. He wanted more than the blacks; he hoped to enlist the active participation of unions, churches, and liberal groups. He said that his group must make "demands greater than Chicago is willing to give . . . so that direct action will become necessary." The trick was to make ultimatums beyond the possibility of being granted, but not to make them so outrageous that they would induce ridicule.

Before July 1, he demanded that Daley and the Board of Aldermen grant: (1) a minimum wage of $2 per hour; (2) total school desegregation within one year; (3) the dispersal of blacks from concentrated areas by building low-income low-density public housing in all of Chicago's fifty wards; and (4) creation of ten "new towns," each with a population of 100,000, of which 30 percent would be black.

The four demands were carefully devised so that they would be impossible to accept or execute. The minimum wage could not be raised above the $1.25 established by Congress without glutting Chicago with a siege of unskilled outsiders and, at the same time, driving consumer prices higher than they were. The dispersal of nearly 1,000,000 blacks was impossible because not more than 10 or 15 percent could be urged to move from their old "home" neighborhoods. The building of low-cost public housing for them would require enormous condemnation proceedings in other crowded sections of Chicago, opening the gates to a municipal protest from blacks and whites. The creation of ten "new towns" was a physical impossibility, unless 30 percent of the blacks were willing to move out of Cook County, in which case Daley would be out of the geographical limits of his power.

King told his advisers that no matter what Daley's response, he was going to make further demands upon Chicago in July. "A riot can always be stopped by superior force," he said, "but they can't stop thousands of feet marching nonviolently." He was planning a huge protest rally for Soldier Field, and he expected to attract 100,000 spectators to listen to the fiery oratory. "If they drain the steam out of the nonviolent movement and give no concessions," he said, "they are planting the seeds for a Watts-like situation." Inexorably, the belligerent direction of the movement was dragging King with it, forcing him, in order to maintain a semblance of leadership, into the position of the janissary who preaches love and prays for violence.

He was still the best known, the most honored black man in the world. At the demonstrations, the press did not follow the Formans, the Wilkinses, the McKissicks, or the Carmichaels. They thronged around Dr. King, begging for statements which would make fresh headlines. He would not pause; he would not give himself rest. He was on top of the mountain. The climb upward had been long and arduous, and he would not permit the swift slide downward.

Chicago fatigued King beyond exhaustion. Three weeks before he publicized his purposefully "impossible" demands, the mayor asked the voters to endorse a new $195,000,000 bond issue for capital improvements. The electorate of Chicago did not want it. The ward politicians told the mayor that the people preferred not to go further in debt for urban renewal. Daley put his prestige on the public block with that bond issue. It won, two to one. The pastor was not elated. He was despondent. The victory would mean that apathy would settle once more on black shoulders like a cloak. They would consider the battle won.

The day of the rally at Soldier Field was hot. Forty thousand people sat in a temperature of ninety-eight degrees. The doctor, seen from the opposite side of the vast stadium, looked like a small dark doll waving tiny arms. He asked the people "to fill up the jails of Chicago, if necessary, in order to end the slums." The people marched in the insufferable sun to City Hall. Dr. King mounted the steps to present his newest demands to Richard Daley. The mayor, as King knew, was out of town. He pasted his demands on the La Salle Street door, and some of the people in the crowd grumbled. There was to be no confrontation with the mayor. The symbolic gesture of the original Martin Luther nailing his ninety-five religious postures on the door of a church was lost on most of the people.

The Roman Catholic Archbishop of Chicago, John P. Cody, sent a message to Dr. King warmly endorsing some of his demands, pledged his archdiocese to abolish the final "vestiges of discrimination," and closed with "Your struggles and suffering will be mine."

Two days later a riot erupted when police turned off two fire hydrants which black children had opened as their "beach." Black men reopened the valve. The police tried to close it as "illegal," and a fight broke out. The vicious gangs, which had been waiting for violence, came out of hiding—some numbering 250 men per unit—and tossed fire bombs into stores and began looting. Hurriedly, Dr. King called a peace meeting. He asked the young gang leaders to speak up from the floor of a church. "This," he said, "will relieve the tension." In silence, the leaders rose and left. There was no kinship between their needs and the pastor's demands: integration of public schools in both student body and faculty; expansion of transit facilities in ghettos; doubling the school budget; withdrawal of all city and Cook County funds from banks which refused blacks mortgages for their homes; the construction of ten new towns, a $2 minimum wage and low-income housing.

When Dr. and Mrs. King emerged from the church, they found young gangs on the far sidewalk; up the street there was shouting and the sound of gunfire. James Orange and Bernard Lee told the Kings to get in the car and get out of the area. The car threaded its way through gangs of young men who peered into the car and rapped its sides. The Kings decided that it would be dangerous to return to the ghetto flat and spent the night at Mahalia Jackson's home.

The riots followed the customary pattern. The gangs interpreted the conciliatory attitude of the police as weakness, which led to fire bombing in other areas. Looting was rampant. The smashing of windows and the arson spread over 140 blocks. Deep into the hot night, the lonesome sporadic crack of gunfire could be heard.

Dr. King drove tirelessly night and day to the riot areas, persuading, pleading with young men to surrender their weapons and go home in peace. Some listened. Others laughed. Not even his growing and formidable list of enemies could deny that he did more than any black in trying to stop disorder. He must have slept somewhere, sometimes; but there is no record of it, and the testimony shows that by day and by night he was present. On the third night, 4,000 national guardsmen returned to the scene of the first riots. The gangs dissipated into dark hallways. The show was over.

King called another conference of gang lords. Once more, by listening to the boiling vituperation of unreasoning young men, by hearing them out and then pitching his preachment toward the value of nonviolence, he achieved a handshake agreement. It is doubtful that Dr. King believed that they had been converted. They knew they hadn't.

Journalists who had been assigned to Dr. King's campaigns began to detect a pattern: (1) Hold staff meetings to select a target city where white racists will react violently for the greatest news media coverage; (2) send advance men as a team to investigate the city, its strengths and weaknesses and submit a report; (3) have Dr. King solicit assistance from local civil rights groups and churches; (4) have King move to target city with staff; (5) make public announcements, enumerating deplorable conditions for blacks; (6) hold church meetings to arouse local blacks; (7) draw up list of demands and present to city authorities; (8) schedule nonviolent demonstrations; (9) preach peace and nonviolence when whites react violently; (10) should blacks retaliate with violence, indict white authorities; (11) demand meeting with mayor and authorities as riots continue; (12) agree to meet white authorities and businessmen; (13) appear publicly to stop rioting; (14) meet with the Establishment and hammer out an agreement; (15) accept terms and proclaim victory; (16) return to SCLC headquarters and hold meetings for selection of next target city. With slight variations, this was the King recipe for success.

The staff now proposed a few marches into all-white areas to stir some action into the Chicago campaign. The long hot summer had materialized in Cleveland, New York, and Detroit, but not in Chicago. The doctor led a procession of 250 blacks out of the ghetto in what King called an Open City March. The thin little group walked across Ashland Avenue, where real estate groups had contained the blacks for years. The march had been publicized, and jeering whites stood along the line of march. The plan was to stop for lunch, then go on to Marquette Park, where Martin Luther King would picket a white real estate agent. At Marquette Park, the blacks were shocked to find, in the heart of liberal Chicago, the leader of the American Nazi Party, George Lincoln Rockwell, with some men standing in conical Ku Klux Klan robes.

This was the kind of publicity the campaign needed, but it stunned the marchers. The confrontation attracted white residents, most of whom armed themselves with rocks. The air was filled with missiles and epithets when the police arrived. A brick hit Dr. King on the side of the head. He stumbled, pulled himself up, and continued to march. Television camera trucks recorded the scene. Police attacked white people. The marchers fled back to Ashland Avenue and beyond, ducking stones all the way. The episode had accomplished what the SCLC staff said it would: expose Chicago whites as vicious racists and, when the scenes were shown on television that night, arouse the blacks to action. There was another march to the Gage Park section, east of Chicago's Midway Airport. Belligerent whites swarmed over the blacks, fists swinging. The whites overturned five automobiles owned by blacks and set them ablaze.

There was another march into the Belmont-Cragin area. Thousands of whites waited on the curbs, screaming "White Power! White Power!" Summer rain was pouring, but the marchers continued. It required 500 policemen to restore order. In the fifth march, priests in Roman collars and nuns in black habits kept step with the black marchers. A roar emerged from the white hecklers. Chicago was the largest Roman Catholic diocese in America. Parishioners yelled that the place of priests and nuns was in church, and they would not contribute unless the clergy stopped working for "niggers." Placards began to appear: "Archbishop Cody and His Commie Coons."

Black gang leaders were at police headquarters demanding more police protection from whites. They were met by Hugh Osborne, deputy director of the Commission on Youth Welfare. He was black. "There are people in your community who are afraid of you," he said, "God-fearing people who are afraid. If I were a police officer, and I saw four or five of you coming down the street, believe me, I would get ready. There is something to say on both sides." Thereupon the gangs appointed themselves march protectors and walked on both sides of King's column, warding off charging whites, deflecting bricks and boards. "I've never seen anything like this in my life," Dr. King said. "I think the people from Mississippi ought to come to Chicago to learn how to hate." It had taken him seven months to precipitate it, but at last he had cracked the safe of white violence.

The mayor, who had always displayed a public attitude of fearlessness, began to worry. The demonstrations were becoming dangerous. Word had reached him that Martin Luther King was seriously thinking of marching west to the vicious little town of Cicero. A black youth had been killed there while merely walking their streets looking for a job. Daley was worried, and worried, he made a mistake. He thought that all politicians and crusaders have a price, and he was prepared to pay the price to get peace. An emissary was sent to Dr. King's apartment with a proposal. If King would stop the marching demonstrations, the mayor would give 300 jobs to blacks at once. They would be public-housing guards, recruited from the tenants in the buildings. King, on his side, made a mistake. He interpreted the move as a sign of weakness. He declined the offer and promised more demonstrations. It had required almost eight months of searching for the tender nerve of the city, but now that he had learned it was real estate that the white man with his little house on his little plot of ground with his little lawn feared the black man as a neighbor—then that was the nerve to irritate until it became raw. The slum riots, as terrifying as they were, had not frightened the whites. The blacks burned their own buildings and looted slum shops. The black enclaves were as tightly insulated as they were in the South. The white nerve could be rubbed raw by leading an innocent march into a white neighborhood. The hate which it induced had a different accent, but it was as white-hot as in the South.

A meeting at St. James Episcopal Cathedral took place on August 17. It involved ranking clergymen, business leaders, real estate boards, union leaders, politicians, and the SCLC. The whites were present to find an agreeable formula for stopping the demonstrations in white neighborhoods. The blacks were there to find a means of declining the agreement. The meeting lasted ten hours, as though each side were trying to prove good faith through endurance. No matter how pleasant the attitudes, how gallant the personal salutes, the whites did not want the blacks in their neighborhoods, and the blacks were determined not to be dissuaded by extraneous evidence of goodwill. The meeting adjourned sine die with no agreement.

On Sunday, the twenty-first, Archbishop John P. Cody endorsed a march through a white neighborhood. Five hundred blacks followed Dr. King; but the police escort outnumbered the marchers, and the hate could not show itself. The City of Chicago went to chancery court and swore out an injunction against King and his men. Judge Cornelius J. Harring ordered that demonstrations be limited to one per day, the marchers limited to 500, the leaders to send notice to the police superintendent twenty-four hours before the demonstration, stating the march route, the number of marchers and, as an added restriction, limiting such marches to the periods between 7:30 and 9 A.M. or between 4:30 and 6 P.M.

The result of the injunction was predictable. Dr. King called it "unjust, illegal and unconstitutional. We are prepared to put thousands in the streets if need be. The city hasn't seen the number of people we can put there." He decided not to defy the injunction but to fight it on appeal.

Daley appeared on morning television to charge that the convulsion in which Chicago found itself had been caused by "extremists of the left and right." They "live out of the community, out of the county and in many instances out of the state." The mayor said that he had warned Dr. King at the Wednesday meeting that the demonstrations "would only serve as a magnet to the hate groups. . . ." To this, the SCLC responded that it would make its next march to Cicero, which, after all, was not Chicago and therefore not subject to the injunction. The last time a black family moved into Cicero had been fifteen years earlier; a mob of 5,000 maddened whites had burned the family's furniture and clothing and damaged the apartment house.

It may not have been Chicago, but Cicero, which was just across the street from Lawndale, was Cook County. Sheriff Richard Ogilvie dourly announced that if King marched, the National Guard would have to be called up a third time. No police department could protect marchers in Cicero. The little town, once the home away from home for Al Capone and other gangsters, had a 100-man police force. The town attorney, Christy Berkos, was wrestling with the problem when an application fell on his desk from the American Nazi Party to hold a rally on the same day in front of the town hall.

One of the strongest advocates of ever-increasing pressure on the white structure was the Reverend Andrew Young, a volatile young man who prodded King toward more militant paths. Young, who had been second or third in command at many a campaign, said that the SCLC couldn't make any progress in Birmingham until the whites were ready to declare martial law, and that it might be necessary to go that far in Chicago. Mayor Daley's hand was being forced. He could no longer deplore lawlessness and wait for it to occur. He had to think of all Chicago and all Cook County. The mayoralty election was due in November, and Daley, boss of a big taut political machine, had to maintain a balance between the blacks (one-quarter of the voters) and the whites (three-quarters).

Two days before the Cicero march, the mayor called King to confer with Ross Beatty, head of the Board of Real Estate of Chicago. The pastor and his assistants on the one side, and Daley, Archbishop Cody and Beatty on the other, reached a positive agreement about open housing. Beatty promised to make a public announcement that the Real Estate Board would withdraw all opposition to the philosophy of open occupancy legislation at the state level, provided it was applicable to owners as well as brokers. Action was to be directed against brokers who failed to comply, with an eye to brokerage suspension or revocation, and the Chicago Housing Authority would begin placing families in the best housing without regard to the racial character of the neighborhood. This would also apply to families on relief, regardless of color. There were also a bankers' pledge "to lend mortgage money to all qualified families without regard to race"; a statement from the Department of Justice that it would reexamine Federal Deposit Insurance Corporation guarantees to institutions guilty of discrimination; pledges from the Roman Catholic Archdiocese, the Church Federation of Greater Chicago, the Chicago Board of Rabbis, and the Union of American Hebrew Congregations to use their good offices "in effecting equal access to housing for all people"; and pledges from commerce, industry, banking, and labor to secure their support of the real estate program.

The blacks left the meeting elated. King said the agreement was "the most significant program ever conceived to make open housing a reality in the metropolitan area. We are still a long way from our goal," he said. He also stated that he would be busy ending discrimination in employment and education in Chicago and therefore would "defer" the march on Cicero. It was a shrewd trade on both sides—nonviolence in return for guarantees and pledges. It was a progressive step if only because it changed the white structure from a belligerent antiblack position to a weak defensive one. Some of the militants in CORE and SNCC called it a "sellout" by Martin Luther King. So long as he proposed to "defer" the march on Cicero, CORE stated, its organization would march on Sunday, September 4. On that day 200 blacks walked west across Route 50 and, in spite of 2,000 marching national guardsmen, were hit by so many flying bottles and rocks that they retreated in disarray to Lawndale. Dr. King showed his shock when he stated, "We can walk in outer space, but we can't walk in the streets of Cicero without the National Guard." It was worse. Blacks couldn't march in Cicero *with* the National Guard.

The 2,000 black militants in Chicago could not believe that a real estate agreement could affect the battle to spring out of the ghetto. "Let's face the fact," King told them, "most of us are going to be living in the ghetto five, ten years from now. But we're going to get some things straightened out right away. I'm not going to wait a month to get the roaches out of my house."

Sometime during his Chicago stay, King came to realize that each small, hard-fought gain in each town brought his people only a little closer to "Freedom Now." When he proclaimed that people would be living in ghettos "five, ten years from now," he was uttering something which he had recently learned. The domination of the black by the white was a matter of numbers, economics, power, and separate cultures. None of the new and liberal laws could convince most whites that blacks were equal. His SCLC treasury had duly noted that, when King marched in the South, Northern liberals contributed generously; when King moved to Chicago, contributions fell off. No matter which way he moved, supporting groups were alienated—sometimes white ones, some-times black. All along, Martin Luther King was certain that all he had to do was march into the ghetto and dramatize what the white man had done to the black and what the black had done to himself, and the conscience of the nation would be aroused. America in its fairness, in its acute sense of justice, would do something to correct the exposed evils. He knew now he had been wrong.

There were big prices on small victories. He won an open housing declaration in Chicago, but the gentlemen of the House of Representa-tives and the United States Senate saw the films of the riots, the flying bottles, the looting, and the fires, and on September 19, the Senate Majority Leader, Mike Mansfield of Montana, withdrew the Lyndon Johnson 1966 civil rights bill from consideration. There was a serious question of how many victories the Movement could afford. In addition, King was most conscious of the fact that the harder he fought for civil rights, the more white people were moved from a neutral, passive posi-tion to one of active opposition to the black.

There was one victory that could not be spoiled for him: With the assistance of federal registrars, the Voter Registration Drive had been a phenomenal success in the South. When the drive began, in 1960, only 29 percent of blacks in the eleven Southern states had been voters. The highest was in Tennessee, with 59 percent; the lowest, Mississippi with 5.2 percent. Within six years, almost 50 percent of eligible blacks had been registered. The highest was Tennessee with 72 percent; the lowest, Mississippi with 28 percent. Thus, within a period of six years, the Southern black (provided he would vote en bloc) held the balance of political power. Also, for the first time, the black's enclave gave him an advantage because the voters in many Southern ghettos outnumbered the town whites. This, in turn, could elect black mayors and Congress-men. In 1940, the total black vote in the South was 100,000. In 1966, it was 2,500,000 and growing. In that year a white Alabama reporter wrote that he had been covering political rallies for a long time, and in this campaign, he had yet to hear a white candidate use the word "nigger."

Al Lingo, running for sheriff in Birmingham, lost. Jim Clark, running in Selma, lost. Before election day, Jim Clark took a look at the registra-tion lists and learned that 11,000 of 23,000 voters would be black. He hid his "Never" button and invited the blacks to a barbecue and beer at a political picnic. Twenty-eight sat with him.

✿ ✿ ✿

The man racist America should have been watching was Stokely Carmichael. Whatever was viable and vibrant in the movement was in his confident, fearless hands, and he confined his work to one intractable county, Lowndes of Alabama. He was seldom seen in the newspapers or on television, but he worked from farm tenant to farm tenant, racking up votes one by one. He had located and verified an old Alabama law which stated that any group of citizens could form its own political party if it drew 20 percent of the vote in any county. If it achieved the 20 percent, it could go on and nominate candidates for state office. Carmichael and his assistants formed the Freedom Party in ten Black Belt counties. He set up a school to teach blacks the duties and responsibilities of the sheriff, the tax assessor, the mayor, the councilman in Alabama; 150 graduated.

The more people he got to register, the more he proselytized to go out and find more blacks in the backcountry. Stokely Carmichael didn't have much time to argue, to persuade; his credo was "Believe in me, please—we're working for the same thing," and the people put their trust in him. Of the 15,000 people living in Lowndes, 81 percent were black. He was determined to elect blacks on the first effort. Seven months before election, the whites began to worry. They dispossessed blacks as tenant farmers and ordered them off the land.

Carmichael asked SNCC for money, lots of it, for tents to be erected on black-owned ground. Black families would live in them and that would be their voting residence. A month before election day, 2,681 blacks had been registered to vote, against a list of 2,519 whites. Carmichael was a merciless fighter, and he had a majority in Lowndes County. He ran his black candidates under the emblem of a black panther. He wanted ferocity and blackness, and it was the most potent animal he could think of. However, his people did not vote en bloc, as he hoped, and his candidates lost by an average of 400 votes. When it was over, the white racists realized that they had been in a closely fought bitter battle and might easily lose the next election. Word was sent to Stokely Carmichael: "We think we're ready for a little integration."

Daley won reelection in Chicago. The forces opposed to Martin Luther King became vocal. The Reverend Henry Mitchell of the North Star Missionary Baptist Church convened with fifteen other ministers, who said they represented 50,000 blacks. Mitchell told the press that

Dr. King's marches "created hate." King, he stressed, was an "outsider" whose work had failed in Chicago and he advised the doctor to "stay in Alabama." The NAACP announced that it was withdrawing from Martin Luther King's Chicago program. The Reverend Carl Fuqua, executive secretary of the local NAACP, referred to King's demonstrations as "useless." Other black organizations stated that they had divorced their activities from the SCLC months earlier but had made no public announcement of it.

Nor was there a public announcement of how the Chicago Board of Aldermen proposed to implement the open housing agreement. They planned to spend hundreds of millions building low-cost public housing solely in the ghettos. This would confine the black to his old slum in new housing.

The campaign in Chicago began to crack. It was difficult enough to fight the devious whites, but King could not afford all the enemies he found in his own camp. The preachers—his brethren—urged him to go back home; the militants accused him of selling them out; the racial antagonisms in Chicago were far worse in November, 1966, than when he sent his advance agents there in October, 1965. He still headed a viable organization, but it was painful to know that after thirteen months of work, he was being dismissed by both sides as a loser. And yet he did not see himself as defeated. Loss of power in the civil rights movement only confirmed his belief that he had outgrown it and that he was ready for a bigger mission: world diplomacy.

At the time that the Chicago campaign was dying a fresh flame was brightening the skies of the West Coast. In Oakland and the San Francisco Bay area a group of supermilitants organized in October, 1966, and called themselves the Black Panther Party. They owed the name to Stokely Carmichael, but the mystic idea of a black nation within a white one was entirely their own. It was a black Ku Klux Klan. Almost open warfare was declared against the police, and in turn, the police ferreted out and shot the Panthers in ultimate confrontation.

The rise of the Black Panthers did not improve Dr. King's disposition. The movement was beyond his control. Nor did it elate him that on the opposite end of the spectrum, Edward W. Brooke of Massachusetts was elected to the United States Senate, the first black man since Reconstruction days. Brooke's skin was pale, his hair straight. He had married an Italian girl whom he met while in service in World War II.

Brooke's origins related to the black middle class, which as far as the average black is concerned, is closer to the White Establishment than to the Black.

The trial and torture of the mind continued when Dr. King saw the "confidential report" of the Chicago Freedom Movement. Daley and his archbishop and his real estate boards had made solemn commitments, but black members of the Chicago Freedom Movement had tested them and found them, not wanting, but totally absent.

"In the past five weeks, the follow-up committee has tested brokers in areas such as Hyde Park, South Shore, Bogan, Gage Park, Belmont-Cragin, Austin and Rogers Park. In every case, the white family was served and the Negro family discriminated against." The report was specific and incisive. It named names and places and people. The Chicago Commission on Human Relations countered the report by claiming it had "done every one of the specific things" in the agreement except inspection of real estate offices and, presumably, practices. Daley's response was a political cliché: "The story of foot-dragging was leaked to the press for purely political purposes."

Martin Luther King closed his Chicago slum apartment and journeyed to make a speech at the University of Pittsburgh. In it there was no mention of Chicago. He was ready for more portentous matters. He leveled a public charge at Lyndon Johnson that 40 percent of the combat troops in Vietnam were American blacks, whereas the black was only 10 percent of the country's population. Blacks were dragooned to war through draft boards, he charged, because most of them did not have sufficient education to ask for a college deferment.

There was no response from the White House. President Johnson's strategy was not to publicize attacks against his Vietnam policy. After a suitable period of waiting, Dr. King made one of his sudden decisions to travel. Before Christmas, he and his wife and Bernard Lee and Dora McDonald, his personal secretary, left for the hot sand and warm laving waters of Jamaica. They relaxed in the hot sun, walked the empty beaches, and the doctor worked at night on his next book: *Where Do We Go from Here: Chaos or Community?* When his editor saw the chapters, she was stunned. Dr. King had simply rewritten part of the text from his book, *Why We Can't Wait* and had filled out other sections with the text of sermons.

When the book was published, Andrew Kopkind of the *New York Review of Books* wrote of Martin Luther King: "He has been outstripped by his times, overtaken by the events which he may have obliquely helped to produce but would not predict. . . . Conventional commentators these days like to speak of King's 'nobility' and the purity of his humanism, and they sigh that the world is not ready for him. But it is more accurate to say that King is not ready for the world."

Another winter, another New Year arrived in Chicago on time. Heavy snows on gale winds came in off Lake Michigan and scrubbed the buildings, the streets, the trees, the lawns, but not the people. Everything was white and bright except the people. The whites were gray; the blacks were gray, but no one noticed the similarity. Both sides were entrenched in a war neither could win. Martin Luther King, in the early months of 1967, was to Chicago what Lyndon Johnson was to Vietnam and what, a long time ago, Napoleon had been to Moscow. In each case, it was fruitless to stay, impossible to leave.

King could make trips, but he was on a self-fashioned leash which always snapped him back to Chicago. At black tie dinners, when he was asked to speak, he swept Chicago from his thoughts and discussed bigger targets. "The promises of the Great Society," he shouted, "have been shot down on the battlefields of Vietnam. The pursuit of this widened war has narrowed domestic welfare programs, making the poor white and Negro, bear the heaviest burdens. . . . It is estimated that we spend three hundred twenty-two thousand dollars for each enemy we kill, while we spend in the so-called War on Poverty only about fifty-three dollars for each person. . . . We must combine the fervor of the civil rights movement with the peace movement." The plea to combine a war with a domestic issue was King's newest ambition. His followers still contributed money, but they patted their hands politely when he spoke, whereas they had once stood and stomped and cheered a new world in the womb.

Chicago would not go away. It stood tall and implacable, with a lopsided grin, facing the doctor with its immovable planes of black and white; white and black. Three and a half million people waited for him to jump one way or the other. He spent less and less time in the dingy four rooms and more and more in the sunnier places. He read the headlines of the New York *Times* and they too hurt:

DR. KING PLAGUED BY RESISTANCE
AND APATHY IN CHICAGO SLUMS
Rights Leader's Aides Cite Some Gains
But Find Problems of Northern Ghetto
Tougher Than Those in the South

The report from Hosea Williams was more discouraging. "The Chicago Negro isn't concerned about what the power structure is doing to him. It's cold here and I'm having a lot of problems." This was defeatist talk from a trusted field marshal. Leon Hall tried to recruit some people on one street. He went back to SCLC field headquarters shaking his head in disbelief. "One lady came at me with an ice pick," he said. "This is worse than Alabama. . . ." Each report was more dismal than the previous one. The SCLC could not permit itself to absorb a fact: They were fighting blacks, not whites. It was as though Jehovah had come to Sodom and the good people did not want to be saved. Worse, they were prepared to destroy Jehovah. Television commentator Frank McGee said, "His disappointment is verging on bitterness."

People outside King's inner circle could only guess the agony of the man. The Southern Baptist preacher's earnest plea "I Have a Dream," a plea which had aroused the heart of a nation, was now worth chiseling on a tombstone. "We Shall Overcome" was rarely sung. The names Montgomery, Albany, Birmingham, Selma evoked no more accolades. Not too long ago, no civil rights rally was complete without the presence of the pastor. He was no longer invited to the councils. In pomp and circumstance he had been a guest at the White House. Today his plea for help went unanswered. Once he had been summoned to Norway to receive the most prestigious award a man might aspire to. Once millions of fearful silent blacks prayed for him, wept unshamedly when they saw his face on television. Now he could not arouse one-half of one percent of the blacks of Chicago to march with him, to listen to him. Some were rude; they waited until he arose to speak and then kicked back their chairs noisily and walked out.

And yet this was a time of budding for the black rose. This was a year, a day when white men South and North edged toward an amiable dialogue; a time when blacks were in the ascendancy; a time when it was shameful to display racial consciousness by word or deed. The halls of the United Nations were filled with tall black men, many in dashikis, who represented new nations in Africa. The black citizens of the 700 Bahama Islands voted the whites out of office and assumed the government of the colony. The United States, through John W. Gardner of the Department of Health, Education, and Welfare, announced that federal assistance for Alabama welfare programs would cease unless the state stopped racial discrimination.

Lyndon Johnson, beaten in Congress in a fight for his 1966 civil rights bill, sent a special message to the Capitol that a 1967 bill had been prepared and that this one would end discrimination in housing and stop discrimination in the selection of juries for trial. The U.S. Civil Rights Commission urged legislation that would make racial balance in all public schools mandatory. Biracial committees were being selected by mayors all over the South to see if both sides could be accommodated without affronting either. Within a few months, President Johnson would name Thurgood Marshall, a black man, to the United States Supreme Court. For the first time, black doctors and lawyers began to enjoy a practice that was on a par with white professionals. Black mayors were being elected. Judges were being appointed. A black man, on retirement from the U.S. Army, was upped in rank from major general to lieutenant general. It was not in any sense equality, as Dr. King had pointed out, but it was a long progressive step from the day when Rosa Parks refused to stand up for a white passenger because her feet hurt. More had been accomplished in eleven years than in the previous hundred.

Dr. King was working within the Movement, but he wasn't *the* Movement anymore. His detractors said, "What King did—if you really want to know—was light the fire. Nobody can take that away from him. He lit it, and he made everybody see it; but he didn't change anything. Now we are in stage two, the changing stage. You don't change the system with prayer. He lit the fire; we're going to put the logs on it."

In Oakland the Black Panthers wished they could be rid of Martin Luther King. To them, he was a hindrance. They wanted him to step down and out. The Black Panthers, meeting in a place called The Black House, also criticized Eldridge Cleaver. The charge was that he was in love with a white woman. This was not true. He was having an affair with a white woman, but he would eventually marry a black one. Many were saying that Cleaver wasn't in the movement with Bobby Seale. Others said he was, secretly. Cleaver and Stokely Carmichael had completed a journalistic tour for *Ramparts* magazine, and Cleaver returned to the Bay Area with the same solution to racial problems that Martin Luther King had originated years ago: "one unified organization for the Black Liberation Movement." The difference between King and Cleaver was a gun. King would not permit the gun in the movement; Cleaver would not join it unless everybody had one. In March, he won his point. Black Panthers began to carry guns. The chapter in Los Angeles insisted that Panthers wear a black leather jacket, a black beret, and black slacks so that they could identify each other. They were an elite corps, but their membership was very small indeed.

God and moral right had been the weapons of Martin Luther King. The Black Panther replaced them with a gun and hate. God, as opposed to a gun, does not work as quickly or directly. Moral right requires reasoning and reasonableness. Hate doesn't. It is a emotion requiring little thought and no rationalization. It also works in concert with a gun. Thus the appeal of the Bobby Seales, the Cleavers and Carmichaels was more potent, more virile, and gave the militant black the thing he had and his forebears lacked—power. The Black Panthers restored testicles to the black man.

King was caught between the contending forces. The verbal shots which whistled past his ears were coming from guns held by blacks. He tried to rise *above* the Movement by combining a fight for world peace with civil rights. He argued with Bayard Rustin that he was entitled to play a part in the fight for world peace because he had won the Nobel Peace Prize. Rustin begged the doctor to stay out of the peace marches, but King refused to and continued to contrast the amount spent on the war and the amount spent to fight poverty and better civil rights.

To maintain his public image, to enhance it, he spurned the counsel of his lieutenants and turned more and ever more toward his role as a critic of the United States government. On March 25 he spoke at a peace rally at the Chicago Coliseum. He addressed himself to the cruel irony of black and white killing and dying "for a nation that has been unable to seat them together in the same schools." Furthermore, he stated, he had a responsibility in this matter as a Nobel Peace laureate and as a Christian minister.

In Atlanta, someone, or some group, hit the pastor a low blow. He found a blank envelope on his desk. How it got there, he did not ask. Once he opened it, Dr. King understood the message. Inside were photographs of him in compromising situations; the pictures were accompanied by tapes, taken from "bugs" in his motel rooms. Dr. King was to curb his opinions or face public exposure. Perhaps it is a sign of character that the threat did not change Dr. King at all. He went on living his life as he pleased. At least now he was aware that he was being spied on electronically.

King was invited to speak at the big gray Riverside Church in New York on April 4. It had been built by the Rockefeller family and hewed to a tradition of Christian liberalism. The doctor was going to speak on war and peace. He had chosen this month to break away from civil rights—not to blend the racial struggle with Vietnam. Part of his staff opposed his new attitude; his supporters within the inner circle were

Coretta King and James Bevel. Mrs. King was a strong advocate of world peace. She wrote later:

"Then, when he made the statement on Vietnam, I had the strong feeling that this was the beginning of a larger work for him which would develop into something greater than we could conceive at the time. All along in our struggle one phase had led to another. As the years unfolded, it was like watching a scroll unfolding, you see more and more as you unroll it. There was a pattern and a process at work for the development of mankind; and though I had said it so often before, I felt at the time of the 1967 statement on peace, that Martin was an instrument of a Divine plan and purpose."*

At the Riverside Church, Dr. King made it apparent at once that he was not there to preach the kingdom of God. An audience of 3,000, including his father, listened enraptured as the doctor thundered that China's involvement in the war was a certainty unless a negotiated peace could be arranged. This, in turn, would lead to World War III. If the war continued, he threatened, the next phase of civil disobedience would be a massive antiwar protest. When the talk concluded, it was obvious that he had converted his father: "When he finished his speech, I knew—the whole audience knew—the man was right," he said. One of his proposals was for a unilateral cease-fire on the part of the United States to create a *climate* for negotiations. He also urged the United States to look realistically at the popularity of the National Liberation Front, which was the North Vietnamese arm in South Vietnam.

The week after the speech, King was in Louisville, Kentucky for the annual meeting of the SCLC. Black leaders were angry and said they were angry. Roy Wilkins criticized King to his face. So did Whitney Young and Ralph Bunche. The NAACP board, composed of sixty members, voted unanimously to condemn King's effort to blend the civil rights and peace movements. Dr. Bunche, who had also won the Nobel Peace Prize, said: "In my view, Doctor King should positively and publicly give up one role or the other." The Washington *Post,* which had reported favorably on King's activities, noted that he had deleted some paragraphs from the prepared text of his speech to the SCLC and had added others. The *Post* assessed this as "last minute attempts by Doctor King to tone down his sharp criticism of U.S. actions in Viet Nam." But he was by no means pulling his punches in the speech. The doctor told his audience that he often counseled young men and advised them that

* *My Life with Martin Luther King Jr.* (New York, Holt, Rinehart & Winston, 1969).

they should be nonviolent. "But they asked, and rightly so—'What about Vietnam?' Their question hit home and I knew that I could never again raise my voice against the violence of the oppressed in the ghettos without having first spoken clearly to the greatest purveyor of violence in the world today—my own government."

Ten days later, the doctor, hatless, led a march of 125,000 people from Central Park, in New York, to the United Nations Building. The parade was sponsored by the Spring Mobilization Committee, whose sole purpose was to end the war in Vietnam. The march had been organized during Christmas week of 1966 at a meeting at the University of Chicago, and attended by some 257 people. The speakers at the Chicago meeting were Bettina Aptheker, sometimes referred to as "probably the most widely known Communist in the United States"; Charles Cobb of SNCC; and the Reverend James Bevel of the SCLC. Among the 257 gathered were members of the Communist Party, the Progressive Labor Party, the Socialist Workers Party, the Young Socialist Alliance, and Youth Against War and Fascism, as well as large numbers of simply concerned people. When this group organized the Spring Mobilization Committee, it strains credibility to believe that Martin Luther King, presiding over the dying Chicago campaign, did not know the company he was keeping.

It is probable that at this point he was thinking seriously of devoting himself entirely to world peace. This seems even more likely because he proposed to the SCLC board that an "heir apparent" in the Southern Christian Leadership Conference be named—Ralph Abernathy. He asked for this, and the board granted it. No one voted against the choice, even though Andrew Young, Hosea Williams, or Jesse Jackson would have made stronger leaders. As Peter among the disciples, Abernathy was amiable and slow-speaking. He was neither a dynamo nor a generator, but Dr. King proved he was still master of the SCLC when he proposed his successor and looked around the table to find no adversaries.

The finest achievement of the Spring Mobilization Committee occurred when it attracted 125,000 to the march. Except for the few in the front ranks, these were average apolitical people who were opposed to the war, parents and youths opposed to the draft, leaderless pacifists who found a catalyst in the Spring Mobilization Committee. It is safe to speculate that most of the marchers were pro-peace, anti-Communist.

The march, well protected by the New York Police Department, moved across town to the United Nations Building, where Dr. King and four other leaders presented a formal petition for peace to Dr. Ralph Bunche. King, who had walked with Dr. Benjamin Spock and Harry Belafonte, had a smile for his old friend Ralph. But Dr. Bunche could not summon one for King. The printed appeal stated simply: "We rally at the United Nations in order to affirm support of the principles of peace, universality, equal rights and self-determination of peoples included in the charter and acclaimed by mankind, but violated by the United States." Bunche accepted the statement and had little to say. Dr. King then made a speech stating that there were at least twenty Vietnamese casualties from American firepower for each one Vietcong casualty. He spoke of the hatred the South Vietnamese feel for Americans and of the destruction done to their crops and water by bombings. He had become the total critic of America in Southeast Asia.

The following morning the Field Foundation called a meeting of civil rights leaders, government officials, and foundation executives. Dr. King was among the guests. However, when they began to discuss black voter registration and better jobs for blacks, the doctor pleaded for a postponement of nine days before resuming the discussion. It is a measure of the esteem in which King was held that the entire body agreed. King promised to spend no more than 5 percent of his time on international affairs, to devote the rest to civil rights.

Two days before the Field Foundation met again at the request of Dr. King, the pastor and Dr. Benjamin Spock issued a joint declaration that they would spend their time working on a Vietnam Summer. The two men expected to enlist 10,000 volunteer workers who would spread the gospel of opposition to the war across the United States. The Field Foundation did not meet. In one week, Dr. King's estimate of spending only 5 percent of his time on international affairs had jumped to nearly 100 percent. "It is more important that I should be concerned with the survival of the world," he said, "than with integration." In a single sentence, he turned his back on his life mission. He sympathized with his people, he hoped they realized their goals; but they could no longer expect him to work solely for them.

James Earl Ray escaped from prison. On Sunday morning, April 27, he reported for duty in the bakery. That night, he was free.* It was not a

---

* For a comprehensive account of James Earl Ray's life, see William Bradford Huie's *He Slew the Dreamer* (New York, Delacorte Press, 1968). Huie is the only author who was in direct communication with Ray after his capture and, as a careful author-investigator, checked and rechecked Ray's statements, sometimes exposing untruths.

newsworthy event, even in Jefferson City, Missouri. The town hugged
the south shore of the muddy Missouri River, and there wasn't much on
the opposite shore except the meeting of Routes 63 and 54 and an
airport.

Ray was now thirty-nine years old, and it bothered him that every
time he tried to escape the State of Missouri had added more time to his
sentence. He had spent thirteen years behind bars—a long time for a
young convict—and he figured that with no good behavior on his record
and with a history of escape attempts, he might be living in this river
cage until the year 1980. He would be fifty-two years of age, an old man
in his eyes, unwanted, unloved, unsung.

As a baker he was permitted to eat in the prison kitchen. He devoured
six eggs, not because of hunger, but because he figured that he might
have to hide inside or outside the prison for a while. He also had a
transistor radio, soap, a mirror, a comb, a score of candy bars, and a
razor. He wasn't expected for duty until 11 A.M., so he allowed himself
from 8 A.M. on to implement his plan. He donned a white shirt he had
hidden and green prison slacks which he had dyed black. On top of
those, he wore the green prison uniform.

Then he walked out into the warming sunshine on the loading dock
and looked around. He carried a four-foot baker's hook in one hand.
Ray knew better than the warden that the prison wall was twenty-three
feet high. At the bottom of the wall was a tunnel for trucks. Inside the
tunnel, the convicts who had agreed to help him were waiting. The guard
in the tower was squinting in the sunlight. James Earl Ray, if he did any
thinking at all, had plenty of material for meditation. He had served
seven years. His brother Jerry and his brother John had come to see him
about once a year. Those were his only visitors, and they were as taciturn as he. No woman visited James Earl Ray because he never had one.
He used them as casual sexual vessels, and he was willing to pay for
what he got.

Recently, Ray had been released from solitary confinement for his
previous attempt to escape, and he spent his comparative freedom
purchasing forged identification cards and selling his prison commissary
cigarettes to prisoners to obtain money—which he hid in his shoe—to
get away from Jefferson City as fast as possible. He had clocked the
actions of the guards on the walls and noticed that they called in by
phone every fifteen minutes. Some, after making the call, sat dozing until
the next call was due. Ray stood on the loading dock watching the guard
squinting into the sun. He figured he had the right one. In a few minutes,

Ray watched him pick up the phone and make his call. Then the man sat back and relaxed.

Ray opened a storage box for the bread baked for the inmates of a nearby prison farm. The box was four feet long, three feet wide. He sat on the fresh loaves of bread and crushed them. A prisoner pushed the top back down on the box. It was loaded onto a truck with the other storage boxes and was passed through the tunnel by the guard. As soon as the truck was off prison grounds, Ray began to pry the lid loose. He emerged to find the truck rolling down a road. When it stopped for a red light near the Missouri River Bridge, at West High Street and Route 54, the prisoner removed his penitentiary costume, and dropped off the tailgate in white shirt and black slacks. In addition to the pleasure of freedom, it must have been a source of satisfaction to Ray to know that, just this once, he had planned something and succeeded.

He had $300, an ID card, and a Social Security number issued to him as "John L. Raynes" years earlier. The prisoner walked quietly along a railroad track until he came to an overpass. There he crouched underneath all day, listening to his transistor radio. He had to keep posted on police statements about his escape and where they would be looking for him. He tuned in on news announcements all day and all night, munching on candy bars. There wasn't a word about the triumphant escape of James Earl Ray. He couldn't believe it. Neither could the warden. The reason the escape was not quickly publicized was that Swensen was sure that Ray, once more, was somewhere inside the prison.

When it became certain that the all-time loser had indeed left the premises, the warden wrote this report to his superiors: ". . . Based upon records in my control, one James Earl Ray, alias Eric Starvo Galt, W. C. Herron, Harvey Lowmeyer, James McBride, James O'Connor, James Walton, James Walyon, John Willard, was sentenced on February 19, 1960, of the crime of robbery first degree by means of a dangerous and deadly weapon and was received by the Department of Corrections on March 17, 1960, from which he escaped custody on April 23, 1967, leaving an unexpired term with legal expiration of March 16, 1980." The prison's response to the escape was to reduce the size of the bread boxes. It offered a reward for the capture of James Earl Ray: $50.

In the night, alone and on foot, Ray walked eastward toward the great city of St. Louis. It is an additional index to his intelligence that he had walked some distance before he realized that the police would be looking for him in that direction, because he had been reared near East St. Louis. He reversed his trail and walked westward, looking at the stars and eating candy. He spent the third day hiding in reeds watching police cars. Ray was certain that they were prowling for him. His feet began to swell. On the third night he stole a bottle of wine and some food from an unoccupied trailer. The night was cold, so he took a blanket and warmer trousers.

He slept in woods under the blanket and awakened in a heavy downpour. On the fourth night he walked and walked, not daring to take the painful shoes off, because he was afraid he couldn't get them on again. Once he built a small fire for warmth and was caught by railroad detectives. Sheepishly, he said he had been hunting and got wet. He was trying to dry out. They left him without bothering to ask how a man goes hunting without a gun. On the sixth day he washed and shaved near a clear stream and, at night, went into a town, bought two cans of beer and some sandwiches. On the seventh day James Earl Ray arrived by bus in Chicago, a furtive, frightened man looking for a job.

> Kitchen man and dishwasher. 6-day wk. $94.
> For North suburban restaurant. Call Indian
> Trail at HI 6-1703.

The restaurant was in Winnetka, Illinois, twenty miles north of Martin Luther King's flat in Lawndale. Ray's name was now John Larry Raynes. The two sisters who ran the restaurant admired their new dishwasher because he was quiet, efficient, uncomplaining. Within a week, he was promoted to the steam table. As a loner, he did not mind spending the nights in a furnished room, drinking a little beer, reading the Chicago *Tribune* or listening to his little transistor set.

Social Security deductions were made from his salary under the name of Raynes. James Earl Ray figured that the job would be worthwhile for two months. After that, he was certain that the Federal Bureau of Investigation would check his number against his aliases and begin to hunt him down. In this, Ray was wrong. They were not looking for him, nor did they have notification of his escape. Still, Ray played the running man. He needed a plan, and after considerable cogitation, he evolved one. He would save and buy a car. He would drop the name Raynes in favor of Eric Galt. Then he would establish identification under the new name, go somewhere far off, and get a job. There he would again save money, this time to make a trip abroad to some nation which did not have an extradition treaty with the United States and remain there for life.

Far, far away.

The June issue of the *Reader's Digest* reached Martin Luther King's desk in Atlanta like a ticking time bomb. It featured an article titled "Martin Luther King's Tragic Decision." It was written by Carl Rowan, a black journalist who had once been American ambassador to Finland. It was written with a velvet hatchet. King, who had been standing tall with medals and honorary doctorates given to him by the white man, was editorially dissected. There was a reference to the infiltration of the SCLC by Communists; the gargantuan effort King was making to swing his followers away from supporting the war in Vietnam; his short stays in jail while his followers served long terms; his unconquerable ego; his alienation of the White House. All of it added up to a solid, telling blow to the lowest part of the belly. A week later another blow landed hard on Dr. King. The United States Supreme Court, which had been his friend through so many trials over so many years, upheld the conviction in Birmingham for demonstrating without a permit. The court in Birmingham blandly informed him, Ralph Abernathy, Fred Shuttlesworth, Wyatt Tee Walker, and four others that they could start serving their four-day jail sentences in October.

King fell into a deep depression. He refused to see the press. Mrs. King did her best to lift her husband's spirits, but it wasn't easy. Dr. King was laden with honors; he was an international celebrity; somehow he confused this with immunity to attack. He considered himself above the swirling chaos of the Movement, serene and peaceful. Suddenly, he was being scorned and attacked. He had predicted a long hot summer for the nation, but not for Martin Luther King.

His book *Where Do We Go from Here? Chaos or Community?* was published by Harper & Row. The reviews were so exasperating to Dr. King that he began another, *The Trumpet of Conscience,* making him one of the few authors to have two books published in the year 1967.

He did not want to discuss the Chicago campaign or the exorbitant losses it incurred. He wanted to get out of Chicago permanently, without having to say officially that he was doing so. More and more duties and more and more authority fell to the Reverend Jesse Jackson, who had the time and the following to advance a step at a time.

Stokely Carmichael of SNCC moved in on Dixie Hills, a black ghetto in Atlanta, King's backyard. He attended church meetings in Dixie Hills, and those discerning eyes of his saw the hopelessness of the people. He noticed that although the churches usually held nearly 200 people, the faces were changing all the time. It was not possible to hold their attention for more than a few minutes. Some wandered out. Others, carrying babies or leading children by the hand, came in. The middle-aged preachers extolled the virtues of patience from the pulpits and deplored the intransigence of the white government of Atlanta. They had no remedies, nothing to erase the pain from worn faces.

Carmichael nodded. He sent claques to sit in the front pews to chant and interrupt the services by calling for him. The ministers looked around confused. They had their homes, their cars, their television sets, and paying jobs. Carmichael and his SNCC had taken the floor away from them. He told the people that they were going to need more than petitions, more than patience. He spoke of the crimes of the "honkies" downtown who lived fat. They might read a petition. But they wouldn't do anything.

The Dixie Hills area was at present surrounded by police. Therefore, he said, "cool it," wait until they leave—today, tomorrow, the next day, then do something to hurt them and bring them back. The more Carmichael spoke, the more older faces he saw turn away from him and leave, the more teen-age boys remained to listen to him. The ministers and the civic leaders of Dixie Hills were shocked and powerless. As the meeting ended, a SNCC man yelled, "Remember Watts. Burn, baby, burn!"

That pulled the trigger. Fifty growing boys, mostly in sneakers, ran down both sides of the street. They picked up stones. They set up a holler, and when they came to the shops, the stones flew through plate-glass windows. They had been told to "cool it," but they could remember only "Burn, baby, burn!" The police of Atlanta tore through Dixie Hills before the first torch was lit. They came in squad cars, equipped with riot guns, and followed by two ambulances, prison vans, and an armored car. Big television lights glared from street corners.

A black woman leaned out of a window and said, "They're going to come up here and kill us like flies." When peace was restored, a hundred uniformed men were left to maintain order. Order number one was "Everybody off the street." The night was hot and breezeless; residents who could not afford air conditioning were accustomed to sitting on front stoops. The story made the front pages: RIOT IN DIXIE HILLS. Dr. King remained silent. On the second night a boy threw a fire bomb which landed near a policeman. The crack of guns and the whine of bullets were heard in the dark streets. A black man and a boy of nine, sitting on a stoop watching, were hit. One bullet killed the man; another wounded the boy.

It wasn't Watts. It wasn't a full-scale riot. The older people who lived in Dixie Hills remained indoors. They did not want violence. Some of their sons did. They got it. On the third night police were on rooftops with carbines. Boys raced from backyard to backyard, cursing the police, hopping fences, taunting, but the Dixie Hills protest was over. It went back to living the same dismal life; on Sunday they listened once more to their preachers counseling more and more patience. Stokely Carmichael had gone.

King flew to New York to appear on an ABC network program called *Issues and Answers*. Again he spoke about the need for government spending to raise the standard of living of the black man, the need for money to dismantle the jungle of slums and to move the blacks into other sections of towns and cities. "Many of the allies who were with us during the first phase of the Movement," he warned, "will not be with us now because it does mean dispersing the ghetto; it does mean living next door to them; and it does mean the government pouring billions of dollars into programs to get rid of slums and poverty and deprivation. I think this is why the civil rights movement has to restructure itself, in a sense to gear itself for an altogether new phase of struggle."

On the same day, race riots were in their third day at Cincinnati, Ohio. National Guardsmen patrolled the streets. In Tampa, race riots and fires were starting. Cassius Clay, heavyweight boxing champion of the world, was in Houston, Texas, sentenced to five years in prison and a fine of $10,000 for refusing to be inducted into the armed services of the United States. He claimed he was Muhammad Ali, a Black Muslim minister, and therefore exempt on religious grounds.

In the last week of June, James Earl Ray bought a secondhand Chrysler for $450 and left Chicago to head southwest. In East St. Louis, he traded it for a secondhand red Plymouth and paid $150 in cash. He told the dealer his name was Raynes.

Riots had broken out in many cities. It amounted to mass crime in the name of civil rights. Most of them were planned by young blacks, who roamed the streets, smashing, beating, looting, and setting fires. At home in Atlanta, Martin Luther kept careful track of the disorders. He saw the bright flames and the running silhouettes on his TV screen. "Winters of delay," he said to Mrs. King, "bring about our summers of riots." Her sympathy was with him in everything he did and said, not only because he was her husband, but because Coretta King believed that he was a great man. "People expect me to have answers," he said, "and I don't have any answers." She understood the despondency. She knew that many of the civil rights leaders had turned away from her husband, but she also knew that there was a great mass of mute people who believed in him as she believed in him. "There are millions of people who have faith in you and feel that you are our best hope." There was a sadness in this sentence. Until recently she would not have had to remind him of people who had faith in him.

He said nothing. He who desired above all to have an ever-expanding mission in life saw it ever-diminishing. She said, "I believe in you, if that means anything."

In some cases, wifely devotion at this time would reduce the husband to tears. He looked up from his chair. "Yes," he said, "it means a great deal."

On the days when Bernard Lee stopped at the front door, tooting the horn, to take him to another flight to another city, reporters would be waiting at the airport to ask Dr. King what he thought of this riot, and that riot, and had he heard—

King usually replied that he condemned the violence of the riots, but that he understood the conditions that caused them. He added that he thought that Americans should be just as concerned about correcting those conditions as they were about punishing the guilty.

The "Burn, baby, burn" credo was in the ascendancy; King and his philosophy of nonviolence were history. The predicted summer riots came. Detroit was a shambles. Detroit showed America what a full-scale riot can do to a metropolitan area. The city of Newark, once the pride of New Jersey with its sedate skyscrapers at Broad and Market streets, raged in flames. Riots plagued the racially torn town of Cambridge, in Maryland. H. Rap Brown, the new head of SNCC, was there, while the deposed Stokely Carmichael conferred with Fidel Castro in Havana. Brown had aroused the blacks to a fever pitch by his description of the killing of a white policeman in Plainfield, New Jersey. "Look what the brothers did in Plainfield," he raged. "They . . . stomped . . . a . . . cop . . . to . . . death. Good. He's dead. They stomped him to death. They threw a shopping basket on his head and took his pistol and shot him and then cut him." Brown waved his arms. "Detroit exploded!

Newark exploded! Harlem exploded! It is time for Cambridge to explode, baby! Black folks built America. If America don't come around, we're going to burn America down, brother. We're going to burn it if we don't get our share of it." Brown was arrested in Alexandria, Virginia, fleeing Maryland. SNCC paid the bail of $10,000, and Brown emerged from jail condemning the President for ordering "Cracker troops into Negro towns to kill black people." He referred to the President of the United States as "a wild, mad dog, an outlaw from Texas."

For a reason which no one could understand, Congress suddenly passed an antiriot law by a vote of 347 to 70, then declined, by a vote of 207 to 176, to spend $40,000,000 to rid the cities of rats. This was no more incongruous than the statement of Governor George Romney of Michigan that, in the riots, Detroit had scored a first in having "integrated looting." Dr. King was asked if he would go to the cities of insurrection. He said, "I will not." After the last ember had cooled, and thirty-one persons had been accorded decent burials, Rap Brown went to Detroit. "The honkie is your enemy!" he told cheering blacks. "You did a good job."

The Smiler was sure the summer would be cooler in Canada. He drove to Montreal, which was in a bubble of excitement called Expo '67, and leased a small apartment at 2589 East Notre Dame Avenue. The rent was $75 a month. He signed as Eric S. Galt and paid the first month's lease and the last. James Earl Ray was left with $70 and a gun. Soon he would have to get some money—either legally or illegally. So, in mid-July, he chose to hold up a store in Montreal and got away with $1,700. It was not the "big lick" of which he dreamed, but it gave him time to think about it.

He spent $300 for clothes at the Tip Top Tailors. Two days later he ordered a suit to be tailor-made at the English and Scotch Woolen Company. He asked the company to mail the suit to him at 2608 Highland Avenue, in Birmingham, Alabama. He had never had any such address. But he was to have a room in that house at a later date. The mystery is who it was who told Ray that he would be staying at that address in the future. Ray, who was always a penny pincher was spending money lavishly, as though it were impossible for him ever again to be broke. He needed women the way a car needs new spark plugs, and with about the same frequency. He needed one now and drove to the Laurentian Mountains to find one, and find one he did at Gray Rocks

Inn. The woman was suing an aggressive husband for divorce and found something appealing in the shy Smiler. They had drinks, and she managed to get "Mr. Galt" on the dance floor once.

Ray had phoned a travel agency and was told that if he claimed Canadian citizenship (as he did), he would require a witness who had known him in Canada for at least two years. This was incorrect. To get a visa to travel to another country on a Canadian passport, all he would have to do was swear that he was a Canadian citizen. He didn't need a witness. He spent considerable time cultivating the lady, and it is to be assumed he was planning to ask her to be the witness he thought he needed. Although he did not work, he did not go broke.

Ray had a great deal to say later about a man named "Raoul," but he did not know "Raoul's" last name or why he had advanced him sums of money without asking for something in return. His Montreal apartment faced the St. Lawrence River, and he visited taverns and the docks, talking to sailors. He was looking for Canadian identification cards. There is no doubt that he was seeking a quick safe way to leave Canada someday, by either plane or ship, but it seems equally certain that he would first go back to the United States to live in a city he had never visited for a purpose never disclosed.

He visited his newfound lady friend in Ottawa, but this time he was even more shy than the last. To her, he looked like a man about to blurt something, but afraid to talk. The woman in Canada did not know that Eric S. Galt was James Earl Ray, nor did she know that she was the first woman he had slept with in seven years. Her anonymous critique to William Bradford Huie was: "I would say he was normal; rather complimentary." He was no wild lover in full cry.

James Earl Ray was simpleminded and sly. The combination made him a half cipher, difficult to read, depending upon which way one turns it. He has been described as a "nigger hater," but Ray was never known to be cruel to blacks, never joined the Ku Klux Klan or White Citizens Council, never took part in a demonstration against blacks, and, so far as is known, never held up a black filling station or store. He was not addicted to drugs, cigarettes, women, or liquor. His innate shyness made him a loner inside prison and outside. The thirty-nine-day psychiatric evaluation at Missouri State Penitentiary points him up as one whose main concern in life was "money," which brings the observer back full circle to the "one big lick."

The only fear he nurtured secretly was that he would end back in the penitentiary. Now that he was free, he imagined a sinister pursuit by the authorities; he feared that the FBI might close in on him. And yet someone or something had sufficient power to pull him to Birmingham from the safety of Canada. He put Alabama license plates on his car. Without a job and no visible source of income, James Earl Ray luxuriated in Mexico before going to Birmingham. He had photographs taken and decided to have a doctor alter the tip of his nose and the prominence of his right ear.

He bought a year-old white Mustang. At the Hotel Rio, in Puerto Vallarta, he signed in as "Eric S. Galt, 2608 Highland Avenue, Birmingham, Ala." He passed himself off as an author, patronized two prostitutes, and lazed through November. When he arrived in Birmingham, it seems magical that he found a room at the place he had told the Canadian clothing company to ship his suit—2608 Highland Avenue. From the day he left prison, his traceable cash is itemized at $300 when he escaped, a net of $670 working at the Indian Trail restaurant, $1,700 from the holdup in Montreal—total, $2,670. With this, he had managed to live for six months, frequent bars, pay prostitutes, buy clothing, own three cars in succession, and live well in Mexico and Birmingham. He said later that "Raoul" had given him $700 to help smuggle small packages across the boarder from Canada to the United States, but anyone terrified of returning to prison—even a simpleminded one—is not going to risk the remainder of his life for $700 when he found it so easy to stand behind a gun and get $1,700.

No, it is much more credible to believe that someone in Birmingham —or some group of affluent personages—was willing to pay a large sum of money to have Dr. Martin Luther King killed. That would be the "one big lick," and to protect the man or men behind the murder, a middleman was used to contact Ray and keep him under daily orders, with a promise that he could travel to a far and safe country afterward. Better heads than his would tell him where to go, when to go, that he had bought the wrong rifle at the Aeromarine Company and send him back for the right one. There are incredible facts. When he bought the white Mustang for $1,995, he had, only a week before, rented a safe deposit box in the Birmingham Trust bank. The morning he bought the car from a private owner, he drove up to the bank, walked in, and, though the records prove he did not go to his safe deposit box, he came out with $2,000 in cash and drove off with the car. He had no Eric S. Galt driver's license; to get one from Alabama, he claimed that he had lost his Louisiana license. Ray was hardly the sort of man who would have been aware that Louisiana does not maintain records of old licenses. The middleman was at work again. It was easy to get an Eric S. Galt "renewal" from Alabama.

In September, while living at the Economy Grill and Rooms on Highland Avenue, a package arrived for Eric S. Galt form Canada: the suit. The man who owned the rooming house, Peter N. Cherpes, had a high opinion of Ray: "You couldn't imagine a nicer guy to have around— quiet, neat, paid his bill promptly every week, looked at television in the lobby, talked mostly about the weather." It would strain the imagination to think of a nicer guy.

The long hot summer was almost over. Black thunder and blue bolts of lightning swept the South in late August. Rain plastered the fields and the woodlands. Automobiles slowed, and headlights swept the highways in the afternoon. Martin Luther King sat in his den in the brick house he bought in Atlanta and thought. The depression had left him, but he sought a role, a niche, in the field of American politics. He needed a goal, an idea, which would sweep and touch everything, like this rain.

In August, Dr. King announced the start of a nationwide campaign to get voters to sign petitions so that a referendum could be placed on the ballot to stop the war in Vietnam. Summer volunteers, the doctor explained in his statement, were getting signatures in New York, San Francisco, Cleveland, Seattle, Portland, and the state of Wisconsin. In the same week the National Mobilization Committee to End the War in Vietnam made the front pages. Without King's assistance, the body announced that it would demonstrate in Washington in October and "shut down the Pentagon." The Reverend Thomas Lee Hayes, an Episcopal minister, said, "We will gather in a massive anti-war presence, and some will take on the serious responsibility of direct dislocation of the war machine." Of the Pentagon, he said, "We will fill the hallways and block the entrances. . . . In the name of humanity we will call the war makers to task."

Dr. King withheld his support from the group, as did most clergymen identified with the civil rights movement. Rabbi Richard G. Hirsch spoke for many when he conceded that most of the clergy, while opposed to war, "are not prepared to go along with these people who think that everything the United States does is wrong and everything Hanoi does is right."

After Labor Day, there was a convention of a group called the National Conference for New Politics. It was in actuality a beef stew of youthful organizations which sent 3,000 young people to the Palmer

House in Chicago. Among the 200 organizations represented were some older active participants, SNCC and the SCLC, as well as Dr. Benjamin Spock. The goals of the convention were simple: Defeat Lyndon Johnson in the 1968 elections by creating a third political force within the nation.

Dr. King, who had once acknowledged that Lyndon Johnson was the greatest friend the American black ever had, joined the convention as keynote speaker. Obviously referring to Johnson, he declared, "The American people must have an opportunity to vote into oblivion those who cannot detach themselves from militarism, those who lead us not to a new world but drag us to the brink of a dead world." Those behind the scenes who imagined a King-Spock ticket misgauged the temper of the delegates. A reporter for the *New Republic* penciled that Dr. King's keynote address "was such a bore to the delegates that they started to walk out of the hall ten minutes before it was finished." A writer for the *New Leader* typed "support for Doctor King as a third-party candidate dissipated after his opening night speech. He not only failed to fire emotions, but the black militants and white radicals wrote him off as passé. . . ." The *New Yorker* stated: "As he spoke, some local Negro teen-agers shouted threats and insults at him from the back of the room." The pastor left, dejected, in the morning. The repetitive phrases, the Biblical allegories, the preachments for peace and love were now out of date. Once 200,000 people in Washington had come to their feet at the sound of those rolling words, applauding and weeping. To the shrewd sophisticates of the next generation, the words had improved nothing, had not encouraged either peace or love.

In front of the hotel, as Dr. King departed, an assemblage of bongo drummers were chanting: "Kill Whitey! Kill Whitey!" King knew as well as any student of politics that if nominated, he could not win. But it would have been the greatest honor he ever received to have been nominated for the highest office in the land. But Martin Luther King— the man of Montgomery—could not have lent himself to the convention philosophy. These were the people he had called the "crazies." Black Power dominated the convention. What had been called a convention of groups of whites and blacks, members of 200 affiliates, were soon transmuted into mute sheep adhering to the shouted demands of black militants. James Forman of SNCC took the podium. Speaking for the black delegates, he drew a Malcolm X line between whites and blacks: "We and we alone have the responsibility to wage our own war of liberation as we see fit. No one, absolutely no one in the world or the

United States, has the right to dictate to us the forms of our struggle. We insist in our right to define the manner in which we will fight our aggressors. It is our right, our responsibility, and anyone who does not like it can go to hell."

A young white woman stood and called for "a point of order."

James Forman shouted, "There are no points of order."

A delegate yelled, "Is this a dictatorship?"

The round face of James Forman froze in a frown. "Yes," he said, "and I'm the dictator." This indeed was the "new politics."

King divorced himself from the new politics, which was, in any case, stillborn. He sat home meditating, writing bits and pieces of the next book. The SCLC people suggested many ideas, but one by one, they were discarded. The doctor needed inspiration and drama, and it came from an unusual quarter. Marian Wright Edelman had spent time working among the poor of Mississippi and also on poverty programs in Washington. She was talking to Martin Luther King about her work, and she said that she was both impressed and distressed at the number of programs which Congress had passed to assist the down-and-out and how few people knew anything about these programs or how to avail themselves of government aid. King listened fascinated. Mrs. Edelman said that she had spoke to many Congressmen about it, and they agreed that it was time that the government lifted the rock-bottom poor to a point where they could feed their families and keep a roof over their heads. There were many avenues already open to the poor—if they but realized it—and Congressmen were ready to grant more, if someone would ask.

Enthusiasm spread across the features of Martin Luther King. He asked more and more questions, then hurried across Atlanta to speak to the leaders at the SCLC. He asked dozens of questions and barely waited for the responses. He came home in the evening, and Coretta King found him bubbling. "This is it," he said. "This is really it." He was excited. He spoke about organizing a march of poor people, people who would walk to Washington from all over the nation to plead their own case to the government. The more he talked about it, the more he honed the idea. "We should get people from all the poverty areas, from the South and from the North, people who don't have jobs or resources. We must get them marching toward Washington. I think it would really dramatize this issue. It must not be just black people; it must be all the poor. We must include Indians, Puerto Ricans, Mexicans, even the poor whites . . ."

A Poor People's March on Washington would do exactly what Martin Luther King required. It would help the poor, it would dramatize the forlorn character of the forgotten, it would bring together complexions of all shades united in hardship, and it would reestablish Martin Luther King at the top of what he called Phase Two of the Movement. Let the violent ones shout their heads off. Let the crazies set their fires and shoot their guns. Let the lawyers file their staid briefs in the marble halls of the Supreme Court. A million eyes, large with hunger, standing suppliant before the power structure, begging a crust of bread, was a gesture worthy of a Gandhi. It had been present, all along, and he had not seen it. Now it was his to hold, his to announce, his to recruit, his to lead, his to feel that he was doing something for "the least of these."

Dr. King was busy with details of the march. He placed the matter before the SCLC and won approval at once. In conference, it was decided to concentrate the drive for recruits to ten cities and five outlying areas. King figured if he got 200 poor from each place, he would lead a march of 3,000 to Washington. It was a small goal. And yet it was not as simple an idea as King thought. His staff reminded him that there would be a great deal of detailed work in providing a place to camp in Washington, tents or other temporary structures for housing, food for 3,000 for the march as well as at the encampment, doctors, nurses and medicines, water, toilets, cooking facilities—the list was long. Martin Luther King was in his element as a stage manager. He saw the Poor People's March, as Coretta King wrote later "as the answer to a pressing need for further programs." Her husband saw it as more than that; much more. "This," he said, "is a mammoth job. Before, we mobilized one city at a time. Now we are mobilizing a nation."

Psychologically, King may have had a compulsion to be a bigger, better man than his father. The things which Dr. King was trying to do with cities and a nation "Daddy" King had been doing all along with individuals. It is not overstating it to say that he may have been one of the most profound father figures in the black South. He spoke bluntly, but not insolently. He was pastor of his church, but he was also the "Daddy" of the thousands of men and women and children who worshiped there. He spoke for Jesus Christ; but he did not speak in "tongues," and he had no time for fancy figures of speech. When he stood in the pulpit and said, "You people in De Kalb County, your taxes are due January 15 and I want you to know that," he was a father reminding children of a duty which may have escaped their attention. If they did not pay the taxes, he did not want them to come whimpering to him that the sheriff was serving notice of foreclosure on a house or a farm.

On days when no church services were scheduled, he would sit behind a big desk in a parlor office on the left side of the corridor. There he would listen to the problems of the poor, the misguided, the neglected children, the jobless, the hurt. He asked incisive questions and gave his best counsel. He was the final arbiter at Ebenezer Baptist Church and the neighborhood. The headquarters of the SCLC was diagonally down the street from his church, and when he walked into the office, which was infrequent, receptionists, secretaries, and staff directors hugged the walls to let him go by. The respect which was accorded to "Daddy" King was never asked; it belonged to him.

Throughout October, as the son was working on his new inspiration, the father was working with a group of Atlanta ministers on Operation Breadbasket. This was a campaign he could support. He wanted to get jobs for blacks. He had no time to talk to the shiftless and lazy, but if a man had a family and wanted to work, there should be a position for him somewhere and a salary commensurate with the work. A delegation of ministers appealed to the new governor, Lester Maddox, for an appointment to talk about state jobs. Governor Maddox had been a restaurateur and, rather than permit blacks to eat in his place, threatened them with pick handles. The black clergy wanted to talk to the archsegregationist, and they knew they had to invite "Daddy" King to participate, but the question was how to keep the Reverend Mr. King's mouth shut or jeopardize whatever Maddox was willing to grant. It wasn't easy. Tactfully, they approached "Daddy" King and said that so-and-so would do the talking, and the rest of us are just going to sit there—nice and quiet. He nodded.

The old man was ushered into the governor's office and sat in his chair. He studied the small, smiling, patronizing face and the eyes behind the glasses. He put one huge palm on one heavy knee, listened to the dialogue, then shifted and put the other palm on the other knee. His glance went from the minister who was speaking to the governor and back to the speaker. Suddenly, his mind reached the point of no return, and his tongue tripped over it.

"Now, Governor Maddox," he said, "I want you to know we didn't come here begging." The hush represented a total abstinence from breathing. "We want our rightful share of jobs in this state, and if you don't let us have them, we're going to get them anyway." Two men stared at each other through glistening glasses. Maddox didn't move.

"Furthermore," said King, "I've been reading about you in the paper, and you say you believe in segregation. You call yourself a Christian? You're a deacon of your church. What kind of preachers have you been listening to?" He took a deep breath of indignation. "I'd like to invite you to come down to Ebenezer and hear me preach. I think I can help you."

The governor did not press a buzzer for a state trooper to show the blacks out. He did not respond in anger. The governor smiled in delight at "Daddy" King and said, "I expect you can, Reverend King." The ministers began to breathe. And smile. When they stood to take their leave, the governor got up from behind his desk and walked over to the old man. "Can you come back to see me sometime?" he said. "I'd like to talk to you some more." When Maddox tendered his first formal reception at the Governor's Mansion, "Daddy" King was invited. And accepted. The governor also allotted a proportion of state jobs to blacks.

Someone gave James Earl Ray $2,000 and a New Orleans phone number. He was told to call that number from time to time for orders. Whatever the orders were, James Earl Ray understood the nature of the assignment, because his Birmingham boss told Ray that he would get an additional $12,000 in cash and a visa to a foreign country, including an escape route through Canada. The ex-con must have been happy—perhaps for the first time in his life—because he was making that "one big lick." As he stated later to William Bradford Huie: "I had fifteen hundred when I got to Birmingham. There I was given three thousand. I spent twenty-five hundred for the car and photo equipment. Another thousand on living expenses. . . . So I was a lot better off than I had ever been. . . ."

It is logical to assume that no one would give Ray that kind of money without a detailed discussion of the assignment: the murder of Martin Luther King. The total of the sums he received, in addition to what was promised, comes to about $20,000. James Earl Ray was never more than what is called in the trade a "two-bit crook." He was unintelligent, unimaginative. Somewhere between Birmingham and East St. Louis, there is an underworld character who was asked to find a man who could commit the murder, someone who would obey orders to the letter. It is preposterous to place credence in Ray's story that someone named "Raoul," a Canadian smuggler, made the original contact in Montreal. No one there knew Ray's real name, and the authorities were not sufficiently interested to track him down. It is much more likely that, enroute to meet his brothers in the Midwest, after he crossed the border from Canada to the United States, that he was taken to a middleman for casual discussions about Ray's feelings regarding blacks and, in particular, Martin Luther King.

Certainly Ray's backers must have convinced him that they would have him killed if he exposed the plotters. In addition, it is reasonable to asume that, even though James Earl Ray's "base of operations" was set in Birmingham, that the person or persons willing to pay $20,000 to see Martin Luther King dead did not live in Birmingham. It is possible that only the middleman was there. The money could have come from anywhere.

James Earl Ray probably was selected because: (1) he had never committed a crime of violence; (2) as long as the money kept coming his way, he would not ask questions; (3) he hated blacks; and (4) he was a boob with the nerve to squeeze a trigger when told. These are not Class A recommendations. There are hundreds of accomplished felons North and South who would have done the work for less; some for love.

It must also have crossed the mind of the prime mover in the plot that Ray might be caught. Anyone who will spend $20,000 or more to have someone slain must think of airtight protection. This is possible only if the money man is unknown to the assassin. It is also necessary to employ a go-between whose identity is unknown to the killer and who keeps him happy with cash. Thus, if the killer is apprehended, or if he fails to execute his assignment, the chain of characters is broken and untraceable.

In the middle of November, Ray moved to Los Angeles. He was safe in Mexico, but whatever fear he had of being tracked inside the United States must have dissipated. He rented an apartment at 1535 Serrano and enjoyed himself doing as he pleased. At the end of November he called the New Orleans phone number. The voice on the other end was not one he recognized, but the voice asked if he could visit New Orleans around Christmas. He said he would be there.

One of the more sensible thoughts he had was that, no matter what country he fled to, he would have to earn a living. After much thinking, he decided that the one job a qualified man could fill anywhere in the world would be as a bartender. Whiskeys and mixed drinks are universal; in cases where there are special native preferences, these are easily learned.

His nightly pleasure was to sit on a barstool near the door of the

Rabbit's Foot Club. He ordered vodka and orange juice but did more staring than drinking. Sometimes he started a conversation with a girl on an adjoining stool, but mostly he watched and listened. Once in a while, when the conversation became political, James Earl Ray would speak up in favor of Governor George Wallace of Alabama for President. He spoke up and sometimes got into endless wrangles about blacks and civil rights. One night he was followed into the parking lot, beaten up and robbed. The old-time burglar was as vulnerable as the store he had robbed in Canada. He did not dare complain to the police. His assailants got $60 and his Alabama driver's license. The license was important.

Someone told him that an American could go to Colombia, South America, and live there without a passport. Ray's reaction was to enroll in a dance school that taught Latin dances. The newspaper advertisement said that the cost was $32, but Ray was halfway through the course before he realized that the full course would actually cost more than $900. It was another failure, the robber being robbed. He enrolled in a course for bartenders at $125, a course which would include a diploma. His self-esteem was often monumental. He made an appointment with a Los Angeles plastic surgeon and said he wanted the tip of his nose leveled off because he had a job "doing TV commercials." The doctor, listening to that country boy diction, refrained from asking what kind of commercial.

The doctor anesthetized the nose and did the work. James Earl Ray paid for the alteration and remembered that the tip, which had been elevated, had also pointed slightly to one side. He went back to his apartment and, while the nose was still numb, removed the dressing and pushed the tip to the opposite side. This, as he stated later, would prevent the doctor from ever being able to identify him. He went to another plastic surgeon to have one ear pinned back, but Christmas and New Orleans were approaching. He did not have time for anything except his bartender's course.

The big press announcement occurred on December 4. Dr. King told the world about his Poor People's March on Washington. It received all the publicity he hoped for, but it wasn't all friendly. The announcement of the convergence of 3,000 poor to request help from its government was not alarming. The pastor feared that an announcement "too tame" in character would result in apathy from the poor and disregard on the part of President Johnson and the government. As a result, he put some dynamite in it. It was not just a Poor People's March, it was a "massive civil disobedience campaign." Although Indians, Mexicans, Puerto Ricans, and Americans had been invited to participate, Dr. King said that the "extended" campaign would represent the "last desperate demand" by blacks to prevent "the worst chaos, hatred and violence any nation has ever encountered."

The threat received more attention than the march. The Establishment learned that Dr. King said his followers "might" tie up transportation in Washington, overcrowd all hospitals, boycott the schools, and stage sit-ins at all government buildings. The press asked him if he had abandoned Chicago? Had he renounced his Christian ethic? Was he now one of the "crazies" he had reviled for years? Was he at last pitting race against race?

King was in no mood to make explanations or even to enumerate his demands. "I think we have come to the point where there is no longer a choice between nonviolence and riots," he said. "It must be militant massive nonviolence, or riots." When the date of the march was announced as "April," word went out from the White House to have 10,000 troops and police ready to "protect the marchers." From whom? one may ask. The 10,000 armed men, to the contrary, would be present to confine the marchers to nonsensitive areas along the Potomac. It was the government which needed protection.

"We welcome help from all civil-rights organizations," Dr. King said. "I think both the NAACP and the Urban League play a significant role. I also feel that CORE and SNCC have played very significant roles. . . . Some of the Black Power groups have temporarily given up on integration. We have not. So maybe we are on the bridge, in the middle, reaching across and connecting both sides."

The doctor was asked about the aims of the march. What he wanted, he said, was a sort of economic Bill of Rights. Sometimes that "would guarantee a job to all who want to work and are able to work. It would also guarantee an income for all who are not able to work. . . ."

The staff at the SCLC reported that it was not going to be easy to recruit 3,000 whites, Indians, blacks, Puerto Ricans, and Mexicans. At once, King set off on a people-to-people tour of several states, outlining his Poor People's March and asking for volunteers. Where his staff failed, he did not. He found the poor, and he convinced them. Then he enlarged the original conception of the march. The 3,000 people were to be marshals, appointed to watch over and protect the scores of thousands of poor he expected to see in Washington. He told his wife that

he would like to see a mule train and a wagon start out from Mississippi
to join the march to the Potomac.

The duration of the encampment was fixed at one week. His inspiration fired more inspiratons. He asked the SCLC to arrange to build a
real shantytown along the edges of the reflecting pool so that the Establishment could see what poverty looked like. He wanted those big men
in those high offices to see it and smell it. Someone said that government
troops might stop them from building and occupying the shanties. It
didn't alter King's enthusiasm, because he could see the cameras
watching as the poor were evicted, weeping, and the troops tore the
shacks apart. It had happened once before, in the Depression years,
when soldiers of World War I had formed a Bonus Army and had been
run off government property by General Douglas A. MacArthur and the
succeeding generation of soldiers. The resultant publicity had caused the
government to hang its head in shame. It could be done again.

The bright spangling ornaments of Christmas and the ho-ho-ho of
Hollywood Santas seem, to the non-Californian, as artificial as plastic
Christmas trees, but downtown Los Angeles was in full cry for Christmas early in December. The canned voice of Bing Crosby warbling "I'm
Dreaming of a White Christmas" threaded the palm trees and the
poinsettias from Union Station to the Beverly Hills Hotel. This Christmas season was tourist weather, warm and sunny with lampposts
festooned with pine branches and silver tinsel and flickering colored
lights.

It was time to go. James Earl Ray had the white Mustang tuned up
and ready. He was going to New Orleans to meet his boss and get some
new orders. He was to meet his man in a certain bar. He thought the
nose surgery made him look younger. Two people were going with him,
Charles Stein and his sister, Rita Stein. They were innocents who were
drawn in sympathy toward the lonesome Smiler. "Eric," as they called
him, told them practically nothing about his past except what he was
able to invent in conversation, and they proved their trust in him by
allowing him to convert them to the cause of George Wallace. They
went to Wallace headquarters in North Hollywood and signed a petition
for the governor of Alabama to run for President.

The Steins thought that they would enjoy seeing the sights of New
Orleans. They had heard about the French Quarter and the Dixieland
bands. Ray said that they could have some fun while he transacted a
little business and then they could drive back to California together. It

was a vacation lark—a change of scenery—for the Steins. The Mustang chewed up Route 10 eastbound, picking up state roads where 10 died off, then coming alive in the next state.

So far as is known, there was no romantic interlude between Ray and Rita Stein. It was a trio of joyriders, two congenial people and one un. They drove day and night, taking turns at the wheel, talking sometimes about the scenery, lapsing into long silences listening to music on a radio station until it faded off in distance and someone tuned in another. In New Orleans the car was parked, a reasonable hotel selected, and the Steins wandered off to see the colorful part of the city.

The day was December 17 on the hotel register of the Provincial. Ray made his phone call and met his man. Apparently, the conference was to the point. The boss wanted a report on what James Earl Ray had been doing with his time in Mexico and California. He listened. One can but deduce from what occurred later that Ray was told that the job he must do would have to wait two or three months. He was also ordered to change his place of residence in Los Angeles to the St. Francis Hotel on Hollywood Boulevard. He was to remain there and await further instructions. He was also to continue to go to the general post office looking for letters addressed to Eric S. Galt.

He was handed $2,500 in $20 bills. Whoever was investing in Ray as a gunman now had expended a total of $8,500 in his future. He was also reminded that when the job was satisfactorily completed, he would get an additional $12,000 and a passport to a "safe" country. Ray, who knew little of geography and less of international politics, asked what would be a "safe" country. The answer was Rhodesia. He was told that it had been part of the British Empire in Africa, but that it had left the Commonwealth because the whites in Rhodesia were the ruling class and were pledged to dominate the native blacks. This must have sounded admirable to Ray. He may also have been told that at this particular moment in history, Rhodesia was a pariah among nations and wasn't recognized by the United States. Little Rhodesia would be perfect for James Earl Ray. Absolutely perfect. He was sure that he could live like a king among whites who subscribed to his racial views, and once he had mastered the art of the cocktail shaker and the mixed drink, he could do the quick little job which had to be done, meet the boss in Birmingham, get on a plane to Canada, and be off to a lifetime of easy living and freedom as a bartender in the former British colony.

He met the Steins. After some New Orleans sight-seeing, the three drove back to Los Angeles. Dutifully, Ray moved from Serrano Avenue to the worn and respectable atmosphere of the St. Francis. His room was above the Sultan Bar, and there, in the evenings, he could spend a little money, shove an ice cube deeper into a glass of vodka and orange juice, and glance forgivingly at a world which had, at every turn until now, proved smarter than he. Until now. On December 28, 1967, "Eric S. Galt" sat to a typewriter and typed a letter painfully, slowly, and solely in capital letters.

It was addressed to American Southern Africa Council in Washington. It began: "THE LOCAL JOHN BIRCH SOCIETY PROVIDED ME WITH YOUR ADDRESS." The letter acknowledged that the United States did not issue passports to Rhodesia, but the applicant was interested in emigrating to Rhodesia. Could they please tell him how this could be arranged? It was signed "ERIC S. GALT" and the return address was his recent apartment on Serrano. In time a reply arrived. And when Ray was sure that there would be no complications, he called for the letter. It told him that the council was concerned mainly with emerging southeastern African nations and then only in tourism. Ray found time to visit a local library and read a little about Rhodesia. Except for the hot river basins, Rhodesia was largely lofty plateaus and had a comfortable climate. In the middle of the twentieth century, it had a population of more than 4,000,000 of which 220,000 were white. The remainder were mostly Bantu natives. Salisbury, the capital, had a population of 300,000 with well-paved streets, ornate buildings, and a European atmosphere. The language was English, and it would be an ideal place for the Smiler.

The New Year came cold and clear to Atlanta, and dead Christmas trees shuddered in the gutters along Auburn Avenue. The metropolis of the South, churning out goods and services, was primarily interested in earning more dollars in 1968 than in 1967. This was the common denominator of American cities and towns. The nation, exalted in its fascination with scientific progress, computers, automation, the exploration of space, technology, coupled with an ingrained faith in its materialistic power, had no time to search for its soul. An Oriental, looking at it in retrospect, might have called it the Year of the Rolling Heads.

This was the hour Martin Luther King chose to turn to God. He had been away on a long mission. At the age of thirty-nine, he had spent more time out of his church than in it. No one knows why he chose this moment to go back to the pulpit, to don the vestments of his father, to preach. Week after week after week, the pastor spent his hours in the Ebenezer Baptist Church, as though to make up in a short time the neglect of a long time. Or as though he knew he had an appointment to keep. The big brown eyes danced with joy; smiles dimpled the round face. His words came from the pulpit in the deep, slow cadence that was the Martin Luther King of old.

He did not neglect the political aspects of his life. He still announced, from the pulpit, the weekly casualty figures of Vietnam, and he blamed President Lyndon Johnson for permitting himself to be drowned in the vortex of the military-industrial complex of the country. King was conscious of world peace and his self-appointed role to seek it, to find it, to force it upon the diplomatic gentlemen of the several nations. Nor had he renounced his Poor People's March. The Movement was in chaos, but he said cheerfully, "I'm going for broke." He would attend the Movement, flog the war makers, and still find time for the Supreme Court of his calling.

In Washington, Stokely Carmichael found himself without a campaign. He had returned from visits to Cuba and North Vietnam, but his opinions on international matters struck no responsive chord in the nation. Wandering around a hotel, he too had an inspirational idea. Why not have a secret Black Power meeting—by invitation only? Why not? Perhaps they could come up with an idea for a campaign, worthy of time and energy—and Carmichael had plenty of both. The meeting was held at the New School for Afro-American Thought. A hundred civil rights leaders attended. Martin Luther King flew up from Atlanta to solicit help in his Poor People's March from the group advocating an outlook he publicly feared the year before—Black Power.

King and Carmichael had time to talk. The seminar lasted but two hours. The pastor felt that the Black Power wing, violent though it was, could ensure the success of his march. Whatever number of people King could cajole into marching, SNCC and CORE groups could treble it. Stokely Carmichael, at the secret meeting, coaxed the militant leaders into joining in King's march. He gave the temporary organization a new title: Black United Front. In addition to enlisting support for King, the young man did more; he promised that SNCC would help with the housing and food requirements in Washington. Dr. King left the meeting jubilant. He said that all groups in the Black United Front would have to pledge themselves to nonviolence in the week that the poor would be in Washington. The lions, he felt, were joining with the lambs. Those who attended the meeting were certain that the lambs were joining the lions.

The pastor hurried back to Atlanta to preach at Ebenezer Baptist Church, a matter which had become a compulsion with him. On that first Sunday in February, King chose his own death as the subject for his sermon. Privately, he had discussed the possibility of his being killed many times. The tone was never morbid, no matter how low his spirit. He spoke of death as one who walks with it in silence. The killer or killers might miss, but again—

"Every now and then," he said from the pulpit, "I guess we all think realistically about that day when we will be victimized with what is life's common denominator—that something we call death." From the crowded pews he heard the murmur: "Noo-o-o." "We all think about it. And every now and then I think about my own death, and I think about my own funeral. And I don't think of it in a morbid sense," the pastor said brightly. The flash of the handsome smile was on his face. "Every now and then I ask myself: What is it I would want said? And I leave the word to you this morning.

"If any of you are around when I have to meet my day, I don't want a long funeral. And if you get somebody to deliver the eulogy, tell them not to talk too long. Every now and then I wonder what I want them to say. Tell them not to mention that I have a Nobel Peace Prize, that isn't important. Tell them not to mention that I have three or four hundred other awards, that's not important. Tell them not to mention where I went to school.

"I'd like somebody to mention that day that 'Martin Luther King tried to give his life serving others.' I'd like for somebody to say that day that 'Martin Luther King tried to love somebody.' I want you to say on that day, that I tried to be right on the war question. I want you to be able to say that day that I did try to feed the hungry. And I want you to be able to say that day that I did try, in my life, to clothe those who were naked. I want you to say on that day that I did try, in life, to visit those who were in prison. I want you to say that I tried to love and serve humanity.

"Yes, if you want to say that I was a drum major, say that I was a drum major for justice. Say that I was a drum major for peace. I was a drum major for righteousness." Some of the women bowed their heads and wept. "And all of the other shallow things will not matter. I won't have any money to leave behind. I won't have the fine and luxurious things of life to leave behind. I just want to leave a committed life behind. And that is all I want to say . . . if I can help somebody as I pass along, if I can cheer somebody with a word or song, if I can show somebody he is traveling wrong, then my living will not be in vain. If I can do my duty as a Christian ought, if I can bring salvation to a world overwrought, if I can spread the message as the Master taught, then my living will not be in vain. . . ."

It had been intended as a cool assessment of his death. The people in the church were solemn and saddened as they left. They too knew that his mission in the Movement could bring sudden death. They had known it all along, as "Daddy" King had known it, as Coretta King had been aware of it, as his disciples knew.

The morning after the sermon, King was in Washington at Arlington Cemetery for a memorial service for the Vietnam war dead. Later, in a speech he made the observation that: "We have developed an under-class in this nation, and unless the underclass is made a working class, we are going to continue to have problems. . . . We of the Southern Christian Leadership Conference . . . feel that it is time now to take a Selma-type or Birmingham-type movement to bear on the economic problems confronting the poor people of our nation."

The International School of Bartending, at 2125 Sunset Boule-vard, offered a six-week course in the preparation and dispensing of alcoholic beverages. It was a legitimate enterprise and was administered by Tomas Reyes Lau, a dark intense man who was also the principal teacher. In the middle of January, the Smiler was ready to begin study. He paid for his tuition and impressed Mr. Lau as "a nice fellow with a slight Southern accent—very intelligent—with ability to develop in this type of service." If, by this, he meant that James Earl Ray was diligent, tried hard, and seldom opened his mouth, either to teacher or customer, he was right.

His written application, on the other hand, was a masterpiece of confusion. He wrote the date "1-19-68" in the upper-right-hand corner, then wrote his name as "Eric S. Galt." Where the application asked for his Social Security number, he left it blank. Address was marked in as "15 35 N. Serrano"; then a line was drawn through it. Under, he wrote: "55 33 Hollywood Blvd." For phone number, he penned, "4698096," then drew a line through that and penned, 464-1131." He gave his age as "36"—wrong. His birthday was "7-20-31," making Ray a little younger. He said he was a U.S. citizen; wrote "single"; "none" under the word "children." It is possible, even probable, that Ray was nervous filling out this application, because he altered it several times. Under former employers, he wrote something indecipherable which looks like "T. S. Shaft," then scratched it out and wrote "Mr. Willer, 751-S-Figeroa, salary 50.00." There was no Mr. Willer.

The bartenders' school asked for three character references. He wrote: "Moris Deninno, 5533 Hollywood Bl. Hollywood; Rita Steen, 5666 Franklin, Hollywood, Calif; Charly Dennino 5666 Franklin, Hollywood, Calif." It is certain that, in the second and third cases, he intended Rita Stein and her brother, but it came out "Steen" and "Deninno." Ray further stated that he had a "high school" education. Thoughtfully, in the space where it asked "What work do you do best?" Ray left it blank. He wrote that he was "5-10," weighed "175," and, when asked about physical defects, wrote "none." Ray must have turned on that tiny grin when, at the bottom where he had to sign, the application stated: "I hereby grant permission to investigate any of the information included in this application." Obviously, he was confident that there would be no checkup; he was right.

Lau, a short precise man, invited his student to examine the premises. The school looked like a smart cocktail room. It had a curved bar, dim lights, a heavy carpet, and a three-tiered array of liquor bottles, filled with colored water. There were shot glasses, cocktail glasses, highball glasses, stemmed martini glasses, champagne glasses, and brandy snifters. The teacher set an obvious example to students in his neatness: His hair glistened; his clothes were carefully draped; his shoes gleamed; his crayon mustache was carefully trimmed.

Ray sat with his teacher and was told that in six weeks he would be a qualified bartender, would know how to mix 110 types of drinks, and would, as a matter of course, be taught confidence, coordination, personality, poise, hygiene, and fundamental psychology. At graduation, in March, the student would get a bona fide diploma and have his photo taken in a tuxedo jacket, lacy shirt, and black tie. James Earl Ray intended to avail himself of the teaching, but he would not want the job promised. Bartenders in big cities usually have to register with the police and are often fingerprinted.

Ray was busy. By day he was studying to be a bartender, how to chuckle at a bad joke, what to do about a fractious customer who might try to wreck the bar, how to be attentive to lady customers without alienating their escorts. By night he was visiting hypnotists, scientologists, and charlatans in an effort to escape the periodic depressions which plagued him. Most of all, Ray was going to need confidence if he got to Rhodesia. He fretted that this was what was lacking in him.

A meeting of the top officers of the Southern Christian Leadership Conference was called for February 12. There was a growing opposition within the ranks to King's Poor People's March, and he was determined to have a showdown. The directors and the staff knew that King would win his fight. If they were united against him—and they weren't—King could hint at resigning and the SCLC would cease to exist. They knew this. He knew it too. On the cold, clear morning of Lincoln's Birthday, he parked at the curb beside the old Masonic Building and swept through the warren of cardboard-partitioned offices.

They were waiting. He was late. King nodded, and there was a chorus of mild hellos. He sat behind the desk, in the big leather-back chair and teetered back on its legs. He glanced at Bayard Rustin, who had officially severed his affiliation with the SCLC long ago. There was opposition there. There was opposition from Michael Harrington, who received a nod of recognition. Dr. King said that the minutiae of the Poor People's March had been drawn up—he took a sheaf of papers from his briefcase—and he proposed to go over it so that everyone would be acquainted with it. If anyone could substitute a better idea, he was willing to listen.

This was a different meeting. Dr. King had always ruled with a gentle hand, sometimes interspersing "down-home" jokes in the order of business. This time there was rebellion among his officers. Did any one believe the march would help President Johnson's new civil rights bill to get through Congress? Did anyone think that the presence of blacks in government halls, sitting in, lying in, would solicit the sympathy of the United States government? The truly poor—black and white—were illiterate and lived in miserable shacks. If the press asked them why they were in Washington would they know? Besides, did the doctor know that recruiting was moving so slowly that it would be necessary for him to go on another people-to-people trip to get enough volunteers to make an impression? And after the impression was made, how would the SCLC get those people back to Mississippi or Massachusetts or wherever they came from?

Abernathy sat quietly, always ready to subscribe to anything Dr. King proposed to do. But they weren't all Abernathys. Andrew Young was an independent thinker, and a good one. Rustin was a master of political in-fighting. Harrington and some of the others couln't bear one more failure. They would prefer to postpone or devise a campaign with success ensured. Dr. King listened to them calmly and quietly. Then he told them he would proceed with the plans he had made.

King was in command. Slowly, he began to talk. He could think of nothing more worthy—nor could anyone else—than helping the poor. To clothe the naked, to feed the hungry were an aspiration worthy of a saint. The trouble with the board, he said, was that it feared the retaliation of the Establishment. Couldn't everyone see that the impoverished, the disenfranchised were above politics? The presence of the skeletons on lawns facing the well nourished, would shame the administration; it would render the power structure incapable of retaliation. What could Congress or the President do? Evict them? Burn the shacks of "Resurrection City"? Throw them into prisons? Use soldiers and tear gas? Oh, no. This was one campaign which no one dared oppose. Hadn't Franklin D. Roosevelt said: "I see one third of a nation ill fed, ill housed . . ."? Had the situation changed for the better? No. The helpless had been caught in a cycle of hunger, lack of education, lack of well-paying jobs, despair, lassitude. Even the will to fight had been taken from the poor.

That was exactly where the SCLC would come in. It would provide the leadership, the will to do battle for the poor. If there was any weakness in the plan, it was this: The poor were resistant to getting off their knees to march. That, said Dr. King, was why it would require all their efforts between now and April 20 to enlist a sufficient number of marchers. The doctor had some fresh ideas about that, too. He would make another people-to-people trip to recruit volunteers. And no one in the room doubted that with his gifted powers of persuasion, King could get them. The march was going to be bigger, much bigger, than originally outlined. He would like it to surpass A. Philip Randolph's March on Washington. The SCLC was going to need at least 300,000 people in the opening phase of the encampment. Help was pledged from SNCC and CORE and other organizations which would give money and recruit volunteers, too. The directors must understand that this thing would have to be big, very big, and potent. He toyed with the idea of expanding the encampment from the original one week to a period of three months. That would carry it up to July 20.

Consulting the plans before him, Dr. King said that the original groups would come from Roxbury, Massachusetts, Chicago's Lawndale, the state of Mississippi, the West Virginia mining districts. This would be only the beginning. The doctor hoped that when the publicity ball got rolling, the poor, white as well as black, would converge on the capital from all directions. Part of the plan, he said, was for camp marshals to accompany crowds of the poor to the front of the White House, to the halls of Congress, to such government departments as Health, Education, and Welfare; Agriculture; and Housing and Urban Development. This would have to be done daily. Unless the poor were stopped, they would clutter the halls, the aisles, sit in the reception offices—shame the government.

Someone asked if King could define the goals of the march. Yes, he could. "We want a twelve billion dollar bill of rights," he said. The money was to be used to destroy ghettos and allow them to spring up, fresh and bright and new, with small homes, apartment houses, green trees, playgrounds and modern shops. Second, he expected the government to guarantee work for everyone able to work; if sufficient employment was not available, then let the government create jobs—it was Lyndon Johnson's dilemma, not King's. Third, a guarantee from the government of a dole to those unable to work because of age or sickness. King didn't want a token pittance, but a "viable" income.

Suppose, one of the directors said, that the government did not respond favorably. King had thought of that. "Then we will bring more people in. More and more." If his demands were met, he expected the government to guarantee their implementation. He was tired of promises. The plan, he said, looking up from the "blueprint," would go much further. In time, he expected to organize the poor of the West Coast, the poor of the North, the East; there would be separate protests, a sort of appendage to the main effort in Washington. He also proposed to organize the poor into unions—tenants, domestics, janitors, store clerks, seasonal crop workers, sanitation workers.

The men in the room glanced at one another. What had begun as a protest of 3,000 people for a period of one week now had overtones of a national rebellion, a contained civil war between classes. Their idol, they realized, was really "going for broke" this time. If the thing succeeded, Martin Luther King must, in time, become the single most powerful man in the country. The scheme had become so monumental that it boggled the mind. There was some dissent, but it was mild and polite. The SCLC was itself a creature of poverty at this time. Expenditures were up, donations down. Dr. King wanted to impress upon these trusted men, in absolute secrecy, that the Poor People's March was much more than a hungry horde of campers. They realized how much more when he said that it must be "powerful enough, dramatic enough, morally appealing enough, so that people of goodwill, the churches, labor, liberals, intellectuals, students, poor people themselves begin to put pressure on Congressmen."

King and Young, both ministers, knew that they would lose the support of black churchgoers in the opening gambit. They were the tame ones, the come-to-Jesus crowd. This applied also to the middle-class blacks who had good jobs and nice homes in the suburbs. These would not ally themselves with the poor. King felt that it didn't matter. He had written off his own "class" long ago. Some would call him a Communist, but that didn't matter either. When he bent the poor of the nation to his will by promising them good food, good housing, good jobs at government expense, it was no longer a consideration what the leader of the revolution was called. The pastor said that the movement had been "bogged in the paralysis of analysis." He enjoyed the sound of that. The Movement would now move from black rights (without abandoning any of the original goals) to a class struggle between those who have and those who have not. He would like to hear no more about "analysis." From now on, he said, the word would be "action."

The meeting continued all day, with phone service cut off from his office. Sandwiches and coffee were brought in. Before it broke up, Dr. King announced that he was going to visit Birmingham, Selma, and Montgomery. It would be a quick round of appearances, beginning on the fifteenth and ending the next day. After that, he and Mrs. King proposed to go to Jamaica for a week of rest. Meanwhile, he expected the directors of the SCLC and his staff to restart the rusty gears of recruiting marchers. "Action."

Memphis was drenched. It was rain and more than rain. The cold black sky opened and the inundation blackened the stone buildings downtown. Icy freshets ran the gutters from Thomas Street to Mendenhall Road. It was so thick that it defeated swift-snapping windshield wipers and dimmed headlights. There was little early morning light on January 31. It was not a day for children to play in the schoolyard at recess time. It was a bad day for telephone linemen, for policemen on foot, for garbage men, for installment collectors, postmen, door-to-door salesmen—a bad day.

The supervisor of the Sanitation Department called the garbage trucks back to their depots. The Wednesday collection of refuse would have to wait until Thursday, because this kind of rain would remain in Memphis all day and perhaps part of the night. The sanitation men, mostly blacks, stood around the yards until the word came to go home. When the word came, they hurried off because, even under the ponchos and the overcoats and slickers, they were soggy with the icy rain.

On Friday, Memphis was clear and cold and dry. Mayor Henry Loeb's auditing department had made up the weekly paychecks for municipal employees. The blacks frowned at what they got. It was less than usual. When they asked, they were told that they were being paid for two hours' work on Wednesday—that's all. It hurt, but they supposed it was fair. A few of them talked with white garbage men in the hall. The whites had been paid for a full day. This was not fair. It was more than that. The blacks thought that this was the mayor's way of revenging himself on them because they had voted against him, as a racist.

The garbage men were paid $1.70 an hour. The loss of six hours' pay meant $10.20. Multiplied by the 1,375 black members of Local 1733 of the American Federation of State, County and Municipal Employees, Henry Loeb had, with a single stroke of the pen, saved the city $14,000. The issue dragged for a week. On the day that Martin Luther King was holding his all-day meeting at SCLC headquarters—Lincoln's Birthday—the black union went out on strike. It wasn't an alarming matter. Other cities had sustained similar strikes to the point where sleek gray rats nested in the neglected garbage cans.

The strike couldn't last. After all, $1.70 an hour was above the national minimum. If a man worked only five days a week, he had $68. For six days, he earned $81.60. No one was going to get rich on it, but the city had offered 10 cents an hour more and 5 cents an hour additional in the summer. The garbage men were ready to accept. But money was not the issue. Race was. The deduction of six hours' pay from the many blacks, while granting a full day's pay to whites was racism. The municipal attitude was that the workers could come back to the trucks or starve.

As always, the white structure misgauged the anger and courage of the black man. This is attributable to the fact that the white experience with his dark brother was almost always on a person-to-person basis. The individual "darky" was an easily managed, and easily intimidated person when alone in the presence of the white man.

So it was in Memphis. On the day the strike was called, the Reverend and Mrs. Samuel B. Kyles were returning to Memphis by car. The radio was on. Sam Kyles was a tall, bushy-haired black with a mustache and glasses. He was pastor of the Monumental Baptist Church at 704 South

Parkway East. Kyles had two missions in life: to save souls and to bring his black brethren to the level of the whites. He was the antithesis of the suppliant black man. He did not advocate violence, but as a board member of the Memphis NAACP he had vowed to fight for civil rights, and such a fight was being mentioned on his car radio.

A news announcer said that Local 1733 of the sanitation workers had gone out on a "wildcat strike." The Reverend Mr. Kyles kept driving. Without taking his eyes off the road, he said, "Well, they finally got up the nerve to walk out." Mrs. Kyles said nothing. Whatever the problem, she was certain that the garbage men would not remain on strike long. Sam Kyles had the same feeling. Still, it would prod Mayor Loeb and the white residents toward the realization that garbage is garbage and blacks are people.

When Mrs. Kyles had been dropped off at home, Sam Kyles went directly to the NAACP. The leaders of the strike wanted the NAACP to keep out of the fight; they insisted that this was a union matter. It is a racial matter, the NAACP insisted. Couldn't the union see that it amounted to discrimination? The meeting was joined by James Lawson. He was a Memphis member of the SCLC, although Memphis did not have a chapter. He too argued that the pay deduction was made along racial lines. The union argued. The disagreement started loud and assertive; it closed with Local 1733 agreeing to make a racial battle of the matter.

Demands were sent to Mayor Loeb, and they transcended the original problem: (1) recognition of Local 1733 as bargaining agent for the garbage collectors and sanitation workers; (2) establishment of a biracial grievance committee; (3) the City of Memphis to deduct union dues from salaries; (4) an equitable system of promotion without regard to race; (5) health, hospital and life insurance for workers; (6) a pension system to match those of other municipal departments such as the Police and Fire Departments; (7) sick leave pay, overtime pay, and a paid vacation; and (8) an increase in wages.

A small matter, involving $14,000 became a racial war. The blacks were asking for more than they would settle for, but they would not step down in their demand to have Loeb recognize their union and arrange a dues checkoff system. It was these points which irritated the mayor most. Never, he said, would he recognize Local 1733. Never. In common with most municipal chieftains, he did not believe it proper for police, firemen, and other municipal employees to have unions, to be permitted to bargain, or to have the right to strike. Each side worked hard to place the other in an untenable position and, in so doing, fell into one itself.

Eleven days later the NAACP and James Lawson led a march of protest down Main Street. It was peaceful. Sanitation workers held placards delineating their eight demands on Memphis, pleading for support. Groups of whites stood on the curbs jeering. A solitary police car in low gear followed the line of marchers moving slowly ahead as the driver inched the car to the right, herding the marchers tightly to the curb. As the vehicle neared the front of the line, the car stopped. Several policemen jumped out. Two grabbed a black man. A third one sprayed a can of Mace, an irritant which causes temporary blindness and skin rash. The other policemen ran into the ranks. One cop brought his nightstick down on the head of a black. The crack was plain to hear. The man fell unconscious. The regional director of the Civil Rights Commission, Jacques Whitmore, hurried to the side of the police and flashed his identification card. A cop squirted Mace in his face.

It seems impossible to underestimate white intelligence. Most of the blacks of Memphis did not believe that the strike was a racial matter until a police superior ordered the Mace attack. They were supported in this by their conservative ministers. The establishment and the press could always be counted on to magnify a small issue into something impossible to control. The newspapers clucked over what the Memphis police had done to the blacks. Certainly, the white citizens applauded it. Overnight, the black ministers and their congregations were converted. This was not a union disagreement; it was a racial fight for life.

Blacks handed out leaflets from door to door; some stood in W. C. Handy Park passing them out. The leaflets asked the blacks to boycott the white newspapers and to buy nothing from the Loeb family stores in Memphis. A mass meeting was held at the African Methodist Episcopal Church, and the old pattern began to become discernible. Dr. Ralph Jackson shouted, "We're going to march until the Sanitation Workers say 'Satisfied!' But I have news for you. We're going to march after that!" The black community had a separate list of grievances: police cruelty; closed housing; job opportunities; low wages; segregated schools. Six hours' pay was about to escalate into seven days of death and destruction.

Martin Luther King was in Jamaica with his wife and Andrew Young when the garbage men's strike started, and he knew nothing of it. Every man has a place where his spirit quiets, his heart slows, his body refreshes and recharges. For King, it was Jamaica with the deep-green mountains, the peaks trailing imitation bridal veils; the rivers running fresh and swift between the banks of bamboo jungle; the call of wild birds unseen; the rhythmic hand of the sea washing rocks.

At this time of his life, nothing lasted long. He was in Birmingham by February 15, exhorting masses of blacks to join the Poor People's March. He told them not to worry about how they got there, but to be there on April 20. They could walk, go on muleback, by train, plane, or car—it didn't matter. Their presence was important. The poor were tired of being poor, but the government would not take the word of a country preacher; those men up there in Washington had to *see* the poor. He was in town. Out of town. The calendar was replaced by the watch. He made speeches in Montgomery and in Selma on the same day. Get up, people. Get out. This may be your last chance. He begged. He pleaded. He wanted names and addresses of those who would recruit others. He went to Mississippi and back home. And out.

He was a busy man. On February 23 he was in New York; he was due in Miami for a ministerial conference the following morning. Dr. King was running harder, faster, more breathlessly than ever. The New York appearance was important to him and politically dangerous. The radical left was gathering at Carnegie Hall to observe the "100th Anniversary of the Birth of Dr. W. E. B. Du Bois—Special Keynote Address by Dr. Martin Luther King, Jr." Du Bois was a professed Communist in his later years. The observance was sponsored by *Freedomways* magazine, which had been denounced by J. Edgar Hoover as a periodical used by "Communists" for propaganda purposes.

The hall was filled with the well-dressed when Dr. King was introduced. Applause was heavy. The question in most minds was: Would King dare to commit himself in public on the subject of Communism? He teased his audience with a dissertation on the life of Du Bois. They were aware of the statistics, the facts. Where did King stand in politics? That is what they had come to hear.

Toward the end, he said: "Du Bois was a restless militant black genius . . . a model of militant manhood and integrity . . . a radical all his life." Then came the words they had hoped to hear. "So many would like to ignore the fact that Du Bois was a Communist in his last years." A roar of approval came from many throats. ". . . our irrational obsessive anti-Communism has led us into too many quagmires. . . . All over the world, we must live together as brothers or we will all perish as fools."

People stood, stomped, whistled, applauded. King tried to speak of "the senseless cruel unjust war in Vietnam," but the radicals were giving him a standing ovation. His mouth moved; but the deep bell tones were overwhelmed by the accolade of the audience, and only a tape recorder caught the end of the speech, when he said "Du Bois will be with us when we go to Washington in April. . . ."

The Ford Foundation supplied the money. The Sheraton Four Ambassadors Hotel supplied the rooms. The City of Miami furnished the sunshine, the palm trees, the zephyr breezes of February. The Ministers Leadership Conference had been in session four days before Martin Luther King arrived, ebullient and buoyant, with a briefcase full of plans for the Poor People's March. Those who had been invited—all expenses paid—were black ministers from cities of 150,000 population or more. At the seminars, each speaker talked of the complexity of racial problems in his municipality. Everyone agreed that no matter how far the nation's lawmakers progressed in civil rights, the white man in his home was still the white man of old.

The week-long series of meetings had been arranged by the Southern Christian Leadership Conference to fuse this ministerial power, to give it direction and purpose. A clergyman from each city was elected as city convener, one who would meet regularly with other black ministers to discuss their problems and unite their people. The city conveners, in turn, would write reports to the SCLC in Atlanta. There, the staff would study, sift, and make recommendations. In this way, all the black strength in the South could, at times, be directed against one recalcitrant town. There were some disputes. Militant preachers accused others of "playing it safe," being "too soft" and "afraid to risk" their positions of affluence and well-being in the black community. Others stated that, under no circumstances could they subscribe to campaigns of violence such as they had read about.

By the time Dr. King arrived, late on Friday, the ministers had completed their work, ironed the wrinkles out of personal disagreements, and were prepared to stand under the umbrella of the SCLC for protection from the white elements. King was cheered by the ministers. He spoke to them of the Poor People's March and how he expected them to bring thousands and thousands more of the poor to Washington.

When the last meeting was concluded, the Reverend Sam Kyles sought King. As always, he was surrounded by a small group, listening and nodding. "Martin," said Kyles, "you know we have a garbage men's strike in Memphis." King looked up, smiling. "You may have to come and help us out," Kyles said. This was jest, or as Kyles said later, "a half jest." He did not expect Dr. King to abandon his big march for the problems of one city. "I phoned home today," Kyles said. "They had a march, just a little one from the auditorium to Clayborne Temple. Know what? They sprayed Mace on the people. Mace."

Dr. King nodded. The disruption of peaceful marches was an old story to him. "Sure," the pastor said. "If you don't get it settled, I'd be glad to go to Memphis." Kyles thanked him and left to say farewell to other groups. But Dr. King was thinking out loud with his staff. His impression was that the Memphis strike would be over quickly—who can bear the smell of garbage for long? In the second place, he was still aching from the defeat of Chicago. If the strike lasted long enough, it might be a good idea for the SCLC to move into Memphis for a short campaign. A local victory would be good publicity to set up public acclaim for the Poor People's March. He wanted to speak to his man in Memphis, James Lawson. If the fight was for narrow goals, union recognition and better salaries and promotions, it could be handled with a couple of massive demonstrations. He ordered Bayard Rustin to go to Memphis in March—"if the strike is still going on."

There was a failure in communications because the violent reaction of the Police Department and the eight black demands had aroused all Memphis. Whites were jeering blacks. Blacks were meeting in temples by the thousands. The young Invaders gang was perpetrating outrages on white merchants; Mayor Henry Loeb was implacable; Memphis was a city in torment. It wasn't Birmingham; it wasn't Selma; it wasn't a union strike either.

The month of March, addicted to changing its mind, was cold. There was snow in Atlanta; in Michigan, a parade of plows curled waves of snow against gutters. Washington, accustomed to warming trends now and then, was freezing thermometrically and politically. Coat collars were up; hands were down deep in pockets. At best, it was an unfriendly month, one of leaden skies and minds, a time of restlessness. There was a long chill in Los Angeles. Tomas Lau graduated James Earl Ray and told him he could easily find him a job. Ray told him he was leaving Los Angeles in a couple of weeks to see his brother so not to go to the trouble.

A photographer was called in, and Lau, dapper in a striped shirt and a mechanical smile, posed with his newest qualified bartender, grim in a black bow tie, holding his diploma against the middle of his chest, his eyes closed. The manager of the Hotel St. Francis was given word that Ray would leave his room on the morning of March 18. He had an optometrist fit him for shell-rimmed glasses even though his sight was good. But the glasses, in addition to the surgery on the tip of his nose, and all the identification he now possessed as "Eric S. Galt" made him certain that no one could study his features and identify him as an escaped convict from Missouri.

Dr. King was in Grosse Pointe, Michigan, to share a platform with black Congressman John Conyers. Episcopal Bishop Richard Emrich introduced the black pastor with an assortment of glittering superlatives and then added that he disapproved of the Poor People's March and of Dr. King's pronouncements on Vietnam. There were 3,000 people out front, and Dr. King realized that they were not all friendly as he listened to the bishop.

He put on his broadest smile as he approached the lectern. Then the catcalls began: "Commie!" "Traitor!" It was rudeness personified. In his defense, many in the audience clapped at times when no applause was elicitated; it was as though they were ashamed. The shouts and howls continued through the talk. The smile faded on the first page of the copy. When Dr. King left for Detroit Airport, he said it was the worst heckling he remembered. He was flying to Los Angeles.

On St. Patrick's Day, James Earl Ray stopped in the main post office in Los Angeles and filled out a change of address card. "Eric S. Galt" stated that all mail should be forwarded to him at "General Delivery, Atlanta, Georgia." On the same day, in the same city, Dr. King addressed the communicants of the Second Baptist Church. He called his address "The Meaning of Hope," but he rendered a dissertation on hate. It was, he said, a national disease, spreading everywhere. "I have seen it on the faces of sheriffs in the South and on the faces of John Birch Society members in California. . . . Hate is too great a burden to bear," he said. "I can't hate."

In the evening, he was on a plane bound for Memphis. The garbage men's strike was still in progress, and James Lawson had phoned King and said there would be a big rally on the eighteenth; all it needed was the doctor's presence to make it a resounding success. He slept on the plane. In the morning, James Earl Ray was wide-awake and off, eastbound, in his white Mustang. He had received a short note from his anonymous boss to drive to New Orleans.

The back of the car was loaded with the impedimenta of a long stay in Mexico and Los Angeles. Everything from a portable television set to extra socks was back there. He also had a few items he planned to give to friends in New Orleans. He drove hard and fast and made it in two days. On March 20, he phoned the boss and was told that he had gone ahead. The new meeting place was the Starlite Motel in Birmingham.

Memphis was quiet when Dr. King arrived. After a short conference with Lawson, Kyles, and other leaders, he went to the Mason Street Temple to speak. There had been talk of a general one-day strike in Memphis to bring Mayor Loeb to the bargaining table. King stepped onstage to the roaring acclaim of 15,000 people. His face broke into a large smile. This was different. This wasn't Grosse Pointe. He turned to Samuel Kyles, and over the din of applause, King shouted joyously, "This is like the old days. How'd you get all those people in here?"

He spoke, but the enthusiasm and respect of the people were so great that King was barely able to complete a paragraph without stopping for a tumultuous ovation. They loved him; he loved them. He had agreed to make only one speech and then return to Atlanta to work on the Poor People's March, but the doctor's ears and mind were bedazzled by devotion. He told the people that they ought to have a one-day stoppage—a complete stoppage—of all work in Memphis. They went wild. He went wild and went beyond what he had planned to do. "You arrange a march for that day," he shouted, "and I'll come back to Memphis to lead it."

"Friday!" they yelled.

"Friday!" he shouted back. But by Friday twelve inches of snow blocked the streets of Memphis, and the march was reset for March 28. Martin Luther King was hurrying faster and ever faster. He chartered a small plane, took young Marty and Dexter by the hands, and flew them around Georgia from one airport to another, talking victory for the masses. The speeches were four hours behind schedule, and Mrs. King was nervous and worried when they arrived home after midnight.

Dexter, weary with sleep, said, "You know, Mommy, I don't see how my daddy can do so much and talk so much to so many people—and not even get tired at all."

On the twentieth, James Earl Ray was out of New Orleans, headed northeast on Route 59 for Meridian, Tuscaloosa, and Birmingham. He met his man at the Starlite; Dr. King was across town at the Gaston Motel. The next morning Ray said he was ordered to Atlanta, which would be Route 78 to the east, but by mistake, so he says, he drove south to Montgomery. Having discovered the error, there was no reason to compound it by driving sixty miles farther off course to a little town like Selma, there to check in overnight at the Flamingo Motel. But then, he tells a second story. In that one, he left New Orleans for Birmingham, but got off Route 59 at the Mississippi-Alabama line and drove on the wrong road a hundred miles to Selma. If so, he could have corrected his error forty miles inside Alabama at Demopolis and have turned north to get back on the road to Birmingham at Eutaw.

Whichever way the truth lies, it is possible that Ray and King passed each other on the road, because King was speaking at Linden, Alabama, and Camden, Alabama, within thirty miles of Selma. The day before, many newspapers published an Associated Press story which stated: "Dr. Martin Luther King takes his recruiting drive for his Poor People's March on Washington back into South Alabama today after spending the night in Birmingham. King and his followers moved into Alabama late Wednesday (March 20th) after a two-day swing through Mississippi. . . . He plans to drive to Linden and Camden today, then fly to Atlanta." James Earl Ray was two days late to see Martin Luther King in Mississippi; two days late to see him in Birmingham; a day and a half late to see him in Camden.

On the evening of the twenty-third, the Smiler left Birmingham with his mentor and drove to Atlanta. He found a cheap place to stay, but the manager was drunk and couldn't show him to his room. The boss remained in the parked Mustang until Ray returned with a key and a room number. The boss said he might want to see him again, but he did not want to go through any employee to do it. One of Ray's studious pursuits in California was to subscribe to a correspondence course to become a locksmith. He said he would make a duplicate key for his employer within a few minutes. He made it, "but it didn't work too good." So Ray left his room door unlocked, and the manager sobered sufficiently to test the doors and lock that one. Ray had to get out of bed to unlock it. Someone returned and locked it again. This went on for one night and one day.

Dr. King spun off to New York in time to see a big story in the Harlem newspapers. Congressman Adam Clayton Powell had announced "The white man is finished" and "the day of Martin Luther King has come to an end." Two days later, on March 27, Dr. King was in riot-swept Newark, New Jersey, addressing 1,600 students at South Side High School. "I wish old Adam could see me now," he said happily. He was shouting: "Build, baby, build!" and the students were in a pandemonium of ecstasy. He moved on to speak in Jersey City, from there to Orange, New Jersey. At the close of the day, he was back in Newark, exhorting the people of the Abyssinian Baptist Church to walk to Washington and watch the doleful expressions on the faces of the white Southern Congressmen as they were confronted by a black sea of the poor. Later he phoned SCLC headquarters to ask for the next several items on his schedule. His secretary begged Dr. King to stop, to pause for breath. His pace was a killing one. He laughed; he still felt strong. "You all are going to kill me anyway," he said, "and I'd just as soon die at an early age."

Ray spent a week in the small Atlanta motel. He spent time studying a street map of Atlanta. In pencil he circled places designated as the home of Dr. Martin Luther King, the headquarters building of the SCLC, the Ebenezer Baptist Church, and a parking lot in the Capitol Homes public housing development. At one time, the manager of the hotel stopped by to exchange greetings and asked Ray what he did for a living. "Oh," said Ray, "I'm a sort of jack-of-all-trades." He spent daylight hours driving around Atlanta to locate Dr. King's home and SCLC headquarters and the roads leading both ways from them and "Daddy" King's church to the swift superhighways.

On Sunday, the thirty-first, the map was discarded. The middleman had arrived, and he ordered James Earl Ray to pack and clear out. The two men drove to Birmingham. There they checked the classified directory and located the Aeromarine Supply Company. Ray was ordered to phone the store and ask if it sold rifles. The response was yes. He was given $700 in cash and told to purchase a "large-bore deer rifle." When the middleman saw the gun, he said it was the wrong kind; Ray would have to return it in the morning, exchange it for the heavier one, and buy new ammunition.

Within a few days, James Earl Ray was on his way to 422 South Main Street in Memphis. Within a few days, Martin Luther King, determined as never before to stop violence from taking place, was on his way to the Lorraine Motel. Across a weedy vacant lot, with the aid of rifle sights, one man studied another. There was an earsplitting crack of noise, which one of them heard. The man who fought so hard for peace was lost to violence. The man who never had anything to give to the world gave it a martyr.

Zeitgeist.

We must love our white brothers, no matter what they do to us. We must make them know that we love them. Jesus still cries out across the centuries: "Love your enemies." We must learn to meet hate with love.

MARTIN LUTHER KING, JR.
January 30, 1956

Sources

Books

ALTSHULER, ALAN A., *Community Control.* New York, Pegasus, 1970.

ANTHONY, EARL, *Picking Up the Gun.* New York, Dial Press, 1969.

The Autobiography of Malcolm X. New York, Grove Press, 1964.

BARTLEY, NUMAN V., *The Rise of Massive Resistance.* Baton Rouge, Louisiana State University Press, 1969.

BENNETT, LERONE, JR., *What Manner of Man.* Chicago, Johnson Publishing Co., 1968.

The Black Panthers Speak, Philip S. Foner, ed. Philadelphia, J. B. Lippincott, 1970.

BLAIR, CLAY, JR., *The Strange Case of James Earl Ray.* New York, Bantam Books, 1969.

CLAYTON, ED, *Martin Luther King: The Peaceful Warrior.* Englewood Cliffs, N.J., Prentice-Hall, 1964.

CLEAVER, ELDRIDGE, *Soul on Ice.* New York, Dell Publishing, 1968.

COHEN, JERRY, and MURPHY, WILLIAM S., *Burn, Baby, Burn!* New York, E. P. Dutton & Co., 1966.

Congressional Record. Vol. 113, No. 158.

Dictionary of American Biography.

Editors of Time-Life Books, *I Have a Dream (The Story of MLK in Text and Pictures).* New York, Time, Inc., 1968.

FRY, JOHN R., *Fire and Blackstone.* Philadelphia, J. B. Lippincott, 1969.

HERSEY, JOHN, *The Algiers Motel Incident.* New York, Alfred A. Knopf, 1968.

HUIE, WILLIAM BRADFORD, *He Slew the Dreamer.* New York, Delacorte Press, 1968.

KING, CORETTA SCOTT, *My Life with Martin Luther King, Jr.* New York, Holt, Rinehart & Winston, 1969.

KING, MARTIN LUTHER, JR., *The Measure of a Man.* Christian Education Press, 1959.

————, *Strength to Love*. New York, Harper & Row, 1963.

————, *Stride Toward Freedom*. New York, Harper & Row, 1968.

————, *The Trumpet of Conscience*. New York, Harper & Row, 1967.

————, *Where Do We Go from Here? Chaos or Community*. New York, Harper & Row, 1967.

————, *Why We Can't Wait*. New York, New American Library, 1963.

KOCH, THILO, *Fighters for a New World*. New York, G. P. Putnam's Sons, 1969.

LEWIS, DAVID L., *King: A Critical Biography*. New York, Praeger Publishers, 1970.

LOKOS, LIONEL, *House Divided (The Life and Legacy of MLK)*. New Rochelle, N.Y., Arlington House, 1968.

LOMAX, LOUIS E., *To Kill a Black Man*. Holloway House, 1968.

Malcolm X, The Man and His Times, John Henrik Clark, ed. New York, Collier Books, 1969.

Martin Luther King, Jr., 1929–1968. Chicago, Johnson Publishing Co., 1968.

MILLER, WILLIAM ROBERT, *Martin Luther King, Jr.* New York, Weybright & Talley, 1968.

The Negro Almanac.

PRESTON, EDWARD, *Martin Luther King: Fighter for Freedom*. New York, Doubleday Signal Books, 1968.

Report of the National Advisory Commission on Civil Disorders. New York, Bantam, 1968.

Seven on Black, William G. Shade and Roy C. Herrenkohl, eds. Philadelphia, J. B. Lippincott, 1969.

VIVIAN, OCTAVIA, *Coretta*. Philadelphia, Fortress Press, 1970.

WATTERS, PAT, *The South and the Nation*. New York, Pantheon Books, 1969.

WHITE, THEODORE H., *The Making of the President 1960*. New York, New American Library, 1967.

————, *The Making of the President 1964*. New York, Atheneum, 1965.

WILLIAMS, JOHN A., *The King God Didn't Save*. New York, Coward-McCann, 1970.

WOLFF, MILES, *Lunch at the 5 & 10*. New York, Stein & Day, 1970.

World Almanac.

Miscellaneous

FEDERAL BUREAU OF INVESTIGATION
MIAMI LIBRARY FILES
NATIONAL ARCHIVES
Personal interviews in Albany, Georgia; Atlanta; Birmingham; Memphis; Montgomery; Selma, Alabama; Washington, D.C.

Periodicals and Newspapers

Jet magazine
Los Angeles *Herald-Examiner*
Los Angeles *Times*
Miami *Herald*
New York *Times*
Newsweek magazine.
Time magazine.
Washington *Post*

INDEX

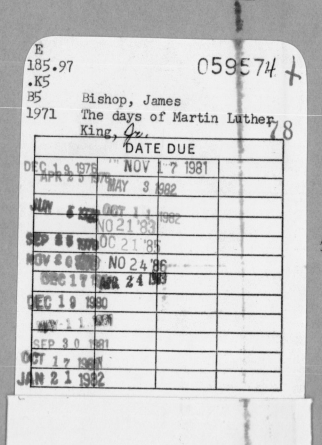

DATE DUE		
DEC 18 1976	NOV 17 1981	
APR 29 1978	MAY 3 1982	
JUN 5 1978	OCT 11 1982	
	NO 21 '83	
SEP 15 1978	OC 21 '85	
NOV 8 1978	NO 24 '86	
DEC 17 1978	AR 24 '89	
DEC 19 1980		
MAY 11 1981		
SEP 30 1981		
OCT 17 1981		
JAN 21 1982		